THE PUNJAB

Praise for the book

Ahmed brings us closer to both the political and human story of partition with all its paradoxes and meanings.

—Nonica Datta in *The Indian Express*

There are four unique contributions that Ishtiaq Ahmed makes to the large corpus that studies Partition. One, he provides a theoretical underpinning to understand why people living peacefully for many generations can become so aggressive and hostile to each other all of a sudden. Two, he gleans much important information from official communications. Three, he interviews a large body of people who witnessed the carnage of Partition, evaluates their memories for veracity, provides us with one of the most comprehensive archive of what people went through at the time of Independence. Finally, he brings together all this information to provide us with, perhaps for the first time, a comprehensive account of what the people of the Punjab went through during Partition. [...] Ahmed writes lightly yet manages to remain magisterial.

—M. Rajivlochan in *The Sunday Tribune*

Describing how 32 days demolished the vibrant Punjabi legacy of pluralism and composite-hood of 500 years affecting even the grassroots level is a story rewoven and told with scientific precision. This story is recorded blow-by-blow in this well-researched work. This makes this voluminous work one of the most informative–discursive resource for yesteryears as well as today and indeed for tomorrow. [...] The outstanding feature that this book presents lies in its use of an extensive repertoire of oral history, thus making a difference; this ultimately makes it a masterpiece.

—Dilip Malik in *India Quarterly*

Ahmed may not win agreement in India or in Pakistan (the book has been published in both countries) for every conclusion of his [...] But I doubt that anyone will question Ahmed's empathy with all sides in 1947's Punjab tragedy [...] A search for the facts has resulted in this book, and the honest way in which the search was carried out may have imparted to the book a role in the healing process for which the subcontinent waits.

[...] The great many in Pakistan and India who wish to preserve a society where freedoms are mutually respected should [...] be all the more thankful for Ishtiaq Ahmed's landmark study.

—Rajmohan Gandhi, in *IIC Quarterly*

THE PUNJAB

Bloodied, Partitioned and Cleansed

Ishtiaq Ahmed

RUPA

Published by
Rupa Publications India Pvt. Ltd 2011
7/16, Ansari Road, Daryaganj
New Delhi 110002

Sales centres:
Bengaluru Chennai
Hyderabad Jaipur Kathmandu
Kolkata Mumbai Prayagraj

First published in hardcover in 2011
First published in paperback in 2013

P-ISBN: 978-93-5520-578-0
E-ISBN: 978-93-5520-579-7

Fourth Impression 2025

10 9 8 7 6 5 4

Printed in India

To my wife Meliha.

She is the bedrock of our family, from whom I and our boys, Sahir and Selim, and their partners, Ice and Helena, always draw strength and support. My granddaughter (Sahir and Ice's daughter) Celeste Yasmin (born 21 August 2017) is the latest member of the family.

CONTENTS

Stage 3: Ethnic Cleansing
15 August–31 December 1947

PREFACE
MARKING THE 75TH ANNIVERSARY OF THE PARTITION OF THE PUNJAB

The publication of the new edition of my book on the 75th anniversary of Partition is a great milestone. Some more oral histories have been added to the main text; a few are presented in this article. Most of the oral histories on Partition that I recorded between 1999 and 2011 are now available for hearing as a part of the Partition Archives of the Lahore University of Management Sciences (LUMS) website. Some are available at the Amritsar Partition Museum.

Over the years, interest in knowing what happened in 1947 has only grown and is likely to grow even more. New generations of Punjabis want to know why the violence unleashed in their province dwarfed the violence elsewhere in the subcontinent when the curtain on the British Empire was finally drawn.

I cannot say with certainty when the idea of researching the partition of the Punjab first occurred to me, but it was something that had piqued my curiosity from early childhood. I grew up listening to elders describing some of the events that took place on Temple Road, Lahore, where I was born. That canvas expanded over time as I went around Lahore on my bike, because I was deeply in love with my city of birth and always thirsted for more knowledge about its past. The bike rides inevitably took me to localities which were once Hindu–Sikh majority areas but from where virtually all traces of Hindu–Sikh presence were now gone. Even as a teenager, I could figure out that such people would not have left their homes and localities willingly or happily. Only in the famous shopping locality of Anarkali, almost entirely studded with shops owned by Hindus before Partition, did Beliram and Brothers continue as major dispensers and chemists till the '70s. It is still a mystery how that shop and its Hindu owners survived so long.

Post-Partition Lahore also had many examples of Muslim suffering. My earliest memory of it is associated with an old man who lived in a small shop in front of our house. He had no proper home. He was a refugee from the other side of the old Punjab. He spoke a rough type of Urdu in an accent I later learnt was typical of what is now Haryana. Prior to Partition, it constituted the easternmost portion of the united Punjab. Every evening, he would start cursing and abusing the whole world. Street urchins would taunt him and knock at his door. When he came out, they would run away. He was known as Chacha Churanji Lal, suggesting that he was a Hindu. Actually, he was a Muslim. Some said his real name was Lal Din, others, Lal Mohammad.

I learnt that he had married late, his wife had died at childbirth and he had brought up his only son all by himself. That boy had been killed in front of him during Partition. The trauma rendered him a mourner forever, but also, obviously, led to some serious mental problems. In 1953, when sectarian disturbances against the Ahmadiyya community (a religious community claiming to be Muslims but constitutionally classified as non-Muslims in Pakistan since 1974) took place, curfew was clamped on Lahore. Every evening, soldiers sitting in trucks would patrol Temple Road. The vehicles moved very slowly. They had guns ready to shoot at miscreants. It was a scary scene. However, the old man was oblivious to the danger they posed and continued with his daily barrage of abuses. That greatly angered the military, who wanted to teach him a lesson, believing his invective to be directed at them. However, elders of the area intervened just in time and told the soldiers about his grief. Thereafter, they ignored him. Eventually, he died.

In 1947, the lives of millions of Punjabis were shattered. Perhaps those who survived paid a heavier price. I am not sure how such suffering can be fathomed or measured.

Nothing epitomizes the tragedy of the Punjab partition more profoundly than the fact that it created a large pool of derelict women. Their treatment by their families and society in general varied. Hindus and Sikhs had greater difficulty in accepting them because according to their caste system such women had been defiled, having been held in Muslim custody. In mid-July 1947, a Hindu girl from Rawalpindi somehow landed up at our Temple Road house. My parents helped her seek refuge at Preet Nagar, a commune founded midway between Lahore and Amritsar by the famous Punjabi writer Gurbaksh Singh, famously known as Gurbaksh Singh Preet Lari. Preet Nagar was frequented by leftists and secular-minded liberals.

On the whole, Muslim women who were recovered from Hindu–Sikh custody fared comparatively better because no theological grounds for their rejection existed, though there were certain social and cultural prejudices.

It was not, however, always the case that men who captured women of the enemy religion became their tormentors. In a few cases, it kindled deep feelings of love and affection. However, the Indian and Pakistani governments agreed to help each other in recovering abducted women and restoring them to their original families. The bureaucracies tasked to undertake such missions tended to be apathetic to cases of mixed marriages. Nothing symbolized such insensitivity more starkly than the story of Boota Singh, who married his much-younger Muslim wife Zaina after having bought her from her captors. They began living as husband and wife, and Zainab bore him two daughters. Then one day, she was taken away and returned to her family, who had relocated to a village near Lyallpur (now Faisalabad) in West Punjab. A kindly Muslim who knew her whereabouts kept Boota informed about Zainab, who had taken their infant daughter with her but left the elder one with him. Boota converted to Islam, became Jamil Ahmed and arrived in Pakistan, bringing his daughter with him.

Boota was harassed by the police for not reporting his whereabouts as required by law, but he managed to convince a magistrate to order Zainab to be produced before the court. She had, meanwhile, been married off to someone else. Zainab disowned Boota in court. Did she do it voluntarily or had she been coerced? Heartbroken, Boota threw himself before a train. This incident aroused great passion among Muslims for what they perceived to be the collective guilt of their community. They atoned for the great tragedy by giving him a befitting Islamic burial, with thousands of people taking part in his funeral rites. Such is the culture of Punjabi Muslims—easily excitable, but generous and forgiving to a fault. This culture may be on the way to destruction if the 'Arabization' of the Punjabi Muslim identity takes root under the juggernaut of petrodollars from the Persian Gulf and State-sponsored Islamization measures that have been brutalizing society for a long time.

Fictional Writings

Albert Camus, the French-Algerian Nobel Prize winner for Literature in 1957, observed most succinctly, 'Fiction is the lie through which we tell the truth.' Indeed, the stark reality of the partition of the Punjab was such that Punjabi short story writers and novelists such as Saadat Hasan Manto, Krishan Chander, Rajinder Singh Bedi, Balvant Singh, Khushwant Singh, Ramanand Sagar, Ashfaq Ahmed, Qudratullah Shahab, Ahmad Nadeem Qasmi, Anwar Ali, and many others have composed the most outstanding genre of Urdu/Hindi/Punjabi literature on the theme of Partition, combining masterfully fact and imagination. Manto's 'Toba Tek Singh' is perhaps the ultimate indictment of the Punjab partition.

As far as I know, the Punjab partition did not receive the same degree of attention by poets. I sometimes wonder why. Perhaps the parameters of poetry did not provide the same degree of freedom to capture profoundly complex situations. But some outstanding exceptions to the rule do exist. Amrita Pritam's 'Ajj Aakhaan Waris Shah Nu (Ode to Waris Shah)' is undoubtedly the most famous of all. Addressing the great Sufi poet of the Punjab, Waris Shah (1722–1798), whose epic *Heer* is one of the most famous renderings of Punjab's indigenous Romeo–Juliet folktale, Amrita Pritam deplored and implored:

'Ajj Aakhaan Waris Shah Nu'

Ajj Aakhan Waris Shah Nuu, Kiton Qabraan Wichon Bol, Tey Ajj Kitaab-e-Ishq Daa, Koi Agla Warka Phol.
Ikk Royi Sii Dhi Punjab Di, Tu Likh Likh Maarey Wain,
Ajj Lakhaan Dhiyan Rondiyan, Tenu Waris Shah Nuu Kain.
Uthh Dard-Mandaan Diya Dardiya, Utth Tak Apna Punjab
Ajj Bailey Lashaan Bichiyaan Tey Lahoo Di Bhari Chenab.
Kisey Ne Panjaan Paaniyan Wich Diti Zahar Rala,
Tey Unhan Paniyaan Dhar Toun Ditta Paani Laa.

'Ode to Waris Shah'

Today, I call to you Waris Shah 'Answer me from your grave!'
And, then, in that Book of Love of yours Move on to a new page.
Once cried a daughter of the Punjab and you composed that narrative of pain Today countless daughters are wailing And say to you, 'O Waris Shah'.
Rise, you the soother of the hurt Wake up, and look at your Punjab
Today the corpses are scattered everywhere And blood runs deep in the Chenab.
Someone has poured in the five rivers A venom very potent
And with that deadly concoct Has watered all our fields.
(Translated from Punjabi by Sain Sucha)

Many years later, when famous poet, writer, director and filmmaker, Gulzar, crossed the border between Amritsar and Lahore at Attari–Wagah to visit his hometown Dina, he was overwhelmed by that experience. Those pent up feelings and emotions were expressed by him in the following poem:

'Zero Line'

Naa'pe Qadmon Se Chalte Chalte Wagah Par
Main 'Zero Line Par Aakar Khada Tha Jab
Meri Perchhaien Pakistan Me Thi!
Mere Peechhe Tha Sooraj
Mere Aage Mere Abbu Khade The
Mujhe Dekha
Chhadi Tteki Zameen Par
Muskuraye Aur Bole:
'Wahan Jab Mitti Chhodi Th
Main Apne Ghar Chala Aaya Tha, Punni!'
Mere Abbu Mujhe 'Punni' Bulaate The
'Mujhe Umeed Thi Tum Aaoge Punni,
Ke Mere Ant Ki Tum Ko Khabar Pahunchi Nahin Thi!
Yakeen 'Tha Tum Aaoge Mujhko Widaa Karne!'

Bas Ik Waqfa Thither Ke Rah Gaya Tha
Chhadi Ko Khattkhattayaa Phir Zameen Par
Badha Kar Haath Bole…
'Chalo "Dina" Chalen 'Ge!'

Mere Ehbaab Jo Wagah Pe Lene Aaye The Mujhko
Pakad Ke Haath Mera Le Gaye Lahore Mujhko
Wahan Ke Shor–O–Gul Me Phir Koi Aawaaz Kaano Me Nahin Aaie
Magar Sannatte Ka Ik Raastaa Tha Jo Dikhai De Raha Tha
Vo Rasta 'Dina' Jaata Tha!

Bahut Chhotta Sa Qasba Tha, Kabhi Wo
Bahut Chhotta Sa Gatton Ka Banaaya Ek Station Tha
Wahan Sab Gaadiyaan Rukti Nahin Thin
Magar Wo 'Laam' Ke Din The
Wahi Rukti Thin Jin Mein Faujiyon Ke Dibbe Hote The
Dhuaan 'Dikhta Tha Gaadi Ka, Tho Doud Aata Tha Station Par
Us Me Abbu, Hatti Ke Liye Saamaan Lekar Lautta Karte The!

Bas Ik Bazaar Tha
Ik 'Ttaalihyon' Waali Sadak Bhi Thi
Wo Ab Bhi Hai
Madrasa Tha Jahan Main Ttaatt Ki Patti Bichhaa Kar Takhti Likhta Tha
Gali Bhi Hai
Wo Jis Ka Ik Sira Kheton Me Khulta Tha
Wo Deewarein Ttattolein, Koyele Se Jin Pe Urdu Likhaa Karta Tha

Mujhe Umeed Thi Koi Meri Ungli Pakad Lega
Mujhe Hijje Sikhaayega
Magar Koi Nahin Aaya
Main Shaayed Chhod Aaya Tha, Wahin Wagah Pe Unko
Main Lautt Aaya

Main Zero Line Par Aakar Khada Hoon
Mere Peechhe Meri Perchhaien Hai, Aawaaz Deti Hai
Wahan Jab Mitti Chhodoge
Chale Aana Tumhaara Ghar Yahin Par Hai
Tumhaari Janam Bhoomi Hai! Watan Hai!!

'Zero Line'

Walking up to Wagah with measured steps
When I came to stand at the Zero Line
My shadow fell in Pakistan!
The sun was behind me
And my Abbu was standing in front
He saw me
Resting his stick on the ground
He smiled and said,
'When I had left my body there
I came back home, Punni!'
Abbu used to call me 'Punni'.
'I had hoped you would come,
For you had not received the news of my death
I knew you would come to bid me farewell!'

Startled, the moment paused
He tapped the ground with his stick
Stretching his hand, he said:
'Come, let us go to Dina!'

My friends who had come to receive me at 'Wagah'
Held me by the hand and took me to 'Lahore'
In the din of the city no voices came back to me
But I could see a trail of silence
That led to 'Dina'.

It used to be a 'qasba' once
With a tiny cardboard railway station

Not all trains stopped there
Those were the days of the war
Only trains carrying soldiers stopped there
I would run to the station whenever I spotted the smoke
Abbu used to return with goods for the 'hatti'.

There was just a 'bazaar'
And a track lined by banyan trees
It's still there
And a 'madrasa' where, sitting on a piece of sackcloth,
I would write on my wooden board
That alley exists still—
Which opened into the fields
I caressed those walls on which
I used to write in Urdu with a piece of coal.

I hoped someone would hold my fingers
And teach me to spell every syllable correctly
But no one came—
Perhaps I had left him behind at 'Wagah'
So I returned—

I am back at the Zero Line
My shadow whispers from behind me,
'When you give up this body
Come back to your home
Your birthplace, your motherland.

(Translated from Hindustani by Rakhshanda Jalil)

Faiz Ahmad Faiz famously described the dawn of freedom as stained and incomplete because a mere transfer of power from British colonialism to Indian and Pakistani states had taken place. In that process, the communal riots that broke out profoundly shocked him. The leftist ideal of true liberation of humankind from class oppression and exploitation was still a distant goal.

'Subh-e-Aazaadi'

Yeh Daagh Daagh Ujaalaa, Yeh Shab Gazidaa Seher
Woh Intezaar Tha Jiska, Yeh Woh Seher To Nahin

Yeh Woh Seher To Nahin, Jis Ki Aarzoo Lekar
Chale The Yaar Ki Mil Jaayegi Kahin Na Kahin
Falak Ke Dasht Mein Taaron Ki Aakhri Manzil
Kahin To Hogaa Shab-E-Sust Mauj Ka Saahil
Kahin To Jaa Ke Rukegaa Safinaa-E-Gham-E-Dil

Jawaan Lahu Ki Pur-Asraar Shahraahon Se
Chale Jo Yaar To Daaman Pe Kitne Haath Pade
Dayaar-E-Husn Ki Besabr Kwaabgaahon Se
Pukaarti Rahi Baahein, Badan Bulaate Rahe

Bahut Aziz Thi Lekin Rukh-E-Seher Ki Lagan
Bahut Qareen Tha Haseenaa-E-Noor Ka Daaman
Subuk Subuk Thi Tamanna, Dabi Dabi Thi Thakan

Suna Hai, Ho Bhi Chukaa Hai Firaaq-E-Zulmat-O-Noor
Suna Hai, Ho Bhi Chukaa Hai Wisaal-E-Manzil-O-Gaam
Badal Chukaa Hai Bahut Ehl-E-Dard Ka Dastoor
Nishaat-E-Wasl Halaal, O Azaab-E-Hijr Haraam

Jigar Ki Aag, Nazar Ki Umang, Dil Ki Jalan
Kisi Pe Chaaraa-E-Hijraan Ka Kuch Asar Hi Nahin
Kahaan Se Aayi Nigaar-E-Sabaa, Kidhar Ko Gayi
Abhi Charaag-E-Sar-E-Raah Ko Kuch Khabar Hi Nahin

Abhi Garaani-E-Shab Mein Kami Nahin Aayi
Najaat-E-Deedaa-O-Dil Ki Ghadi Nahin Aayi
Chale Chalo Ki Woh Manzil Abhi Nahin Aayi
15August 1947

'The Dawn of Freedom'

This stained, pitted first light,
this daybreak, battered by night,
this dawn that we all ached for,
this is not that one.

Sure, in the belief
that we would, eventually,
reach the last station of the stars
somewhere in the sky's arid plains,
sure that night's sluggish wave
would eventually make beachhead,
sure that the ship of our sorrows
would find land, somewhere,
our yearnings drove us all on.
But this, is not that dawn.

Down mystifying highways
that only the young can take,
together we made our way, only
to be accosted a thousand times,
while, from Beauty's nocturnal domain,
from her impatient bedchambers,
hands beckoned, reached out for us,
bodies craved our presence.

But more enticing by far
was the pull of dawn's demeanour.
How close were we,
close enough to touch the hems
of the maidens of light,
how delicate were our desires,
how restrained our exhaustion.

We have heard that the darkness
has already separated from the light.
We have heard that the weary footstep
has already found its way home,
that the lot of the anguished multitudes
has changed, very substantially,
that the rapture of union is celebrated lawfully,
the pains of separation, completely proscribed.

The antidote of severance
has had no effect on the burning heart,
on the longing of the waiting gaze,
on fires raging in the gut.
From whence did this zephyr
manifest itself, where did it zip past?
Even the lamps lining our streets
are hard pressed to know.

There has been no easing
of the full weight of night.
Parched eyes, aching hearts
are yet to find their moment of deliverance.
Walk on, walk on,
the home we seek has still to arrive.
15 August 1947

(Translated from Urdu by Mustansir Dalvi)

It is important to underline that Faiz and many other leftists had obliquely accepted the divisive logic of the two-nation theory because top theoreticians of the Communist Party of India had passed a resolution in its favour based on the right of self-determination of oppressed nationalities. That resolution upheld the right of linguistic nationalities to self-determination, including their right to form independent states, but when it came to Muslims and Sikhs, the right of self-determination was to be extended to them on a communal basis. Such convoluted reasoning had in practice resulted in horrific riots and pogroms in the

Punjab, between Muslims on the one hand and Hindus and Sikhs on the other. That agony and shock pervades Faiz's verses composed to mark the 'dawn of freedom'.

The greatest indictment of Partition by a Punjabi poet was undoubtedly 'Mufahamat (Compromise)' by Sahir Ludhianvi.

'Mufahamat'

Nasheb-E-Arz Pe Zarroñ Ko Mushta.Il Pā Kar
Bulandiyoñ Pe Safed-O-Siyāh Mil Hī Ga.E
Jo Yādgār The Bāham Satīza-Kārī Kī
Ba-Faiz-E-Vaqt Vo Dāman Ke Chaak Sil Hī Ga.E
Jihād Ḳhatm Huā Daur-E-Āshtī Aayā
Sambhal Ke Baith Ga.E Mahmaloñ Meñ Dīvāne
Hujūm Tishna-Labāñ Kī Nigāh Se Ojhal
Chhalak Rahe Haiñ Sharāb-E-Havas Ke Paimāne
Ye Jashn Jashn-E-Masarrat Nahīñ Tamāshā Hai
Na.E Libās Meñ Niklā Hai Rahzanī Kā Julūs
Hazār Sham-E-Uḳhuvvat Bujhā Ke Chamke Haiñ
Ye Tīrgī Ke Ubhāre Hue Hasīñ Fānūs
Ye Shāḳh-E-Nūr Jise Zulmatoñ Ne Sīñchā Hai
Agar Phalī To Sharāroñ Ke Phuul Lā.Egī
Na Phal Sakī To Naee Fasl-E-Gul Ke Aane Tak
Zamīr-E-Arz Meñ Ik Zahr Chhor Jā.Egī

'The Compromise'

Finding the elements on earth agitated
In the skies black and white have joined hands
Those that were reminders of our quarrels
Due to need of time those collars have been mended
Jihad has ended and time of peace has come
The wild ones are now sitting in marriage palanquins
Hidden from the eyes of those dying of thirst
Wine of lust's goblets are overflowing
This is not a celebration of joy but a farce
In a new uniform has come the gang of robbers

After extinguishing a thousand candles of love have glowed bright
These chandeliers of separate houses
This seed of light which is born from darkness
If it sprouts it will bring us flowers of fire
And if it fails to grow then
Till the next cycle of crops it will
Poison the conscience of this land
(Translated from Urdu by Dr Aamir Butt)

Sahir was one of the few dissenting voices among Muslim leftists who could foresee that the underlying logic on which the partition was based was theoretically flawed and ethically regressive—that Hindus and Muslims constituted two communal nations who could not form a single political nation of equal citizens. I talked to his childhood friend Hameed Akhtar who told me that Sahir used to warn him and other comrades that Jinnah's Pakistan would easily fall prey to the clerics and Islamist ideologues because the movement for Pakistan was heavily immersed in communalist and religious imagery and terminology. Such an ideology was the antithesis of class liberation and the emancipation of the oppressed from reactionary beliefs and prejudices. Hence, Sahir described Partition as a phenomenon that would sow hatred and poison the minds of coming generations. That proved prophetic. Not only did Pakistan succumb to Islamism from the time of Independence, but Nehru's secular India was challenged from the late '90s onwards by burgeoning Hindu nationalism thriving on majoritarianism and demonization of minorities, especially Muslims.

Such a standpoint made Sahir unpopular with Pakistani leftists, and he left Lahore for Nehru's India a year after Partition. It was a most courageous decision, because it contradicted the underlying logic of Partition: Muslim Punjabis going to Pakistan and Punjabi Hindus and Sikhs to India. Sahir was not only a Muslim Punjabi but was born in Ludhiana, from which all traces of a Muslim presence was erased in the wake of the horrific riots at the time of 1947 Partition. In India, Sahir got the freedom to express himself. His secular, humanist poems were sought after by filmmakers for film songs; they became a powerful medium for conveying enlightened social messages.

The Objective and Results

Academic research hesitated for too long and was seriously handicapped because the truth of the partition of the Punjab could not be told with the help of the sources that the historians of Partition were used to—archival material maintained by the State and its functionaries, biographies and high politics concentrating on political personalities like Gandhi, Jinnah, Nehru, Mountbatten, Patel and Azad, to name a few.

More importantly, official reports even after power was transferred to the Indian and Pakistani Punjab administrations on 15 August 1947 remain classified on both sides for no other reason than the obvious one—that both were complicit in the expulsion of unwanted minorities.

This book set out to achieve the opposite of what Camus associated with literature: to tell the truth concealed by governments and thus expose the lies about the partition of the Punjab. In doing so, it took me 12 years to collect evidence from Hindus, Muslims and Sikhs, which is presented in the book not simply as stories but as a depiction of events as they transpired once the violent attacks and communal riots began, culminating in ethnic cleansing on both sides of the divided Punjab.

After the publication of the book in both India and Pakistan, I have been receiving a steady and growing body of emails, Facebook and WhatsApp messages and telephone calls pertaining to Partition. I share here with the readers some of the most extraordinary stories told to me.

Harbhajan Kaur/Shahnaz Begum

This proved true in a larger-than-life and stranger-than-fiction ordeal of Harbhajan Kaur/Shahnaz Begum and her children. It was brought to my notice by Nasim Hassan, an engineer who lives in Hockessin, Delaware, United States (US). We came in contact when he read one of my articles in Lahore's *Daily Times* in which I had taken up the issue of Partition. He had a story of his own to tell.

In 1947, Nasim was a small child who escaped with his family from Shimla. Eventually, they set up home in Lahore and visited Shimla many years later. How he describes his feelings when returning to his roots is best read in the book. A Sikh gentleman named Romy Singh read his story, which he had shared in an online community magazine. While Romy had his business in Virginia Beach, his family lived in Baltimore, Maryland, US. Romy wanted Nasim to help his stepmother, Harbhajan Kaur, locate her five children in Pakistan. Nasim wrote to me for help. Harbhajan Kaur had the following to say about her past:

'My name is Harbhajan Kaur. I am now 82 years old. My father, Sher Singh, was a landlord of Rajasansi town near Amritsar. I was married to Sardar Harbil Singh in Lahore in 1946. In 1947, while migrating from Lahore to Amritsar, our truck was attacked, and the mobsters killed everyone except the girls. I was one of the surviving girls. After changing hands, a person named Afzal Khan married me and renamed me Shahnaz Begum. Afzal Khan was 16 years older than me. We moved to Karachi and had five children. Afzal Khan manufactured face cream and we lived in the Koyla Godam (Coal Storage) area of Karachi. The names of my children are Khurshid, Jameela, Zubeda, Bala and Rizwan.

In 1962, visa restrictions between India and Pakistan were relaxed and I decided to visit Rajasansi as I longed for my parents. Two people, Bashir Ahmed and Zahoor Ahmed of Akbari Mandi, Lahore, helped us get the visa. In fact, their mother-in-law was like a godmother to me. So, I, Afzal Khan and our five children visited Rajasansi. The youngest, Rizwan, was a baby then, born in 1960. My parents did not allow me to go back to Pakistan, but Afzal Khan and the children were sent back to Pakistan. Thus, I became a victim of Partition for the second time.

In 1969, I was married to Sardar Gurbachan Singh, whose wife had died and he needed someone to take care of his son Romy, who was five years old. My Romy migrated to the US in 1989. After he had established a business, he brought me and my husband over to the US, in 1997. My husband passed away in 2007. Although I never revealed my past to Romy, he found out from other sources. Romy asked me if I wanted to contact my kids in Pakistan. Now they must be grown up and God knows where they live at this time. Please let me know if anyone can help in locating my children in Pakistan.'

In my article, 'Help a Mother Find Her Children' in the *Daily Times,* Lahore, dated 16 December 2012, I appealed to all good people to help. I left for India on 30 January for a lecture tour. However, on the morning of 17 February when I checked my emails, one dated 13

February from Jameela Begum (63) greatly surprised me. She wrote that she was Shahnaz Begum's (Harbhajan Kaur's) daughter. She had read an Urdu translation of my *Daily Times* article published in the *Daily Jang* of Karachi. The journalist had given my email at the bottom and therefore she wrote to me. I talked to her on the phone on the contact number she had given. Her elder sister, Khurshid Begum (66), was at that time in Canada with her son. She flew out to meet her mother in the US.

From the time of my departure to India, the following had happened. Nasim Hassan talked to Tufail Uppal, who turned out to be from Rajasansi originally before moving to Pakistan at the time of Partition. He not only knew Harbhajan Kaur but had also attended her marriage in 1946. They met in Baltimore, where both had been living without knowing about one another. Mr Uppal and Harbhajan Kaur recognized each other after 65 long years. Mr Uppal's daughter, Fazilat, and his son-in-law, Waseem Sheikh, arranged, with the help of Bashir A. Tariq, the publication of the story in the Karachi Urdu-language *Daily Jang*; hence, Jameela Begum contacted me.

Apparently, the publication of the story in *Jang* coincided with a family friend of the Uppals, Khalid, locating the shop where Afzal Khan used to manufacture his face cream. The shop owner's son remembered his father talking about Afzal Khan, who had died years ago. He also knew Rizwan, the youngest child of Harbhajan Kaur, who was only two when he was separated from his mother. Just then, the story was published in *Jang*. The shop owner's son called Rizwan, who did not believe it. He thought it was a hoax. Then modern technology worked wonders and mother and children not only talked but also saw each other.

Romy Singh then obtained a visa for himself and Harbhajan Kaur to visit Pakistan. On 13 April, they flew to India, met the family and paid their respects at the Golden Temple. After one week, on 20 April, they crossed the border at Wagah and entered Pakistan. Khurshid, the eldest daughter whom they had already met when she had come from Baltimore, Canada, was waiting for them. Together they visited the birthplace of Guru Nanak at Nankana Sahib. Finally, on 22 April, they arrived in Karachi and the family met after more than 50 years. Later, they shifted to Hyderabad as it was much safer than ethnic violence-ridden Karachi where Khurshid had a much bigger house for the whole family and relatives to congregate easily. Then on 30 April 2013, Romy and his stepmother returned to the United States. The family has grown. Harbhajan Kaur now has many grandchildren.

Sadly, Mr Uppal died soon after initial contact between Harbhajan Kaur and her children had been made. He was then in hospital and lived long enough to know that the family had met. However, he and his children and family friends, Romy Singh and Nasim Hassan—all participated in the healing and uniting process the Punjab book set in motion. Religion and politics were set aside, and humanity prevailed.

This was further illustrated when, in 2014, I narrated the story of Harbhajan Kaur/Shahnaz Begum to my students at the LUMS. To my very great surprise, one of the students, Aamna Ali, told me that her grandfather belonged to Rajasansi and he and Tufail Uppal were lifelong best friends. They were like brothers, she told me. So, Partition connected with my class, literally, after all these years!

Lalit Mohan Jain

Another story, less dramatic but important to share, originated in Stockholm. Just before I left Stockholm for India on my lecture tour, my late friend Riaz Cheema, whose account of his family leaving Delhi for Pakistan on 16 March appears in the book, requested me to meet Mr Lalit Mohan Jain, his father Abdullah Cheema's colleague's son. The two families had reconnected by chance after more than 60 years. I rang up Mr Jain, a retired senior civil servant, who invited me for lunch at the office of The Bharat Scouts and Guides office in New Delhi, where he continued to render voluntary service. I met him in his office on 11 May 2013. This is the fascinating interview Mr Jain granted me:

'We are originally from Rohtak, now in Haryana, but before Partition, it was part of the united Punjab. My father, Mr Pritam Singh Jain, and Mr Abdullah Cheema were class-fellows at the Lahore Law College. They were from the first batch which joined the Punjab judicial service called PS Judicial, after successfully passing the first competitive exam held either in 1928 or 1929. Earlier, judges were nominated by the government. My father and Cheema Sahib were great friends and my father used to speak volumes about him. In the early '40s, my elder brother developed a serious kidney problem and needed to be operated upon. My father wanted to be posted to Gurgaon (now Gurugram) so that the operation could be carried out in a nearby Delhi hospital. However, just then, my father was posted to a hamlet in northern Punjab, Pind Dadan Khan, while Cheema Sahib was posted to Gurgaon. Cheema Sahib learnt about my father's predicament and offered to switch the postings, saying that he would give in writing to the Punjab and Haryana High Court that he wanted to be posted to Pind Dadan Khan. Thus, my father got the Gurgaon posting and my brother was successfully operated upon in Delhi. That was such a great favour, which we, to this day, remember in our family.

Years later, I met Abdullah Cheema Sahib in Delhi, I believe in 1960 when I was studying at Delhi University for my master's exam in English Literature. My father phoned me and told me that Cheema Sahib would be coming to see me. My father retired in 1957, so Cheema Sahib must have also retired by that time. He used to come to Delhi probably to meet his old Hindu and Sikh colleagues. He very kindly visited me at my hostel and gave me his blessings.

Now, it so happens that the SAARC member states by turn arrange the annual Scout-Guide Jamboree, and boys and girls from the member states visit one another. In 2009, the Pakistani scouts and guides were led by a gentleman who belonged to the judicial service. He, too, had retired and like me continued to take part in such activities on a voluntary basis. I told him that my father was in the Punjab judicial service and about his friendship with Abdullah Cheema Sahib. Luckily, he knew the family and said that one of his sons lived in Rawalpindi and he would let him know about me. Then one day, his son, Colonel (retd) Aslam Cheema, phoned me and we had a long chat. A few months later, his elder brother Riaz Cheema called from Stockholm.'

There is a very sad and tragic story from the Punjab Partition to which I am witness. A West Punjabi Hindu family called the Batras was transferred to Karnal, where my father was then posted. It was soon after Partition. Their children were our age, very beautiful and well-groomed. We used to play together. One day, their elder sister threw herself in the canal that flows through Karnal and died by suicide. That was a great shock to all of us. She had probably been traumatized by some horrific experience in West Punjab. A few days later, one evening, we and her brothers were playing when suddenly they said they wanted to go home. It was still not really dark, so we told them that there was no need to go so early, but they left. The next day we learnt that the whole family—father, mother and the children—had died by suicide. Something devastating must have happened in their life that first their beautiful girl died by suicide and then the whole family decided to end their lives as well. Partition destroyed many lives.

Beliram and Brothers of Lahore

On 2 November 2021, I received an email from Dr Tribhavan Kumar, PhD Physics, who introduced himself as an 'Old Lahori'. He informed me that he had read many of my books and watched many of my videos. He pointed out that in my book *The Punjab Bloodied, Partitioned and Cleansed* (Rupa Publications, 2011), I had mentioned the name of their shop as 'Beliram and Sons'. The correct name was 'Beliram and Brothers'. I had corrected that mistake in subsequent editions of the book published by Oxford University Press, Karachi, and the mistake is being rectified in this new edition of the book by Rupa Publications, India.

I remember, when in September 2011, the book was launched at the India International Centre by Rupa Publications I had informed them that I have heard that the Beliram family owned a shop in Connaught Place, New Delhi, and someone from the family should be invited to the book launch. On that day, however, nobody turned up from the Beliram family.

A friend of mine in Lahore, the late Pervez Razi, told me that his family was distributors for Beliram and Brothers products for Karachi and other towns. Therefore, the Beliram and Brothers saga had continued to be mentioned one way or another whenever old Lahore and its people were the subject of conversation with my friends.

Therefore, Tribhavan Kumar's email to me was a most welcome arrival out of the blue. I requested him to write down the extraordinary story of his family. In several emails during 2–5 November and later in December 2021 exchanged between us, Tribhavan Kumar shared with me the following sketch of his family's roots in Lahore.

'The offspring of Beliram and Brothers now span the whole world. I moved to the US 56 years ago. I did my PhD in Physics and have lived most of my life in the San Francisco Bay Area in northern California.

My great-grandfather Bishan Das Mehta started producing medicines from his home inside the walled city of Lahore way back in 1890. In 1904, the famous shop in Anarkali Bazaar was built at 10 Anarkali Road. Bhisan Das had three sons, Beliram, Kirpa Ram and Balak Ram, hence, the name of the shop: Beliram and Brothers. It was the retail shop of our firm. My grandfather was Kirpa Ram. We supplied medicines to Punjab and the North-West Frontier Province.

During Partition, when Hindus and Sikhs had to flee from Lahore and elsewhere in Pakistan, Mahatma Gandhi persuaded the family to stay on in Lahore and provide medicine to all as previously done. The Pakistan government also gave us full protection. Beliram went to Bombay and others in the family to Delhi and other parts of India. However, my grandfather, Kirpa Ram, stayed on with his family and five children. Grandfather died in May 1948.

My father Roshan Lal continued with the business in Lahore. I was born on 10 November 1947. Beliram and Brothers in Anarkali was the retail part of the pharmaceuticals and drugs business that Beli Ram and his two brothers along with their father owned. They had two manufacturing companies. One was British India Drugs situated in Mughalpura area and the other was National Pharmaceuticals near Sheikhupura. These two supplied the pharmaceuticals of the time to a large swath of the area now in Pakistan. My grandfather was asked by Gandhiji to stay in Pakistan and keep supplying the essential medical and pharmaceutical supplies. My father stayed with my grandfather during the killing months of May 1947 onwards. During those months, all their store supplies were given out free to anyone in need.

I do not know what Lahore was like before 1947 as a sleepy town of Muslims, Hindus and Sikhs. My memories of religious differences began in 1953 when I suddenly found that a few families had moved into our house. They were Ahmadiyyas. An Ahmadi medical doctor who was an old customer and friend of my father sought refuge with us. I remember a lot of crying and late-night conversations that I could not understand.

One thing led to another, and my grandfather died in May 1948 and my father, my mother and their five kids found themselves staying in Lahore as the last vestige of Hindus, as you put it, in the city of Lav [according to a Hindu legend, one of the sons of Lord Ram was Lav]. The rest of the family had moved to India. Times changed and people changed, and the changes accelerated after the Hazratbal incident in December 1963 [an incident originating in Srinagar, Kashmir, where hair believed to belong to the beard of Prophet Muhammad was stolen. That relic was recovered soon afterwards]. Soon thereafter, activities took place, which lead to the 1965 India–Pakistan war.

We found ourselves living among people who were now ashamed to speak in Punjabi, and most claimed their ancestors came from Central Asia or the Middle East; hardly anyone from Punjab. It was time for us to leave, and we did, in 1975.

I was told by my father that the father of my great-great-grandfather had been hanged outside the walled city of Lahore along with his Muslim and Sikh compatriots by the British for opposing their annexation of Lahore in March 1849, while many other Lahore Muslims, Hindus and Sikhs had ridden off in the service of the British to suppress the 1857 war against the British. Those who supported the British were amply rewarded, and many of them became the powerful feudal class of the Punjab.'

Lala Mela Ram and Rai Bahadur Ram Saran Das

I did a video on the story of Beliram and Brothers, which I shared on my YouTube channel as the beginning of a new series: *The Story of Lahore*. Social media provides scope for unprecedented instant communication with the big wide world. Thousands of people watched that video and implored me to tell more such stories.

The latest video I did in the series before submitting the manuscript to Rupa Publications was the story of another famous Hindu family of Lahore—that of a Lala, later Rai Bahadur Mela Ram, and his son Rai Bahadur Ram Saran Das. Their services in the development of Lahore and their philanthropic engagements are proverbial, and despite all efforts to erase the contributions of these non-Muslims, the people of Lahore continue to remember them and talk about them.

To my very great surprise, as soon as the videos on YouTube were uploaded, I immediately received messages from the descendants of that family—famous Indian journalist, news presenter and interviewer Karan Thapar and his sister Shobha Banerjee.

In one sense then, the Punjab Partition saga is not over yet and never will be. It was not only the bloodiest episode in the saga of the British Empire ceasing to exist in mid-August 1947 but of British rule terminating in all other parts of the world: 500,000–800,000 people were killed and 10 million were forced to flee their homes only in the Punjab. I feel privileged and redeemed to have recorded it in print at the twilight moment in history when some from the generation who witnessed and suffered it are still around to talk about it.

Researching Partition

With a few exceptions of Indian feminists such as Urvashi Butalia, Ritu Menon and Kamla Bhasin, I found the existing research on the partition of Punjab woefully limited in its scope because conventional historians trained to rely on official documents almost invariably stopped their enquiries on 14 August 1947 when the British governors or the Punjab chief secretaries ceased writing fortnightly reports of the events taking place in the province. Some ventured a little further by including police FIRs of some districts, but police FIRs are notoriously unreliable because the police are known for concealing true figures about law-and-order violations and concomitant violent incidents to evade reprimand from their superiors for incompetence and ineffectiveness.

As a political scientist, I was keen to extend the frontiers of my knowledge about forced migration, ethnic cleansing and genocide that wreaked havoc on Punjabis in 1947. In one sense, the Jewish holocaust, ethnic cleansing in former Yugoslavia, genocide in Rwanda and Darfur and Partition are manifestations of the same irrationality and aggression that have bedevilled civilizations in antiquity, in the Middle Ages and in our own time. In this study, I bring forth abundant evidence to underscore that.

However, the main focus is on identifying and highlighting the peculiarities of the specific Punjab situation and explaining it in theoretical terms. Such an undertaking furnishes a basis for testing theory. In other words, theorizing the Punjab case should be useful and relevant for scholars studying the Punjab as well as similar phenomena elsewhere.

I consider myself privileged for having talked to many different Punjabis and recorded their experiences. As a result, vast ethnographic material was collected, which I now share with my readers. We get glimpses into the Punjabi ethos, its strengths and weaknesses. Naturally, customs and traditions—some good and some bad—which permeated their lives in the '40s, shaped their sympathies, passions and prejudices. These, in turn, impinged upon their responses to the completely novel situations that cropped up in 1947. What this study demonstrates amply and forcefully is that no particular group or religious community was the embodiment of either pure evil or good.

Punjabi Spellings

There is no standard English spelling of Punjabi titles, names, surnames and places. I have accepted the spellings used by the person in question. In some cases, the spellings of names have changed. For example, in the Punjab governors' reports, the first name of the last Punjab premier was spelled as 'Khizar', but now it is spelled as 'Khizr'. I believe Sir Khizr himself used the latter spelling. On the other hand, 'Liaquat' has become current for the first name of the Muslim League leader and later Prime Minister Nawabzada Liaqat Ali Khan while he himself spelled his name as 'Liaqat'. I have used this form as well.

A majority of the people whose testimony is included in the book neither speak nor write English. I have, therefore, exercised my own discretion in using the English spellings. However, for places I have used the spellings prevalent in 1947: Jullundur (now spelled as Jalandhar), Ferozepore (now spelled as Firozpur); there are other examples as well. Then there are some places whose names have been changed, such as Lyallpur in West Punjab, now called Faisalabad, and Montgomery, now known as Sahiwal.

The 1947 Calendar

I have included the 1947 calendar for readers to help them identify the day of the week that correspond to the dates given in the book. I was myself curious to know about the day when a certain event or episode took place, because dates are opaque and impersonal. Knowing the particular day in the week when they happened can convey deeper meaning to them. This should be especially true of those elders who were part of that historical experience, as well as to their families and children, who have been hearing stories from those days.

Indigenization of the Administration

Emphasis is laid in the book on the indigenization of the administration, which had begun to pick up pace in the '40s. I do not have exact figures because there is not much material available in the official records and reports. Naming officials was definitely not standard practice. Towards the end of my research, I began to look for the names of the main linchpin of the administrative machinery, the deputy commissioner. I could never obtain a complete list. It includes names of Hindus, Muslims and Sikhs. I corrected it in the light of reliable information that I had collected and added the names of some British officers who were also serving at that time. It is worth presenting, even though it is incomplete and may include some inaccuracies.

On the whole, it underscores the point that by 1947, Hindus, Muslims and Sikhs had preponderated. The old Punjab comprised five divisions, which in turn consisted of districts. There were 29 districts altogether. From July onwards, deputy commissioners and other senior officials began to be transferred to the other side if their religion was not compatible with the religious majority of the divided Punjab in which they had been serving at that time. The list below refers to the period 1 January to roughly 30 June 1947.

Rawalpindi division	
Attock	Swaroop Krishan till 22 March 1947; H.J.V. Taylor till 31 July; K.S. Sheikh Muhammad Rashid from 11 August 1947 till 14 November 1948.
Rawalpindi	C.L. Coates; S.A. Haq took over on 14 August 1947.
Jhelum	S.B. Balwant Singh Nalwa till 15 April 1947; Zafar-ul-Ahsan from 16 April till 5 August 1947; A.D. Arshad from 8 August 1947 to 21 March 1950.
Gujrat	Wazir Chand from 1946 to August 1947; Sardar Abdul Samad from 14 June 1947 to 9 April 1948.
Mianwali	(Khan Ghulam Hasan Khan Leghari) Ch. J. Naryal Singh from 18 March 1946 to 15 August 1947; Said Zaman Khan from 15 August 1947 to 27 October 1947; Mohammad Tufail Hussain Buttar from 27 October 1947 to 20 February 1949.
Shahpur	Kewal Singh Chaudhry from 24 April 1946 to 31 May 1947; Ch Ghulam Ahmed from 1 June 1947 to 15 August 1947; Ghulam Hassan Khan Leghari from 16 August 1947 to 1948.
Multan division	
Montgomery (now called Sahiwal)	Said Zaman Khan from 17 December 1946 to 6 August 1947; Raja Hassan Akhtar from 6 August 1947 to 21 October 1948.
Lyallpur	A. K. Malik from 8 July 1945 till 26 April 1947; Nukal Sen from 26 April 1947 till 6 August 1947; Agha Abdul Hameed from 6 August 1947 to 12 January 1948.
Multan	A.J.V. Arthur from 18 October 1946 till 5 August 1947; A.G. Raza from 8 August 1947 to 20 September 1947; M.S.A. Baig from 21 September till 30 August 1949.

Jhang	S.P. Narendra Singh from 1 January 1947 to 30 June 1947; Chaudhry M. Akram from 1 July till 13 July 1947; Zafar-ul-Haq from 14 July 1947 till 11 September 1947; Mushtaq Ahmed Cheema from 12 September 1947 till 25 May 1948.
Muzaffargarh	Raja Sultan Lal Hussain from 1944 till 18 August 1947; Syed Ejaz Hassan from 19 August till 8 November 1947; C.H. Disney from 8 November 1947 till 1 January 1948.
Dera Ghazi Khan	B.M.K. Slater till 15 March 1947; J.A. Biggs Davidson from 16 March till 22 May; J.H. Buttar from 25 May till 23 October 1947; J.H. Biggs from 24 October till 10 February 1948.
Lahore Division	
Gujranwala	Sunder Das Midha from 6 July 1944 to 6 July 1947; Pir Mubark Ali Shah from 2 August 1947 to 19 August 1947; M.H. Mahmud from 19 August to 1 November 1947; S.S. Jaffery from 5 November till 12 April 1948.
Lahore	J. Mifearne till 23 January; J.C.W. Eustace took over on 23 January; Zafar-ul-Ahsan took over on 14 August 1947.
Sheikhupura	Dewan Sukkha Anand November 1946 till 3 March 1947; apparently no DC for several months; C.H. Disney from 14 August 1947 to 29 October 1947; Ch. Ghulam Ahmed from 30 October 1947 to 7 March 1948.
Sialkot	Nukal Sen from 8 July 1944 to 18 February 1947; Raja Muhammad Afzal from 18 February 1947 to 26 August 1947; Mirza Muzaffar Ahmad from 27 August 1947 to 21 February 1949.
Amritsar	J.D. Frazer till 22 May; G.M. Brander took over on 24 May and remained in office till 22 August; from 23 August onwards, Nukal Sen was appointed.

Gurdaspur	K.D. Regress from 25 May 1946 to 13 August 1947; Mushtaq Ahmed Cheema from 14 August 1947 to 17 August 1947; Chanaya Lal from 18 August 1947 to 9 October 1947; Saroop Krishan from 10 October 1947 to 17 December 1950.
Jullundur Division	
Ferozepore	R.B.L. Vishnu Bhagwan from 1947 to 20 January 1948.
Jullundur	Ahsan-ud-din till 1 July 1947; Sunder Das Midha took over on 7 July 1947.
Ludhiana	Sardar Abdul Samad Khan from 23 July 1946 to 3 August 1947; R.N. Luthra from 4 August to 23 September 1947; N. Sehgal from 24 September 1947 to 18 July 1948.
Hoshiarpur	R.S. Harbans Lal Khanna from 13 October 1944 to 12 February 1948.
Kangra	Zafarul Ahsan from May 1946 to May 1947; Kapur Singh from 3 August 1947 to 8 February 1948.
Ambala Division	
Ambala	B.S. Grewal in 1947.
Hissar	S.A. Haq till 13 August 1947.
Rohtak	Alauddin till Partition.
Karnal	R.L.B.V. Bhagwan from 6 October 1945 to 8 January 1947; E.J. Cocks from 11 February 1947 to 5 August 1947; R.S. Roshan Lal from 8 August 1947 to 21 June 1948.
Simla	Sheikh Fazal Illahi; Kewal Singh Chaudhary from 5 July 1947 to 17 May 1948.

Most of the native deputy commissioners were Indian Civil Service (ICS) officers. The highest police officer in the district was the superintendent of police (SP). Most of them were natives. Some Punjabi Christians also held senior posts in the '40s. What happened to them once power was transferred to India and Pakistan is not clear. There is enough scope for research connecting the developments in the two Punjab(s) since Partition. I hope the story of Punjab will continue to be told because time did not stop at the end of 1947.

Ishtiaq Ahmed
Solna Municipality, Stockholm
7 June 2022

CALENDAR 1947

January 1947–December 1947

January 1947

S	M	T	W	T	F	S
			1	2	3	4
5	6	7	8	9	10	11
12	13	14	15	16	17	18
19	20	21	22	23	24	25
26	27	28	29	30	31	

February 1947

S	M	T	W	T	F	S
						1
2	3	4	5	6	7	8
9	10	11	12	13	14	15
16	17	18	19	20	21	22
23	24	25	26	27	28	

March 1947

S	M	T	W	T	F	S
						1
2	3	4	5	6	7	8
9	10	11	12	13	14	15
16	17	18	19	20	21	22
23	24	25	26	27	28	29
30	31					

April 1947

S	M	T	W	T	F	S
		1	2	3	4	5
6	7	8	9	10	11	12
13	14	15	16	17	18	19
20	21	22	23	24	25	26
27	28	29	30			

May 1947

S	M	T	W	T	F	S
				1	2	3
4	5	6	7	8	9	10
11	12	13	14	15	16	17
18	19	20	21	22	23	24
25	26	27	28	29	30	31

June 1947

S	M	T	W	T	F	S
1	2	3	4	5	6	7
8	9	10	11	12	13	14
15	16	17	18	19	20	21
22	23	24	25	26	27	28
29	30					

July 1947

S	M	T	W	T	F	S
		1	2	3	4	5
6	7	8	9	10	11	12
13	14	15	16	17	18	19
20	21	22	23	24	25	26
27	28	29	30	31		

August 1947

S	M	T	W	T	F	S
					1	2
3	4	5	6	7	8	9
10	11	12	13	14	15	16
17	18	19	20	21	22	23
24	25	26	27	28	29	30
31						

September 1947

S	M	T	W	T	F	S
	1	2	3	4	5	6
7	8	9	10	11	12	13
14	15	16	17	18	19	20
21	22	23	24	25	26	27
28	29	30				

October 1947

S	M	T	W	T	F	S
			1	2	3	4
5	6	7	8	9	10	11
12	13	14	15	16	17	18
19	20	21	22	23	24	25
26	27	28	29	30	31	

November 1947

S	M	T	W	T	F	S
						1
2	3	4	5	6	7	8
9	10	11	12	13	14	15
16	17	18	19	20	21	22
23	24	25	26	27	28	29
30						

December 1947

S	M	T	W	T	F	S
	1	2	3	4	5	6
7	8	9	10	11	12	13
14	15	16	17	18	19	20
21	22	23	24	25	26	27
28	29	30	31			

CHRONOLOGY OF EVENTS DURING 1947

24 January – Premier Khizr bans the Muslim National Guard and RSS; direct action launched by the Muslim League against the Khizr ministry.

20 February – British government announces end of British rule in the Indian subcontinent by June 1948.

26 February – The Muslim League calls off the civil disobedience movement, all detainees are released.

2 March – Khizr resigns, causing a major political and constitutional crisis.

3 March – Master Tara Singh waves his *kirpan* on the steps of the Punjab Legislative Assembly in Lahore, denouncing the idea of Pakistan. Hindu and Sikh leaders pledge their opposition to the creation of Pakistan in a public meeting in Lahore.

4 March – Violent clashes break out in Lahore and Amritsar between Hindu–Sikh agitators and Muslim opponents.

5 March – Rioting spreads to Multan and Rawalpindi; on a lesser scale to Jullundur and some other towns in central Punjab.

5 March – Punjab Governor Sir Evan Jenkins imposes governor's rule in the Punjab. It lasts till power is handed over to the East and West Punjab governments on 15 August.

6–13 March – Predominantly Sikh villages in Rawalpindi, Campbellpur (Attock) and Jhelum districts are attacked by armed Muslims. Some 2,000–5,000 Sikhs and Hindus are killed in the riots. Thousands of Sikhs seek refuge in the eastern districts and princely states of the Punjab.

8 March – Congress party endorses the Sikh demand for partition of the Punjab.

24 March – Lord Louis Mountbatten takes over as the last Viceroy and Governor-General of India.

April–June – Recurring, gradually escalating incidents of stabbings, arson and crude bomb explosions take place in Lahore and Amritsar. Hindus and Sikhs in large numbers begin to migrate from western Punjab to safe havens eastwards.

15–16 May – Jinnah and Liaqat Ali Khan meet Maharaja of Patiala and other Sikh leaders to discuss the possibilities of Sikhs joining Pakistan; the talks fail.

3 June – Partition Plan announced by Mountbatten; power to be handed over to the Indian and Pakistani governments by mid-August 1947.

23 June – Members of the Punjab Legislative Assembly meet as East and West Punjab groups and vote in favour of partitioning the Punjab.

8 July – Sir Cyril Radcliffe arrives in India to preside over the Boundary Commission.

18 July – India Independence Act 1947 passed by the British Parliament.

21 July–31 July – The Punjab Boundary Commission examines the conflicting territorial claims in the British-administered Punjab put forth by the Congress, Muslim League, the Sikhs and some minority groups.

July onwards – The old Punjab disintegrates as rioting spreads to the rural areas; the government writ rapidly diminishes; Sikh *jathas* begin to attack Muslims of the eastern districts.

1 August – The poorly-manned and badly-equipped Punjab Boundary Force (PBF) under Major General Rees takes over to monitor events in twelve districts of the British-administered Punjab. It has no jurisdiction over the Punjab princely states.

12 August – The first large-scale movement of Muslims from the eastern districts to the Muslim-majority areas westwards is reported by Governor Jenkins.

15 August – Power is handed over to the East and West Punjab governments and British rule in the subcontinent ends.

17 August – The Radcliffe Award, demarcating the international boundary between India and Pakistan, is made public. It results in sharp escalation of violence as millions of Hindus, Muslims and Sikhs are on the wrong side of the new boundary.

1 September – The PBF is disbanded; Indian and Pakistani governments form joint units to escort caravans and convoys of refugees across the India–Pakistan border.

17 August–31 December – Ethnic cleansing takes place on both sides of the divided Punjab.

31 December – Most of the ten million unwanted Punjabis have crossed the border; some 500,000 to 800,000 are killed.

GOVERNMENTS OF PUNJAB
(1 JANUARY–31 DECEMBER 1947)

Governor:	Sir Evan Jenkins, Indian Civil Service (ICS)
Chief Secretary:	Akhtar Hussain (ICS)
Inspector General of Police:	Sir John Bennett, Indian Police (IP)
Prime Minister* (Premier):	Sir Khizr Hayat Khan Tiwana (1 January 1947–2 March 1947)

Ministers (ministry dissolved after Governor's Rule was imposed on 5 March 1947)

Public Works:	Chaudhri Lahri Singh
Education:	Mian Muhammad Ibrahim Barq
Finance:	Bhim Sen Sachar
Revenue:	Nawab Sir Muzaffar Ali Qizilbash
Development:	Sardar Baldev Singh

Government of West Punjab (15 August–31 December 1947)

Governor:	Sir Francis Mudie, ICS
Chief Secretary:	Hafiz Abdul Majeed, ICS
Inspector General of Police:	Khan Qurban Ali Khan, IP

*The head of elected government in the united Punjab was called prime minister. In some other provinces, too, this was the practice.

Premier:	Nawab Iftikhar Hussain Khan of Mamdot

Ministers

Finance:	Mumtaz Muhammad Khan Daultana
Revenue:	Sardar Shaukat Hayat Khan
Education:	Sheikh Karamat Ali
Refugees and Rehabilitation:	Mian Muhammad Iftikharuddin (18 September 1947–15 November 1947)

Government of East Punjab (15 August 1947–31 December 1947)

Governor:	Sir Chandulal Madhavlal Trivedi, ICS
Chief Secretary:	Mulk Raj Sachdev, ICS
Inspector General of Police:	Sant Prakash Singh, IP
Premier:	Dr Gopi Chand Bhargava

Ministers

Home, Irrigation and Power:	Sardar Swaran Singh
Revenue and Rehabilitation:	Ishar Singh Majhail
PWD, Buildings and Public Works:	Chaudhri Lahri Singh
Social Welfare:	Prithvi Singh Azad

INTRODUCTION

THE PARTITION OF THE PUNJAB TOOK PLACE AS PART OF AN OVERALL agreement brokered by the British government between the main India-level political parties—the Indian National Congress, the All-India Muslim League and also the Sikhs of the Punjab—to partition India. The Mountbatten Plan was announced by the British government on 3 June 1947, and was endorsed by the representatives of the main political parties and Baldev Singh, the representative of the Punjab Sikhs. In mid-August, the British Indian Empire ceased to exist. The international boundary between the two States was drawn, through the Punjab in the northwest and Bengal in the northeast of India, a couple of days later.

According to the 1941 census, the total population of the Punjab (Figure 1), including British Punjab and the princely states, was 33,922,373. The Muslims were in an absolute majority of 53.2 per cent, Hindus were 29.1 per cent (caste Hindus 23.8 per cent and 5.2 per cent Scheduled castes and tribes), Sikhs 14.9 per cent and Christians 1.4 per cent.

British Punjab (Figure 2) comprised 29 districts with a total population of 28,418,819 of which Muslims were 57.1 per cent; Hindus 28.8 per cent (including 6.6 belonging to the Scheduled castes or 'Untouchables'); Sikh 13.2 per cent and Christians 1.7 per cent.

There can be no denying that if India had not been partitioned the Punjab also would not have been divided. The demand for the partition of the Punjab was made by the Sikh leaders in reaction to the demand by the leaders of the Muslim League for a separate Muslim-majority Pakistan that would include the Punjab as well. However, it was not inevitable that the Punjab must necessarily have been partitioned if the leaders of the three main communities—the Hindus, Muslims and Sikhs—had agreed to remain together.

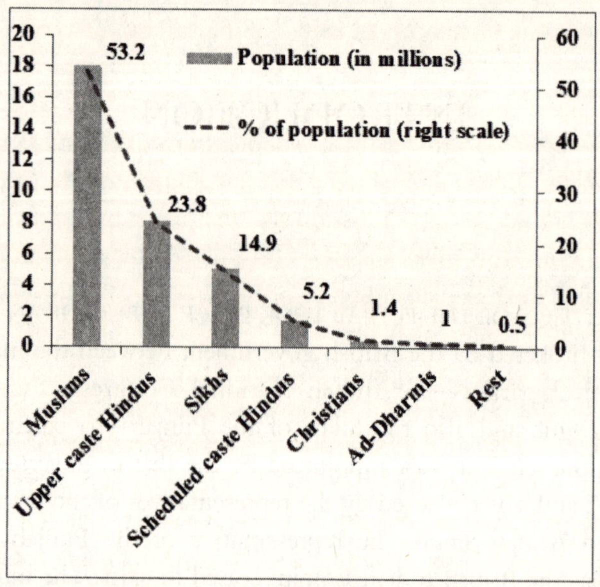

Figure 1: Pattern of population in the Punjab Province including princely states, 1941
Source: Census of India, Punjab, 1941

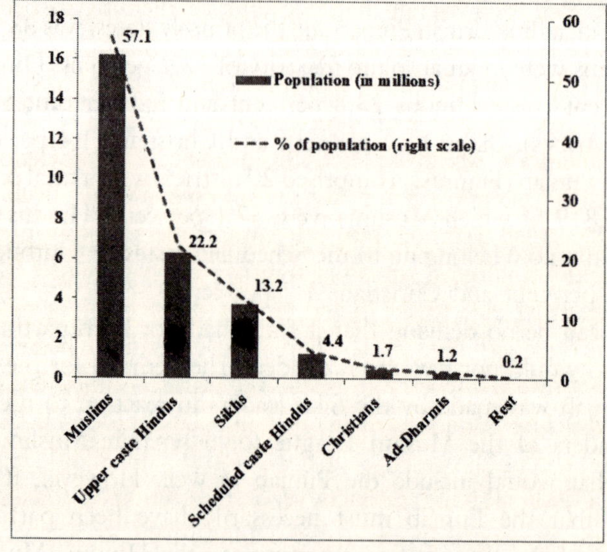

Figure 2: Pattern of population in British Punjab in 1941
Source: Census of India, Punjab, 1941

The decision to partition the Punjab applied to British Punjab: an administrative unit directly under British administration. However, the great commotion and upheaval that attended the partition process inevitably enveloped the princely states of the Punjab as well. The culmination of the partition process resulted in the obliteration of all traces of Muslim presence in the Indian Punjab; the sole exception was the tiny princely state of Malerkotla (total population 88,109) ruled by a Muslim nawab. Equally, Hindus and Sikhs became conspicuous by their absence from the Pakistani West Punjab and the princely state of Bahawalpur (total population 1,341,209).

The intriguing aspect about the Punjab was that pre-colonial Punjab had a rich tradition of liberal and pluralist interpretations of the three major religions – Islam, Hinduism and Sikhism – as they interacted with Sufi, Bhakti and Sant movements, which preached harmony rather than confrontation. There can be no denying, however, that the history of the Punjab was also one of frequent warfare, as invaders used to arrive in the subcontinent through the north-western mountain passes and establish their rule in the Punjab and beyond, in northern India and even further. Before the British annexed it militarily in 1849, the Punjab was under Sikh rule, though half a century earlier it had been one of the provinces of the Mughal Empire.

On the other hand, the three communities could invoke a long list of grievances against each other, with all of them deploying their 'historical memory' selectively. Yet, the evidence is overwhelming that most Punjabis, till almost before the end of colonial rule, lived in peace. A shared sense of common Punjabi cultural identity was prevalent in the thousands of villages, towns, and cities of the province. That bond would later prove too weak, in the face of divisive forces that became active in the twentieth century. The Punjab administration began reporting from 1945 onward the establishment of 'private armies' by the three communities. The Sikhs bore arms, a sword called the ***kirpan***, as a matter of religious right. Moreover, Punjabi Muslims and Sikhs, and Hindus from the Hindi-speaking districts of eastern Punjab, constituted the largest single provincial group in the colonial army. Nearly one million of them returned to their villages because of general demobilisation after the Second World War. In addition, gangs of strongmen or criminals known as *badmashes* and *goondas* were to be found throughout the length and breadth of the Punjab. They, in turn, had links with the politicians and the police.

It was under these circumstances that the provincial election campaign began in the Punjab in the second half of 1945, and culminated in the election of February 1946. It resulted in a highly volatile situation. The Muslim League, which stood for a separate Pakistan through the partitioning of India on the basis of contiguous Muslim and non-Muslim majority areas, won the largest number of seats in the Punjab legislature. However, it did not win a majority and therefore, could form a government only by entering into a coalition with other parties. That did not happen. Its opponents formed a coalition government under the leadership of Sir Khizr Hayat Khan Tiwana, whose party had been routed in the election. Such a situation created a classic problem – that of distinguishing legality from legitimacy. The coalition government was undoubtedly legal, according to parliamentary procedure, but among the Muslim majority of the Punjab, it was not perceived as the legitimate representative government. That resulted in agitations and demonstrations by the Muslim League, culminating in the fall of the Khizr ministry on 2 March 1947.

Almost immediately, the Punjab Congress party and the Sikh parties took to the streets to protest the fall of the government, vowing not to let the Muslim League form a new one. The agitations triggered violent riots, particularly in the villages in Rawalpindi district, where the Sikh minority was attacked with unprecedented savagery by Muslim hordes. It resulted in thousands of Sikhs fleeing to safety in the eastern districts, where their community was present in significant numbers.

The government brought matters 'under control', yet only barely, as the old harmony could not be restored again. Everyone wanted an answer to the crucial question: Will Punjab as a whole be awarded to Pakistan, as the Muslim League was hoping, or will it be divided between Pakistan and India, as the Sikh leaders and the Indian National Congress demanded? Neither one, obviously, would have satisfied all the three groups.

Starting from the middle of May 1947, there was a revival of attacks, becoming more frequent and more organised as the weeks passed. The riots continued well into the end of that year, reaching their peak in early August, while a British governor was still in power. After power was handed over to India and Pakistan in mid-August, the violence spiralled dramatically, continuing at a very high level for some three months. It is widely acknowledged that what happened in the Punjab dwarfed the violence of the communal rioting that happened in Calcutta, Bihar, and some other places in 1946. In the end, it would prove to be the first large-scale experiment in population cleansing after the Second World War.

It must be stressed that the decision to partition the Punjab was taken not by the Punjabi masses or even their elite, but at the central level, by the colonial government at Delhi, the high commands of the Indian National Congress, and the Muslim League; only the Sikhs from the Punjab were consulted by the viceroy, where they put their case forward for special treatment. They claimed that their religion and cultural identity was rooted in the Punjab more than those of Hindus or Muslims. The fact was that they were a minority in the Punjab, and in the context of India, a miniscule minority. Yet, that they were employed in huge numbers in the colonial army rendered them an important community. The Punjabi people, in general, were not consulted on this issue and most of them had no inkling that they would be required to leave their homes and ancestral abodes. (This point comes across forcefully and unequivocally, over and over, in my interviews with a cross-section of Hindus, Muslims, and Sikhs.) The worst aspect of the Partition process was that the much-discussed Radcliffe Award, which demarcated the international border between India and Pakistan, was made public on 17 August after Pakistan and India, on 14 August and 15 August respectively, had become independent. Its timing was most inappropriate, as suddenly, millions of people were on the wrong side of the line. The colonial government that could have maintained order was removed from the scene, and the displaced people became sitting ducks who could be easily targeted by men who had, in the preceding months, prepared to inflict violence on the other side.

The slaughter of innocents that followed was horrific, described to me with immense pain by the veteran journalist, writer and art critic Reginald Massey, during our interview on 5 July 2006 in his home in Llanidloes in mid-Wales. Massey belongs to a Punjabi Christian family in Lahore, among the few that decided to leave for India. His father, an officer in the Royal Indian Air Force, felt that Pakistani leaders, after the new country's founder, Jinnah's death, would succumb to the temptation of experimenting with an Islamic state. Such a state would inevitably set in motion processes that would put religious minorities in a vulnerable position. He put more faith in Indian Prime Minister Jawaharlal Nehru's secularism and decided to move to India in the beginning of September 1947. It was not easy for Massey's family to leave Lahore, though, as he portrays in his own words:

'Saying goodbye to Lahore in September 1947 was not easy. My mother was in tears. We left, not by train, because trains were being looted and burnt, but by *tonga*, a horse-drawn buggy. Flying from the *tonga* was a red cross. By proclaiming that we were Christians, we were safer. A few Hindus and Sikhs used the same ploy. Some employ the trappings of religion to kill, others use the trappings of religion to save their skins. I leave it to the moral philosophers to argue the pros and cons.

'The scenes on the road going past the Shalimar Gardens, Jallo, Batanagar and Burki were horrific. We were held up for hours. Hundreds of thousands were fleeing to India and hundreds of thousands were streaming into Pakistan. I saw corpses and mutilated limbs on either side of the road. The lamentations and the wailing were scenes from Dante's *Inferno*.

'After crossing the Wagah–Attari border into India the scenes were, if truth be told, even worse. Master Tara Singh's Akali cohorts massacred the poor Muslims of East Punjab indiscriminately. Muslim girls were raped by the thousands. Gandhi's cries and fasts for communal harmony made no impression whatsoever. The Punjab was convulsed with insanity.

'I can never, till my dying day, forgive the British who, in their utter panic, lost their nerve and left my country in such a blood-soaked mess. The Punjabi poet Amrita Pritam has said it all in her graphic and memorable verses.'

Such an appraisal has been repeatedly confirmed in interviews that I conducted, both before and after speaking to Massey. In this connection, I must acknowledge with great humility the meeting I had with Sikh elders in Gujjarwal village near Ludhiana, in January 2005. Their narration of events in Gujjarwal will be presented in a latter part of the book. Suffice it to say that a couple of them had shifted to Gujjarwal from areas left in Pakistan. They confirmed that the crimes committed against the Muslim minority in eastern Punjab were on a much greater scale. However, it remains a matter of dispute as to how many Hindus, Muslims, and Sikhs perished during the partition of the Punjab.

A Muslim Plan to eradicate Hindus and Sikhs from West Punjab

Two reports from the Indian side, on the Punjab, are currently available. Sardar Gurbachan Singh Talib collected data for the Sikh religious organisation, the Shiromani Gurdwara Prabandhik Committee (SGPC), and presented them in a 453-page book, *Muslim League Attack on Sikhs and Hindus in the Punjab 1947*. The report served to refute allegations that the Sikhs had a plan to eradicate Muslims from East Punjab. It argued that the main Muslim communal party, the Muslim League, wanted the whole of the Punjab and planned the expulsion of Sikhs and Hindus from the areas that were assigned to Pakistan. It blamed not only the Muslim League, its leaders and cadres, but virtually the whole Muslim community for participating in that project. The report contains a great deal of data but omits to mention the instances of Sikh actions that provoked the chain of events, that finally ended in the bloodbath at the time of the partition of the Punjab. The SGPC report stated:

> The Sikh (and Hindu) revenge was violent, swift and terribly destructive. Muslims of East Punjab had to pay for the misdeeds of their co-religionists in West Punjab and other parts of India. This was unfortunate and not very logical either, but in human affairs it is not always logic which governs conduct, and the mass mind, once it is roused to the pitch of fury, will grow terribly revengeful, unreasoning and hysterical. That is what happened to Muslims in East Punjab after the terrible sufferings undergone by Sikhs and Hindus at the hands of Muslims in West Punjab and in the North-Western Frontier Province (1991: 243-4).

Meanwhile, the other main Indian compilation of data is the 349-page long *Stern Reckoning*. In the report, Justice G.D. Khosla, formerly of the Punjab High Court, traced the history of Hindu–Muslim tension and mutual suspicion to at least the beginning of the twentieth century. He asserted that the events of 1947 had deep historical and religious roots. His findings affirmed that the Muslim League, its leaders and cadres, initiated the riots that continued as a one-sided affair until mid-August.

A Sikh Plan to eradicate all Muslims from East Punjab

The idea of a Sikh Plan to drive all Muslims out of East Punjab has been mentioned by many individuals who were directly involved in the events of that period. The late Harkishen Singh Surjeet, of the Communist Party of India (Marxist), witnessed the events and said in our interview:

'The communal attacks on the minorities were definitely planned. I know more about the persons involved in the eastern wing because I was there. I saw those dreadful acts with my own eyes. In that conspiracy, the Maharaja of Patiala was involved. The idea was that if the Muslims were driven out, the Sikhs could form their own state in eastern Punjab.'

No report comparable to those by SGPC and Khosla was published in Pakistan in the immediate years after the Punjab partition. However, the government published in 1948 three short reports: *Note on The Sikh Plan; The RSS in the Punjab*; and *The Sikhs in Action*. They were based on data collected by the Criminal Investigation Department while rioting was going on in the Punjab. They alleged that the Sikhs had a definite plan to eliminate Muslims from East Punjab and that the Hindu group, Rashtriya Swayamsevak Sangh (RSS), was behind many heinous bomb blasts and other assaults on Muslims. *Note on The Sikh Plan* says:

> The ultimate goal which the Sikhs had set before them seems to have been the establishment of Sikh rule in the Punjab. Their preparations to this end were aimed directly and exclusively against the Muslims. Whether the Hindus who formed the bigger minority in the Punjab, would ultimately have acquiesced in the fulfilment of Sikh ambitions at their expense, is doubtful; but for the time being they made common cause with the Sikhs. The activities and preparations of the two, therefore, run parallel to each other and even where active conspiracy between them is not evident, the fact that they regarded the Muslims as their common enemy created

mutual disposition towards collaboration which virtually amounted to a conspiracy and let [sic] to concerted effort (1948: 1-2).

Chaudhri Muhammad Ali, who represented Pakistan in the Steering Committee of the Partition Council set up by the colonial government, and was later Prime Minister of Pakistan (1955–56), alleged in his book, *The Emergence of Pakistan*, that the Sikh leadership at the highest level, especially the Maharajas of Patiala and Kapurthala, were involved in a macabre conspiracy to wipe out all Muslims from East Punjab.

The former Chief Justice of the Pakistan Supreme Court, Muhammad Munir, one of the two members nominated by the Muslim League to the Punjab Boundary Commission, admitted in his book, *From Jinnah to Zia,* that the first large-scale communal attack in Punjab occurred in the Rawalpindi region in March 1947 against Sikhs and Hindus, and its perpetrators were Muslims (1980: 17). He reiterated the charge that the Sikhs had a plan to eradicate all traces of Muslim presence in the eastern parts of Punjab.

Ian Coupland has also provided relevant insights in *The Master and the Maharajas: The Sikh Princes and the East Punjab Massacre of 1947* (2002: 657-704), about the elimination of Muslims from the princely states. The Sikh *jathas* were ideologically motivated to seek revenge for the excesses of Muslims in March 1947 in the Sikh villages of northern Punjab. Some of the *jathas* used Bren guns and even machine guns. He also asserts that the Muslims of the tiny Malerkotla state in East Punjab escaped annihilation because a kinsman of the nawab and office-bearer of the Ludhiana Muslim League encouraged the Muslims to arm themselves to face the Sikhs planning to attack Malerkotla (ibid.: 684).

It is very different from the prevalent theory, and one which the Sikhs proffered, that some three hundred years ago, Gobind Singh, the tenth guru of the Sikhs, had blessed the then Muslim ruler of Malerkotla for having opposed the torturing and bricking up alive of the guru's *sahibzadas* (sons). Therefore, the Sikhs would never attack Malerkotla or harm its Muslims. I heard this many times when I interviewed Sikhs who stood outside the boundaries and attacked Muslims trying to enter Malerkotla, but did not pursue them once they crossed the road into its territory.

It is also interesting to note that the Punjab Boundary Force (PBF) which was established (it lasted only for a few days from 1 August to 1 September 1947) to maintain law and order, was a poorly-equipped and undermanned body of Hindu, Muslim and Sikh troops, with very few British officers. It did save some lives in the twelve districts where it operated, but it had no jurisdiction in the princely states (Jeffrey, 1974: 491-520). That might also explain the high Muslim casualties in some of the princely states.

How many fatalities?

Sir Penderel Moon, a veteran of many years of service in the Punjab, noted that more Muslims perished as compared to Hindus and Sikhs put together (1998: 293). G.D. Khosla, who collected data on the Punjab riots mainly narrating the Hindu–Sikh suffering, also conceded that more Muslims could have died as a result of Hindu–Sikh retaliation against Muslim violence at the earlier stages of the communal violence (1989: 299). He said:

> The loss of Muslim life was not less than the loss of non-Muslim life in West Punjab. Indeed, there are many who boast that the total number of Muslims killed was more than the number of Hindus and Sikhs who perished in West Punjab, though the latter suffered greater losses in property. ... It must, however, be remembered that the attacks on the Muslims were by way of retaliation and began only after several months of a determined and sustained effort to drive the non-Muslims out of West Punjab, (Khosla, 1989: 289-90).

In an article presented at the thirty-fifth session of the Punjab History Conference, held in Patiala in March 2003, Bhai Aridaman Singh Jhubal confirmed that more Muslims died than Hindus and Sikhs. His assessment is based on the evidence presented in the *Encyclopaedia of Sikhism*, *Vol. III,* compiled by Professor Harbans Singh (2002: 122-23). Penderel Moon estimated 180,000–200,000 fatalities for the undivided Punjab and Bahawalpur state (1998: 293). G.D. Khosla suggested a figure of 500,000 (1989: 299). Lieutenant General (Retd) Aftab Ahmad Khan of the Pakistan Army, who was part of the Punjab Boundary Force and later of the joint operations of the Indian and Pakistan armies to supervise the transfer of people across the borders, wrote on 2 February 2007 that at least 500,000 Muslims died in East Punjab. He believed that Hindu–Sikh casualties were far less in the western Punjab.

Over the years, the estimate for fatalities has been climbing and some people have suggested a figure as high as two million (Talbot, 2008: 420). The exact figure will never be known, but one million is now considered a reliable estimate for the whole of India. Figures of 600,000, 800,000 and 1,000,000 have been suggested by Britons who were present in India at that time (Roberts, 1995: 129-130). Whatever the truth, the overwhelming majority of deaths took place in the Punjab.

How many crossed the border?

About the numbers of people who crossed the international border Penderel Moon wrote:

> Reliable figures are not available in regard to all matters, but it can be stated compendiously and with certainty that while Muslims lost the most lives, Hindus and Sikhs lost the most property. As regards the numbers of persons compelled to migrate, reasonably accurate figures are available. Between August 1947 and March 1948 about four and a half million Hindus and Sikhs migrated from West Pakistan to India and about six million Muslims moved in the reverse direction. A great part of this massive migration took place within only three months, between the middle of August and the middle of November (Moon, 1998: 268).

Shahid Javed Burki has calculated that a total of 14 million crossed the borders but he also includes non-Punjabis in the estimates (Burki 1980: 11). Ian Talbot, who has devoted his life to studying the Punjab, especially its partition in 1947, mentions 18 million for Muslims, Hindus and Sikhs of all nationalities, not just Punjabis (2008: 420). With regard to my query about how many could be from the Punjab alone he replied by email on 19 March 2010, saying that it was between nine and ten million. In 'A Note on the Statistics of Refugees and Evacuees' Problem', dated 31 October 1947, M. Hassan, Secretary, West Pakistan Board of Economic Inquiry, estimated that if all Muslims left East Punjab, West Punjab would receive 5.9 million Muslims. On the other hand, if all Hindus and Sikhs were to leave West Punjab, East Punjab would receive 3.8 million Hindus and Sikhs from West Punjab (Hassan, 1993: 16). It meant that potentially, at least 9.7 million Punjabis would be dislocated and forced to cross the new international border as a result of the partition of the Punjab alone. How many of them would perish was another question. Consequently, 9 to 10 million is a fairly accurate figure with regard to forced migration in the Punjab. Muhammad Waseem gives a figure of 5.3 million for Muslims from East Punjab who made their way to West Punjab and consequently constituted 25.6 per cent of its population (Waseem 1999: 211).

There was another angle to the Punjab partition: how particularly unsafe the situation was for women. For example, at least 90,000 of them were abducted by men of the enemy religions; some were recovered but not all. Author Ayesha Jalal believes that the assaults on women during those times were a display of masculinity. She writes, 'Men of all three religions delighted in their momentary sense of power over vulnerable women' (1998: 13).

Existing literature

Journalists Larry Collins and Dominique Lapierre published *Freedom at Midnight* (1975), a highly moving account of oral histories of the Partition riots all over India. It contains heart-wrenching accounts from the Punjab. The fiftieth anniversary of the partition of India, Punjab and Bengal in 1997 worked as a catalyst, as if voices long suppressed under the deadweight of emotions and strong feelings could not be suppressed any longer. Many interviews or oral histories were published after that in both India and Pakistan. In the same frame, Indian feminists of Punjabi origin made some path-breaking contributions. Urvashi Butalia's *The Other Side of Silence: Voices from the Partition of India* (1998); and Ritu Menon and Kamla Bhasin's *Borders and Boundaries* (1998) presented the trauma suffered by victims of Partition. They focussed on the suffering of women but because of visa constraints, could not collect data from the Pakistani Punjab, although their work was by no means meant to portray the agony of only one side.

Ian Talbot has pioneered several publications on the Punjab partition. He and Gurharpal Singh have edited *Region and Partition: Bengal, Punjab and the Partition of the Subcontinent* (1999), in which my own contribution on the arguments advanced by the various Punjabi parties and groups is included. Along with Shinder Thandi, he has also edited a collection of essays on the Partition – *People on the Move: Punjabi Colonial, and Post-Colonial Migration* (2004). Anders Bjorn Hansen's *Partition and Genocide: Manifestation of Violence in Punjab 1937-1947* (2002) looks at the fortnightly reports submitted by the chief secretaries of the Punjab to the viceroys between 1937 and 1947. Ahmad Salim has collected already published first-person accounts in *Lahore 1947* (2003). It is a useful compilation.

Kirpal Singh's *The Partition of the Punjab* (1989), provides a very useful overview by a historian of the machinery and mechanisms set up to bring about the partition of the province and the main decisions taken during that period. He mentions various estimates but does not take a stand himself. His collection, *Select Documents on Partition of Punjab–1947*, contains rare interviews that he conducted during his research on the Punjab partition. I met him in Chandigarh on 2 January 2004.

The government of Pakistan, for its part, published in 1993 *The Journey to Pakistan: A Documentation on Refugees of 1947,* a collection of first-person accounts by Muslim refugees. Another publication is *Disturbances in the Punjab,* published in 1995. Khawaja Iftikhar published in 1980 a report on the events of his former hometown, Amritsar. *Jabb Amritsar Jall Raha Tha* (*When Amritsar was Burning),* is the title of a painstaking effort to present the Muslim point of view on Amritsar. There is no doubt that it is written with deep emotions. I have yet to meet an Amritsari Muslim who does not mourn the loss of his beloved city, and Iftikhar captures that emotion very well. It was written at a time when General Muhammad Zia-ul-Haq was in power and Islamism was being promoted as state ideology. Moreover, in Afghanistan a jihad (holy war) had been launched with all the trappings of religious zeal, though its sponsors were not only Saudi Arabia but also the United States. Not surprisingly, the narrative is suffused with triumphant wording deriving from a belief in the inherent superiority in the battle of Muslims over

Hindus and Sikhs. Some of the language and description of events can be shocking, but the strength of the work lies in tracing witnesses all over Pakistan to build up the narrative.

In an extensive interview granted to me in April 2003, Iftikhar appeared a changed man. He began our discussion by saying that the people of Amritsar always believed in *muhabbat* and *shafqat* (love and affection). When I asked him if this applied to the Hindus and Sikhs of the city of his birth, he claimed that before the riots, the three communities lived in peace and harmony. The fact is that even when writing in a manner that makes Hindus and Sikhs appear cruel and crafty, and attacks on them justified, throughout the book Iftikhar had the integrity to mention by name Hindus and Sikhs who protected Muslims and thus saved many lives. He told me that he has been to Amritsar a number of times and taken his children with him as well. His old Hindu friends and their children showed him and his family respect that proved that Amritsaris are personifications of *muhabbat* and *shafqat*.

Muhammad Ayub Khan has written an account of what happened in Jullundur at the time of the Punjab partition. The book, one-sided though it is, provides fairly adequate details and includes much useful information. He states that when Prime Minister Nehru visited Jullundur, he ordered that the beleaguered Muslim community not be attacked. As soon as he left, however, Home Minister Sardar Patel arrived and reversed Nehru's instructions. It was then that a massacre of Muslims took place. In 2003, Hakim Muhammad Tariq Mehmood Abqary Mujadidti Chughtai published another collection of first-person accounts of East Punjab Muslims: *1947 ke Muzlumon ki Kahani Khud Muzlumon ki Zabani* (*The Story of the 1947 Atrocities from the Victims Themselves*).

Pakistani scholars have been slow to step into the field of Partition studies because unlike in India – where lamenting Partition is an essential element of the national psyche – in Pakistan, any mention of Partition as a human tragedy is viewed with suspicion. What is deplored by Hindus and Sikhs is presented as the liberation of the Muslim nation from the tyranny of Hinduism and the economic exploitation of the Muslim masses by Hindu and Sikh moneylenders. Still, even Pakistanis see 1947 as a tragedy too profound to be ignored, especially by the Punjabis. They, too, have begun to bring forth stories of Muslim suffering during that period.

Generally, Indian scholars, in consonance with the anti-colonial nationalist ideology of the Congress, emphasise a British hand in the division of India and of the Punjab. Pakistani scholarship also deplores the 'British conspiracy' by pointing to an example: the decision of the Radcliffe Award to give to India some Muslim-majority areas in the Punjab, especially district Gurdaspur, so that a direct road link could be established between India and Kashmir.

Partition studies, including those of the Punjab, have been undertaken mainly by historians. In recent times, though, social scientists have begun to take interest. They have focussed on the experiences of the survivors and observers of the partition events and incidents, rather than on the political game.

Contribution of this study

This is the first holistic and comprehensive case study of the Punjab partition. I crosschecked, when possible, important episodes in which eyewitness accounts have been collected from both sides. The main argument set forth is that the partition of India was a necessary but not sufficient basis for the partition of the Punjab. Placing this study in the context of the partition of India, the dynamics of the partition of the Punjab are identified primarily as conflicts and contradictions emanating among the leaders of, on the one hand, Hindus and Sikhs and, on the other, Muslims. A theoretical framework is propounded to examine the partition process as interplay between apprehensive religious groups, especially their leaders, fearful of an uncertain future; a waning colonial state authority; and the partisan role of state functionaries after the transfer of power to the Indian and Pakistani governments.

This book also sheds light on the merits of the allegations that both Muslims and Sikhs had a grand plan to eradicate unwanted groups from their territory – the Muslim League, against the Hindus and Sikhs from a united or divided Punjab, and the Sikhs, against the Muslims from East Punjab. In reality, this is what happened when the Punjab was partitioned. How and why? Secondly, the study addresses the much deeper question of identity, both individual and collective. Was the old Punjab a deeply divided society or a composite-plural one? To find an answer, the post-Partition politics of communal identity in East and West Punjab are briefly reviewed. The investigation also addresses the conceptual question as to whether the tragedies of the Partition should be described as genocide, or ethnic cleansing.

Research in both Punjabs against all odds

It is almost impossible for a Pakistani researcher to do fieldwork in the Indian Punjab, and likewise for an Indian in the Pakistani Punjab. Being a Swedish citizen has helped me escape the same treatment of Indian and Pakistani citizens by their bureaucracies. I could, therefore, travel to both India and Pakistan and talk to people, and have been able to present my findings based on fieldwork in both the Punjabs.

During my field visits, I was assisted in Pakistan (2003–05) by Ahmad Salim; in India (March 2004 and January 2005) by Mahinder Pal Singh (Vicky); and in East Punjab (November 2005) by Hitesh Gosain and Virender Singh.

Primary sources

The British have maintained extensive information on the Punjab situation as seen by their administrators and functionaries. The following official sources have been used extensively for this publication:

1. There is a complete record of the classified fortnightly reports (FRs) written by the Punjab governors and chief secretaries to the viceroys. They begin from April 1936 and the last one was written on 13 August 1947, the second last date for an officer of the colonial government to exercise authority in the Punjab. The governors were always British, while the chief secretaries were sometimes Indian. I have relied heavily on the FRs and special reports from the governors. They provide not only information on the political situation and riots, but also a clearer understanding of the thinking of the highest British officer posted in the Punjab. As the level of secrecy was total, Indian politicians were not privy to them at that time. Fortunately, all the FRs of the Punjab governors

were published by Lionel Carter of the British Library in several volumes between 2004 and 2007. Also including telegrams and special reports, this book series on the Punjab governors' FRs is a mine of information, now easily accessible. The FRs of the chief secretaries are mainly records of events, which are often available in the governors' FRs as well. I have used the latter sparingly. From 15 August 1947, the Indian and Pakistani governments took over, and from that time onwards, no such reports are known to have been kept, or at least they remain classified. The FRs filed by the Punjab governors are based on information gathered by intelligence agencies. Thus far, the FRs of the chief secretaries are available only on microfilm.

2. The British published the twelve-volume *The Transfer of Power 1942-7* during 1970–1983. Those volumes constitute the most exhaustive government record of events and negotiations dealing with the transfer of power to Pakistan and India. Documentation on the Punjab is a major portion of the twelve volumes. Most of the Punjab governors' FRs, telegrams, and special reports are also included in the twelve volumes. Moreover, Carter's collections of governors' FRs exclude the replies or comments from the viceroys or other British officials. Those have been accessed from the transfer-of-power volumes.

The problem is, of course, that from the time the authority of the British government over united India ended, official records of events subsequently in the two parts of the Punjab are still not available. This I checked by consulting colleagues in the two countries. The main killings took place after 14–15 August and were the product of coordinated activities of biased officials in the police and other government departments, activists of political parties, religious fanatics and criminal gangs. It is understandable that both the states, and especially the governments in the two Punjabs, are unwilling to divulge inculpating evidence against their functionaries.

There were various daily newspapers published from Lahore, the capital of undivided Punjab (and now of Pakistan Punjab). Fires raged in Lahore in 1947, destroying precious records, including periodicals. I have relied primarily on the pro-Congress English-language *The Tribune* and the pro-Muslim League, the *Pakistan Times*. Their files are available, though not always in complete form. However, we need to bear in mind that the press could report only under severe restrictions from the Punjab administration. In one sense, virtual censorship existed during the most critical periods when rioting was at its height. Besides these primary sources, I have benefited from a number of secondary sources that deal with the partition of India, as a whole, and the Punjab situation in particular.

Oral histories

Oral history, or personal narrative in the form of an open-ended, extensive interview with individuals directly witness to or victims of traumatic events, was employed effectively as research technique in several recent works on Partition. The present study utilises it amply too. In my opinion, the outstanding virtue of this technique is that it presents a personal, perhaps emotive, insight into the life story of the interviewee. He/she is not treated merely as a source or object of information, but as a subject who is intrinsic to the story he/she tells. Each such story is a living history to be read on its own merits.

The problem, of course, is how to choose the interviewees; each strategy has its strengths and weaknesses. It was easy to decide against the distribution of a questionnaire to a representative sample of the various Punjabi communities. People have great difficulty in talking about tragic and traumatic experiences, and are not likely to answer a set of questions with exclusive answers like 'Yes/No', or in terms of some continuum of intensity of an experience. Moreover, respondents cannot be expected to write down well-thought-out answers to questions posed by a stranger in a questionnaire.

In order to gain an in-depth response, it was important to collect oral histories. The main questions posed were the following:

1. Where and when were you born?
2. Was it a religiously mixed area or village or not?
3. How do you recall your relationship with people from the other communities?

4. When did the Muslim and Hindu–Sikh communities begin to be drawn away from each other?
5. Tell us what happened in 1947.
6. Did you know that you would have to abandon hearth and home?
7. What was the pattern of attacks; were outsiders involved or neighbours?
8. Can you name people from the political parties or the police and other functionaries who played some important role in fomenting communal conflict?
9. Can you name people who played an important role in saving lives of members of the other communities?
10. How do you explain the reasons for the partition of Punjab?

I let the interviewees narrate their story at their leisure. The average length of the interview was one hour. Questions were kept to a minimum. By comparing Hindu, Muslim and Sikh versions of the same events and relating them to other sources, such as newspaper reports, one can present a fairly reliable account. This has not been possible always, and in most cases, I have relied on the testimony of a single person if I felt that it was vital to shed light on some crucial event. I have been extremely careful in selecting only those examples which I intuitively felt were an honest attempt to recall the past. The observations of body language and the spoken word cannot be transferred to written text. Ideally, the interviews should have been video-recorded, though it was not possible mainly because of logistical constraints. Interviews were recorded on audio-cassettes instead. The aim was to interview as broad a selection of people as possible. Among the interviewees are individuals who even admit to having taken part in violent attacks, that led to many deaths. I have taken their permission to give their real names. In some cases, the respondents wanted to remain anonymous, and their request was respected.

We began by talking to people we knew. As we listened, new vistas opened up and we expanded our net to include more diverse opinions. We started in the cities and towns and then decided to visit some villages. Two colleagues, Ahmad Salim and Mahinder Pal Singh, would visit some villages and make initial enquiries, and then I would fly in from Sweden. We then visited, day after day, different towns and villages in the two

Punjabs. Considering that thousands of villages are to be found in both Punjabs, the selection was based partly on convenience, and partly on our understanding of the importance of certain areas during the riots. Contacts tend to produce more contacts, and that is how we went about looking for interesting respondents to our questions. Sometimes, I would just stop our vehicle in the middle of nowhere and talk to some old man.

Getting close to women in the Punjab is never easy for men, and even less so for complete strangers. Thus we spoke mostly to men. I believe women researchers have a definite advantage in approaching other women. Nevertheless, to try to compensate for the lack of women interviewees, the study draws on secondary literature to examine their sad plight during that period.

We were able to talk to politicians, retired senior bureaucrats, as well as other government functionaries, teachers, lawyers, peasants, members of the proletariat, writers, wrestlers, political workers, etc. Most of the people in the rural areas were illiterate. Almost all the interviews took place in Punjabi, which is my mother tongue. It was not unusual for old men to start weeping and I, too, was sometimes moved to tears; at other times I felt embarrassed and ashamed to be prying into such personal, harrowing experiences. Our interviewees belonged mostly to the age group of sixty-five to eighty-five. On a number of occasions I was simply in awe that people, then as young as three to five years, remembered the events of Partition most vividly and in detail.

This is not unthinkable, given that traumatic experiences register on the mind even at a very tender age. I accepted as true the accounts given by interviewees who were very young in 1947. Sometimes, when I checked the same story with the elder brothers or other members of the family, I found that the younger ones could give even more details and the elders would then confirm the memory.

I sincerely believe that almost all those people who volunteered to talk to us spoke with great honesty. To be sure, there were a few interviewees who were distorting facts or lying about something; they likely had a political agenda to advance. I believe an experienced researcher cannot be easily deceived in an interview. Others, perhaps, had more vague memories, and so tended to mix up dates and events. After all, there has been a long time lapse from 1947 to the year I conducted the interviews. (My earliest interviews are from 1997 and the latest from when this book was submitted for publication.)

Structure and organisation of the book

The investigation is organised in chronological order, on the assumption that actions and reactions over it amongst the contestants became a chain of intended and unintended consequences. The book first presents the conceptual and theoretical frameworks as well as historical background. Thereafter follow the events in the Punjab: both within it and pertaining to it, in Delhi, where the future of India was negotiated between the Congress party, the Muslim League and the Sikh leaders. The events are structured in three stages, representing the most crucial periods in the unfolding of the division of the Punjab. Stage One, The Punjab Bloodied, covers the period January 1945–March 1947. During this period, processes were initiated which set in motion polarisation between, on the one hand, Muslims and, on the other, Hindus and Sikhs. Such polarisation culminated in bloody rioting in March 1947. It was the first indication of the fissures that were developing, as well as of the colonial administration's inability to pre-empt the riots in time. Stage Two, The Partition Endgame, covers the period April 1947 to 16 August 1947, during which initially, the government managed to establish law and order but not peace, as incidents of killing and arson continued to take place in some places. Gradually, such incidents became more frequent, more gruesome and pitiless, escalating from the end of May. Sir Evan Jenkins ended his term as the last British Governor of the Punjab on 14 August. Stage Three, Ethnic Cleansing, covers the period 15 August to the end of December 1947. However, the Radcliffe Award, which fixed the international boundary between India and Pakistan in the Punjab, was made public only on 17 August. Immediately, violence increased dramatically, because now there was no doubt which town or village was in which country. Thereafter followed slaughters on both sides of the divided Punjab that reached genocidal proportions. By the end of 1947 or soon after, religious cleansing had been achieved in the two Punjabs.

References

Ali, Chaudhri Muhammad. *The Emergence of Pakistan,* Lahore: Research Society of Pakistan, 1973.

Burki, Shahid Javed. *Pakistan under Bhutto, 1971-1977*, New York: St. Martin's Press, 1980.

Butalia, Urvashi. *The Other Side of Silence: Voices from the Partition of India,* New Delhi: Penguin Books, 1998.

Chughtai, Hakim Muhammad Tariq Mehmood Abqary Mujadidi (compiler and editor). *1947 ke Muzalim ki Kahani khud Muzlumon ki Zabani* (The Story of the 1947 Atrocities from the Victims Themselves), Lahore: Ilm-o-Irfan Publishers, 2003.

Collins, Larry and Dominique Lapierre. *Freedom at Midnight*, New York: Avon Books, 1975.

Coupland, Ian. 'The Master and the Maharajas: The Sikh Princes and the East Punjab Massacres of 1947', *Modern Asian Studies*, Vol. 36, No. 3, Cambridge: Cambridge University Press, 2002.

Hansen, Anders Bjorn. *Partition and Genocide: Manifestation of Violence in Punjab 1937-1947,* New Delhi: India Research Press, 2002.

Iftikhar, Khawaja. *Jabb Amritsar Jall Raha Tha (When Amritsar was Burning).* Lahore: Khawaja Publishers, 1991.

Jalal, Ayesha. 'Nation, Reason and Religion: The Punjabis' Role in the Partition of India', *Economic and Political Weekly, Vol. xxxiii, no. 12, August 8, 1998*, Mumbai, 1998.

Jeffrey, Robin. 'The Punjab Boundary Force and the Problem of Order, August 1947', *Modern Asian Studies*, Vol. 8, No. 4, Cambridge: Cambridge University Press, 1974.

Jhubal, Bhai Aridaman Singh. 'Partition of Punjab: Role of Sikh Leadership; S. Amar Singh Jhubal and his Family', *Journal of Sikh Studies, Vol. XXVII, No. 2*, Amritsar: Guru Nanak Dev University, 2002.

Khan, Muhammad Ayub. *Tarikh-i-Pakistan Aur Jullundur* (The Pakistan Movement and Jullundur), Lahore: Asatair, 2002.

Khosla, Gopal Das. *Stern Reckoning: A Survey of the Events Leading up to and following the Partition of India,* New Delhi: Oxford University Press, 1989, first published in 1949.

Menon, Ritu and Bhasin, Kamla. *Borders and Boundaries: Women in India's Partition,* New Delhi: Kali for Women, 1998.

Munir, Muhammad. *From Jinnah to Zia,* Lahore: Vanguard Books Ltd, 1980.

Robert, Andrew. *Eminent Churchillians*, London: Phoenix, 1995.

Salim, Ahmad (ed.). *Lahore 1947*, Lahore: Sang-e-Meel Publications, 2003.

Singh, Kirpal. *The Partition of the Punjab*, Patiala: Patiala University, 1989.

———. *Select Documents on Partition of Punjab – 1947*, Delhi: National Book Shop, 1991.

Talib, S. Gurbachan. *Muslim League Attack on Sikhs and Hindus in the Punjab 1947,* New Delhi: Voice of India, 1991, first published in 1950.

Talbot, Ian and Gurharpal Singh (eds). *Region and Partition: Bengal, Punjab and the Partition of the Subcontinent,* Karachi: Oxford University Press, 1999.

Talbot, Ian and Shinder Thandi (eds). People on the Move: Punjabi Colonial, and Post-Colonial Migration, Karachi: Oxford University Press, 2004.

Tanwar, Raghuvendra. *Reporting the Partition of Punjab: Press, Public and Other Opinions*, New Delhi: Manohar, 2006.

Waseem, Mohammad, *'Partition, Migration and Assimilation: A Comparative Study of Pakistani Punjab'* in Talbot, Ian and Singh, Gurharpal (eds). *Region and Partition: Bengal, Punjab and the Partition of the Subcontinent,* Karachi: Oxford University Press, 1999.

Official documents

Carter, Lionel (compiler and editor). *Punjab Politics 1936-1947, Governors' Fortnightly Reports and other Key Documents*, all volumes, New Delhi: Manohar, 2004–2007.

Disturbances in the Punjab, Islamabad: National Documentation Centre, 1995.

The Journey to Pakistan: A Documentation on Refugees of 1947, Islamabad: National Documentation Centre, 1993.

Note on the Sikh Plan, Lahore: Government Printing Press, 1948.

The RSS in the Punjab, Lahore: Government Printing Press, 1948.

The Sikhs in Action, Lahore: Government Printing Press, 1948.

Mansergh, N. and E.W.R. Lumby (ed.). *Transfer of Power* (in twelve volumes), vol. 1–4; Mansergh, N. and P. Moon vol. 5–12.

Interviews

Harkishen Singh Surjeet, New Delhi, 21 October 1999

Professor Kirpal Singh, Chandigarh, 2 January 2005

Reginald Massey, Llanidloes, mid-Wales on 5 July 2006; also via email on 4 August 2007

Lieutenant General Aftab Ahmad Khan, letter from Lahore, dated 2 February 2007

Ian Talbot, email response from Southampton, UK, 19 March 2010

1

A THEORY OF ETHNIC CLEANSING

FORCED MIGRATION, ETHNIC CLEANSING, AND GENOCIDE ARE processes whose inter-connections are elaborated in this chapter, in order to develop a theoretical framework for analysing the events in the Punjab in 1947. An ethnic group, it may be noted, comprises individuals who believe they share a common ancestry. It may not be strictly true but putative common ancestors tend to generate emotive feelings of solidarity. When similar feelings exist between people who share the same religion or language, or some other such attribute, it is considered to be an ethnic group distinct from others. When two or more such groups – deriving from ethnic, religious, sectarian or any such criteria – clash with one another, the generic term to describe such events is 'ethnic conflict' (Ahmed, 1998: 19-38). Suffice it to say that ethnic cleansing is a generic term that covers removal of a distinct population – on the basis of ethnic, religious, sectarian and other such factors – from a specific territory. In the case of the Punjab conflict, it was the religious factor which became the basis of politically-relevant ethnicity.

The Punjab partition puzzle is that the division of the province was agreed at the all-India level as part of the overall agreement to partition India. It was not, however, a decision that, once agreed at the level of high politics, became an ordinary administrative task. In the Punjab itself, the Sikh leaders were adamant that if India is divided on a religious basis, so must the Punjab. The Sikhs were, however, a small minority of the population of the Punjab. Any division of the Punjab – that was negotiated and not simply imposed by the Sikhs – would have divided them. On the other hand, the Muslims constituted a slight majority of the Punjab population. The Muslim leaders wanted the whole of

Punjab in Pakistan but agreed to its partition because otherwise there would not have been any Pakistan. The partition of the Punjab could have been averted if the three major communities of Hindus, Muslims and Sikhs had shared a Punjabi cultural identity that was strong and resilient enough to transcend their religious identities. Another possibility was of the Muslim majority and the Sikh minority agreeing to keep the Punjab united. That would have created the substantial majority needed to oppose the partition of the Punjab. It may still have been partitioned, but much farther to the east, where the Hindi-speaking Hindu Jats were a majority. The colonial authorities at the centre, headed by the viceroy, did not believe that wholesale transfer of power on ethnic grounds would take place, though the Punjab government had been warning about large-scale violence if the Punjab was partitioned. When the Partition process culminated, unwanted religious minorities had been eradicated on both sides. Why did that transpire?

A preliminary answer would be that the large-scale attacks on predominantly Sikh villages in northern Punjab in early March 1947 by armed Muslim mobs generated enough bad blood between these two communities to prove inadequate the initiatives that were taken later to mend the harm done to their relationship. Rather, the Hindus and Sikhs closed ranks, spelling doom for the prospects of a united Punjab.

This study seeks to advance the frontiers of knowledge on the partition of the Punjab by approaching it as a process, with a beginning and an ending. It comprised actions and reactions that produced both intended and unintended consequences in the context of contested nationalism and conflicting claims to territory. The alienation of communities began to take shape with the introduction of violence in March 1947. It triggered forced migration from unsafe and vulnerable places to safer havens. Such movements of people intensified and multiplied over the weeks and months that followed. The final outcome was 'ethnic cleansing' on both sides of the divided Punjab.

Forced migration

Migration of individuals, groups, communities and even whole societies have taken place throughout the ages and across all the regions and continents of the world. Across world history, the search for food, desire for conquest, escape from poverty and persecution, and a host of other reasons have resulted in migratory movements of people. It is useful to distinguish between forced and voluntary migration, although in some cases it is difficult to do so. Normally, the decision to uproot one's self from one's homeland is emotionally taxing, even when the decision has been freely made. Nowadays, this is perhaps less true of the industrialised urban cities of the West, where people move quite frequently. The fact of community 'rootedness', however, is still alive. Historically, even nomadic people moved within familiar surroundings and followed seasonal cycles. They resisted being forced to move out of those natural habitats in which they roamed. This sentiment has continued to prevail, and perhaps even been strengthened, since territorial states and other modern inventions have begun to restrict the free movement of naturally wandering peoples.

In agrarian societies, like the Punjab at the time of Partition in 1947, mobility was rather limited. Most people lived in rural communities in which close identification with the village and the local *biradari* (kinship lineage) ties constituted their universe of activity and thought. The relationship with local entities was organic, and for the landowning castes especially, an inalienable part of their identity. The situation in the towns and the cities of the Punjab of 1947 was not very different. Although Punjabis from several districts were enlisted in the British Indian army and served in different parts of the subcontinent – many even in foreign lands – the connection with their ancestral homes remained steadfast. Therefore, when people were forced to leave their homes at the time of Partition, this proved to be a shattering experience. This comes out vividly in the interviews I conducted: most people continued to identify with the locality or house where they were born, and which their families had taken pains to build. Even among poorer people, the attachment to their ancestral *mohalla* (neighbourhood or locality) remained strong over the years. Many of the interviewees would inevitably give in to crying when talking about their lost homes.

Ethnic cleansing

Ethnic cleansing is the epitome of forced transfer of a population, but of a special type. It is derived from a concern to purify the assumed 'exclusive homeland' of a people or religious community, or a nation of extraneous or alien elements. Behind such an urge is the problem of conflicting ethnicity: whereas an 'ethnic group' is a group of people who believe they share a common descent and culture, the term 'ethnicity' is a generic description for such strong feelings and emotions deriving also from a common religion, sect, or language (Ahmed, 1998: 26). It is a subjective feeling and derives from real or felt discrimination and injustice. 'Ethnic cleansing' is also a generic term or blanket concept, which covers not just racially-motivated removals of population, but those motivated by religious, sectarian, racial, linguistic or any such ascriptive factors. In the case of the Punjab, the 'cleansing' was based on religion because most of the people were of the same highly mixed and variegated ethnic pool. In other words, religion became the problematic ethnicity that needed to be cleansed in order to establish an imagined pure nation.

Andrew Bell-Fiakoff's book is called, *Ethnic Cleansing* (1999), yet the discussions use 'population cleansing' as the generic term because of the misunderstanding which the term 'ethnic' can cause. Bell-Fiakoff finds population cleansing a recurring phenomenon throughout history and well into modern times. As early as the ninth century BC, the Assyrians, during the reign of Assurnasirpal II (883–859) resettled up to 4.5 million conquered people. Indeed, the Assyrians seemed to have indulged in ethnic cleansing on a grand scale and as a constant policy. The practice was continued by many later dynasties in the Middle East during antiquity. At that time, the main consideration was to forestall rebellion (ibid.: 7-10). During the Middle Ages, religious concerns with purity and adherence to dogma, rather than the fear of rebellion by deviant groups, resulted in the state attempting ethnic cleansing in the form of religious cleansing (ibid.: 11).

In this regard, we can mention the expulsion of Jews and Muslims from Spain at the end of the fifteenth century – a religious cleansing carried out with great determination and motivated by a fanatical concern for the purity of the Catholic Church (Mann, 2005: 45-48). We find similar attempts in the Islamic world. At the beginning of the sixteenth century, the Safavids came to power in Iran and imposed Shi'ism as a state religion, requiring the Sunni majority to convert or leave. While most people converted to Shi'ism, there was also an exodus to neighbouring Afghanistan and the Indian subcontinent (Abisaab, 2004). For their part, Shias had been subjected to forced assimilation in Egypt and North Africa during the time of Saladin.

Bell-Fialkoff asserts that in order for a forced transfer of population to be classified as cleansing, it must additionally be based on some particular trait or traits that make it undesirable. He employs the more neutral concept of 'population cleansing' to cover all sorts of deliberate removal of a particular group of people from a territory. He does not include the use of force as a necessary condition to achieve ethnic cleansing and suggests that where two or more groups cannot agree to live peacefully in the same territory, some formula for transferring them should be attempted (which one and on what basis, he does not discuss). The essential point of his argument, however, is that the cleansing of a people from a territory requires action on the part of the state and its functionaries. He writes:

'Population cleansing is a planned, deliberate removal from a certain territory of an undesirable population distinguished by one or more characteristics such as ethnicity, religion, race, class, or sexual preference. These characteristics must serve as the basis for removal for it to qualify as cleansing' (Bell-Fialkoff, 1999: 3).

In his major work on ethnic cleansing, Michael Mann (2005) asserts that in the modern era, the practice represents the 'dark side of democracy'. It takes place 'where ethnicity trumps class as the main form of social stratification, in the process capturing and channelling classlike sentiments towards ethnonationalism' (ibid.: 5). It is the result of the idea of majority rule, or the power of the people, being confused with the power of the ethnic group. When two or more ethnic groups lay claim to the same territory and want to establish their exclusive state over it, the result is murderous ethnic cleansing. Organised violence is employed in the name of some exclusive ethno-nationalist version of democracy. Thus, democracy assumes an ethnicised character and the weak group has to give way or face mass slaughter. This observation of Mann is significant. However, in the conceptual framework of his book, he further distinguishes between the following: ethnicity (a group defining itself or defined by others as sharing common descent and culture); ethnocide (destruction of the culture of a people); genocide (the intentional killing by the majority of a minority); and ethnic cleansing. Mann seems to consider ethnic cleansing and genocide as interchangeable terms, especially if ethnic cleansing becomes what he calls 'murderous ethnic cleansing' (ibid.: 10-18). Indeed, the distinction between ethnic cleansing and genocide is not easily drawn in concrete situations. We shall address this problem later.

It is notable that since the worldwide rise of nationalism in the nineteenth century, ethnic cleansing has often been the result of an ultra-nationalist party or movement employing force to achieve congruence between state and nation. What most researchers emphasise is that ethnic cleansing is not possible without state functionaries exploiting their power and authority to rid the country of people considered alien and unwanted because of their race, religion, sect, or language (Naimark, 2001). The American journalist Roy Gutman (1993) notes that Serbian ultra-nationalists invented the term 'ethnic cleansing' as a euphemism to conceal the random slaughter, arbitrary executions, systematic rape and castration, and wholesale deportations, which they committed in Bosnia–Herzegovina during 1992–3, mainly against Muslims but also against Croats (ibid.: vii). Some 200,000 to 250,000 Muslims perished during that period, and many times more were driven from their ancestral homes. Hitherto, notwithstanding conflicting interpretations of history and of religious faith, a certain degree of actual intermixing had occurred between communities through inter-marriage and, in the Communist era, the adoption of cosmopolitan values and ideological notions. The Serbian ultra-nationalists directed their fury towards attempts to demolish all traces of such hybridisation. Their intention was undoubtedly to eradicate all traces of a people from a region considered fit only for 'pure' Serbs (ibid.: xxvii-xxxi).

Genocide

The term 'genocide', like 'ethnic cleansing' is of recent origin; it is, however, an equally ancient vice of human civilisation. First coined by the Polish jurist Raphael Lemkin in 1944 to designate the destruction of a nation or an ethnic group, the term 'genocide' was given legal recognition at the Nuremberg Trials of 1945 to '47. The subjects of those trials were members of the Nazi Party who participated in mass murder and other atrocities against civilian populations and racial and ethnic minorities before and during World War II. The cruel exactions committed by Japanese forces in China and other parts of eastern and south-eastern Asia during roughly the same period also led to key Japanese figures in authority being tried and punished after the war. International law gave proper legal recognition to the concept of genocide on 9 December 1948, when the United Nations Convention on the Prevention and Punishment of the Crime of Genocide was signed (a treaty ratified in 1951 by the required number of member states).

The Genocide Convention proffers a wide definition of genocide, taken to mean 'any of the following acts committed with intention to destroy, in whole or in part, a national, ethnical, racial or religious group as such:

1. Killing members of a particular group;
2. Causing serious bodily or mental harm to members of that group;
3. Deliberately inflicting on the group such conditions of life calculated to bring about its physical destruction in whole or in part;
4. Imposing measures intended to prevent births within that group;
5. Forcibly transferring children of the group to another group.'

Franck Chalk and Kurt Johansson (1990) find evidence of genocide even in pre-history, in violent conflict between nomads and settled agrarian peoples. Thus, the defeated people were killed or sold in slavery. The aim was to eliminate a threat. These authors call the excesses of the Assyrians acts of genocide, while Bell-Fialkoff calls the same phenomenon ethnic cleansing. Other reasons for committing genocide include terrorising and subjugating a people. The Mongol warlord Genghis Khan is said to have perfected this technique. A third type of genocide is committed to acquire economic wealth; once again, this was practised in the distant past. A fourth type of genocide has to do with the implementation of the beliefs, theory or ideology of the perpetrators; their victims are their fellow citizens rather than outsiders. It has been used against heretics and other social hate-figures, such as witches, who were burnt in thousands by church authorities. All these four types of genocide reached full development during the period of nation-states (ibid.: 33-40).

Distinguishing ethnic cleansing from genocide

It is not always possible, in a given historical situation, to determine whether the intention was to rid unwanted people from a territory or to destroy them physically. In practical terms, extreme violence may result from the resistance put up by the opposite group, or the perpetrators in the field may employ excessive force, or the undesirable people may not be able to cross over to safety into another area or country. In all such situations, the result may be veritable genocide. On the other hand, whereas the intention may be physically to exterminate an unwanted group, the agency that wants to achieve it may not have the resources and capability to put such a plan in action. Consequently, the target group may escape by crossing over to safe territory. In all cases of ethnic cleansing and genocide, the type of weapons and technology accessible in a conflict plays an important role.

Even the most notorious case of genocide – the Jewish holocaust – is viewed by some scholars as a policy initially aimed to drive Jews out of Germany and Europe (Gellately, 2003: 246-52; Melson, 1992). It resulted in genocide when the possibilities for Jews to seek refuge were denied by unsympathetic governments of other states. In ideological terms, there is no doubt that the Nazis' 'final solution' unmistakably aimed at the liquidation of the Jews and gypsies as unwanted races. Therefore, their organised and systematic annihilation in the concentration camps is indicative that genocide was closer to their real intention (Lang, 2003). It is therefore possible to get some clue about intentionality from ideological statements and propaganda. But genocide is often carried out in great secrecy, and terms like 'ethnic cleansing' may be used to deceive the world. Some scholars do not think that genocide needs to be determined only by declared intention. They focus on the end product – if the deaths caused by concerted violent action against a people are massive and incontrovertibly barbarous, then genocide has occurred (Jonassohn and Björnson, 1999).

In this regard, we also need to keep in mind that ethnic cleansing and genocide may be the end product of the complete breakdown of law and order, after protracted negotiations between contestants fail to reach an agreement on a power-sharing formula within the established boundaries of the existing state system. In other words, ethnic cleansing and genocide may be the unintended consequences of failed negotiations, rather than of premeditated plans to achieve them. In any case, it is important that ethnic cleansing and genocide be kept apart conceptually. 'Ethnic cleansing' can be understood as the wider and more general term relevant to understand the implications of contested nationalism. It has more to do with the security concerns of apprehensive groups and their notions of state and nation building. On the other hand, genocide ideologically aims at the destruction of a people rather than simply forcing them to exit from a territory. However, as argued above, the borders between the two can be blurred and they can also be placed along a continuum with forced migration at one end and genocide at the other, and ethnic cleansing in the middle.

The following definition of ethnic cleansing can be useful to distinguish it from genocide:

> Ethnic cleansing is a more or less coordinated coercion employed by an agency to empty a specific territorial space of unwanted individuals and groups marked by some ethnic, religious, sectarian and other such cultural factors. Ethnic cleansing can be achieved peacefully through transfer of populations but in case such an arrangement is not in hand terror, including burning, killing, raping and other such extremist means are widely employed to achieve it. Such measures are employed because the undesirable people normally resist forced expulsion from their ancestral abodes and homes. Whereas all acts

of genocide aim at the destruction of a people and include ethnic cleansing the latter is focused on the removal of a people from a territory by all means.

Why does group conflict take place and when does it become violent?

While forced migration, ethnic cleansing and genocide are terrible misdeeds, we need a psycho-sociological explanation as to why groups are formed and why they are drawn towards tension and conflict against one another, and indeed the circumstances in which such relations result in ethnic cleansing and/or genocide. Beginning with the individual, we note that human beings are normally gregarious, and shared identity caters to their psychological or emotional needs to build solidarity and feel secure. Tribe, clan, language, belief in common ethnic origin, religion, caste and so on, have been the factors around which collective identity has been formed and continues to be, at present. The propensity to associate with those that one identifies with simultaneously involves the exclusion of exogenous groups and peoples. Such identification and classification has been practised in almost all known human societies, whatever their level of development and stratification (Ahmed, 1998: 4). In ontological terms, groups are not simply the sum-total of members. They possess a personality and identity of their own, and the survival of the group in relation to individual members and vis-à-vis other groups is innate to that personality and identity. However, groups expand and contract through the incidents of population growth or disease and defeat.

Now, individual action rarely suffices to make effective demands on state and society. Therefore, human beings almost invariably act together in groups in the pursuit of their political objectives. Shared identity plays an important role in connecting them to each other. It thus helps build solidarity networks. In terms of politics, the study of identity is interesting as it explains how individuals and groups invoke it to justify their claims to power within a state or as separate nations entitled to independent statehood. The question, however, remains: is group formation a voluntary choice or are individuals born into groups and remain in them permanently? In social science literature, one can conventionally locate two contrasting perspectives to group-formation and identification: the primordialist and the instrumentalist.

The primordialists argue that ethno-centrism is natural to human beings; individuals have always been grouped together on the basis of shared objective characteristics such as common descent, skin colour, tribe, and religion; each group develops a sense of identity and ethnicity as it faces, in different historical contexts, challenges to its survival. Thus the collective memory of such experiences becomes the reference-point for developing strategies to ensure the security of the group (Connor, 1994; Geertz, 1963; Shils, 1957). On such a point of view, ethno-centrism and tribalism is intrinsic to human nature. A stronger version of the primordialist conception of groups known as sociobiology is premised on the normality of ethno-nationalism. It holds a pessimistic view about durable peace between disparate groups (Kecmanovic, 1996; Kellas, 1998: 13-14). Such arguments suggest even more forcefully that separating them and consolidating them as exclusive nation-states is the best recipe to preserve the peace. However, the principle of separate states for discrete groups would mean thousands of states, as more than 8,000 ethnic groups have been identified in the world population.

In contrast, the instrumentalists assert that identity is fluid and easily pliable, and therefore contains no permanent boundaries. Rather, competition over power and resources between the elite and elite factions makes political entrepreneurs exploit shared cultural factors to create a new identity, in order to mobilise support for their agendas. On the latter view, therefore, ethnic identity is merely a political instrument rather than some objective and intrinsic property of human nature. It is when political leaders manipulate the so-called objective factors and cultural groups are animated with hostile propaganda that they develop subjective awareness about their differences and are drawn into conflict (Brass, 1991; Steinberg 1981; Young 1976). The instrumentalists view identity as constructed (though not invented). Ethnicity, according to this view, does not have an independent role or standing and can be made sense of only in the wider political context. It is not different from other political affiliations, such as ideology, economic interests, and so on. The instrumentalist approach is critiqued for ignoring the relational nature of identity.

Moreover, critics say, individual identity is almost never unidimensional. Each individual bears several identities and the context determines which factor is relevant at a given time. For example, a person can be a Punjabi by language and ethnicity, a Muslim in terms of inherited religious affiliation and Sunni in terms of the sectarian divisions within the Muslim community. Someone wanting to categorise all speakers of Punjabi together will include him and thus objectify his identity as a Punjabi. However, for him, his religion, sect, or caste could be even more important, or, alternatively speakers of the Punjabi language may not pay special attention to the fact that he is a native speaker of their language. They may like to classify him according to some other criterion. Thus, individual identity is relational and varies from situation to situation. Consequently, the type of trust and solidarity an individual can invoke in different situations also varies.

One can extend the same logic to the relational and multidimensional nature of ethnic groups. Relations between them are situational and contextual as well, and the importance of their attributes also vary at different times and in different places. Thus, the Catholic and Protestant distinction once wreaked havoc on European societies, but such differences have declined in most places because of secularisation. It does not mean that Catholics and Protestants have ceased to exist as cultural entities, but that such distinctions no longer result in discriminatory citizenship or persecution of one group by the other. In Northern Ireland, some vestiges of the recent animosity do from time to time burst into violence, but it seems that if power-sharing stabilises, their religious differences need not spiral out into violent conflict.

One can also imagine that after the 11 September 2001 terrorist attacks on the United States, tension and mutual suspicion between Christians and Muslims have sharpened, but that does not mean that within the world of Islam, all Muslims have begun to close ranks or build solidarity. The notoriously harsh treatment of Muslim workers in the oil-rich Arab states can easily belie any naïve belief in Muslim solidarity. Similarly, Hindus probably share the fear of a terroristic attack by Muslim groups based in Pakistan, but among themselves their caste and regional differences continue to produce volatile situations. The attacks on migrants from northern India to Mumbai by the hardcore Shiv Sena, that represents rabid Maharashtrian nationalism, are cases in point.

Thus, the relational, contextual and multidimensional nature of group identities is important to keep in mind, even when religious differences seemed to be the organising criteria for group identities in the pre-partition Punjab. In other words, notwithstanding the overwhelming evidence of communal killings that took place in the Punjab in 1947, there is no reason to believe that such a gory outcome was inevitable.

The context of ethnic conflict

Assuming that ethnicity is relational, the situations or contexts in which violent ethnic conflict takes place is also important, in that diversity of identities does not automatically mean they will clash. David A. Lake and Donald Rothschild focus on the historically embedded social conditions in which ethnic conflict assumes extreme forms. They observe:

> We argue that ethnic conflict is not caused directly by intergroup differences, "ancient hatreds" and centuries-old feuds... Instead, we maintain that ethnic conflict is most commonly caused by collective fears of the future. As groups begin to fear for their physical safety, a series of dangerous and difficult-to-resolve strategic dilemmas arise that contain within them the potential for tremendous violence. As information failures, problems of credible commitment, and the security dilemma takes hold, the state is weakened, groups become fearful, and conflict becomes likely. Ethnic activists and political entrepreneurs, operating within groups, reinforce those fears of physical insecurity and cultural domination and polarise society. Political memories, myths and emotions also magnify these fears, driving groups further apart. Together, these between-group and within-group strategic interaction produce a toxic brew of distrust and suspicion that can explode into murderous violence, even the systematic slaughter of one people by another (1998: 4).

They emphasise that such pathological situations trap not only individuals and groups but also their leaders (ibid.: 3-23). The historically embedded social conditions can vary across cases, but in the context of the Punjab, Lake and Rothschild's description comes very close to the situation in the Punjab in 1947.

The plural society

Leo Kuper (1982) put forth the idea of a plural society as the structural base for explaining why apparently peaceful multi-ethnic and multi-religious societies implode into violent conflict accompanied by genocide. A plural society is one which is characterised by the presence of identifiable groups and persistent and pervasive cleavages between those groups, deriving from racial, ethnic and religious differences. Often the cleavages are concomitant with inequalities in economic advancement and opportunities, and in political clout. For example, Hindus and Sikhs, on the one hand, and Muslims on the other, would draw water from different wells. The untouchables would use a different well too. Also, because of the strict Hindu dietary regulations, they would ordinarily not eat with Muslims. Even orthodox Sikhs who were vegetarians would not eat with Muslims. Such differences, apparently, were accepted as given rules of conduct based on tradition and therefore not resented.

Such societies may remain peaceful for long periods of time, but under stress they can suddenly implode. The result can be genocide of the vulnerable group. Kuper maintains that plural societies predate the colonial intervention but colonial policy and the processes of change exacerbate communal tensions, and when the colonial power withdraws, they explode into genocidal violence (ibid.: 57-59). Such structural basis for violent conflict has been described by other writers as deeply-divided societies, or segmented societies, and so on.

Kuper further observes that massive acts of violence are impossible without the involvement of state functionaries. But even ordinary members of society can be galvanised into committing atrocities against groups perceived to be enemies and threats to their existence. This is true of even the Punjab situation, but the circumstances in which such desperate pathological behaviour occurs need to be probed and understood. He presents the Punjab as a typical case of a plural society which erupted violently in 1947 (ibid.: 65-67). He does, however, mention that not all people acted in a brutal manner against members of rival groups.

In order to avoid confusion, we need to keep in mind that a plural society is not the same as a pluralist society; the latter carries positive connotations and is often used as a synonym for stable multicultural societies. The pluralist society is supposed to be based on equal rights of citizenship accompanied by cultural or communal diversity, and is celebrated as an accomplishment of the post-war democracies in the industrialised West. Kuper's plural society is the opposite of the pluralist society.

Punjab: A composite, traditional multicultural society

The description of the Punjab as a plural society is not accepted by some scholars. They point out that from the time of the Mughals (1526–1857) the Punjab had been developing a distinct composite identity whose resilience is attributed to shared culture and traditions of mutual accommodation being strongly entrenched in the social practice of the various religious communities (Ballard, 1999:7-24; Grewal, 2004: 12). A stringent definition of a composite Punjabi culture has not been developed, but it seems to mean that shared language and common festivals mitigated the divisions of religion and caste (Williams, 2004). In fact, sometimes, common patrimonial lineages such as among the very large agricultural caste of Jats (Jatts in Punjabi) who were both Muslim and Sikh, or Rajputs who were both Muslim and Hindu, helped create ties of sympathy. However, this was not universally true: it could also create resentment and alienation, especially among upper-caste Hindus whose relatives may have converted to Islam. But, as mentioned earlier, none of these factors applied universally throughout the Punjab or even in local conditions such as villages.

My own understanding of the pre-Partition composite Punjabi culture is that because none of the three religions were organised in terms of national ecclesiastical bureaucracies, the priests were also local people rooted in the immediate communities. Their role was largely ceremonial for performing the rituals of worship, marriage, births and deaths. Additionally, belief in holy men and evil spirits was widespread and that meant that people sought blessing across religious divides. Moreover, traditional medicine men and doctors – the Hindu and Sikh *vaids* and the Muslim *hakims* – always received patients from all communities. The treatment was cheap and often even free. This tradition continued even when modern, educated doctors established their practices. Finally, teachers – Hindus, Muslims, Sikhs, Christians – were held in great respect by all pupils.

The organic nature of pre-Partition Punjab society helped people circumvent the strictures of orthodoxy and relate to each other in a friendly manner. Therefore, although Punjab society was plural in that the different communities were identifiable, it was also cemented together by strong emotional and cultural bonds deriving from shared spiritual and moral traditions. Consequently, the factors that led to an implosion within that composite Punjab have to be identified within the power struggle and political ambitions of elite leaders in the context of fast deteriorating state authority, and not among the masses.

Paul Brass has described the very large loss of life in the Punjab as 'retributive genocide'. However, it was not the product merely of some spontaneous or natural urge for revenge, asserts Brass. Rather, it comprised a complex interplay between, on the one hand, identity, prestige, culture and on the other, the planning and diverse objectives that the different actors involved in the crimes sought to achieve. The chain of events were several and different subjects and objects perceived them in very different and diverse ways (Brass, 2003: 77-97).

Towards a theory of ethnic cleansing

We start with a situation in which uncertainty, anxiety, fear and suspicion begin to have adverse effects on relations between communities conscious of their differences despite common cultural traits. While there are various circumstances in which relations between different groups change from peaceful to conflict-prone, some of the more significant factors that lead them to violent conflict are negative historical, socio-economic and cultural factors converging and the old order on which their peaceful co-existence rested, no longer being able to reproduce it along the established lines.

In such circumstances, some degree of planning becomes necessary to meet the threats and challenges that have emerged. On such a basis alliances may be formed between different groups, if more than two are involved in the contested claims to territory and national rights. If nothing is done to assuage the apprehensions of individuals, they are likely to seek closer contact with their co-religionists or sectarian affiliates or whatever else is the binding tie for presumed social solidarity. But consciousness of changed circumstances may not suffice to produce politically significant behaviour. In most cases, such behaviour requires action on the part of leaders, activists and cadres backed by some degree of organisational coordination. Their combined efforts are necessary to bring about mass mobilisation of members.

Group anxieties accentuated by political entrepreneurs and ethnic activists

It is impossible to say whether all members of a group automatically feel anxiety, or a band of ethnic activists in that group are particularly prone to such angst and play a pivotal role in expressing it on the group's behalf, or whether 'political entrepreneurs' – ambitious leaders and intellectuals who may not share the zeal of the activist – excel in articulating such feelings. In this regard, the roles of propaganda and especially rumours have to be particularly studied to understand what activities and processes are generating anxiety and fear. If the adversaries are unable to counter such propaganda effectively, the side which is able to whip up fear and mass hysteria enjoys a strategic advantage. No other platform presents better scope for deploying zero-sum strategies against one another than protracted election campaigns. Equally, a partisan press can play a very pernicious role in such circumstance (Tanwar, 2006: 8-15).

Sensational news reporting and articles are therefore a source of fomenting fears and prejudices, thus paving way for conflict. If the state does not impose a strict code of conduct on the election campaign and media reporting, the processes of demonisation and dehumanisation of the 'enemy' can prove to be very effective and can further deplete the already declining mutual trust. Such processes greatly aggravate subsequent efforts to cull out a framework for power-sharing between rival parties. The cumulative impact of such processes is that individuals and groups become even more insecure and suspicious. The overall discourse that evolves in such situations sharpens differences and deepens cleavages. As the situation worsens, agreements, if any, may begin to be broken or ignored.

Suffice it to say that without an effective leadership, neither activists nor ordinary members can convert such fears and anxieties into activities and movements purporting to combat the perceived threats; this means that political entrepreneurs have the advantage of exaggerating and manipulating such fears in the pursuit of their political ambitions. Often, selective narratives of real or imagined grievances from the past are invoked in such circumstances.

However, political entrepreneurs are able to exert influence only through existing networks and thick social webs in which they are embedded, along with their groups and group members. Such connections circumscribe the extent to which they can exploit a situation. Thus, while leaders may exercise influence and power over group members, they do not ordinarily invent the circumstances from which conflicts emanate. Moreover, their ability to manipulate a given situation in the direction of violence is contingent on objective circumstances – something they may not be able to control. Given such uncertain contexts and situations, the actions and reactions of leaders and cadres carry both intended and unintended consequences and ramifications. As the situation worsens, communication between estranged groups are adversely affected.

Communication failures between groups

Communication failures and depletion of trust exacerbates relations between estranged groups. Once the normal or routine pattern of politics does not suffice, new, volatile forms of action begin to take place, which affect communal (ethnic) groups and indeed individuals in different ways. Some feel elated and powerful while others, weak and vulnerable; it all depends on the context. As the ongoing political contest moves out of closed chambers and onto the public sphere and into the streets and other public arenas, the established mechanisms for defusing tension and conflict become increasingly ineffective. The overall impact of such change in the context of an uncertain political future can be quite profound and disorienting. Demonstrations, processions, slogans – all acquire different meanings during such periods, even if violence is absent or minimal. What may be viewed as legitimate and peaceful expression of a group's political dissatisfaction may be perceived as threatening by adversarial groups.

Consequently, the end result may be very different from the objectives set up by the competing parties. In other words, it is not necessary that ethnic cleansing and genocide be desired goals or objectives. But in case of lack of trust, the failure to negotiate a peace and power-sharing deal within given territorial boundaries, or to arrange a peaceful transfer of populations can set into motion processes which are no longer controllable by social and political factors. The result can be the outbreak of violence, or rather, retaliatory violence.

Anarchy and chaos

As state authority becomes increasingly ineffective or biased and partisan, and anarchy prevails, individuals and communities have no choice but to manage their survival on their own. The social capital and goodwill that may have existed depletes even further as threats to life begin to be real and immediate. If the conflicting groups are evenly balanced and strongly motivated to defend their interests, then the stage is set for violent conflict, often giving birth to the politics of reaction. Here, 'reaction' is used in a double sense: as a mechanical action-reaction relationship, as well as an unenlightened mode of thinking and behaving towards one another by two or more ethnic groups. In such circumstances, gut reactions take over. Revenge becomes the typical manifestation of such reaction. As the situation worsens, the imperative of survival renders striking first the best option, as Hobbes so vividly described in his *Leviathan*. The 'Enemy' becomes a faceless, indiscriminate lump of individuals, an ethnic mass, a target requiring and justifying punitive preemptive action.

However, spontaneous aggression does not automatically escalate into organised pogroms and massacres. Some amount of demonising and dehumanising of a target group must take place before massive violence can be deployed against it. It has been noted that apparently sound and balanced human beings with no record of participating in hostile group activities have been, at times, noted as participants in such crimes. It seems reasonable to assume that they, too, have in some ways been exposed to processes of demonisation and dehumanisation. We are familiar with notions of mob psychology, but such psychology also derives from imperceptible processes of indoctrination that are underway in societies. Therefore, even gut reaction is a product of processes of brainwashing that may have begun a long time ago.

Most ethno-nationalist rhetoric and ideology given vent to by political entrepreneurs can impact upon the collective anxiety and neurosis of group members, thus galvanising them into action against the perceived threat. In extreme situations, a release of collective psychosis can take the shape of systematic and organised mass killings and other atrocities. Gut reaction takes over and as part of a crowd or a gang, individuals feel obliged to act together against the enemy.

Dusan Kechmanovic (1996: 101-50) has elaborated how nationalism works on the psychology of individuals and groups and prepares them for aggressive behaviour. They feel weak vis-à-vis the group and feel obliged to conform to the behaviour the crowd has assumed. Christopher R. Browning shed light on this phenomenon when he described how some individuals from the German police battalions, drafted to carry out the massacre of Jews, took part in the killings only not to earn the ire of their group members (1992: 169-83). In other words, group or mob psychology requires conformity to a set pattern of behaviour, and most individuals adhere to it. But even more crucially, those who are prepared to commit the crimes need to have the means and capability to use force.

Forewarned is forearmed

Those groups that are attacked first and remain at the receiving end for a fairly long period of time can be expected to take precautionary measures and prepare for the worst. Such preparation would include not only defensive measures but also offensive ones. Such subjective awareness is a necessary, though not sufficient, basis for beginning to organise for future conflict. The extent to which a group has access to weapons and the training and motivation to use them also plays an important role in such circumstances. As long as state and government are able to exercise some degree of control, the preparation for conflict remains latent. As soon as the established state authority terminates, and anarchy and chaos prevail, the stage is set for the warring groups to put into operation their defensive and offensive capabilities. Under the circumstances, those forewarned are forearmed.

Communication failures within groups and casualties

Whereas communication failures between conflicting groups exacerbate a fast deteriorating situation, communication failures within groups are also crucial in determining how the different groups will fare in such situations. Assuming that group leaders are in a much better situation to be aware of the impending danger in a highly volatile and explosive situation, such as the bitterly contested partition of a territory, if they fail to inform and prepare their ordinary members to take precautionary measures, such as exit from trouble spots before the attacks occur or arm themselves or both, the chances of suffering casualties increase. A situation can also be imagined where the leaders are oblivious to the dangers involved in the division of territory because of total uncertainty or lack of previous experience in hand to orient themselves in such a situation. That, too, would result in heavier losses being suffered than by groups that are aware of the danger because of direct experience or warnings from their leaders.

Ethnic cleansing: A recapitulation

Even if the division of a territory has been agreed on beforehand, but the borders between its divided parts not determined and demarcated, ethnic violence, already endemic to such a situation, will escalate. As soon as a new administration that is partisan and sides with some group or groups takes over, the ability to attack the alienated and demonised group or groups increases dramatically. It is not uncommon that the process of carving new states out of empires or bigger states involves wholesale expulsion under duress of people the victorious group does not want to include within the imagined nation. Such an objective is achieved successfully and efficiently when so-called civil society actors, political cadres, and state functionaries join forces to eliminate an unwanted population.

Unless an elaborate and organised plan to physically exterminate all members of a demonised and dehumanised groups exists, and it is backed by a powerful and effective state bureaucracy and military apparatus determined to realise such an objective, chances are that removal from a territory of an unwanted population can take place without the wholesale murder or genocide of a target group. This is, of course possible, if exit routes remain open. It is possible that some members of a demonised and dehumanised group will be able to remain behind if they convert and change their identity or are protected by powerful patrons, although such exceptions would still not prevent ethnic cleansing from taking place. On the other hand, the prerogative of sovereignty, which states enjoy under international law, enables them to make, with the help of international borders and border control systems, forced migration and ethnic cleansing permanent and irreversible. The final result can be a complete destruction of the demographic structure and traditional culture upon which rested the previous, traditional balance between communities.

References

Abisaab, R. *Converting Persia: Religion and Politics in the Safavid Empire*, London: I.B. Tauris, 2004.

Ahmed, I. *State, Nation and Ethnicity in Contemporary South Asia,* London and New York: Pinter, 1998.

Aziz, K.K. *The Murder of History,* Lahore: Vanguard Books, 1993.

Bell-Fialkoff, A. *Ethnic Cleansing,* New York: St. Martin's Press, 1999.

Brass, P. *Ethnicity and Nationalism: Theory and Practice,* New Delhi: Sage Publications, 1991.

Brass, Paul. 'The partition of India and retributive genocide in the Punjab, 1946-47: means, methods, and purposes', *Journal of Genocide Research*, London: Taylor & Francis, Cartex Publishing, 2003.

Browning, C.R. *The Path to Genocide,* Cambridge: Cambridge University Press, Canto edition, 1995.

Chalk, F., and K. Jonassohn, *The History and Sociology of Genocide: Analysis and Case Studies,* New Haven and London: Montreal Institute of Genocide Studies and Yale University Press, 1990.

Connor, W. *Ethnonationalism: The Quest for Understanding,* Princeton: Princeton University Press, 1994.

Geertz, C. (ed.). *Old Societies and New State,* New York: The Free Press, 1963.

Gellately, R. 'The Third Reich, the Holocaust, and Visions of Serial Genocide' in Robert Gellately and Ben Kiernan (eds), *The Specter of Genocide: Mass Murder in Historical Perspective,* Cambridge: Cambridge University Press, 2003.

Gutman, R. *A Witness to Genocide,* Shaftesburg, Dorset: Element Book, 1993.

Hansen, A. B. *Partition and Genocide: Manifestation of Violence in Punjab 1937-1947,* New Delhi: India Research Press, 2002.

Hobbes, T. *Leviathan,* London: Puenguin Classics, 1985.

Jonassohn, K., and K.S. Björnson, *Genocide and Gross Human Rights Violations*, New Brunswick and London: Transaction Publishers, 1999.

Jonsson, G. (ed). *East Timor: Nationbuilding in the 21st Century,* Stockholm: Center for Pacific Asian Studies, 2003.

Kellas, J.G. *The Politics of Nationalism and Ethnicity,* New York: St Martin's Press, 1998.

Kecmanovic, D. *The Mass Psychology of Ethnonationalism,* New York and London: Plenium Press, 1996.

Kuper, L. *Genocide,* New Haven and London: Yale University Press, 1982.

Lake, D.A. and D. Rothchild, (eds). *The International Spread of Ethnic Conflict,* Princeton: Princeton University Press, 1998.

Lang, B. *Act and Idea in the Nazi Genocide,* Syracuse: Syracuse University Press, 2003.

Mann, M. *The Dark Side of Democracy: Explaining Ethnic Cleansing,* Cambridge: Cambridge University Press, 2005.

Melson, R. *Revolution and Genocide: On the Origins of the Armenian Genocide and the Holocaust,* Illinois: University of Chicago Press, 1992.

Naimark, N.M. *Fires of Hatred: Ethnic Cleansing in the Twentieth Century Europe,* Cambridge Mass., London: Harvard University Press, 2001.

Shils, E. 'Primordial, personal, sacred and civil ties', in *British Journal of Sociology*, 1957.

Steinberg, S. *The Ethnic Myth: Race, Ethnicity and Class in America,* New York: Atheneum, 1981.

Tanwar, Raghuvendra. *Reporting the Partition of Punjab 1947*, New Delhi: Manohar, 2006.

Williams, H. 'Freelance', *Times Literary Supplement,* 13 February, 2004.

Young, C. *The Politics of Cultural Pluralism,* Madison: The University of Wisconsin Press, 1976.

2

PRE-COLONIAL AND COLONIAL PUNJAB

THE PUNJAB OF MODERN TIMES IS PRIMARILY A POLITICO-administrative unit. Although the descriptions used have not always corresponded exactly to the same unit, they have nevertheless overlapped. The oldest is the Rigvedic *Sapta Sindhu*, or 'land of seven rivers', of which the river Indus was the most important. A more popular theory is that the name (Persian *panj ab*, five waters) refers to the five rivers, Jhelum, Chenab, Ravi, Sutlej, and Beas. It began to be used by the Mughals for their possessions in the five interfluvian zones. Maharaja Ranjit Singh considered his kingdom to include Punjab as well as Multan in the south and Kashmir in the north. The British extended the boundaries of their Punjab Province to the banks of the Yamuna in the east. Reviewing some of the descriptions, J.S. Grewal observes:

> Though there is no uniformity in the territorial entities we have noticed, not even when the term used is the same, they tend to overlap. The river Yamuna is never crossed and the Himalayas and Sindh remain outside. The region thus appears to emerge as the area surrounded by the Himalayas on the north and north-west, the river Yamuna on the east, and the Aravalli hills and Thar Desert on the south and south-west (2004: 2).

Ethnic composition of the Punjab

Regarding the earliest inhabitants' ethnic and religious characteristics, the aboriginal proto-Australoids and later, the Dravidians, are believed to have been present at the time of the influx of the Indo-Europeans from around 1500 to 1000 BC. The Hindu four-fold *varna,* or caste cluster as it has come to be known, comprising Brahmins, Kshatriyas, Vaishyas and Sudras, took shape after the intruding Aryans and Indo-Aryans defeated the indigenous people. The so-called untouchables were those sections of society that were reduced to sub-human status by the Hindu hierarchy. However, the caste system did accommodate later arrivals such as the Greeks, Scythians, Huns, Shakas, Kushanas and many other minor groups in different caste positions, but some remained peripheral to it and retained their tribal and clannish identities. Both Hinduism and Buddhism had their adherents in this region in the eleventh century, when invasions led by Turco-Afghans started from the north-western mountain passes. Arabs had been settled in Multan and adjoining areas since the early eighth century. A convenient point, therefore, to begin with the cultural diversity and syncretic tradition of the Punjab would be the conquest of Lahore by Mahmud of Ghazni in AD 1021. From that time onwards, a Muslim presence in this region became permanent.

Communal relations

Conversions to Islam in the Punjab were gradual, picking up pace only from the sixteenth century onwards, although some tribes began to convert from even earlier as a result of Sufi influence. The usual pattern was that first Muslim rule was established and consolidated and then the Sufis began to preach Islam and were able to win over people peacefully. The theological concept of the equality of all human beings entered as a value into the subcontinent through the Islamic contact, though whether it helped create a more egalitarian social structure is doubtful.

A synthesis between Hinduism and Buddhism was underway in the Punjab because of the efforts of Gorakhnatha, who was probably born in this region sometime between the tenth and thirteenth centuries AD. The Gorakhnathi *yogis* or wandering sages retained features of the Shaivite Hindu cult, while accepting Buddhist and Islamic influences. According to Vaudeville, the Gorakhnathis were able to form a bridge between Muslims and Hindus because of their monotheism and opposition to caste distinctions and ritual purity (Alhaq, 1996: 286). Another Hindu reform process, which gained a foothold in the Punjab, was the order of the Sants, or itinerant sages, often of humble status. The Sants were associated with the Bhakti movement, which originated in south India among Hindus, mainly of lower-caste origin, who were opposed to caste oppression. The Bhaktis made great headway into northern India and the Punjab. This movement too gained followers from among Muslims. Among them, the name of Kabir is the most important. Their philosophy was that there was one God and His creation was inseparable from Him. The Bhaktis made vows of poverty and purity of conduct. In the Punjab, the movement had a profound impact on the evolution of Sikhism, as we shall examine presently.

Sufism and a composite culture

The Sufi brotherhoods that arrived in south Asia from either the Middle East or central Asia had already been influenced by the pantheistic traditions of south Asia, and in some cases the result was theist fusion or a unitarian view of God. Within Islam, the main Sufi schools of Suhrawardia, Chishtia, Naqshbandia and Qadriyya adhered to Sunni doctrines and upheld observance of the *sharia* or Islamic law as important, even while they adapted local traditions and customs. However, individual Sufis sometimes evolved non-conformist positions that made adherence to the *sharia* practically, if not formally, redundant. The basic idea that gained acceptance in such circles was that ultimately there is one Great Spirit or God holding together the cosmic and earthly systems (ibid 1996: 283-464).

Such a train of thinking reached its apogee under Bulleh Shah (1680–1758). Bulleh Shah's master, Shah Inayat, belonged to the Qadriyya Shattari school of Sufism, which readily borrowed Hindu philosophical ideas of reaching individual salvation and incorporated them into Sufi beliefs (ibid.: 634). Bulleh Shah, however, surpassed his teacher and guide in terms of openly questioning religious dogmas (Ahmad, 2004). To quote a couplet, which, from a dogmatic point of view, is heretical:

Gal samajh laee te raolaa keeh
eyh Raam, Raheem te Maulaa keeh

(Why this commotion if you claim understanding?
Why all this fuss about calling Him Ram, Rahim or Moula?)*

*Ram is a Hindu god; Rahim and Moula are designations for Allah

There were also Sufis who were strict followers of dogmatic Sharia. The Naqshbandi Sufi, Ahmed Sirhindi or Mujadid Alf-Sani, who lived during the sixteenth century and is buried at Sirhind in the Indian East Punjab, played an important role in the revival of strict Islam in the Mughal Empire.

The Punjabi language

It is not clear when Punjabi evolved as a distinct language, but its various dialects seem to have preceded the arrival of the Turco-Afghans. The Brahmins used Sanskrit, while Muslim clerics used Arabic for religious purposes. Farsi (Persian) and even Turkish were spoken by the Muslim upper classes, while the common people spoke different dialects of Punjabi. The Gorakhnathis addressed the people in the vernacular (Grewal, 2004: 11). The thirteenth-century writer and Sufi, Amir Khusrau, called the central Punjab language Lahauri (ibid.: 10). There were other dialects, too, which persisted into modern times. Punjabi began to be used for literary and religious composition from the time of Shaikh Fariduddin Ganjshakar of the Chistia Sufi Order, and Shah Hussain, Sultan Bahu, Bulleh Shah, Mian Muhammad and Khawaja Ghulam Farid wrote in Punjabi in its various dialects.

Love and heroic epics such as *Heer Ranjha, Puran Bhagat, Sohni Mahiwal* – and even stories from the Arabian and Sindh deserts such as *Laila Majnu* and *Sassi Punnu* – were recited with great devotion. The two most famous works on *Heer* are by Damodar, a Hindu, and by the Muslim Sufi, Waris Shah. The symbiosis between Hinduism and Islam comes out strongly in *Heer*, when the heroine's lover Ranjha joins the Gorakhnathi *yogi* order. These epics were recited and sung in the villages and towns among gatherings of men. This is not to deny that dogmatic rules and regulations were observed at all levels of society, especially by the clerics and upper strata of each community, or that communal boundaries were marked clearly through manifest rites, rituals, and practices. Orthodox Brahminical Hinduism, for example, had its adherents among the upper castes, while Islamic orthodoxy was represented by Sunni orthodoxy among Turks, Afghans, Mughal and other elements claiming descent from holy lineages – that is, putative Arabic ancestors (Ahmed, 1999).

Undoubtedly, the biggest impetus to Punjabi as a language of religious and literary expression was the advent of Sikhism. In the late fifteenth century, Nanak Chand (1469–1539), by caste a Khatri Hindu, born in Talwandi (now Nankana Sahib, in the Pakistani Punjab), initiated a religious reform movement which came to be known as Sikhism. Guru Nanak expressed his thoughts in what has been described as Lahauri Punjabi. This tradition continued and flourished in the writings of his spiritual successors. The fourth guru, Ram Das, even devised the Gurmukhi script, which is an adaptation of the Devanagri script. Sufis and other Muslim writers wrote Punjabi in the Persian script, while the Devanagri script continued to be used by Hindus. Hence, in the evolution of the popular Punjabi cultural identity, the oral tradition played a key role, whereas the written word remained inaccessible across communal lines. In any case, Punjabi was never the state or government language at any stage of the Punjab's history. Even the Sikh ruler, Ranjit Singh, used Persian as the language of government.

Sikhism in the Punjab

Influenced by the Gorakhnathi, Bhakti and Sufi movements, Guru Nanak, as he came to be known, rejected untouchability and stressed the worship of one God. He condemned the corruption rampant in the Muslim and Hindu religious and political establishments. Founding a system of free community kitchens, he was able to persuade his followers, who came largely from Hindu ranks, to eat together (Singh, 1986: 49). Sikhism made headway largely among the agricultural and artisan castes of the Punjab – castes otherwise assigned a lowly station in the Hindu social order. Among them, the Jats were the most numerous (Singh, 1963: 89). The Sikhs remained a peaceful reformist sect during the time of the first four gurus, almost undistinguishable from other reformist brotherhoods. Some permanent centres of Sikh faith and influence were established early in its history; the most important is the Golden Temple established at Amritsar by the fourth guru, Ramdas. Among those who laid its foundations was the leading Muslim Sufi, Mian Meer, of Lahore. The

Mughal Emperor Akbar, known for his tolerant views, was impressed by the learning of the fifth guru, Arjan (1563–1606), and honoured him with expensive presents and grants in land and revenue.

The Akal Takht (Throne of the Immortal) was added to the Golden Temple complex by the sixth guru, Hargobind, who wore two swords signifying a linkage between spiritual and temporal authority (Ahmed, 1990: 108). Gradually, Sikh power based on peasant and petty-trader support, began to emerge in northwestern India. It was viewed with concern by the later Mughal emperors, who ordered military action against some of the later Sikh gurus. The ninth guru, Teg Bahadur, took up the cudgels on behalf of the pandits of Kashmir who alleged that they were being forced to embrace Islam. This resulted in his and some of his followers arriving at the Mughal court and entering into a religious debate, in which the guru refused to embrace Islam. Dared by Emperor Aurangzeb to prove his superior spiritual powers by performing a miracle, the guru failed, and was publicly executed on royal orders along with some of his followers (Singh, 1963).

Teg Bahadur's son, the tenth and last guru of the Sikhs, Gobind Rai (1666–1708), maintained a well-trained and disciplined regular army. Most of his soldiers came from the poorer sections of the peasantry and artisan castes. The Sikhs began to collect revenue and other taxes in areas under their control, and soon Sikh power became a dominant force in the politics of northern India. Gobind Rai fought many battles against both Muslim and Hindu chiefs. His campaigns, it seems, were not viewed necessarily as religious crusades by the Punjab populace: many Muslim notables opposed to Mughal supremacy sided with him, and both Muslim and Hindu soldiers were to be found in substantial numbers in the Sikh armies. In 1699, Gobind Rai summoned his followers to collect at Anandpur in northern Punjab. At this gathering, he decided to organise the Sikhs along distinctive lines and institute the system of baptism. They were given one family name: Singh, which means 'lion'. Baptism signified that they had given up their previous castes and means of earning a living and become soldiers of the Khalsa, 'the Pure', abandoning all other social ties. They also adopted distinctive emblems, such as unshorn hair and beards, and the sword or *kirpan,* which was to be carried at all times.

The Mughals persecuted Gobind Singh to the end of his life, and ordered two of his sons to be put to death. In 1708, he died of stab wounds inflicted by Muslim assassins. In Sikh communal memory, therefore, the Muslims or Turks (as the Mughals were also known) came to be particularly associated with the persecution of their gurus. An exception was the Muslim ruler of the small princely state of Malerkotla, who objected to the torture and murder of Gobind Singh's sons. The guru thereupon instructed his followers never to harm the Muslims of Malerkotla (Kholi, 1986). Some Sikhs, however, considered it their duty to avenge the wrongs done to them at their Muslim rulers' hands by embarking on massive killings of Muslims. Banda Bahadur let loose a reign of terror not only against the Muslim ruling class of the Punjab, whose land was confiscated and redistributed among Sikhs, but also against ordinary Muslims such as artisans and farmers. His atrocities became part of the Muslim historical psychology as recalled by their spokespersons (Ahmed, 1990: 108-9; Singh, 1963: 118).

As regards the relationship between Sikhism, Islam and Hinduism, it is significant that Sikhism was considered a Muslim sect by the British historian Cunningham. In terms of monotheism and other egalitarian practices, indeed, Sikhism was closer to the popular versions of Sufi Islam, but historically, the lines between it and Hinduism were never drawn so distinctly, and many people continued to subscribe to a popular religion combining Hindu and Sikh beliefs. Also, among some Punjabi Hindus of the western and central districts belonging to the Khatri and Arora castes, raising one son as a Sikh, often the eldest, was an established tradition. Intermarriage between Hindus and Sikhs of the same caste was quite common. These traditions continued on to modern times, the exception being that Sikh and Hindu Jats did not normally marry (Akbar, 1985: 131-33). In the British census records, the Sikhs were entered sometimes as Hindus and sometimes as Sikhs. At the beginning of the twentieth century both Hindus and Sikhs, however, were minorities in the Punjab region.

In any event, during the eighteenth century, the Mughal empire was delivered severe blows by a series of attacks led by Persian and Afghan invaders. First came the Persian Nadir Shah (in 1738 and 1739) who laid waste the Punjab and the areas around the Mughal capital, Delhi.

A series of invasions followed under Ahmed Shah Abdali, an Afghan adventurer. This caused havoc within the social order of the entire Punjab and northern India. Muslims, Hindus and Sikhs all became victims of the slaughter that followed Afghan victory. No Mughal administrative or military structure worth the name survived the repeated onslaughts (Ahmed, 1990: 108-111).

The Sikhs, who had taken to the forest with their mobile military formations intact, emerged as the strongest military force in the Punjab. The pinnacle of Sikh power was the establishment of the Kingdom of Punjab under Ranjit Singh in 1799, but for as long as thirty years before that the Sikhs had gained political clout in different parts of the Punjab. A Sikh trio of warlords, for example, had established their power in and around Lahore and was collecting taxes and other dues (Sheikh, 2005). The Sikh rise from a minor sect to the ruling community of Punjab was consummated in the creation of an independent kingdom. This was most unusual so far as the majority Muslim population was concerned. As was the established tradition in the subcontinent Ranjit Singh used excessive force to crush all opposition – which meant mainly against Muslims who served the Mughal Empire or were allied to the rulers of Afganistan. In some cases, the Sikh armies desecrated Muslim sacred places to express their pent-up anger over the treatment of their gurus by the Mughals. However, Ranjit Singh quickly moved away from such policy into the South Asian fiction of the ruler being a protector of all communities.

He proclaimed himself Maharajah (supreme king) of the Kingdom of Lahore in 1801 and began a long reign of expansion and consolidation. After crushing all opposition, he embarked upon a policy of reconciliation. Accordingly, Muslim and Hindu Punjabis were included in his council of ministers and advisers. Muslims, Hindus and Sikhs were to be found at all levels within the army, including in positions of command. Over the years, Ranjit Singh earned the reputation of a just and wise ruler. Many reforms were introduced in his reign, including free medicine and separate courts for the three main communities of the Punjab (Singh 1985: 48-50). Apparently, during his reign, literacy in the Punjab was higher than in any other part of India. Community schools run by Hindus, Muslim and Sikhs imparted not only religious knowledge but also a sound basis in mathematics and the sciences. Punjabi was the main medium of instruction, but the pupils also learnt Arabic, Urdu, Persian and Sanskrit. A strong Punjabi identity shared by people from all walks of life flourished during his rule (Sheikh, 2010). However, notwithstanding an emphasis on Punjabi cultural identity, the Sikh kingdom retained Persian as the official language of state (Chaudhry, 1977: ii).

At the time, the British were expanding rapidly in northern India. Ranjit Singh died in 1839, and a struggle for the throne erupted among different claimants. Some Sikh chieftains began to extort heavy taxes and other dues from areas in which they maintained military presence. Chaos ensued. The British took advantage of the situation to invade the Punjab. Several battles were fought between the British and Sikh armies.

British rule

On 29 March 1849, a treaty was signed between Dalip Singh, Maharaja Ranjit Singh's younger son, and the British, whereby the kingdom was passed on to the possession of the British East India Company. At that time the capital, Lahore, was in a state of chronic dilapidation, economic misery, and overall decay; the buildings, streets, sewage system and other infrastructure were in complete disrepair. Under British patronage, the Punjab and particularly Lahore, flourished, as the British wanted to safeguard their Indian empire from Afghan raiders and the Czarist Russian Empire beyond.

Accordingly, many Sikh chieftains were won over through bribery and confirmation of their proprietary rights over estates and princely states. It is important to note that not only Sikhs from the Punjab, but also many Muslim and Hindu chiefs who helped the British crush the Sepoy Mutiny or the uprising of 1857, were generously rewarded with lands and titles. Later, the system of granting land to loyal notables continued and as a result, a powerful class of landowners, called *zamindars*, was established all over the Punjab. In this regard, it must be said that the British very skilfully co-opted religious leaders from all three communities. In particular, religious figures and heads of Sufi shrines were brought under direct patronage, and in return they ensured that peace was kept locally and soldiers were recruited to the army. That class remained loyal to British rule until the end (Ali, 1970: 193-240; Leigh, 1922).

The Punjab was considered strategically a key province to the defence of the British Empire. The British therefore decided to introduce Urdu as the medium of instruction in municipal and government schools, which replaced the educational system that existed prior to the annexation of the Punjab. This issue was keenly debated among the senior members of the Punjab administration. The opinion prevailed that Punjabi was a kin language to Urdu, and since the British had already been using it in northern India in schools and as the official language at the lower levels, it should be extended even to the Punjab. Thus, all those Punjabis who wanted to join government service in either the civil or military branches had to be conversant with written Urdu (Chaudhry, 1977).

Punjab during the colonial period

The British conquest resulted in an end to further invasions from the north-western passes, from which most invaders and conquerors had entered the subcontinent. The British directly administered large parts of the Punjab, but also took princely states under their paramountcy through treaties with local rulers. From the second half of the nineteenth century onwards, the western part of the Punjab was rapidly transformed, under British planning and patronage. A vast network of canals and waterworks was established, resulting in the biggest irrigation system in the world. With the American civil war disrupting Britain's supply of cotton from the southern states, the Punjab benefited, as farmers were encouraged to grown cotton. People from the over-populated East Punjab were settled in the canal colonies. Thousands of Sikhs and Muslims were among the new settlers (Ali, 1989; Bhatia, 1987: 83-89; Singh, 1966: 116-18). However, the change in the western districts took place within a framework which, while promoting the privatisation of land-ownership and commercialisation of the economy, restrained independent industrial enterprise (Ali, 1989).

Despite these new economic opportunities, northern and eastern Punjab continued to suffer from over-population, a scarcity of fertile agricultural land, and fragmentation of land-holdings. In the past, such pressing circumstances had forced Punjabis from these regions to seek employment in the armies of both native rulers and invaders. British policy supported this trend: Sikhs, Punjabi Muslims and Hindu Rajputs, considered 'martial races', were encouraged to seek employment in the British Indian army. In fact, colonial policy deliberately prevented economic development in northern Punjab so that a continuous supply of soldiers could be ensured.

Moreover, an institution which developed rather quickly and became an important appendage of the growing commercialisation of agriculture was that of the moneylender, the *bania*, who almost invariably was a Hindu or Sikh. Roughly, the division of functions within the colonial economy was such that trade, retail as well as large-scale, and modern firms and companies were in the hands of Hindu and Sikh trading castes. Thus shops all over the Punjab in the rural and urban areas were in the hands of these castes. Most of the peasantry, including agriculturalists and pastoral tribes, were either Muslims or Sikhs, except in eastern Punjab, where the Hindu Jat peasantry predominated. Most big landowners were either Muslims or Sikhs but Hindus were also to be found in different parts of the Punjab. All sections of society were indebted to the moneylender, but Muslims in particular resented his power over their economic circumstances. In his classic work, *The Punjab Peasant: In Prosperity and Debt*, Malcolm Darling shows that nearly fifty per cent of indebted peasants in the Punjab were Muslims (1978: 21). Bulaki Shah of Lahore personified the typical moneylender. There was hardly any landlord worth his name who was not indebted to him. The image of the moneylender as a greedy extortionist seems, nevertheless, to be a creation of political propaganda, because in the eyes of many of my Muslim interviewees, the behaviour of individual moneylenders varied considerably, with some proving helpful to people in distress.

On the whole, the stratum that gained most was that of Hindu trading castes of Khatris and Aroras and, indeed, Sikhs of the same stock. Hindus and Sikhs were the first to take to modern education and establish modern business enterprises. From the beginning of the twentieth century, urban Hindus and Sikhs established a firm hold over the modern economy. Hindu–Sikh partnerships and joint business ventures were noteworthy but Muslims were almost invariably excluded (Moon,

1998: 288). In government services, too, the Hindus and Sikhs were more advanced than Muslims. Thus Muslims held only twenty per cent of government jobs in 1931, whereas they made up more than half of the total population of the Punjab (Talha, 2000: 9). This pattern remained until Partition. D.N. Malhotra writes:

> Years later, possibly in 1944, Jinnah visited Lahore on a tour and addressed a very large gathering of Muslims on the grounds of the Islamia College. I went there with a few friends to listen to him – the new apostle of the Muslim community. His speech was clear and loud in pooh-poohing the notion of India being one nation composed of both the Hindus and the Muslims. He gave a clarion call to the Muslim youth to get together and be ready for sacrifices to achieve Pakistan. He gave examples from daily life and said: 'Do you know that there is a great banking institution in the Punjab called the Punjab National Bank. This is a wrong name. It is actually Punjab Hindu National Bank. You will find that there is no Muslim employee in this bank. It is a Hindu National Bank. Muslims will have to carve out their destiny separately (2004: 58).

Religious revivals

While the British authorities continued the tradition of religious neutrality, the various Christian churches which accompanied their rule began to establish themselves in the Punjab. Conversions to Christianity in the Punjab took place mainly among the poorer sections of society, mostly the untouchables, but some leading families and upper-caste individuals were also attracted to the Christian missions. Some members of the ruling family of Kapurthala, for instance, converted to Christianity. Such developments prompted Hindu, Muslim and Sikh leaders to contemplate the question of social reform. Each of them indulged in introspection, which led to a revival of idealised Hinduism, Islam, Buddhism, Sikhism and other religions (Bhatia, 1987: 114-20; Farquhar, 1967). Among Hindus, the aggressive campaigns of Christian missionaries in the late nineteenth century, and continuing conversions to Islam, led to a number of reformist initiatives.

The decline in the proportion of Hindus in the Punjab population between 1881 and 1941, and the increase in the proportion of Muslims in particular, but also of Sikhs and Christians, caused upper-caste Hindu Punjabis a great deal of worry. Not surprisingly, the Arya Samaj (pure Aryan-Vedic society) movement originating in distant Gujarat (not in the district of the same name in the Punjab) found the upper-caste Punjabi Hindus most receptive to its message. Seeking to rid Hinduism of idol-worship and caste prejudices through a revised interpretation of scripture, ancient history and folklore (Jones, 1989a), it was mainly successful in removing social taboos among the upper three 'twice-born' castes and in winning back some recent converts to Islam and Christianity (Bhatia, 1987: 114-20: Farquhar, 1967).

The Arya Samaj gained supporters among urban sections of Hindu society while the majority continued to adhere to traditional Hinduism with its myriad gods and goddesses. The Hindus introduced the novel idea of 'reconversion' of Muslims and Christians and even of Sikhs. The *shuddi* campaign, as reconversion came to be known, resulted in turn in Muslim *tabligh* (proselytising) counter-moves. Another Hindu reform movement was the Brahmo Samaj, originating in Bengal, which pressed for greater adaptation to Western rationalism. Its supporter base in the Punjab was more elitist and upper class, and it won some converts such as the founder of the Dayal Singh College and Library in Lahore.

Among Punjabi Muslims, while upper-class families responded favourably to Sir Syed Ahmed Khan's educational reforms, the more radical elements were attracted to the Wahhabi movement, which had reached the Punjab in the early nineteenth century as part of the militant movement of Syed Ahmed Shaheed Barelwi. Later, the radical Deobandi movement of Sunni Islam also gained adherence in the Punjab (Ahmed, 1999: 218-222). The Ahmadiyya sect, founded at Qadian in Gurdaspur district of eastern Punjab in the early twentieth century, broke away to establish itself independently. It opposed any idea of *jihad* or holy war against the British and was generally regarded as loyalist to British rule. Although Mirza Ghulam Ahmad began his religious career as a keen Sunni debater who confronted both Christian missionaries and Hindu reformers with clever doctrinal arguments, he later staked a claim to being a prophet ('The Promised Messiah') and made several other controversial pronouncements not easily reconciled with mainstream Sunni doctrines (ibid.: 233-234). Both groups accused each other of heresy. Upon Ahmadiyyah's request, its followers were shown as a separate sect in the population census.

Among Sikhs, the Akali Dal and Singh Sabha represented Sikh religious and communal interests. It is also to be noted that in the 1920s, a bitter conflict broke out between Hindus and Sikhs when some Arya Samaj leaders described the Sikhs as merely a Hindu sect. The Sikhs responded by asserting that they were not Hindus. Several heterodox Sikh sects also emerged during this period (Bhatia, 1987: 121-202).

Communal conflicts before the Partition riots

On various occasions, the radicalisation of religious identity did spill over into communal tensions, and even violence. In the main city and provincial capital, Lahore, two cases stand out. One was the publication of the book *Rangeela Rasul (The Pleasure-Loving Messenger of God)*. Its Hindu publisher Rajpal was sentenced on 18 January 1927 to eighteen months' imprisonment and slapped a fine of ₹1000 for provoking enmity between Hindus and Muslims. The book was judged to be a scurrilous satire on the Prophet of Islam.

However, that did not placate the Muslims of Lahore. On 6 April 1929, a Muslim youth of eighteen or nineteen years of age, Ilam Din, stabbed Rajpal to death (Malhotra, 2004: 4). Rajpal's son, Dina Nath Malhotra, told me that the author of the book was a Hindu, Pandit Chamupati, who had written it in retaliation for one written by a Muslim in 1920 denigrating Lord Krishna and Swami Dayananda, the founder of the Arya Samaj. Malhotra's father, having promised not to reveal the author's name, had attracted the wrath of the enraged Muslims onto himself (ibid.: 2). The Hindus of Lahore took part in large numbers in the funeral procession of Rajpal.

When the trial began, the initial defence of Ilam Din was prepared by Mian Farrukh Hussain. A death sentence was passed on Ilam Din at the sessions court. Allama Iqbal and Mian Abdul Aziz were leading the Muslim effort to save Ilam Din. Iqbal urged Jinnah to come from Bombay and appear before the Lahore High Court on behalf of Ilam

Din. Jinnah agreed. Jinnah's plea was that Ilam Din was an illiterate youngster, who was incensed by the disparaging language against Prophet Muhammad used in the book and therefore should not be sent to the gallows. Jinnah did not endorse what Ilam Din had done, however. On 17 July 1929 the Lahore High Court upheld the death sentence passed earlier by the session's court on Ilam Din for the murder of Rajpal. The High Court judge who upheld the verdict was Kanwar Sir Dalip Singh, a Christian who hailed from the ruling family of Kapurthala. Ilam Din submitted a mercy appeal to the government but it was rejected. He was hanged in Mianwali jail on 31 October 1929 and buried there.

People began to agitate for his body to be brought to Lahore. Two things convinced the British authorities to comply with that demand: persistent processions and demonstrations, on the one hand, and on the other, assurances by the notables of the Muslim community that peace and order would not be disturbed if the request was granted. Ilam Din's father requested Iqbal to lead the funeral prayers for his son, but he excused himself, saying that he was a sinner and therefore a more pious Muslim should lead the prayers. He paid glowing tributes to Ilam Din. Maulana Zafar Ali Khan, too, waxed eloquent in a eulogy to Ilam Din at the graveside. During those two years, Hindu–Muslim relations were very hostile (Nagina, 1988).

The Masjid/Gurdwara Shahidganj dispute

Muslim–Sikh relations in Lahore had been strained in Lahore over a gurdwara that Muslims claimed was a mosque built in the eighteenth century, in whose place a *gurdwara* had been built during Ranjit Singh's time. In the early twentieth century, that controversy gained momentum. Muslim sentiments during those times were vividly described to me by Mian Mustafa Kamal Pasha. He began with a background into his family's role in Lahore politics.

Mian Mustafa Kamal 'Pasha'

'I was born in 1928 in Lahore in a well-known Arain family (a farming caste). I was given the name Mustafa Kamal but people began to add 'Pasha' (in memory of the great Turkish leader) to my name. My grandfather, Mian Nuruddin Kaada, was a famous man. The word *Kaada* in Punjabi means 'one who takes out or finds out'. When no one else could resolve a bitter and complicated dispute, he was chosen as the arbitrator. He would propose a solution which the conflicting parties and others would find fair and acceptable; hence the title Kaada. My father Mian Ferozdin was put in jail in 1919 in connection with distributing a *fatwa* (religious ruling) in the cantonment area to Muslims, to the effect that serving in the British Army was *haram* or un-Islamic. He would disguise himself sometimes as a water-carrier, sometimes as a servant, and enter the different barracks in and around Lahore. He was charged with sedition and sentenced to death but somebody advised him to pretend that he was insane, which he did. My grandfather then pleaded that he had only one son who was mentally unbalanced, and therefore he should be released. The well-known Ahrar leader Shorish Kashmiri wrote an article on my father in which he presented that story.

'My father played a major role in the Masjid Shahidganj dispute. He delivered a speech in which he said that the governor of Punjab, Emerson, was actually Amar Singh. That is why he was favouring the Sikhs. He was sent to Montgomery (currently Sahiwal) where he was put under detention. My father joined the Muslim League around 1937. In opposition to Majlis-e-Ahrar that represented pro-Congress nationalist Muslims, he, along with Maulana Zafar Ali Khan and Ahmed Saeed Kirmani's father, founded the Majlis-e-Ittihad-e-Millat.'

In 1935, the Masjid/Gurdwara Shahidganj dispute between Muslim and Sikh zealots turned into a bloody conflict. Many people were killed, and a veritable threat to law and order reigned for some days. Its echo continued to be heard even in 1936. I was told by a number of Hindus, Muslims and Sikhs, that during the agitation, a number of innocent people were stabbed to death. Professor Chaman Lal Arora, once a resident of Lahore, told me on 4 January 2005 in Jullundur that the Shahidganj agitation created bad blood between Muslims and non-Muslims, especially Muslims and Sikhs. He said:

'One of my neighbours on Brandreth Road, a Hindu, did not close his shop as the agitators demanded of all shopkeepers. He was stabbed to death by Muslim ruffians. The Muslims were in a very aggressive mood in those days and the non-Muslims felt very threatened. The Sikhs were equally adamant but they were a tiny minority in Lahore and were therefore greatly outnumbered. My feeling is that the alienation between Muslims and Sikhs started from that time onwards. The Muslim leaders did not properly assess the consequences of such violent behaviour. Allama Iqbal incited the agitators rather than pacifying them in the interest of communal harmony.'

Governor Emerson wrote in his fortnightly report dated 16 November 1936:

> 'The coming Assembly elections in Lahore have been the direct cause of an attempt to revive the Shahidganj agitation. The body immediately responsible is the Ittihad-e-Millat, an association which was formed in July 1935, when the Shahidganj incident occurred… The Association has put up several candidates for the new Assembly. In ordinary circumstances they would stand little chance of elections, and their influence with the masses has declined as feeling has abated over the Shahidganj affair. In order to improve their election chances they have been engaged for several weeks in an attempt to revive the agitation, and they have talked freely of starting civil disobedience' (Carter, 2004: 58).

The Lahore High Court issued a ruling which confirmed the Sikhs' rights over the Shahidganj property, but Muslim–Sikh relations had been strained, and later, when conflict over the Punjab became acute, such factors played a crucial role in the Sikhs' decision to side with the Congress and the Hindus, rather than with the Muslims. Similarly, Rawalpindi and Multan had a history of Muslim–Sikh and Hindu–Sikh communal clashes. In Rawalpindi, the first clash occurred in 1926, and in Multan, in 1929. In Amritsar, a communal clash occurred in 1940. Jullundur, Gujranwala and other towns also occasionally went through tensions and clashes. Elsewhere, communal skirmishes occurred from time to time, but these were always easily brought under control through government action and the efforts of local leaders and elders to mediate and defuse situations.

Philanthropic activities

The complexity of the Punjab situation can also be judged from the fact that all communities practised philanthropy. The Hindus were leaders in this respect. They built hospitals, free dispensaries, and water tanks for horses and cattle. In Lahore alone, the Sir Ganga Ram Hospital, the Janki Devi Hospital, the Gulab Devi Hospital, and the Dr Khera dispensary in Gawalmandi are well-known. Dayal Singh College was built by a Sikh convert to the Brahmo Samaj. The Muslims and Sikhs spent liberally on providing food in religious shrines and *gurdwaras*. The Christian missions were the most progressive, providing good schools and colleges. In short, there was ample goodwill present among the inhabitants of the modern Punjab.

Social relations between the three communities

At the personal and local level, the three communities interacted routinely with one another. In the agrarian sector, village production was based on a division of labour in which each of the various castes and *biradaris* rendered a particular service. Also, people participated in each other's religious events as well as weddings and funerals. While Muslims ate food cooked by Hindus, the latter accepted only uncooked items from Muslims. In the *mohallas* and villages, social communication and interaction could be friendly. Also, both in the towns and villages, the elders and community leaders met to discuss issues of common interest and take decisions about them. There were some villages in which both Muslim and Hindu landowning and cultivating castes lived together. Shopkeepers were mostly Hindus, or occasionally, Sikhs.

However, perhaps more important is the fact that the lives of the Punjabis were organised in their local milieus. Belief in holy men and fear of evil spirits were widespread. Ordinary village folk would seek help from any quarter and therefore there were intricate, crisscrossing loyalties between them. While Hindus and Sikhs would easily flock to Muslim holy men and shrines, Muslims also went to *pandits* and *sadhus* to seek their spiritual or magical help to solve some problem or find a cure for an illness. Muslims and Hindus held Baba Guru Nanak, the founder of Sikhism, in great respect. Many Hindus and Sikhs were disciples of Muslim holy men. This can be illustrated by this story that I heard in Patiala on 7 January 2005 from Amrik Chand Ahluwalia:

'Our family shifted to Patiala from Sirhind in the time of Banda Bahadur. I was born in 1925. My family were devout Hindus but we also were disciples of the Hazrat Sakhi Sarwar in the western Punjab on the Balochistan border near Dera Ghazi Khan. I remember going there with my parents when I was a small boy. Hindus, Muslim, Sikhs and others lived like a family. There was a lot of *prem-pyar* (love and affection) amongst us. The Muslims would send us uncooked food including meat while they ate our food without any hesitation. We ate meat but only that of goats and lambs slaughtered according to Muslim tradition. There are Muslims who live in Patiala now and we buy halal meat from them.'

Sir Denzil Ibbetson (1994) noted in his *Punjab Castes* that most of the agricultural castes of the Punjab identified among Hindus, Muslims and Sikhs shared the same *gotras* (kinship lineages). However, conversions to Islam from the Hindu trading castes and Brahmins were much less frequent. Things, of course, varied across regions within the Punjab. The landlords were a powerful class who extracted many paid and unpaid services from the peasants, artisans and craftsmen, while they themselves served as linchpins of the colonial order. Most of them were Muslims, with a few Sikhs and Hindus. They exercised their influence in keeping peace and order in the countryside, while simultaneously acting as recruiting sergeants for the British Indian Army.

Remembering pre-Partition Punjab

The veteran revolutionary Dada Amir Haider, describing his childhood at the turn of the twentieth century in the Pothohar area around Rawalpindi, talks not only about the Sikh and Hindu moneylenders to whom the Muslim peasants were indebted, but also of how kindly he was treated by orthodox Hindu families, including one of Brahmin priests in charge of a temple. They gave him refuge when he ran away from his stepfather. Though given a lot of affection and treated kindly, Dada Amir was served food in separate vessels, as Muslims were not allowed into the Hindus' kitchen. However, he specifically attributes such treatment to the Hindus' dietary purity as laid down in their religion, rather than some conscious policy to discriminate against Muslims (Gardezi, 1989: 22-33).

Prakash Tandon (1988: 73), who hailed from the northern district of Gujrat, notes that Brahmins were not a privileged class among Punjabi Hindus; they were simply priests and given charity. He confirms that Punjabi Muslims and non-Muslims did not eat together. Hindu eating habits were governed by rules of pollution and were applied by the superior castes against the lower castes, not only against adherents of other faiths as such. Indeed, Hindus and Sikhs of the same caste could eat together and even marry. Cross-community marriages took place, especially among the trading castes of Khatris and Aroras. Some villages and areas were entirely Muslim or Hindu–Sikh, but there were mixed villages and urban localities, too. Sikh and Hindu landowners and cultivators employed Muslim tenant cultivators, artisans and the lower service castes. The *jajmani* system applied to some hereditary Muslim castes serving Hindus (ibid.: 76).

On the whole, peace and amity were prevalent. Former Pakistani Prime Minister Nawaz Sharif's was the only Muslim family in village Jati Umra, some twenty kilometres from Amritsar, in Taran Taran *tahsil*. He said:

> 'Well, my father tells [me] that they had [a] very sincere and friendly relationship with Hindus and Sikhs. They never practised any religious discrimination against us; on the occasions of marriage, death or social gatherings, we were treated as equals. We used to visit one another without any prejudice or discrimination. The non-Muslims always treated us the same as they did all other villagers' (Warraich, 2008: 29).

The famous Indian filmmaker O.P. Dutta has vividly described how, in the northern Punjab town of Chakwal, inter-communal relations were friendly and respectful. One example from his narrative on Chakwal vivdly illustrates that. He writes:

> It is said that social laws are not enacted – they evolve themselves. The society of Chakwal in early thirties [1930s] proved it. It all

> started with an attempted suicide by the grown-up daughter of a schoolteacher named Ramsarandas. The daughter was driven to desperation looking at the plight of her beloved father who could not meet the dowry demands of the prospective husband. She decided to end her life to spare her father further embarrassment. Ramsarandas, with his meager salary, could hardly provide his family with two meals a day; where would a dowry come from?
>
> The 'Chakwal' commune got together and under the guidance of the wise ones including Harbans Singh Seestani, Master Gyanchand, Trilokinath Advocate, Burhannudin Khoja, Amin Qureshi (he ran the only mutton shop in town) Qazi Omar and Master Budhram, the citizens of Chakwal passed a resolution unanimously to put a limit of Rupees five hundred on dowry to be given to a bride irrespective of the status of her father. (That would avoid comparisons and keep the disparities under cover). Anyone violating the order would be ex-communicated. A seemingly conservative society, steeped in traditional beliefs, was actually a progressive one (Dutta, 2000: 4).

Rao Abdur Rashid, ex-Inspector General of Police, Punjab, Pakistan, has provided a very interesting sketch of the social conditions in the hamlet of Kalanaur, in the eastern district of Rohtak. He writes:

> Our hamlet (Kalanaur) was the stronghold of Muslim Rajputs. They were very strict Rajputs. They preserved the purity of their blood with great care. They would agree to a marriage proposal after considerable inquiry [to ensure that proper Rajput blood is mixed with theirs]…. Kalanor was a big hamlet. Its population was some 10,000. Muslim Rajputs constituted more than half its population. All the land was owned by Muslim Rajputs. Hindu merchants who had their businesses in Calcutta and farther away had built houses on land belonging to Muslim Rajputs. They used to pay a token rent of Rs. 1 or 1.25 per year. When a wedding took place among such Hindus they would bring their son [bridegroom] mounted on a horse to the house of the Rajput landowner to pay respect. They would also bring sweets and other such things. This was a custom without which their wedding ceremony was not completed. This was the only

time when a Hindu could ride a horse in our streets. Otherwise no non-Rajput was allowed to ride a horse in our village.

We had blood relations with Hindu Rajputs. We belonged to the same *biradaris*. In the *panchayats* [village councils] Muslim and Hindu Rajputs would sit together and make decisions and give verdict. Before the Pakistan movement started there was no distinction of Hindu or Muslim, the distinction was between Rajputs and non-Rajputs. The Rajputs [Hindus and Muslim] considered themselves superior and were also because they own all land.... However, as the Pakistan movement gained momentum, Hindu–Muslim tension also developed. In one village some Hindu Rajput boys set a mosque on fire. Their elders were deeply saddened. A panchayat was called in which both Hindu and Muslim Rajputs participated. The Hindu Rajput elders begged forgiveness and offered to repair the mosque. So, again the fraternal spirit was restored. However, a Hindu Rajput said in an emotional manner: 'We are the decendants of the same mother. A revolution took place and we took different paths [that is, some converted to Islam while others remained Hindus]. Now again another revolution is about to take place. Why don't we become one again? Why do you want to leave your own blood relatives and go to another country?' The appeal was made with great sincerity.... Some of our elders who were strict Muslims but equally mindful of old traditions and etiquette said to them, 'Brothers we will think over your invitation and give you an answer later'. My late elder brother got up and said to our elders, 'Are you willing to change your religion?'.They said 'no'. Then he said, 'What is the point of thinking over this matter?' Then he said before the whole panchayat that since for both sides their religion is very dear, 'Neither we shall change our religion nor do we expect you to do so' (Rashid, 2010: 15-19).

Chaudhri Muhammad Bashir

'I was born in village Makhanpur, *tahsil* Pathankot, district Gurdaspur in 1932. Our village was half-Muslim and half-Hindu. We were the leading

Muslim family of Arain farmers. There were Muslim Gujjars too living in our village. The Hindus were Brahmins and Khatris. We helped each other in all possible ways. There was never ever any friction. On the contrary, there was genuine love and sympathy. I particularly remember our next-door neighbour Pandit Bua Ditta. He was a moneylender, but with a golden heart. Once, because of an allergy my eyes became very red and swollen. I was crying. He heard me from his rooftop. Panditji said, "Son, don't cry. I will help you". He came over with some medicine which he put in my eyes and soon I had recovered completely. I have done very well in Pakistan but my heart still belongs to my village [in India].'

Rana Muhammad Rashid

'I belong to the Rajput *biradari*. I was born on 21 December 1928 in my maternal grandparents' house in Moza Mughia Rajput, Hoshiarpur district. Ours was a Muslim village entirely, with Arains being the largest *biradari*, but we owned most of the land and were the *chaudhris*. I studied in *tahsil* Banga, Kapurthala. Most of the pupils and teachers were Hindus. The teachers were truly saintly people. When we were preparing for the matric exam our teacher Pandit Sham Swarup said to me that if five or six students got together he would coach us. So five of us, all Muslims, got together. Masterji would come everyday in the morning and continue helping us till afternoon. He never charged anything. Between his home and our village there was a graveyard where we met. After I came over to Pakistan [during Partition] I wrote to him from Chichawatni and informed him about my parents' death on the way, saying we were completely without any support. After twenty days I received a reply in which Masterji wrote that when his mother heard of what had happened to us she was so sad she would not cook food all day.'

Ahad Malik

'I was born in 1936 in Jullundur city. My father was originally from *tahsil* Dasyua of Hoshiarpur district belonging to the Dogar *biradari*. My mother was a Jullundur Arain. We lived in Mohalla Iqrar Khan, Kucha

Hashimpura. I grew up in a town in which political activities were very hectic. Hindus and Muslims lived in separate *mohallas*. Lala Bihari Mal had his milk business in our locality. He was actually the main supplier of milk to Jullundur. He was a very good man and treated us very well. He had some medicine which he would give anyone having toothache. He would put it on cottonwool and place it on the gum and the pain subsided miraculously. If, during Ramazan, any poor child from a Muslim family would go to his shop, he would give him milk free of charge. He was really a very God-fearing person. His son was employed in some senior position in the defence department. My father was serving in Palestine during World War II. My mother was very worried so she sought help from Bihari Lal's son in getting him transferred to India. This he arranged in a matter of few days. There were other good Hindus too. Some of them were close friends of my elders such as Prem Saigal, who was a brother of the great singer K.L. Saigal.

'But most Hindus kept a physical distance from us. When we went to Hindu shops to get sweets they would avoid touching us. Once in 1945, we returned from Lahore on the Frontier Mail. It was night time when we reached Jullundur. There were only *tongas* in those days as the means of transport. A Muslim *tonga*-driver, a Jat known to our family, told us to climb on. A young Hindu couple also came by the same train. They needed to come to town and wanted to rent the *tonga* alone as they would not like to travel with Muslims. The *tonga*-driver told them that they will have to travel in the same *tonga* or go on foot. Reluctantly, they agreed, and sat in front while avoiding any contact with us. Although Hindus were economically the strongest in town and owned factories and businesses, there were also prominent Muslim families who owned agricultural land and various food and fruit markets. Many Muslim landowners, however, were indebted to Hindus.'

Syed Ejaz Husain Jafri

'I belong to a family of *hakims* (traditional doctors) of Mehatpur Kasba, *tahsil* Nakodar, district Jullundur. Ours was an idyllic little hamlet where Hindus, Muslims, Sikhs, Christians – all lived in peace and amity. There was no enmity, only love. Eye-operations were also done by our elders.

All weddings coming to our village were entertained in our *haveli* (mansion) and could stay there for one day. There was no question of charging any rent or anything. The Hindus and Sikhs took part in the Moharram ceremonies while we took part in Hindu and Sikh festivals. In fact Hindus and Sikhs ate at our house and we ate at theirs.

'Some years before Partition, my father requested my teacher Gurdas Ram Pundit to help me learn some trade. He sent me to Lahore to Harnam Singh, who lived in the locality of Dharampura in Lahore, to learn the art of watch repairs. It was only at the time of Partition that people realised that India will be divided. While in Lahore I sensed that things would be getting bad very soon. So I came back to bring over my family and relatives to Lahore. Nakodar was a Muslim-majority *tahsil* but I still felt that it would be good to be in Lahore because here the Muslims were strong and felt secure. When we were leaving our village the Hindus and Sikhs came and said to my father, "Hakim Sahib you should not go. Those who come to attack you will have to kill us first". My father thanked them and said that he will come back once the inflamed passions subside and law and order are restored. Alas, that never happened. When we reached Lahore, I went to see Harnam Singh, only to discover that he and his family had been killed only a few days earlier. He was a good man, who used to recite the Sikh scriptures all the time, and treated me like his son. Those were good days and the people were good, too. I still long for my village but now I am nearly blind. I will never be able to go and see it again. That longing will go with me in my grave.'

Muhammad Feroz Dar

'We are originally from Wazirabad, where my grandfather had shifted from Kashmir in 1870, but my father was employed in the railway and was posted in Rawalpindi where I was born on 1 April 1936 in the Railway Colony. My father was a train driver. I had three older brothers and two elder sisters. The Railway Colony was close to the railway station. We all lived as one family – Hindus, Muslims, Sikhs, Christians and even Britishers. All communities used to send sweets to their neighbours on religious festivals. My brothers' Hindu and Sikh friends would come to our house and there was never a feeling of any difference. The only rule everybody observed was not to approach the kitchen of Hindus. I used to take my Hindu, Sikh and Christian friends to the mosque at the time of Eid and all children got some sweets. Then we used to go to the church on Christmas and were given chocolates. Similarly children would go to *mandirs* and *gurdwaras* and receive sweets on festivals.

'There was uncle Sher Singh and his wife Leela Kaur who were our next-door neighbours. Leela *chachi* used to often visit our house and she was like an elderly sister. *Chacha* Sher Singh did not keep good health. My father and I visited him in the railway hospital in Lahore. So, close were we to them. Leela Kaur was cooking food in the corridor. There was Bau Sri Ram. His son Hamesh was a very close friend. When I visited him then I had to avoid going to the kitchen. You would be surprised that his mother used to say to me, "Fauzi when you cook meat do give it to Hamesh also. He needs to become strong". I told this to my mother and thereafter he sometimes ate meat at our place.

'When my mother died, all the communities had come to express their condolences and for a long time the Hindu and Sikh women who knew my mother would stop me and put their hand on my head, which was the traditional gesture for expressing sympathy for an orphan. They always talked about her with sadness. It never occurred to anyone that one day, blood would flow in the streets of Rawalpindi and the Hindus and Sikhs would leave forever. But from 1945 onwards, something strange had begun to happen. We used to hear that India is going to become independent but after the Second World War, stories began to circulate about miraculous signs of a Muslim state called Pakistan coming into being. Sometimes it would be a calf born in some village with Pakistan written on its body, sometimes it was reported that a child had been born in a village with Pakistan written on his head. Another strange thing which started happening was that Hindus and Sikhs began to be transferred to places in East Punjab and elsewhere and many of our non-Muslim neighbours were already gone from Rawalpindi by 1947. I remember my father used to wonder what was happening. For example, Babu Sri Ram and other Hindu officers were transferred to Delhi while some Muslims and British officers were suddenly being sent to Rawalpindi. I think someone somewhere knew what was going to happen. Even Hindu teachers in schools were leaving for India. Despite all this, nobody could anticipate the type of bloody killings and division that would eventually take place.

'Hindus and Sikhs in Rawalpindi began to sell their properties and leave. This started some time in 1946. The election campaign of 1945–46 did not have much impact in the railway colony but I remember my father went to Wazirabad to cast his vote because we had property in that town.'

Rakshat Puri

'I was born on 24 February 1924, in Shahalmi Gate area of Lahore. We are Radha Swamis. We do not belief in organised religion but have faith in spirituality and the common humanity that connects us human beings. The stronghold of the Radha Swamis was the Beas region, now in East Punjab. When the head of our mission, Babaji, visited Lahore one-third of his followers were Muslims. Yes, people of all religions had joined the Radha Swami movement. We followed the teachings of Bhagat Kabir, Guru Nanak, Bulleh Shah and other such Sufis. When the Beas Muslims left for Pakistan, Babaji sent his Muslim followers to Pakistan but instructed them not to reveal their identity. This was necessary because the situation in East Punjab had become totally unsafe for anyone with a Muslim name. It was similar for us with Hindu names to leave West Punjab in 1947.'

Another very interesting syncretic movement in the Punjab was that of the Hussaini Brahmins. The Hussaini Brahmins, also known as Mohyal Brahmins with their famous clans of Dutts, Balis, Chibbers, Vaids were once found all over Punjab. Unlike other Punjabi Brahmins they were engaged in agriculture and sought employment in the police and military services. According to their family legend, their forefathers had settled in Arabia and one of their ancestors, Rahab Sidh Dutt, and his sons fought on the side of Prophet Muhammad's grandson, Imam Hussain, at the battle of Karbala in AD 680. They died fighting along with Hussain and his other followers. Some member of the family survived and returned to the Punjab.

This story was narrated to me in slightly different versions by three members of that group: the Bombay mega-filmstar Sunil Dutt, Professor

V.N. Datta and veteran journalist Jamna Das Akhtar. The Hussaini Brahmins remained Hindus but observed the rituals associated with the tragedy of Karbala. In the pre-Partition Punjab, the dual identity of the Hussaini Brahmins was expressed in the following verse:

Wah Dutt Sultan,
Hindu ka Dharm
Musalman ka Iman,
Adha Hindu Adha Musalman

(O! Dutt, the king
Follower of the religion of the Hindu and the faith of the Muslim
Half Hindu, half Muslim)

The writer Mashkoor Sabri told me that as a young man, he used to play the role of Lord Ram in the annual Ram Leela drama festival in Toba Tek Singh. Initially, the orthodox Hindus were somewhat irked, but he played the role so well that later he was selected every year to play Ram.

At a village school, known as a *dharamsala*, in the remote Campbellpur (Attock) district of northern Punjab, a young Muslim girl, Noor Bhari, in the 1930s who wanted to educate herself was allowed by her teachers to attend classes, but she had to sit outside along with the Hindu girls as it was a boys' school. At that time it was an extraordinary achievement because women in general and Muslim women in particular from the rural areas getting an education was unheard of.

Pre-Partition Lahore

Agha Ashraf's autobiography, *Aik Dil Hazaar Dastan* (*One Heart and a Thousand Stories*) (1989: 16-24), begins with a detailed description of his childhood in the 1920s within the walled city of Lahore. Children of all communities studied together in the local schools. He portrays in saintly terms some of his Hindu and Sikh teachers at the Dayal Singh School. He played truant, he says, along with his Hindu, Muslim and Sikh class fellows. They went around, among other things, visiting Hindu temples all over Lahore on such occasions. Drinking, taking opium, gambling, and other such deviations were widespread in the inner city. Ashraf himself indulged in drinking bouts along with his friends.

In another major autobiography, *Mera Shehr Lahore* (*My City of Lahore*), Yunas Adeeb covers mostly the society within the old walled city and the period from the late 1930s onwards. As a young lad, he could casually enter orthodox Brahmin homes and go to the temple with his neighbour Pandit Bhagat Ram's older, unmarried sister. He notes that the people had evolved their own peculiar ways and means of circumventing the strictures of orthodox Hinduism, Islam and Sikhism; in the process a composite, heterodox way of life had emerged (1991: 36-40). In the local *mohallas,* help and sympathy was given to the poor and distressed without reference to the various prejudices, although communal pride could sometimes prevent members of one group from taking help from the other community. Commenting upon the multiculturalism of Lahore, he recalls that Hindus would shower flowers on the Muharram procession, while Muslims flocked to the great Ram Leela festival held in Minto Park behind Badshahi Mosque, and many Muslims also took part in the Diwali and Dusshera celebrations. For those seeking exit from the conventions of regular society, the various Sufi shrines and abodes (*takkias*), the Hindu and Sikh non-conformist groups, the wrestlers' training centres (*akharas*), the courtesans' quarters, and various hideouts of opium-eaters and users of other intoxicants offered a range of possibilities. In these marginal enclaves, orthodox beliefs and practices were ignored. Adeeb personifies traditional multiculturalism in the following inimitable words:

> I remember in particular Lala Ganpat Rai because of his typical Hindu dress and appearance. He wore narrow pajama-type trousers, a kurta [long shirt], a waistcoat, and a black pointed cap on his head. Looking at his face one knew that he was extremely cordial and friendly. It was his routine that when he passed the mosque in Kucha Darzian (locality of the tailors) he would stop, bend down to touch the steps of the mosque with his hands, and then with both hands pressed together paid his respect (ibid.: 163).

I spoke to a former resident of the pre-Partition walled city of Lahore, the well-known Pakistani educationist, Professor Shaukat Ali, on 29 July 2002, at his son's residence in Mansfield, Massachusetts, US.

Professor Shaukat Ali

'I was born in 1923 in a very poor Muslim family in the slums of Bhati Gate. We lived in the predominantly Hindu locality of Mohalla Jallotian, Kucha Nakarchian, inside the walled city. We were five brothers and sisters with no earning member of the family except my widowed mother who used to perform various domestic chores such as stitching and needlework for others. Of the 250 or more families living in that locality, only five were Muslim. Our Hindu neighbours were very gracious and God-fearing. Almost all of them kept a cow at home. Knowing that my mother was a poor but hardworking woman, they would give us milk, butter and curd free of charge. At the time of Hindu festivals such as Holi and Diwali we would receive sweets from them. I don't remember a single instance when they made us feel unwelcome in their homes. The only restriction was the kitchen which the women kept only for themselves and Muslims were not allowed there. This was part of their religious practice and had nothing to do with discrimination as such. The Hindu women would come and spend hours talking to my mother.

'I studied at the Dayal Singh High School. Most of my friends at school were Hindus. There was no discrimination at school, our teachers were fair and kind and very helpful. The school was located in Said Mittha Bazaar and I had to walk that distance from Bhati Gate. It was my great desire to become an academic, but my circumstances were most discouraging. However, my mother took on more work and my maternal uncle who lived in Said Mittha Bazaar also helped me financially to get admitted to Dayal Singh College where I did well and gradually gained admission to the BA honours class.

'Two of my Hindu teachers took special interest in me and inspired me to work hard. One was Professor Prem Kirpal who had studied at Oxford University. His father, Rai Bahadur Ishwar Das, was the registrar of Punjab University. They lived on Race Course Road. Professor Kirpal would invite some of us home for extra coaching. The other boys came from well-to-do backgrounds. I was the only one who was humbly-dressed in *shalwar-kurta* and a Turkish fez on my head. We were treated to coffee and Western delicacies, things I had never tasted before. The same was true of Professor Lajpat Rai Nayyar. I used to go to his house too which was located near Miani Sahib off Mozang Chungi. He also treated me very kindly.'

Kuldip Kumar Chopra

'My maternal grandfather (*nanaji*) Bali Ram Khullar was a big landlord of Kahna Kachha, Lahore district. He owned seven villages. Two of his cousins, Daulat Ram Khullar and Jagan Nath Khullar, were well-known lawyers of Lahore. Nanaji owned a number of *sarayes* (resting places, where travellers could rest and stay free of charge and food was also served for free). Most people who worked on our land were Muslims. They were provided housing, appropriate wages and food grain. They also worked in my *nanaji's haveli*. *Nanaji* used to smoke waterpipes with his Muslim landlord friends and sometimes those friends stayed overnight in the haveli and took food and drinks together. My nani fell ill and could not breastfeed my mother. So, a Muslim maid breastfed her for at least two months. Since Kahna Kacha was not far from the Indian border, my mother's family crossed safely into India in August 1947. My *mama (*maternal uncle), Inder Sain visited Kahna Kacha in 1956. One of my *nana's* peasant retainers had taken possession of our haveli. He greeted my *mama* with respect and affection urging him to come back. My mother who was a student of Hans Raj Mahila collage Lahore, still claims that her best time in life was spent in Lahore'.

'On the other hand, things went bad for my paternal grandfather, Milkhi Ram Chopra, who lived in Hafizabad, Gujranwala district. He was an officer in the Indian railways. He was stabbed to death during the Partition riots. His children ran away in different directions is sheer panic when they saw their father die before their own eyes. My father was only eighteen at that time. He somehow managed to reach a camp at Ferozepore on the Indian side of the Punjab border. He could not sleep for months and constantly had nightmares and anxiety. Yet, on both sides of my family, the elders did not brook any deep hatred for the people of Pakistan. They realised that it was a moment in history when insanity had prevailed on all sides. They still keep saying that the Partition should not have taken place.'

Som Anand, the author of *Lahore: A Lost City*, stayed behind in Pakistan after Partition with his father, Faqir Chand, a banker who had married a Muslim woman. I talked to him in Delhi about pre-Partition days and the events of 1947 and later. Here, I quote passages from his book. He remarks that the Hindu and Muslim communities 'lived like two streams, flowing side by side but never meeting at any point' (1998: 3). He goes on:

> To keep themselves away from the Muslims' 'polluting touch', the Hindus had set up many barriers in their daily life. My mother, for example, would never allow any Muslim to enter her kitchen. No cooked food was accepted from them. I remember how, if any of our Muslim neighbours even sent any special dish for my father, it never went beyond the dining table, a place where she did not take her own food. While eating she would never allow any of her Muslim friends or neighbours to touch her. During my childhood such inhibitions were generally not observed by male members of educated Hindu families. (Women have always been more conservative in these matters.) Some decades earlier these rules formed a strict code of conduct for all, no matter how educated or enlightened a person might be....
>
> The absurdities of such Hindu restrictions notwithstanding, the Muslims had come to accept them as a law of nature. Their older generation knew the limits of a relationship with the Hindus and considered it improper even to offer them drinking water from their utensils.... The Hindus have always complained of Muslim fanaticism but they have never understood that the walls they raised around themselves could have not resulted in any other attitude....
>
> It took many centuries for the Hindus of Punjab to realise how absurd and harmful their anti-Muslim prejudices were. In this respect the first current of change was felt during the Khilafat movement in the early twenties. Though the spirit of Hindu–Muslim amity received many reverses in later years, at the social level the urban elite had changed its code of conduct for the better. This was due, in part, to Western education. What this change meant was evident in my father's attitude. When he was young, my mother used to

> recall, he would come back to change his clothes if a Muslim had touched him while walking in the bazaar; but during my childhood in Model Town, father had several Muslim friends and he considered my mother's inhibitions a sign of backwardness (ibid.: 3-5).

Dina Nath Malhotra, whose father Rajpal was the publisher of the controversial book *Rangeela Rasul* referred to earlier, talked to me at great length about the Lahore of the 1940s. He confirms Som Anand's observation that Muslims must have felt insulted by some Hindu practices. Here I quote from his book:

> During the summer months in Lahore, young Hindu volunteers from good families used to haul trolleys of cool water, scented with *kewra* and *sandal,* on Nisbet Road and other areas, offering water in silver tumblers to every passer-by with courtesy. But it was limited to Hindus only. When any Muslim, even if decently dressed, came forward to get a glass of water, he was given water in a specially reserved inferior glass, the water being taken out from a bamboo funnel more than a yard long. This was most humiliating and repulsive. Such acts effectively made the Muslims feel discriminated against. Under the circumstances, it was inevitable that the exhortations of Jinnah had a telling effect on the mind of the Muslim community (Malhotra, 2004: 59).

In his autobiography, *Truth, Love and a Little Malice,* the famous Sikh writer, journalist and historian Khushwant Singh has provided many glimpses into Punjab society from the early twentieth century. He has a whole chapter on Lahore, where he was trying to establish a law practice. Khushwant Singh was born in 1915 in a tiny hamlet called Hadali, an area in the Shahkot district. His village had the reputation of having provided more soldiers proportionately than any other village in India in the First World War. Many of the men had served as bodyguards of British viceroys. Singh mentions that most of the three hundred or so families were Muslims. Hindu and Sikh families were about fifty. The non-Muslims were engaged in trade, shopkeeping and moneylending. His own family was the richest in the village; they lived in a house made of bricks while most people lived in mud houses. He writes: 'We

Sikhs and Hindus of Hadali lived with the Muslims in an uneasy but peaceful relationship. We addressed their elders as uncles or aunts as they did ours, we rarely went to each other's homes except on marriages and deaths' (2002: 5).

Writing about Lahore before Partition, Khushwant Singh provides many interesting anecdotal accounts of life within the upper-middle-class families. He observes that while Hindus and Sikhs made friends routinely and their families socialised happily, Sikhs or Hindus with close Muslim friends or family contacts were rather rare. He writes:

> Despite our friendship with the Manzur Qadirs I had no illusions about the general Muslim-Hindu/Sikh divide. Even in the High Court Bar Association and Library, Muslim lawyers occupied different corners of the large lounge and library from Hindus and Sikhs. There was a certain amount of superficial mixing at weddings and funerals, but this was only to keep up appearances. After the Muslim League resolution demanding Pakistan, the cleavage became wide and continued to grow wider (ibid.: 105).

Prem Dhawan, the veteran songwriter and music-director of the Mumbai film industry, told me that as a young man he came into contact with revolutionaries in the Lahore jail, where his father was a superintendent. By the time he graduated from the famous Forman Christian College. Lahore in 1942, he had been converted to Marxism. About the Lahore of the 1930s and early '40s he remarked:

'The atmosphere in F.C. College was cosmopolitan. The students came from all the communities. Most of us got along very well. Things were the same in most other parts of Lahore. It was indeed a city of tolerance and light. I left for Bombay in 1943. That four years later Hindus and Sikhs would have to leave Lahore forever never occurred to me. It could never have occurred, could it?'

The same feeling about congeniality at college was shared with me by the late Communist leader of Pakistan, Sardar Shaukat Ali, a class fellow of Prem Dhawan, who shed tears when I mentioned that I had met Dhawan in Mumbai in 2001. He said:

'From the fifth class I studied in Kasur. In 1939 I joined Ram Sukh Das College in Ajnala Tehsil, Amritsar, where my brother was a revenue official holding the position of Qanungo. It was a very good experience. Muslims were in the majority but there were Hindus and Sikhs. We ate the same food. Later I joined the F.C.College in Lahore and I was in the same class as Prem Dhawan. I and some of my friends were attracted to the Communist movement.'

Tahira Mazhar Ali Khan, daughter of Sir Sikandar Hayat Khan, the first Premier of the undivided Punjab and leader of the Unionist Party, had the following to say:

'I was born in Wah in northern Punjab which is our ancestral town, but I grew up in Lahore. I studied at the Queen Mary's School, where girls from the upper-class families of the Punjab studied. We never thought of each other as Hindus and Sikhs. We would celebrate each others' festivals. Raja Narendra Nath, leader of the Hindu Mahasabha, called himself my father's brother and he was a very, very nice family friend. We had two kitchens, one for Muslims and one for Hindus and Sikhs. It is true Hindus would not let us enter their kitchens. Later I joined the Communist wing of the Congress party and there we had friends from all the religions and there was no feeling of communal differences.'

The well-known Punjabi singer and actress, Pushpa Hans had fond memories of Lahore to recount:

We lived on Fane Road. My father was a barrister. I started my singing career from Lahore Radio Station. The famous Bollywood actor, Om Parkash, used to play Fateh Muhammad and a Muslim gentleman, whose name I now forget, played the character of a Hindu in a Punjabi skit that was relayed regularly from Lahore Radio. It was the most popular programme of that time.

Mian Hameedudin from Ferozepur lived on 13 Fane Road. He was a brilliant lawyer. His daughter Kishwar was one of my best friends. I used to keep *roza* (fast) along with her. Among educated people religious differences were never a problem. We got along very well. We kept in touch for a long time but now I don't know where Kishwar should be. I hope she is alive and in good health.

When I sang the famous Punjabi songs, *'Sari Raat Taknia teri reh'* and *'Channa khetey guzari a raat wei'* listeners from Pakistan sent requests for it to be played many times on All-India Radio. In fact I once performed for Indian *jawans* (soldiers) on the Jammu border. The

Pakistani troops on the other side requested that one of the loudspeakers should be turned in their direction. This was done and we all had a very good time.

References

Adeeb, Y. *Mere Shehr Lahore (My City of Lahore)*, Lahore; Atish Fishan Publications, 1991.

Ahmad, S. *Great Sufi Wisdom: Bulleh Shah*, Islamabad: Saeed Ahmad, 2004.

Ahmed, I. 'Sikh Separatism in India and the Concept of Khalistan' in Haellquist, K. R. (ed.), *NIAS Report 1990*, Copenhagen: Nordic Institute of Asian Studies, 1990.

———. *State, Nation and Ethnicity in Contemporary South Asia*, London and New York: Pinter Publishers, 1998.

———. 'South Asia' in David Westerlund and Ingvar Svanberg (eds.), *Islam Outside the Arab World*, pp. 212-252, Richmond: Curzon Press, 1999.

Alhaq, Shuja. *A Forgotten Vision: A Study of Human Spirituality in the Light of the Islamic Tradition*, Chippenham, Wiltshire: Minerva Books, 1996.

Akbar, M. J. *India: The Siege Within*, Harmondsworth: Penguin Books, 1985.

Ali, I. *History of the Punjab (1799-1947)*, Delhi: Low Price Publication, 1970.

———. *The Punjab under Imperialism 1885-1947*, Karachi: Oxford University Press, 1989.

Anand, S. *Lahore: Portrait of a Lost City*, Lahore: Vanguard Books Ltd, 1998.

Ashraf, A. *Aik Dil Hazaar Dastan (One Heart and a Thousand Stories)*, (Lahore; Atish Fishan Publications, 1989.

Bhatia, S. *Social Change and Politics in Punjab: 1898-1910*, New Delhi: Enkay Publishers Pvt Ltd, 1987.

Carter, L. *Punjab Politics 1936-1939, The Start of Provincial Autonomy: Governors' Fortnightly Reports and Other Key Documents*, Delhi: Manohar, 2004.

Chaudhry, N. A. *Development of Urdu as Official Language in the Punjab (1849-1974)*, Lahore: Government of the Punjab, 1977.

Darling, S. M. *The Punjab Peasant in Prosperity and Debt*, New Delhi: Manohar Book Service, 1978.

Dutta, O. P. 'Chakwal Fondly Remembered', *The South Asian*. Available online at http://www.the-south-asian.com/July-Aug2000/Chakwal_memories_4.htm, 7 August 2000.

Farquhar, J. N. *Modern Religious Movements in India,* Delhi: Munshiram Manoharlal, 1967.

Gardezi, H. N. *Chains to Lose, Life Struggles of a Revolutionary: Memoirs of Dada Amir Haider Khan,* New Delhi: Patriot Publishers, 1989.

Grewal, J. S. 'Historical Geography of the Punjab' in *Journal of Punjab Studies,* vol. 11, no. 1, Spring, 2004.

Ibbetson, S. D. *Punjab Castes,* Lahore: Sang-e-Meel Publications, 1994.

Jones, K. W. *Arya Dharm: Hindu Consciousness in 19th-Century Punjab,* Delhi: Manohar, 1989a.

Kholi, S. S. *The Life and Ideals of Guru Gobind Singh,* Delhi: Munshiram Monoharlal, 1986.

Lahori, Tahir. *Sohna Shehr Lahore (The Lovely City of Lahore),* Lahore; Sang-e-Meel Publications, 1994.

Leigh, M. S. *The Punjab and the War,* Lahore: Government Printing Press, 1922.

Malhotra, D. N. *Dare to Publish*, New Delhi, 2004.

Moon, Penderal. *Divide and Quit,* New Delhi: Oxford University Press, 1998.

Nagina, Z. I. *Ghazi Ilam Din Shaheed,* (Lahore; Jang Publishers Press, 1988.

Sheikh, M. 'The 30-year rule of the "three hakeems"'. *Dawn,* Karachi, 25 June 2005.

Sheikh, M. 'When the 'wild' proved more educated'. *Dawn* (Lahore edition), 24 January 2010.

Singh, G. *Religion and Politics in the Punjab,* New Delhi: Deep & Deep Publications, 1986.

Singh, K. *A History of the Sikhs, vol. 1, 1469-1839*, Princeton: Princeton University Press, 1963.

———. *A History of the Sikhs, vol. 2, 1839-1964,* Princeton: Princeton University Press, 1966.

———. *Ranjit Singh: Maharajah of the Punjab 1780-1839*, New Delhi: Orient Longman, 1985.

———. *Truth, Love & a Little Malice,* New Delhi: Viking, 2002.

Talha, N. *Economic Factors in the Making of Pakistan,* Karachi: Oxford University Press, 2000.

Warraich, S. *The Traitor Within: The Nawaz Sharif Story in his own Words,* Lahore: Sagar Publishers, 2008.

Interviews

Jamna Das Akhtar, Delhi, 20 October 1999
Prem Dhawan, Mumbai, 22 October 1999
Sunil Dutt, Mumbai, 20 October 2001
Professor Shaukat Ali, Mansfield, Massachusetts, USA, 29 July 2002
Noor Bhari, Lahore, 17 April 2003
Chaudhri Muhammad Bashir, Lahore, 18 April 2003
Rana Muhammad Rashid, Lahore, 18 April 2003
Syed Ejaz Husain Jafri, Lahore, 22 April 2003
Tahira Mazhar Ali Khan, Lahore, 23 April 2003
Sardar Shaukat Ali, Lahore, 3 May 2003
Dina Nath Malhotra, 15 March 2004
Pushpa Hans, New Delhi, 31 March 2004
Mashkoor Sabri, Multan, 22 December 2004
Professor Chaman Lal Arora, Jullundur, 4 January 2005
Amrik Chand Ahluwalia, Patiala, 7 January 2005
Raskhat Puri, Delhi, 10 January 2005.
Professor V. N. Dutta, veteran historian, New Delhi, 10 January 2005
Ahad Malik, Stockholm, 13 January 2006
Muhammad Feroz Dar, Solna, Sweden, 18 February 2007
Kuldip Kumar Chopra, Stockholm, 20 April 2011
Mian Mustafa Kamal Pasha, Lahore, 14 January 2005

3

GENESIS OF THE PUNJAB PARTITION 1900–1944

The larger context

The British Indian Empire came directly under the Crown in 1858, after the English East India Company successfully crushed an uprising in 1857, when some Indian sepoys of the Company's 'Bengal Army' revolted. Some disgruntled Indian princes and religious figures also joined that movement. Even in the Punjab, mutinies and rebellions took place but were successfully contained. Hindu–Muslim cooperation ensued during the uprising but began to wane as the British devised a system of patronage that made the different communities compete against each other. The British Indian Empire comprised primarily two distinct types of political arrangements – territories directly administered by the British and hundreds of princely states that under treaty accepted British paramountcy. From the end of the nineteenth century, Hindu, Muslim and Sikh religious revivalism began to take place. This generated a further sense of alienation between the two communities.

Hindus constituted roughly two-thirds of the Indian population. Upper-caste Hindus were concerned lest pan-Islamism arising elsewhere in Asia would sweep into India and with the help of Indian Muslims, break up the subcontinent. Already, in the late nineteenth century, apprehensive Hindus had begun to suggest that without Muslims being reconverted to Hinduism a coherent Indian nation could not be achieved. Some wanted Muslims to be driven out into west Asia but most advocated forced assimilation or *shuddi* (Jones, 1989b). The Muslim minority of India made up 24.9 per cent of the total Indian population. Most of them were converts, largely from the lower castes and pastoral and peasant tribes, while a tiny minority claimed descent from forebears who had migrated to the Indian subcontinent from central, southwest and west Asia. Ideas of creating one, or several, separate Muslim states held an attraction for some Muslims. The most prominent Muslim to demand a separate Muslim state was the poet-philosopher Iqbal, also a Punjabi but of Kashmiri Brahmin descent, who took up the issue at the annual session of the All-India Muslim League in Allahabad in 1930. In his famous address he declared:

> The Muslim demand for the creation of a Muslim India within India is ... perfectly justified ... I would like to see the Punjab, North-West Frontier Province, Sind and Balauchistan amalgamated into a single State. Self-determination within the British Empire or without the British Empire, the formation of a consolidated North-West Indian Muslim State appears to me the final destiny of the Muslims, at least of North-West India (Pirzada, 1970: 159).

Choudhary Rahmat Ali, another Punjabi, was a more determined advocate of Muslim separatism. In 1933, he and some other students at Cambridge University produced the pamphlet 'Now or Never', in which the idea of a separate Muslim state, called Pakistan, was presented. This name was an acronym derived from the five Muslim majority regions of north-western India: Punjab, 'Afghania' (the North-West Frontier Province), Kashmir, Sindh and Baluchistan. Rahmat Ali began to lobby conservative British politicians to support his political schemes, writing in 1935 to a British peer:

> We, the Pakistanians, have lived from time immemorial our own life and sought our national salvation along our own lines. PAKISTAN has retained, during the whole of its existence, its own law and has cherished its own religious, spiritual and cultural ideals, which are basically different from those of HINDOOSTAN. We have, as a nation, nothing in common with them, nor they with us. In individual habits, as in national life, we differ from them as fundamentally as from any other civilised nation in the world (Aziz, 1978: 23-4).

The Government of India Act 1935

It is clear from the Government of India Act 1935, which served as the basis of the 1937 election, that the British had no intention of letting go their Indian Empire. For example, the Government of India Act 1935 envisaged the following, among other points:

1. India was to be a federation comprising provinces directly under British suzerainty as well as the princely states.
2. The Governor-General remained the head of the central administration and enjoyed wide powers concerning administration, legislation and finance.
3. The provinces were given autonomy with respect to subjects delegated to them.
4. With regard to the provinces, although wholly elected ministries were to be formed, Section 93 provided for the governor to issue proclamations in consultation with the Governor-General (Viceroy) to take over the civil administration should he feel that the constitutional machinery was no longer functioning satisfactorily. Such a proclamation was to cease to operate after 6 months, but the British parliament could prolong it for another 12 months by passing a resolution to that effect.

The 1937 provincial elections

The two main political parties, the Indian National Congress (founded 1885) and the All-India Muslim League (founded 1906), contested the provincial elections in early 1937. The Congress tested its claims of being the representative of all Indians and pressed for greater self-government while the Muslim League contested on the claim to represent the Muslim community of India. The Congress also announced an intention to abolish big landlordism in independent India, something which did not go down well with the big landowners. In the Muslim-majority provinces of north-western India, such as the Punjab, the Muslim landlords were greatly perturbed. In any case, Congress did well in the Hindu-majority provinces, winning 711 general seats out of a total of 1,585. It also contested fifty-eight reserved seats for Muslims but won only twenty-six. The Muslim League fared miserably in the Muslim-majority provinces (Punjab, Sindh and the North-West Frontier Province [NWFP] in north-western India) winning only one seat in the Punjab, and none in Sindh and NWFP. In these provinces, regional parties dominated by Muslim leaders won most of the reserved Muslim seats. On the other hand, the Muslim League did well in Hindu-majority provinces, and won 108 reserved Muslim seats out of a total of 485 (Allana, 1977: 149).

The Congress formed ministries in six provinces, and then in two more. There is some evidence that an agreement existed between the United Provinces (now known as Uttar Pradesh) Congress and the Muslim League to form a coalition government. However, after the Muslim League was routed all over India, the Congress reneged on that agreement. Commentators generally agree that this was a major blunder on the part of the Congress (Jalal, 1985; Seervai, 1989; Wolpert, 2002). Whatever the truth, it was surely a short-sighted decision which raised the fear that in a future united India, Congress would set up one-party rule. The Muslim League, alleging that the Congress governments adopted policies which adversely affected Muslim interests and cultural identity, especially in the United Provinces, now embarked on a concerted policy to rouse Muslim opinion in favour of a separate Muslim state. It asserted that a 'Hindu Raj' should be prevented from taking over. Jinnah, the leader of the Muslim League, began to argue that the Muslims were a separate nation and not a religious minority, and therefore entitled to the right to self-determination. Thereafter, the Muslim League abandoned its elitist approach and began to prepare for mass politics. On 20 March 1938 the Muslim National Guard, a volunteer corps, was established. Its members were to wear a green uniform with a badge comprising a crescent and star in white (Allana, 1977: 175).

For its part, the Congress took the view that the Muslim League was a stronghold of pro-British Muslim landlords rather than the representative party of the Muslim masses, and so it launched counter-campaigns of its own, seeking mass contact with Muslims. It deployed Muslim nationalist parties, such as the Jamiat-ul-Ulama-e-Hind, in the field against the Muslim League and, in the Punjab, the radical Muslims of the Ahrars were mobilised against both British rule and the Muslim

League, which was attacked as a party of toadies (*Report of Court of Inquiry*, 1954: 254). The League retaliated by repeating the warning of a Hindu Raj under the Congress. Additionally, the idea was fostered that Hindu traders and moneylenders would cause further ruin to Muslims. From 1937 onwards, Jinnah embarked on a relentless campaign to emphasise that the Muslims were not simply a minority but a separate nation altogether from the Hindus. Such extreme polarisation ultimately culminated in the partition of India as well as of Bengal and the Punjab in mid-August 1947.

The Punjab

In 1901, the five frontier districts of Peshawar, Kohat, Bannu, Hazara and Dera Ismail Khan were separated from the Punjab to constitute the new North-West Frontier Province (NWFP). The district of Delhi was separated from the Punjab in 1911 when the colonial power moved its capital there from Calcutta. Since then and until 17 August 1947, the British designated the whole of Punjab including 'British territories' that they directly administered as well as the princely states as the Punjab Province. The total area of the Punjab Province was 138,105 sq. miles (357,692 sq. kilometres). The British Territories constituted 99,089 sq. miles (256,640 sq. kilometres) and remained so until 1947.

The following were the main administrative units, known as divisions and districts, that constituted the British territories:

1. Rawalpindi division: Attock, Rawalpindi, Jhelum, Gujrat, Mianwali and Shahpur districts.
2. Multan: Montgomery (now called Sahiwal), Lyallpur (now called Faisalabad), Multan, Jhang, Muzaffargarh and Dera Ghazi Khan districts.
3. Lahore: Gujranwala, Lahore, Sheikhupura, Sialkot, Amritsar and Gurdaspur districts.
4. Jullundur: Ferozepur, Jullundur, Ludhiana, Hoshiarpur and Kangra districts.
5. Ambala: Ambala, Hissar, Rohtak, Karnal, Gurgaon and Simla districts.

The Lahore and Jullundur divisions comprised the central districts, where the Muslims were in a slight majority. In these two divisions, plus the Jhelum and Gujrat districts of the Rawalpindi division and the Lyallpur district of the Multan division, Lahori Punjabi with its local variations was spoken. The Sikhs were concentrated in these two divisions but were also to be found in significant numbers in the otherwise predominantly Muslim district of Rawalpindi. In the Multan division, the local language/dialect was known as Multani or Seraiki, and in the Rawalpindi division, Pothohari. It is a matter of debate whether they are different languages or just dialects of Punjabi. Meanwhile, in the eastern Ambala division, Hindi and not Punjabi was the main language. Even the Muslims of Rohtak, Hissar, Gurgaon and Karnal, known as Meos, spoke a Hindi rural dialect and did not eat beef. Hindus were in a clear majority in the Ambala division. Thus the British territories were an administrative unit rather than the homeland of a compact Punjabi-speaking people. Hindus were to be found everywhere, but their numbers in the Rawalpindi division and in the Multan division were small.

The Punjab enjoyed the reputation of being the 'loyalist' province of British Raj. The British administration, with the governor as pivot, established an elaborate system of patronage extending across religious communities and castes. A clear bias in favour of the rural classes underpinned such a system. Thus the Land Alienation Act of 1901 categorised Punjabi castes into 'agriculturalist' and 'non-agriculturist'. Under the terms of the act, the non-agriculturalist castes were legally prohibited from acquiring agricultural land. As a consequence, the power and influence of the rural agricultural castes and classes was consolidated over the Punjab. They, in return, helped supply soldiers to the army from their areas of influence. The Punjab supplied nearly half of all soldiers of the Indian Army. It also made handsome financial contributions to the war efforts during both wars.

Punjab census reports

The Census of India reports provide vital information and constitute fascinating source material for research on India. The reports were, no doubt, written from a colonial perspective and what is intriguing is the special emphasis given to the British territories as a distinct category when comparisons are made over time in the population variation of the religious communities. Rather, consistent tables are available only for the whole of Punjab or the Punjab Province. It has been quite a frustrating task trying to find comparable tables for the British territories as an entity. This approach of the census authorities is rather peculiar because most of the activities of the British were carried out in the territories that they directly administered. The emphasis is mainly on the castes and detailed descriptions are provided.

It is worth noting that insofar as the partition of the Punjab in 1947 is concerned, the British territories were directly discussed and disputed before the Boundary Commission by the parties involved. The princely states were not represented except in the case of Bahawalpur and Bikaner states, but their points of view were admitted only in connection with the irrigation systems and water heads that would affect them. The statistics listed below are important to bear in mind.

Population percentages for the Punjab Province 1901–1941

Year	Muslims	Hindus*	Sikhs	Christians	Others
1901	49.6	41.3	8.6	0.3	0.2
1911	51.1	35.8	12.1	0.8	0.2
1921	51.1	35.1	12.4	1.3	0.1
1931	52.4	30.2	14.3	1.5	1.6
1941	53.2	29.1	14.9	1.5	1.3

Source: Census of India, 1941, vol. 6, Punjab table, page. 46.
*includes caste Hindus as well as scheduled caste Hindus. The scheduled castes comprised the lowest castes and included the so-called untouchables.

Population percentages of Muslims, Hindus and Sikhs for British territories 1881–1941

Year	Muslims	Hindus	Sikhs	Christians
1881	51.72	40.29	6.56	–
1931	56.54	26.83	12.99	1.74
1941	57.06	26.56	13.22	1.77

The above table has been worked out from two sources. One, the Census of India, 1931, vol. 17, part 1, where the percentages' variation between 1881 and 1931 have been given on page 291 for Muslims, Hindus and Sikhs. I have added the figures from the 1941 census given under the heading 'Sample tables VII, XI & XIII' on page (65). While an official census of the Christian population of the British territories could not be found, my guess is that it was slightly higher than 0.03 per cent for 1881 the Punjab Province. The figures for Hindus include both caste Hindus and the scheduled castes, but from 1931 onwards and until the last census of 1941, sections of the untouchables began to register themselves with the census authorities as Ad-Dharmis. The Ad-Dharmis did not consider themselves Hindus in any sense.

The Muslim percentage of the British territories increased very gradually. The following figures have been given in *The Partition of the Punjab 1947* vol. 1 (1993: 151), which is a compilation of the official documents by Mian Muhammad Sadullah.

1881	52.75
1891	51.83
1901	52.31
1911	55.29
1921	55.27
1931	56.98
1941	57.06

We notice that in the Punjab, the proportions of the Hindu population between 1881 and 1941 declined rapidly but it did not mean any spectacular gains for the Muslims, whose numbers rose very slowly and naturally. Much of the loss in Hindu numbers was because of the sharp increase in the Sikhs' proportion of the Punjab population. As we have argued earlier, Hindu and Sikh identities were not so sharply differentiated in the Punjab, but during the twentieth century, this began to change. Others who gained from the Hindu population were the Christians and Ad-Dharmis: both were movements that attracted the most despised and degraded sections of the scheduled castes known as the untouchables. Notwithstanding, the slight increase of the Muslim population particularly worried the Hindu minority. The Punjab administration noted that the various religious communities and their political organisations deliberately exaggerated their proportion of the population. Upper-caste Hindus, in particular, complained that the census returns were biased and that the functionaries of the state took partisan positions in the collection of data.

Ideas of partitioning the Punjab

In November–December 1924, Arya Samaj leader Lala Lajpat Rai wrote a number of articles in *The Tribune* of Lahore, in which he said: 'My suggestion is that the Punjab should be partitioned into two provinces, the Western Punjab with a large Muslim majority to be [a] Muslim-governed province; the Eastern Punjab with a large Hindu–Sikh majority to be [a] non-Muslim-governed province' (Aziz, 1995: 145). He also suggested that Muslim provinces be established in the NWFP, Sindh and East Bengal.

According to Kirpal Singh, Lajpat Rai had been shocked by ferocious attacks on the Hindu minority by Muslims in Kohat in the NWFP in September 1924. It resulted in Hindus and Sikhs being evacuated to Rawalpindi in northern Punjab (1972: 9). Singh asserts that Lajpat Rai was not thinking in terms of sovereign Muslim states but some sort of autonomous Muslim-majority arrangement within India (Singh, 1989: 10). K.K. Aziz argues, however, that in his 14 December 1924 article in *The Tribune*, Lajpat Rai clearly and categorically advocated the partition of India (Aziz, 1995: 145-146).

When it came to the predominantly Hindu-majority and Hindi-speaking Ambala division, some prominent Muslims were in favour of it being separated from the Punjab. The British were also thinking of solving the problem of communal tension by separating Ambala division from the Punjab and thus making the Muslim community predominant in the Punjab. Allama Iqbal had supported such an idea. Other notable Muslims who supported this idea in different forms included Nawab Sir Mohammad Shahnawaz Khan (Singh, 1989: 12). Such suggestions were resented not only by Hindus, whose numbers in the Punjab would decrease drastically if such a scheme were to be adopted, but also by the Sikhs. At the Indian Round Table Conference held in London in

1930–1931, the Sikh delegates tried to confront the idea of making Punjab a conclusively Muslim-majority province by using the following argument:

> If the Muslims refuse to accept in this province, where they are in a slight majority in population anything but their present demand of reserved majority, we ask for a territorial rearrangement which would take from the Punjab, the Rawalpindi and Multan Divisions (excluding Montgomery and Lyallpur districts). These Divisions are overwhelmingly Muslim as well as racially akin to the North West Frontier Province (quoted in ibid.: 11-12).

As mentioned in the introduction, in the Punjab tangle, the aspirations of the Sikhs need to be taken note of, particularly because as the third major community of the Punjab, and one with complete identification with the Punjab as their religious and cultural homeland, the position of their leaders on the shape of the Punjab mattered. They had a very large presence in the British Indian Army and were, therefore, an important community of the province. In the 1920s, a bitter conflict broke out between Hindus and Sikhs when some Arya Samaj leaders described the Sikhs as merely a Hindu sect. The Sikhs responded by asserting that they were not Hindus, though in political terms they considered the Muslims as their main rivals in the Punjab.

An important feature of the evolution of political parties during the colonial period was the emergence of the Indian National Congress and the All-India Muslim League as the two main parties representing conflicting versions of nationalism. The Congress claimed to be a secular party of all Indians while the Muslim League was a party exclusive to the Muslims. There were strong regional parties in different parts of India as well.

The Punjab Unionist Party and Punjabiat

The Punjab Unionist Party (hereafter referred to as the Unionist Party) was founded in 1923, dominating the politics of pre-Partition Punjab till the election of 1946. It based its support on a sense of Punjabiat (shared Punjabi cultural identity). Punjab was considered the loyalist, 'sword arm' of the British who recruited half the soldiers of their imperial army from among its so-called martial races comprising various Muslim, Hindu and Sikh castes. Its founder, Sir Fazl-i-Hussain (died 1936), had established the basis of communal harmony, but one that preserved the interests of the Muslim and Hindu landowning and agricultural classes vis-à-vis urban Hindus. The Sikhs were not part of it (Oren, 1974: 397; Ali, 1970: 425-81; Husain, date of publication unavailable). I interviewed at length the veteran Muslim Leaguer, Syed Afzal Haider, and the well-known historian Professor V.N. Dutta in Delhi about Sir Fazl. Both agreed that Sir Fazl was an outstanding Punjabi leader.

Sir Fazl was not himself a feudal landowner, having attained his prominent position in politics through education and merit. As education minister of Punjab province, he introduced quotas for the educationally backward Muslims in some leading educational institutions. This was resented by the Hindus, but Sir Fazl was able to carry through his policy through excellent speeches in the Punjab legislative assembly. He was strictly opposed to politicisation of religion and to any suggestion of the division of the Punjab and was therefore highly respected by all the communities. His successor, Sir Sikandar Hayat Khan, was one of the biggest landlords of the Punjab and a more pragmatic politician, although he remained a steadfast opponent of the division of the Punjab on communal grounds (Ali, 1970: 425-81; Husain, date of publication unavailable). I also interviewed his son Azim Husain in London.

From 1909 onwards, Indian Muslims, including Punjabi Muslims, voted separately for a reserved number of seats. The 1935 Act introduced wholly-elected ministries in the provinces, though the governor, who was always British, continued to enjoy overriding executive powers. The right to vote was gradually expanded but even in 1937, when the elections were held, it was limited to around ten per cent of the Indian population. Sir Sikandar Hayat Khan was elected the first Premier of Punjab province (some British-ruled provinces had premiers while others had chief ministers). Sir Sikandar despised the Congress party's radicalism. The Congress leader Jawaharlal Nehru had threatened to carry out land reforms to abolish landlordism and that was unacceptable to the Unionist Party. Sir Fazl and Sir Sikandar had even kept the Muslim

League at arm's length but later, fearing growing Congress popularity, Sir Sikandar entered into the so-called Jinnah–Sikandar Pact of 1937 by which Muslim members of the Unionist Party in the Punjab legislature agreed to become members of the Muslim League and thus strengthen the hands of the central Muslim League on the national level. On the other hand, the Unionist Party was to continue freely to decide its political priorities in the Punjab (Carter, 2004: 142-7).

Sir Sikandar believed that the Punjab's best interests lay in the continuation of the British connection. For a short period, he served as acting governor of the Punjab, a rare occurrence during the British Raj. Under the rule of the Unionist Party, the Muslim proportion of the government services rose sharply, although in the 1940s, Hindus and Sikhs were still ahead of them. However, in some key services such as the police, Muslim representation was disproportionately higher than the population strength of Muslims in the Punjab. When the Second World War broke out, Sir Sikandar came out strongly in support of the British. Governor Sir Henry Craik wrote in the FR of 13 September 1939 to Viceroy Linlithgow that Sir Sikander was hoping to supply half a million soldiers recruited for the British war effort. Like the moderate Hindus of the Punjab, he was hoping the Congress would also support the war effort, in which case he intended to include two Congress members in his ministry and thereby broaden the basis of communal amity in the Punjab (ibid.: 378). Tahir Lahori notes that whether Hindu, Muslim or Sikh, the politicians of the 1930s observed high standards of honesty. He remarks:

> The finance minister was Sir Manohar Lal. His only son was an employee in a bank, but he did not hold any high position. If the finance minister had wanted he could have found him any high position. Sir Choutu [sic] Ram owned some agricultural land before he became a minister. When he left that job he still had the same piece of land. All leaders were of strong character. Muslim leaders were also of firm and exemplary patriotic character. Sir Sikandar Hayat's son was a major in the army (1994: 223-4).

In political terms, it would seem, Punjabis of all communities, or at least their elite, were committed to some vague feeling of Punjabiat or

Punjabi unity transcending communal differences. The Congress party, however, decided not to co-operate with the British war effort and its ministers resigned in 1939. Things began to change thereafter, as the competition between the Congress party and the Muslim League on the national level inevitably impinged on Punjabi politics. Until then, the Indian National Congress and the all-India Muslim League have had a negligible influence among Punjabis.

The third prominent leader of the Unionist Party was the dynamic Hindu leader from the Hindi-speaking Ambala division, Sir Chhotu Ram. He was the leader of the Haryana Jats and his sympathies lay with the oppressed peasantry rather than upper-caste Hindus. He took a number of measures to provide legal relief to the indebted agricultural sector of society (Gopal, 1988). The British had already introduced the Punjab Alienation of Land Act in 1901, whereby legal restrictions on agricultural land passing into the hands of moneylenders and other non-agricultural castes were introduced. However, that alone did not prevent the moneylenders from acquiring control over land through the use of front-men and other deceptive measures. Thus, the peasant continued to be heavily indebted to the moneylender. The veteran Communist leader and former General-Secretary of the Communist Party of India (Marxist), Harkishen Singh Surjeet, explained the situation at that time in the following words:

'In the 1940s the Congress party in the Punjab was the stronghold of the urban Hindu trading class. It had little influence in the countryside. In 1936 when Sir Chhotu Ram introduced a bill to remit the debts to the moneylenders the Punjab Congress refused to support such a bill. Mahmud Ali (uncle of the Trotskyist writer Tariq Ali) and I came to Delhi and met Maulana Azad, who instructed the Congress members of the Punjab legislature to support that bill. Of the 13 Congress members of the legislature, 7 were Communists. They voted in favour of the bill but the 6 who were not abstained. The bill was passed without the support of the main Congress leaders. Of course remission from the loans was granted, but still the cultivator always needed to borrow money and the moneylenders continued to do business in informal ways.'

The Punjab Congress

The Indian National Congress had marginal support in the Punjab until the last election of 1946. Whatever support it had was confined to the urban areas and attracted nationalists from all communities. However, communal revivals, not broad-based national awakening in the Punjab, served as the route to politicisation and mobilisation and this applied to the Congress, too. Paul Wallace makes this insightful remark:

> Communal groups served as the initial change agents for both social mobilization and politicization rather than the nationalist movement. They, rather than the Congress Party, produced the bulk of the leadership and the cadre, as well as orientation towards communal issues which comprised the core elements for nationalist politics during the first two decades of the twentieth century (1976: 390).

He identified two Hindu factions in the Punjab Congress: the Lala Lajpat Rai–Bhargava factions, which saw the nationalist movement as inseparable from a Hindu orientation and considered concessions to Muslims as appeasement; and the Satyapal faction which sought close co-operation with Muslims in the Punjab in the interest of national freedom. Dr Satyapal, with Dr Saifuddin Kitchlew, was instrumental in welding together Hindus, Muslims and Sikhs in Amritsar before the Jallianwalla Bagh massacre in 1919. The Lajpat Rai–Bhargava faction was closely aligned to the Hindu Mahasabha in the Punjab and with Sardar Patel at the national level. Both Hindu factions were urban-based and upper-caste, and came from central Punjab. It was the same base from which the Hindu Mahasabha recruited its members.

On the other hand, the Satyapal faction tried to bring in nationalist Muslims. They were supported at the national level by Jawaharlal Nehru and Maulana Azad. Later, when Lala Lajpat Rai died in 1928, the Congress right-wing continued to be led by Gopi Chand Bhargava, while after Satyapal's death, Bhim Sen Sachar become the leader of the Congress left-wing in the Punjab (ibid.: 389-402). Many Congress members of the Bhargava group were leading moneylenders and involved in other financial activities.

However, the Congress did represent the broad-based anti-colonial sentiment all over India. Therefore anti-colonial Muslims from all over the Punjab were attracted to the Congress in the wake of the Jallianwala Bagh massacre and the Khilafat Movement. Some prominent Muslims in the Punjab Congress were Maulvi Abdul Qadir Kasuri (president), Mian Iftikharuddin (president), Dr Saifuddin Kitchlew (president), Dr Mohammad Alam (general secretary) and Sheikh Muhammad Hayat. Sheikh Muhammad Hayat was very close to Maulana Abul Kalam Azad. His daughter Mahmooda Begum talked to me at length in December 2004 about her father's long association with the Congress party. The famous people's poet, Ustad Daman, was also associated with the Punjab Congress.

To my great surprise, when I spoke to elderly Punjabis all over the Pakistani Punjab, I learnt that several anti-colonial Muslims were active in the Congress in many districts such as Jhelum, Gujrat, Ludhiana, Amritsar, Multan, Gujranwala, and Jullundur. Moreover, the Congress had its allies among the radical *ulema* of the Punjab belonging to the Ahrar, Deobandi and Ahl-e-Hadith schools. Only after the 1940 Lahore resolution, which proposed the creation of Pakistan as a separate Muslim state, did sections of the Muslims desert the Congress to join the Muslim League. In the various governors' fortnightly reports from the late 1930s and early 1940s, the Congress was described in contemptuous terms and visits of Gandhi and Nehru viewed with dismay. Surprisingly, the Harrovian Nehru was described as more dangerous than Gandhi by Governor Emerson (Carter, 2004: 69).

The Punjab Muslim League

The Punjab Muslim League did not have a proper office until 1938. Thus for example, in his first fortnightly to Viceroy Linlithgow dated 19 October 1936, Governor Emerson mentions neither the Muslim League nor the Congress as important parties in the Punjab. They receive only cursory mention (Carter, 2004: 47-56). However, some of the leading all-India level figures of the Muslim League were from the Punjab. Sir Muhammad Shafi (died 1932), a big landowner and a leading barrister, was a leader of the stature of Jinnah (Shahnawaz

2002). Shafi represented the right wing which believed in co-operation with the British and strongly supported separate electorates. Iqbal was another all-India level Punjabi leader of the Muslim League. However, the Muslim League remained marginal in Punjab politics and won only two seats in the 1937 elections.

Thereafter, the Muslim League engaged in hectic activities across India. Indeed, in the Punjab, it began to attract the intelligentsia. In 1940, when the idea of a separate state was floated from the platform of the Muslim League, the Muslim intelligentsia and urban classes flocked to it. The leading Muslim landowners remained with the Punjab Unionist Party until at least 1943. After World War II, when they sensed that the British were increasingly bestowing recognition on the Muslim League as the sole party representing Indian Muslims, they rapidly changed sides and joined it (Talbot, 1996).

The Sikh Panthic parties

The Sikh had been granted separate electorates in 1919 and some extra seats, more than their proportion of the Punjab population (Grewal, 2000: 132). Sikhs entered Punjab politics through the revolutionary Ghadr Party but it was the mass agitation for acquiring control of Sikh *gurdwaras* from Hindu priests in 1925 which brought most Sikhs into the political arena and led to the founding of the Akali Party. The Akali or Panthic Sikhs began to represent Sikh communal interests although they co-operated with the Congress on many issues until 1942. There were various factions of the Akalis, collectively referred to as the Panthic parties. The Sikhs broke away from the Congress when the Congress party began a movement against recruitment to the British Indian Army. Soldiery provided the Sikhs with employment and a large percentage of the Indian Army consisted of Sikhs who supported the Akalis. This conflict came to a head at the time of the Quit India Movement which was launched by Congress in 1942 (interview, Kirpal Singh).

Minor political organisations and parties

Anti-British Muslims infused with Islamic zeal tended to join the Majlis-e-Ahrar (1929), a party closely allied to the Congress, while some others joined the Khaksar movement (1931), based on semi-military organisation inspired by fascism, but basically anti-British in orientation (Hafiz, 2001: 167-200; 217-34). On the other hand, the Hindu Mahasabha and later the Rashtriya Swayamsevak Sangh (RSS), both India-level organisations, were active in the Punjab but remained minor players. Their ire was reserved for the Muslims. At the time of the Punjab partition, the RSS was actively engaged in terrorism in the province (Ali, 1970: 674-79). It specialised in manufacturing bombs and exploding them indiscriminately.

The Punjab Communists worked through the left wing of the Congress party as open activities were banned. In 1941 when the Soviet Union was attacked by Hitler, the Communists in the Punjab, as elsewhere in India, began cooperating with the war effort. In return, they were allowed to open an office and begin their activities. The government, however, continued to monitor their activities with no less vigilance. The Punjab Communists (Hindus, Muslims, Sikhs and even some Christians) had some influence among writers and the railway union (Josh, 1979).

The Lahore resolution of 23 March 1940

Although the idea that the Muslim League should demand a separate state had been floated by Iqbal in 1930, it was taken up in earnest only in 1938 when a number of resolutions were proposed and discussed, mainly by Punjabis. It culminated in the 23 March 1940 resolution, already mentioned in a previous chapter, being moved publicly at the annual session of the Muslim League in Lahore (Malik, 2001). It stated:

'Resolved that it is the considered view of this session of the All-India Muslim League that no constitutional plan would be workable in this country or acceptable to Muslims unless it is designed on the following principle, viz., that geographically contiguous units are demarcated into regions which should be grouped to constitute "independent states" in which the constituted units shall be autonomous and sovereign.' (Allana, 1977: 226-7)

According to Wali Khan, Sir Muhammad Zafrulla Khan, a leading stalwart of the Ahmadiyya community and member of the Viceroy's Executive Council, was instructed by Linlithgow to prepare a memorandum advising the Muslim League to demand a separate state (Khan, 1987: 29-30). At that time, World War II was raging in full fury and Britain wanted to exert pressure on the Indian National Congress, which was not cooperating, to support the war effort. At that time, the Ahmadiyya community was under instruction from their religious head, Mirza Bashiruddin Mahmud Ahmad, to not join the Muslim League. Governor Sir Henry Craik noted in his FR dated 25 March 1940:

> I had an interesting talk this morning with Pir Akbar Ali, a Unionist member of our assembly, who belongs to the Ahmediyya community...Pir Akbar Ali gave me two items of information, which may interest you. The Ahmedis, he said, have always considered the Khaksar Movement a dangerous one and not a single Ahmedi has joined it. The second item was that the Ahmedis as a body have not been allowed by the religious head of their movement to join the Muslim League. Akbar Ali himself has been allowed to join as a member of the Unionist Party for a term of six months only. The question whether his followers should be allowed to join the League is, I understand, shortly to be considered by the head of the community (Carter, 2005: 101).

Subsequent research clearly shows that the Lahore resolution was a turning point in the destiny of the Punjab, as well as of India as a whole. The Punjabi Hindus and Sikhs reacted with great alarm to the idea of a separate Muslim state. It was dubbed as the 'Pakistan Resolution' by Hindu and Sikh newspapers. On the other hand, the popularity of the Muslim League increased rapidly, according to accounts of C.R. Aslam, Ahmad Bashir, Ramanand Sagar, and Amarnath Sehgal, in our interviews. Tahir Lahori records that when the Muslim League passed the Lahore Resolution in March 1940, demanding the creation of a Muslim state, there began the parting of ways between Hindus and Muslims. The former reacted with great alarm to the idea of a separate Muslim state, but the Muslim League became very popular among the Muslims (1994: 224-5).

However, the Shia and Ahmadiyya communities were apprehensive about a Sunni-dominated Pakistan coming into being. This is obvious from the correspondence between the Shia leader Syed Ali Zaheer and Jinnah in July 1944 (Allana, 1977: 375-9). The Council of Action of the All-Parties Shia Conference passed a resolution on 25 December 1945, rejecting the idea of Pakistan (Bakshi, 1997: 848-9). However, most Shias shifted their loyalty to the Muslim League in the hope that Pakistan would be a non-sectarian state. Initially, the Ahmadiyya were also reluctant to support the demand for a separate Muslim state. It was only when Sir Zafrulla was won over by Jinnah that the Ahmadis started supporting the demand for the creation of a Pakistan. The decision to support Pakistan was taken only prior to Partition in 1947 (*Court of Inquiry*, 1954: 196-7). Thereafter, the Ahmadis also put all effort behind the demand for Pakistan. To such groups, Jinnah gave assurances that Pakistan would *not* be a sectarian state.

In any event, after the 23 March 1940 Lahore Resolution, the focus of Muslim politics shifted decisively from the Muslim-minority provinces to the Muslim-majority ones of north-western India. Craik observed in a long telegram of 1 April 1940 to Viceroy Linlithgow: 'Muslim opinion is now, outwardly at least, in favour of the partition of India. Only a very courageous Muslim leader would now come forward openly to oppose or even criticise it' (Carter, 2005: 108-9).

It is well known that Sir Sikandar Hayat Khan was opposed to such an idea. However, he was the chief host to a gathering of Muslim notables from various provinces of India and therefore did not resist the idea categorically. In any case, the Punjab now became the key province in the struggle for a separate Muslim state. Not surprisingly, the Sikhs perceived the creation of such a state as inimical to its deepest interests in the province. They began to clamour against an impending majoritarian tyranny of the Muslims, and continued their agitation and propaganda throughout 1940 and 1941. When Sir Stafford Cripps came with his mission in early 1942, they presented a memorandum to him on 31 March in which they complained that Sikh interests would be sacrificed if the British government conceded the creation of Pakistan.

They said that the Muslim majority of the Punjab was unreal and made out a case that the Hindu–Sikh proportion of the population was greater than the Muslim. Some areas in the western region of the province had been included only for administrative reasons. They wrote, 'We shall resist, however, by all possible means the separation of the Punjab from the All-India Union. We shall never permit our motherland to be at the mercy of those who disown it' (Mansergh and Lumby, 1970: 582-8; Kirpal Singh, 1972: 26-7). It was signed by Baldev Singh, President of the Sikh All Parties Committee and included the signatures of Master Tara Singh, Jogendra Singh, Ujjal Singh and Mohan Singh (ex-adviser to the Secretary of State for India). They also appended a note in which they developed their argument further, though somewhat shoddily, saying that instead of total opposition to the partition of India, they proposed the creation of two provinces in the Punjab, with the river Ravi being the boundary between a Muslim-majority province to the west and a Hindu–Sikh majority province to the east. (ibid.: 27-31).

The Khizr ministry

The Quit India Movement begun by Congress on 9 August 1942 did not have much of an impact in the Punjab, but as elsewhere, its leaders and activists in the Punjab were arrested and put in jail. Surprisingly, there is no mention in the governor's fortnightly reports of the impact of the Quit India movement on the Punjab. Meanwhile, the sudden death of the redoubtable Sir Sikandar on 26 December 1942 created a political crisis. His successor, Sir Khizr Hayat Khan Tiwana was, like his predecessor, opposed to the division of India on religious grounds, and especially to suggestions about partitioning the Punjab on such a basis. He was also a firm believer in the benefit of continued British rule. However, he lacked the political skills of Sikandar and faced leadership challenges from within the Unionist Party (Talbot, 1996).

Khizr clashed with Jinnah in 1943 and 1944 when the latter, in contravention of the 1937 Jinnah–Sikandar Pact, tried to expand his direct influence in the Punjab. Khizr offered considerable resistance to Jinnah's increasingly communal rhetoric and demand for a separate Pakistan. But challenges from within to his leadership by Sir Sikandar's son Sardar Shaukat Hayat, in 1943, and later defections of other powerful landowners greatly weakened his position. (ibid.: 113-124). As the moment of British departure came closer, the landlords shifted their support to the Muslim League, not wanting to live in a united India ruled by the Congress. After all, the Congress had declared that it will prioritise the abolition of the *zamindari* system when it came to power.

On the other hand, the Muslim League presented the idea of Pakistan as a panacea for all economic and social problems afflicting Muslims (ibid.). Already, as early as in 1944, the Punjab Governor, Sir Bertrand Glancy, noticed such a trend gaining pace in the Punjab. In the FR dated 26 October 1944, he remarked:

> I would lay very great emphasis on a point that I endeavoured to make recently at Delhi – and that is the intense danger in the crude Pakistan theory. The more one considers this theory the more fantastic – and the more ruinous to Muslims and all other interests – does it appear. No one can deny the possibility of political unrest after the end of the war, but I can think of no more alarming menace to peace, so far as the Punjab is concerned, then the pursuit of the Pakistan doctrine. Any serious attempt to carry out into effect this idea in the Punjab with its bare Muslim majority and its highly virile elements of non-Muslims means that we shall be heading directly towards communal disturbances of the first magnitude. Hence I maintain that we should try to wean Muslim opinion into acceptance of equal or adequate representation at the Centre, while endeavouring to persuade Hindus that they should be prepared to pay this premium for unity and security (Carter, 2006: 106-7).

References

Ahmed, Ishtiaq. *'Let's not forget Jallianwala Bagh'*. *Daily Times,* 13 April 2003.

Ali, I. *History of the Punjab (1799-1947),* Delhi: Low Price Publications, 1972.

Allana, G. (ed.) *Pakistan Movement: Historic Documents*, Lahore: Islamic Book Service,1977.

Aziz, K. K. (ed.) *Complete Works of Rahmat Ali*, Islamabad: National Commission on Historical and Cultural Research, 1978.

Aziz, K.K. *History of Partition of India,* vol. 1, New Delhi: Atlantic Publishers and Distributors, 1995.

Bakshi, S. R. (compiler). 'Resolution adopted by Council of Action of the All-Parties Shia Conference', held at Poona, 25 December 1945, in, *The Making of India and Pakistan: Ideology of the Hindu Mahasabha and other Political Parties,* Vol. 3, New Delhi, Deep & Deep Publications, 1997.

Batalvi, A. H. *Hamari Qoumi Jidojehed (Our National Struggle),* Lahore: Pakistan Times Press, (no year of publication given).

Gopal, M. *Sir Chhotu Ram: A Political Biography,* New Delhi: B.R. Publications, 1988.

Grewal, J.S. 'Punjabi Muslims and Partition' in Amrik Singh (ed.), *The Partition in Retrospect,* Delhi: Aanamika Publishers & Distributors (P) Ltd, 2000.

Haafiz, Takiuddun. *Pakistan ki Syasi Jamaaten Aur Tehriken* (The Political Parties and Movements of Pakistan), Lahore: Classic, 2001.

Husain, A. *Mian Fazl-i-Husain: Glimpses of Life and Works 1898-1936,* Lahore: Sang-e-Meel Publications, (no date of publication given).

Jalal, Ayesha. *The Sole Spokesman*, Cambridge: Cambridge University Press, 1985.

Jones, K.W. *The New Cambridge History of India: Socio-Religious Reform Movements in British India*, Cambridge University Press, Cambridge, 1989b.

Josh, Bhagwan. *Communist Movement in Punjab (1926-47)*, Delhi: Anupama Publications, 1979.

Wali, Khan. *Facts are Facts: The untold story of India's Partition,* New Delhi: Vikas Publishing House Pvt Ltd, 1987.

Lahori, Tahir. *Sohna Shehr Lahore (The Lovely City of Lahore),* Lahore; Sang-e-Meel Publications, 1994.

Malik, M.A. *The Making of the Pakistan Resolution,* Karachi: Oxford University Press, 2001.

Oren, Stephen. 'The Sikhs, Congress, and the Unionists in British Punjab, 1937-1945', *Modern Asian Studies*, Vol. 8, No, 3, Cambridge: Cambridge University Press, 1974.

Pirzada, Syed Sharifuddin (ed). *Foundations of Pakistan: All-India Muslim League Documents, 1906-1947, vol. II,* Karachi: National Publishing House Ltd, 1970.

Seervai, H.M. *Partition of India: Legend and Reality*, Bombay: Emmanem Publications, 1989.

Shahnawaz, Begum Jahan Ara. *Father and Daugher: A Political Biography,* Karachi: Oxford University Press, 2002.

Singh, Kirpal. *The Partition of the Punjab*, Patiala: Publication Bureau Punjabi University, 1989.

Talbot, Ian. *Khizr Tiwana: The Punjab Unionist Party and the Partition of India*, Richmond, Surrey: Curzon, 1996.

Wallace, Paul. 'Communalism, Factionalism and National Integration in the Pre-Independence Punjab Congress Party' in Harbans Singh and N. Gerald Barrier (eds), *Punjab Past and Present: Essays in Honour of Dr Ganda Singh*, Patiala: Punjab University, 1976.

Wolpert, Stanley. *Jinnah of Pakistan*, Karachi: Oxford University Press, 2002.

Official documents

Carter, Lionel., (ed.). *Punjab Politics 1936-1939, The Start of Provincial Autonomy: Governors' Fortnightly Reports and other Key Documents*, Delhi: Manohar, 2004.

———. *Punjab Politics 1940-1943, Strains of War, Governors' Fortnightly Reports and other Key Documents*, Delhi: Mahohar, 2005.

———. *Punjab Politics, 1 January 1944 – 3 March 1947, Last Years of the Ministries, Governors' Fortnightly Reports and other Key Documents*, New Delhi: Manohar, 2006.

Census of India, 1931, vol. 17, Punjab Part 1. Lahore: "Civil and Military Gazette" Press, 1933.

Census of India, 1941, vol. 6, Punjab, tables. Simla: Manager of Publications, Delhi, 1941.

Mansergh. N. and E.W.R. Lumby, (eds). *The Transfer of Power*, January-April 1942, vol. 1, London: Her Majesty's Stationery Office, 1970.

Sadullah, Mian Muhammad (compiler) *The Partition of the Punjab 1947, vol. I, official documents*, Lahore: Sang-e-Meel Publications, Lahore, 1993.

The Punjab Alienation of Land Act, 1901. Lahore: Government Printing Press, 1901.

The Report of the Court of Inquiry constituted under Punjab Act II of 1954 to enquire into the Punjab Disturbances of 1953 (also known as Munir Report), Lahore: Government Printing Press, 1954.

Interviews

Amarnath Sehgal, Delhi, 20 October 1999

Ramanand Sagar (famous Mumbai writer and filmmaker), Delhi, 25 October 1999 and Mumbai, 18 October 2001

C.R. Aslam, (veteran Communist leader), Lahore, 14 December1999

Syed Afzal Haider, Lahore, 13 April 2003

Ahmad Bashir, 22 April 2003

Harkishen Singh Surjeet, General Secretary Communist Party of India (Marxist), Delhi, 21 October 1999

Mushtaq Raj member of Congress in Gujranwala, 9 December 2004

Mahmooda Begum, 9 December 2004

Professor Kirpal Singh, Chandigarh, 2 January 2005

Professor V.N. Dutta, veteran historian, New Delhi, 14 January 2005

Azim Husain (son of Sir Fazli-i-Husain), London, 6 June 2005

STAGE I

The Punjab Bloodied

INTRODUCTION

The first stage in the partition of the Punjab extended from January 1945 to March 1947. Religious revivals had been taking place from the beginning of the twentieth century, emphasising the differences between communities and promoting inter-communal tensions. In some cases, such tension resulted in violent incidents. The processes of revivalism received a boost during the 1945 election campaign, with the Muslim League launching a virulent communal campaign directed mainly against the Punjab Unionist Party, and demonising the Hindus and Sikhs as well. It generated fear and anxiety among these religious minorities while generating complacence among the Muslim majority. The election result further compounded the communal tangle: While the Muslim League emerged as the clear choice of the Muslim voters, its astounding success still fell short of the parliamentary majority needed to build a government. The defeated Punjab Unionist Party joined hands with the Punjab Congress and the Sikh parties to form a coalition government. This was unacceptable to the Muslim League, which threatened direct action. When in January 1947, the Khizr ministry banned the Muslim League National Guards, it resulted in mass demonstration which grew bigger and more frequent by the day.

On 20 February, the British government announced its intention of handing over power to Indians by June 1948. Khizr Tiwana felt that such an announcement had created an entirely new situation and therefore he resigned as Punjab premier on 2 March. The Muslim League tried to find coalition partners but failed. That resulted in communal clashes in Lahore on 4 March. Similar clashes took place in Amritsar, Multan and Rawalpindi. On a lesser scale, some other urban centres were also affected by communal violence. Whereas in Lahore and Amritsar, the initial clashes were between more or less equally balanced Hindu–Sikh and Muslim protestors and agitators, in Multan the Hindu minority was no match for the Muslim majority. In Rawalpindi city, the initial contest was even-handed. In fact, the Sikhs had the upper hand, but once the violence spread to the villages, the armed Muslim mobs wreaked havoc on the Sikh villages. The government seemed to have been caught off-guard, in spite of the fact that in the fortnightly reports based on intelligence reports that the Punjab governor and chief secretary wrote, warned of 'private armies' being raised by the Hindu, Muslim and Sikh communities. Within ten to fifteen days, the government was able to restore law and order, although hardly normality or peace.

The hundreds of deaths and injuries and the destruction of property through looting and arson meant that the politics of violence – emerging in Calcutta in August 1946 and spreading to other parts of India – had also reached the Punjab. The underlying logic of the Punjab partition had begun to form at this first stage: If India is partitioned, then Punjab would suffer the same fate.

8 March Congress resolution supporting the Sikh demand for partition of the Punjab

Such logic was formalised when, in a meeting held in Delhi on 8 March 1947, the Congress Working Committee came out categorically in support of the Sikh standpoint on the Punjab. It adopted a resolution which observed that in view of the tragic events in that province, a way out involving the least amount of compulsion should be found. 'This would necessitate a division of the Punjab into two provinces, so that the predominantly non-Muslim part may be separated from the predominantly Muslim part' (*Pakistan Times*, 10 March 1947). With the passage of such a resolution, the Punjab question no longer remained a provincial matter. Not only the Sikhs, but henceforth even the Congress was going to link the future of the Punjab inextricably to the future of India. However, the final word on the future of the Punjab was still to come.

References

Pakistan Times, Lahore, 10 March 1947.

4

PUNJAB ELECTION AND COALITION GOVERNMENT 1945–1946

The larger context

The Conservative Party lost the July 1945 UK general elections and a post-war Labour Government came to power. Prime Minister Clement Attlee was reconciled to the fact that Britain would have to pack up and leave India soon. He had begun to set in motion the process which aimed at the transfer of power to Indian hands, preferably united and as a member of the British Commonwealth. If that failed, India and Pakistan were to be advised strongly to remain in the Commonwealth. Consequently, elections for India were announced in Delhi on 21 August. Electioneering was immediately underway all over India, though the Congress was under a huge disadvantage because its leaders had been behind bars since August 1942 on account of the Quit India Movement that Mahatma Gandhi had launched, in the hope of forcing the British to transfer power to the Congress. It sought a mandate to keep India united while the Muslim League stood for a separate Pakistan.

The elections were held in two stages: first for the Constituent Assembly and then for the provincial assemblies. The latter were more relevant for the future of the Punjab, as the Muslim League did not take part in the proceedings of the Constituent Assembly and focussed its attention instead on the demand for Pakistan. The results vindicated the contradictory claims of both parties. Congress secured 905 general seats out of a total 1,585 in the provinces, while the gains of the Muslim League were even more impressive at 440 seats out of 495 reserved for Muslims (Allana, 1977: 396). Thereafter began intense activities to find a constitutional formula that would be acceptable to the two main antagonists, the Congress and the Muslim League. That was to prove impossible.

The top-secret breakdown plan of 27 December 1945

The intelligence services and the Commander-in-Chief of the British Indian Army, General Auchinleck, were of the opinion that widespread unrest could be expected by the summer of 1946. Moreover, Viceroy Wavell was pessimistic about a negotiated settlement between the various parties and therefore wanted the government to announce a constitutional award. In a top-secret communication of 27 December 1945 he sent a 'breakdown' plan to the Secretary of State for India at the India Office, Lord Pethick-Lawrence. In it, he asserted that the law-and-order situation could deteriorate to a dangerous level because of 'excessive requirements by the Muslim League for representation and safeguards; or a demand by Congress for the abolition or weakening of the Governor-General's powers of veto' (Mansergh and Moon, 1976: 700). In order to avoid that from happening, he suggested a plan in which the government would be ready to announce an award to settle the constitutional problem. He noted:

> We should base ourselves on two points of principle:
>
> a) If the Muslims insist on self-determination in genuinely Muslim areas this must be conceded.
> b) On the other hand there can be no question of compelling large non-Muslim populations to remain in Pakistan against their will (ibid.).

Proceeding along such a line of reasoning, Wavell observed:

> If these principles were followed, the effect would be that at least two divisions of the Punjab [Jullundur and Ambala] and almost the whole of Western Bengal including Calcutta would have to be allowed to join the Union [i.e. an India ruled by Congress]. The attractiveness of Pakistan to the Muslims would largely disappear. Only "the husk", in Jinnah's own words, would remain (ibid.).

He urged the British government to authorise him to open negotiations in which he could threaten Jinnah with announcing an award dividing both Bengal and Punjab. He added:

'It is likely that Jinnah would press for an exact statement showing how H.M.G. would demarcate the "genuinely Muslim areas" ... To meet such a request we should, I think, be ready with a detailed demarcation. This is difficult, and any line will involve grave trouble with the Sikhs in the Punjab, but I will put forward proposals shortly' (ibid.: 701).

Wavell thought such a strategy would induce Jinnah to work towards the best possible terms for his Muslim supporters within a united India. At the same time, while conceding the principle of Pakistan, he opposed its area being left undefined. He asserted that an award from the government would be considered as fair by the world, but the Muslim League was unlikely to accept it as the consequence could be serious communal conflict (ibid.).

Wavell's boundary-demarcation plan of 7 February 1946

On 7 February 1946, in continuation of his breakdown plan, Wavell submitted to Pethick-Lawrence his idea that if compelled to give an award, the demarcation of 'genuinely Muslim areas' (ibid.: 912) should include:

1. (a) Sind, North-West Frontier Province, British Baluchistan, and Rawalpindi, Multan and Lahore divisions of Punjab; less Amritsar and Gurdaspur districts.
   (b) In Bengal, the Chittagong and Dacca divisions, the Rajshahi division (less Jalpaiguri and Darjeeling), the Nadia, Murshidabad and Jessore districts of Presidency division; and in Assam, the Sylhet district.
2. In the Punjab, the only Moslem-majority district that would not go into Pakistan under this demarcation is Gurdaspur (51-per cent Moslem). Gurdaspur must be attached to Amritsar for geographical reasons and Amritsar, being sacred city of Sikhs, must stay out of Pakistan. But for this case for [of] importance of Amritsar, demarcation in the Punjab could have been on divisional boundaries. Fact that

much of Lahore district is irrigated from upper Bari Doab canal with headworks in Gurdaspur district is awkward but there is no solution that avoids all such difficulties.

3. Greatest difficulty is position of Sikhs with their homelands and sacred places on both sides of the border. This problem is one which no version of Pakistan can solve (ibid.).

Wavell then presented the population figures of Sikhs in the Punjab, including the princely states, as 5,116,000. Of these, 1,461,000 would be in Pakistan and the rest in India. He stated further that Rawalpindi – with its large Sikh population of 64,000 and the canal colonies of Lyallpur with 263,000 and Montgomery with 175,000 Sikhs – would have to remain in Pakistan because they were placed in Muslim-majority areas. With regard to Calcutta (twenty-three per cent Muslim population) in Bengal, it should also remain in India or be made into a free port if negotiations between the parties could successfully reach such an arrangement (ibid.: 913). Wavell's plans to discourage the Muslim League from demanding partition through the announcement of an award, rather than a negotiated settlement were, however, ignored by the British government in London. It has never been explained why this happened.

The Cabinet Mission Plan

The next attempt to find a solution to the impasse between the Congress and Muslim League was a high-powered British parliamentary delegation consisting of three cabinet ministers, Lord Pethick-Lawrence, Sir Stafford Cripps, and Mr A.V. Alexander, who arrived in India on 23 March 1946. They conducted extensive discussions and negotiations about the transfer of power, preferably to a united India. Not surprisingly, the British ministers found the Congress unwilling to make concessions on its goal of a united India with a strong centre, and the Muslim League holding out for a separate Pakistan constituted of two wings: one in the north-western and the other in the north-eastern zones of the subcontinent. Consequently, the Cabinet Mission announced its own scheme on 16 May 1946. It rejected the demand for Pakistan because such a state would still have considerable non-Muslim minorities: 37.93 per cent in the north-western and 48.31 per cent in the north-eastern areas (Mansergh and Moon 1977: 584). Additionally, twenty million Muslims would be left behind, out of a total population of 188 million for the rest of India. The Mission then considered a smaller Pakistan from which non-Muslim areas in the eastern Punjab and western Bengal would be excluded. It rejected that, too, making the following observation:

> We ourselves are also convinced that any solution which involves a radical partition of the Punjab and Bengal, as this would do, would be contrary to the wishes and interests of a very large proportion of the inhabitants of these Provinces. Bengal and the Punjab each has its own common language and a long history and traditions. Moreover, any division of the Punjab would [out] of necessity divide the Sikhs leaving substantial bodies of Sikhs on both sides of the boundary. We therefore have been forced to the conclusion that neither a larger nor a smaller sovereign State of Pakistan would provide an acceptable solution for the communal problem (ibid.: 585).

The report continued along such lines, giving administrative, economic and military reasons for rejecting the partition of India. That the two wings of Pakistan would be separated by some 1,500 kilometres would make Pakistan extremely vulnerable and indefensible in a war with India. Additionally, the report asserted, such a separation would make it difficult for the princely states to associate themselves with a divided British India (ibid.).

The solution offered by the Cabinet Mission Plan comprised the following items:

1. There should be a union of India, embracing both British India and the princely states, which should deal with foreign affairs, defence, and communications, and have the power to raise finances required for those three areas of government activity.
2. All other areas of policy would be delegated to the provinces.
3. The princely states would retain all powers other than those ceded to the union.
4. Provinces would be free to form groups with executive and legislatures, and each group could determine the provincial subjects to [be] taken up in common (ibid.: 587).

5. 'The constitutions of the Union and of the Groups should contain a provision whereby any Province could, by a majority vote of its Legislative Assembly, call for reconsideration of the terms of the constitution after an initial period of 10 years and at 10 years intervals thereafter' (ibid.).
6. Representation should be given to three groups – General (Hindus and others), Muslim and Sikh representatives in the provincial legislatures, each group electing its own members.
7. Three sections or groups should be constituted by the provinces. Group A should include the Hindu-majority provinces of Madras, Bombay, United Provinces, Bihar, Central Provinces and Orissa. Section B should include Muslim-majority provinces of the north-west: Punjab, North-West Frontier Province and Sind (Sindh). Group C should include the Muslim majority provinces of the north-east: Bengal and Assam.

Thereafter followed a number of clauses on the Constituent Assembly, which was to frame a constitution for the federation. The Congress, in a resolution of 24 May 1946, stated that it was not agreeable to the proposals since it believed that an independent India 'must necessarily have a strong central authority capable of representing the nation with power and dignity in the councils of the world' (ibid.: 679-80). The Sikh leader Master Tara Singh sent a letter dated 25 May 1946 to Secretary of State for India, Pethick-Lawrence, in which he said:

> The Sikhs have been entirely thrown at the mercy of the Muslims. Group B comprises the Punjab, the N.W.F. Province, Sind and Baluchistan ... The Cabinet Mission recognises "the very genuine and acute anxiety of the Muslims lest they should find themselves subjected to a perpetual Hindu majority rule." But is there no "genuine and acute anxiety" among the Sikhs lest they should find themselves subjected to a perpetual Muslim majority rule? If the British Government is not aware of the Sikh feelings, the Sikhs will have to resort to some measures in order to convince everybody of the Sikh anxiety, in case they are subjected to a perpetual Muslim domination (ibid.: 696-7).

For its part, the Muslim League passed a resolution on 6 June 1946 in which it expressed regret that the demand for Pakistan had not been conceded fully – but nevertheless accepted the proposals because the idea of Pakistan was inherent in them 'by virtue of the compulsory grouping of the six Muslim Provinces in Sections B and C' (ibid.: 837). It also agreed to take part in the constitution-making process. On 16 June the Cabinet Mission proposed that an interim government be formed. Jinnah demanded fifty-fifty representation for the Muslim League in the interim government (Moore, 1983: 556-7). However, since major differences existed between the two main parties, they were unable to agree on the formation of an interim government. For this reason the Cabinet Mission decided to issue an invitation to prominent members of the two parties and some minorities to join the interim government. It stressed: 'The ... Interim Government is in no way to be taken as a precedent for the solution of any other communal question. It is an expedient put forward to solve the present difficulty only and to obtain the best available coalition government' (ibid.: 954).

On 25 June, the Congress party's Working Committee rejected the idea of forming an interim government, but accepted the constitutional proposals and suggested it would put its own interpretation on the Cabinet Mission Plan. The same day the Muslim League accepted the proposals for an interim government but rejected the idea that the Congress could place its own interpretation on the British plan (ibid.: 1032-49). On 10 July, Nehru stated in a press conference in Bombay that the Congress would enter the Constituent Assembly 'completely unfettered by agreements and free to meet all situations as they arise' (quoted in *Azad*, 1989: 164). The text given in the government papers is worded slightly differently (Mansergh and Moon, 1979: 25). In a statement of 29 July, the Muslim League declared itself greatly perturbed by Nehru's remarks, on the grounds that it made the future status of the minorities in India uncertain. Some days later the League took the decision to withdraw its support for the Cabinet Mission Plan, and threatened to resort to direct action to achieve Pakistan (ibid.: 135-9). It fixed the date for direct action as 16 August.

To the great surprise and disappointment of the Muslim League, Wavell invited Jawaharlal Nehru to form an interim government. On

13 August, Nehru wrote to Jinnah inviting his cooperation in the formation of a provisional national government. However, the direct-action call resulted in communal rioting of exceptional barbarity, leading to a temporary suspension in building a national government.

The Great Calcutta Killings

Although the rivalry between the Congress and the Muslim League was pivotal to the partition of India, the full significance and shattering impact of communal riots on mass psychology in terms of the brutalisation of social relations has not been properly assessed. Sporadic clashes between Hindu–Sikh and Muslim gangs had been taking place since the 1946 elections but communal harmony was largely preserved. Matters in Calcutta had begun to turn from bad to worse several days before the 16 August Direct Action Day announced by Jinnah. There is sufficient evidence to suggest that both Congress and Muslim League leaders made inflammatory speeches. Bengal Premier Husain Shaheed Suhrawardy of the Muslim League declared 16 August a public holiday when he and other leaders were going to address a public gathering in the town centre, while the Congress leader K. Roy urged Hindus to open their shops. Sikh leaders instigated their rather large Sikh community to give Muslims a thorough thrashing (Tuker, 1950: 154-56). The situation was volatile and explosive.

On the morning of 16 August 1946, Muslims in large numbers began to enter the city, while Hindus formed barricades to try and stop them. Minor scuffles took place. A huge crowd gathered at the Ochterlony Monument, from where Suhrawardy and other Muslim League leaders addressed them. After the meeting, Muslims began to loot Hindu shops and attack run-down Hindu localities. Hindus resisted but initially Muslims, led by well-known *goondas* (gangsters) went on the rampage. Later, Hindus and Sikhs retaliated with great ferocity, resulting in a higher number of deaths among the Muslims. Altogether, some 2,000–4,000 people were massacred, at least 15,000 were injured, and 100,000 rendered homeless. It was the first occasion when criminal gangs of the underworld from all the communities took part in the slaughter (Mansergh and Moon, 1979: 239-40; 293-304). The Calcutta killings proved a contagion; soon, communal riots were breaking out in many parts of India. In Bombay, Muslims and Hindus clashed and deaths in the hundreds were counted on both sides. In Noakhali, East Bengal, Muslims attacked Hindus and killed some 400.

The butchery of Muslims in Bihar

Communal frenzy then turned to Bihar, where the Muslim minority was subjected to barbaric revenge attacks on 27 September and then again on 25 October, continuing into the first week of November. According to some observers, it was the Hindu workers who had escaped Muslim fury in Calcutta who returned to Bihar and wreaked havoc on Muslims. The Governor of Bihar, Sir H. Dow, however, pointed out that the Congress government in Bihar did little to stop the carnage, which claimed up to 2,000 victims by 9 November (Mansergh and Moon, 1980: 38-9). Later, Pethick-Lawrence gave the figure as high as 5,000 dead for Bihar (ibid.: 188), almost all of them Muslims. The Head of the Eastern Command, Sir Francis Tuker, provided harrowing details of the Bihar attacks. He remarked:

> Of all the terrible doings of 1946 this fearful carnage was the most shocking. Its most dastardly side was that great mobs of Hindus turned suddenly, but with every preparation for the deed, upon the few Muslims who had lived and whose forefathers had lived in amity and trust all their lives among those very Hindu neighbours. It has never been ascertained who was the organising brain of this well-laid widely-planned plot of extirpation. All that we do know is that it went to a fixed plan and schedule. Had it not been so, such large mobs fully armed with prepared weapons, would never have collected in the time and moved with such obvious, fiendish intent from victim to victim (1950: 181-2).

Tuker believed that the Hindu Mahasabha masterminded the slaughter and Marwari Hindus whose businesses had been attacked in Calcutta financed it (ibid.: 182). In early November, Nehru visited Bihar. According to Tuker, 'Pandit Nehru's own influence, his ubiquity and the speeches that he made, had a most quietening effect on the large masses of people whom he addressed throughout the disturbed areas (ibid.: 186). With regard to the military operations that were ordered, Tuker noted that the men who took part in that operation under Colonel Venning were 'nearly all Hindus and they fought against great odds with great determination against their co-religionists' (ibid.: 190).

Carnage of Muslims in Garhmukteswar

Another series of slaughters of Muslims started at a fair in Garhmukteswar in western Uttar Pradesh, near the Punjab border, on 6 November. Muslim stall-holders were attacked and killed to the last man. On 6 November, Muslims were again butchered by Hindu Jats from Rothak and Hissar in the Punjab. Later, more Muslims in neighbouring villages were attacked. The killings continued until 15 November. The reasons were not political; rather, Hindu Jats resented Muslims for slaughtering cows at the time of the religious festival of Eid-ul-Zuha which fell at that time (Tuker, 1950: 195).

On 15 November 1946 Jinnah was quoted in the Muslim League mouthpiece, the English-language daily *Dawn,* as saying that the only solution to the fast-deteriorating situation was to create two separate states of 'Pakistan and Hindustan'. He said, 'The exchange of population will have to be considered seriously as far as possible, especially after this Bihar tragedy' (Mansergh and Moon, 1980: 73-5).

Interim Government

In the meantime, an interim government had been formed with Jawaharlal Nehru as vice-president, while the viceroy remained its chief executive. It took office on 24 August 1946. The government renewed efforts to convince the Muslim League to join it. The League made its membership in the Cabinet conditional, on the recognition of its status as the sole representative of Indian Muslims. This was agreed and on 15 October, the League took the decision to join the Cabinet. The names submitted were those of Nawabzada Liaqat Ali Khan (whose landed estates were situated on the Indian side of what would eventually become the Indo–Pak border); I.I. Chundrigar (Bombay); Abdur Rab

Nishtar (NWFP); Raja Ghazanfar Ali Khan (Punjab); and Jugandra Nath Mandal (a scheduled caste Hindu from Bengal) (ibid.: 729-30). On 25 October, the Cabinet was reconstituted and a government was formed, consisting of the Congress, the Muslim League, and the religious minorities, including the Sikhs. It appeared to give a chance to the efforts of keeping India united. The Muslim League was allotted five cabinet positions, including the crucial finance portfolio, which was given to Liaqat Ali Khan.

However, mutual suspicion and animosity among the members of the interim government proved too strong. Although they were members of the same cabinet, Muslim League and Congress ministers worked at cross-purposes. For example, the budget proposal from the Finance Minister, the Muslim League's second-in-command Nawabzada Liaqat Ali Khan, was deliberately drafted to hit hard against industrial and commercial classes which were supportive of the Congress (Azad, 1964-94). In the absence of a power-sharing formula being agreed on at the centre, the partition of India became inevitable and the greatest price was paid by the Punjab.

The Punjab

The British government's announcement that elections would be held in early 1946 was received in the Punjab with mixed feelings. The Muslim League was upbeat and enthusiastic; the ruling Punjab Unionist Party was not. At the time the Punjab Premier, Sir Khizr, was in Europe, having sailed for Paris to attend the peace conference of allied nations which opened on 29 July. He spent several weeks abroad and returned to the Punjab in the middle of September. The Congress was poorly equipped to participate in a hectic election campaign. Its leaders, both at the central and Punjab levels, had been in jail since August 1942 when the Quit India Movement was launched; additionally it was plagued by factionalism of the right and left. The ban on the Congress party was lifted shortly before the announcement of the elections. The Sikhs were, as usual, vociferous in their denunciation of the Pakistan demand. The Punjab Unionist Party, for its part, was beset with defections. The most severe blow it would yet receive was the death of Sir Chhotu Ram on

9 January 1945. Without him, the solid standing it enjoyed with the Hindu Hindi-speaking Jats of the Ambala division could not be taken for granted. The Sikh Panthic Party, a group of Sikh parties among whom the Akalis were the biggest group, contested the elections by demanding a mandate from their co-religionists for the creation of a Sikh state should India be partitioned.

Tables turn in favour of the Muslim League

On the other hand, the tables had turned completely in favour of the Muslim League, which, in the absence of the Congress and the large influx into its ranks of landowners and spiritual divines from the Unionist Party, had virtually the whole field open to disseminate its message to the Muslims: that the creation of Pakistan would liberate them from all types of exploitation and discrimination. In his fortnightly report of 16 August 1945, Punjab Governor Glancy observed:

> Muslim Leaguers have been indulging in much propaganda, wholesale vilification of Congress and of the Unionist Government in the Punjab. Jinnah and his supporters are clamouring for general elections, a matter about which Congress appears to be comparatively lukewarm.... I must confess that I am gravely perturbed about the situation, because there is a very serious danger of the elections being fought, so far as Muslims are concerned, on an entirely false issue. Crude Pakistan may be quite illogical, undefinable [sic] and ruinous to India and in particular to Muslims, but this does not detract from its potency as a political slogan. The uninformed Muslim will be told that the question he is called on to answer at the polls is – Are you a true believer or an infidel and a traitor? Against this slogan the Unionists have no spectacular battle-cry... if Pakistan becomes an imminent reality, we shall be heading straight for blood-shed on a wide scale; non-Muslims, especially Sikhs, are not bluffing, they will not submit peacefully to a Government that is labelled "Muhammadan Raj". Hence it appears to me to be of vital importance to take action, before it is too late, to deflate the theory of Pakistan (Carter, 2006: 141-2).

Glancy belonged to the school of British administrators who strongly believed that the Punjab should remain aloof from the politics of the Congress and Muslim League, and considered the Punjab Unionist Party's inter-communal approach the best formula to maintain peace and order and the province's unity. He suggested that the government make an authoritative statement to the effect that if India was divided on the basis of contiguous communal areas, then the Punjab could also be divided on a similar basis. Such a statement would discourage the Muslim League from continuing with its demand for a separate Pakistan. He went on:

> For in the Punjab there are two neighbouring Divisions (Ambala and Jullundur) out of our total of five, in which there is no single district with a Muslim majority, and to this extensive area can be added the adjoining and very important district of Amritsar. The citation of this practical illustration might be of great help. Action on these lines would at least provide the Unionist Party with a rallying cry against Pakistan – something on which the elector could definitely bite. No Punjabi, however, uninformed, would contemplate with equanimity so shattering a dismemberment of the Province involving in effect the disappearance of the word "Punjab"... I am of course entirely in favour of Muslims being given adequate representation and all possible safeguards at the Centre. This, it seems to me, will amount to true Pakistan as opposed to the sinister and insensate variety which Jinnah and his supporters advocate (ibid.: 142).

At that time, roughly only eleven per cent of the Punjabi population was enfranchised. Moreover, the Punjabis were not going to vote as a single electorate, but virtually as separate communities, since both Muslims and Sikhs enjoyed reserved seats, while the Congress would compete for the general votes as well as put up Muslim and Sikh candidates for the reserved seats. Perhaps more important to note is that the possibility that the Punjab could be partitioned was never submitted to a vote. It therefore did not figure in the election manifesto of any of the political parties, although the Sikhs had been threatening for many years that if Pakistan was conceded, they would demand a partition of the Punjab. Therefore, no public ventilation of opinion and discussion took place on the most critical aspect of the partition of India – that the Punjab, too, could be divided.

Islam as election slogan

According to veteran journalist Aziz Mazhar, Dr Muhammad Baqir, a writer and historian, advised Jinnah to use Islamic slogans if he wanted to rouse mass support among Muslims. The proletarian writer, Qamar Yurish, was of the opinion that Dr M.D. Taseer was the one who suggested that Islamic slogans be raised to galvanise the Muslim masses around the Muslim League. Asghar Sodai, a poet and academic from Sialkot in the Punjab, coined one of the slogans raised in those days: '*Pakistan ka na'ara kya? La Illaha Il-lilah*' (What is the Slogan of Pakistan? It is that there is no god but Allah). In the 1970s, the motto was revived but with a slightly different wording, '*Pakistan ka matlab kya? La Illaha Il-lilah*' (What is the Meaning of Pakistan? It is that there is no god but Allah).

It is possible that a number of Muslim intellectuals in the Punjab made this suggestion to Jinnah. The influence of the poet Iqbal, for instance, was considerable in the Punjab. For a long time, Punjabi Muslims had been fed on his romantic poetry about an idealised Islamic past which needed to be revitalised and resuscitated to re-establish that glory and power. Consequently, his followers had probably made the assessment that deploying Islamic slogans in the election campaign would raise the stock of the Muslim League.

It is not surprising that Jinnah, a politician of considerable political acumen, who hitherto had strictly confined his political campaign for Pakistan to constitutional arguments, began to sense that emotive Islamic appeals and slogans could prove crucial to winning mass support among Muslims. Aziz Mazhar, Hukum Qureshi, Syed Ahmed Saeed Kirmani, and many others who were young students at that time and active in the Muslim Students Federation affiliated to the Muslim League confirmed that slogans such as '*Pakistan ka na'ara/matlab kya? La Illaha Il-lilah*' (What is the meaning/slogan of Pakistan? It is that there is no god but Allah) were loudly shouted at public rallies and marches. Thus Islamic slogans were profusely used at campaign rallies. In the FR of

13 September, Glancy described the Muslim League campaign in the following words:

> Muslim Leaguers are doing what they can in the way of propaganda conducted on fanatical lines; religious leaders and religious buildings are being used freely in several places for advocating Pakistan and vilifying any who hold opposite views. Communal feeling is, I fear, definitely deteriorating. Sikhs are growing distinctly nervous at the possibility of Pakistan, and I think there is no doubt that they will forcibly resist any attempt to include them in a Muslim Raj (ibid.: 145).

In the FR of 29 September, Glancy provided more descriptions of a highly tense and combative election campaign. The Muslim League accused the coalition government of interfering in the election campaign to discourage Muslims voting for it, while the Hindus complained that Muslim officials have been indulging in active propaganda on behalf of the Muslim League. With regard to the two Muslim organisations hostile to the Muslim League – the Khaksars and Ahrars – the governor remarked: 'Khaksars and Ahrars have also entered the lists, and the Ahrars in particular, who include some very effective speakers among their ranks, have been unrestrainedly vituperative about the Muslim League' (ibid.: 148).

In the FR of 27 October Glancy took up the employment of Islamic threats by the Muslim League to non-Muslims in the election campaign:

> 'Communal relations continue to deteriorate. Baldev Singh, our Development Minister, spoke to me a few days ago about the effect produced by Muslim League supporters in the Ambala Division declaring that Pakistan would soon be a reality, that the only laws that would prevail in a short time would be the Muslim laws of the Shariat and that non-Muslims would have to bring their complaints to the mosques for settlement (ibid.: 151).

Glancy also reiterated his earlier suggestion that the government should announce that the Punjab would be divided on contiguous communal lines if India was divided on such a basis, as it would 'provide a most timely, and surely an entirely unexceptionable, corrective to the fanatical and highly dangerous doctrine of "Islam in danger" that is now being preached by advocates of the League' (ibid.). It is intriguing that the British government never responded to this suggestion. No communication is to be found in the documents so far published by the British in which is recorded the response of Viceroy Wavell or that of the Secretary of State for India and Burma, Lord Pethick-Lawrence, to Glancy's pleas.

Apparently, Glancy never ventured to give such advice to Sir Khizr himself, which is indicative of the strict discipline the British followed in securing clearance from their superiors in the colonial hierarchy before expressing their views to Indian colleagues. With regard to the Punjab Congress, Glancy observed that its orators were wasting time on issues other than the election campaign. They were busy espousing the cause of the rebel Indian National Army (INA) that had been formed by the Japanese from amongst Indian soldiers who had been taken as prisoners of war in Burma. The Congress was also busy denouncing British intervention in Indonesia.

One of the biggest feudal lords and formerly a leading member of the Unionist Party, Sir Firoz Khan Noon, who held the defence portfolio in the Executive Council of the Viceroy until 15 September, spoke to Glancy and told him frankly that he 'did not believe in Pakistan as preached by the Muslim League' (ibid.: 152). He refused to take such a position publicly, however. In the FR of 27 December, in fact, we learn that Noon had joined the fray and was pleading the cause of the League in Islamic terms:

'Among Muslims the Leaguers are increasing their efforts to appeal to the bigotry of the electors. Pirs and Maulvis have been enlisted in large numbers to tour the Province and denounce all who oppose the League as infidels. Copies of the Holy Quran are carried around as an emblem peculiar to the Muslim League. Firoz and others openly preach that every vote given to the League is a vote cast in favour of the Holy Prophet. These deplorable tactics, as I have frequently said, were only to be expected; they provide a grim augury of the future peace of India and they are certainly not easy for the Unionists to counter' (ibid.: 160.).

Regarding the shifting loyalties to the parties, Glancy reported:

> An example is that of Syed Amjad Ali, the son of Sir Maratib Ali, the well-known military contractor; he was for a long time a Secretary in the Unionist Party and received the Party's support in the election campaign, but went over a few weeks ago to the Muslim League on being given the assurance that he would be nominated by them for his constituency in the Ferozepore district. This assurance was overruled by the Central Parliamentary Board of the Muslim League with the result that he immediately endeavoured to get back in the favour of the Unionists, though without success (ibid.).

The same FR reported that negotiations had stalled between the Congress and the Akalis on how to avoid a direct clash of interests during the elections. In some constituencies, however, the Sikhs agreed that either Congress or Akali candidates should contest against Communists. Moreover, the Hindu Mahasabha support base had virtually disappeared, and the Congress was now supported by almost all Hindus. Additionally, the Congress had decided to put up Hindu Jats instead of the Banias (traders and moneylenders) in the Ambala division. That meant it was trying to appropriate support from the late Sir Chhotu Ram's constituency that previously was the preserve of the Punjab Unionist Party.

The Muslim League campaign in the Punjab comprised three specific groups of activists. The first was of Muslim students from Aligarh Muslim University in the United Provinces, who came in large numbers as volunteers to tour the towns and villages propagating the idea of Pakistan as an escape for Muslims from the slavery of caste Hindus. The exact date or month on which the Aligarh students visited the town of Sheikhupura in West Punjab is not remembered by Chaudhri Nazir Ahmed Virk, whom we interviewed on 30 December 2005, but he distinctly remembered what was said on that occasion:

'One day some 200–250 students wearing pajamas and sherwanis from Aligarh University had come to Sheikhupura and gathered in the main bazaar. They blew a bugle and changed their dress to the Muslim League National Guards. Then their leader addressed the public and said: "Friends, the place from where I come will never be a part of Pakistan but Sheikhupura will definitely become Pakistan. O Khizr Tiwana –

you listen to me. We have come to Sheikhupura with *kaffans* (Muslim burial shrouds) tied around our heads. We will get Pakistan. Our heads and chests are ready for you to fire at us". Then they walked away in groups of two because at that time Section 144 had been imposed. They boarded a train shouting, "*Le ke rahein gai Pakistan, dena hoga Pakistan, Pakistan Zindabad*" (We will get Pakistan, you will have to give Pakistan, long live Pakistan). They left, but we students from Sheikhupura were galvanised by their performance and kept shouting those slogans. Some of our boys were also arrested.'

The second group to carry out the Muslim League's campaign in the Punjab was the Muslim Communists, who had joined the League after the Communist Party of India concluded that the demand for Pakistan was consistent with the Leninist right of self-determination for an oppressed nation, as the Muslims were an economically-backward nation. The dynamic president of the Punjab Provincial Congress Committee, Mian Iftikharuddin, who was the main patron of the Punjab Communists, joined the Muslim League on 25 August 1945. The veteran Punjabi Communist Abdullah Malik talked to me at length on this topic on 19 December 1995 in Lahore. He explained that the Communists delivered speeches in the Muslim League public meetings, projecting the idea that Pakistan would be a state free from the exploitation of man by man.

The third and perhaps the most crucial group drafted by the Muslim League to win Muslim support was that of the ulema and *pirs* (religious divines). A Mashaikh Committee consisting of some leading *pirs* was formed to lead the propaganda campaign in favour of Pakistan. Among them were Pir Jamaat Ali Shah of Alipur Sharif, Pir Ghulam Mohiyddin Shah Gilani of Golra Sharif, Pir Fazl Shah of Jalalpur in Jhelum district, Pir Nazimuddin of Taunsa Sharif, and Makhdum Reza Shah of Multan. Some lay politicians also played the charade of associating holy suffixes to their names: Nawab Mamdot became Nawab Mamdot of Pir Mamdot Sharif, and Sardar Shaukat Hayat Khan was Shaukat Hayat Sajjada Nashin of Wah Sharif. There were also Firoz Khan Noon of Darbar Sargodha Sharif and Nawab Muhammad Hayat Qureshi as Sajjada Nashin of Sargodha Sharif (*Court of Inquiry*, 1954: 255).

Moreover, the conservative ulema of the biggest Sunni sub-sect of Brelawis, who were close affiliates of the *pirs*, were also deployed in the field (Gilmartin, 1989; Talbot, 1996). The type of campaign and propaganda varied from place to place, though the emphasis was on the creation of an Islamic state. The Muslim League was able to muster such a large body of *pirs* and *maulvis* (lower-level clerics) that the Unionist supporters sent frantic appeals for help to Khizr. A desperate plea was expressed in a telegram sent from Multan to Unionist headquarters: 'Kindly send more Maulvis' typifying the predicament (Gilmartin, 1979: 515). Several Hindus and Sikhs that I talked to reported that they were told that non-Muslims would have to pay the protection tax, *jizya*, and they would be tried in Islamic courts for civil and criminal offences.

The famous Hindi writer, playwriter and actor Bhisham Sahni, spoke to me on 23 October 2001, about the election campaign in Rawalpindi city and adjoining areas about the activities of Pir Jamaat Ali Shah on behalf of the Muslim League. Jamaat Ali Shah told the non-Muslims that Pakistan will be an Islamic state but non-Muslims would live in peace and security by paying *jizya*. Apart from the Brelawi ulema and *pirs*, some prominent Deobandi dissidents such as Shabbir Ahmed Usmani and their factions also joined the Muslim League and campaigned vigorously for the creation of Pakistan. The Muslim League applied an inclusive strategy to maximise its support among Muslims. Thus all those who had been entered in the census records as 'Muslims' were mobilised for its campaign. Even the Shias and the Ahmadiyya, considered heretics by orthodox Sunnis and Shias, were included.

The Unionists belatedly tried to counter the religious offensive by deploying ulema from the Ahrars as well as Khaksar orators in the electoral campaign, even though in the past both groups had been hostile to them. Premier Sir Khizr also began to quote verses from the Quran in his public speeches, though the tactics failed as the party's otherwise non-communal ideology did not fit in with its use of religion in the election campaign (Talbot, 1996: 147).

In the FR of 2 February 1946, Glancy wrote to Viceroy Wavell:

> The ML [Muslim League] orators are becoming increasingly fanatical in their speeches. Maulvis and Pirs and students travel all round the Province and preach that those who fail to vote for the League candidates will cease to be Muslims; their marriages will no longer be valid and they will be entirely excommunicated ... It is not easy

> to foresee what the results of the elections will be. But there seems little doubt the Muslim League, thanks to the ruthless methods by which they have pursued their campaign of "Islam in danger", will considerably increase the number of their seats and unionist representatives will correspondingly decline (Carter, 2006: 171).

In the following FR of 28 February, Glancy reproduced a translation from an Urdu poster circulated by the Muslim League candidate, Raja Khair Mehdi Khan from Jhelum *tahsil,* that unequivocally appealed to religious differences to solicit votes. It was written by Abbas Ali Shah, a *khateeb* (leading cleric) of Jhelum:

> Muslim League Zindabad Pakistan Zindabad
> In His name
> Muslims, the time of your test has come.
> In this battle of righteousness and falsehood, you have to choose between *Din* (religion) and *Dunya* (wordly possessions).

Din (the faith)	**Dunya (the world)**
On one side is your belief in the Almighty and your conscience	*On the other side you are offered squares and Jagir.*
Righteousness and faithfulness are on one side	*The other side has to offer Lambardari and Zaildari*
On one side is the rightful cause	*On the other is Sufedposhi (economic advantage and status).*
One side has Pakistan for you	*The other has Kufiristan (reign of infidels)*
On the one side is the problem of saving the Muslims from the slavery of Hindus	*As opposed to this, there is only consideration of personal prestige of one man*
On one side you have to bring together	*On the other side is the idol worship, bradri [sic] (clan) and caste*

all those who recite the Kalma (the basis of Islam)	*consideration*
On the one side you have the Holy Muhammad and Ali	*On the other side Baldev Singh and Khizr Hayat.*
On the one side is the consideration of the unity and brotherhood of all Muslims	*On the other side is the Danda (big stick) of bureaucracy and terror of officialdom.*
On the one side are the lovers of Muslim League and Pakistan	*On the other side are the admirers of Congress and Unionists.*
On the one side is the honour of the Green Banner.	*On the other side is the Government of Khizr Ministry.*

With this in view, leaving aside your party feuds and personal grievances for the sake of your religion, you have to decide in the light of your strength of faith, that in Tehsil Jhelum the rightful claimant of your vote is the Muslim League candidate, i.e, Raja Khair Mehdi Khan (ibid.: 174-5).

In the Khosla report, a long passage is quoted from a well-known journalist, Brailsford, published in *The Tribune*, Lahore, of February 1946. It confirms the view that religious fanaticism was employed extensively by the Muslim League to garner votes. Brailsford wrote:

> Three great powers confront the Muslim peasants – the feudal landlord, the Government and the League. Of these three only the League can reach his emotions, and it has been in action everywhere on behalf of the Muslim League. It has created a fear that Islam is in danger. The clergy tells the peasants that their hope of salvation depends on their voting for the League, and sometimes they enforce this appeal by parading the roads with a copy of the Quran. I have heard the loudspeaker on their cars shouting the slogan 'A curse on the infidel Hindus.' The result is that a wave of communal feeling has gripped the Muslims of this province, who form a slight majority

> of its population, and, with rare exceptions, they have rallied to the demand for Pakistan (1991: 94).

Not surprisingly, such a campaign struck terror among Hindus and Sikhs who were scattered across the western districts in small numbers. In my interviews, it comes out vividly that the first time they sensed that their lives might be in danger was during the election campaign. In the rural areas of Jhelum, Gujrat, Mianwali, Dera Ghazi Khan and Attock, Hindu and Sikh shopkeepers and traders began to sell their businesses and leave or dispatch their women and children to relatives in east Punjab from as early as the second half of 1945. Most stayed put, hoping that some constitutional solution would be agreed upon by the politicians.

Results

The fears of the governor were borne out by the election results announced on 24 February 1946. In the 175-member Punjab Legislative Assembly, the Muslim League won seventy-five seats and thus became the biggest single party in the assembly, though ten short of an overall majority. Later, two members elected on the Unionist ticket crossed over to join the Muslim League, thus bringing its overall strength to seventy-seven. All its gains were made at the expense of the ruling Unionist Party, whose strength was reduced to eighteen seats. The Congress party also performed well and won fifty seats, while the Panthic Sikhs won twenty-three seats. Seven seats were captured by independents. The Communists lost the four seats they held previously while the Ahrars, who contested reserved Muslim seats with Congress support, won no seat at all. It was clear that the Muslim voters had rallied behind the Muslim League, Hindus (including the Jats who previously under the leadership of Sir Chhotu Ram voted for the Unionist Party) had backed Congress, and Sikhs voted for the Panthic parties, of which the Akalis were the biggest group.

Coalition government formed

Punjab Chief Secretary H.D. Bhanot (an Indian Christian) wrote in his FR for the second half of February, dated 28 February, that Sardar

Vallabhbhai Patel, the Congress strongman at the centre, was deeply perturbed and remarked, 'We will have no truck with the League' (L/P & J/5/249). In any event, parleys between the Muslim League, Congress and the Akalis on power-sharing started immediately, but unsurprisingly did not result on an agreement to form a coalition government. In a confidential note dated 7 March 1946, Glancy reported that the leader of the Punjab Muslim League, Nawab Mamdot, met him the day before to discuss prospects for forming the government, since his community constituted the majority in the Punjab and his party had won the largest number of seats in the Punjab Legislative Assembly. He told the governor that negotiations with the Sikhs had broken down because 'the Panthic Party had asked him to define the area to be set apart as "Khalistan" – a demand with which he found it impossible to comply' (ibid.: 176). Mamdot claimed to enjoy the support of eighty-seven members of the Punjab Assembly. That included seventy-eight members from his party, including three others that had joined the Muslim League, two caste Hindus who had been elected on Unionist tickets, four scheduled caste representatives, two Indian Christians, and one Sikh.

Glancy expressed doubts about Mamdot's claims. He showed him a letter signed by Hindus, of both castes saying that they continued to adhere to the Unionist Party. When confronted on the question of support of the four scheduled caste representatives, Mamdot admitted he was not definite about their support. With regard to the Indian Christians, Mamdot said that he could be sure of the support of only one of them (ibid.: 176-7). The governor estimated that the Muslim League had only the support of eighty legislators. On the other hand, when he met Sir Khizr, Bhim Sen Sachar and Baldev Singh, they claimed to have a clear majority of ninety-four members. Glancy, however, felt that it was an exaggerated number and that their actual strength in the Punjab Assembly was only ninety, which was, in any case, at least ten more members than those of the Muslim League. Glancy then invited Khizr to form the government.

Hence a coalition government came to power on 11 March 1946, with Sir Khizr Tiwana as the premier and comprising the following: three Unionist Muslims (Sir Khizr, Muzaffar Ali Qizilbash and Muhammad Ibrahim Barq); two Congress men (Bhim Sen Sachar and Lahri Singh);

and one Panthic Sikh (Baldev Singh). The Muslim League responded with a campaign that portrayed the new government as unrepresentative of the Punjab situation, since it excluded the biggest party representing the majority community of the Punjab. Consequently, the government imposed section 144 of the Code of Criminal Procedure, which disallowed an assembly of more than five persons, the holding of public meetings, and the carrying of firearms.

On 8 April 1946 Sir Evan Jenkins, an old Punjab hand from the civil service, took over from Sir Bertrand Glancy as Governor of the Punjab. Jenkins was a pragmatist who, like all other British administrators, including his predecessor Glancy, despised the Congress. Such antipathy had grown enormously when the Quit India Movement was launched by the Congress party. On the other hand, Jenkins' views about the Muslim League were coloured largely by considerations of law and order and maintenance of communal peace – both of which he believed were being threatened by the League. Like Glancy, he too believed that the best interests of the Punjab were served by it remaining united and under a representative coalition government of the three main communities. In his first FR dated 15 April, Jenkins remarked:

> '[I]n the rural areas, the average man probably troubles himself very little about politics and the future of the Punjab, but if there were really serious trouble in Lahore and Amritsar, there is no saying how fast or how far it would spread. The Sikhs, in particular, could adapt the techniques of their religious mass movements (in which the villagers join wholesale) to a political offensive' (ibid.: 182).

We also learn in the same report that the Congress leader in the Punjab Assembly, Bhim Sen Sachar, did not like the Unionists and wanted to strike a deal with the Muslim League, but regretted that it could not be worked out (ibid.: 183). Regarding such a deal between the Muslim League and the Sikhs, Jenkins wrote:

> 'Master Tara Singh... demanded either Khalistan, with transfer of population, or a new State stretching from the Jummna to the Chenab, in which he said that the Sikhs could not be oppressed: I told him to keep as calm as he could, and asked him (as I have

asked others) whether he really wanted to break the Punjab up into a lot of petty Provinces – a question to which one never gets a rational answer' (ibid.).

In the same FR he mentioned that although senior staff had maintained impartiality, eighty per cent of the Muslim employees at the lower level had secretly campaigned for the Muslim League. However, the Inspector-General of Police Mr Bennett was satisfied with the morale of his men, but he pointed out that, 'The Force as a whole is 70 per cent Muslim, and that the non-officer grades are 73 per cent Muslim. The inference is fairly obvious' (ibid.: 186). In other words, the new governor was pointing out that an over-representation of the Muslims could be a problem if at some point the Punjab was destabilised and law and order is compromised. The Hindus and Sikhs were to later complain that the Muslim police sided with their co-religionists during agitations and rioting.

In the next FR of 2 May, Jenkins drew attention to the fact of communal incidents in Hissar, Kartarpur (Jullundur district), Amritsar, and Multan. He noted: 'All communities are said to be preparing for widespread rioting, and there is much talk about "volunteers" who constitute the "private armies" of the various communities' (ibid.: 186). The role of the communal press in aggravating communal tension was also noted. As far as the Congress ministers in the Khizr ministry were concerned, Jenkins remarked that Bhim Sen Sachar and Lahri Singh openly criticised the administration. He wrote: 'Here again they fail to realise the political implications of what they are doing. Muslim officials here, including the great majority of the police, dislike the Congress and sympathise with the Muslim League' (ibid.). On the whole, one gets a clear impression that the ministers did not conduct themselves as a team.

In a special secret letter to Wavell dated 27 May, Jenkins informed the Viceroy that the Sikhs were disappointed with the Cabinet Mission Plan of 16 May as it prescribes for them to belong to Group B provinces with Muslim majorities without listing down safeguards for their interests. The Sikh leader Baldev Singh told Jenkins that he believed in a strong centre and feared that the Muslims would seek to make Group B a strong union, leading to the creation of Pakistan. Jinnah had approached him for Sikh co-operation in writing a strong 'Group Constitution', in return for which the Muslims would concede generous weightage to the Sikhs in the civil services. Group B would also claim forty per cent of the total strength of the defence services, and Jinnah had promised to ensure that Sikhs got their share in such an arrangement. Baldev Singh, however, considered such terms only superficially attractive, and thought that it would be impossible to convince the Sikhs to accept them at the time, given their apprehensions about Muslim domination. The governor asserted that if the Sikhs did not co-operate, the Group B constitution could not be agreed. The chances of any settlement between the Sikhs and Muslims were becoming less likely because of the intemperate statements of the Sikh leaders as they tried to outdo each other in claiming to represent their community (ibid.: 204-7).

In the 15 June FR, the governor reported that intelligence had been obtained about the meetings of Sikh leaders in Amritsar on 9 and 10 June. Two factions were identified among the Akalis: the 'Giani Group' led by Giani Kartar Singh and Master Tara Singh, and the 'Nagoke Group' headed by Udham Singh Nagoke and Ishar Singh Majhail. A third group consisted of nationalist or Congress Sikhs. Serious efforts had been made before the meetings to secure unity, but they met only with partial success. The Cabinet Mission statement was unanimously condemned in extraordinarily violent speeches. Threats of guerrilla war against the British were voiced. Certain Sikh newspapers had been suggesting that the Sikhs should seize one or two districts. 'I have no doubt,' the governor concluded, 'that wild ideas of this kind have occurred to Udham Singh Nagoke and his friends' (ibid.: 217).

The more sensible Sikhs realised that it would be wise to wait and see how events developed and that 'direct action' against the British could lead only to conflict with the Punjab government and large-scale communal disturbances. In the end, an advisory committee was set up to negotiate with the Cabinet Mission, the Congress and the Muslim League, and a council of action was to prepare for an offensive against the British. It would not move, however, until the advisory committee had done its best to reach a settlement protecting Sikh interests (ibid.).

In the 29 June FR, the governor wrote, 'The Sikhs are busy raising their new private army, recruits to which are required to sign the standard pledge in their own blood' (ibid.: 226). On the other hand, the Congress and the Muslim League had been rather quiet. The governor notes increasing discontentment among ex-servicemen unable to find employment. In the 15 July FR, Jenkins noted that the Sikhs continued to make the most violent speeches. However, the leaders of the Congress Sikhs, Narinjan Singh Gill and Pratap Singh Kairon, were going to ensure that the Sikhs kept in line with Congress. Jenkins further noted that the Muslims were angry that negotiations between Congress and Muslim League had broken down. They felt that since the Muslim League had accepted the Cabinet Mission Plan, it should have been invited to form a government without Congress. He wrote:

'In this they have the sympathy of many British civilians and Army officers and some educated Hindus who think that the Muslim League had been badly treated, although they were glad at the outcome. Hindus generally were jubilant and believed that Jinnah has suffered a severe defeat' (ibid.: 250).

The 29 July FR of the governor took up the party manoeuvrings in the Punjab Assembly. The Congress had stirred up an agitation in Gujranwala, while strikes were reported from Amritsar and Lahore. Punjab Chief Secretary Bhanot noted in his FR for the first half of July, dated 31 July that one of the most ominous characteristics of the current situation was the marked increase in the activities of the RSS and of the Muslim League National Guards. The membership of the RSS had doubled since November and was estimated to be over 28,000. The Sangh members had been involved in communal violence, which included instances of murder. Some branches of the Sangh were believed to be armed. The strength of the Muslim League National Guards had increased from 3,000 at the end of 1945 to over 10,000. The League announced its intention to increase the number of Guards to half a million in the remaining months of the year. Both these organisations had branches in many places, including rural areas, and were therefore to be considered potentially very dangerous. Bhanot also noted that a nationalist Muslim, Maulana Daud Ghaznavi, who was president of the Provincial Punjab Congress Committee, had crossed over to the Muslim League (L/P & J/5/249).

In a special report to Wavell dated 31 August, Jenkins refers to Nehru's provocative statement of 10 July in Bombay, in which he declared that the Congress would not be bound by any commitment when it entered the Constituent Assembly. Jenkins said that such a statement had incensed Punjabi Muslims, while at the same time feeling alarmed by the 'revolutionary changes' Nehru threatened about. Some of them were also dismayed by the decision of the Muslim League central committee to launch 'direct action'. The majority had accepted the idea of a 'Direct Action Day' and would be prepared to break the law, while the Provincial Muslim League had decided that the observations were to be peaceful. The idea was to observe this day in religious places. Therein lay the danger. Slogans of 'Islam in danger' would be raised and would excite the masses. As regards the Congress, the Forward Bloc and the Socialists continued to use objectionable language.

In an FR dated 31 August, Jenkins informed Viceroy Wavell that law and order problems had taken up most of his time in the second half of August. We learn that the Muslims complained that the coalition government did not take action when agitators from Bihar, such as Jayaprakash Narayan, a Congress socialist, visited the Punjab and made provocative speeches against the British, but Muslim League speakers who made violent speeches were immediately taken to task (ibid.: 268-9). He feared that resentment among the Muslims would grow if the government did not conduct itself in a neutral manner. Referring to the Muslim League leaders, he wrote: 'We must not forget that the Muslim leaders are on the whole people who for generations have been friendly with the Government of the day and with the British officials. If they had been professional agitators of the Congress type, we should have had trouble before now' (ibid.: 270).

In the Punjab Secretary's FR dated 31 August and covering the second half of August, it was noted that the Muslim League's 'Direct Action Day' on 16 August was observed peacefully in the Punjab. No mass movement was launched, although calls for jihad were being given from the mosques. The Sikhs had moved closer to the Congress but interest has been aroused by the invitation extended by Jinnah to Master Tara Singh for a meeting. Tension was most palpable in towns and districts in which the communities were equally represented. The reporting of the Calcutta riots had worsened the situation instead of making the communities pause and reflect on the consequences of conflict, leading to bloodshed and perhaps civil war (L/P & J/5/249).

In a special report on the Punjab situation, also dated 31 August, the governor reviewed the overall situation and pointed out that the differences between the Hindu–Sikh group and the Muslim group were increasing rapidly, thereby generating anxiety and apprehension among them. The Muslims considered the formation of the interim government at the centre by the Congress as an unconditional surrender of power to the Hindus and completely in contravention of parliamentary practice. While the Congress rejected the Cabinet Mission Plan and the Muslim League accepted it, the former was invited to form the government, and not the latter. They feared that the Hindus would exploit their newly-acquired power for the systematic suppression of the Muslims. Such an attitude of the British government had given birth to the suspicion that there was a deep-rooted plot between the British and the Congress against Muslims (ibid.: 272-3). The communal carnage in Calcutta had greatly aggravated their strained relations. About the Hindu reaction to the Calcutta riots and the Muslim response to it, Jenkins wrote:

> Hindu propaganda on the Calcutta riots was extraordinarily prompt and effective and received weighty support from the *Statesman* (newspaper). Punjabi Muslims have not relished cartoons of Muslim League leaders washing in blood, cutting off the breasts of Hindu women and committing other atrocities; nor are they ready to believe that the Muslims of Calcutta were entirely to blame, as the news and articles of the Hindu Press imply.
>
> The Hindus are jubilant – they are bad winners, and will do all they can to taunt and humiliate the Muslims. They are foolish enough to believe that here in the Punjab they will be able to suppress the Muslims once [and] for all with British aid, and loose talk to this effect is going on among Congress leaders. The Congress pact with Sikhs is welcomed as ensuring protection for the Hindus, especially in the Central Punjab. The Hindu papers are arrogant and most bitterly communal. Underneath the bluster there is (as always with the urban Hindu) an undercurrent of fear; nothing is more likely

> to bring about a physical conflict than this pitiful combination of arrogance and timidity (ibid.: 273).

He noted that the Sikh community was divided into at least three factions, and although now Sikhs were officially linked with the Congress, some influential Sikhs would be reluctant to break with the Muslims. However, the chances were that in any serious conflict the Sikhs would side with Hindus. The tone of the Sikh press and speakers was anti-British and anti-Muslim, and Sikh speakers were among the most violent in the Punjab. At the same time, Jenkins noted: 'We have the material for a vast communal upheaval. The Muslims will not submit to dictation from the Congress High Command' (ibid.: 274).

The governor suggested that the Punjab needed a government representing all three communities, strongly supported in the Assembly, and with a marked rural bias. Such a government could be formed by a coalition based on genuine common interest, or by a revived and strengthened Unionist Party. The current ministry had no genuine common interest, and commanded only a bare majority in the Punjab Assembly (ibid.). Jenkins then assesses the way the administrative machinery is likely to deal with a communal conflict:

> The sympathies of Muslim officials (including about 70 per cent of the police) are mainly with the Muslim League; and the British officials are most reluctant to be drawn into a common struggle on behalf of the Congress. How far can we count on the loyalty of Muslim officials holding key posts, and of the Police, it is impossible to say... The attitude of the average British official in the Indian Civil Service or the Indian Police must be clearly understood. He will do his work, and, if assured of support, will deal with any emergency which does not involve taking sides. But he will not lend himself to any policy which he believes to be immoral and unjust. Provided the Punjab is left to itself, and there is no outside dictation, he may stand firm; but if HMG promotes, or acquiesces in, any systematic suppression of our large Muslim population, he will not .... How far the Muslim soldiers of the Indian Army would support the present regime in an emergency is at least doubtful. A report of the pro-League resolution of Muslim airmen of the RIAF at Ambala was

> promptly denied but civil intelligence gives reasons to think that the denial was not wholly accurate. It is known that Muslim soldiers on leave were being approached in at least one district, and even Muslim soldiers of unimpeachable loyalty are being affected. The danger with the soldiers as with the rest of the Muslim population is the religious appeal; Friday sermons and the influential *Pirs* will inevitably stress the danger in which Islam now stands, and few Muslims can resist an appeal of this kind (ibid.: 276-77).

In administrative terms, if a communal bloodbath was to be avoided, argued Jenkins, then the Congress high command and the interim government should keep out of Punjab politics and administration. With regard to the Punjab itself, trouble could be avoided if the Hindu–Sikh and Muslim newspapers and journals were ordered to climb down from their constant provocative propaganda against each other; stringent action was taken against all violent speakers irrespective of their party affiliations; the private armies were suppressed, of which the Muslim National Guards and the Rashtriya Swayamsevak Sangh (RSS), were the most important; and the district officers were supported in their use of statutory law and order powers' (ibid.: 278).

However, if these steps were not taken, the situation would get out of control. Jenkins observed perceptively:

> If an upheaval occurs it will I believe begin with communal rioting in the towns on an unprecedented scale. The Sikh villages of the Central Punjab and the Jats of the East will join in before long, and the Muslim villagers of the North and West will follow suit. A very experienced Intelligence Officer thinks that the main upheaval will be preceded by a series of political assassinations, but this is a matter of opinion (ibid.: 279).

In the FR of 14 September, the governor reported small communal clashes at Multan and Jullundur which were dealt with quickly. Elsewhere, there was no outbreak of violence, although tension was very high. The Punjab Muslim League were waiting for instructions about launching a prolonged direct action, though their own ideas seemed to be non-cooperation on the model of the Congress, directed against the government and not

Hindus or Sikhs (ibid.: 280.). However, Bhim Sen Sachar had expressed fears to the governor about a Muslim conspiracy to start killing Hindus on 9, 10 and 11 September. The Lahore Congress was constantly feeding him with such horrible rumours (ibid). Sachar wanted the INA drama on communal harmony to be sent to all the districts so that people could appreciate the beauty of communal harmony. Moreover, he wanted a defence committee established in every *mohalla* of every town with a police inspector in charge of it. On the other hand, the Governor was of the view that the League intended to use the Congress tenderness for the INA as a means of winning over the loyal Muslim soldiers of the Indian Army.

Jenkins wrote:

> I assured Bhim Sen Sachar that our civil intelligence is very good, and though there may be bad trouble at any time, I do not think the League leaders want communal riots now, and we should almost certainly know of any elaborate plan for disorder. But the whole province is burning with rumours, and the Hindus are capable of frightening themselves into a fit (ibid.: 3).

Temporary Chief Secretary (who was actually Punjab Home Secretary), A.A. MacDonald wrote in the FR dated 14 September that the Working Committee of the Provincial Muslim League met on 1 and 2 September and gave thought to the practical forms that a civil disobedience movement could take. Strategies that were discussed included non-payment of taxes and revenues, the violation of control measures and law, and boycott of a social kind, as well as of non-Muslim trade and goods. It also considered the cost of casualties and evacuees and the raising of funds for the provision of relief to dependents of those incapacitated by injury or imprisonment. The provincial Muslim League president was given dictatorial powers and his successors were named. It passed a resolution assuring the central Muslim League that it would not recognise the interim government. A programme for arranging meetings in every district and major town had been drawn (L/P & J/5/249). Muslims, practically in every town, had been adversely affected by the ML propaganda which continued in ML papers, in public meetings and in mosques. He remarked:

> There is an increasing threat of 'Jehad' and there is more response to religious exhortation ... Along with organised, open propaganda quieter persuasion is taking place and it has been reported that deliberate attempts are being made to affect men on leave from the Army. It has also come to notice that in certain rural areas the message is being passed from mouth to mouth that the Hindus are in power, the Muslims have been betrayed, that Islam is in danger and that Muslims must fight. The result of all this is an increase in Muslim determination and disregard of consequences (ibid.).

In the 30 September FR, the governor noted that the preparation for direct action had not been deferred, and notably negative speeches had been made by Mulim League leaders such as Raja Ghazanfar Ali Khan and Ghulam Mustafa Gilani. About Raja Ghazanfar Ali Khan, he noted:

> Raja Ghazanfar Ali Khan is one of those people, far more numerous in India than in any other country, whose survival in public life is a kind of permanent surprise. It would be impossible for any sane man to respect or trust him either in private or in public affairs; but a talent for speaking and a remarkable faculty for laughing off discreditable episodes have kept him afloat, and he is one of the more dangerous members of the League. His line is scurrilous attack on the British, combined with vivid communal invective. His recent speeches have certainly been actionable, but the Premier does not wish to prosecute him until it is clear that no settlement between the League and Congress is possible. There is no doubt that Ghazanfar Ali and his like intend direct action to be organised like a *Jehad* with the Muslim divines strongly supporting it (ibid.: 284-285).

We also learn that the Bengal Muslim League leader, Khawaja Nazimuddin, had been in Lahore and had advised the local leaders to prepare for direct action that must start when Jinnah issued an order to that effect (ibid.: 285). Khizr returned from Europe and on 16 September reached Simla. Jenkins noted:

> He does not want to prosecute bad Muslim speakers until it is clear there will be no Congress-League settlement. For the same reason he is reluctant to commit himself to the suppression of Muslim

> League National Guards and the Rashtriya Swayamsevak, or to ban the entry of Jayaprakash Narayan and his immediate associates to the Punjab (ibid.: 286).

The FR of the governor of 14 October noted that the first half of October was quiet except for disturbance at Hansi in the Hissar district. It caused about thirty casualties, including one death. The peace elsewhere in the Punjab had been kept because of a tough and well-officered police force and very effective understanding with the army. The Muslim League's preparation for direct action continued and meetings in the districts were being attended by large crowds (ibid.: 289). About preparations for any outbreak of violence, Jenkins provided the following information:

> The Premier and I had a Conference on 14 October with G.O.C-in-Chief Northern Command about the location of British troops in the Punjab. According to present plans there are to be four Battalions which it was proposed to place at Sialkot, Lahore, Ferozepore, and Jullundur. The Punjab view is that the vital stations at present are Rawalpindi, Lahore, Jullundur and Ambala. Amritsar is covered by a detachment from Lahore, and Multan is covered by the British troops at Karachi, some of whom could in a real emergency be flown to Multan. General Gracy, who was on his way to Delhi, took note of our views, and said he would try to meet them. Khizr said he would like at least two more British Battalions, making six in all, but it is very doubtful whether there will be more British troops to spare (ibid: 290).

Moreover, the premier had objected thrice to interference from the interim government in the Punjab's affairs. In a meeting with the administration he suggested three measures in order to counter loose talk about 'civil war'. One, the British government or viceroy must issue a statement that the British government remains ultimately responsible for India until their responsibility is formally terminated by an Act of Parliament, or the Constituent Assembly propounds a new constitution and the British government accepts it. Two, the uneasiness among members of the higher services, both British and Indian, could be mitigated by a timely announcement as to the terms on which they will be allowed to go and the terms on which the provincial governments will be prepared to keep them. The premier had heard that British army officers had been saying that they would soon leave if 'Nehru Raj' takes over. There was a similar tendency of British officers on the civil side (ibid.: 291).

The chief secretary reported in his FR of 14 October that the Muslim League propaganda had intensified the call for jihad. The interim government was being presented in negative terms. It is being called a 'Hindu government'. Since colleges had opened after the summer recess, the Punjab Muslim Federation had come up with rules and regulations for a corps of guards which, among other duties, would prepare Muslim students to sacrifice their lives and keep their honour through the achievement of Pakistan. Women were also being organised for action. Nurses, and first-aid training courses were being organised (L/P & J/5/249). He remarked:

> Reports which have been received also show that strong appeals continue to have been made based on religious sentiment, both in mosques and in public places. Apart from an increasing mention of *Jehad* it is believed that some preachers are proclaiming the dangers of Hindu domination and are saying that it spells the ruination of all mosques and will inevitably result in the forcible conversion of Muslims to the Hindu religion (ibid.).

The chief secretary also noted that the Sikh leader Master Tara Singh had given a statement belying the allegation that Jinnah was a British agent. This had been taken as an indication that the Akalis wanted to work out a deal with the Muslim League. It was believed that if things progressed with the constitutional plan, Sikhs and Muslims would be drawn together because of common interests in the Group B, and by the fact that they were both martial people (ibid.). From such depictions, it is clear that at that point in time, Punjab politics were in a state of flux and no stable alliances were being formed.

From the governor's FR of 31 October, it is learned that the positive effect of acceptance of office by the Muslim League in the Interim Government had been neutralised by the disturbances in East Bengal (Noakhali). Moreover, there was an outbreak of communal violence in

Ludhiana on the night of Diwali on 24 October. It started that night with a row over traditional gambling: A Hindu (or Sikh, it is not exactly known) won a lot of money and was attacked by Muslims who had lost; he was then chased and fatally stabbed. There were further incidents in October, on 25, 26 and 27, resulting in injuries to thirty people, of whom seven died (Carter 2006: 292-3).

On the other hand, Hindu students of DAV and Sanatam Dharam Colleges in Lahore had celebrated 'Noakhali Day' on 29 October, and in Lahore, they marched in a procession while chanting the most provocative slogans, including one which may be translated as 'Blood for blood'. Sir Gokul Chand Narang, a former Punjab minister, was whipping up anti-Muslim sentiments. The Hindus in Lahore felt they were well-prepared and wished to provoke a conflict. He writes: 'I can hardly believe that this is true; but the intemperance and irresponsibility of educated people, including I am afraid some members of the teaching staff of the university, are almost incredible' (ibid.: 293-4).

In the FR of 13/14 November, Jenkins wrote from Sialkot instead of from Lahore, where he was usually based:

> Communal tension is now worse than ever. I agree with Your Excellency that the responsibility for this rests with Congress. They have for years encouraged, and are still encouraging, contempt of authority and a violent attitude of mind.... The slightest incident might now touch off very serious disorders in any big cities, and there is quite a chance that once disorders began, the villagers though naturally non-communal, might join it (ibid.: 296).

In the same report is mentioned a minor incident in which Hindu students in Lahore beat up a Muslim butcher who was carrying goat meat on the carrier of his bicycle. The only serious trouble reported so far was from Rothak in the Ambala division. The story was that some Hindus had desecrated a Muslim shrine which resulted in stabbings on 11 November. The Hindu Jats began to swarm the area in large numbers, armed with axes and *lathis* (batons). 'They attacked a small railway station and murdered the Muslim Assistant Station Master and forced the Hindu Station Master to hand over such money as he had.' (ibid.: 297).

With regard to the Congress members of the ministry, Lahri Singh was reported to have made a speech in which he boasted that the Congress ministers were running the Punjab. During the tour to various parts of Punjab, the governor noted that the old supporters of the government were far from happy. They thought that the future now lay in the hands of the political parties, which they disliked and were not interested in joining (ibid.: 298).

Viceroy Wavell had gone to England at the end of November, so Jenkins' FR of 30 November was addressed to the officiating viceroy, Sir John Colville. The most significant event from that period was the promulgation of the Punjab Public Safety Ordinance, on 19 November. It had been drafted by the governor and was promulgated under Section 89 of the Government of India Act of 1935. The premier advised the governor to exercise his special powers and not submit it for approval to the Punjab Assembly, where delays and amendments could damage its impact and render it ineffective (ibid.: 302). Under the new ordinance, the government banned drills and carrying of arms and other forms of militancy. As a result, some Muslim National Guards were told to go home and take off their uniforms, and some members of the RSS in Lahore were arrested. Jenkins writes, 'This is perhaps the first major case in which a Governor has used his discretionary powers with the support and encouragement of his Ministers' (ibid.).

We also learn that during his visit to Delhi, the Punjab premier was shocked by the communal outlook of the members of the interim government. He thought that the only solution was the dismissal of the interim government and a return to firm government under British authority. 'In the last resort he thinks that the Punjab should be declared a Dominion and maintain direct relations with the Crown' (ibid.: 303). About Shaukat Hayat's intemperance, Jenkins remarked that he recently had advocated the murder of the premier. 'Shaukat is a small man and, I think, dishonest; but he can be very mischievous' (ibid).

The new Chief Secretary, Akhtar Hussain, took over in the Punjab and noted in his FR dated 30 November that the communal situation had deteriorated further. The reasons were the communal disturbances outside Punjab. In particular, Hindus seemed to be in a more provocative mood because trouble had prevailed in districts where they were in a majority (Rothak). Some of the murders of Muslims were committed by Hindu villagers, using firearms. There were also reports of Muslims being forced to convert to Hinduism. The news about the Garhmukteswar riots had spread to all the districts. However, the Punjab Safety Ordinance had had a positive effect since it prohibited marches and the carrying of arms. Communal disorder persisted in Rothak. On the other hand, the Shia ceremony of Muharram passed without serious incident, and only in one place was the procession banned due to disagreements between Muslims, as well as for communal reasons. The chief secretary writes: 'A satisfactory feature of Muharram was the good work done by peace committees, and in many places Hindus served appreciative Muslim processions with refreshments' (L/P & J/5/249).

The chief secretary noted that following rioting against non-Muslims in some districts of the NWFP, frightened Hindus had arrived in the Punjab from there (ibid.). On the other hand, the RSS had arranged impressive displays of their presence in the Punjab districts when their chief organiser visited the province. A detailed report of the intelligence agencies is given in the booklet, *RSS (Rashtriya Swayam Sewak Sangh) in the Punjab,* published by the Government of Pakistan in 1948. It was noted that:

> The strength of the Rashtriya Swayam Sewak Sangh was demonstrated in November 1946, during the extensive tour of the province, but its chief organiser and the head of the All-India Rashtriya Swayam Sewak Sangh – Madho Rao Golwalkar. He visited Multan, Montgomery, Rawalpindi, Jhelum, Dharamsala, Amritsar, Hoshiarpur, Jagraon, Lyallpur, Sheikhupura, Sialkot and Lahore. The number of volunteers who greeted him on parades, at these places was estimated to be 25,000. The number of Hindu and Sikh visitors who were issued special invitations to witness the rallies, during this tour, was estimated to be over 40,000. At some of the centres, where the District Magistrates had prohibited public gatherings under section 144, Criminal Procedure Code, he held secret meetings. ... The Congress was held responsible for the sufferings of the Hindus in Bengal and elsewhere and it was affirmed that if the Hindus wished

to survive, they would have to fight the Muslims without mercy (1948: 5-6)

Referring to the past activities of the RSS in the Punjab, the same report makes the interesting remark that 'The movement was not anti-government and its workers did not participate in the Congress civil disobedience movement of 1942' (ibid.: 5).

In the 14 December FR, Jenkins reflected on the impact of the constant wrangling of politicians in Delhi on the people of the Punjab. He wrote – unusually for a bureaucrat – with feeling: 'The average man, whether Muslim, Hindu or Sikh is deeply concerned about the future – it seems that there can be no settlement without widespread disorder, which will cause no loss to the political leaders, but will be disastrous for the mass of the population' (Carter, 2006: 307).

He toured the Rawalpindi division, visiting Rawalpindi, Campbellpur and Mianwali, from where the bulk of the Muslim portion of the British Indian Army was recruited. Rawalpindi district alone provided 70,000 men and the other districts another 40,000. In these areas, support for the British was still strong and the people felt they should not abandon India. 'The feeling is growing that India is heading for chaos, and the British must do something about it (ibid.: 308).

In the FR of 30 December, Jenkins notes that close allies of the Congress, the nationalist Muslims of the Ahrar, were discussing their future course in a meeting in Lahore and, according to intelligence reports, were very uneasy:

'They [nationalist Muslims] are convinced that the Bihar massacres were arranged by the Bihar government and that Jayaprakash Narayan was one of its organisers. They have no desire to join the Muslim League, but they do not see that they can continue for very long with the Congress'. (ibid.: 310).

With regard to the Punjab Muslim League, Jenkins observed that a challenge to the leadership of Nawab Mamdot had been launched by his rivals, Shaukat Hayat Khan and Firoz Khan Noon. They were conspiring to oust him, but had not succeeded thus far because Mamdot had been able to secure the support of district office-bearers and organisers (ibid.). Similar leadership contests were going on among the Sikhs. In the *gurdwara* elections, the Akalis had won by an overwhelming majority and a struggle was going on between Kartar Singh and the Nagoke group (ibid.) During his trip to Shahpur in the Rawalpindi division, which was the stronghold of the Premier's Tiwana clan, Jenkins talked to several people and addressed a large gathering of ex-servicemen. He remarked:

'They will not tolerate domination by a Hindu Centre; but they are not in their hearts particularly keen on Pakistan, nor do they want an immediate severance of the British connection. I was repeatedly asked why we were determined to leave India and what was so wrong with the old regime that we must suddenly break with it' (ibid.: 311). He noted that Rawalpindi city was always a danger spot. 'There was a bad communal riot there about 1926 and, and as far as I remember, a large number of rural Muslims joined on that occasion' (ibid.: 311).

Chief Secretary Akhtar Husain noted in his FR of 30 December that the National Guards and the RSS had gained in importance. National Guards numbers had risen from 1,500 in December 1945 to approximately 22,000 at the end of 1946. RSS were 14,000 in December 1945 and were now estimated to be some 46,000 (L/P & J/5/249). The Governor's FR of 14 January 1947, covering events from the second half of December 1946, took up the disturbances in Hazara district of the NWFP on the border with northern Punjab. As a result, a large influx of mainly Sikh, but also Hindu refugees to Rawalpindi, had taken place. At first, Khizr was inclined to let them fend for themselves because he thought that if any arrangements were made, he would be accused of helping Frontier Hindus and ignoring Bihari Muslims, who had also sought refuge in the Punjab following the bloody rioting in that province. However, the governor persuaded him that those who had entered Punjab on foot without any means to support themselves could not be ignored. Khizr agreed to establish refugee camps for them (ibid.: 321).

With regard to Khizr, Jenkins expressed disappointment that the Punjab premier had not addressed a single public meeting since he, Jenkins, became Punjab governor in April 1946. His passivity greatly weakened the authority of the coalition government. On the other hand, Khizr had given him a dismal picture of a Punjab without the British. Jenkins presented the premier's views in the following words:

> 'He said the other day that the present Central Government was in his opinion incompetent and incapable of administering the country: that the Indian Army without British officers would be reduced rapidly to a rabble.... He has some hazy idea about the conversion of the Punjab into a Dominion and has told me this could be done' (ibid.: 323-4).

On 15 March 2004, I was given an eyewitness account by two Sikhs, Amar Singh and Madanlal Singh, originally from Rawalpindi and now settled in Delhi, on the influx of the refugees from Hazara into Rawalpindi. They recalled:

'The Sikhs and Hindus came to Rawalpindi and narrated hair-raising stories of the utter inhumanity with which they had been treated by the Muslims. Many women and children were abducted and never returned. Some of the women had been raped. In some truly shocking cases their breasts had been cut off and their vaginas pierced with sharp metal objects. We were able to provide them help in the *gurdwaras* and *mandirs,* and some were even taken to the Sikh-Hindu *mohallas* and they stayed with relatives or even strangers. Not all of them stayed in Rawalpindi. Some moved to east Punjab, especially Amritsar and Patiala, Kapurthala and other Sikh states. Later, more and more people were to join them when Muslim attacks began to occur from March 1947. When the retribution attacks of Sikhs started in August 1947, those from the Hazara district were among the first to take part in them.'

References

Allana, G. *Pakistan Movement: Historic Documents,* Lahore: Islamic Book Services, 1977.

Azad, M.A.K. *India Wins Freedom,* Lahore: Vanguard Books Pvt Ltd, 1989.

Gilmartin, David. 'Religious Leadership and the Pakistan Movement in the Punjab' *Modern South Asian Studies, vol. 13, No. 3*, Cambridge: Cambridge University Press.

Gillmartin, David. *Empire and Islam: Punjab and the Making of Pakistan,* Delhi: Oxford University Press, 1989.

Khosla, G. D. *Stern Reckoning: A Survey of the Events Leading up to and Following the Partition of India*. New Delhi: Oxford University Press, 1991.

Moore, R. J. 'Jinnah and the Pakistan Demand', *Modern Asian Studies, Vol. 17, No. 4,* pp. 529-561, Cambridge: Cambridge University Press, 1983.

Talbot, I. *Khizr Tiwana: The Punjab Unionist Party and the Partition of India,* Richmond, Surrey: Curzon, 1996.

Tuker, Sir Francis. *While Memory Serves*, London: Cassell and Company Ltd., 1950.

Official documents

Carter, Lionel. *Punjab Politics 1 January 1944–3 March 1947: Last Years of the Ministries (Governor's Fortnightly Reports and other Key Documents).* New Delhi: Manohar 2006.

Mansergh. N. and P. Moon, (eds). *The Transfer of Power, 1 August 1945-22 April 1946, vol. 6,* London: Her Majesty's Stationery Office, 1976.

———, (eds). *The Transfer of Power, 23 March-29 June 1946, vol. 7,* London: Her Majesty's Stationery Office, 1977.

———, (eds). *The Transfer of Power, 3 July-1 November 1946, vol. 8,* London: Her Majesty's Stationery Office, 1979.

———, (eds). *The Transfer of Power, 4 November 1946-22 March 1947, vol. 9,* London: Her Majesty's Stationery Office, 1980.

RSS (Rashtriya Swayam Sewak Sangh) in the Punjab, Lahore: Government Printing Press, 1948.

Microfilm

Fortnightly Reports of Punjab Chief Secretary for 1946 (which also include reports of the Punjab Governor) in the Political Department Miscellaneous (also known as Political and Judicial records) under the designation L/P & J/5/249. London: British Library.

Interviews

Bhisham Sahni, Delhi, 23 October 2001

Abdullah Malik, Lahore, 19 December 2001

Aziz Mazhar, London (based in Lahore), 18–19 May 2002

Amar Singh, Delhi, 15 March 2004

Madanlal Singh, Delhi 15 March 2004

Hukum Qureshi, Lahore 30 October 2005
Syed Ahmed Saeed Kirmani, Lahore, 31 October 2005
Chaudhri Nazir Ahmed Virk, Sheikhupura, 30 December 2005

5

DIRECT ACTION
24 JANUARY–26 FEBRUARY 1947

THE PUNJAB PREMIER, SIR KHIZR HAYAT KHAN TIWANA, HAD BEEN hesitant in dealing firmly with the Muslim League's challenge to his government, and Governor Jenkins described his attitude as indecisive and slow. That ended in January 1947, when a dramatic change took place in his approach to the Muslim League's persistent threats to bring down his government. He decided to clamp down on what he sensed was a growing insurgency, as arms had reportedly been collected by the private armies under the direction of political parties. On the other hand, nothing had happened in parliamentarian terms to indicate that the Muslim League commanded a majority of its own, had won over independent members, or had found a coalition partner that would provide it with a majority. Equally, none of its popular actions during December or January suggested that the Muslim League was about to order the direct action it had been threatening to launch for months, to bring down the Punjab government. Nevertheless, it is possible that following the rioting in NWFP's Hazara district, Khizr felt that Punjab could be heading in a similar direction. He therefore decided to take pre-emptive action (Moon, 1998: 75).

On 24 January, the government issued orders banning the Muslim National Guard and the RSS. A police force arrived at the Muslim League National Guard Headquarters in Lahore, with search warrants. The leaders present were about to hand over the keys when Mian Iftikharuddin arrived and stood in front of the door, refusing to give the police permission to enter. Other leaders also arrived and obstructed the police (Nawab Mamdot, Malik Sir Firoz Khan Noon, Syed Amir Hussain Shah, Begum Shahnawaz, Shaukat Hayat Khan and Mian Mumtaz Daultana). They were arrested (Carter, 2006: 328). Inside the National Guard headquarters, the police found 1,000 steel helmets. The Punjab Home Secretary visited them at the Civil Lines Police Station and found them, 'bitter and angry and determined to out [oust] Khizr at all costs' (ibid.).

The arrests of the Muslim League leaders triggered a spontaneous mass civil disobedience movement across the province. Direct action became a fact. The government responded with the imposition of restrictions on all Punjab's newspapers to report on the demonstrations and protests. To quell the protests, the government already had at its disposal Section 144 of the Criminal Procedure Code, as well as the Punjab Public Safety Ordinance. In the days and weeks that followed, however, such measures were to prove ineffective in curbing the agitation. The provincial capital, Lahore, naturally became the hub of Muslim League activism. Demonstrations and *hartals* (closures of shops and businesses in protest) broke out in different parts of the city. The same day, Muslim students, mainly from the Islamia College, a Muslim League stronghold, were arrested at Nila Gumbad near Anarkali when they tried to lead out a procession (interviews, Aziz Mazhar; Hukum Qureshi).

Raja Ghazanfar Ali Khan, a member of India's interim government in Delhi, visited the detainees and later remarked that the atmosphere inside the prison was akin to that of a picnic! Another member of the interim government, Sardar Abur Rab Nishtar, issued a statement saying: 'It appears to me another attempt on the part of the Punjab Government to kill Muslim League Organisation by force, but let me tell them that by the grace of God, they shall not succeed. Muslim India will never take it lying down' (*Dawn*, 26 January 1947). The acting president of the Punjab Muslim League, Sheikh Sadiq Hasan, told the Associated Press of America that the struggle was non-violent and non-communal. He asserted that he had received instructions from his leaders to break Section 144 whenever necessary: 'Even if people are shot they are not to retreat' (ibid.).

At the same time, the government feared that weapons were being kept in the private homes of some leading politicians. The same day, therefore, the police surrounded the Birdwood Road residence of Syed Amir Hussain Shah, *Salar-e-Suba* (Commander of Province) of the Punjab Muslim League National Guard. They wanted to search the house. Women members of the Punjab Muslim League Women's Committee, such as the elderly Lady Shafi, Fatima Begum, Lady Zulfikar Ali and Begum Kamaluddin, were inside, along with Begum Nasim Amir Hussain Shah (*Dawn*, 26 January). They refused permission. In extended interviews, Begum Nasim Amir Hussain Shah and Raja Tajammul Hussain, who had been outside along with other students, recounted to me how the ladies defied the police for several hours, until finally the acting president of the Muslim League, Sheikh Sadiq Hassan, persuaded them to allow entry. In the meantime, some weapons had been quickly wrapped in a cloth and sent away from the back door. Tajammul Hussain and another student were arrested.

Raids were also conducted on the same day in Rawalpindi, Jullundur, Lyallpur, Ferozepur, Simla and Rohtak at the offices and residences of some of the leaders of the National Guard and RSS but nothing incriminating was found. In Amritsar, provocative literature and some daggers and uniforms were recovered from the Muslim League office. In Ludhiana, too, some objectionable printed material was impounded (*Dawn,* 26 January). Protests and demonstrations continued all over the province. Muslim students were arrested in Jullundur for defying the ban on processions and use of loudspeakers (interview, Malik Abdul Ahad). In Multan, Muslim students demonstrated to demand the release of their leaders and shops remained closed. Similarly, in Ferozepur, Muslims observed *hartal*. Nawabzada Liaqat Ali Khan, a member of the interim government, issued a statement that any description of the National Guard as a private army was preposterous and a comparison with the RSS, wholly unwarranted (*Dawn*, 27 January; interviews Malik Abdullah, Khursheed Abbas Gardezi).

From Karachi, Jinnah issued a very strong condemnation of the ban, fully supporting Liaqat Ali Khan's contention. He warned that the consequences of such high-handed and unwarranted action would be 'terrific all over Muslim India and I appeal to the Viceroy to immediately intervene and save the situation which otherwise may take a very serious turn for which the entire responsibility will rest with the Viceroy and

H.M.G.' (*Dawn,* 28 January). The message undoubtedly registered with the Punjab premier, who ordered the release of the leaders on 26 February. However, they refused to leave the Lahore Central Jail unless other men and women arrested during the campaign were also set free. The government virtually threw them out of jail. Mamdot said that the Muslim League would not rest content unless the ban on the National Guard was withdrawn unconditionally (ibid.). The women leaders were also released but they too protested that all other men and women should be freed. It was clear that the Muslim League had no intention of calling off the agitation short of achieving some major gain.

The government then rearrested, at midnight on 27–28 January, the Muslim League's top leaders. On 28 January, the ban on the National Guard was lifted. However, the Committee of Action of the Muslim League decided to continue its 'non-violent mass struggle against the reactionary Punjab regime' (*Dawn,* 30 January). More people offered themselves for arrest. Firoz Khan Noon's Austrian-born wife was arrested while leading a women's procession. The Punjab Governor, Sir Evan Jenkins, explained in a telegram dated 28 January to Wavell, why only the Muslim League National Guards and RSS have been banned:

> Congress volunteers are not an organised body in the Punjab and are not suitable object for ban. R.S.S. is real Hindu private army... Akali Jathas [Sikh militias] have existed for many years but are usually formed *ad hoc* and are not now active. ... Object of bans was to deal simultaneously with only two active communal private armies (Carter, 2006: 331).

At that stage, then, according to the Punjab administration, only two 'private armies' were in such an advanced level of preparation that their arrest was deemed important to obviate communal trouble. In any case, *hartals* and processions continued in the eastern city of Ludhiana, where some 1,000 *burqa*-clad women also took part in the procession. In Amritsar, the Senior Superintendent of Police, S.F. Robinson, was grievously injured while controlling a Muslim League procession on Tuesday, 28 January, when he was attacked with a flagpole by an agitator (Carter 2006: 334; *Dawn,* 30 January). This incident resulted in a number of arrests in Amritsar. At Rawalpindi too, some local leaders were arrested, as well as fifty-seven Muslim Leaguers in Ferozepur.

It was now clear that the Muslim League had decided to bring down the Khizr ministry. Thus on 30 January, a crowd of several thousand gathered in Mochi Gate, one of the main gathering points in Lahore, to form a procession. Begum Shahnawaz writes that after that meeting, she and other leaders went to the provincial civil secretariat, joined by a crowd of some 100,000. She took the people inside the gate and was about to address the meeting, when European police began to charge the crowd, armed with batons. She claims to have quickly come between the opposing sides and stopped the attack, assuring the authorities that the people would remain peaceful and disperse quietly after she had addressed them. The police retreated to a distance. She recounts what happened next:

> I spoke for about forty minutes, calling upon the Government, the Governor, and the officials to see the upsurge of the Muslim nation, and realize that they were standing united under the flag of the Muslim League and that Pakistan had to be given to them. Muslims would never tolerate Hindu majority rule, because they did not wish to become part and parcel of the 'depressed classes' (Shahnawaz 2002: 196).

Later, sixty people from the assembled crowd deliberately sought arrest, following which they were taken to the Civil Lines police station. Arrests continued to mount, including that of the uncle of the Punjab premier, Major Nawab Mumtaz Tiwana, and the premier's spiritual guide, Pir Sahib Golra Sharif. The president of the Muslim League in Wazirabad was also arrested. Arrests were also made at Bhalwal and Ferozepur. People spontaneously began to court arrest.

On 29 January, the government banned for fifteen days the circulation of the Delhi-based newspaper *Dawn*, the English-language mouthpiece of the Muslim League in the Punjab. On 30 January, the *pir* of Taunsa Sharif, Khawaja Shujauddin, was arrested. Some leading men from the powerful family of Gilani *pirs* were also arrested, along with the poet Ishq Lehar, who recited rousing poems at the start of Muslim League public meetings. At Jullundur, the *hartal* continued for the eighth day.

In Gujrat, Jahan Khan Bhusal and Nawabzada Asghar Ali Khan were arrested. It was reported that thousands of villagers were trekking towards Gujrat to court arrest. The first death was reported from Simla, in a police baton-charge. In Jullundur the Muslim League prisoners went on hunger strike to protest ill treatment by the authorities.

The most dramatic event was the hoisting of the Muslim League flag over the gates of Government House in Lahore on 1 February by Zahida Hayat, daughter of the late Sir Sikandar Hayat Khan, amid shouts of 'Down with the Khizr ministry' (*The Tribune,* 3 February). In Multan, Gardezi *pirs* and others from the Gilani family were also arrested. At least 100,000 people were reported to have taken part in the protest march in Multan against their arrests. Nawab Muhammad Khan Leghari and many other landlords and notables of Dera Ghazi Khan also courted arrest. There was little doubt that the agitation was spreading, and Muslim notables who hitherto had never taken part in agitational politics were now courting arrest. In a statement issued from Karachi on 2 February, Jinnah made a plea to the viceroy to restore civil liberties in the Punjab. He advised the Muslim youth in the Punjab 'to avoid communal conflicts and keep the movement absolutely peaceful' (*Dawn*, 4 February). The main slogan adopted by the Muslim League at this time was 'restoration of civil liberties'. However, since direct action had been announced, resort to extra-constitutional methods had begun to take new forms. In Lahore, the demonstrators began to disrupt traffic and in some cases Hindus and Sikh motorists were forced to fly Muslim League flags on their cars. Some non-Muslim bystanders were also harassed, but by and large the agitation remained peaceful (*The Tribune* ,5 February).

In Gujrat, under the leadership of Syed Amir Hussain Shah, *Salar-e-Suba* of the National Guard, batches of demonstrators entered the court rooms of the local magistrates and paralysed their work by shouting 'Civil liberties *zindabad!*' (Long live civil liberties!), 'Muslim League *zindabad!*', and 'Khizr ministry *murdabad!*' (Death to the Khizr ministry). On Sunday, 2 February, a large police force under a Deputy Superintendent of Police raided Syed Amir Hussain Shah's village, Moinuddinpur, to arrest him, but was turned back by thousands of supporters from the village belonging to his Syed *biradari* (clan). Next day, the police returned, but thousands of men and women blocked their way. Syed Amir Hussain Shah then gave himself up, urging his followers to continue their struggle along non-communal and peaceful lines (*Dawn*, 6 February; interview with elders in village Moinuddinpur on 5 April 2003).

In Dera Ghazi Khan the Baluch leader, Sardar Haji Jamal Khan Leghari, who had renounced titles such as 'nawab' and 'sir', led a procession of 60,000 tribesmen, 1,000 of whom were armed with rifles and pistols. They marched past the house of the Deputy Commissioner in the Civil Lines, but the authorities made no attempt to arrest them. Reports also started coming in of Muslim police refusing to take firm action against women. Some 13,000 people had been arrested by the first week of February (*Dawn*, 7 February). Many *pirs* had joined the movement. Pir Sahib Sial Sharif was arrested in Sargodha on 6 February. Muslims from minority districts and towns of the Punjab also joined the movement and offered themselves for arrest. In Ambala and Gurgaon, Muslim League office-bearers and even MLA Chaudhri Mehtab Khan of Gurgaon were arrested. On 6 February, it was reported that seventy-four of the seventy-nine Muslim League MLAs were in jail. Hunger strikes in Sonepat, Jullundur and Simla jails were reported. 7 February, the fifteenth day of direct action, was observed throughout the Punjab as 'Simla Martyr's Day' to mark the death of a Muslim in the normally quiet hill-station from a *lathi* blow to the head. On 6 February, the Punjab government ordered a ten-day pre-censorship of all news and commentaries related to the agitation. It substituted for the earlier order of 27 January a fifteen-day ban on all communiqués, except official ones. The new order was served on all newspapers of Lahore including the British-owned *Civil & Military Gazette* (*Dawn*, 9 February).

A three-man delegation of high-ranking Muslim League members from outside Punjab, Khawaja Nazimuddin, Muhammad Ismail Khan and Siddiq Ali Khan, arrived in Lahore on 7 February. Their arrival gave a further fillip to the struggle against the ministry. At the Badshahi Mosque, they addressed a gathering of 100,000 people. In sympathy with the Muslim League movement, the Lahore Butchers' Association, the Fruit Market Association and the Vegetable Market Association decided to suspend their business from Monday, 10 February (*Dawn*, 9 February). The 10 February issue of *Dawn* mentioned police baton-charges against women, prisoners and students in different parts of the Punjab. In a telegram dated 8 February to Pethick-Lawrence, Jenkins noted that the mob in Lahore was growing more aggressive. The Hindus and Sikhs were terrified; he felt that the Muslims wanted to establish a Muslim Raj. He then remarked that the agitation was likely to accentuate the Sikh demand for a partition of the Punjab:

> It is quite impossible for one community to rule the Punjab with its present boundaries. Long-term alternatives are therefore reversion to Unionist principles with Muslim domination or partition which would create intolerable minor[ity] problems. Effect of agitation is to force second alternative on non-Muslims and to impair very seriously long-term prospects of Muslim League and Muslims generally. Muslim League are in fact wantonly throwing away certainty of Muslim leadership in a United Punjab for uncertain advantages of a partition which Sikhs will gradually now demand. But nobody has the brains to understand this (Carter 2006: 343).

The situation in the Punjab had clearly become unmanageable and the Punjab Safety Ordinance of (October) 1946 was being openly defied. Students squatted on the Mall and all vehicular traffic stopped on 10 February. The same day, the Union Jack was removed from the High Court Building in Lahore and in its place, the Muslim League flag flew for two hours. This incident resulted in the arrest of Dr Omar Hayat, the principal of Islamia College, and many students. The day before, 9 February, a funeral was held for Abdul Maalik, a Muslim student killed the previous day as a result of a brickbat thrown from a house in Beadon Road. Thousands of *tonga*-drivers, college students, women and children took part in the funeral procession to Miani Sahib Graveyard, and a record crowd of 200,000 took part in the funeral prayers. News also arrived that a Muslim boy, Mohammad Sharif, had died in Jhelum as a result of injuries sustained in a police baton-charge. *Hartals* were observed in other Punjab towns.

On 10 February, Police Constable No. 1751, Nasiruddin, came forward to be arrested, along with fifty others in Lahore. Among them were five scheduled caste Hindus (*Dawn,* 13 February 1947). A report from Jhang, in western Punjab, suggested that a Muslim youth had succumbed to police brutality (ibid.). Acting Muslim League Punjab president Malik Shaukat Ali was arrested on 13 February.

The *Civil & Military Gazette* editorial of 12 February observed:

> [The Muslim League's] agitation ... is dangerous ...to the peace of the province and the constitution security of Government in the Punjab as far as can be seen in the future. Tempers are daily wearing thinner ... and the time is not far off when bullets may replace tear-gas bombs.... The present policy of drift [of the government] is playing into the hands of the agitators and it is preparing the way for goondaism [hooliganism].

The Punjab campaign was now cited by Nawabzada Liaqat Ali Khan, Secretary of the All-India Muslim League, as an example of what the Muslim League could do on an all-India scale. The struggle, he said, would remain non-violent. He deplored the Muslim League's exclusion from the Khizr ministry, despite the fact that it represented the largest community in the province and formed the biggest single party in the Punjab Legislature. He expected the Ministry to fall as a result of the continuing Muslim League campaign (*Dawn*, 15 February).

In a telegram to Wavell dated 12 February, the Punjab governor made the following assessment:

> Hindus and Sikhs will not stand Muslim agitation much longer. Gopi Chand Bhargava has written personally to the Premier saying if he does not suppress agitation with all resources at his disposal Hindus must act on their own. Tara Singh has issued statement to Press to effect that Sikhs are in grave danger and must revive their "Army" immediately under his command... we are suppressing Tara Singh's statement. But we can only delay active non-Muslim intervention which in my opinion is now almost certain. Lahri Singh who saw me this morning said that Hindus could not be kept quiet for long (Mansergh and Moon, 1980: 680).

In Amritsar on 13 February, Saifuddin Kitchlew, President of the Punjab Provincial Congress Committee, declared: 'Pakistan is unfeasible – it is unworkable and impracticable, politically, economically and socially' (*Pakistan Times*, 15 February 1947). He regretted that the Congress had not seriously pursued the plans of Jawaharlal Nehru to establish contact with the Muslim masses. That was why, he asserted, they had fallen into the lap of the Muslim League. As a Muslim, he felt his community stood to gain more in a united India. He warned Muslims not to fall prey to the League's propaganda that 'Islam was in danger'. Rather, he emphasised, 'If Islam has thrived on its own merits and purity it can never stand in danger from anyone, much less from our own countrymen. In fact, the greatest danger to our religion is through slavery and from the imperialist Churchill group' (ibid.).

Tensions continued to rise in the Punjab. On 14 February, police fired at a procession of some 100,000 demonstrators in Amritsar. Nobody was killed but injuries were recorded. The demonstrators were heading towards the Civil Lines when they encountered the police, who tried in vain to stop them. The procession surged forward to plant Muslim League flags on the deputy commissioner's courtroom and the general post office. Petition-writers' papers were damaged. In the *lathi*-charge which followed, some of the rioters were injured.

On 16 February, the Sikh Panthic Board Working Committee met to express disapproval of the agitation, which it feared could be turned against the Sikh community. It demanded that the government take firm action. Acting Muslim League President Daud Ghaznavi commented: 'If the Government ceased to ban processions and meetings, the movement will stop, I hope.' (*Dawn*:18 February 1947). On 17 February, the police not only used tear gas and *lathi*-charges but also fired live rounds. Many people sustained injuries, and at least one died. (*Dawn*: 19 February). On the same day, Muslim League saboteurs made an attempt to wreck the Frontier Mail train near Rawalpindi (*Civil & Military Gazette:* 18 February 1947). Riots were reported from Sialkot and Gujranwala.

On 17 February, Raja Ghazanfar Ali Khan and Khawaja Nazimuddin in a joint press conference in Lahore, warned Muslims not to 'let their movement assume forms which have not yet been authorised or sanctioned by [your] leaders' (*Dawn*: 19 February 1947). They went on to say:

> It appears that in certain parts of the Punjab, particularly in Gujrat, Jhelum, Rawalpindi and Sargodha Districts, large numbers of people have started a campaign to delay railway trains. This, it is said, is being done by National Guards under the impression that the

> authorities of the Provincial Muslim League have sanctioned this form of activity, as a part of the Civil Disobedience Movement in this province.
>
> We have ascertained from people now in charge of Punjab Muslim League Organisation and wish to make it clear that the delaying of railway trains or interference with the railway traffic in any way, has not so far been sanctioned by the Provincial Muslim League or any higher authority' *(Dawn*: 19 February).

Meanwhile, the editors of the Muslim newspapers in Lahore, Faiz Ahmed Faiz (*Pakistan Times*), Akhtar Ali Khan (*Zamindar*), Hameed Nizami (*Nawa-e-Waqt*), Noor Ilahi (*Ehsan*) and Abdul Hameed (*Eastern Times*), issued a statement protesting that since 28 January, Lahore newspapers had all been directed 'not to publish any material except that supplied by the Government regarding progress of the movement. ... This was to lapse on Feb. 16, but on the evening of February 15 a fresh Order was served with the result that the gag Order which was originally intended to remain in force for 10 days will now be effective for a full month' (*Pakistan Times*: 19 February).

20 February announcement of British government to transfer power

While the Muslim League's direct action in the Punjab was in full swing, the British government announced in London on 20 February its plan to transfer power to Indians by the middle of 1948 at the latest. The statement expressed emphatic regret that the Cabinet Mission Plan had not been allowed to serve as the basis of government and that the Constituent Assembly had failed to agree on a constitutional formula. Further, 'His Majesty's Government wish to make it clear that it is their definite intention to take the necessary steps to effect the transfer of power into responsible Indian hands by a date not later than June 1948' (Mansergh and Moon 1980: 774).

The reactions to the statement were varied. The Muslim League felt it was winning the battle of Pakistan; Congress, for their part, was of the view that such a statement would compel Jinnah and the Muslim

League to become more realistic and flexible. The Sikhs were particularly perturbed because no guarantees had been given to them with regard to their special claims on the province (*The Tribune*: 4 February). As for Khizr, he expressed his disappointment in no uncertain terms, calling the statement 'the work of lunatics'. On 21 February, he appeared to backtrack, describing the statement only as a threat which the British did not mean seriously. Jenkins, however, advised him to take it as a conclusive decision which would be carried out.

Agitation turns violent in Amritsar on 24 February

The civil disobedience movement began to acquire an increasingly unruly character with every passing day. Nowhere was this more vivid than in Amritsar. Khawaja Iftikhar noted in his book, *Jabb Amritsar Jall Raha Tha* (When Amritsar was Burning) that Muslim protestors would gather first in the compound of the Muslim Anglo-Oriental (MAO) College. The principal, Dilawar Husain, would provide them all the help and encouragement. On one occasion he angrily protested to a British police officer who was obstructing the procession to leave the college. The daily marches would go round the city and on the way the police would try to disperse them by firing tear gas shells and sometimes through *lathi*-charges. The tension between the protestors and the police continued to heighten, until one day when Muslim women also joined the agitation and loudly shouted anti-British and pro-Pakistan slogans. Superintendent of Police Robinson let loose his wrath on the procession. He lashed out with his whip at some women marchers when they were proceeding towards the Town Hall. A young man, Ayaz Mahmood, retaliated by snatching a *lathi* from a policeman and hitting Robinson on the head with its metal part. Robinson fell to the ground. He was in a coma for a week in a hospital in Amritsar; part of the skull had been smashed, and his recovery was slow. Ayaz Mahmood was tried for attempted murder but was released on 14 August when India and Pakistan exchanged prisoners (1991: 73-79).

The agitations continued, becoming more frequent and turning out bigger crowds by the day. On 24 February, the movement completed one month of continuous civil disobedience. It was celebrated with *hartals* in most towns and serious disturbances in Amritsar, Jullundur and Rawalpindi. In Amritsar that day, the levels of violence escalated. Jenkins remarks in the fortnightly report of 28 February 1947:

> Events at Amritsar deserve special mention. A large crowd of demonstrators moved on the Civil Station and began making murderous attacks on the Police. A Sikh constable, who was apparently on point duty and was certainly not actively engaged against the rioters, was beaten to death, and other Police Officers were attacked. The Police suffered about 55 casualties including one killed and three seriously injured. They were obliged to fire several times. There were about 110 casualties among the demonstrators, including one killed and eleven injured by revolver fire. The man who was killed was attempting to beat to death a Police officer who had been knocked down, and it is fortunate he was shot dead. The Additional District Magistrate (a Muslim) sustained a fractured skull. During these incidents a Company of troops stood by, but was not, I understand, engaged at all (Carter, 2006: 365-6).

The gruesome murder of the Sikh constable led the Sikh leader, Master Tara Singh, to describe the Muslim League campaign as 'communal' and not 'political'. Three days later, he warned of the risk of a civil war and demanded that the British return the Punjab to Sikh suzerainty. At that point, intelligence reports were already warning that recruitment to the private armies was proceeding at a brisk pace (Talbot, 2004: 82). Regarding the death of the Sikh constable, Khawaja Iftikhar gave a different version of the events leading to the murder. He asserted that the Muslim crowds had swelled by the day and had become increasingly assertive and bold. They put the administration virtually on the retreat; some government functionaries were even manhandled by the demonstrators. As a result, policemen would panic and run away upon seeing the protestors. Some would fire at them from behind bushes and from the trees they had climbed onto. The emboldened Muslims began to pull down the Union Jack and in its place hoist the Muslim League flag. In one such attempt a young man, Muhammad Sharif, climbed the wall of the Amritsar Jail and began to wave the Muslim League flag. He was shot dead (Iftikhar, 1991: 82-83). His death resulted in the protestors going berserk. They went about shouting *'Ley key rahen gey Pakistan, Daina parey ga Pakistan'* (We will take Pakistan, Pakistan will have to be given) and *'Pakistan ka matlab kya? La Illaha Il Lillah'* (What is the meaning of Pakistan? It is: there is no God but Allah). It was in such an inflamed situation, asserts Iftikhar, that a Sikh constable, who happened to find himself surrounded by a mob, was killed.

Neither the governor nor the chief secretary mentions the death of a Muslim who had climbed the jail wall. However, several interviewees – Hindus, Muslims and Sikhs – recalled a Muslim youth being killed while planting the Muslim League flag atop the wall of Amritsar Jail, but did not link it to the death of the police constable; it is only in Iftikhar's book that such a connection is made. It is therefore difficult to ascertain if both deaths happened on the same day and if the second death was an immediate reaction to the killing of Muhammad Sharif. Incidentally, on 30 December 2004, I interviewed an elderly man, Ali Baksh Mochi, in Rang Mahal in the old walled city of Lahore. He told me that Sharif belonged to his *biradari* of shoemakers. He described him as the first Muslim to die for Pakistan, but did not remember the date.

On 25 February, serious trouble was reported at the eastern town of Ambala, which previously had been quiet. A crowd of some hundreds of women and thousands of men attacked the police with brickbats and *lathis*. The police opened fire and injured several demonstrators. Several policemen were also injured in the violence (ibid.). The *Pakistan Times* of 28 February reported that two women were killed in the *lathi*-charge in Ambala. In Lahore the same day, demonstrators drew out knives. One of them tried to stab the Superintendent of Police but was knocked down by a constable. The same day the Secretariat was invaded by a crowd of women, children and youth. The youth who took part in that agitation included Mian Muhammad Salim and Arif Khokhar from Mozang, Lahore.

Efforts to end the agitation

Notwithstanding direct action that was raging in the Punjab and the several months of estrangement between Khizr Hayat Khan Tiwana and the Muslim League leaders, communications between them had not completely severed. Until recently, many of the new stalwarts of the Muslim League – such as Malik Sir Firoz Khan Noon, Sardar Shaukat Hayat, and Begum Shahnawaz – had been leading members of the Unionist Party. On a personal level, the Muslim landed gentry were known to maintain cordial relations. A political impasse had occurred, however, and the good offices of Khawaja Nazimuddin, the Bengali Muslim Leaguer who was on friendly terms with Khizr, were sought out for a resolution. However, it was the governor and not the premier who met him on 18 and 19 February. They discussed at length different possibilities. The governor observed in the fortnightly report of 28 February: 'At our first discussion Khwaja Nazim-ud-Din admitted candidly that he did not know what Pakistan meant, and that nobody in the Muslim League knew, so that it was very difficult for the League to carry on long-term negotiations with the minorities' (Carter, 2006: 366-7). However, both agreed that a settlement could be possible if the Punjab Public Safety Ordinance was replaced by another legislation and the prohibition on meetings was lifted (ibid.: 367). The premier was hesitant to comply and the negotiations ended inconclusively.

In the meantime, the Deputy Inspector General of Police, Jenkin, received a letter from Firoz Khan Noon informing him that Mamdot and Noon were in a position to make a settlement on behalf of the Muslim League. Under authority from the Premier, Jenkin visited Mamdot and Noon at the Kasur sub-jail. They sounded reasonable but wanted Daultana to be present. Daultana was brought to Lahore and they all met at Jenkin's house. Daultana took a more hard-line position and carried the other two with him to demand a meeting of the whole Punjab Muslim League council. Even this was arranged at the Kasur Sub-Jail, where the council met on 20 February, deciding to send Maulana Daud Ghaznavi, who was not under arrest, to seek instruction from Jinnah (*Pakistan Times*, 25 February).

In a public statement issued on 24 February, Jinnah suggested a settlement of the Punjab dispute. He supported the Punjab Muslim League's demand that the ban on public meetings and processions be removed, and that the Punjab Public Safety Ordinance be placed before the Legislature; all those who had been arrested, detained, imprisoned or convicted under the campaign should be released. He noted that the

Muslim League was not insisting on an immediate removal of the ban on processions, but declared that the other three points were important for the government to fulfil if the Punjab situation was to be brought back to normality. He believed that the settlement he offered was just (*Pakistan Times,* 26 February). Jinnah offered the same terms which Governor Jenkins and Nazim-ud-Din had discussed previously.

Agitation called off on February 26

As a result of the various overtures, a settlement was reached sometime late on 25 February but announced only the next day: the agitation was called off. Next, a statement from Khizr said that it had never been his government's intention to restrict political activities except to ensure that communal tension and conflict did not erupt as a result of them. The Punjab Public Safety Ordinance had been introduced to avoid the communal violence which had led to bloodshed in Calcutta, eastern Bengal, Bihar, the western United Provinces and Rohtak in eastern Punjab. Moreover, the British government's declaration on 20 February, stating its intention to leave India by June 1948, had created an entirely new situation 'in which leaders of all parties and communities must be in a position to confer with one another and to decide how the Punjab should face the future' (*Pakistan Times*: 27 February 1947).

The agitation lasted for thirty-four days, from 24 January to 26 February, and on the 27th, the government began to release Muslim League leaders. Instead of dispersing, however, the Leaguers addressed a public meeting at Kasur on the same date. This turned out to be a large manifestation of growing Muslim support for them and their aims. It was announced that the 2 March would be celebrated throughout the Punjab as Muslim League Victory Day. On 29 February, Mian Iftikharuddin addressed a large gathering in Amritsar. He demanded that Khizr resign and that fresh elections be held. Others joined him in calling for Khizr's resignation.

Premier Khizr resigns

The agitation had stretched the Punjab premier's patience. Shortly before midnight of 2 March, he resigned, and Governor Sir Evan Jenkins invited the leader of the Punjab Muslim League, Nawab Iftikhar Hussain Mamdot, to seek a parliamentary majority which would enable him to form a government. Mamdot opened negotiations with the Congress and Sikh members of the Punjab Assembly but failed to assuage their apprehensions. They were determined not to let the Muslim League come to power. In an interview on 28 February with a *The New York Times* reporter in Amritsar, the Sikh leader Master Tara Singh sounded clearly belligerent, disclosing that the Sikhs were organising their private army. He said:

> I do not see how we can avoid civil war. There can be no settlement, if the Muslims want to rule the Punjab. We cannot trust the Muslims under any circumstances. The Sikhs had the ability to keep the Muslims out of Eastern Punjab but why should we stop there? We would drive them out of the Punjab entirely (quoted in the *Pakistan Times*, 2 March 1947).

Perceptions of the Muslim League's direct action

In an editorial on 27 February, the *Pakistan Times* of Lahore described the settlement as a victory of civil liberties for the common man. The pro-Congress Hindu newspaper *Milap*, on the other hand, portrayed the political agitation, which had led to the settlement as a 'movement of goondas, which despite its very provocations did not receive any similar response from Hindus and Sikhs' (*Pakistan Times*, 1 March).

Neither the governor's secret reports, nor Muslim League sources, mention the type of slogans that were raised during the agitation. My Hindu, Sikh, and Muslim interviewees, who were in Lahore at the time, recalled the use of the following slogans:

> *'Pakistan ka na'ara kya? La Ilaha Il-lilah!'*
> ('What is the slogan of Pakistan? There is no God but Allah')

[The first part of this slogan was sometimes worded *'Pakistan ka matlab kya?'* *i.e.*: What is the meaning of Pakistan?]

'Seenay par goli khayengey, Pakistan banayengey!'
('We will create Pakistan even if we have to be shot in the chest.')

'Le key rahengey Pakistan, jaisey liya tha Hindustan!'
('We will get Pakistan the way we got Hindustan.')

'Khoon se lenge Pakistan!'
('We will acquire Pakistan with bloodshed.')

'Maareingey marjaangey par Pakistan banayengey!'
(We will die and we will kill but we will create Pakistan'.)

Some slogans directed against the premier were in the most offensive Punjabi parlance: *'Khizr dalla hai hai!'* (Down with Khizr the pimp); *'Khizr kanjar hai hai'* (Down with Khizr the procurer); *'Khizr kutta apni maa nal sutta'* (The dog Khizr slept with his mother).

According to Lt Colonel (Retd) Nadir Ali, the slogan raised in Gujrat went even further in humiliating Khizr:

Chalo bhayee chalo, ikk cheez meley gi
Kya bhayee kya? Khizr ki beti,
wah bhayee wah!

(Come let's go, we will get something.
What? Khizr's daughter. O, what fun!)

Muslim women, most of them clad in traditional *burqa*, also joined the demonstrations. On one occasion, Lady Shafi and some other women arrived at the residence of the premier and performed *siapa* (mourning ritual) to symbolise that he was dead. However, the mood of the Muslim League agitators changed rather dramatically in the opposite direction when Khizr resigned on 2 March. The slogan then changed to: '*Tazi khabar aiye hai, Khizr saadha bhai hai*' (The latest news is, Khizr is our brother).

There was no doubt in the mind of my Muslim interviewees that they expected the Muslim League to come to power. In the popular mind, the creation of Pakistan was going to be the 'magic moment' when they will be liberated from caste oppression and economic exploitation, and an era of Islamic justice and solidarity will be ushered in. For their part, the Hindus and Sikhs recalled seeing the Muslim League agitation as being ominous of a reign of terror to be let loose against them by fanatics in a Pakistan under Muslim League rule. In the SGPC report, the author, Sardar Gurbachan Singh Talib notes: 'All these slogans, as the Sikh leaders rightly pointed out, were really attacks directed against Hindu and Sikh minorities, who to a man were opposed to the establishment of the Islamic Republic of Pakistan' (Talib:1950: 59-60).

Khosla remarks: 'The agitation was ostensibly against the Khizr Ministry but, as this Ministry was supported by Congress and the Akali Parties, it assumed a communal shape' (1989: 96). He mentions some of the violent slogans, quoted above, that the crowd chanted. On the other hand, he alleges that the administration was lenient towards the protesters; most of them were driven out of Lahore and then set free. At any rate, following the death of the Sikh constable in Amritsar on February 24, Master Tara Singh described the Muslim League agitation as communal and not political and in a conference in the city, he warned about the risk of a civil war breaking out in the Punjab. He demanded that the Punjab be returned to the Sikhs who were the rulers from whom the British annexed the Punjab (Talbot 2004: 82). He even began to threaten with a counter direct action against the Muslims (Carter, 2006: 350).

A Christian Punjabi, A.T. Chaudhri, veteran press photographer of the *Pakistan Times,* recalled the Muslim League direct action in the following words:

'The first issue of the *Pakistan Times* was published on 5 February 1947, but we had started taking pictures of the Muslim League agitation right from the start. On 24 January, when the police tried to break into the Muslim League office at Lakshmi Chowk, Mian Iftikharuddin came forward and blocked the way. It resulted in an exchange of hot words and Mian Iftikharuddin slapped the SSP. I took a picture of that event. It was published in the gazette of 5 February. The agitation was largely peaceful, with the numbers swelling everyday and showing it clearly that Pakistan was on the cards. The speaker of the Punjab Assembly, S.P. Singha, tried his best to mediate between the Muslim League and Congress-Sikh politicians. Things went out of control, however, after 3 March, when Tara Singh waved the *kirpan*. Nobody anticipated at that early stage that, in the end, so many people would be killed and maimed and rendered homeless. There was a British CID officer, Mr Savage, who instigated Muslims to attack Hindus, and vice versa.'

Governor's views on the agitation

In the fortnightly report of 15 February 1947, Governor Jenkins set forth an in-depth assessment of the Muslim League direct action. Some of the points were merely a reiteration of the observations he had made in the past. With the help of the 1941 population census of the Punjab, he presented a simple table which showed the following breakdown of the population, community wise, in the five divisions constituting the British-administered Punjab Province.

Punjab Population 1941

(in Millions)

Divisions	Muslims	Others
Rawalpindi plus Multan	9	2
Lahore (alone)	4	3
Jullundur plus Ambala	3	7
Totals: community wise	**16**	**12**

Total population of the Punjab [British Punjab] 28

He then wrote:

> It is obvious on [sic] these figures that no one community can rule the Punjab with its present boundaries, except by conquest. The peaceful alternatives are a united Punjab under a Government representing Muslims, Hindus and Sikhs, or a partition into two or possibly three separate States.... The Muslim League have been determined – so far as their published policy is concerned – to establish undiluted Muslim rule all over the Punjab. This can certainly not be done by consent, and I am very doubtful whether it could be done by conquest. Members of the Muslim League are in fact much more liberal in private conversation than they are in public, and some of them realise the difficulties inherent in the official policy. But the fact remains that they fought the general election of 1946 on the extreme demand of Pakistan, and have not since said a word to reassure the Hindus or the Sikhs. Even among the more liberal of them the line seems to be that having established undiluted Muslim rule they will be generous to the minorities.
>
> The failure of the Muslim League to take office after the general election was due more to their uncompromising communal outlook than to any other cause. I believe that the local Congress broke with them on the old question of the inclusion of a nationalist Muslim in the Cabinet [the reference is to the opposition by the Muslim League to allow the Congress party to nominate a nationalist Muslims to the interim government] (Carter, 2006: 345).

On the other hand, Jenkins was of the opinion that in the negotiations between the Muslim League and the Sikhs, the immediate terms offered by the Muslim League were acceptable, but it bluntly refused to discuss the future of the Sikhs or to give them any assurances. The Sikhs felt that they could not support a party which would treat them as inferiors in a Muslim state (ibid.: 345-6). The governor noted that in his visit to twenty-five of Punjab's twenty-nine districts, he heard complaints from the Muslim League district and local leaders that the Khizr government had victimised them during the election campaign. While such complaints may have had some truth to them, Muslim officials in large numbers favoured the Muslim League. The fact that the League had won so handsomely was proof enough that the alleged interference on behalf of Khizr had no influence on the outcome. Therefore, the governor asserted, it was untenable to allege that curbing the civil liberties of the Muslim League had played a major role in determining its political support.

In a supplementary top-secret note dated 16 February, Jenkins made the following assessment:

> There are three parties – the Muslim League representing the great majority of Muslims, whose avowed aim is to undiluted Muslim rule; the Panthic Sikhs who will resist undiluted Muslim rule *a outrance;* and the Congress who, like the Muslim League, are part of an all-India organisation, but would provincially side with the Sikhs. No one community can rule the Punjab with its present boundaries except by conquest, and the only peaceful alternatives are (a) a Government formed by a coalition of all parties or by a non-communal party; or (b) a partition. If the Punjab were dealt with in isolation it might be possible to persuade the parties to take one or the other of these alternatives on the understanding that in due course the all-parties or non-communal Government would take over from the British, or that the Governments of the partitioned state would do so. But the statement [of February 20 to transfer power by June 1948] makes it impossible for the Punjab to take a line of its own, and even encourages the Muslim League and the Congress to set off all-India interests against provincial interests. The Muslim League in the Punjab will be encouraged by the Muslim League High Command to avoid a compromise, so as to increase its bargaining power in the Muslim minority Provinces; and the Punjab Congress will be expected to work (so far as is possible) for a *de facto* Central Government dominated by Hindus (ibid.: 353).

A few months later, this assessment would no doubt inextricably link the partition of the Punjab to the partition of India. However, Jenkins had very perceptively anticipated the trouble that was in store when the decision to partition India was taken in June; it also resulted in a decision to partition Bengal and the Punjab. He wrote:

> The decision of H.M.G. to leave India by a stated date is a 'breakdown' decision, involving the abandonment of all we have worked for many years. It is a very dangerous decision, amounting to an invitation to the warring parties to make real war upon one another. It is an impossible decision unless the authorities who are to receive power in 1948 are clearly defined now, and are assisted to prepare themselves for the task (ibid.: 354).

In other words, the governor was saying that at the time of the transfer of power in 1948, a functioning government was imperative in a united or divided India to avoid bloodshed in the Punjab. We will presently learn that the unfolding of events would render that possibility a non-starter.

In the next FR of 28 February, submitted immediately after the direct action had been called off, Jenkins noted that the agitation had widened the cleavage between Muslims on the one hand and Hindus and Sikhs on the other. After talking to Sardar Swaran Singh on 27 February, Jenkins made the following remark about his thoughts:

> The Sikhs have been profoundly moved by the obvious desire of the Muslims to seize the Punjab for themselves and would not permit them to do so. The agitation has shown Pakistan in all its nakedness and was a fair example of the kind of treatment that the minorities, including the Sikhs, might expect from Muslim extremists. He [Swaran Singh] admitted that civil war would lead to widespread misery, but he could not see how the Sikhs could be partners with the Muslims on any terms in the absence of some effective sanction. He disliked the idea of partitioning the Punjab, but felt that a partition with all its disadvantages might prove to be the only remedy (ibid.: 369)

Jenkins was of the opinion that in the event of a settlement between Khizr and the Muslim League, the Hindus and Sikhs should be satisfied, because only a ministry comprising the three communities could keep the peace in the Punjab. On the other hand, Premier Khizr believed that if the Sikhs could be brought into line, the Congress leaders would not create any difficulty, but the Muslim League wanted to go all alone with the help of some scheduled caste members. Khizr believed that the Punjab Muslim League would not decide anything independent of Jinnah; they were not free agents. Khizr had advised Mamdot through a mutual friend to refrain from provoking Sikhs but he believed that the Muslim League would not heed his advice (ibid. 370).

However, Jenkins noted, the agitation was not all that successful as the Muslim League claimed it to be. Many districts 'gave practically no trouble, and serious trouble was confined to half a dozen districts, notably Gujrat, Lahore, Amritsar and Jullundur. The agitation was essentially communal – most of the rank and file believed they were out to establish Muslim Raj' (ibid.: 368).

Chief Secretary Akhtar Hussain's comments

In his fortnightly report of 4 March 1947 covering the second half of February, Chief Secretary Akhtar Hussain wrote that the agitation had affected all districts, even creating serious situations in some places: 'The campaign is of deliberate disobedience and defiance of law conducted with a definite undemocratic political motive' (L/P & J/5/250). In the report of 24 March (covering the first half of March), he remarked: 'Although many were shocked by the vulgarity of the League's tactics and behaviour, the agitation undoubtedly attracted the sympathy of most Muslims' (ibid.). The Nationalist Muslims and Khaksars remained opposed to the campaign, while the Congress socialists ridiculed it as 'a circus of British toadies.' He noted:

'Of all reactions, however, the most marked, and the most dangerous, were those of Sikhs. Their resentment was bitter and their feelings inflamed by their understanding of the League's objective and by incidents involving Sikhs and furnished what they accepted as proof of Muslim mass animosity directed against the Sikh community' (ibid.).

Akhtar Hussain blamed the Muslims of Amritsar particularly for their brazenly aggressive attitude towards Sikhs. He continued:

'Muslims in their stupidity disgraced Sikhs, singled out Sikh policemen for their attacks and brutally murdered a Sikh Constable. The effect of this was grave in the extreme and, as has been already been stated, communal strife between Sikhs and Muslims was almost inevitable if the League movement of defiance had continued' (ibid.).

It is clear from these various accounts that while the Punjab situation was volatile, by no means did it preclude some sort of understanding between the three major communities if their leaders could make compromises and adjustments. In the case of the Muslim League and Congress, the freedom to decide was severely curtailed by what their high commands would decide. Under no circumstances were the Sikhs going to accept Muslim domination. Thus, the Muslim League had to develop a strategy to placate the Sikhs.

References

Iftikhar, Khawaja. *Jabb Amritsar Jall Raha Tha* (When Amritsar was Burning). Lahore: Khawaja Publishers, 1991.

Moon, Penderel. *Divide and Quit,* New Delhi: Oxford University Press, 1998.

Shahnawaz, Jahan Ara. *Father and Daughter: A Political Autobiography,* Karachi: Oxford University Press, 2002.

Talbot, Ian. 'Violence, Migration and Resettlement: The Case of Amritsar' in Talbot, Ian and Thandi, Shinder (eds). *People on the Move: Punjab Colonialism, and Post-Colonial Migration.* Karachi: Oxford University Press, 2006.

Khosla, Justice G.D. *Stern Reckoning,* Delhi: Oxford University Press, 1989.

Talib, S. Gurbachan Singh, *Muslim League Attack on Sikhs and Hindus in the Punjab 1947*, New Delhi: Voice of India, 1991.

Official documents

Carter, Lionel. *Punjab Politics 1 January 1944 -3 March 1947: Last Years of the Ministries (Governor's Fortnightly Reports and other Key Documents).* New Delhi: Manohar 2006.

Mansergh. N. and P. Moon, (eds). *The Transfer of Power , 4 November 1946-22 March 1947, vol. 9,* London: Her Majesty's Stationery Office, 1980.

FR of Punjab chief secrtary for 1947: 10RL/PSJ/5/25C

Newspapers

Dawn, Delhi, 1947.

Pakistan Times, Lahore, 1947.

The Tribune, Lahore, 1947.
The Civil and Military Gazette, Lahore, 1947.

Interviews

Aziz Mazhar, London, 18–19 May 2002
A.T. Chaudhri, Lahore, 23 April 2003
Begum Nasim Amir Hussain Shah, 25 April 2003
Raja Tajammul Hussain, 27 April 2003
Hukum Qureshi, Lahore, 30 October 2005
Ahad Malik, Stockholm, 13 January 2006

6

THE MARCH RIOTS: LAHORE

LAHORE HAD ALWAYS BEEN THE PREMIER CITY OF THE PUNJAB SINCE at least the sixteenth century, when the Mughals made it their provincial capital. Its roots go back to antiquity; legend has it that it was founded by Lav, a son of Lord Rama. It was also the capital of the Sikh kingdom founded by Maharaja Ranjit Singh in 1799. Lahore city was undoubtedly the most spectacular post-1857 accomplishment of the British Raj in urban planning and development. The governor and senior civil and military officers were based in Lahore. It was, therefore, the seat of British power and prestige. Under British patronage, Lahore expanded rapidly outside the ancient walled city, especially in an easterly direction. A moat from earlier times encircled the old city, but the British had added a green belt on its exterior, comprising parks and gardens. As the city expanded, many adjoining villages and hamlets were assimilated. The most modern and luxurious locality was the Civil Lines, located in an easterly direction from the old city. The leading educational institutions included the Punjab University and many arts, science, commerce, engineering and medical colleges. The Mall and Anarkali Bazaar were busy shopping and commercial areas. Then there were the food, grain and fruit markets, and the railway workshops at Moghulpura.

A budding film industry had also sprung up and was being considered a rival to those based in Bombay and Calcutta (interview, B.R. Chopra, 4 January 1997). The British were considering restructuring Lahore on the pattern of a presidency such as had been conferred on other modern urban centres of Calcutta, Delhi, Bombay, and Madras (Daeshsel, 2004: 26-27). Successful people from all over the Punjab settled in Lahore, and it was there where the princely families maintained their houses.

Many retired officers, successful traders, and businessmen set up home in the premier city of Punjab.

Demographic profile according to 1941 census
Total population of Lahore City (including the Lahore Municipality and Lahore Cantonment):

Community	Number	Share (%)
All communities	671659	100
Muslims	433170	64.50
Hindus (including the scheduled castes)	188222	28
Sikhs	34021	5
Others (including Christians, Ad Dharmis, Jains and Parsees)	14245	2.50

Lahore District:

Community	Number	Share (%)
All communities	1695375	100
Muslims	1027772	61
Hindus (including the scheduled castes)	287351	17
Sikhs	310646	18
Others (including Christians, Ad Dharmis, Jains, Parsees)	69606	4

The population percentages for both Lahore city and district show a clear Muslim majority, but a casual visitor to the city could easily form the impression that Lahore had a Hindu majority, as some seventy-five per cent of the property – buildings, businesses and new development schemes – were owned by Hindus. Even the tiny Sikh minority in the city was economically better off than the Muslims (Ahmed, 1999: 127).

Many Lahore Hindus believed that they formed a majority together with the Sikhs.

When it came to Lahore district, the Muslims were once again in clear majority although in the villages, the Sikhs were in substantial numbers. Thus, while the Hindus were essentially an urban community, the Muslims were distributed both in the urban and rural areas and the Sikhs were predominantly a rural community. The district administration was headed by Deputy Commissioner Mr J.C.W. Eustace.

2 March 1947: Victory Day and Khizr's resignation

The settlement of 26 February between the Khizr ministry and the Muslim League did not restore the Punjab to normality. The Hindu and Sikh leaders were badly shaken, and among their co-religionists anxiety and fear had grown over the weeks, as prospects loomed large for a Muslim League government. At the same time, Muslims in the urban areas, where the civil disobedience movement had raged for the past weeks, felt there was no longer any doubt that Pakistan would come into being. It was only a matter of 'when', rather than 'if'. Their leaders, while less certain, were elated that the masses had mobilised in such large numbers behind the demand for Pakistan, and for their part were disinclined to slacken the pressure. In any event, Lahore remained volatile, and hectic political activism continued. The coalition government was still in power and the Muslim League was out of it. Nothing changed substantially after direct action was launched. 2 March 1947 was a Sunday, and the Muslim League chose to celebrate it as Victory Day.

Mian Maqsood Ahmed, Mian Muhammad Salim and Arif Khokar were young men at that time. During my interviews, they gave a vivid account of the confidence infused into the Muslims by the direct action mass movement. The Muslim Student Federation had played an important role both in the 1945–46 election campaign and in direct action. I interviewed a leading figure of that organisation, Aziz Mazhar. In 1947, he recounted, he was Joint Secretary of the Islamia College Student's Union. Later, on my behalf Ahmad Salim interviewed Syed Ahmed Saeed Kirmani, who in 1947 was Organising Secretary of the Muslim Student Federation. He subsequently became Punjab Law Minister in Pakistan.

Both confirmed that the establishment of Pakistan had become a burning passion among the Muslim youth. However, at that time nobody could anticipate that communal rioting and bloodshed would cause hundreds of thousands of fatalities, and that masses of people would have to flee in search of safe havens. They also recalled that among the students there was never any discussion on driving Hindus and Sikhs out of Lahore and Pakistan. They admitted, though, that Islamic slogan-mongering was a regular feature of their protest marches.

In any event, people began to assemble in the Mochi Gate Park outside the walled city to celebrate the huge success of their direct action. It was a Sunday. There was a mammoth gathering of excited Muslims present when Muslim League leaders told them that the successful mass movement of the previous weeks was the first step in the direction of achieving Pakistan. Among those who addressed the crowd were two scheduled caste leaders, Sardar Hari Singh Nirbhay and Chaudhry Sukh Lal, who assured the Muslims of their support. Those who addressed the crowd included Mian Iftikharuddin, Firoz Khan Noon, Shaukat Hayat, Begum Shah Nawaz, and even Raja Ghazanfar Ali Khan, Health Minister in the Interim Government of India. Ghazanfar said that as far as the Muslims were concerned, they would like the British to quit in June 1947 instead of June 1948 (*Pakistan Times,* 4 March 1947). The speakers assured the minorities of proper protection in a future Pakistan. In the evening, Muslim houses, shops and institutions were brilliantly illuminated to celebrate Victory Day (*Pakistan Times,* 4 March 1947).

Khizr met Jenkins on the morning of the 2nd, telling him of a conversation he had had with Sir Zafrulla Khan, a leading member of the Ahmadiyya community, who was in Lahore at the time. Both men felt that the Muslim League must be made to realise the gravity of the situation that had been created by direct action. Khizr later met the Congress leader Bhim Sen Sachar and the Sikh leader Swaran Singh and informed them of his intention to resign. They were both surprised and disappointed. Sachar told Jenkins that 'the Congress could not cooperate with the Muslim League unless it was clear that the minorities would be treated as equals and not as inferiors' (Carter, 2007a: p. 51). The same day, at 10.15 p.m., Khizr called upon the governor and tendered his resignation as well as that of his colleagues. He reiterated that the

20 February statement of H.M.G. had created a new situation and therefore the Punjab leaders and their parties needed to discuss anew the future of their province' (*Pakistan Times,* 4 March 1947).

March 3: Master Tara Singh's bravado

The news of Khizr's resignation was received next day by the Lahore Muslims with great jubilation. Instead of the coarse insults of the previous days, they now started chanting slogans in his praise. For quite some time, an inner party struggle had been going on within the Muslim League as Firoz Khan Noon and Shaukat Hayat tried to wrestle power from the hands of Nawab Mamdot, but he was supported by most other leaders and the office-bearers of Muslim League offices in the Punjab. Consequently, he was unanimously re-elected leader of the Muslim League Assembly Party. Shaukat Hayat and Mian Nurullah were elected as the party's deputy leader and secretary, respectively. The governor invited Mamdot to form a government. Mamdot approached Sardar Swaran Singh, leader of the Panthic Assembly Party, asking him to cooperate in forming a Muslim–Sikh coalition. He assured Hindus and Sikhs that the Muslim League had never intended to impose Muslim domination on non-Muslims in the Punjab, 'It will be our endeavour to secure the willing co-operation of all for the purpose of building up a happy and prosperous Punjab' (*Pakistan Times,* 5 March 1947).

Governor Jenkins noted in a telegram dated 5 March to Wavell that in order to form a coalition, Mamdot was banking on the support of the scheduled castes and Christian members of the Punjab Assembly. Such a government, the governor felt, was certain to meet stiff opposition from the Congress and Sikhs, who would launch a civil disobedience movement, with the result that communal disturbances would break out throughout the Punjab (Carter, 2007a: 57).

Negotiations failed between the Muslim League and the Sikhs. The Punjab Congress reaffirmed its faith in a united India, declaring 'its firm determination not to submit to any Government based on communal or sectional domination' (*Pakistan Times,* 5 March 1947). The Sikh Members of the Legislative Assembly (MLAs) also met and decided not to cooperate with the Muslim League. Without the help of one of these factions, the Muslim League would not be able to form a coalition that could command a stable majority in the Punjab Assembly.

Muslim crowds outside surrounded the building, shouting slogans demanding that the Muslim League form the government, at all costs. The situation only worsened when the Sikh leader Master Tara Singh came out on the stairs of the Assembly, accompanied by other Sikh leaders, and facing the crowd, unsheathed his ceremonial *kirpan* and waved it in the air. The infamous *kirpan*-brandishing has been reported by almost everyone I interviewed for this study who were present that day. While there are different versions of what the master exactly said, the message was a crystal-clear rejection of Pakistan. Justice Khosla (1989: 99) says that the master shouted, '*Kat ke deynge apni jan maggar nahin deyinge Pakistan*' ('We will let ourselves be cut to pieces and die but will not concede Pakistan'). *The Tribune* described the scene slightly differently:

> Master Tara Singh came out of the Party Room and raising loud shouts of 'Pakistan Murdabad' [Death to Pakistan] and 'Sat Sri Akal' [True is Holy God] went out of the main entrance of the Punjab Assembly Buildings from where they would have dispersed. As the Sikh M.L.A's [sic] under the leadership of Master Tara Singh and in response to his call raised their slogans they were greeted by a hostile crowd of Muslims who were standing in front of the Assembly Buildings and they began to raise counter slogans. A large number of them made hostile demonstrations against the Sikh Leaders and some of them employed improper epithets. The police intervened and kept the supporters of the various slogans apart. In the meantime Mian Iftikhar-ud-din and Mian Mumtaz Daultana arrived on the spot and they successfully asked the Muslim crowd to go away and not hold any counter demonstrations (*The Tribune*, 4 March 1947).

In the whole saga of the Punjab partition, no other moment has been described as more dramatic than Master Tara Singh's display of bravado outside the Punjab Assembly. Muslims, Hindus, Sikhs, and Christians – all those who witnessed the episode and shared their recollections with me – testified that the Sikh leader's theatrical belligerence served to unleash wild passions that had, until then, been kept under control by the administration. Nanak Singh Broca happened to be present at the spot. A large Muslim crowd had assembled on the Mall Road. They were shouting slogans against Master Tara Singh but nobody bothered him despite his Sikh identity being apparent.

Not surprisingly, the SGPC report omits any mention of this episode in the main text, as its several hundred pages had been written with a patently partisan objective to pin all blame on the Muslims and the Muslim League. Yet the historical significance of that event in the process leading to the partition of the Punjab is highly significant. The report instead mentions it in passing in an additional chapter, 'Postscript', but that too as part of evidence given during cross-examination in a Pakistani court, pertaining to a case in which Mamdot had been charged with corruption and misappropriation of funds of the Punjab Muslim League (1991: 446).

The Tribune, continuing to narrate the events of the 3rd, noted that soon after the commotion at the assembly buildings, Sardar Dalip Singh, advocate and MLA, issued a resolution the party had adopted declaring their resolve to oppose 'by every possible means the establishment of a Muslim League Government in the province so long as its objective is Pakistan or Muslim domination in the Punjab – the Homeland of the Sikhs' (*The Tribune,* 4 March 1947).

Later that day, Hindus and Sikhs gathered on the grounds of the Kapurthala House near Purani Anarkali to listen to their leaders. The speeches, delivered in Punjabi, were vitriolic. Their English translations from Volume II of the compilation of official documents by Mian Sadullah are quoted below. Master Tara Singh said:

> O Hindus and Sikhs! Your trial awaits you. Be ready for self-destruction like the Japs and the Nazis. Our motherland is calling for blood and we shall satiate the thirst of our mother with blood. We crushed Mughlistan and we shall trample Pakistan.... The world has always been ruled by minorities. The Muslims snatched the kingdom from the Hindus, and Sikhs grabbed it out of the hands of the Muslims and the Sikhs ruled over the Muslims with their might and the Sikhs shall even now rule them. We shall rule them and shall get the government fighting. I have sounded the bugle, finish the Muslim League (*The Partition of the Punjab, Vol. II*, 1993: 138).

Another Sikh leader, Giani Kartar Singh, said, 'This day the crusade starts. One hundred years ago today our yellow flags were flying on the fort of Lahore. The same flag shall fly again. Our battle-axe shall decide if the Muslims shall rule. The Sikhs shall never disgrace the name of Guru Gobind Singh' (ibid.: 351). A Hindu leader, Chaudhri Krishan Gopal Dutt, declared, 'Is there the man who dare snatch us from our mother and place us in the lap of Mamdot? Create such an atmosphere that the League may find it impossible to form a ministry' (ibid.: 35).

Congress leaders were also present at the Kapurthala House meeting in the evening of 3 March. In their address, they were no less resolute in opposing a Muslim League government, though they did not take recourse to communal invective. Thus, for example, the veteran Congress leader Dr Gopi Chand Bhargava, MLA, called on all Punjabis 'who did not subscribe to the ideology of Pakistan to celebrate Anti-Pakistan Day by staging strikes on their shops and business premises, holding public meetings and hoisting the national flag' (*Pakistan Times*, 5 March 1947). It was also announced that 11 March was to be celebrated as anti-Pakistan Day.

While walking around the walled city of Lahore, Ahmed Salim and I were tipped off by an elderly gentleman to contact Haji Abdul Rahman Gill, a resident of Shahalmi Gate whose family lived in the same place before the Partition. We met up with Gill on 30 December 2004; later clarifications to some of his assertions was sought on my behalf by Ahmad Salim on 29 September 2005, and again on 15 October the same year. Gill was a key witness to the events that transpired in Lahore in 1947. He asserted that Hindus and Sikhs were the aggressors in the rioting that took place in Lahore. His account is presented chronologically in several chapters. Gill was himself involved in a conspiracy to set Shahalmi Gate ablaze to drive Hindus and Sikhs out of Lahore in the end of June.

Haji Abdul Rahman Gill

'On 3 March 1947, Master Tara Singh waved his *kirpan* on the steps of the Punjab Legislative Assembly, shouting slogans against Pakistan; later that day he addressed a public meeting in which other Hindu and Sikh leaders made inflammatory speeches. Afterwards, the Hindus and Sikhs formed a procession and chanted provocative slogans as they headed towards the Hindu–Sikh stronghold of Shahalmi. When they reached Bansanwala Bazaar, just outside Shahalmi, they looted the shops selling bamboo poles and other long sticks. With those crude weapons they attacked the Muslim potters and vegetable-sellers who had their shops in the park outside the Shahalmi Gate. Then they entered the gate and turned towards Papar Mandi. A Muslim ration-depot owner, Nawab Butt, and some labourers were busy unloading sacks of wheat flour. The rioters attacked and killed Nawab Butt. The labourers and bullock-cart owners were also badly injured.

'The mob then attacked a Muslim *pakora* (spicy savoury made of chickpea flour) maker in Nawan Bazaar, who managed to throw boiling oil at them and thus managed to escape. This was described to me by many people who saw it with their own eyes. In another attack, I was witness to an attack on a Muslim *tonga*-driver. I was coming back home from school and had collected my younger brothers also from the Rang Mahal Mission High School. The *tonga*-driver was going towards Machi Hata, but the Hindus pounced on him and stabbed him several times. He collapsed on the road. I can still see him in the eye of my mind lying on the road face down. Third murder was that of a musician who worked for Gama Wajjainawala (a professional band playing on wedding occasions) near the Choura Khu. So, three Muslims met martyrdom on 3 March. The whole area was now disturbed. I saw Muslim youths from Nawan Bazaar taking the dead bodies of Nawab Butt and the musician to Mayo Hospital. They also helped the injured labourers get to the emergency ward. I don't know what happened with the dead body of the *tonga*-driver.

'My father, Billa Jatt (Jat) was at his *deira* (a sitting or socialising place associated with *pehlwans,* or prominent figures in a locality), outside the Shahalmi Gate. He had been involved in a number of inter-communal conflicts in the past and was viewed as a threat by Hindus, although he had some close friends among them. In any case, some Hindus decided to finish him off in the heat of the emerging communal unrest in Lahore. One of them shouted from a house-top, "Billey *Pehlwan*, I am sorry to tell you that your family has been murdered." My father shouted back: "If my children have been killed then no Hindu mother and father will find their children alive." By that time my paternal and maternal uncles had collected at our *deira*.

'The Hindus wanted to lure him back inside the gate, where an armed party was waiting to kill him. Father sensed the danger and instead went to the nearby police *chowki* (post) at Mochi Gate to talk to the officer in charge, Dildar Ali Shah. Dildar Ali Shah was a very good and brave man, always helping people in distress. Father wanted to find out whether Dildar Shah could provide him with a police escort when he entered Shahalmi Gate. He wanted to take all the precautions because he had been involved in criminal cases many times, including those concerning murder; now that he had a family and small children he wanted to avoid entering into a conflict with the law. Dildar Shah told him that at the moment he did not have enough rifle police at his disposal. So my father returned to the *deira*. By that time, hefty Muslim youths from Mochi Gate had assembled in the park. My father told them that he was going to go into Shahalmi since his family had been killed; would they like to come along? No one did.

'So my father and my uncles began to prepare themselves for the worst. They tied turbans on their heads and armed themselves with *dandas* (long sticks) and other weapons. Just then, two Hindus who were bosom friends of my father, Hans Raj, a cigarette-seller, and Lala Chuni Lal, an *acharfrosh* (pickle-seller), came and pleaded with him not to make that blunder. Some Hindus wanted to kill him. They said, "It is our duty to find out what has happened to your family and relatives, but you should not come in." He agreed to let them try. They came to our house and shouted loudly, "*Kaka* [son], are you all right?" I replied, "Yes, *chachaji* (dear uncle), but where is my father?" They replied that he was all right too. Meanwhile, my father and uncles had decided to go in at any cost, but just before they entered Shahalmi Gate, armed police despatched by Dildar Ali Shah arrived. They fired in the air and people ran in all directions seeking safety. My father and uncles reached our house and heaved a sigh of relief to find us alive.

'During the night of 3 March, the whole of 4 March, and until the evening of the 5th we remained in our home. Night curfew had been imposed on the 3rd but from the 5th it applied even during the day. On the 5th, the same two Hindus came in the afternoon and told father that a plot had been hatched to attack our *mohalla*, Katra Susian, and kill all Muslims. Therefore we must vacate our homes and go elsewhere until things returned to normal. My father, stubborn and defiant man that he was, responded that first they would have to kill him and then his children. Realising that my father would not listen to them, they went to my grandfather, Chaudhri Fazal Din, who lived next door. They put their caps at his feet and implored, "Tell Billa to vacate the house and take all of you away". My father never defied grandfather, so when he ordered him to vacate our homes father obeyed. At the time of *asr* (afternoon prayers) we locked our houses and went to live with our relatives in the nearby Muslim-majority, Navan Bazaar. We left in the clothes we were wearing, hoping to come back in a day or two. However, our return was not possible till many months later after Pakistan had come into being. We were thus the first refugees of Shahalmi Gate!'

I mentioned to Gill that government sources and the Lahore newspapers mention 4 March as the day when the clashes took place. The SGPC report makes no mention of the 3 March incident and neither does the Khosla report. Gill explained that regular clashes between agitators from both sides broke out on the 4th, but on the 3rd it was only the Hindu and Sikh mob returning in the evening from the public meeting at Purani Anarkali that attacked some Muslims causing a few fatalities and injuries. He suspected that the concerned Station House Officer (SHO) at the Lohari Gate Police Station, Pandit Devi Das, probably did not register the First Investigation Report (FIR) and therefore those murders were not reported to the higher authorities. This is in principle possible because while collecting data on the Punjab riots the figures the people remembered tended to be far greater than what one found in the police reports and the fortnightly reports.

On the other hand, the telegram of 5 March mentioned below, sent by the Punjab governor to Viceroy Wavell, suggests that curfew was imposed on 4 March and not a day earlier. I found finally incontrovertible proof that the incident that Gill was referring to took place on 4 March. In a note dated 4 March by Jenkins of an interview with Mamdot he recorded:

> Khan Iftikhar Husain Mamdot saw me at his request at 6.05 p.m. this evening. During the afternoon reports had come in of communal rioting in the Lohari Gate and Shahalmi Gate area of the city, It is believed that a number of Muslims have been killed, but the facts are not yet known. Police reinforcements have gone in, troops are moving up to the Kotwali and a curfew is being imposed in the City area from 8.00 p.m. to 7.00 a.m. (Carter, 2007a: 232-3).

It is, however, possible that Gill erred about the dates. This would be quite understandable of one who is being asked to recall events of more than half a century ago. It is equally possible that Gill did not make a mistake at all; he could have purposefully fixed 3 March as the date for the beginning of rioting, in order to put the blame on the Hindus and Sikhs for starting the clashes. There is no doubt, however, that except for the date the overall narrative of Gill is reliable as we kept probing it with him over a number of meetings. His main story can be accepted as accurate.

Communal clashes break out on 4 March

The morning of 4 March 1947 undoubtedly brought in the open the frustrations and aggressions that had simmered in the Punjab for months. It had been announced in the 3 March evening meeting of Hindus and Sikhs that the next day, students would meet in Gol Bagh, situated near the District Courts and the Government College, to express their grievances. Jenkins sent a telegram to Secretary of State for India and Burma, Lord Pethick-Lawrence, with a copy to Wavell:

> Yesterday March 3rd Muslims in Lahore were jubilant and noisy. Non-Muslims especially Sikhs were correspondingly exasperated and at night very large non-Muslim meeting was held at which violent speeches were made by Congress and Sikh leaders.
>
> Today, March 4th there has been much communal violence. During the morning Student procession mostly Hindu clashed with Police and later raided Police office damaging property and injuring about 30 Policemen of whom two have since died. Police opened fire and three demonstrators are reported to have gunshot wounds. This

> afternoon communal rioting has broken out in Lahore City. So far six members of public reported dead and 59 treated in hospital of whom 20 injured seriously. Police are still engaged and I have no complete report. Troops are standing by.
>
> Congress and Sikhs are determined to resist Muslim rule. Mamdot has made no progress in forming Coalition and now wants Muslim Ministry supported by a handful of Scheduled Caste and Indian Christians. Situation is grave and without Coalition communal trouble on a large scale seems inevitable. I have told Mamdot that he must convince me of firm Parliamentary majority before I consider putting him in and that his Muslim government will be short-lived that it might be impossible to put him in at all. Alternative is Section 93 which would not be satisfactory but might possibly be preferred by Punjabis generally (Carter, 2007a: 55).

Vimal Issar, who was then of school-going age, recalled that she and other Hindu girls from the walled city had as usual climbed onto the *tonga* to go to school, but were turned back as the agitation had begun. Likewise, Iqbal Singh was on the way to Dayal Singh College when he got caught up in the clashes, but managed to return safely to his home in Kila Gujjar Singh. Amarnath Sehgal was inside the Government College when the police fired at the Hindu and Sikh protestors.

In a telegram to Wavell the following day, Jenkins reported that curfew had been imposed in Lahore between 20.00 to 07.00 hours, and public meetings, processions and general gatherings of five or more people were banned. The nights of 4 and 5 March were quiet but communal rioting broke out again in the morning of the 5th. Outside Lahore, a Hindu–Sikh mob near Kamoke, Gujranwala district, stopped a train and burned the signal cabin. In the same telegram, he informed the viceroy that trouble was expected in Amritsar on the 6th and 7th, the days the Sikhs had planned aggressive demonstrations in connection with the Holi and Hola festivals. Reports of serious communal rioting were also coming in from Multan.

The Tribune of 5 March 1947 reported that on the previous day – the very first of the minorities' demonstration against the perceived imposition of a communal majority rule on the Punjab – the police resorted to firing seven times and *lathi*-charged the demonstrators about a dozen times. Rattan Chand, a student of the fourth-year class of the Dayanand Anglo-Vedic College (DAV), was killed by a police bullet while standing in one of the hostel rooms. In the evening, police opened fire from the front of the Lajpat Rai Hall. Another student died in hospital from bullet wounds received in the Gol Bagh area, where police opened fire five times. About sixty persons were injured, of whom twenty-seven were admitted to the Mayo and Sir Ganga Ram Hospitals. Near Chauk Matt, a procession of Hindu and Sikh demonstrators was attacked; a fight broke out in which *lathis*, hatchets, knives and brickbats were used. About sixty to seventy persons were injured, of whom six were later reported dead in hospital. Two constables were also reported to have been killed. The communal situation eased a little in the evening, following the announcement by the District Magistrate (also Deputy Commissioner), Mr Eustace, of a Curfew Order between the hours of 8 p.m. and 7 a.m. for the next ten days. Mr Eustace told *The Tribune* representative a little before midnight that the situation was 'well under control'. The military was called in during the evening and kept their positions.

Khosla gave another account. He wrote that on 4 March at 10 a.m., Hindu–Sikh students began to move in a procession from the Anarkali Bazaar towards the Gol Bagh shouting, '*Pakistan Murdabad*' (Death to Pakistan). The police had already cordoned off entry to the district courts. When they were denied access to the courts, the students began to gather in the square in front of the Government College with a view to organising a strike. The principal of the college, Mr Bukhari, called the police, who quickly opened fire at the crowd, killing a number of them. Another procession of non-Muslims clashed with the National Guards in the afternoon. Later, non-Muslims were attacked – mostly stabbed – in different parts of the city. The riots began. A number of Hindu shops were set on fire in Sua Bazaar and Chowk Rang Mahal in the walled city. By the evening, the Mayo hospital had registered thirty-seven cases of non-Muslim casualties (Khosla, 1989: 101).

Governor's rule imposed on 5 March

In consultation with Wavell, Jenkins assumed direct control of the Punjab under Section 93 of the Government of India Act, 1935, which prescribed governor's rule during emergency situations. The Punjab continued to be ruled under Section 93 till British rule ended. Much controversy has surrounded Jenkins' refusal to allow the Muslim League to form the government. The governor's stand was that the Muslim League leader Nawab Mamdot failed to convince him that he enjoyed a stable majority in the Punjab Assembly. Correspondence between Mamdot and Jenkins on the 5th was brisk, with Mamdot trying to convince the governor that he had the support of eighty Muslim League MLAs, four members of the scheduled castes, one European and two Indian Christians. He claimed that the support was likely to increase to a hundred before the legislature resumed its sessions. Jenkins replied that he would have to show he had a stable majority to run the government. He demanded that Mamdot submit the names of his supporters in writing; those who were not from Mamdot's party should give written pledges that they were prepared to support his government in the House on all questions of confidence (Carter, 2007a: 57). Mamdot reiterated that he enjoyed the support of more than ninety members and that was likely to go up to a hundred. The governor responded on 5 March:

> My personal belief is that no Government which does not command the confidence of Punjabis generally can solve our present problems, and it is for you to consider whether in the additional time now available you should not resume negotiations with the other communities. May I also suggest that at the present juncture a statement by yourself and the leaders of the Hindus and Sikhs condemning the present communal outbreak would have an excellent effect. I have reason to believe that a move on your part for the issue of such a statement would be well received (Carter 2007a: 238).

This was immediately heeded by Mamdot, who issued an appeal for peace. Mian Iftikharuddin and Mumtaz Daultana then called upon Bhim Sen Sachar and Swaran Singh to build up a foundation of a peace committee representing all sections of public opinion. They agreed. They met on 6 March at the residence of DBSP Singha, the Christian leader and speaker of the Punjab Assembly. Other members were Master Tara Singh and Gopi Chand Bhargava. C.E. Gibbon (Anglo–European MLA) was nominated to act as the committee's emissary to go to Amritsar and meet Tara Singh. The police, however, informed them that because of serious rioting in Amritsar it was not possible to contact him. Later, Tara Singh came to Lahore and met the peace committee, but the estrangement between the Muslim League and the Congress and Sikhs was undiminished.

The telegrams sent by Jenkins to Wavell on subsequent days spoke of the situation being brought under control, despite some isolated cases of stabbings. By the 6th, the Lahore area commander had put two British battalions into the city at 14.00 hours, with instructions to restore order and disarm rioters. He reported that as soon as the military appeared, the mobsters ran away. The curfew was extended, to continue unbroken for forty-eight hours. In a number of interviews recorded with Hindus and Sikhs, the point most emphasised was that the predominantly-Muslim police engaged in handling the thirty-four-day direct action by the Muslim League did not fire a single shot, while non-Muslim students in Lahore were fired at from the very first day, suffering casualties including deaths.

From 5 March, violence quickly spread to many parts of the walled city of Lahore. Looting and burning of shops began to take place in Kinari Bazaar, Kasera Bazaar, and Rang Mahal. When the non-Muslims offered resistance, a Muslim sub-inspector with a police party arrived at the scene and opened fire. A Hindu youth who tried to stop the sub-inspector was shot dead by him (Khosla, 1989: 102). Consequently, tension and anxiety increased on all sides. Schools were closed down and children were kept at home by parents. The Sikh–Congress decision to celebrate 11 March as a day of protest did not materialise as the government banned all processions and marches. Notwithstanding the clashes and concomitant violence and bloodshed, much of Lahore remained relatively peaceful. Elders in the various localities met and agreed not to allow violence to prevail. A number of Hindus in Lahore also issued the following appeal:

> We, the undersigned Hindu residents of Kucha Mela Ram, inside Bhatti Gate, Lahore, do hereby condemn the state of affairs created by the resignation of the last Ministry and the consequent bloodshed and arson since March 4, 1947, as a result of political differences

> among Hindus, Muslims and Sikhs. We thank our Muslim neighbours that they protected us and kept us safe in their areas even though we are in a minority. They also provided us with all facilities that we needed. We hope that in the future too they will give proof of the same generosity.
>
> We appeal to our Hindu and Sikh brethren that wherever they are in a majority, they should give the same protection to the Muslim minorities. This behaviour and treatment will not only be beneficial to the community but will also foster Hindu–Muslim–Sikh unity, and thus lead to the progress of our Province.
>
> (Signed) Manohar lal, Banarsi lal, Ram Rattan Anand, Vishwa Suri, Madan Gopal, Jhandu Ram, Sardari Lal Chaddha, Ram Lubaya Suri, Mool Chand and others' (*Pakistan Times,* 8 March 1947).

The Muslim League leaders repeated their call for calm, assuring the minorities that Muslims would protect them. The Punjabi leaders received the news of the Congress Working Committee in Delhi deciding, on 8 March, to throw its weight behind the Sikh demand for partition of the Punjab with mixed feelings. While the Punjab Muslim League considered it just a pressure tactic and a challenge, the Congress and Sikh leaders at Lahore issued a strong statement expressing their opposition to the Pakistan demand. In a joint statement they said that they were 'in no circumstances willing to give the slightest assurance or support to the Muslim League in the formation of a Ministry', and they 'were opposed to Pakistan in any shape or form' (Carter 2007a: 71). On 14 March, Nehru and Baldev Singh visited Lahore and toured the affected areas. They expressed great concern at the growing violence in the Punjab capital.

References

Ahmed, Ishtiaq 'The 1947 Partition of Punjab: Arguments Put Forth before the Punjab Boundary Commission by the Parties Involved' in Ian Talbot and Gurharpal Singh (eds), *Region and Partition: Bengal, Punjab and the Partition of the Subcontinent*, Karachi: Oxford University Press, 1999.

Daeschsel, Markus. 'De-urbanizing the City: Colonial Congnition and the People of Lahore' in Talbot, Ian and Thandi, Shinder, *People on the Move: Punjabi*

Colonialism, and the Post-Colonial Migration. Karachi: Oxford University Press, 2004.

Gujral, S. *A Brush with Life: An Autobiography,* Delhi: Viking Books, 1997.

Khosla, G.D. *Stern Reckoning,* Delhi: Oxford University Press, 1989.

Talib, S.G.S. *Muslim League Attack on Sikhs and Hindus in the Punjab 1947,* New Delhi: Voice of India, 1991.

Newspapers

Pakistan Times, Lahore, 1947.

The Tribune, Lahore, 1947.

Official documents

Mansergh, N. and P. Moon, (eds.), *The Transfer of Power 1942-47,* vol. 9, November 4 1946 to March 22 1947, London: Her Majesty's Stationery Office, 1980.

Carter, Lionel, (ed), *Punjab Politics, 3 March – 31 May 1947, At the Abyss, Governors' Fortnightly Reports and other Key Documents,* New Delhi: Manohar, 2007a.

Census of India, 1941, Volume 6, Punjab, Simla: Government of India Press, 1941.

Interviews

B.R. Chopra, Mumbai, 4 January 1997

Amarnath Sehgal, Delhi, 20 October, 1999

Nanak Singh Broca, Mumbai, 23 October 1999

Aziz Mazhar, London, 18–19 May 2002

Mian Maqsood Ahmed, Lahore, 3 April 2003

Mian Muhammad Salim, Lahore, 4 April 2003

Arif Khokhar, Lahore, 4 April 2003

Vimal Issar, Delhi, 13 March 2004

Iqbal Singh, Delhi, 13 March 2004

Haji Abdul Rahman Gill, Lahore, 30 December 2004; 29 September 2005; 15 October 2005

Hukum Qureshi, Lahore, 30 October 2005

Syed Ahmed Saeed Kirmani, 31 October 2005

7

MARCH RIOTS: AMRITSAR AND JULLUNDUR

PRE-PARTITION AMRITSAR WAS THE SECOND LARGEST CITY OF THE Punjab and the major business centre after Lahore. One hundred years earlier, it had even more inhabitants than Lahore. In historical–religious terms, it was the most important city of Sikhism, as the holiest shrine of the Golden Temple was located there.

Sikhs were to be found in large numbers in the villages around the city. The Hindus and Sikhs predominated inside the walled city, while Muslims lived around the gates and in large localities such as Sharifpura near the railway line. Although the Hindus and Sikhs were the richer communities, the Muslim traders were also prominent, making the economic balance less tilted in complete favour of non-Muslims. Thus, the Muslim and Hindu–Sikh groups were more or less equal in number at the level of the city, while Muslims were a minority in the district as a whole. It was the only district in the Lahore division which had a non-Muslim majority. The distance between the two cities was some thirty miles or slightly more than forty-eight kilometres. There was regular interaction between them through trade and commerce and brisk road and railway traffic. In March 1947, the administration in Amritsar district was headed by J.D. Frazer.

Demographic profile according to 1941 census Amritsar City (including Amritsar Municipality and Amritsar Cantonment):

Community	Number	Share (%)
Total population of all communities	390,930	100
Muslims	183850	47
Hindus including the scheduled castes	144010	36.80
Sikhs	58769	15
Others, including Christians, Ad Dharmis, Jains, Parsees	4319	1.10

Amritsar district:

Community	Number	Share (%)
Total population of all communities	1,413,876	100
Muslims	657695	46.50
Hindus including the scheduled castes	216778	15.30
Sikhs	510845	36.10
Others, including Christians, Ad Dharmis, Jains, Parsees	28540	2

The news of the fall of the Punjab ministry on 2 March, followed by the high drama the following day with Master Tara Singh waving his *kirpan* outside the Punjab Assembly in Lahore, reached Amritsar the same day as many of its dwellers returned from Lahore after the day's work. The Sikhs, highly emotional and excitable people like the Muslims, had for several weeks been watching with great anxiety the demonstration of Muslim street power. With Master Tara Singh having given the call to take the Muslims head-on, the situation reached boiling-point. All that was needed at that point was a provocation that would make the two groups lock their horns. Such an occasion arrived on 4 March, when some Akalis went around in a *tonga,* beating drums at the main squares of Amritsar. According to Iftikhar (1991: 95), the author of a major work on the 1947 situation in Amritsar, the Sikhs were shouting:

Jo maange Pakistan
Uss ko deinge Qabristan.
Nahin baney ga Pakistan
Bann key rahe ga Sikhistan.

(Those who want Pakistan
Will get instead the graveyard.
There will be no Pakistan
But Sikhistan will come into being.)

When they reached Gol Hatti in the main town centre at Hall Bazaar, they beat the drums again and soon, a crowd collected. One of them made a speech against Muslims. The owners of a shop that specialised in making *kirpans* began distributing them among Sikhs. The Muslims responded by shouting:

Bann ke rahe ga Pakistan
Le ke rahen gey Pakistan (ibid.: 96)

(Pakistan will be made
We will get Pakistan)

The result was the first of the many violent contests between the two groups in the Gol Hatti square. The Muslims threw stones, bricks, and soda-water bottles while the Sikhs attacked with their *kirpans*. The police arrived and ordered the bazaar to be closed. Rumours began to circulate, however, that the Sikhs had killed seven Muslims at another place, at the Fountain Square, and cut off the arm of a Muslim tonga-driver near the Golden Temple. While such rumours were doing the rounds, a Muslim passerby was killed by Hindu fanatics. Such news infuriated the Muslims. As a result Mehraj Din alias Bhola, Anwar Minto, Mus Pehlwan, Naseer Khan, Bashir Paharia, Maulvi Hasan, Rafiq Gotaywala, Jawa, Gogi and Gami went about in search of revenge. A melee soon broke out in which bricks, knives, swords and soda-water bottles were used. According to Iftikhar, the non-Muslims ran away. The Muslim strongmen brought back the dead bodies of their co-religionists killed by the Sikhs. As they were returning, they met Sikh and Hindu counterparts and another fracas started. This time the Muslims took their revenge for the deaths and injuries of their co-religionists. The dead bodies of the non-Muslims were thrown into wells or put on carts and thrown into the stream near Baij Nath High School (ibid.: 97).

The contest at Mahan Singh Gate and Chowk Farid

Amritsar was now ripe for a showdown between armed Muslim and Hindu–Sikh gangs. The Akalis of Phula Singh's Burj, armed with guns and daggers, attacked Muslims of Mahan Singh Gate on 5 March but were repelled by the joint efforts of Muslims from Katra Mahan Singh, Kucha Dabgran, and Cheel Mandi. Both sides suffered death and injury, but the Sikhs allegedly suffered greater losses, according to Iftikhar. The next day, the Sikhs attacked the Muslims of Chowk Farid. The well-known Akali leader Udham Singh Nagoke and Madan, son of the famous Hindu *goonda* of Amritsar, Bijli Pehlwan, armed with guns, spears and other weapons, led the assault from the Golden Temple. From the Muslim side, too, came full resistance, in which even women took part. When returning from the combat at Chowk Farid, the Sikhs and Hindus set ablaze the shops and other buildings of Muslims at Katra Jamail Singh. The damage ran into millions of rupees (Iftikhar, 1991: 100-107). Ian Talbot, who conducted research in Amritsar some years ago, has written a vivid account of the incidents. Referring to both Iftikhar and another writer, Chaudhri Mohammad Said, Talbot mentioned that by 6 March, Amritsar city was ablaze (2004: 83-4).

SGPC report

The SGPC report, for its part, presented a different chronology of events. It claimed that Muslims of the Amritsar Muslim League formed a committee on 3 March to provide first-aid to the injured. It was indicative of planning for a long-drawn showdown. Further, that the Muslims had been storing weapons and petrol and were assisted by the police and other government functionaries. The Muslims wanted to break Sikh morale in their most important city. If that were to happen, the resistance to the greater goal of establishing Pakistan by force would weaken and fail. The report alleged that preparations for an attack were completed by the Muslim League on the 4th and the date given for the outbreak of violence was 5 March. The report also asserted that three or four Sikhs went around announcing, on behalf of the Shiromani Akali Dal, a public meeting to be held in the evening to discuss the Muslim League's bid to establish Pakistan. They were attacked at Chowk Moni by Muslims with brickbats and one Sikh, Bhai Mangal Singh, was killed (1991: 144-6). Thousands of Muslims began to form small units all over town and closed all points of entry to the city.

At four o'clock (presumably in the afternoon) unsuspecting Hindus and Sikhs were attacked by Muslims and many of them at Hall Bazaar, the main business centre, were killed. Thereafter, the Muslims began to loot property everywhere. The police did not take action, even though all of that occured close to the City Kotwali Police Station. Later, at five o'clock, several Sikh workers were killed when they came out of the factories. Some eighteen bodies were sent to the mortuary besides those killed earlier, but many more were burnt or thrown in wells and dirty ponds (ibid.: 147-8).

It is asserted in the SGPC report that since the Hindu and Sikh population lived in the centre of town, they were encircled by the Muslims living on the *mohallas* on the outer ring of the city. Therefore, when the troubles started, the Muslims enjoyed a distinct advantage in attacking the beleaguered Hindus and Sikhs. Moreover, many who took part in the attacks were wearing the Muslim League National Guard uniform and steel helmets. The mainly Muslim administration in Amritsar – including doctors and other staff – also denied care to injured non-Muslims brought to them.

Attack on train

A vicious attack on an incoming train took place just outside Amritsar at the Muslim suburb of Sharifpura, in which Hindus and Sikhs were hacked to pieces. It was another trigger for communal violence in Amritsar in early March. I talked to many people in Amritsar and Lahore about the carnage on the train. They remembered that the incident took place at

Sharifpura, a Muslim locality in the outskirts of Amritsar city, and one which escalated the violence in the subsequent days, though surprisingly it is not mentioned in any government reports of either the governor or the chief secretary. The SGPC report gave 6 March as the date of attack on the train. It alleged that the Muslims killed not only Hindu and Sikh men but also women and children (p. 151). Justice Khosla (p. 102) and *The Tribune* (8 March 1947) of Lahore also mentioned 6 March as the day on which this atrocity occurred.

Iftikhar described the train incident in more detail. According to him, it was a reprisal for the massive onslaught on the Muslims of Chowk Pragdas that took place on the night of 6–7 March (Iftikhar 1991: 110). Yet, when he describes the events leading to the attack, he alludes to another alleged atrocity by non-Muslims and not the events at Chowk Pragdas. He asserts that the Muslims of Sharifpura used to practise military drill and fighting techniques on a piece of land near the railway line as a preparation to provide protection for the nearby Sharifpura locality. He wrote that when the train from Dera Baba Nanak approached Sharifpura, Hameed, who had boarded the train, pulled the emergency lever to bring it to a halt. He yelled to the men who were exercising nearby that in some of the compartments were Hindus and Sikhs who had used violence against Muslims at the Dera Baba Nanak Railway Station. Upon hearing this, they jumped on to the train and one of them thrust a spear into the body of the driver while the others began to slaughter the Hindu and Sikh culprits from Dera Baba Nanak. Iftikhar added that women and children were spared in the best traditions of Islamic valour! (1991: 135-6).

I have searched in vain for any reference to attack on Muslims at Dera Baba Nanak; none of my interviewees remembered it, either. In accordance with the above description, one can conclude with some certainty that the attack on the train preceded the attack on Chowk Pragdas and took place on 6 March. It is possible that Iftikhar confused the dates. It can also be an attempt to put the blame on the Hindus and Sikhs for the breakout of violence.

Muslim carnage at Chowk Pragdas

The situation in Amritsar quickly deteriorated, and soon, the Chowk Pragdas carnage of Muslims happened. Iftikhar wrote that on 5 March, an emergency meeting was held at the MAO College under the chairmanship of Sheikh Sadiq Hasan, the chief Muslim Leaguer in Amritsar. It was attended by the city's notable Muslim personalities. It was decided that Muslims living in Hindu and Sikh-majority areas should be brought to safer areas. Many families heeded the call and shifted to Sharifpura. Among them were also those living in Chowk Pragdas and Chowk Manna Singh which were surrounded by Hindu and Sikh localities. However, Maulvi Muhammad Yusuf, the Imam of Unchi Masjid, and some others refused to leave because they had reached an agreement with the Hindus and Sikhs of those areas to maintain the peace. These people were nationalists who belonged to the Majlis-e-Ahrar and had good relations with the non-Muslims (1991: 105-6).

Iftikhar alleged that their trust was betrayed by two Sikhs, Mahender Singh and Dhian Singh, both members of the local peace committee who succeeded in convincing the Muslims to surrender their weapons. The Sikhs also searched the houses of those Muslims they considered unreliable. In the end, the Muslims of Chowk Pragdas had no weapons with which to defend themselves. Later, the Hindus and Sikhs held a meeting in which the reverses in the combats with Muslims in the previous two days were discussed and speakers narrated the cruelties suffered by Hindus and Sikhs during earlier Muslim-rule eras. As a result, crass emotions were whipped up into mob fury. In the early hours of 7 March, the Hindus and Sikhs, among whom were also volunteers from the Sikh princely states and ex-servicemen, launched a full-fledged attack on the Muslims of Chowk Pragdas (Iftikhar, 1991: 110). Guns, daggers, spears, and *kirpans* were employed and Muslim houses were set ablaze. Many Muslims were shot or stabbed, while others were burnt to death. Even elderly women were not spared. Some Muslim women were paraded naked and then hacked to pieces. Others killed themselves rather than let the Sikhs touch them. Similarly the Muslims of Chowk Manna Singh were dealt with extreme savagery. Altogether, fifty-five charred bodies were found and buried in various graveyards (ibid.: 120).

Shining examples of humanity

It has often been said that it is in times of crisis that humanity shines. Indeed, amidst all the carnage in the Punjab, there were non-Muslims who displayed their humanity and, at great risk to their own lives, saved those of Muslims. Iftikhar offers the example of Bawa Ghansham, a Sikh belonging to the Communist Party of India, who saved hundreds of Muslims by giving them refuge in his house. Another compassionate person was Babey Daktarni, the elderly wife of a Sikh doctor, who saved many lives (ibid.: 118-9). Although Iftikhar blames the Hindu and Sikh staff at the various hospitals for being heartless and unmoved by the suffering of injured Muslims, he records with gratitude and respect the conduct of two Hindu doctors, the brothers Dr Proshottam Dutt and Dr Narain Das. Both men raised their guns and stopped a Hindu–Sikh mob from attacking the Muslims who were being attended to in the hospital. Dr Dutt addressed the miscreants in the following words:

> This behaviour of yours is very cowardly. Communal prejudices and political enmity has made you mad. You have forgotten that something called humanity also exists in this world. You have stooped so low that you do not consider it degrading for your manhood to attack those who are in pain and ill. You should be ashamed of your disgraceful behaviour. One day you will regret your behaviour but humanity will never forgive you. You can even now repent and leave otherwise as long as we two brothers are alive and our rifles have bullets we will never let you touch the Muslim patients in this hospital (1991: 140-41).

Iftikhar tells the story of two Sikh girls who, having fallen into the hands of Muslims at Hathi Gate, were saved by the General Secretary of the Amritsar Muslim League, Mir Anwar Saeed. Another story is that of a Muslim doctor, Abdur Rauf, of Katra Karam Singh, who played an equally laudable role in saving the lives of non-Muslims. Iftikhar writes:

> Dr Sahib played a prominent part in training the Muslims of that locality in military skills. His house was the centre of the mujahideen (Islamic warriors) organisation in that locality. One day some 200

> non-Muslim men, women and children were surrounded in front of his house by the mujahideen. A controversy started among the inhabitants of that *mohalla* as how to treat the non-Muslims who were now captive. The problem was brought before Dr Sahib. He gave the ruling that they should be disarmed, their other belongings and money should not be touched and the women and children should not be harassed. The mujahideen argued that Muslims captured by the non-Muslims were treated in a beastly manner. Therefore they should be allowed to ravage the attractive non-Muslim females. Dr Sahib urged them to practise exemplary Islamic moral conduct and large-heartedness. As a result notwithstanding their anger they did no harm to the non-Muslims (1991: 141-2).

Master Tara Singh escapes assassination plot

The Amritsar authorities were hugely perturbed at the way violence had spiralled and expanded in scale. Leaders of all the communities were quickly summoned to a meeting to discuss the worsening situation. According to Iftikhar's account, Mir Anwar Saeed brought the two Sikh girls with him to the meeting where their father Thakur Gian Singh was also present. He was surprised to see them alive and thanked Saeed for having saved his daughters. At that moment Master Tara Singh arrived at the meeting and, in an attempt to exploit the situation, alleged that the two girls had been manhandled. The girls made a firm denial. Shortly, many Muslim leaders arrived, and a spirited discussion took place in which both sides negotiated the safe return of women and girls who had been abducted. This was successfully achieved and the female captives on both sides were released.

The meeting ended and Tara Singh prepared to leave. Abdullah Khan, in a conniving manner, suggested to Mir Anwar Saeed that he should convince Tara Singh to hitch a ride with him in his car. Madhi Gheewala quickly retorted that under no circumstances would he allow his 'dear leader' to fall into the hands of Muslims. Iftikhar remarked, 'As a result Abdullah Khan's plan failed; otherwise the chief killer of Muslims would have been finished off that very day' (ibid.: 122).

Such acts of treachery do not receive any comment from Iftikhar and the book is full of shocking incidents in which the ghastly behaviour of Muslims is presented almost in entertaining language. He also deplores the fact that while Jawaharlal Nehru saw for himself the horrors of Chowk Prag Das when he visited Amritsar soon afterwards, he failed to show sympathy for the victims. Instead, Iftikhar says, Nehru proclaimed all sides to be guilty of heinous crimes. He also blamed the Amritsar administration for having done nothing to punish biased and partial officials (ibid.: 144-46).

SGPC report alluded to the Chowk Pragdas outrage

As already noted earlier, the SGPC report gives ample attention to alleged Muslim atrocities in Amritsar, while glossing over or distorting similarly atrocious attacks on Muslims. Thus the report depicts the Chowk Pragdas event in the following words:

> On the first day of attack, several Muslims got killed by an infuriated Sikh crowd in a locality which was at the junction of a Muslim and non-Muslim zone, not very far from the centre of the Sikh influence. More than one hundred Muslim women and children whose menfolk had either been killed or had run away for safety, fell into the hands of the Sikhs. Sikhs kept them safe and fed them for two or three days that the fighting lasted and all communications in the town were cut off, and later sent them under escort to the City Police Station. These women acknowledged the chivalry and courtesy of the treatment of the Sikhs towards them (1991: 156).

This passage refers to the 'first day of attack'. It can be assumed that from the SGPC's perspective, it signifies the first occasion when a 'proper' Sikh-Hindu attack on Muslims took place.

Eyewitness Account of the March Riots

Professor V.N. Dutta

'I was in the new hostel of Government College, when Tara Singh lifted the *kirpan* outside the Punjab Assembly. My Muslim friends told me that now there will be trouble. A man had died in Mozang, someone has put a dagger into his body. I went to Prof. Sirajuddin, whose father Meraj Din was a close accquaintance of our family in Amritsar. He was lying on a bed and a Pathan was standing by his side. He asked me why I had come. I told him that *The Tribune* has reported that Hall Bazaar and the adjoining localities had been gutted and I want to go to Amritsar because my house is just in that place, but Sec. 144 has been imposed. "What should I do?"

'"Can you help me?" I asked. He paused for a moment and said "We will not forgive the Sikhs for what they have done. When I saw you Vishwa I got quite angry. Go if you can risk your life". The Pathan's eyes were full of hate and that sent shivers down my spine. I left crestfallen. I went to a Muslim friend of mine, Yakub. He took me to the Student Federation who gave me the Red Cross badge. I put it on my chest and went to the station and took the Frontier Mail which used to leave at about 9.15 a.m. I went to Amritsar where I found that the house next to ours had been badly burnt. I did not find my father. I met a lawyer, Gian Chand Kapoor, who told me that father was safe. I went to my sister's house and found my father there. He told me that Babbo, a Muslim friend of his, who owned a shoe-shop, had come to our house stealthily by passing over the roofs of several buildings. He said to my father that his life was in danger and he should leave, but my father refused to do that. Later Dilawar Hussain [principal of MAO College in Lahore after Partition] came to my father. He was a close friend of his. He said, "Please leave, otherwise Manto and Mutto, two Muslim *goondas,* will not leave you alive". On the Hindu side Bijli *pehalwan* was the ringleader. My sister, who lived on Majithia road, then sent her husband to fetch Father. Rai Bahadar Badri Nath, SP police, sent some policemen to my father and brought him. The localities of Katra Sher Singh, Hall Bazaar were gutted. Some of the most distinguished lawyers lived there. My father had his business on Hall Road.'

Ripudamman Singh

'Trouble started in Amritsar on 4 March when some Sikhs went around beating a drum and urging Sikhs to resist the Pakistan demand.

Already that day some casualties took place and the whole town was panic-struck. The violence kept escalating by the hour and reports of murder and bloodshed kept pouring in from all directions. There were surely exaggerations on both sides of the cruelty they had committed. However, I was witness to the Chowk Pragdas carnage. It is true that Muslims were butchered without mercy being shown to the old, women or children. Notorious Akali leaders such as Udham Singh Nagoke and Hindu–Sikh criminal gangs were involved in those atrocities. There is no doubt that Amritsar was the stronghold of criminal gangs of all the major communities. In the past they would cooperate with each other and avoid conflict. It seems that some implicit understanding existed about the division of the different zones in the town for their activities. Therefore, once they were mobilised to defend their religion and the honour of their communities they proved to be the worst type of wild beasts that tried to outscore each other in the cruelty they exercised in dealing with hapless, totally innocent people of the "enemy" community they could lay their hands on. I saw mutilated bodies of some Hindus and Sikhs on the 5th and 6th. However, the attack on the Muslims of Chowk Pragdas was totally out of proportion. It was truly a bloodbath. It had been planned in detail. I am not sure, but I heard that Sikh troops of some princely states were involved in the Chowk Pragdas assault.

'The Akalis did not save any Muslim girls and women. Rather, they were at the forefront of the whole operation. It was Bava Ghansham Singh, a Sikh leader of the Communist Party who had saved the lives of many Muslim men, women and children. In one street, some 300 Muslims were saved.

'I was a young boy in those days. The Chowk Pragdas events deeply traumatised me as I saw humanity being debased in the worst possible manner. For many months I could not cope with what I had seen. Ultimately I found spiritual refuge in the secular view of humanity presented by Marxism. I joined the Communist Party and have remained a member of it. Killing innocent human beings cannot be condoned under any circumstances.

'I can also tell you that bomb factories were established in Amritsar through secret funding by Sardar Patel. I am not sure if other Congress leaders were aware of it but the involvement of Sardar Patel is beyond any doubt. I have met many people who confirmed that he used to finance such bomb factories. I have always wondered why the British were so poorly prepared to deal with the Partition riots. There is no doubt that the Indian members of the administration had become partisan; instead of helping people in trouble some of them actively participated in the crimes against other groups.'

Devi Das Mangat

'The attack on the Muslims of Chowk Pragdas was in retaliation to what the Muslims had been doing from the evening of 4 March. The worst incident was the attack on the train at Amritsar station. Men, women and children who were just passengers in a train were butchered by militant Muslims. When that news reached us, the anger among the Hindus and Sikhs knew no bounds. Our elders were sure that if they did not act now atrocities against our people would only multiply. The Muslims were in a very aggressive mood. I am not aware of the betrayal of an agreement with nationalist Muslims by Mahender Singh and Dhian Singh not to touch the former; but it is true that it was an unequal fight. Those Muslims who had remained in their *mohallas* and not pulled out became easy targets. I am ashamed by what was done to women and children and the old. You know, previously we always addressed elders of the Muslim community as *chacha* (uncle) or *chachi* (aunty), the same way we greeted our own elders. On the whole, the people of Amritsar were friendly with each other, even the gangsters showed respect to the elders, and molesting of women was severely punished by them. However, once a communal war had begun, human beings had been transformed into wild beasts.'

Mohan Singh Rahi

'Trouble started on 4 March 1947 when Sikhs went around beating drums and calling for resistance to the Pakistan demand. 6 March was Holi and while the Hindus and Sikhs were preparing to begin their festivities, Sikh workers in the railway workshops were attacked by Muslims and some were killed. There was also an attack on a train in which Amritsari

Muslims mercilessly killed innocent Hindus and Sikhs. Later, Muslims set fire to Hindu–Sikh buildings, and in retaliation Sikhs and some Hindus attacked the Muslims of Chowk Pragdas. A day earlier, the Muslims had thrown *lottas* (small mud pitchers) at Hindus and Sikhs who were passing by. The Sikhs attacked the Muslims with *kirpans* and knives and indeed acted brutally towards Muslims of Chowk Pragdas.'

Gurcharan Das Arora

'The Muslim League was determined to wipe out Hindus and Sikhs from the Punjab, but in Amritsar they met with very strong resistance. It is true that hostilities started on 4 March when excited Sikhs went around beating a drum and inviting people to oppose the Muslim League, but that was a reaction that should have been expected. Since the spectacular victory in the 1946 elections the Lahore leadership of the Muslim League was constantly shuffling between the two cities. It is they who were responsible for creating a situation which exploded into killing and burning. The attack on Chowk Pragdas came only after the Muslims had slaughtered Hindu and Sikh passengers in a train outside Amritsar. The Muslim *badmashes* waylaid innocent people and butchered them mercilessly. They paid a heavy price ultimately but in March it was an even contest.'

Aftar Singh Judge

'I was born in Amritsar but educated at Government College, Lahore. Our house in Amritsar was located in [Chowk] Pragdas. We lived next door to Kashmiri Muslims, known as Lakhras [those who had ₹100,000 or more]. They had made a lot of money in the shawl business. Some of the Amritsar Muslims were quite wealthy. The rioters came to set fire to the Lakhras' house. My grandfather, who was deeply religious, protested that if they burnt the Lakhras' house they will set his house ablaze as well. Let them go. The rioters came again, armed with pickets, axes, spears, but my uncle Sujjan Singh had brought the Muslims over to our home and thus while the house was destroyed they were saved.'

Khawaja Iftikhar's book is based on extensive interviews with Muslims who relocated to Lahore and other places in Pakistan. One can consider it the presentation of the pro-Muslim League point of view. I managed to track down and talk to a number of people mentioned in the book; they mostly agreed with Iftikhar's version of events. The few deviations in their accounts are not significant and relate to small details about specific events.

Below are excerpts of two interviews: the first is with a Muslim of the Ahrar party which was not in sympathy with the notion of Pakistan, and the second, a non-political person.

Qamar Yurish

'It is true that the Sikhs provoked a clash on 4 March, but provocations had been going on for a long time on the part of the Muslim League which drafted Muslim gangsters into its political campaigns. Aggression against the non-Muslims intensified in January and with every passing day they felt threatened. We lived in a non-Muslim area, but there was never a single threat or insult issued to us. After 4 March, grand old Amritsar's strong traditions of anti-colonialism were superseded by communalism. The slaughter of Hindus, Muslims and Sikhs in early March was the outcome of months of incitement. Muslim League leaders from Lahore were frequently in town and carried only one message for the Amritsar Muslims: challenge the Hindus and Sikhs and defeat them.'

Sheikh Abdul Wahab

'We lived in a mixed locality, where all the elders agreed that come what may, they would stand by each other and not let any intruders bring violence into our midst. During the March riots, the *badmashes* were involved from all sides. They usually attacked innocent people – some workers from the nearby villages and towns who had no clue as to what was happening. I had a Christian friend, Arthur, who used to visit me almost daily. He was killed by the Muslim criminals even when he pleaded with them that he was a Christian. There was no bravery involved on any side. Nobody died in our *mohalla* but Arthur was murdered in a street that connected us to a Hindu *mohalla.* His father worked in a mission school. I remember to this day, his parents were simply petrified. They did not know what to do. They had shifted to Amritsar from Gurdaspur and went back after his death. He was killed either on 6 or 7 March. I felt terribly guilty and to this day I have not overcome the shock. The Muslim League had been provoking the Hindus and Sikhs since the election of 1946. It was not surprising that bloodshed took place in March. Our family was originally from Gujranwala so we returned to our hometown at the end of June.'

Jenkins on Amritsar

In a telegram dated 6 March, Jenkins informed Wavell about violent incidents in different parts of the Punjab. About Amritsar, he noted that the situation was 'very grave with main business streets in flames; rioters using firearms and general looting. Known casualties up to 10.30 today [presumably in the evening] were about 65 with 10 dead' (Carter 2007a: 59). On 8 March, he sent Wavell a telegram saying Amritsar was still disturbed and completely disorganised. Two British battalions sent after the riots broke out were still there (ibid.: 68-9). In a longer report, dated 9 March, he informed that the civil surgeon had counted one hundred dead in Amritsar: 64 Muslims; 31 Sikhs; 4 Hindus; and 1 Christian (ibid.: 73). On 13 March, Jenkins visited Amritsar. He said: 'I visited Amritsar this afternoon. City was quiet under curfew. Damage was extensive and special organisation will be necessary to remove debris, demolish unsafe buildings and take care of unclaimed property. Amritsar casualty now 127 dead and 175 seriously injured' (ibid.: 78).

No mention is made of Chowk Pragdas till much later, on 30 April: 'During the earlier rioting a mosque in a quarter known as Chowk Prag Das had been burnt, and a number of Muslims had been murdered there' (Carter 2007a: 152).

Jullundur

My research led me to discover some major events in Jullundur in March. Jullundur city and cantonment had a fifty-nine per cent Muslim majority. The SGPC report of 1991 contained a facsimile between pages 20 and

21, of a certificate allegedly issued by the Jullundur Muslim League to a woman for completing training as a National Guard volunteer, which was not only about drill but also training in fighting and using weapons including firearms. It was a stronghold of the Muslim League, though both the Congress and the RSS were also well-organised and active. Muhammad Ayub Khan, a resident of that city has recorded the events that transpired in Jullundur in his book, *Tarikh-i-Pakistan Aur Jullundur* (*The Pakistan Movement and Jullundur*). According to Ayub Khan, the situation in Jullundur deteriorated soon after Master Tara Singh's speech on 3 March 1947. The Hindus and Sikhs in Jullundur went out on a procession on the night of 4 March, walking through Muslim areas while shouting slogans against Pakistan and the Muslim League. They shouted: '*Jo koi mange ga Pakistan uss ko milay ga qabristan*' (Those who demand Pakistan, they will get the graveyard) and '*Raj karey ga khalsa, akee rehey na koi*' (The pure will reign and nobody will remain opposed to them) (Khan, 2002: 258).

Continuing with his narrative, Ayub Khan says that at that time, the Muslims were sleeping and they kept their cool. The provocation continued on the next day. A bus carrying Muslim female students of Islamia College was surrounded by Hindu and Sikh students who threw stones and hurled abuses at the civilians. Many of the girls were injured, along with the driver, but they managed to reach the civil hospital. The Hindu doctors were not very helpful, but soon Muslim doctors from all over the city arrived and attended to the injured. The Muslim youths of Jullundur wanted to take revenge but were dissuaded by the elders. Later that day, the miscreants killed a number of Muslims (ibid.: 259-60).

The murder of Labh Singh

The Akali Sikh leader of Jullundur, Sardar Labh Singh, however, visited the Muslim localities along with another Akali leader, Darbara Singh. He went around various Muslim localities and asked for forgiveness from the Muslims for the shameful behaviour of the Sikhs. The police had received intelligence of a conspiracy to kill Labh Singh but failed to act in time. Labh Singh was killed by a Muslim youth, Bashir Julaha. The police arrested a number of Muslims who were tried and sentenced to death in the lower court. An appeal was entered before the High Court in Lahore, but before a decision could be given, Partition took place. All those men were later released after an exchange of prisoners took place between the two governments.

The murder of Labh Singh is mentioned in a telegram dated 10 March that Jenkins sent to Wavell. He wrote that two police officers who met Master Tara Singh in Amritsar found him in a very excited state after the former president of the SGPC in Jullundur, Labh Singh, was murdered. Master Tara Singh asserted that 'Civil War' had already begun. He threatened raids on police stations and a mass Sikh uprising (Carter, 2007a: 76).

References

Iftikhar, Khawaja. *Jabb Amritsar Jall Raha Tha* (When Amritsar was Burning), Lahore: Khawaja Publishers, 1991.

Khan, Muhammad Ayub. *Tarikh-i-Pakistan Aur Jullundur* (The Pakistan Movement and Jullundur), Lahore: Asatair, 2002.

Khosla, G. D. *Stern Reckoning*, Delhi: Oxford University Press, 1989.

Talbot, Ian. 'Violence, Migration and Resettlement: The Case of Amritsar' in Ian Talbot and Shinder Thandi (eds.), People *on the Move: Punjabi Colonial, and Post-Colonial Migration*, Karachi: Oxford University Press, 2004.

Talib, S.G.S. *Muslim League Attack on Sikhs and Hindus in the Punjab 1947*, New Delhi: Voice of India, 1991.

Newspapers

Pakistan Times, Lahore, 1947.

The Tribune, Lahore, 1947.

Official documents

Carter, Lionel, (ed). *Punjab Politics, 3 March–31 May 1947, At the Abyss, Governors' Fortnightly Reports and other Key Documents*, New Delhi: Manohar, (2007a).

Census of India, 1941, Volume 6, Punjab. Simla: Government of India Press, (1941).

Interviews

V.N. Dutta, Delhi, 10 March 2004
Gurcharan Das Arora, Amritsar, 24 March 2004
Mohan Singh Rahi, Amritsar, 25 March 2004
Devi Das Mangat, Amritsar, 25 March 2004
Ripudamman Singh, Amritsar 26 March 2004
Sheikh Abdul Wahab, Lahore, 24 December 2004
Qamar Yurish, Lahore, 26 December 2004
Aftar Singh Judge, Delhi, 10 January 2005

8

THE MARCH RIOTS: MULTAN

THE THIRD MAJOR URBAN CENTRE TO EXPERIENCE SAVAGE COMMUNAL rioting was the ancient city of Multan. Located in southern Punjab, the city's topography is part of an arid desert belt that covers Sindh, and extends to the opposite side into India as well as the Indian state of Rajasthan. The weather is essentially hot and dry. Multan is believed to have been the capital of an empire at the time of the *Mahabharata* war in antiquity. Like many other towns and cities of the Punjab, Multan went through a great deal of warfare against invaders from Greece, Arabia and central Asia. The famous Hindu festival of Diwali (the festival of lights) is believed to have originated in Multan. In early eighth century, Multan was conquered along with Sindh by the Arabs, under the leadership of Muhammad bin Qasim.

Multan was, for some time, the seat of government of the Ismaili sect of Shias. In the eleventh century it was captured by the Sunni Turco–Afghan, Mahmud of Ghazni. Later, many Afghan and Baluch tribes also established their presence in Multan and adjoining areas. Multan gained great fame for the presence of a large number of sufis who settled and established their lodges. Many Sufi shrines are to be found in Multan. It enjoyed peace and prosperity during Mughal rule, experiencing prosperity under Maharaja Ranjit Singh (1799–1839) and under the British too.

The British dug many irrigation canals and waterworks in southern Punjab. As a result, agriculture prospered in Multan district. A large number of settlers from the overpopulated eastern districts and some from northern Punjab were allotted lands in the canal colonies in the district, of which the one at Montgomery (now called Sahiwal) is the most famous. The locals spoke Saraiki, which some believe is a separate language, while others consider it a dialect of Punjabi. Punjabi-speaking people settled in Multan during the British period as well as after the partition of the Punjab, as the Hindus and Sikhs left for India and Muslims crossed the border into Pakistan. Multan division, like Rawalpindi division, was overwhelmingly Muslim in religious composition.

Demographic profile according to 1941 census
Multan City (including Cantonment area):

Community	Number	Share (%)
All Communities	142768	100
Muslims	81383	57
Hindus (including scheduled castes)	56258	39.41
Sikhs	2665	1.87
Others (including Christians, Ad Dharmis, Jains, Parsees, Buddhists and Jews)	2462	1.72

Multan district:

Community	Number	Share (%)
All Communities	1484333	100
Muslims	1157911	78
Hindus (including scheduled castes)	242987	16.37
Sikhs	61628	4.15
Others (including Christians, Ad Dharmis, Jains, Parsees, Buddhists and Jews)	21727	1.46

Riots started in Multan on 5 March, mostly involving Muslims who attacked Hindus and Sikhs. The attacks were confined to the city, although one area on the outskirts, Basti Nau, was raided, resulting in considerable losses of life and property amongst the Hindus. There were very few Sikhs in the city. The district administration was headed by Deputy Commissioner A.J.B. Arthur, ICS.

The Multan Hindus were a peaceful people with no tradition of militancy. While the RSS was active among them, it had only a limited following. The March rioting was thus largely one-sided. Neither the *Pakistan Times* nor *The Tribune* covered the events in Multan in any detail. The Khosla and SGPC reports, as well as the government reports, are given later. The events of those days are reconstructed using the accounts of interviewees: those of Muslim inhabitants of present-day Multan, and then of Hindus who fled the town.

Interviews with Muslims

Syed Khurshid Abbas Gardezi

'Before the riots of 1947, things were quite peaceful in Multan. The total population of Multan was only 90,000 [Mr Gardezi was presumably making a rough guess]. There were very few Sikhs in Multan. Although Hindus were concentrated in trade and commerce and were well-off, Muslims who constituted the majority dominated political and cultural life of this town. The strong Sufi traditions of the local culture encouraged peaceful co-existence and mutual respect. Hindus visited Muslim shrines as frequently as Muslims did. Muslim landlords had Hindu accountants called *dumbirs*. Punnu Ram was our *dumbir*. They would always address us with a lot of deference using honorific expressions such as "*Pir ji*" (dear spiritual master). There were also some big Hindu landlords as well as some tenant-cultivators. The Muslim landlords were indebted to Hindu moneylenders. Hindus spent money in building big houses and on lavish weddings. Such practice was imitated by Muslims who would ruin themselves in such exhibitionism. However, there were also some very successful Muslim businessmen. So, in Multan not only big Muslim landlords and custodians of religious shrines exerted a great deal of influence there was also a significant trading community among Muslims.

'The beginnings of political activism in Multan can be dated from at least the 1946 elections. Before that, Muslim landlords were members of the Punjab Unionist Party and loyalists of the British. Then, sometime around 1945, defections to the Muslim League began to take place rapidly and by 1947, hardly any landowner worth the name was outside the Muslim League. Our Gardezi clan belongs to the Shia sect, but with roots in Sufism. We joined the Muslim League as did many other Shias, because Jinnah was a Shia and we believed that Pakistan will be a non-sectarian state. About twenty-five per cent of the Muslim population of Multan was Shia. The Congress did not have a strong presence in Multan.

'In March 1947, I was studying at Emerson College. Priya Warat and Ashok Kumar Khanna were two Hindu classfellows of mine that I was close to. They were good, gentle people. Some of them ate *halal* meat. There was a prominent Hindu shopkeeper who had goats slaughtered according to Islamic ritual before he ate the meat. At that time, the deputy commissioner was an Englishman called Arthur. The police in Multan were mainly Punjabi Muslims who hailed from other parts of the Punjab. Our local language and culture derives from Saraiki which is also known as Multani. Very few Saraiki-speakers were in the police.

'After Tara Singh unsheathed the *kirpan* outside the Punjab Assembly in Lahore, Multan was gripped by restlessness. The first clash was at Borh Gate where the Gardezis were settled. A procession of Hindus came shouting anti-Pakistan slogans. Abdul Karim, who sold ice slabs, another man called Mustakeen, and Allah Diwa *kumhar* (the potter), challenged the demonstrators. A butcher, Muhammad Ramzan, brought knives to the scene and thereafter a bloody encounter took place. Two of the protesters were killed. A Sikh started shouting hysterically "*Tu zinda hai, zinda hai*!" (You are alive, you are alive) while pointing at one of the dead bodies. Such a reaction intensified the rioting. Since the Hindus owned big houses and had fortified them from inside, the Muslims resorted to arson and set Hindu properties ablaze; as a result many died. The Hindus also set some Muslim properties on fire. For example, the buildings of the prominent trading family of Muslim Khwajgans, who were in the skin and tannery business, were torched by Hindu gangs. They also attacked Muslims in their strongholds, causing fatalities on the Muslim side too. On the other hand, Hindus and Muslims also helped each other, but the situation never returned to normality again. I must say that the local Multanis never understood who was manipulating and masterminding the riots. There seemed to be a "hidden hand" at work that let the situation worsen. The Hindus indeed lost a lot of property during the March fires and rioting. Some Hindus converted to Islam. They are known as Deendar Muslims.'

Ataullah Malik

'There was no problem in Multan before the 1940s. Hindus were concentrated in the city but the majority population in greater Multan was Muslim. We lived in peace and harmony. Hindus would distribute sweets at the time of Diwali and other festivals and we responded with friendly gestures too, during Muslim festivals. The Muslim *jagirdars* (feudal lords) were loyal to the British and opposed any movement that challenged the Raj. The Congress had a presence here, but the most active anti-British organisation was the Majlis-e-Ahrar to which belonged all nationalist Muslims. We believed that the Congress and Majlis-e-Ahrar had a common cause against colonial rule. The *jagirdars* were indebted to Hindu moneylenders and in many cases their property was under Hindu control. Sir Chhotu Ram's reforms had weakened the hold of the moneylenders, but they carried out their transactions through Muslim front-men. During the 1945–46 election campaign, the Muslim League drafted Brelawi *maulvis* into the campaign. They popularised slogans such as '*Pakistan ka Na'ara kiya, La Ilaha Il-lilah!*' Beating drums and giving calls of *Allah-ho-Akbar* (God is great), they would gather people and preach the cause of Pakistan. This was something new. The Brelawis had always kept out of politics and were known to be in the pay of *pirs* and *jagirdars*. Now, they were promising heaven and earth to Muslim voters and damning the Hindus and Sikhs as infidels. They described the future state of Pakistan as the citadel of Islam, which will launch jihad to establish true Islam on earth. All this was pure fakery because in their past conduct they only stood for docility towards the British Raj and the landowning classes.

'Many *jagirdars* such as Ali Hussain Gardezi, Mumtaz Daultana and Alamdar Hussain Gilani [father of later Pakistani Prime Minister Yousaf Raza Gilani] joined the Muslim League, but a few remained in the Unionist Party. Only Ibrahim Barq, a minor landowner, was elected on the Unionist Party ticket but he contested the reserved Muslim seat from Multan district and not from the city. All other seats were won by Muslim League candidates. The Muslim League employed *goonda* (strong-arm) tactics to crush the resistance offered by nationalist Muslims. It is true that the Ahrar orators challenged the Muslim League's credentials as representatives of Islam. Our point of view was that the *jagirdars* had never participated in the anti-colonial struggles and were now in the field to subvert Hindu–Muslim unity against the Raj, rather than to create an egalitarian society in accordance with Islamic teachings.

'I was a student at Emerson College in 1947. It was a co-educational institution. In the first attack on non-Muslim protestors at Borh Gate on 5 March, a Sikh, Nanak Singh, was killed by Muslims. The demonstrators did shout anti-Pakistan slogans, but during the civil disobedience movement in January 1947 the Muslim League had without any hindrance shouted communal slogans against the Congress, but no Hindu or Sikh had dared raise a voice. Now, when the non-Muslims came out in the streets to protest the fall of the Khizar ministry the Muslim League's supporters resorted to violence forthwith.'

The murder of Seth Kalyan Das

Ataullah Malik continued his narrative:

'The most regretful and shameful murder that took place in March 1947 was that of Seth Kalyan Das, a prominent Hindu, who was also a landlord. He lived near the railway station. He had excellent relations with Muslims. He enjoyed the respect of all communities. Sometimes he was approached by Muslims to arbitrate in disputes within the Muslim community. But in March the Muslim League National Guards, many of them being former police touts and criminals, brought to naught all those relationships. They surrounded his house and mercilessly killed him and his entire family.

'At that time, the Congress President of Punjab, Dr Saifuddin Kitchlew, was in town and staying with him. Somebody recognised him and said he was a Muslim. They started abusing him, but were hesitant to kill him. They made him take off his clothes to make sure he was circumcised. He was told that if he signed the membership form of the Muslim League, he would be spared, otherwise they would kill him.

Just at that moment, we nationalist Muslims arrived on the scene. The dead bodies of Seth Kalyan Das and his family were lying in pools of blood. It was a ghastly sight indeed. We found the thugs examining Dr Kitchlew. He was completely naked and was trying to reason with them. Our entry on the scene saved his life. We nationalists and the Muslim Leaguers knew each other, because Multan was, after all, a small town in those days. Some had earlier been with the Ahrar but had joined the Muslim League. Some of our elders were able to convince the National Guards that killing a Muslim is not permitted in Islam. This way Dr Kitchlew's life was saved [this incident was also narrated to me by Dr Kitchlew's son, Toufique Kitchlew, in 2005. He lived on the outskirts of Delhi. Dr Saifuddin Kitchlew remained in India and died there in 1963].

'In Basti Nau, outside Multan city, Hindus were killed in large numbers. They owned considerable land in that area. At least 10–20 of them lost their lives. The Hindus also retaliated; the RSS had been practising military drill in the Hindu areas. Some Muslims were killed by the RSS. From the Muslim League side, Mian Abdullah Arain and Zanu Shah spearheaded most of the attacks on Hindus and Sikhs. Nehru visited Multan soon afterwards. He first came to the Muslim camp where a young man cursed him. He listened patiently and then ordered the medical staff to give him all the help he needed. Then he visited the camp set up for Hindu survivors of the bloody mob attacks. A young Hindu girl shouted at him for letting his community be brutalised and humiliated. He listened with a bowed head and then quietly walked away.'

Arshad Multani

'Before Partition, there was no real trouble between the communities. Multan had many Hindu philanthropists while the Muslim feudal lords were interested in preserving their privileges. Trouble started in March 1947. I remember the first person who was killed was a Sikh, although there were not many Sikhs in our city. It was mostly Hindus. Most of them were devotees of the Sufis and visited the Sufi shrines. It is true that most property was with Hindus. That was one very strong motivation to attack them. I think the police was involved in instigating attacks on Hindus. They used to take a share in the loot. Since the Hindus were in a minority in Multan, they were not very strict about ideas of pollution but it is true we did not sit and eat together. Multan was a better place before the riots of 1947.'

Former Hindu inhabitants of Multan

Premchand Khanna

'Multan was a peaceful town, full of affection and good people. Saraiki language and culture are beautiful. Never for a moment could we believe that one day it will all end up in our exit from that city of Sufi piety. Our elders were original inhabitants of Multan and lived under Muslim rulers for centuries, but what happened in 1947 had few parallels except for the occasional excesses of Muslim invaders. We had good relations with our Muslim neighbours. We even ate together. My father had great faith in Muslim *pirs* and regularly visited Sufi shrines. I was a Congress worker at that time. Until the 1946 election campaign, the environment in Multan was not strained, but the Muslims used abusive language against the Unionists. They used *mullas* (clerics) during the public meetings to incite the crowds against non-Muslims. I took part in the procession in Multan on 5 March. It was mostly Hindu students who took part in the procession. It is true that slogans such as '*Quaid-i-Azam murdabad*' (Death to Quaid-i-Azam) were raised by some of the anti-social elements amongst us. At Borh Gate, there was a violent confrontation in which the Muslims used knives and axes. Some people were injured and a few died. All the losses were sustained by us. The Muslims then went on a rampage and set fire to Hindu shops, and many of them were gutted. The murder of Kalyan Das created a stir and some of the well-to-do Hindus decided to move their families to East Punjab. We left Multan in April and came and settled in Jullundur. I have always wanted to go back and see Multan, but the fear that was generated in March 1947 still grips me.'

Girdhari Lal Kapur

'I can see even today before my eyes the dead bodies of Nanak Singh and some Hindu students who were brutally murdered at Borh Chowk. My father had a shop in that area and we lived in a street behind the shop. The Hindus and Sikhs were peacefully protesting the fall of the government in Lahore when they were pounced upon by Muslims, many of them known criminals. I was not part of the 5 March procession, but when the attack took place and the Hindus and Sikhs panicked, they ran into the streets all around. I and my cousin Amrit Lal also ran with them because Muslims were pursuing all Hindus. It was very frightening, but we were helped by some Muslims who hid us. The police was certainly hostile to the Hindus and Sikhs and did nothing to stop the aggressors.

'The situation improved from the middle of March as the elders from all the communities met and an understanding was reached to maintain the peace. However, after March, the Hindu and Sikh minorities were always worried about what would happen if Pakistan comes into being. They knew that the Multan division as well as Multan district were predominantly Muslim, and if the Punjab is divided they would be on the wrong side of the border. Some of them started sending their families to safer places in the eastern parts of the Punjab. My mother, my two sisters, and I were sent in early April to Saharanpur, now in Haryana, but which was a part of the old Punjab at that time. My father and uncles stayed on. They came over in the end of July. Some of our relatives, however, were killed in August.'

Bhola Nath Gulati

'We had a retail shop close to Borh Bazaar. Most of our customers were Muslims. The ladies would come fully veiled but once inside the shop they did not hesitate to show their face. We would call them '*bibiji*' as many of them were from *pir* families. One of them had tied *rakhi* on my father. She had no children and often told my father that she wanted to adopt me. Father would say in return, "He is your son, *bibiji*". On 5 March there was suddenly a lot of commotion. I was in my shop at that time. I heard shouts and cries after a while. I had no clue that it would be the saddest day of my life. My mother had died when I was an infant and I was the only child of my parents. Somebody killed my father, though he did not take part in the procession. He had just gone out to have a look. A Muslim friend of mine, Sarwar, proved to be an angel. He took me home. His father knew my father, so they took care of me, but then my father's younger brother, Kishan Chacha, who was in the railways and posted in Ludhiana came to Multan when he heard about the trouble. We sold our shop and left Multan in early April. I did not take part in attacks on Muslims though I know many Hindus and Sikhs who had been uprooted and taken refuge in Ludhiana were involved in a great deal of raids on Muslim *mohallas*. They said they wanted to avenge the wrongs done to their families. I did not take part because I was too afraid of bloodshed. Sometimes I do dream of Multan and especially my father. He used to wear a *pagri* (turban) and loved me a lot. I was thirteen when the riots took place in Multan. I can still speak Seraiki because my *chachaji* used to speak it to me.'

Khosla and SGPC reports

The Khosla report gives a vivid account of the attacks on non-Muslims in Multan. It says that Hindu and Sikh students went out on a peaceful procession on 5 March in protest of the shooting of peaceful Hindu–Sikhs students in Lahore the previous day. Given particular mention are the events that took place specifically in Multan, including the pitiless murder of the Hindu philanthropist, Seth Kalyan Das, and the humiliation of his guest, the Muslim president of the Punjab Congress Committee, Dr Kitchlew (1989: 104-5). The SGPC does not take up the events in Multan (probably because few Sikhs lived in that district) but mentions it as one of the areas affected by the violence carried out by Muslims.

Governor Jenkins

In a telegram to Wavell dated 6 March, Jenkins reported a hundred dead and a large number injured. Two days later, on 8 March, he mentions that one hundred and forty dead bodies had been recovered in Multan but the deputy commissioner estimated that the number was closer to two hundred dead and five hundred injured (Carter 2007a: 69) On 10 March, the governor visited Multan and reported about the quiet there. Some incidents were reported from the villages around Multan. On the following days, he reported that trouble was again brewing in Multan. In the FR dated 14 March, he wrote about Multan: 'Multan is also bad, but the country is easier, and yesterday or the day before a small party of Indian troops, who had been surrounded by a riotous mob and were obliged to open fire seriously, did considerable execution. This should have a good effect' (Carter 2007a: 81). On 17 March he wrote to Wavell, 'At Multan the trouble was started by a sudden procession of non-Muslim students shouting "Quaid-i-Azam murdabad". Between 12 noon and 3.15 p.m. it is estimated that about 150 people – nearly all Hindus – lost their lives. There was much incendiarism, but the damage as compared with that in Amritsar is small' (ibid.: 85). Thereafter, the governor started reporting improvement from Multan. In the FR dated 31 March written to Mountbatten, Jenkins reported that the province has come under control.

References

Khosla, Gopal Das. *Stern Reckoning,* Delhi: Oxford University Press, 1989.

Talib, Sardar Gurbachan Singh. *Muslim League Attack on Sikhs and Hindus in the Punjab 1947 (SGPC report),* New Delhi: Voice of India, 1991.

Official documents

Carter, Lionel, (ed). *Punjab Politics, 3 March–31 May 1947, At the Abyss, Governors' Fortnightly Reports and other Key Documents,* New Delhi: Manohar, 2007a.

Census of India, 1941, Volume 6, Punjab, Simla: Government of India Press, 1941.

Interviews

Syed Khurshid Abbas Gardezi, Multan, 21 December 2004

Arshad Multani, Multan, 22 December

Ataullah Malik, Multan, 22 December 2004
Premchand Khanna, Delhi, 9 January 2005
Girdhari Lal Kapur, Delhi, 9 January 2005
Bhola Nath Gulati, Delhi, 9 January 2005

9

THE MARCH RIOTS: RAWALPINDI AND ADJOINING RURAL AREAS

LOCATED ON THE POTHOHAR PLATEAU OF NORTHERN PUNJAB, Rawalpindi is on the direct route from the Khyber Pass in the north-western mountains to the Indian subcontinent. Most incomers followed that path in their march eastwards and in southerly directions. Archaeological findings reveal that Vedic and Buddhist civilisations flourished in the Pothohar region. The famous seat of Buddhist learning at Taxila is only some twenty kilometres from Rawalpindi. Thus Rawalpindi has been of cultural, strategic, and military importance throughout history, despite its enduring character of a small town.

It gained considerable importance when the British made it their main garrison in north-western India, establishing it as the headquarters of the Northern Command. Rawalpindi served as the hub of intelligence-gathering operations during the notorious 'Great Game' played out between Britain and Russia and other great powers for influence in the tribal areas, Afghanistan and central Asia. In 1947, a large contingent of the British Indian Army, including several hundred British troops, was present in Rawalpindi. According to the 1941 census, of the total population of 185,042 of Rawalpindi City, more than 49,000 were concentrated in the two cantonments known as Rawalpindi Cantonment and Chaklala Cantonment. It is not clear if in March 1947 a formal decision had already been taken that British troops will not be committed to quell communal riots. The first definite decision in this regard was taken when Field Marshal Auchinleck wrote to Mountbatten about it in a note dated 26 June 1947. Referring to Jinnah's wish that British troops should not be withdrawn too quickly; he wanted the government to make it crystal-clear to the Muslim League leader that 'British Troops will NOT be available in communal disturbances' (Mansergh and Moon, 1982: 660-61). It is possible that in March 1947, some secret decision had already been made, or a tacit understanding existed, that their main mission was to protect British and other European lives in the event of an eruption of large-scale violence. There were several hundred British and European families in Rawalpindi at that time.

Rawalpindi city also served as the divisional and district headquarters of the civil administration. The Rawalpindi division was overwhelmingly Muslim in communal composition; the same was true of Rawalpindi district. However, in the city, the Hindus and Sikhs were in a majority. The Sikhs constituted the richest community, as most of the trade, commerce and money-lending activities were in their hands. They owned most shops, commercial buildings, and residential localities. They had converted to Sikhism only a few generations earlier from Hindu Khatri and Arora sub-castes. Sikhs from eastern Punjab called them 'Bhappas'. Hindus, meanwhile, were mostly petty traders though many of them were goldsmiths. The Muslim population of Rawalpindi city was poor; the majority were artisans and low-paid workers.

It is interesting to note that the Muslim component of the 'martial races' of the Punjab recruited in the British Indian Army comprised men of the Rajput, Ghakkar and Awan tribes of Rawalpindi division, especially Rawalpindi district (Tan, 2005). During the interviews in the city and district, I learnt that soldiering was the only profession that the people could turn to because agriculture as a livelihood was poorly developed. Rainfall was the main source of irrigation for the barren, stony and tough Pothohar land, and it was rarely enough to produce a bumper crop. Landholdings were small. Some people told me that the British discouraged economic development in the rural areas so as to ensure a steady supply of cannon fodder for the army. On the few occasions when building of dams and extending irrigation facilities was mooted, the plans were abandoned due to pressure from the military. Trade and shops in the rural areas were owned mainly by Sikhs and a smaller number of Hindus. The Muslims of Rawalpindi city and district were heavily indebted to Sikh moneylenders.

By 1947, demobilised soldiers from the Rawalpindi division were arriving in thousands from South-east Asia, the Middle East, and elsewhere. Some were still abroad. Those who returned to their villages found that economic hardships had increased rather than diminished. Hence, many ex-soldiers would hang around Rawalpindi in search of work and other means of earning a livelihood (interview, Feroz Dar). Many of them were involved in the raids on Sikh villages in the Rawalpindi district and the adjoining Campbellpur (now named Attock) and Jhelum districts.

Demographic profile according to 1941 census Rawalpindi city (including Rawalpindi municipality and cantonment and Chaklala Cantonment):

Community	Number	Share (%)
All Communities	185,042	100
Muslims	81,038	43.79
Hindus, including scheduled castes	62,397	33.72
Sikhs	32,054	17.32
Others, including Christians, Ad Dharmis, Jains, Parsees, Buddhists and Jews	9,957	5.38

Rawalpindi district:

Community	Number	Share (%)
All Communities	785,231	100
Muslims	628,193	80
Hindus, including scheduled castes	82,453	10.5
Sikhs	64,127	8.17
Others, including Christians, Ad Dharmis, Jains, Parsees, Buddhists and Jews	10,448	1.33

Unlike other parts of the Punjab, Rawalpindi had already dealt with an influx of refugees when, in December 1946, Hindus and Sikh from the nearby Hazara district of NWFP arrived in large numbers. News of Master Tara Singh's call to arms given in Lahore reached Rawalpindi by the evening of 3 March, and incited hectic activities in Muslim, Hindu and Sikh *mohallas*. Some brawls in the neighbourhoods took place on 4 March but the first clash in the centre of town took place on 5 March. The *Pakistan Times* of 10 March reported that a mob from Hazara district invaded the Murree hills and the bazaars of Jhikka Galli, Ghora Galli and Lower Topa. On 12 March it reported that incendiarism had occurred in Kahuta, Gujarkhan and Mandra areas. Further, that trouble had spread to Fatehjung, Hassanabdal and Cambellpur. *The Tribune* of 7 March took up the clashes in Rawalpindi and then reported almost daily till about 14 March, that mob raids had engulfed many areas outside Rawalpindi city and its suburbs. The district administration in March 1947 was headed by Deputy Commissioner C.L. Coates, OBE.

Ahmad Salim and I spent several days in Rawalpindi city and district in December 2004 talking to a cross section of people who were witness to the events of March 1947. Among them was the veteran educationist Khawaja Masud, a *tonga*-driver, two shopkeepers and two Sikhs whom I had met earlier in March 2004 in Delhi. Another interviewee was a Khaksar activist in March 1947, whom I met in London in May 2002 at the World Punjabi Conference.

Khawaja Masud Ahmed

'I was a young, newly-married lecturer of mathematics in Gordon College in 1947. On 5 March Hindu–Sikh and Muslim mobs clashed in the centre of town. The principal, Dr Stuart (an American), went in the evening to see the Deputy Commissioner Mr C.L. Coates, who refused to see him. Dr Stuart came back very worried and told the staff that the government was not willing to help. The next day, an RSS activist went around shouting that this time Holi [6 March 1947 was the day of the Hindu festival of colours] would be a *khooni* (bloody) Holi. I came out from the college and found Muslims on one side of the Murree Road and Hindus and Sikhs on the other. Both sides were armed with spears and long knives. They were shouting provocative slogans, but since I was a college teacher and was known to them, nobody harassed me. I walked between them and came to the office of the Communist Party. Comrade Gurbaksh Singh and others chided me for not being careful.

Later, Gurbaksh escorted me home. For a number of days we had no food at home because the shops had closed and people preferred to remain indoors. Comrade Vishwanath Sehgal, who belonged to one of the richest Hindu families of Rawalpindi, would bring food for both of us from his home.

'On 5–6 March, suddenly loose pages of the Quran were found strewn all over the town. A Khaksar collected them and put them in a well. This happened just outside the college. He had good friends among Hindus and Sikhs. So, he went into a Hindu–Sikh *mohalla*. A loud shriek was heard. Somebody had stabbed him. He was found lying dead in a pool of blood. There is no doubt that the RSS was behind that heinous crime. It triggered rioting, arson, looting and stabbings which took place in many parts of the town. The only exceptions were the cantonment areas, where the upper-class people had their residences.

'Although Rawalpindi was politically a lively place, violence among communities was rare. Elders of all the communities had good relations with one another and their influence and goodwill sufficed to maintain normal relations among people. Gordon College was a haven of cultural and intellectual diversity. Intellectuals, academics, journalists and other socially-aware people assembled every day in the college canteen and spirited discussions used to take place. Supporters of all the main political parties would be present, but since they knew each other well, no acrimony was involved in the exchange of views. Also, the college was truly multi-religious. Both faculty and students belonged to different religions. Quite a few Hindu, Muslim and Sikh students lived in the college hostel. I was a member of the Communist Party. In 1946 the famous Indian actor, Balraj Sahni, who hailed from Rawalpindi but was living in Bombay, visited his hometown. He was very impressed by our activities. He himself was a Marxist. We believed India would be independent soon and we would chart out a progressive future for our people. Not even after the March 1947 riots did we believe that India will be partitioned.'

Sheikh Noor Din

'I have been a *tonga*-driver all my life. Violence broke out when the Sikhs organised a procession shouting anti-Pakistan slogans. Rawalpindi's strongman Chaudhry Maula's son told the Sikhs to stop using provocative language, but they would not listen. A scuffle took place. A Sikh attacked him with a *kirpan* and inflicted a deep wound on his thigh. When Chaudhry Maula learnt what had happened he came quickly to the spot with his men. Thereafter for several days riots took place. Many people died or were injured. There was considerable loss of property as well as looting and arson. I have no idea which side lost most, but the Sikhs were definitely better armed and fired guns.

'Later, of course the non-Muslims had to flee from here but in the beginning the contest was even-handed. I have lived all my life in Rawalpindi working as a *tonga*-driver. Before the rioting of 1947, this place had a very large Hindu and Sikh population. They were generally good and kind people. One family of Dutt Brahmins always rode in my *tonga* and the lady of the house called me her brother. They always gave me presents at the time of Hindu as well as Muslim festivals.'

Sheikh Muhammad Ishaq

'My ancestors converted to Islam from the Thapar sub-caste of Aroras some generations earlier. We had a shop in the city centre in 1947. Our business connections were spread all over the Punjab and my father and I would travel to the eastern districts to collect merchandise for our retail shop. Until the 1946 election there was no real political activity in this town. The Unionist Party was the main party, while the Congress party was the stronghold of anti-British elements. The Khaksars and Ahrars were also active. The Communists were a small group. The RSS had some presence as well. The Muslim League gained a foothold some time in 1945–46 when the elections were held.

'Trouble broke out in the evening of the 4th though mostly in the form of slogan mongering. The first clash took place on the 5th when a Sikh–Hindu procession clashed with Muslim League supporters. Thursday, 6 March, coincided with the Hindu festival of Holi. Instead of the general festivities, the trouble from the previous day continued and firing took place on Nehru Road [now called Ghaznavi Road]. Both sides fired upon each other. There were incidents elsewhere too. Sikhs and Hindus fired on some Muslims in Kartarpura. It resulted in some deaths. On the other hand, in Ratta some Sikhs were killed and in Dhok they were forcibly converted and their hair and beards shaved. Some of them who resisted were killed by Muslim mobs. On the other hand, in Bagh Sardaran, which was a Sikh stronghold, the Muslims were subjected to terrible atrocities. The Sikhs used guns and *kirpans*. Fighting in Rawalpindi was essentially between Muslims and Sikhs. It was, however, in the villages around Rawalpindi that non-Muslims were treated most brutally. Some of them escaped and came to Rawalpindi. That is when we learnt about their ordeal.'

Haji Sher Ahmed

'On 5 March, our Sikh neighbours warned us not to open our shop here in Raja Bazaar because trouble could be expected as some members of their community were planning to hit back if the Muslims resorted to violence. On 6 March the clashes were more serious. The Muslims fired gunshots from inside the Jama-i-Masjid and Sikhs fired from the opposite side of the road. Some deaths occurred. It is true that Sikhs and Hindus were forced to convert to Islam in some localities such as Dhok. Their beards and locks were forcibly shaved. Some Sikhs committed suicide because they could not bear the shame of having their religious symbols desecrated. Most of the rioting subsided quickly, but in villages outside Rawalpindi the level of violence was much greater. Many Hindus and Sikhs ran away from the villages and came to Rawalpindi. Their situation was pitiable indeed. Treating them in that way was not consistent with true Islamic teachings.'

Rashid Nisar

'The trouble in Rawalpindi started with slogan-mongering by both sides. On 6 March, a peace committee was formed by the elders of all communities in Lal Kurti, a *mohalla* of Rawalpindi. However, one of the Muslim members of the committee, Sheikh Barkat, proved to be treacherous. A meeting was held on 7 March in the sitting room of Sheikh Barkat. When the Hindu and Sikh members arrived, they were viciously attacked and Sunder Singh *halvai* (maker of sweets) tried to escape but he was pursued by a mob carrying hatchets and axes. He sought refuge in the local mosque and declared his intention to become a Muslim and recite the *kalima*. However, the mob threw him on the floor near the spot where worshippers perform their ablutions before prayers. Then they hacked him to pieces with hatchets and long knives. They pulled out his tongue, shaved his beard and dragged his dead body out of the mosque. His blood mingled in the water around the ablution pond. As his corpse was dragged out in the street, a thick brownish paste was formed because of blood mixing with dust. It was a ghastly sight. To this day I remember that outrage. The police were in the know about the meeting and it seems they were aware of a plan to kill the non-Muslims. Therefore, instead of intervening to help the victims, they saw to it that the killers finished off their job without any obstruction.

'A Sikh family who were our neighbours took refuge in our house. A crowd gathered outside and wanted us to surrender them, but we refused. My family belonged to the Khaksar movement. Our leader Ashraf Khan had taken a vow from us that we would do all we could to protect whosoever was in distress. Therefore, the Khaksars were always in the forefront and saved many non-Muslims. This we did in spite of the fact that a Khaksar had been murdered in a Hindu *mohalla* on 5 March. Most probably the RSS was behind that gruesome murder, but we kept the pledge we had given our leader and put our own lives at risk to help people in distress. We continued rendering such services even after the Punjab had been divided. Some Hindus and Sikhs were still in Rawalpindi after Partition. We escorted them to the refugee camps. Our activities were confined to the city. Whatever happened in the villages was beyond our reach.'

Harkishen Singh Mehta

'We are from village Kontrila, *tahsil* Gujjar Khan, but had shifted to Rawalpindi when I was small. We lived in the street known as Mai Veero di Bani, near the Khalsa High School. Our house was actually built in March 1947. It was an exclusively Hindu–Sikh area. I remember, guns were used in the March riots by both sides. The real killings took place in the villages around Rawalpindi. I remember that refugees from

Hazara had been given shelter in our locality. My father was a Travelling Ticket Examiner in the railways. A Muslim tribal chief, Gullu, saved his life as he was surrounded by a mob who wanted to shave his hair. Gullu brought him to Rawalpindi. He was the chief of an armed tribe of Mianwali. We shifted to Delhi in June.'

Amar Singh

'The news of Master Tara Singh's speech outside the Punjab Assembly reached Rawalpindi the same day and tension began to rise from the evening. 5 March was the first day of open clashes between Hindu–Sikh demonstrators, on the one hand, and Muslims on the other. Hindu–Sikh demonstrators who were shouting slogans against the formation of a Muslim League government in the Punjab were challenged by Chaudhri Maula's son. In the first clash the Sikhs and Hindus suffered heavy losses, but from the evening of the 6th we had put the Muslims on the run. We fought back with great courage. In one case, the Sikh owners of Eros Cinema shot dead more than thirty Muslims. Elsewhere too, the Muslims were repulsed. We had a strong presence in the city.

'A Hindu who worked in the police told me that he overheard some Muslim colleagues saying that the British had given them three days to do whatever they wanted against non-Muslims. However, our side had guns and ammunition and the Muslims had to pay dearly with their lives for fomenting riots. When they could not win the battle in the town they turned their wrath towards the villages. In the rural areas, the Sikhs and Hindus were badly outnumbered. Therefore in those assaults, massacres of Sikhs and Hindus took place. I must, however, pay tribute to the Khaksars, especially their leader, Ashraf Khan. He and his comrades saved many Sikhs and Hindus. However, they were an exception. The Muslim League *goondas* showed no mercy to completely helpless people in the villages.

'I must admit that the Muslims ultimately paid a very heavy price for the crimes they committed against the Sikhs in Rawalpindi. I myself participated in attacks on Muslims all over East Punjab after mid-August 1947. Please don't ask me for details, but we felt justified in taking revenge because the Muslims had behaved like beasts against our people.'

Madanlal Singh

'6 March was definitely the day when Rawalpindi became the venue of bloody rioting. An exchange of gunfire between Sikhs and Muslims near the Kalyan Das Mandir resulted in heavy casualties on both sides. The Sikhs were in a good position to defend themselves in the city and in fact proved that they were better fighters. The leaders of the Muslim miscreants were Chaudhry Maula and his brother Chaudhry Haqqa. The Sikhs had set up prize money of fifty thousand rupees for their heads and they had announced the same for the head of any Sikh leader. It is true that the Khaksars did whatever they could to prevent loss of life, but the Muslim police remained passive, and only when the military was deployed did things come under control.

'When trouble started in Rawalpindi the Sikhs started making bombs in a secret place near a Muslim shrine. Baba Gurbaksh Singh, an accomplice of the legendary freedom fighter, Bhagat Singh, was involved in that activity. One day a device exploded while Gurbaksh Singh was working on it. His stomach burst open and his intestines were flung out. He was in great pain, but did not want to be arrested by the police. He asked my father, Ram Singh, to kill him, but Father could not summon the nerve to do that. So, Gurbaksh Singh thrust his *kirpan* into his own chest and died.'

The SGPC report gives a vivid account of the Sikhs' upper hand at the beginning of the violent contest in Rawalpindi city:

> On March 5 1947, on hearing of the firing on the Hindu and Sikh students in Lahore, the Hindu and Sikh students of Rawalpindi took out a procession protesting against the Muslim attempt at the formation of a communal (Muslim League) Ministry in the Punjab, and the police firing on the non-violent procession of Hindu and Sikh students. This procession was attacked by Muslim Leaguers. There was a free fight in which the Muslims got the worst of it. Then a huge Muslim mob from the countryside, incited by the Pir of Golra, a Muslim religious head and a leader of this area, fell upon the town. But the Hindus and Sikhs fought them back from their *mohallas* in trenches, and the Muslims again lost this battle (p. 78).

Attack on villages

The situation outside the city was almost entirely in favour of the Muslims. For example, *The Tribune* of 9 March reported that a train was stopped at Taxila Railway Station by Muslim marauders on 7 March. They killed twenty-two Hindu and Sikhs. The same incident is mentioned in the SGPC report (1991: 86). A police report also mentions the attack on the train (1995: 87). Thus, a 'balanced contest' in Rawalpindi city turned virtually into a one-sided assault on Sikhs and Hindus in the villages of Rawalpindi, Campbellpur (renamed Attock) and Jhelum districts. It is generally acknowledged that the attack on Sikh villages created the chasm between Muslims and Sikhs which could not be closed, notwithstanding the vicissitudes that followed in the weeks and months ahead.

Justice Munir's remarks on Rawalpindi rioting

Justice Muhammad Munir, who represented the Muslim League on the Punjab Boundary Commission and later served as Chief Justice of the Pakistan Supreme Court, had the following to say about the riots in Rawalpindi in his book, *From Jinnah to Zia*:

> The disturbances broke out in March, 1947 in the District of Rawalpindi and the adjoining areas and the Muslims were the aggressors. I spoke to the Quaid-i-Azam [Jinnah] about this telling him that it was a bad augur and he should either go himself to Pindi or send some responsible member of the Muslim League to assure the minorities that in Pakistan, if it ever were established, they will have equal rights with the Muslims as free citizens of the new States. He agreed with me and though it was before the scheme of 5th of June, 1947 [*sic.* – should be June 3rd] was announced or before Partition was decided upon, he replied in a bold and confident manner, 'Let me get into the saddle and you will not hear any nonsense of the kind.' However, he ordered Mamdot to go there personally for the purpose. After the Rawalpindi disturbances, the Sikhs started preparing a plan called the Sikh Plan, with the cooperation of the

Hindus, to exterminate the Muslims in the Punjab (1980: 17). It is to be noted that neither Jinnah nor any other leading Muslim Leaguer issued a public statement condemning the atrocities in Rawalpindi. I have checked the main English-language newspapers, the *Pakistan Times* and *The Tribune* and found no statement by any Muslim Leader on the Rawalpindi riots. In the *Jinnah Papers* as well there is nothing on the Rawalpindi riots. No Punjab-level leader of the Muslim League either issued a condemnation. In the long run such apathy was never forgotten by the Sikhs and later initiatives to develop friendly relations between the two communities failed – a basic distrust had taken deep root. Major General (retd) Shahid Hamid deplored that fact many months later. On September 13, 1947, when the slaughter of Muslims in East Punjab was at its worst he said, 'The Sikhs have sworn to kill every Muslim in India in revenge for the killings in Rawalpindi' (Hamid 1986: 248).

The Khosla, SGPC, and other reports

The heavy loss of life of Sikhs in the Rawalpindi district and surrounding areas is very well recorded in the SGPC and Khosla reports. The SGPC report gives a figure of at least 7,000 dead while Khosla mentions 2,000 as was given in the government estimates. Gyandra Pandey mentions that already by the end of April some 80,000 Hindu and Sikh refugees, especially from Rawalpindi division, had sought shelter in central and eastern Punjab and even beyond in Delhi and UP (2001: 24). He also informs that he saw copies of three First Investigation Reports (FIRs) registered with the police about violent attacks by Muslims in the Hindu Mahasabha papers. Those reports refer to atrocities committed in the villages Mughal, Bewal and Bassali of Rawalpindi district. Hundreds were killed, including the old and infirm, and children. Names of the victims are given and, in some cases, those of local men who joined the raiders are also mentioned (ibid.: 74-9). A collection of photos in booklet form entitled *The Rape of Rawalpindi* was published by a committee consisting of Hindus and Sikhs, in which the cruelty is amply displayed. The government immediately stopped its circulation, as it was feared it would incite reprisals in eastern Punjab against Muslims.

The fact that Sikhs themselves beheaded, shot dead or set ablaze their women and children in large numbers is mentioned in neither the SGPS nor Khosla reports. Would the Muslims have spared them if they had fallen into their hands without forcibly converting them? This is, of course, a moot point. In any case, the fact that in Rawalpindi the initial clash was provoked by the Hindu–Sikh protestors on 5 March 1947 is not mentioned in these two reports. A team of the All India Congress Committee arrived in the affected areas and collected material. It noted the following:

> These were not riots but deliberately organised military campaigns. Long before the disturbances broke out secret meetings were held in mosques under the leadership of Syed Akbar Khan [Shah?] ex-MLA, Captain Lal Khan of Kahuta, Tehsildar and Police Sub Inspector Kahuta, Maulvi Abdul Rehman and Kala Khan MLA in which jihad (an Islamic war) was proclaimed against the minorities and emissaries where sent out to collect volunteers from the rural areas.... The armed crowd which attacked Kahuta, Thoa Khalsa, and Nara etc. were led by ex-military men on horseback... armed with Tommy guns, pistols, rifles, hand grenades, hatchets, petrol tins and even carried field glasses....
>
> The mobs were divided into (the four following categories): 1. Armed with fire arms; 2. Lock breakers; 3. Provided with Petrol and kerosene oil; 4. In charge of donkeys, camels etc. to carry away looted property....
>
> First of all minorities were disarmed with the help of local police and by giving assurances on oaths on holy Quran of peaceful intentions. After this had been done, the helpless and unarmed minorities were attacked. On their resistance having collapsed, lock breakers and looters came into action with their transport corps of mules, donkeys and camels. Then came the 'Mujahidins' with tins of petrol and kerosene oil and set fire to the looted shops and houses. Then there were Maulvis (Muslim religious leaders) with barbers to convert who somehow or other escaped slaughter and rape. The barbers shaved the hair and beards and circumcised the

> victims. Maulvis recited *kalmias* [*kalima*] (attestation of faith) and performed forcible marriage ceremonies. After this came the looters, including women and men. (quoted in Talbot, 2008: 425).

The attacks began on the evening of 6 March, when the Muslims turned away from the city because the Sikhs were heavily armed, and instead headed towards the nearby villages. Between 11–14 December 2004, Ahmad Salim and I visited some villages in the Rawalpindi district that were attacked in 1947. We avoided visiting Thoa Khalsa, whose story has been made unforgettable by Urvashi Butalia in her classic work, *The Other Side of Silence* (2000). Thoa Khalsa is located close to Kahuta, where the principal Pakistani nuclear enrichment plant is located. In *Freedom at Midnight,* Larry Collins and Dominique Lapierre depicted the agony of Kahuta – a rather large village of 2,000 Hindus and Sikhs and 1,500 Muslims – in the following words:

> A Muslim horde had descended on Kahuta like a wolf pack, setting fire to the houses in its Sikh and Hindu quarters with buckets of gasoline. In minutes the area was engulfed in fire and entire families, screaming pitifully for help, were consumed by the flames. Those who escaped were caught, tied together, soaked with gasoline and burned alive like torches. Totally out of control, the fire swept into the Moslem quarter and completed the destruction of Kahuta. A Few Hindu [and Sikh] women, yanked from their beds to be raped and converted to Islam, survived; others had broken away from their captors and hurled themselves back into the fire to perish with their families (1975: 139).

The area is out of bounds to foreigners, and the police and intelligence agencies have a strong presence there. Notwithstanding my Pakistani origins, as a Swedish citizen I thought it wise not to enter such a sensitive area. However, when we visited another village, Duberan, on the border with Azad Kashmir, where an almost complete extermination of the Sikh population took place, we found that it, too, had a very large presence of security agents and police. We thus decided not to conduct any interviews there.

The carnage at Thamali (Dhamali)

I was, however, very keen to visit Thamali (Dhamali a village in the Kahuta *tahsil* of pre-Partition Punjab). I had read about the slaughter there in the reports of Khosla and Talib. In March 2004, I met Moni Chadha, a retired Indian diplomat, at the India International Centre in Delhi. Moni told me the following story about his visit to Rawalpindi and Thamali:

'In 1983, I led an Indian delegation to a SAARC meeting in Islamabad. The visit brought me back to the places from where my immediate family had escaped during 1947. Many of my relatives were brutally murdered, but I had never forgotten those places where we once lived in peace and amity with Muslims. Fortunately, the then Counsellor in the Pakistan High Commission at Delhi, Riaz Khokhar, helped me get permission to visit my ancestral villages – Kullar, Thamali and Gujjar Khan. I was only a small boy in 1947, but setting foot on the same soil brought back so many memories.

'Wherever I went the people went out of the way to help. Their warmth was real and spontaneous. However, a car of the ISI followed me wherever I went, stopping wherever I did. When I stopped at the signboard that read "Thamali", and tried to take some pictures there, they got annoyed and objected, and asked if I had permission to visit this area. I showed them the paper issued by Mr Khokhar that authorised me to do so. They were disappointed, but thereafter did not bother me, though they kept trailing me. The incongruity between the attitude of the ordinary people and that of the functionaries of the state was most striking.

'In Kullar Syedan I was fortunate to meet an old man (he was ninety) who knew my family, remembered their names and showed me their houses in the village. He told me that the marauders who attacked the Sikhs had come from outside. He had tears in his eyes when I left some time later, and he embraced me.'

Later, during our conversation, Moni told me that a relative of his, Ranjit Singh Bhasin, survived the slaughter at Thamali. He offered to arrange for me to talk to him, provided I was willing to travel to Kapurthala, now in India's Punjab state, the former capital of the princely state of Kapurthala, where that elderly Sikh gentleman lived. I was leaving for Stockholm the next day, but expressed a strong desire to meet him on my next visit. Later, in December 2004, I was in Pakistan and then within a couple of weeks, also visited India. I decided to visit Thamali before talking to Mr Bhasin in Kapurthala.

We arrived at Thamali late in the afternoon of 14 December 2004. It was a rather large village with paved, narrow streets running through it. Both sides of the streets were dotted with brick houses that seemed to have been built a long time ago. We went to the village school to meet the headmaster, who had been informed about our visit by Dr Zulfikar, the government physician in that area, who was a relative of Ali Safdar, our main contact in Rawalpindi. Most of the current inhabitants of Thamali, we learned, were Muslim refugees from Kashmir who had been allotted property left behind by the Sikhs and Hindus. However, a few Muslim families from pre-Partition days still lived there. The headmaster very kindly arranged for us to talk to two gentlemen belonging to the pre-Partition Muslim families of Thamali.

Haji Sher Khan

'I was born in Thamali in 1931 and studied in this school. General Tikka Khan also studied here. In 1947, very few Muslims lived in Thamali, just three or four families, but we had a mosque. It was a big and prosperous village of some two thousand people, mostly Sikhs. It had tall multi-storeyed brick buildings and a big *gurdwara* in the centre. Relations between us and the Sikhs as well as with the few Hindus here were very friendly. We were poor and indebted. The Sikhs were very rich. The bazaar in the main street had many shops, including that of goldsmiths. Many people from the areas around this place would come and buy things from here.

'Outsiders began to collect around the village a few days earlier, but the massive attack took place on 12 or 13 March. By that time, several thousand people had surrounded the village. The raiders had many weapons but most of them carried long sticks and spears. The Sikhs were not armed heavily. They sought a peace deal with the attackers. The peace pact was brokered by Raja Muhammad Iqbal, father of General

Tikka Khan. It was written down and signed. It required that the non-Muslims should surrender their weapons and in return they would be given safe passage out of the village. Some Hindus and Sikhs even gave money and were allowed to leave. However, most Sikhs decided to stay put in the hope of the government sending some help.

'Despite the agreement, in the evening of the 12th a mob attacked the village. So, it was a breach of the agreement. Our house was in a side lane. We had stayed in the village because our relations with the Sikhs were very good. They all respected my father. One could hear gunfire and people were shouting slogans, while children and women were crying loudly. The Sikhs defended themselves for some time, but were overwhelmed by sheer numbers. Most of them lost their lives. Two Sikh boys came running towards our home and sought refuge. My father hid them. In the meanwhile, fire broke out in some parts of the village and also in the *gurdwara*. Many loud sounds, as if bombs were exploding, could be heard. The fight continued for the whole of the 12th.

'When the military arrived the next day, we handed over the boys to the soldiers. The soldiers were mostly Hindu Gurkhas. They wanted to kill us, but the Sikh boys said, "Don't kill them; they have saved our lives". Everything had been destroyed by the time the military arrived. The Sikhs had killed most of their women and children. There was a Sikh, Surat Singh, who had a very beautiful wife. A *goonda* from this area, Muhammad Sharif, captured her. He told her to become a Muslim and marry him, but she refused and said that she preferred to die instead. Sharif would not kill her, however, probably because she was so beautiful. When the military came, she left with the others. Some Sikhs and Hindus converted to Islam and stayed on but most left for India. No non-Muslim remained in Thamali after March 1947. I believe the worst attack took place in Thamali. In Kallar Syedan, which is only about two-three kilometres from here, perhaps one or two Sikhs were killed. Many years later, in 1962, the two Sikh boys whom my father, Wazir Khan, had saved visited the village wanting to meet him but he had died some years earlier. I was away at that time serving in the army. They gave some money to people who were staying at our place. It was surely a gesture recognising my father's kindness to them.'

Jan Dad Khan

'I was born in Thamali in 1933. It was a big village of about 2,500 to 3,000 people. Non-Muslims, mainly Sikhs and a few Hindus, were in a majority; only four Muslim families lived there. My family owned land and was not debt-ridden. The villages around Thamali were mainly populated by Muslims. The relations between us and the non-Muslims were friendly. The non-Muslims not only had shops, but some went around on horse cart and bicycles to the villages to sell merchandise. Some Sikhs held officer's rank in the army, others were in the police at the rank of deputy superintendent (DSP) and superintendent (SP). They lived in two- and three-storey brick buildings. Money lending was prevalent on an extensive scale. Many people bought things from them on *udhar* (loan). This way, many Muslims were indebted to them.

'I studied in this school, which was only a primary school in 1947. I would not claim that we were close friends, but our relations with Sikh boys were good. They were rich while we were poor. At Kallar Syedan they went to the Khalsa High School while we studied at the Government high school. We had some Hindus in our school too. I was in the 8th class in March when the trouble started. We had no idea what was happening. Most of our teachers were Hindus. They did not talk in the class about the Pakistan movement. They were good people.

'When the trouble started we ran away into the fields. The people who attacked were outsiders. We were afraid of both the attackers and the non-Muslims. We heard some slogans such as *Allah-ho-Akbar* (Allah is Great) being raised. The Sikhs did not have any weapons. They set fire to their property and killed their own women and children. Our village was the last one to be attacked in this area. I can't tell you the exact date when the raiders arrived.'

Ranjit Singh Bhasin

I interviewed Ranjit Singh Bhasin at his residence in Kapurthala during the late afternoon of 3 January 2005. Mr Bhasin owned a modest motor spare-parts business. He wore a long beard and other Sikh emblems. Before we interviewed him we visited Sultanpur Lodhi, a town some thirty kilometres from Kapurthala, because of a promise I gave to one of its former residents, Maulana Mujahid Al-Hussaini, to go and take some pictures for him from there. We returned two hours later when it had become quite dark. Mr Bhasin began his narrative in his native Pothohari-Punjabi:

'Thamali was a rather large, quiet village of some five hundred families. It was mainly populated by Sikhs of the Khatri castes such as Kandharis, Gandhis, Gujrals, Bhasins, Sahnis and some others. There were some Hindu Brahmins too and three or four Muslim families. The *gurdwara* in the middle of the village was the central place where we congregated. The Thamali primary school was on the eastern outskirts of the village. I studied there up to the sixth class. Afterwards I went to school in Kalar [now called Kalar Syedan], which was only about 1-2 kilometres from Thamali. I either walked to school or sometimes rode on the back of a donkey. One never felt unsafe or insecure. I had a Muslim classfellow whose name was Nasiruddin Haider. I don't remember any other name now.

'We lived in peace and had excellent relations with Muslims. My grandfather owned considerable land, which he had inherited. It was not Muslim property under mortgage to us. We did not practise money-lending. My family served in the army and were awarded land in lieu of their services. The Muslims in this area used to sell goats and buffaloes. We had an orchard in which Muslims were employed to work.

'The first batch of raiders arrived around the village in the evening of 6 March. There was no warning, although we had heard that trouble had started in Rawalpindi a day or two earlier. The first attack on the village was from behind, from the north and not the road in the south. Initially only a few hundred took part in the assault but soon others joined them. Their numbers continued to swell all the time. They were beating drums and shouting "*Allah ho Akbar*". Some were on horses but most were on foot. Our elders took positions on the rooftops, giving the impression that we were well-armed, whereas in fact we had only three double-barrelled shotguns and almost no ammunition. The early attacks were mostly cases of brick-throwing which continued sporadically until the 12th when several thousand men encircled Thamali.

'In the meantime, efforts were afoot to reach some agreement that would terminate the hostilities. On the 12th, finally, an agreement was reached. My father, Subedar Diwan Pal Singh, had retired only six months before the riots. He and retired Superintendent of Police Bal Mukand, a Brahmin, represented our side. The Muslims had Subedar Lal Khan and some other notables representing them. The agreement was that if we surrendered our weapons they would escort us safely to village Pharawan from where we would be able to take the road to Poonch in Kashmir. During the negotiations, the raiders realised that we were poorly armed. So, against all moral and religious principles, the same evening a massive attack took place. Bal Mukand and some other Brahmins had already left for Lal Khan's village under a secret understanding. One Brahmin, Jagan Nath, was killed because he had a rifle and the Muslims had seen him firing at them. About 10–12 Sikhs from our village had gone to village Kaloha and were saved.

'The Sikhs decided not to surrender. Some of them even went out and fought in the fields, but it was clear that we were fighting a lost battle. The women were taken to the *gurdwara*. They brought along their valuable possessions. Then a fire was lit. It had been decided that we will not let the Muslims touch our womenfolk. My grandmother, mother and one of my sisters died in that fire. My brother's wife, her father, and her infant son and her daughter were also burnt to death. My father's uncle, his two sons and their wives and a dozen children from our extended family also died. For some reason my *bhabi* (brother's wife) sent me out of the *gurdwara*.

'My father fell fighting in the fields outside. Before the violence broke out some Muslims had offered to protect my father and our family provided we sought refuge with them, but my father refused saying that if you want to save us save the whole village. Some people remained in their homes and did not come to the *gurdwara*. Most of them were found by the attackers and brought out in the open field. I and some children were also driven out to that spot. By that time, it was early morning of 13 March. About fifteen–twenty of us were now assembled in an open field. It was mostly young men but some elderly men were also rounded up.

'The Muslims ordered us to chant loudly "Allah, Allah". There was a retired policeman, Ram Singh, who must have been seventy at that time. He was repeating loudly, "Allah, Allah" but a man hit him on his bald head with an axe. He fell to the ground. Then he struck me. I received the blow on my shoulder. I was hit again on the right side below my arm [Mr Bhasin lifted his shirt at this point and showed me his ghastly scars]. I fell to the ground bleeding profusely. I was in great pain but held my breath and said nothing. The attackers collected thorns from a *kikar* (Acacia Arabica) tree and put them on the bodies lying in the fields and started a fire. Someone said, "Why do you burn them? They had been chanting 'Allah, Allah'. Therefore they had changed their religion!" For some reason, that argument prevailed and the fire was quenched. This saved me and some others who were pretending to be dead.

'The army arrived at about 11.30 a.m. on the 13th. It had been in the area for some time, but remained passive. The soldiers shouted loudly to find out if someone was alive. A man answered, "Unless you remove the thorns how can we get up?" That they did. Altogether about twelve to fifteen of us were saved. The soldiers were Hindus; I don't remember seeing any Sikh among them. There were no Britishers among them. I and three of my sisters were saved. One of them was completely traumatised and became mad. Another had been burnt, but survived, while the third was saved by a Muslim who returned her one day later to my aunt's husband. One Sikh family that remained in their home and did not come to the *gurdwara* remained undetected and survived. A young woman whom a Muslim tried to abduct refused to go with him [Perhaps it is the same woman whom the *goonda* Muhammad Sharif tried to convert and marry]. When the army came she could also leave. She later settled in Lucknow. I have met her. I don't know if she is still alive.

'I was admitted to the cantonment hospital in Rawalpindi where my wounds were stitched and bandaged. After forty days we went back to Thamali, escorted by the army to perform the religious rites associated with cremation. We collected the bones and other parts of bodies that were still lying around and cremated them according to Sikh and Hindu rites. No local person was allowed to come close to us. We too had no wish to enter the village. Everything had been destroyed.

'Suddenly Thamali had become an alien and hostile place, with the exception of our cattle. Apparently they had been roaming around and nobody had taken care of them. They recognised us and would not leave even when the military tried to drive them away. After a while we were told to climb on to the trucks. As the vehicles started moving, the cows and buffaloes began to run alongside and would not abandon us. However, the trucks picked up speed and in a few minutes left the animals far behind. That is my last memory of Thamali.'

At this point, Mr Bhasin began to weep like a child. I let him be for some time, and then I asked him whether Thamali was still in his thoughts. He regained his composure and said:

'I have never wanted to go back. Our family was nearly wiped out; those who survived never overcame the shock and pain of those days. However, in my dreams Thamali keeps coming back, as if a phantom does not want to leave me alone as long as I live. Every year in March I arrange the religious ceremony of *phhat* to commemorate the death anniversary of my family members. Those few who survived from our village went to Delhi and settled in the locality of Bhogal. I have no contact with them. One thing more, people have often wondered why the Sikhs and Hindus of Kallar were saved. I learnt from some elders that the police officer in charge at Kallar was not on duty. His assistant, a *havaldar* (head constable), was not party to the conspiracy. He fired some shots above the heads of the mob, who ran away. Only a *kolu* (oil-extracting press) was set on fire.

'I served in the Indian Army for twenty-eight years in the Border Security Force. After retirement I settled in Kapurthala. I had three sons and three daughters. One son died when he was only 21. You want me to tell you my theory as to why the Sikh villages were allowed to be attacked for a whole week before the military arrived and stopped the slaughter? My hunch is that the whole problem of 1947 was created by the British. How can you explain the fact that it took so long for the troops to arrive in the affected villages when they were only an hour or two away from the military headquarters in Rawalpindi?'

'Allah, Allah' or the complete kalima?

After my interview with Mr Bhasin, I requested clarification from him if he and other survivors were made to chant only 'Allah' or the complete formula *'La Ilaha Il-lilah Muhammad ur Rasul Allah'* (There is no God but Allah and Muhammad is Allah's messenger) to declare conversion to Islam. He was absolutely certain that they only wanted the victims to recite 'Allah' all the time. It has been noted by many researchers that in the countryside, profession of the Islamic faith does not mean proper knowledge of even rudimentary Islam, and the fact that the raiders were unsure if the dead bodies could be burnt only confirms the suspicion that they did not really know how to handle such a situation in a proper Islamic manner.

Choa Khalsa rioting

The second hamlet that we visited was Choa Khalsa, where we recorded some interviews with Muslims who lived there in 1947:

Syed Nazir Hussain Shah

'Choa Khalsa was a big and prosperous village of some 3,000 in 1947. As elsewhere in Rawalpindi, Muslims were poor while Sikhs and Hindus were rich and controlled the business. There were an equal number of Hindus and Sikhs. Some of them were prominent people with high positions in the military and civil administration. Although one did not normally visit each other's homes, some families were very close to each other. The non-Muslims, especially Hindus, showed great respect for Muharram. The Hindus and Sikhs celebrated their holy days with great zeal. I particularly remember the festival of Ram Lila, in which we also participated. Choa Khalsa was a very peaceful place.

'I was in the Indian Army in March 1947. What I am telling you was narrated to me by my wife and brothers. The attackers were Muslims from the villages around Choa Khalsa. The headmaster of the village school, Thakhur Das Puri, BA, BT, was a saintly person. There would hardly be any Muslim who did not hold him in great reverence. He had great affection for all pupils. He used to help Hindu, Muslim and Sikh students without prejudice. Unfortunately the raiders treated him brutally, but he was saved by a Muslim teacher, Master Sher Zaman, and could later safely leave for India. When the trouble started the Sikh shopkeepers gathered their families in high buildings. The women and children were killed or thrown into the fire. Those who did not do so were killed by the attackers. One or two Sikh and Hindu families became Muslims. They live in the village of Khanada, which is nearby. The Muslims who took part in the attack were of the "wild" type. They just wanted to loot the wealth of the non-Muslims. There was nothing in their conduct which reflected Islamic piety and kindness.'

Raja Muhammad Riasat

'I am the Nazim (chairperson) of the Union Council of Choa Khalsa. In March 1947, Hindus and Sikhs exceeded the population of Muslims in Choa Khalsa but the villages around were inhabited by Muslims. The Hindu and Sikh *mohallas* were separate from those of Muslims. Yet, there was never any enmity or hostility. The elders of the three communities were respected by everyone and people listened to their advice and took guidance from them. There were three or four *mandirs* and the same number of *gurdwaras* and mosques. The town had about three to four thousand inhabitants. At the time of weddings or bereavement all the communities participated, although the Sikhs and Hindus did not eat with us. The Muslims were poor. Because of lavish spending on weddings and other celebrations the Muslims were indebted to the Hindus and Sikhs who charged compound interest. This way the non-Muslims began to acquire Muslim land. The Unionist minister Sir Chhotu Ram introduced reforms that stopped the transfer of land, but Hindus and Sikhs would use Muslim front-men to buy land. After Partition our lands were not returned to us: they were given to refugees from Kashmir and East Punjab.

'On 6 or 7 March the first batch of Muslims started attacking Choa Khalsa. Some Hindus and Sikhs were killed, but mainly the attackers wanted to loot shops. The result was that community leaders met at the main mosque and agreed that they will not attack each other. However, on the 12th or 13th another mob of Muslims came. They were so large in numbers that they overwhelmed us. The non-Muslims were given a choice to convert to Islam or die. The Sikhs in particular refused to become Muslims. Two Sikh brothers who were prominent among their community began to kill their womenfolk and children and throw them into the fire. One of them was called Balwant Singh. Both brothers died ultimately, but the son of Balwant Singh survived and later could leave safely. I believe some 150 Sikhs died. I remember seeing smouldering bodies with their heads severed.

'I, my father, grandfather and some others went to see what was happening in the centre. We saw in one house the charred body of a Sikh teacher. His name was probably Ranjit Singh. I saw other corpses too. My grandfather, who was a *zaildar*, and my uncle went to one of the main trouble-spots to prevent rioting, but soldiers of the Gurkha regiment who had arrived fired upon them. Grandfather's arm was blown off while my uncle died. Among Hindus the loss of life was less, around ten only. Two hundred or more shifted to Mohra Hira, a locality nearby. They had expressed the desire to become Muslims. However, when the army came they decided to leave. Some others were protected by Muslims.

'Of all those who suffered, the humiliation meted out to my beloved teacher Master Thakur Das Puri was the most shameful. The attackers threw him to the ground and kicked him, but Master Sher Zaman saved him. Master Thakur Das Sahib was a very kind and noble soul. There was hardly any Muslim student who did not receive his help. I still think about him sometimes. I know he reached India safely.'

At this point, tears began to roll down Raja Muhammad Riasat's cheeks. He then continued:

'I became a schoolteacher and taught in the same school later for twenty-five years. Some Hindus and Sikhs did visit Choa Khalsa later. Some used to write to my father. A Hindu doctor, who was just a child in 1947, visited some years ago and met my father. I also met him. He was president of the Choa Khalsa Refugees Association in Delhi. He told us that the elders remembered their old *vatan* (homeland) and often discussed the old times with a great deal of nostalgia.'

Ahmad Salim and I visited Chak Beli Khan, a village of Muslim Rajputs, on 11 December 2004. Two days later we visited Parial village in Attock district as well.

Ameer Khan

'In March 1947 there were equal numbers of Muslims and Sikhs in the village. The Muslims were all cultivators. A few Hindus in Chak Beli Khan were jewellers. Some Sikhs were small cultivators but most of them were traders and moneylenders. Most shops were owned by Sikhs. They had big shops. Muslim land was mortgaged to the Sikhs. The reason was that the expenditure of farmers is always greater than their income. The Sikhs on the other hand were thrifty. The bigger the Muslim landowner the greater his debt to the Sikh moneylenders. Our father had mortgaged 8 kanals (roughly 505 sq metres per kanal) of land to the Sikhs but Sir Chhotu Ram introduced a law which required that if the land had been kept for a certain amount of time then it had to be returned to the original owners. That is how we got our land back. The Hindus were poor people in our villages; all the *seths* (businessmen) were Sikhs. We had no enmity towards them, instead there was a lot of goodwill and a sense of brotherhood prevailed. The Sikhs who kept the land of Muslims would serve them and do many services so that they would not turn against them. Because of religious differences, we did not eat together, but they would send uncooked food to Muslims. Sikhs and Hindus took water from one well and Muslims from another. There were only two wells in the village. We did not make a fuss about that. Most of the people here sought service in the army, a few Sikhs and even fewer Hindus from here were in the army. I was in the wireless service in the army. We had Hindus, Sikhs and Muslims in the same unit.

'It all started with rumours. I still, to this day, cannot figure out who spread the rumours. The rumour was that Sikhs had gathered in some place and were attacking Muslims. When this rumour reached us, the Muslims started attacking Sikhs and Hindus. Some Muslims gave protection to them. The men left while the women were left behind with trustworthy friends. After the creation of Pakistan they came back along with the Pakistani and Indian Army and took them back. Those women were not molested. There was no killing here. My father Chaudhri Beli Khan and his brother Chaudhri Mahboob Khan, Ali Safdar's father [our contact in the village], saved many Sikhs and Hindus. They also saw to it that the houses were not destroyed. So no attacks took place, but during the night Sikh shops were looted.'

Haji Muhammad Hanif

'I was in the fourth class. I had gone to Fatehjang, district Attock along with my uncle who was a school teacher to take part in the scholarship exam. After the exam we came back in the afternoon to Rawalpindi, it was probably beginning of March. In those days only one bus left from Liaqat Bagh for our village at 12 noon. When trouble had started in our village the Sikhs and Hindus were gathered in a big building. People were carrying spears and knives and big sticks, the shops of non-Muslims were being looted. This happened here in Chak Beli Khan, but no killing took place. The shops were looted before the army came. The Sikhs and Hindus were told to accept Islam. I remember they were standing in a cue and were taken in small batches to the mosque where they were made to recite the *kalima*. Their hair and beards were shaved. When the military came they left. All the trouble was the result of rumours. There was Muslim League in this area. Perhaps they spread the rumours.'

In these two accounts from the same village we get different versions of what transpired in March 1947 in Chak Beli Khan. Both interviewees, however, said that no killing took place.

Parial

Haji Muhammad Sharif

'Rioting took place in Parial only when we heard that Muslims in East Punjab were being killed in the thousands [He had probably confused it with killings in Bihar in November 1946]. Babu Karam Singh was our teacher. He alone could read English. He was a great human being. One day during Ramazan, a man Bahadur Khan asked him, "Would you like to drink water or something?" Babu Karam Singh said, "O Bahadur Khan, you really dishonour me by saying that. I have never taken water during Ramazan even in my own home".

'The village elders had come to an agreement that if there was an attack on the village they woud all defend it together. Muslims from a neighbouring village came beating drums and with swords and spears wanted to attack our Sikhs and Hindus but we sent them back. Things got out of hand when Muslims from East Punjab arrived and told the local people about their suffering. Some people from our village who were in the army had recently been sent home. They were posted in Patna, Bihar, before that. Fazal Baig, Khan Muhammad, and Lala Shan Muhammad planned the operation. They had grenades and other ammunition with them. The Sikhs had stored ammunition in their *gurdwaras*. The Muslims decided to climb the mosque building and lob hand grenades into the *gurdwara* which was very close to the mosque. All the men were from our village.

'Before retiring from government service I worked in Sindh and noticed that in villages where Hindus were in a majority the low caste were treated very badly. If we offered a *bhil* (Hindu outcaste) tea or something he hesitated because of his low status. The real reason that Pakistan came into being was that the Hindu caste system degraded human beings while Islam stands for equality. Muslims and non-Muslims are two separate people. The Sikhs joined Hindus in inflicting great suffering on Muslims. It does not matter if my ancestors were Hindu Rajputs, the real difference is of faith.'

Faiz Zaman

'I was born in 1929. I served in the Pakistan Army all my life and after retirement came back to Parial. The man who threw the grenade into the *gurdwara* was Akbar Khan, who had left the army. When that happened I was attending the class of Babu Karam Singh. Akbar Khan shouted, *"Na'ara-e-Takbir, Allah ho Akbar"*. After that many others started shouting slogans. Then people started looting the property of the non-Muslims. Babu Karam Singh took me with him to his house. My maternal uncle and Babu Karam Singh were like real brothers. We used to eat at their place and they were also welcome to eat at ours. He told his daughters to accompany me to my uncle's house. The girls were young. I saw people were starting fires. The arsonists were not outsiders. They were from Parial. For two days the fires continued. I saw a young girl who was hiding in a pit. We told her to get out and recite the *kalima*. She refused. She set fire to herself. Babu Karam Singh was saved; his wife and daughters were saved. They stayed at my uncle's place. Nobody attacked them. The army came on the fourth day. When parting, Babu Karam Singh said to my uncle "You can take the money I have", but my uncle replied, "I called you my brother so how can I take your money?" He told Karam Singh, "You become a Muslim and I can assure you that nobody will harm you". He refused and then left. His wife and three daughters were saved.

'One Sikh remained behind. He converted to Islam. He died later at an advanced age. He used to loudly recite the *kalima*. Some of the Sikhs were very rich. Sewa Singh was one of them. When his daughter married my father gave ₹100 to her. The Sikhs used to give us clothes. Some of the Sikhs from this village and those around did come once or twice when visiting Punja Sahib at Hassan Abdal.

'Almost three hundred families were wiped out. Only a few individuals escaped. The Muslims were poor. They looted everything. Altogether some 1,000 or more people were killed. We never thought that we had done anything wrong. In our village they were in a minority, even when they were three hundred families. Pir Mukeem visited Parial before the attack took place. He came and said to our people, "You are doing nothing when Muslims are being killed by Sikhs and Hindus in East Punjab". That surely incited our people. His son, Pir Karam Shah, was later a member of the Islamic Ideology Council of Pakistan'.

It is worth noting that with regard to the timing of the slaugher in Parial, there is some confusion. It is possible that it took place in August rather than in March 1947, an impression I got while listening to both the interviewees quoted, as well as other elders who were present during our conversations.

Dr Jagdish Chander Sarin, whom I interviewed much earlier on 24 October 1999, when I first started collecting oral histories on the Punjab partition, was a volunteer at a camp set up in Jhelum to take care of the people displaced from their villages in the Rawalpindi division. This is what he told me:

'I was based in Lahore in March 1947. I volunteered along with two other doctors to go to camps set up outside Jhelum where survivors of the riots had been assembled. It was a piteous sight. I saw many maimed and disfigured people. In some cases, the mutilation had been carried out with exceptional barbarity. Even I, a pathologist, could not help being profoundly shaken. The assailants had chopped off the breasts of women and raped them many times. The men had also been subjected to bestial acts of disfiguring. Some children, even babies, had been pierced with sharp spear-like things and their bodies were waved in the air. Only a few among them survived. When I talked to some of the survivors, they said that the attackers had been indoctrinated by people who had come from UP and Bihar. The demobilised Muslim servicemen who had returned after serving at various fronts in the Second World War seemed to have planned the whole operation.'

Official reports on attacks in northern Punjab

Enclosure to No. 560
Note by General Messervy

SOME REMARKS ON THE DISTURBANCES IN THE NORTHERN PUNJAB

1. Causes

The first cause was politico-religious. The Muslim League, though a political party, has been framing its main propaganda on religious lines for some time. This has undoubtedly had a great effect on all Muslims in the Punjab. Pakistan and Islam together provide an almost irresistible force on the minds of the mass of comparatively uneducated Muslims. When the intensive Muslim League campaign succeeded in forcing the resignation of the Unionist Punjab Government and was followed by militant anti-Pakistan statements by Master Tara Singh and other Sikh leaders, Muslim feelings were roused to a pitch of fanaticism. It only needed a spark to set alight the raging fires of religious passion. This was provided by anti-Pakistan meetings and processions in such places as Lahore, Amritsar, Multan and Rawalpindi. In Multan the Hindu–Sikh processionists were even so madly unwise as to raise the cry of 'Qaid-e-Azam Murdabad'. In the predominantly Muslim areas of Rawalpindi and Multan divisions the fires spread rapidly to the rural areas.

There have been also two minor causes. The first is the economic element. Scarcity of cloth and some items of food, such as sugar, has undoubtedly been taken advantage of by the Hindu–Sikh bania community to profiteer and indulge in black-market operations. The Govt. controls were also mostly in the hands of Sikh or Hindu agents and clerks. The Muslim peasant and labourer was only too ready to get some of his own back when he got the chance. The second is the 'goonda' element in every community, which is always ready to take full advantage of such disturbances to practise arson, loot and dacoity.

2. The Course of the Disturbances

In the cities events followed the usual course, well known to us for many years, but attacks were fiercer, more sudden, and more savage than ever. In the rural areas attacks were launched by large mobs of Muslim peasants who banded together from several hamlets and villages to destroy and loot Sikhs and Hindu shops and houses in their area. In some areas arson and loot were the main objects, and casualties inflicted on the Hindu–Sikh community were not great. In others savagery was carried out to an extreme degree and men, women and children were hacked or beaten to death, if not burned in their houses. There were also a number of cases of forcible conversion of males and abduction of females. Having served for 34 years, mostly in the Punjab and with Punjab troops I would never have believed that agitation could have aroused the normally chivalrous and decent P.M. [Punjab Muslim] peasant to such frenzied savagery as was widely prevalent. Much of this savagery was undoubtedly deliberately intensified by the wildest rumours, the commonest of which was an impending attack by a large Sikh Army. It is interesting that on no occasion as far as is known has a second major attack been made on any village or area in a village. The passion of the mob burns itself out and the survivors are generally left unmolested. There has also been a widespread desire to rid many areas of all Sikhs and Hindus, entirely for ever. Some former sites of houses have even already been ploughed up.

3. Refugees in the Rawalpindi Division

Refugees in the Rawalpindi Division are likely to amount to some 40,000 homeless and largely destitute persons. This is a big problem. We are planning eventually to form camps to take the whole number at Wah and Kala (near Jhelum). Other refugees, who may amount to about an equal number will either be persuaded to return to their homes or be absorbed in other Sikh-Hindu communities in towns or large villages. Some 4,000 have already been absorbed in Rawalpindi City.

4. Prevention of Outbreaks in Other Districts of the Punjab

I have concentrated all available troops in the Punjab. Flag marches and patrols are being carried out widely wherever tension is greatest. But it must be clearly understood that such preventive action is only a palliative. We are dealing with the symptoms of disease and cannot eradicate the disease by military action. The disease comes from the political leaders of all parties. The only complete cure is for them to come to some agreement. An agreement now between the Sikh and Muslim leaders would result in immediate peace in the Punjab. Failing this unlikely contingency the avoidance of provocative statements and the impressing on their followers of the necessity of avoiding bloodshed and protecting minorities is the only hope.

F.W. Messervy (Lt. General)
General Officer Commander-in Chief, Northern Command

(It is to be noted that General Messervy later served as Pakistan's first commander-in-chief).

Jenkins' reports

The Punjab governor sent almost daily telegrams to Viceroy Wavell indicating that the conflicts in the rural areas were in a class by themselves, not comparable to anything that has previously taken place elsewhere in the Punjab in March 1947. Since his report on the Punjab riots is devoted mostly to Rawalpindi and is based largely on General Messervy's special report, quoted above, there is no point in repeating it here. Besides Lt. General Messervy, who was the GOC-in-C Northern Command headquartered at Rawalpindi, the Commissioner for Rawalpindi division was C. King, the Deputy Inspector General of Police was J.A. Scott, and the deputy commissioner was C.I. Coates. Jenkins was accompanied by the Inspector General of Police, Mr Bennett, when he met these officers in Rawalpindi on 9 March (Carter 2007a: 69-70). In a special report to Viceroy Mountbatten dated 16 April, Jenkins wrote that in one police station alone in Rawalpindi, as many as five hundred murder cases were registered during the March riots. In the same report he presented an estimate of 3,500 dead, though in mid-April the count stood below 3,000. He remarked:

> The communal proportions have not been accurately reported, but I should say that among the dead are 6 non-Muslims for every Muslim. Mr. Liaquat Ali Khan can hardly realise the terrible nature of the rural massacre. One of my troubles has been the extreme complacency of the League leaders in the Punjab, who say in effect that "boys are boys". I have no doubt that the non-Muslims were provocative in the cities, but the Muslims had been equally provocative during their agitation and had in particular murdered a Sikh constable in Amritsar (ibid.: 137).

Jenkins also mentioned that the Rawalpindi police chief, Mr J.A. Scott, publicly expressed his disgust during a press conference he gave on the riots in his district (ibid.: 138). Jenkins's FR dated 17 March provided further details of the March riots but the main emphasis is on the events in northern Punjab, in the Rawalpindi division. Some excerpts, but without the point numbers, are quoted below:

> At Rawalpindi, as in Lahore, the rioting seems to have followed the pattern of earlier communal riots. I have not been through Rawalpindi City, but from the air it does not appear that many buildings have been burnt. Causalities were fairly high.
> There is nothing special to note about the other cities and towns. Jullundur had the worst of lesser outbreaks, and Ludhiana probably came next.

In the rural areas gravely affected there has been extreme savagery. In the triangle Taxila-Murree-Gujar Khan there was regular butchery of non-Muslims, particularly Sikhs. Cruelty and treachery seem to have been common. General Messervy told me that he had seen in hospital a child whose hands had been cut off; there are at least two well-documented stories of non-Muslims being lured into "peace committees" and then murdered; in one village, Sasali, a party of Sikhs, who surrendered to the Muslim attackers on a promise that their lives would be spared, were murdered out of hand. The most brutal killings seem to have been in the triangle to which I have referred, but there has been frightful brutality outside it, and everywhere in the district looting and arson have been common.

In Attock, the Chauntra area which is very close to Rawalpindi, was affected in much the same way. In the rest of the district there seems to have been fewer killings than in Rawalpindi, but quite as much burning and looting. A common method of attack has been for the Muslims in a village to put white flags on their houses and to invite the Muslims of the neighbouring villages to come and deal with property not so marked.

In the Chakwal neighbourhood of the Jhelum district a large village, Dhudial, was sacked, but the police and troops were able to inflict fairly heavy casualties on the attackers.

In Multan, murder, arson and looting were much the same as in the districts of the Rawalpindi Division, but the area affected (the Sadar Police Station and part of the Shujabad tahsil) is relatively flat and easy to control. The troops seem to have inflicted fairly heavy casualties on a mob at an early stage, and the loss of life and property must have been heavy, but it is certainly less than that in the Rawalpindi district.

The affected districts of the Rawalpindi Division are now under the operational control of the 7th Indian Division (Major-General Lovett). By improvisation the Division now includes six Brigades with, I think, two independent forces. It is operating from Campbellpur and Rawalpindi in the north to the line Jhelum–Chakwak–Tallagang in the south, and is extending its operations southward into Shahpur and westward into Mianwali....

It is very difficult to account for this extraordinarily violent rural movement. General Messervy thinks that there are some signs of organisation and conspiracy – in parts of Rawalpindi outbreaks seem to have occurred almost simultaneously, and the raid at Murree, to which I referred in my letter of 9th March, appears to have been carefully planned and carried out. All Muslims in the affected districts seem to be involved in or sympathetic to the movement. The Commander 7th Division told me when I saw him yesterday that attacks on non-Muslims had been led in some cases by retired Army officers – some of them pensioners with honorary Commissioned rank. The Muslim section of the local notables, to whom I spoke at Campbellpur yesterday, were extremely sulky, and though some of them are beginning to be frightened, there is little doubt that they believe that the movement was inevitable and are not prepared to oppose it. The most probable theory is that the growth of the Pakistan idea from 1943 onwards, the extreme communalism of the election campaign of 1945-46, the frustration which followed it, the propaganda against the Coalition Ministry, the Muslim League's agitation, H.M.G.'s statement of 20th February, and Khizar's resignation combined to touch off an explosive mixture which had been forming for some time. The Muslims say that they were influenced by rumours of a large Sikh Army marching on the north; also that the movement is a spontaneous outburst against black-marketing by non-Muslims. It is more likely that they believe that by exterminating non-Muslims now they will make their districts a safe base for operations against the other communities in due course. No educated man could reasonably believe the story about the Sikh army, and though opportunity has been taken to wipe out economic scores, resentment at the controls and the way in which non-Muslims make money out of them was not in my judgment the immediate cause of the trouble.

The non-Muslims are vehemently bitter against the civil services and particularly against the police... There have also been complaints of partiality against troops – the Commander of the 7th Indian Division told the governor that one of the complaints was justified. Demands will now be made to transfer the Muslim officers from the riot-affected areas.

> Damage to property in Amritsar and Multan was exceptionally heavy... Legally I suppose the State is not liable for damage caused by civil commotion, and I do not think that in Section 93 I can do much more than see that damage is properly registered and leave it to a popular Ministry to decide what compensation, if any, should be given.
>
> When I was at Rawalpindi yesterday the total number of refugees was estimated at nearly 30,000 refugees, and we must be prepared to receive at least 35,000 or more from the Rawalpindi Division (ibid.: 85-90).

In the FR of 31 March, which was the first sent to Mountbatten, the governor said, among other things, the following:

> There are various rumblings below the surface, and there may be a recrudescence of serious trouble at any time. The Muslims are fatuously complacent. They say that they were not the aggressors; that Master Tara Singh set things off with his violent statements; and that even now the Sikhs are making a great parade of their *kirpans*, in respect of which they have an exemption on religious grounds. Some bad speeches are being made in the mosques, and intelligence reports suggest that some members at least of the Muslim League would be glad of further trouble.
>
> The Hindus and Sikhs are for the time being acting together. They realise, I think, that their speeches on 3rd March were injudicious; but they hold quite rightly that there was no justification for the general massacre in the Rawalpindi division. They are intent on a partition of the Punjab, and are not inclined for any reconciliation with the Muslims. (ibid.: 102).

References

Chandra, Prabodh (compiler). *Rape of Rawalpindi*, Lahore: The Punjab Riots Sufferers' Relief Committee, 1947.

Collins, Larry and Dominique Lapierre. *Freedom at Midnight*, New York: Avon Books, 1975.

Hamid, Shahid (Maj. Gen Retd). *Disastrous Twilight,* London: Lee Cooper, 1986.

Khosla, Gopal Das. *Stern Reckoning: A Survey of the Events Leading up to and Following the Partition of India,* New Delhi: Oxford University Press 1989.

Munir, Muhammad. *From Jinnah to Zia,* Lahore: Vanguard Books Ltd, 1980.

Pandey, Gayendra, *Remembering Partition,* Cambridge: Cambridge University Press, 2001.

Talib, S. Gurbachan. *Muslim League Attack on Sikhs and Hindus in the Punjab 1947,* New Delhi: Voice of India, 1991.

Talbot, Ian. 'The 1947 Partition of India' in Stone, Dan (ed), *The Historiography of Genocide,* Houndsmill, Basingstoke, Hampshire: Palgrave Macmillan, 2008.

Newspapers

Pakistan Times, Lahore, 1947.

The Tribune, Lahore, 1947.

Official documents

Carter, Lionel, (ed). *Punjab Politics, 3 March – 31 May 1947, At the Abyss, Governors' Fortnightly Reports and other Key Documents,* New Delhi: Manohar, 2007a.

Census of India, 1941, Volume 6, Punjab, Simla: Government of India Press, 1941.

Mansergh, Nicholas and Penderel Moon, (eds). *The Transfer of Power 1942-7, vol. XI, The Mountbatten Viceroyalty, Announcement and Reception of the 3 June Plan, 31 May-7 July 1947,* London: Her Majesty's Stationery Office 1982.

Interviews

Rashid Nisar, London, 18–19 May 2002

Amar Singh, Delhi, 14 March 2004

Madanlal Singh, Delhi, 14 March 2004

Harkishan Singh Mehta, 20 March 2004

Moni Chadha, New Delhi, 28 March 2004

Dr Jagdish Chander Sarin, Delhi, 24 October 2004

Ameer Khan, Chak Beli Khan, Rawalpindi district, 11 December 2004

Haji Muhammad Hanif, Chak Beli Khan, Rawalpindi district, 11 December 2004

Khawaja Masud Ahmed, Rawalpindi 12 December 2004

Sheikh Noor Din, Sheikh Noor Din, Rawalpindi, 12 December 2004

Haji Muhammad Sharif, Parial, Attock (Campbellpur) district, 13 December 2004

Faiz Zaman, Parial, Attock (Campbellpur) district, 13 December 2004

Raja Muhammad Riasat Khan, Chou Khalsa, Rawalpindi district, 14 December 2004

Haji Sher Khan, Thamali, Rawalpindi district, 14 December 2004

Jan Dad Khan, Thamali, Rawalpindi district, 14 December 2004

Syed Nazir Hussain, Choa Khalsa, 14 December 2004

Haji Sher Ahmed, Rawalpindi, 15 December 2004

Sheikh Muhammad Ishaq, Rawalpindi, 15 December 2004

Ranjit Singh Bhasin, Kapurthala, 3 January 2005

STAGE 2

The End Game Unfolds
24 March 1947–14 August 1947

INTRODUCTION

The second stage in the partition of the Punjab began with a change of viceroy in Delhi and ended with power being transferred to the Indian and Pakistani governments on 15 August 1947. With regard to the Punjab, it meant that it was also partitioned, giving birth to two separate provinces with two different administrations. During this period, violence gradually spread from Lahore and Amritsar to other towns and finally, to the rural areas.

The Mountbatten viceroyalty set in motion processes at the level of the state, which culminated in the partition of India. The chain of events at the level of the colonial state comprised interactions between the Punjab governor Sir Evan Jenkins and Viceroy Mountbatten, all-India and Punjab-level politicians and government commissions set up to implement the decisions pertaining to the Partition. At the ground level, the recrudescence of violence and its proliferation and intensification constituted a dynamic on its own, although both processes created an impact on each other and effected intended and unintended consequences.

Quite soon after he assumed the role of viceroy and governor-general, Mountbatten became convinced that India would have to be partitioned. His consultations and negotiations with Indian leaders sought to ensure that British strategic interests in South Asia were not adversely affected. During those discussions he dropped a bombshell: he announced to the Indian leaders that power would be transferred in mid-August 1947, and not in June 1948 as was originally planned. That decision of his remains the most controversial, but it was not the only one; upon his insistence the boundary award was announced a few days after, rather than before Pakistan and India declared themselves independent.

The assumption that the partition of the Punjab would not entail the physical movement of huge populations was totally unrealistic – the

Punjab governors had been warning that it would be violent. From April onwards it revived again, and by the second week of May, it began to worsen almost by the day. The intelligence agencies were reporting it and the Punjab governor passed on that information to Delhi through telegrams and longer reports. But it did not seem to worry Mountbatten. The administrative measures that were put in place, including the establishment of a Punjab Boundary Force, proved grossly inadequate. The Sikhs had been warning that they would not accept a partition scheme that did not comply with their demands. The Muslim leaders remained complacent because in most encounters, their ethnic activists and criminal elements enjoyed the upper hand. The Hindus were mainly shopkeepers and traders who shunned violence. The exceptions were the RSS and Hindus of the Hindi-speaking areas of eastern Punjab where they constituted a peasantry that was prone to violence and resorted to it as well.

With regard to the Punjab, from April to the end of June, it was mainly in Lahore and Amritsar that violence and terrorism persisted. On the whole, the situation remained volatile and explosive though an uneasy peace prevailed in much of the province. However, as long as Jenkins remained in power, the façade of a structure of authority continued to be observed. It constrained both biased officialdom as well as the armed men who went around looking for targets to attack. Consequently, the death count remained small, a few thousands according to official statistics. Such statistics were in all probability low. Movement of Hindus and Sikhs eastwards from the Muslim-majority districts in northern and western Punjab continued throughout April to mid-August and hundreds of thousands crossed over to safer havens in Hindu–Sikh areas. On the other hand, significant movement of Muslims from eastern Punjab in the other direction started only in the second week of August. The reason was that for most of this time the attacks were taking place in Muslim-majority areas. It is also worth noting that the Punjab countryside remained largely unaffected and most crimes that took place were in the cities and towns. The bulk of the population, however, decided to stay put.

Thus, although fear and angst had been multiplying, the people were not willing to leave as long as state authority was not perceived to be totally partisan and hostile.

10

BRITISH POLICY ON THE PUNJAB: 24 MARCH–30 JUNE 1947

ON 24 MARCH, LORD LOUIS MOUNTBATTEN WAS SWORN IN AS THE new Governor-General and Viceroy of India. He had been given a definite brief to bring about the transfer of power from British to Indian hands in a united or divided India by June 1948. Undoubtedly, the most difficult and delicate task ahead was finding a solution to the Punjab problem, where the Sikhs, though comprising only 13.2 per cent of the population, were an important and powerful community. They were substantially represented in the Indian Army and strongly entrenched in the agricultural sector (especially the canal colonies in western Punjab). Moreover, in Rawalpindi city and district, they predominated as moneylenders and held considerable property.

Jenkins on the Sikhs

In a top-secret, undated note on the Sikhs [probably written in early April] to the viceroy, Punjab Governor Jenkins provided a historical sketch of Sikh politics from the early twentieth century, including the formation of the SGPC in the wake of a movement to bring all *gurdwaras* under the control of orthodox Sikhs. The Shirmoni Akali Dal, which was founded as a militant group, had over the years become a populist political party. Jenkins went on to describe the preparations of the Sikhs for an eventual showdown with the Muslims. Such measures included establishment of *jathas* (organised bands of Sikh volunteers, usually on horseback, willing to fight for the community). Hundreds of *jathas* had been established. The Sikhs were aiming for the establishment of their own state after the British had departed. While blaming Master Tara Singh for making an inflammatory speech on 3 March in Lahore, the governor reiterated a point he made earlier, which proved decisive in obstructing reconciliation between the Sikhs and Muslims:

> Unfortunately the Muslims, especially in the Rawalpindi Division, seem to have made a dead set at the Sikhs, and there is no doubt that the Sikh leaders are preparing for retaliation. It is known that they have been in touch with the Rulers of the Sikh States, and a few days ago Giani Kartar Singh addressed a meeting of 300 Jathedars (heads of the *jathas*) and instructed them to make preparations for the defence of the community (Carter 2007a: 111).

Jenkins noted that factionalism was rampant among the Sikhs. Although Master Tara Singh and Baldev Singh (defence minister in the central interim government) were the most important among them, the governor identified three main groupings: mainstream Akali Sikhs led by Master Tara Singh (non-agriculturist) and Giani Kartar Singh (agriculturist). The governor noted, 'Until the recent disturbances Kartar Singh had been inclined to favour an alliance between the Sikhs and the Muslims' (Carter, 2007a: 111). Then, there was a minor Akali wing headed by Udham Singh Nagoke and Ishar Singh Majhail, both agriculturists from Amritsar district. The third grouping consisted of pro-Congress Sikhs led by Pratap Singh Kairon (agriculturalist) and Surjit Singh Majithia, a landed aristocrat. The fourth grouping was that of the Communist Sikhs, whom the Akalis despised. He further noted that caste groupings were also important in Sikh politics. The agricultural Jat Sikhs were the most numerous, though the leadership was with non-agriculturalists. Among other leaders of the Sikhs were Sardar Swaran Singh and Sardar Ujjal Singh. Describing the quality of the Sikh leadership, Jenkins remarked:

> In my negotiations with the Sikh community the persons to get hold of are Master Tara Singh, Giani Kartar Singh and Sardar Baldev Singh – the last named because of his wealth and standing as a Member of the Governor-General's Council. It is seldom possible to get any clear information or decisions out of the Sikhs – up to a

> point the Sikh leaders are clever organisers; but they are weak on the bigger issues and their outlook is extremely narrow (ibid.: 112).

In a separate secret letter of 9 April to Mountbatten, Jenkins expressed concern over an unsigned pamphlet, which exaggerated the atrocities committed against them in the Rawalpindi division, and called upon Sikhs to prepare for a battle with the Muslims. Also an appeal purported to be signed by eighteen prominent Sikhs, including Sardar Baldev Singh and several Sikh MLAs, called for a donation of ₹50 lakhs (five million) to a Sikh 'war fund' (ibid.: 117).

These observations are significant. That the defence minister had put his name to the appeal that talked of war and a fund to sustain it indicated that the normal procedures and practices of legitimate government were no longer being adhered to, and the colonial order was losing its grip notwithstanding the existing formalities. There were many other reports about ministers in the interim government coming to Punjab and openly empathising with their co-religionists. The colonial state apparatus had begun to disintegrate.

In an uncirculated report on a meeting of the viceroy's staff held on 12 April, Mountbatten disclosed that he was thinking along two main lines with regard to the transfer of power: Plan 'Union' was purported to keep India united within a modified version of the Cabinet Mission Plan, while Plan 'Balkan' would leave each province the choice of its own future, with a truncated Pakistan coming into being as a consequence. It would, however, require a centre (at Delhi) until June 1948 to deal with defence and the armed forces (Mansergh and Moon, 1981: 207-9).

In another meeting on 14 April, Jenkins told Mountbatten and other senior British officials that the Muslim aim was to dominate the whole of Punjab, while the Sikhs had decided to frustrate the Muslim plan, by fighting if necessary. He said that there were three alternatives in the Punjab: (a) revision to the unionist model of inter-communal government; (b) partition; or (c) civil war. If the government could not get either (a) or (b) accepted, then the British should withdraw and let the Muslims and Sikhs fight it out (ibid.: 231-2).

The Gandhi–Jinnah appeal of 15 April

Mountbatten exerted his influence to persuade Gandhi and Jinnah to issue a joint statement in favour of the renunciation of violence, in the hope that tension would be reduced. He noted that it required two days of exerting pressure on Jinnah to make him agree, while Gandhi immediately accepted the proposal. A problem now arose because the Congress wanted their president, Acharya Kripalani, to sign on their behalf; this was unacceptable to Jinnah. He would sign only if Gandhi signed. Another three days of negotiations followed and eventually only Gandhi and Jinnah affixed their names to the appeal. Issued on 15 April 1947, the statement read thus:

> We deeply deplore the recent lawlessness and violence that have brought the utmost disgrace on the fair name of India and the greatest misery to innocent people, irrespective of who were the aggressors and who were the victims. We denounce for all time the use of force to achieve political ends, and we call upon all the communities of India, to whatever persuasion they may belong, not only to refrain from all acts of violence and disorder, but also to avoid, both in speech and writing, any incitement to such acts (Carter, 2003: 85-6).

The appeal was directed to the whole of India, but was most certainly reflective of concerns about the situation in the Punjab, where the March rioting had rung alarm bells, the administration could no longer ignore. The appeal, however, had no effect on the situation on the ground and the Punjab continued to experience outbursts of violence mostly in Lahore and Amritsar.

Liaqat Ali Khan's letter to Mountbatten

In a letter to Mountbatten dated 15 April, Liaqat Ali Khan, Finance Minister in the Interim Government, complained that Sir Evan Jenkins was unfairly denying the Muslim League the right to form the government in the Punjab. The Muslim League was the biggest party in the Punjab assembly and represented fifty-seven per cent of the population. In Liaqat's view:

> The disturbed state of the Punjab was made an excuse by the Governor for the imposition of Section 93 in the province, despite the fact that the leader of the Muslim League Party claimed his constitutional right of facing the House after the Governor had invited him to form a Government.
>
> Events in the Punjab since the imposition of Section 93 have made it clear that the present administration has made it a matter of policy to suppress, intimidate and coerce the Muslims and it appears as if the Governor considers it his personal concern to do all that he possibly can to prevent the majority community in the Punjab from having its proper share in the administration of the province (ibid.: 256-7).

Mountbatten sent a copy of the letter to Jenkins who replied with a long note to the viceroy in which he refuted the charges laid against him and his administration. He traced the origins of the trouble in the Punjab to the Muslim League's 'Direct Action' which was meant to bring down a government which enjoyed a majority in the Punjab assembly. Thereafter, law and order began to be flouted by crowds and mobs, and the result had been the proliferation of violence and terrorism. He wrote about the violence in the Rawalpindi division:

> In the Rawalpindi and Attock districts and later in part of the Jhelum district there was an absolute butchery of non-Muslims. In many villages they were herded into houses and burnt alive. Many Sikhs had their hair and beards cut, and there were cases of forcible circumcision. Many Sikh women who escaped slaughter were abducted.
>
> The Muslim League made no efforts to maintain peace and Mamdot made no serious attempt at forming a Ministry. At the time he had no majority and he gave me the impression that he was not anxious to take responsibility for quelling a very serious outbreak of violence ... The total number of dead is not known. The latest figure is just under 3,000, and I believe that the final figure may be 3,500. The communal proportions have not been accurately reported, but I should say that among the dead there are 6 non-Muslims for every Muslim (Carter, 2007a: 137).

Jenkins went on to point out that the cadres in the Punjab services were mixed and it was therefore impossible to ensure that Muslims would have the full share of senior appointments; he could not pass over senior British or non-Muslim officers. Out of twenty-nine districts, ten were held by British officers, nine by Muslims and ten by Hindus or Sikhs. Moreover, there was a Muslim commissioner, though he was on leave. On the other hand, the chief secretary was a Muslim. Also, it was untrue, said Jenkins, that the British officials were hostile to Muslims. He remarked:

'They have been deeply shocked both by the atrocities committed in the rural areas and by the complacency of the League. Scott, DIG Rawalpindi, a good fighter but no politician, gave an interview to some journalist at which he unwisely expressed his disgust' (ibid.: 138).

Jenkins also denied that selective censorship was being applied. He asserted:

> For what object the British officials in the Punjab, including myself, are 'fostering chaos' I do not know. Every British official in the I.C.S [Indian Civil Service] and I.P. [Indian Police] in the Punjab, including myself, would be very glad to leave it tomorrow. With two or three possible exceptions no British official intends to remain in the Punjab after the transfer of power. Six months ago the position was quite different; but we feel now that we are dealing with people who are out to destroy themselves, and that in the absence of some reasonable agreement between them the average official will have to spend his life in a communal civil war (ibid.: 138).

In a separate top-secret letter to the viceroy dated 16 April, Jenkins argued that should the partition of the Punjab become unavoidable, the following steps, among several others, should be taken. First, it should be announced that the Punjab would be divided into two parts: one comprising districts with a Muslim majority, and another consisting of those that are non-Muslim majority. He added, 'Adjustments may be made by agreement in respect of *tahsils* (sub-unit of a district) contiguous to the Muslim and non-Muslim portions and having Muslim and non-Muslim majorities' (ibid.: 134). Second, a Boundary Commission should be set up to effect the adjustments and to determine what portions of the non-Muslim province should be 'released to form a separate Jat Province' (i.e. the Hindi-speaking Ambala division populated mainly by Hindu Jats) (ibid.).

Congress expresses doubt on the impartiality of some governors

On 17 April Mountbatten met Krishna Menon of the Congress party, who expressed the view that his party 'viewed with the gravest suspicion the Governors of N.W.F.P., Punjab, Bihar, and Sind'. Although Jenkins was not accused of deliberate anti-Congress bias, Menon 'held him in part to blame for allowing the critical situation to develop which had resulted in government under section 93' (Mansergh and Moon, 1981: 310).

On 30 April, Sikh leaders Kartar Singh, Harnam Singh and Ujjal Singh met Lord Ismay, the chief of the viceroy's staff, to discuss the Punjab situation. Ismay summed up their position:

> 'The main burden of their representation was the question of the Lahore Division, and particularly Lahore City. They admitted that the Muslims were in a majority, but that it was a matter of life and death for the Sikhs that the Division should not be handed over to them, even as an interim arrangement. They would far sooner all die fighting' (ibid.: 490).

On 1 May, Jenkins wrote a long letter to Mountbatten in which he said that he was going to discuss the security arrangements with the army commander, the Lahore area commander and the Inspector General of Police for an eventual partition of the Punjab. He suggested to the viceroy that he should try to persuade the Indian leaders to accept the Cabinet Mission Plan, but that if that failed, then he and HMG should broadcast to the people of India that if India was partitioned, Bengal and the Punjab would also be partitioned into Muslim and non-Muslim majority areas. Such an announcement should not be made before 15 May but any time after that. Jenkins wanted to know not more than forty-eight hours in advance that such an announcement would be made. He would then meet the Punjab leaders to persuade them to form a coalition ministry while the details and technicalities of the partition were sorted out. However, the Punjab governor did not expect the partition of the Punjab to be peaceful. He wrote, among other things:

(a) A peaceful partition of the Punjab is most improbable. The Muslims want virtually the whole of the Punjab; the Sikhs want all districts from the Jumna to the Ravi, and possibly to the Chenab; the Hindus are likely to follow the Sikhs.
(b) The initial boundary will give the non-Muslims the Ambala and Jullundur divisions *plus* Amritsar, and the Muslims, the Rawalpindi and Multan divisions and the Lahore division *less* Amritsar.
(c) The statement will excite anger among all Muslims and Sikhs, and fear among those of them, and among Hindus, who will live on the wrong side of the boundary. We can expect no rational examination of the statement; nor any united reaction against partition (Carter, 2007a: 160).

Jinnah's stand on Bengal and Punjab

A statement of Jinnah in the *Dawn* newspaper, dated 1 May 1947, demanded the whole of Punjab and Bengal, NWFP, Sindh, Baluchistan, Bengal and Assam. Such a demand was premised on the familiar two-nation theory. However, with regard to Bengal and the Punjab he opined that the demand to partition these provinces was not based 'on any sound principle except that the Hindu minorities in the Punjab and Bengal wish to cut up these provinces and cut their own people into two in these provinces' (Mansergh and Moon, 1981: 543). Jinnah went on to argue that an exchange of population would have to be effected at some stage:

> It is obvious that if the Hindu minorities in Pakistan wish to emigrate and go to their homelands of Hindustan they will be at liberty to do so and *vice versa* those Muslims who wish to emigrate from Hindustan can do so and go to Pakistan; and sooner or later exchange of population will have to take place and the Constituent Assemblies of Pakistan and Hindustan can take up the matter, and subsequently the respective Governments in Pakistan and Hindustan

> can effectively carry out the exchange of population wherever it may be necessary and feasible.
>
> The Congress propaganda is intended to disrupt and put obstacles and obstructions and difficulties in the way of an amicable solution. It is quite obvious that they have put up the Hindu Mahasabha in Bengal and the Sikhs in the Punjab, and the Congress Press is inciting the Sikhs and misleading them. The Sikhs do not stand to gain by the partition of the Punjab but they will be split into two halves. More than half of their population will have to remain in Pakistan even if a partition of the Punjab takes place according to their conception, whereas in Pakistan, as proposed by the Muslim League they will play, as one solid minority, a very big part. We have always been very willing to meet them in every reasonable way (ibid.: 544).

Jinnah's stand that the partition of India between two nations was not comparable to the demand of the non-Muslim minorities of Bengal and the Punjab to partition their provinces did not convince the non-Muslim leaders of the Punjab. It also failed to impress the Punjab governor and the viceroy. In a personal report dated 1 May 1947, Mountbatten remarked:

> I had a long talk with Jenkins about the partitioning of the Punjab. The bone of contention is going to be the area between the two rivers, Ravi and Sutlej, and it is going to be very difficult to produce a demarcation which will be acceptable by both parties. The Sikhs in their endeavours to obtain a real "Sikhistan" are most anxious to take in a large part of the area where most of the land is owned by Sikhs but where the Muslim population predominates. *To this I am absolutely opposed* [emphasis added]. The Sikhs also want their holy places preserved for them, including Lahore itself, the capital-designate of Pakistan! It is significant, however, that when the Sikh delegation saw me they particularly asked that I should not decide whether the Sikhs would join Pakistan or Hindustan, since they had not made up their minds to which side they wanted to go (ibid.: 537).

Mountbatten's remark is significant as he is generally accused of taking the side of the Congress against the Muslim League. The above observation indicates that his disregard for Sikh interests was no less striking. Moreover, he had already begun to refer to Lahore as the capital-designate of Pakistan. It is equally significant that the Sikhs were of two minds at that time about joining either India or Pakistan. As events would eventually unfold, the Hindus and Sikhs continued to believe that Lahore would be awarded to India.

Sikhs meet Jenkins

A delegation consisting of Swaran Singh, Harbans Singh, and Bhim Sen Sachar, met Jenkins on 2 May and reiterated that the partition in the Punjab should designate the river Chenab as the boundary between the Indian and Pakistani Punjabs. They raised many objections to the population factor alone being made the basis for allocation of territory in the Punjab. The governor remarked: 'This partition business seems to be getting out of control' (Carter, 2007a: 162). Unless the communities agreed to a partition formula, there would be trouble in the offing. If the province was partitioned by force through a government award, then a very large body of troops would be needed to implement it. Since such troops were not available, it was impractical. Even if such an enforced solution could be found: 'It would in any case be difficult and unpleasant course, resulting in the establishment of two Governments which would be compelled to rule by massacre' (ibid.). In a separate note dated 2 May, Jenkins observed that the Sikh leaders considered the census records unreliable. The sticking point for them was the Lahore division; they argued vehemently:

> That Gurdaspur was a non-Muslim district; that Amritsar must certainly go to the non-Muslims...; that outside Lahore city the Lahore district was substantially Sikh; and that the Muslims had played a very small part in the development of Lahore city...; that they hoped that nothing would be done to hand the Sikhs over to Muslim domination and oppression (ibid.: 165).

In early May, a draft was prepared of a broadcast statement to be made by the viceroy to announce the partition plan. In that undated statement, the date for the British withdrawal is given as June 1948 (Mansergh and Moon, 1981: 545). Thus at the beginning of May the British had not decided to bring that date forward to mid-August 1947. Sometime around 9 May, Mountbatten began to share with his staff the idea of transferring power in 1947.

Referendum on the Punjab

The Punjab Unionist leader and former premier, Sir Khizr Tiwana, met the viceroy on 3 May. In that meeting the viceroy expressed his idea about the holding of a referendum in the Punjab. Khizr suggested that four options be offered to the voters:

1. A free Punjab, with an agreement (or agreements) with Hindustan and Pakistan about defence;
2. Punjab to join Pakistan;
3. Punjab to join Hindustan;
4. Punjab to be divided.

Khizr, in response to the viceroy, stressed his own strong position that splitting up the Punjab would mean civil war (ibid.: 590).

Mountbatten subsequently sought Jenkins' views about a referendum; the latter declared it would be unhelpful. His contention was that whereas the Muslims would vote for the inclusion of the whole province in Pakistan, the Hindus and Sikhs would oppose it tooth and nail; they would vote for its partition on a religious basis. Under the circumstances, he argued, the referendum would not result in an amicable solution (ibid.: 605-6).

In a meeting with Jinnah and Liaqat on 4 May, Mountbatten told the Muslim leaders that the Sikhs were in a 'truculent frame of mind', an impression he had gathered in a meeting with the Maharaja of Patiala. The viceroy appreciated the fact that Jinnah was going to meet the maharaja (ibid.: 613).

Sikh apprehensions on notional division of the Punjab

The Sikhs learned that the government was thinking of dividing Punjab on a notional basis of communal majorities and minorities in the districts: meaning, seventeen districts including Gurdaspur would be placed in West Punjab, and twelve in the East. Upon learning of the plan, the Sikh community quickly became concerned that such a division would also serve as the basis of the final partition. In a letter dated 5 May, Mountbatten assured Baldev Singh that the notional division was necessary:

'[S]olely in order to create two assemblies for voting purposes on the broad question of partition or unity. It will in no way prejudice the subsequent work of the Boundary Commission which will have to be set up, in order to demarcate the actual limits of the two parts of the Punjab' (ibid.: 619-20).

In another interview dated 6 May, Mountbatten warned Baldev Singh that if the Sikhs created serious trouble or started a communal war, 'I shall crush them with all the power at my command, and would instruct him as Defence Minister to turn out the Army and Air Force to fight them' (ibid.: 632). Moreover, Baldev Singh had demanded that Gurdaspur, Amritsar and Lahore districts be included in East Punjab. Mountbatten consulted Jenkins about the districts, to which the latter replied on 7 May:

'Baldev Singh, like other Sikhs, seems quite unable to understand that the Sikhs are not the only people to be considered. They have no absolute majority of their own in any district, and the new State they contemplate is not really a Sikh State at all, but a non-Muslim State' (ibid.: 643).

The colonial administration's predicaments

It is clear from the above review of the Muslim League, Sikh and Congress standpoints that doubts about the impartiality of the colonial administration were being expressed at the highest level. The highly personal nature of Mountbatten's interaction with the Indian leaders obscured the extent to which anxiety about the ability of the colonial state to act as an honest arbiter of conflicting interests was prevalent among them. However, such leaders were becoming more vocal about the role of provincial governors.

With regard to the Punjab, Jenkins had rebutted at length the Muslim League's charges and probably would have done the same to the misgivings expressed by the Sikhs and the Congress; the important point is that the authority and prestige of the colonial administration was diminishing, and was poised to suffer greater diminution as the date for the transfer of power came closer.

Keeping India in the Commonwealth

Keeping India united or divided within the British Commonwealth was another task that had been assigned to Mountbatten. He deployed all his skills to attain that objective; it seemed that he considered it an objective particularly important to realise. The British did not anticipate that Jinnah would oppose Pakistan's membership of the British Commonwealth. Mountbatten quoted Jinnah:

> All the Muslims have been loyal to the British from the beginning. We supplied a high proportion of the Army which fought in both wars. None of our leaders has ever had to go to prison for disloyalty. Not one member of the Muslim League was present in the Constituent Assembly when the resolution for an Independent Sovereign Republic was passed [passed on January 22 1947]. Not one of us had done anything to deserve expulsion from the Commonwealth. Will the other Dominions agree to us being thrown out against our will? Is there anything in the Statute of Westminster which allows you to kick out parts of the Commonwealth because a neighbouring State which used to be a member wants to leave? Mr. Churchill has assured me that the British people would never stand for our being expelled (Carter, 2003: 127).

Mountbatten told Jinnah that he agreed with him on an emotional level. However, Mountbatten quickly added, he felt that it would create an odd situation if only one part remained in the Commonwealth, and on that basis, retained British officers and received British help. Such a situation would become impossible if it went to war with the other part that opted out of the Commonwealth. He warned Jinnah to be prepared for a refusal to membership for Pakistan if India did not join the Commonwealth. By Mountbatten's account, Jinnah retorted that he would rely on the power of appeal of the Commonwealth over the heads of His Majesty's Government; Jinnah was confident that he would receive support from the British people (ibid.).

Meanwhile, the Congress had thus far resisted the Commonwealth idea, claiming the right to full sovereignty and independence. However, the intense pressure being exerted on them proved too much and by May 1947, the Congress leaders began to come around one by one. In the minutes of the twenty-seventh viceroy's staff meeting dated 7 May it was stated that Sardar Patel had been won over to the idea, and Nehru too would agree (Mansergh and Moon, 1981: 659).

Transfer of power in 1947

An undated report was presumably written in early May about the minutes of the viceroy's twenty-ninth staff meeting. The report recorded: 'HIS EXCELLENCY THE VICEROY said that he considered it most desirable that, if Dominion status was to be granted to India before June 1948, the grant should take place during 1947' (ibid.: 702-3). Mountbatten seemed to have calculated that if the Congress party also agreed to India's staying on in the Commonwealth, it was in the British interest to transfer power earlier, in fact in 1947, and thus avoid further wavering.

Among the practical advantages of an early granting of dominion status would be that it would enable all British troops to leave the country as soon as possible; some, however, would be needed for the interim period (ibid.: 703). Continuing along such lines, the report notes:

> HIS EXCELLENCY THE VICEROY said that in his opinion the solid advantages which the United Kingdom would gain were as follows:
>
> i) An early transfer of power would gain her tremendous credit.
>
> ii) Such a transfer would involve the termination of the present responsibilities.

iii) A request by India to remain in the Commonwealth would enhance British prestige enormously in the eyes of the world. This factor alone was of overriding importance.

iv) Such a request would be of the greatest advantage to the prestige of the present British Government in the eyes of the country.

v) From the point of view of Empire defence an India within the Commonwealth filled in the whole framework of world strategy; a neutral India would leave a gap which would complicate the problem enormously; a hostile India would mean that Australia and New Zealand were virtually cut off (ibid.: 703-4).

By that time, the British government had also accepted the opinion that Partition was inevitable. The report goes on:

> 'HIS EXCELLENCY THE VICEROY said that he fully realised the difficulties involved in transferring power on a Dominion status basis in 1947. He had no doubt, though, that these difficulties could be overcome, in the same way that apparently insurmountable difficulties had been overcome during the war. One of the main difficulties was doubtless the setting-up of administrative machinery to run Pakistan, and constitutional machinery to receive power there. But there were, without question, ways of mitigating these difficulties (ibid.: 704).

Early transfer of power mentioned to Nehru

A highly classified document of a miscellaneous meeting of the viceroy with some of his staff at Simla was issued on 10 May. Nehru was also present in that meeting. The records said that the Reforms Commissioner V.P. Menon, had been working on an earlier transfer of power long before Mountbatten arrived in India. V.P. Menon had apparently explained the scheme to Nehru a day earlier and four months earlier to Patel (ibid.: 731). There was no follow-up on this and therefore we have no way of ascertaining on whose behalf V.P. Menon had been working with such an idea. In the same report it was stated that Nehru had become openly supportive of India remaining in the Commonwealth.

British military prepare memorandum on Pakistan

The final proposals for the partition of India were discussed in a meeting on 12 May 1947 in London, with the RAF Marshal Lord Tedder in the chair and in the presence of the chiefs of staff of various branches of the armed forces, Field Marshal Montgomery, and Lord Ismay. Partition was assumed to be the basis of the political settlement. It was expected that Pakistan would comprise Sindh, Baluchistan, North-West Frontier Province, the western Punjab and Assam, with possibly a part of Bengal. It was also expected that Jinnah would present:

> [A]Moslem application to remain within the Commonwealth. A number of Princes might do the same thing. On the other hand, Hindustan might well stick to the declared intention of Congress to be a free Sovereign State, although there were signs that some Congress leaders had doubts of their ability to continue without some British advisers and administration (ibid.: 788).

According to this document, the chiefs of the armed forces were kept in the dark about the fact that the Congress had already been brought around to the idea of India remaining a member of the Commonwealth. Montgomery asserted, 'It would be a tremendous asset if Pakistan, particularly North West, remained within the Commonwealth' (ibid.: 791). The chiefs of staff agreed that their views should be submitted to the prime minister. They agreed on the following:

> From the strategic point of view there were overwhelming arguments in favour of Western Pakistan remaining within the Commonwealth, namely, that we should obtain important strategic facilities, the port of Karachi, air bases and the support of the Moslem manpower in the future... There was therefore everything to gain by admitting Western Pakistan into the Commonwealth. A refusal of an application to this end would amount to ejecting loyal people from the British Commonwealth, and would probably lose us all chances of ever getting

> strategic facilities anywhere in India, and at the same time shatter our reputation in the rest of the Moslem world. From a military point of view, such a result would be catastrophic (ibid. 791-2).

It was also emphasised that the princely states and Bengal should be encouraged to seek membership of the Commonwealth. Therefore, it was imperative that all the areas, which wanted to join, should be advised to apply for membership.

Punjab to be divided on a notional basis for purposes of voting

In a meeting on 11 May, with Mountbatten presiding and in the presence of Jenkins and Nehru, the viceroy said that the British administration 'would need to work on the basis of Muslim and non-Muslim districts for notional partition for working purposes. But this would not prejudice the subsequent work of a Boundary Commission' (ibid.: 759). Nehru agreed that the principle of property ownership which the Sikhs were emphasising could not reasonably be made the basis of the allocation of areas, 'but there were Sikh shrines in some of the predominantly Muslim areas. This point should be borne in mind' (ibid.).

Jenkins, however, was of the opinion that although there were a number of Sikh shrines in western Punjab, 'the real Sikh Holy Land was in Amritsar, which would in any case fall in the Sikhs' (ibid.). Jenkins could also foresee that both Gurdaspur and Lahore districts could be divided by the Boundary Commission. At that meeting, Nehru mentioned a rumour that arms were being smuggled in the Punjab from abroad. Jenkins denied that such an event was taking place but conceded that some arms had been brought from the NWFP. The government was looking into the matter, he said (ibid.).

Meanwhile, the mechanism for partitioning the Punjab began to be discussed. The idea of notional division was to establish a framework for finding out what views were held by representatives of the Punjabis – or those elected to the Punjab Legislative Assembly – as opposed to the people as a whole. The district was to serve as the unit for notionally grouping the twenty-nine districts of the province into Muslim and non-Muslim-majority provinces. Such ideas were developed further in a draft dated 13 May of the speech in which the Indian people were to be told about the decision to partition India. In a comment on the draft statement, Jinnah declared that the Muslim League had definitely decided not to accept the Cabinet Mission Plan in any form, but reiterated that partition of Bengal and the Punjab was totally unacceptable (ibid.: 852). Mountbatten, however, had in several discussions with Jinnah insisted that the same principles would be applied to the division of these provinces as in the partition of India of a whole. In a further revised draft statement of 17 May, an appendix was included in which the Punjab was divided notionally into seventeen Muslim-majority and twelve Hindu–Sikh-majority districts on the basis of the 1941 census (ibid.: 887).

Jinnah–Patiala meeting

Mountbatten persuaded Jinnah to meet the Maharaja of Patiala to find out if the Muslims and Sikhs could agree on a formula to keep the Punjab united. The meetings were held in Delhi on 15–16 May. Both the *Pakistan Times* and *The Tribune* of 18 May reported that the maharaja had stressed Jinnah's assurances that minorities would be protected in Pakistan, though he would not give any precise proposal or formula. With regard to the international boundary with India, Patiala had repeated the Sikh proposal that it be drawn at the Chenab river while Jinnah wanted the Sutlej river. However, the feeling was that a compromise solution was likely, with the river Ravi as the boundary.

The principal secretary to the viceroy, Sir E. Melville, reported in a telegram to Mountbatten on 20 May that Jinnah and the Maharaja of Patiala had met, and according to the latter, 'he [Maharaja of Patiala] had long talks with Jinnah and tried to make him realise the disastrous consequences of his demand for a division of India but he found Jinnah uncompromising and adamant' (ibid.: 915). Melville noted in the same telegram:

> The Sikhs consider division of the Punjab essential and any division of the Province which does not take into consideration the rights of the Sikh community in respect of their landed property, other assets,

> their holy shrines and does not secure for the major part of the Sikh community a national home is likely to provoke stiff opposition... It will be most unfair to both Sikhs and Hindus if the division of the Punjab is made merely on the basis of the incidence of population by ignoring all other factors such as the relative share of the various communities in the national asset, their relative contribution to the prosperity of the province and the desirability of making the divided units self-contained. (ibid.)

Moreover, the maharaja felt that the authorities followed a pro-Muslim policy, especially in the police force. He pleaded that if power was transferred to a divided India, HMG and the viceroy should 'arrange for a division of the Punjab on a basis which will be fair and just to the Sikhs' (ibid.).

Jinnah's offer to the Sikhs

The above account does not bring forth the complete record of the meetings between Jinnah and the Maharaja of Patiala. In several interviews with informed Pakistanis I was told that Jinnah offered very generous terms to the Sikhs to dissuade them from demanding the partition of the Punjab if India was partitioned. This claim is amply corroborated by the article, 'I remember Jinnah's offer of Sikh state' by the late Maharaja of Patiala, published in *The Tribune* of 19 July 1959. Apparently, Lord Mountbatten was also present as were Liaqat Ali Khan and his wife. Some of the extracts are given below:

> We had a drink and went in to dine. The talks started, and offers were made by Mr. Jinnah for practically everything under the sun if I would agree to his plan. There were two aspects. One was based on the idea of a Rajasthan and the other one for a separate Sikh State – Punjab minus one or two districts in the south. I had prolonged talks with Master Tara Singh, Giani Kartar Singh and other Sikh leaders, and all the negotiations on behalf of the Sikhs were within my knowledge. Indeed, in some ways I had quite a deal to do with them. I told Mr. Jinnah that I could not accept either of his two proposals, and told him a lot of what was on my mind. Liaquat Ali

> and Begum Liaquat Ali were most charming to me, and went out of their way to offer, on behalf of the Muslim League, everything conceivable. I was to be Head of this new Sikh State, the same as in Patiala. The Sikhs were to have their own army and so on.
>
> All these things sounded most attractive, but I could not accept them as being practical, and neither could I in the mood I was in, change my convictions. The talks lasted till past midnight. Lord Mountbatten was a patient listener, occasionally taking part. He eventually said that perhaps Mr. Jinnah and I could meet again at some convenient date. (Quoted in Singh, 1991: 86).

Patiala then talks of Jinnah inviting him over for tea at his residence in Delhi, where he was received with great warmth. Ms Fatima Jinnah was present and Liaqat Ali Khan later joined. They went over the same points and issues as two days earlier, but no breakthrough was achieved.

The former ex-Prime Minister of Patiala, Hardit Singh Malik, was also involved in the discussions between the Muslim League and the Sikh leaders. In the account given below, reference is made to some other meeting, where besides the maharaja, other Sikh leaders were also present. The veteran Sikh historian of the Punjab partition, Kirpal Singh, interviewed Malik about the meeting with the Sikhs. He posed the following question to Malik:

> Question: You accompanied the Sikh leaders for negotiations with Mr. Jinnah and Liaquat Ali Khan. Could you throw some light on it. Why did it fail?
>
> Answer: 'You see at that time Pakistan's formation had not been conceded. Jinnah was very anxious to win over the Sikhs and he sent a message to the Maharaja of Patiala asking him for a meeting. The Maharaja consulted me and I said "By all means have a meeting, but let him come to see you. Why should we go to see [sic] him. He has something to ask from you. He should come to see you.
>
> 'So we sent that message to Jinnah and the reply came that Mr. Jinnah could not do that but we could meet at some neutral place. We agreed and finally met at my brother's house 4, Bhagwandas Road, at New Delhi. Present at the meeting were Jinnah himself,

Maharaja Patiala, myself, Master Tara Singh and Giani Kartar Singh. I was the spokesperson for the Sikhs.
'Jinnah started by saying that he was very anxious to have the Sikhs agree to Pakistan and he was prepared to give them everything that they wanted, if they could accept Pakistan. I said to him, "Mr. Jinnah you are being very generous but we would like to know exactly what our position will be. You will have a Government, you will have a Parliament and you will have Defence forces, what part will the Sikhs have in all [sic] these. He reply [sic] was "Mr. Malik, [sic] Are you familiar with what happened in Egypt? I will deal with the Sikhs as Zaghlul Pasha dealt with the Copts (the Christian minority) when Egypt became independent. "He then went on to tell us the story. According to Jinnah, the Copts when they first met Zaghlul Pasha put forward some demands. After listening to them he advised them to go back, think the whole thing over and come to see him again with a paper incorporating all their demands. They did this. Zaghul Pasha took the paper from them and without reading it wrote on it "I agree." Mr Jinnah added "That is what I will do with the Sikhs."
'This put us in an awkward position. We were determined not to accept Pakistan under any circumstances and here was the Muslim Leader offering us everything. What to do?
'Then I had and [sic] inspiration and I said, "Mr Jinnah, you are being very generous. But, supposing, God forbid, you are no longer there when the time comes to implement your promises?" "His reply was astounding ... He said, "My friend, my word in Pakistan will be like the word of God. No one will go back on it".'
There was nothing to be said after this and the meeting ended (ibid.: 87).

Jinnah demands corridor for Pakistan

On 21 May, Reuters reported Jinnah as saying:

Firstly, the Moslem League will demand a corridor through Hindustan to connect the two groups of Pakistan Provinces in North-Western and North-Eastern India. Second, the League will 'fight every inch' against the partition of Bengal and the Punjab. Thirdly, a 'really beneficial' relationship can be established between Pakistan and Britain. Fourthly, relations between Pakistan and Hindustan should be 'friendly and reciprocal...All the armed forces must be divided completely. I envisage an alliance, pact or treaty between Pakistan and Hindustan in the mutual interest of both and against any aggressive outsider' (ibid.: 929-30).

British government convinced Cabinet Mission Plan will not work

On 22 May, British Prime Minister Attlee issued a memorandum on Indian policy, stating with regret that although Mountbatten had been given a brief to negotiate the transfer of power under the Cabinet Mission Plan, the viceroy was convinced that it would not work. The British government in London still referred to June 1948 as the date for the transfer of power (ibid.: 949).

With regard to the armed forces of India, a detailed note dated 27 May prepared by the British Commander-in-Chief in India, Field Marshal Sir Claude Auchinleck – an outspoken opponent of the idea of partition and especially of dividing the Indian Army – highlighted the enormous difficulties involved in dividing the army (ibid.: 1004-8). The same day, Gandhi warned that the worst type of violence was likely to erupt at the time of dividing India, and the best thing for the British was to transfer power under the Cabinet Mission Plan of 16 May and leave (ibid.: 1037). The Congress president, Acharya Kripalani, issued a statement on 28 May after a visit to the Punjab, in which he said that Congress was opposed to the division of India but that if it was going to take place:

'[R]esponsibility for such a division of the country must rest primarily with the [Muslim] League and then with the British Government. And if partition must come, the division must be fair. Under no circumstance will Congress allow the inclusion of non-Muslim areas in so-called Pakistan' (ibid.: 1038).

The Partition Plan of 3 June 1947

From 19 May onwards, Mountbatten was in the United Kingdom for consultations with the British Cabinet and the India Office and did not return to India until 30 May. In a telegram dated 31 May to all the provincial governors, he informed them of what he had told the Cabinet:

> It was clear to me that if we waited till constitutions for both Hindustan and Pakistan had been framed and all the negotiations about partition settled we shall have to wait a very long time, and things would get more difficult instead of easier. There would be likely to be chaos in June 1948… I therefore pressed that H.M.G. should legislate at once and set up two dominion Governments, if the people voted in favour of partition, each having a constitution based on the Government of India Act 1935, but with the right to frame a new constitution any time (Mansergh and Moon, 1982: 29).

Mountbatten then met the Indian leaders on 2 June. They were handed copies of this latest statement next day at 10 a.m., with the request that they give their replies and comments by midnight, but that the statement was final. Much of the text had in fact been shared with the Indian leaders in various revised forms, but the early date of the transfer of power had not been mentioned. However, Mountbatten went on to circulate a document entitled 'The Administrative Consequences of Partition' in which for the first time, he revealed his plan for a very early withdrawal from India if Partition was agreed. He wrote: 'It is my intention that the Act should be brought into operation at the earliest possible date after enactment, in any case not later than 15th August, 1947' (ibid.: 53). Both India and Pakistan were to be accorded dominion status. In that paper, a comprehensive plan to effect Partition was set forth.

Among the items included were: 1. Final demarcation of boundaries; division of the formations, units and personnel of the Indian Armed Forces; and division of staff, organisations and records of the central civil departments and the assets and liabilities of the Government of India (ibid.: 53-4). With regard to 15 August as the latest date for the transfer of power, the viceroy remarked: 'The severe shock that this gave to everyone present would have been amusing if it was not rather tragic' (ibid.: 163).

Such a remark is most revealing in that it captures graphically the effect it had on the Indian leaders. As noted above, Nehru and Patel had already been taken into confidence about an early British withdrawal from the subcontinent and were themselves in favour of it. However, the exact day of withdrawal being brought forward so radically may not have been intimated to them. There is no doubt that the Muslim League, the Sikhs and possibly other Congress leaders learnt about it only on 2 June and must have been most shocked by it. Partitioning the subcontinent was never going to be an easy task: doing it in less than eleven weeks would be infinitely more difficult because the administrative machinery had not been prepared.

Announcement of the Partition Plan

Months of hectic and intense consultations and negotiations involving the British Government in London, the Government of India, and a broad sector of Indian opinion – with the Congress, Muslim League and Sikh representatives playing centre-stage – culminated in Mountbatten's announcement of the Partition Plan over All-India Radio in the evening of 3 June. In London, Prime Minister Attlee made a statement in the House of Commons at 3.30 p.m. This in turn was broadcast on the radio in India. In his address, Mountbatten said:

> For more than a hundred years 400 millions of you have lived together and this country has been administered as a single entity. This has resulted in unified communications, defence, postal services and currency; an absence of tariffs and customs barriers, and the basis for an integrated political economy. My great hope was that communal differences would not destroy all this.
>
> My first course, in all my discussions, was therefore to urge the political leaders to accept unreservedly the Cabinet Mission Plan of 16th May, 1946. In my opinion, that plan provides the best arrangement that can be devised to meet the interests of all the communities of India. To my great regret it has been impossible to obtain agreement either on the Cabinet Mission Plan, or to any

> other plan that would preserve the unity of India. But there can be no question of coercing any large areas in which one community has a majority to live against their will under a Government in which another community has a majority and the only alternative to coercion is partition.
>
> But when the Muslim League demanded the partition of India, the Congress used the same arguments for demanding in that event, the partition of certain Provinces. To my mind this argument is unassailable. In fact, neither side proved willing to leave a substantial area in which their community have a majority under the Government of the other. I am, of course, opposed to the partition of the Provinces as I am to the partition of India herself and for the same basic reasons.
>
> For just as I felt there is an Indian consciousness which should transcend communal differences so I feel there is a Punjabi and Bengali consciousness which has evoked a loyalty to their Provinces.
>
> And so I felt it was essential that the people of India themselves should decide this question of partition...
>
> It was necessary in order to ascertain the will of the people of the Punjab, Bengal and part of Assam to lay down boundaries between the Muslim majority areas and the remaining areas, but I want to make it clear that the ultimate boundaries will be settled by a Boundary Commission and will almost certainly not be identical with those which have been provisionally adopted.
>
> We have given careful consideration to the position of the Sikhs. This valiant community forms about an eighth of the population of the Punjab, but they are so distributed that any partition of this Province will inevitably divide them. All of us who have the good of the Sikh community at heart are very sorry to think that the partition of the Punjab, which they themselves desire, cannot avoid splitting them to a greater or lesser extent. The exact degree of the split will be left to the Boundary Commission on which they will of course be represented (ibid.: 86-7).

The British government's published statement of 3 June included the following stipulations:

> 5. The Provincial Legislative Assemblies of Bengal and the Punjab (excluding European Members) will … each be asked to meet in two parts, one representing the Muslim majority districts and the other the rest of the Province. For the purpose of determining the population of districts, the 1941 census figures will be taken as authoritative. The Muslim majority districts in these provinces are set out in the Appendix to this Announcement.
> 6. The Members of the two parts of each Legislative Assembly sitting separately will be empowered to vote whether or not the Province should be partitioned. If a simple majority of either part decides in favour of partition, division will take place and arrangements will be made accordingly...
> 9. For the immediate purpose of deciding on the issue of partition, the members of the Legislative Assemblies of Bengal and the Punjab will sit in two parts according to Muslim majority districts (as laid down in the Appendix) and non-Muslim majority districts. This is only a preliminary step of a purely temporary nature as it is evident that for the purposes of a final partition of these provinces, a detailed investigation of the boundary question will be needed and, as soon as a decision involving partition has been taken for either province, a Boundary Commission will be set up by the Governor-General, the membership and terms of reference of which will be settled in consultation with those concerned. It will be instructed to demarcate the boundaries of the two parts of the Punjab on the basis of ascertaining the contiguous majority areas of Muslims and non-Muslims. It will also be instructed to take into account other factors. Similar instructions will be given to the Bengal Boundary Commission. Until the report of a Boundary Commission has been put into effect, the provisional boundaries indicated in the Appendix will be used (ibid.: 90-1).

The Appendix was based on district-wise majorities as recorded in the 1941 census. It showed that Muslims were in the majority in three of the five administrative divisions of the Punjab:

1. Rawalpindi division: Attock, Gujrat, Jhelum, Mianwali, Rawalpindi, Shahpur.

2. Multan division: Dera Ghazi Khan, Jhang, Lyallpur, Montgomery, Multan, Muzaffargarh.
3. Lahore division: Gujranwala, Gurdaspur, Lahore, Sheikhupura and Sialkot districts (ibid.: 94).

Amritsar, which belonged to Lahore division, had a non-Muslim majority and was, therefore, not included among the Muslim majority areas in the appendix. Besides Amritsar district, Hindus and Sikhs were in a majority in the following division and their districts:

4. Jullundur division: Ludhiana, Ferozepore, Jullundur, Hoshiarpur, Kangra.
5. Ambala division: Gurgaon, Rothak, Hissar, Karnal, Ambala, Simla.

Following Mountbatten's address, Nehru, Jinnah and Baldev Singh made speeches endorsing the 3 June statement as the basis of a political settlement for India.

On 4 June, Mountbatten gave a press conference in Delhi in which he made, among many others, the following observations:

> There are two main parties to this plan, the Congress and the Muslim League, but another community much less numerous but of great importance – the Sikh community – have of course to be considered. I found that it was mainly at the request of the Sikh community that Congress had put forward the Resolution on the partition of the Punjab, and you will remember that in the words of that Resolution they wished the Punjab to be divided between predominantly Muslim and non-Muslim areas. It was, therefore, on that Resolution, which the Sikhs themselves sponsored, that this division has been provided for. I was not aware of all the details when this suggestion was made but when I sent for the map and studied the distribution of the Sikh population under this proposal, I must say that I was astounded to find that the plan which they had produced divided their community into two almost equal parts. I have spent a great deal of time both out here and in England in seeing whether there was any solution which would keep the Sikh community more together without departing from the broad and

> easily-understood principle, the principle which was demanded on the one side and was conceded on the other. I am not a miracle worker and I have not found that solution (ibid.: 112).

The next important step was the establishment of the Partition Committee on 12 June. This body, chaired by Mountbatten, included Congress representatives Sardar Patel and Dr Rajendra Prasad and from the Muslim League, Nawabzada Liaqat Ali Khan and Sardar Abdur Rab Nishtar (ibid.: 284).

Jenkins' remarks on the Partition Plan

Punjab Governor Evan Jenkins noted in his FR of 15 June that the partition plan did not at all go down well with Punjabis in general, while the politicians put their own spin on the pronouncement:

> There is a complete absence of enthusiasm for the partition plan – nobody seems pleased, and nobody seems to get on with the job. The plan has had no discernible effect on communal relations, which remain as they were. Nor is there any sign of special anxiety for, or hostility to, Dominion Status (Carter, 2008b: 74).

He further noted that the political parties had acquiesced to the idea of division but for different reasons. The Muslim Leaguers thought it was a master-stroke of Jinnah to accept it because now Pakistan would come into being, while the Congress leaders believed that the insistence on the partition of Bengal and the Punjab had pushed Pakistan itself out of the limelight. Mian Ibrahim Burq (a minister in the defunct Khizr cabinet) claimed to have heard the Congress strongman Sardar Patel say that if Pakistan made any trouble for India, India could easily make an end of its Muslim inhabitants. Jenkins wrote: 'This may be quite untrue, but the story represents the attitude the Hindus hope and the Muslims fear Patel will take up'. As for the Sikhs, they were pinning their hopes on the Boundary Commission. They were fairly well organised in the districts they thought critical, and it was quite likely they would refuse to go very far with Partition until they knew where the boundary would run. They were demanding both exchanges of property and transfers of population (ibid.)

The governor also mentioned that British civil servants were not enthusiastic to serve in the Punjab even if it remained a Dominion. On the other hand, Muslim civil servants were parcelling out the more lucrative Pakistan appointments among themselves while non-Muslims did not think they would be safe in the western Punjab, and hoped to be accommodated in 'Hindustan'.

Members of the Punjab Assembly voting on the partition of the Punjab

The Partition Plan stipulated that the members of the Punjab Legislative Assembly, organised separately into a western and an eastern bloc, would vote on the issue of partitioning the Punjab. Accordingly, members of the Western Section of the Assembly (presided over by the Speaker Diwan Bahadur S.P. Singha) and that of the Eastern Section (presided over by the Deputy Speaker Sardar Kapur Singh) voted on 23 June 1947. *The Transfer of Power volume XI* presented a Reuters report describing the situation when the members of the Punjab Assembly met separately as East and West Punjab entities to vote on the partition of the province:

> With large sections of Lahore and scores of villages throughout the Province fire-blacked ruins, the 168 members of the Punjab Legislative Assembly laughed and joked as they shook hands in the lobbies of the Assembly building on their way to record their votes to decide whether the Punjab should be partitioned.... Approaches to the Assembly building were blocked by barbed-wire barriers and the vicinity was under heavy police guard. The public was not admitted, but foreign and local pressmen filled the press gallery (Mansergh and Moon, 1982: 566-7).

With regard to the voting, seventy-two members from East Punjab met in a separate session. They rejected by fifty votes to twenty-two, a motion by the Muslim League leader the Khan of Mamdot that the province should remain united. On the other hand, in the West Punjab section, a motion to partition the Punjab was rejected by sixty-nine votes to twenty-seven. In communal terms, eighty-eight Muslims, including Khizr Tiwana and seven other members of the Unionist Party, two Indian

Christians and one Anglo-Indian voted for a united Punjab; Hindus, Sikhs and representatives of the scheduled castes, numbering altogether seventy-seven, voted for partitioning the Punjab (ibid.: 567).

Punjab Boundary Commission

Mountbatten began discussions with the Indian leaders about the composition of the Punjab Boundary Commission. It was agreed that the Commission should include an independent chairman and four other persons. Two were to be nominated by Congress (of which one was to be a Sikh) and two by the Muslim League. If possible, all the four nominated members were to be of high judicial standing. Congress nominated Justice Mehr Chand Mahajan and Justice Teja Singh while the Muslim League nominated Justice Din Muhammad and Justice Muhammad Munir. Justice Mehr Chand Mahajan's proposal that Justice Din Muhammad, who was the senior-most among them, should preside over the sessions of the Commission was accepted by the other members. On 27 June, it was agreed that Sir Cyril Radcliffe, a member of the English Bar, would chair the Commission. Radcliffe was going to remain in Delhi and not directly partake in the sessions of the Punjab Boundary Commission. The records of the proceedings were to be flown to him by air.

References

Singh, Kirpal (ed.). *Select Documents on Partition of Punjab – 1947: Indian and Pakistan, Punjab, Haryana and Himachal, India and Punjab – Pakistan,* Delhi: National Book Shop, 1991.

Official documents

Carter, Lionel (ed). *Mountbatten's Report on the Last Viceroyalty (23 March–15 August 1947),* Manohar, Delhi, 2003.

———, *Punjab Politics, 1 June–14 August 1947, Tragedy, Governors' Fortnightly Reports and other Key Documents,* New Delhi: Manohar, 2007a.

———, *Punjab Politics, 3 March–31 May 1947, At the Abyss, Governors' Fortnightly Reports and other Key Documents,* New Delhi: Manohar, 2007b.

Mansergh, Nicholas and Penderel Moon (eds). *The Transfer of Power 1942-47, vol. X, The Mounbatten Viceroyalty, Formulation of a Plan, 22 March–30 May 1947,* London: Her Majesty's Stationery Office, 1981.

——. *The Transfer of Power 1942-7, vol. XI, The Mountbatten Viceroyalty, Announcement and Reception of the 3 June Plan, 31 May–7 July 1947,* London: Her Majesty's Stationery Office 1982.

Sadullah, Mian Muhammad (compiler). *The Partition of the Punjab 1947,* Lahore: Sang-e-Meel Publications, 1993.

11

THE BATTLE FOR LAHORE AND AMRITSAR 1 APRIL–30 JUNE 1947

WHILE THE PARTITION DRAMA WAS SLOWLY UNFOLDING AT THE level of high politics in Delhi, the situation on ground in the Punjab remained bad. Although atrocities committed during March 1947 ebbed from the middle of that month, the situation never returned to normal. During the first week of April, the *Pakistan Times* and *The Tribune* carried reports of isolated cases of ambush and attacks on individuals in different parts of the province. Trouble involving communal mobs flared up again in Amritsar on 11 April, when a large number of Muslims congregated for Friday prayers at the mosque in Chowk Pragdas, where a massacre of Muslims had taken place the month before. The congregation overflowed into the street. After the prayers, the Muslims passed through a predominantly non-Muslim area, shouting slogans against Hindus and Sikhs. In response, bricks were thrown at them from the rooftops by Hindus and Sikhs, and the Muslims retaliated. The melee left thirty-two people dead – seven Muslims, six Hindus, and nineteen Sikhs – while the number of injured was 103, according to the report by Governor Jenkins in his FR dated 30 April.

Jenkins observed that an atmosphere of 'civil war' prevailed throughout the Punjab. Sporadic cases of stabbing were being reported, especially from Lahore. Bombs of a crude type – often with soda-water bottles as containers – were being manufactured freely. Many fires had been started as a result of communal vandalism. People in towns were erecting barriers to protect the streets and lanes in which they lived. Amritsar was rapidly being split into a number of fortified areas. There was a great scramble for arms and the Sikhs were parading with unsheathed *kirpans*. Muslims were protesting vigorously against the exemption in favour of this traditional Sikh weapon. With regard to the Rawalpindi riots of March, Jenkins writes:

> Daultana recently toured in the Attock district, and there is credible evidence that he told the people in at least one village that if they could stick it out for a fortnight or three weeks, all proceedings against them will be withdrawn and the officers who have suppressed the disturbances will be given a hot time (Carter, 2007a: 153).

Rioting intensified in Amritsar and Lahore

In the second half of April and early May, mob violence subsided again, but there was a revivial in Amritsar on 9 May. The *Pakistan Times* and *The Tribune* of 10 May reported five people killed and twelve injured from stabbings. Arson and bomb blasts were also reported, though with no loss of life. The next day the situation deteriorated further when a party of Sikhs and Hindus, who had come to the Hindu cemetery of Daimganj with the body of a dead infant, were attacked by the Muslims, on the order of Mian Mehraj Din. Seven of the mourners were killed and five injured. Controversially, Khawaja Iftikhar asserts that the funeral party did not walk modestly in a Muslim-majority area and behaved in a generally arrogant manner. It is for this reason, he says, that the Muslims, who had not forgotten the outrage of Chowk Pragdas, were infuriated. The mourners' bodies were sprinkled with petrol and burnt. The injured were taken in very bad shape to the hospital. However, even on such an occasion, a woman by the name of Labhi was spared. When the police arranged an identification parade, one of the attackers, Meraj Din, had shaved off his beard. Labhi could not identify him and pointed out another man. Thus, the case collapsed against the Muslims who had been taken into custody (1991: 143-6).

Iftikhar gives the impression that Muslims enjoyed the upper hand in Amritsar. He goes into great detail on many other violent acts, even relating that each day Muslim doctors and other medical staff would give the 'score' of non-Muslim casualties. Iftikhar blames the administration for being 'anti-Muslim' and mentions the names of Hindu police officers, such as *thanedar* Kundan Lal Mehta, who were accused of victimising Muslims. He repeats many times that the Muslim victory over non-Muslims was a foregone conclusion because infidels were no match for the bravery of true Muslims. (ibid.: 146-9)

The heartless nature of the attack on the funeral party was reported on 11 May both by the pro-Muslim League *Pakistan Times* and by *The Tribune*, which put it in bold letters on the front page. Punjab Chief Secretary Akhtar Hussain, in his FR for the first half of May, wrote: 'Some of the acts committed were shocking in their stark brutality and an attack on a funeral party of a child in which six Sikhs and one Hindu were killed has added to an already over-long list of Muslim atrocities.' In the same report he mentioned that Hindus and Sikhs had been making crude bombs, most of which had exploded while being made, causing more injuries to their makers than to the intended victims.

Both the *Pakistan Times* and *The Tribune* reported that on 11 May, cases of arson had proliferated in Amritsar. *The Tribune* gave a figure of ten cases of arson and ten stabbings. On 12 May *The Tribune*'s front-page headline read, 'Regular Pitched Battle between Rival Parties at Amritsar'. It was noted there that home-made bombs had been freely used. The *Pakistan Times* also reported the gravely deteriorating position in that city. The authorities imposed a forty-eight-hour blanket curfew on 13 May.

Lahore

The inter-communal violence in Amritsar spread to Lahore on 13 May. The *Pakistan Times* of 14 May 1947 reported five incidents of shooting and stabbing from Sunday, 11 May and the two days after. *The Tribune* of 15 May reported seventeen stabbings, which resulted in twelve deaths. The report noted:

'Following these stabbing cases schools and colleges were closed and children were seen rushing back to their homes and in many cases people did not go to their offices while most of the offices were closed earlier. Shops were closed in most of the bazaars as also in Anarkali and other places of business.'

My elder brother, Mushtaq Ahmad, and the Punjabi writer, Mustansar Husain Tarrar, were both schoolboys in those days. They recalled the closure of schools in the following words:

Mushtaq Ahmad

'My school was located near the Punjab University Ground close to Chauburji [probably on Lake Road]. It was an English-medium school. It must have been in April when the classes had just started that our school was set ablaze by some miscreants. The Hindu staff, mostly lady teachers, ran away in panic. Some of the older children went home on their own while others were fetched by their families when they learnt about the attack. I did not know what to do, so I sat outside the gate of the school, all alone. I was only six at that time and did not know the way back home. The school was several miles away from our house on Temple Road. By chance *Abaji* (father) was on some official errand in the neighbourhood. His office was not far from there. He saw me and brought me home. The school never opened again. We had to wait till after Pakistan came into being to start school again.'

Mustansar Husain Tarar

'I was only eight in 1947. I studied at the Rang Mahal Mission School. I don't remember but it was sometime in April when our lady teacher told us to go home because curfew had been imposed. I used to come from Gawalmandi to the school. All the teachers had left. Nobody came to fetch me. I started walking back home. Outside Mochi Gate the Circular Road was completely desolate. I was, naturally, frightened and started running. Then I saw a man lying in the middle of the road. When I came close to him I saw him in a pool of blood. I don't know if he was a Hindu or a Muslim. That was the first time I saw blood. I started crying. By sheer good luck my *mama* Ahmed Ali happened to come that way. He brought me home. We were living on Chamberlain Road, which was a Hindu-dominated area. My father then arranged for two constables to remain at our residence all the time. At nighttime the Hindus would fire some shots at Muslim localities. The two constables would also go to the roof and fire some shots to warn the Hindus to keep away. Every evening one heard loud shouts of "*Allah-ho-Akbar*" (God is Great) and "*Har Har Mahadev*" (Glory of God's names).

✧

One anecdote that I grew up hearing is that Muslim *badmashes* in Lahore received from their Muslim counterparts in Amritsar a packet containing *churian* – glass bangles which women wear – and henna as a taunt for their unmanliness and cowardice at not finishing off Hindus and Sikhs, even though Lahore was a Muslim-majority city (1989: 114). This insult had the desired effect, for within a short time the Lahore *badmashes* indulged in a spree of stabbings and killings. *The Tribune* of 16 May reported:

> In the words of the Lahore District Magistrate, Mr Eustace, Lahore had been wiser and better sense prevailed for a long time. But on the basis of information in his possession Mr. Eustace said that trouble had started once again because the Amritsar Badmashes sent bangles to their brethren in Lahore to wear. This meant exciting them to indulge in the trade of goondaism at once.

The 'Lahore *badmashes*', according to Mr Eustace, got upset over this and decided to start trouble. But for this, the district magistrate believes there would have been no trouble again in Lahore.

Eustace, who was also deputy commissioner, did not mention henna in his press conference but that omission is not important. *The Tribune* of 17 May followed up that story and urged the governor, the Deputy Commissioner of Lahore and the Inspector-General of Police to investigate the so-called 'bangle business'. The *Pakistan Times* of 16 May 1947 avoided any direct mention of the story but reported that as a result of the escalation in violence, twenty-two persons died on 14 May. Kaleb Ali Sheikh explained the riddle of how the bangles were presented to the people of Lahore:

'Some [people] from Amritsar used to come daily to Lahore to work. They would take the train or travel on buses. When the trouble started, the Amritsar *goondas* started to come frequently to Lahore. The Lahore Muslims did not really have their heart in practising violence the same way the Amritsaris did. One day in May, a Muslim League procession or some gathering on the Mall was taking place. That is when the Amritsaris approached the Lahoris and said, this is a gift from us. Thereafter, a visible difference in the degree of ferocity of Muslim aggressive behaviour could be noticed. It is well-known that some Muslim League leaders such as Sardar Shaukat Hayat were connected to the *goonda* elements both in Amritsar and Lahore. Such a nexus then began to operate with increasingly violent methods of assaulting Hindus and Sikhs'.

Iftikhar has also described the same incident in the following words:

> Communal violence had spread to the towns and villages of the united Punjab. But it was a strange fact that a city [Lahore] as lively which not only was always the vanguard of political movements but also that all movements originated from it and gained popularity, was completely quiet this time. Some naughty Muslims of Amritsar sent by Babu Train, which daily left for Lahore, henna and bangles in one compartment for the Muslims of Lahore. The purpose was to make the Muslims of Lahore come out in the arena to take revenge for the crimes that had been committed against Muslims. The news that the Amritsar Muslims have sent bangles and henna for the Muslims of Lahore was published by the Lahore newspapers in a prominent manner. As a result the national pride of the Lahore Muslims was provoked. With the cooperation of Amritsaris they set ablaze Lahore's Shah Alam Market [the Hindu-majority Shahalmi Gate locality. The name Shah Alam market was given to it after Pakistan came into being] (1991: 192).

The attack on the Shahalmi Gate took place much later; Iftikhar has confused the dates. At any rate, between midnight, Friday 16 May, and the morning of Saturday 17 May, the total number of people killed since 14 May was given as fifty-five and number of injured as 128 (*Pakistan Times,* 18 May). Thereafter the situation subsided as Gurkha troops were ordered to patrol the troubled areas. The Lahore Congress leader Bhim Sen Sachar and Hindu Mahasabha leader Dr Gokul Chand Narang sent a telegram to the Punjab governor in which they asserted: 'Lahore situation is extremely critical. Strongly urge imposition of 24-hour curfew and calling out of troops on extensive scale. Immediate action can only check further deterioration' (*The Tribune*, 17 May).

However, the RSS was also active in Lahore and violence against Muslims did take place. I was told by Dr Hafeez Ahmad Mughal that his *khalu* (aunt's husband) Chanan Din, who had moved back from

Calcutta in 1939 to Billa Kabutar Baz Street near Rang Mahal, inside the walled city, was stabbed to death on 16 May 1947, in Ksayra Bazaar. The murderers could not, however, be traced. Dr Mughal also told me that throwing of brickbats and waylaying strangers were common occurrences, requiring curfews to be imposed in trouble-spots in the walled city.

Great fire raging in the walled city

The *Pakistan Times* of 18 May 1947 reported that several fires raged in the walled city from the night of Friday 16 May. The situation began to deteriorate, with stabbings occurring soon after 8 a.m., when the curfew was lifted. By afternoon, pitched battles were being fought between rival communal groups in an area extending from Yakki Gate and Taxali Gate. The fires which had begun in the middle of the day spread quickly, engulfing large areas, including Chowk Wazir Khan, Akbari Mandi, and Kucha Wanwattan. Gurkha troops were ordered to patrol the Circular Road.

Attack on Muslim locality of Rajgarh

On 18 May the Muslim locality of Rajgarh suffered an organised attack by Hindus and Sikhs. Rajgarh was surrounded by several Hindu-majority localities such as Sham Nagar, Prem Nagar, and the main stronghold of Krishan Nagar. Akhtar Hussain notes in his report for the second half of May that beginning in 11 April, 460 people had either been killed or injured in Amritsar; in Lahore since 9 May – the day on which the new outbreak occurred – there were 325 dead or injured. He observed:

> Incidents proving better organisation have occurred outside as well as inside the two cities. The best examples are attacks which took place at Rajgarh and Singhpura near Lahore on the 18th and 19th of May and at Rasulpura close to Amritsar on the 24th. Rajgarh and Rasulpura were scenes of large-scale and well-planned onslaughts on Muslims by Sikhs and Hindus armed with modern weapon, grenades, and bombs. Singhpura was different in that it furnished no evidence of an unprovoked aggression but supplied proof of the

> preparedness of Sikh organisation to meet any emergency and to retaliate with brutal effect. In all these three cases in which Muslims suffered heavy casualties, investigation is being conducted and is likely to result in interesting disclosures. Already there is reason to believe that the Rajgarh attackers included men of the Rashtriya Swayam Sewak Sangh. It is known that [sic] that members of the Sangh are concerned with an organisation inside the city which has been functioning under the control of a Defence Committee which is part of the Punjab Relief Committee (20 June 1947, POL. 8501/47).

The report goes on to state that outside Lahore and Amritsar, the most serious communal disturbances had taken place in the Gurgaon district. The disorder had apparently started on 25 May when Hindu Ahirs attacked a Muslim village, causing many casualties and damage to property. The next day another Muslim village was attacked but was met with Muslim retaliation. The district experienced virtually communal warfare, which the authorities had failed to control. Some fifty villages were destroyed and a large number of people either died or were injured. Muslim Meos formed the main community clashing with the Ahirs. The police and military had fired as many as 1,000 rounds in an attempt to reestablish the peace. Arms recovered from both sides included some solidly-made, locally-manufactured mortars (ibid.).

The Punjab governor separately reported on 31 May that armed parties from the Sikh states of Faridkot and Nabha were reported in Lahore, where they had created a scare. They were subsequently warned not to send armed people nor service vehicles to the British Punjab without permission (Carter, 2007a: 222).

Dr Mughal remembers that frightening night very well. He wrote to me:

> I was fourteen and a half at the time our country came into being (born 2 January 1933) and studying in 9th class in Central Model School and living in Mozang.... A battalion of the Indian Army... attacked Muslims residing in Rajgarh. A large number was killed including women and children. The soldiers in jeeps passed on Begum Road before our eyes. It was nighttime and we could hear

the cries of the people being attacked and could see the fire and smoke of burning huts.

Visit to Rajgarh on 13 January 2005

Rajgarh was a Muslim locality on the outskirts of pre-partition Lahore, surrounded by Hindu–Sikh localities, among them Sham Nagar, Ram Nagar, and Prem Nagar, as well as the Hindu stronghold of Krishan Nagar. It was at some distance from the nearest Muslim stronghold of Mozang.

Ahmad Salim and I arrived in Rajgarh when the winter sun was fast setting on the horizon. After a while we met some locals who put us in contact with elders whom we hoped could help us reconstruct the events of 18 May 1947.

Ghulam Haider

'The culprits came from the Hindu-majority locality of Sham Nagar and Krishan Nagar. They had modern firearms and explosives with them. They exploded some bombs and set fire to the thatched huts of Muslim gypsies and also attacked the dairy farm of Gujjars. They killed my uncle and his sister-in-law. After these events, his family moved to the Muslim locality of Ichraa and returned home only after the creation of Pakistan. DSP Tek Singh was party to the conspiracy to attack Rajgarh.'

Muhammad Munir

'I was only 10–12 at that time. The raiders came late in the evening. Some bombs were exploded and several Muslims were killed or injured. The raiders cut off both legs of Gaam Nai. We sought protection with our relatives in Mozang. Many Muslim leaders, including Begum Shahnawaz, subsequently visited Rajgarh. Then the military and police came and some Hindus and Sikhs suspected of the crime were rounded up and taken to the Mozang police station. It was the Hindus from Krishan Nagar who attacked Rajgarh. Some five to seven Muslims were killed.

My uncle Jalal Din, his wife Ghulam Fatima, and their son Muhammad Yusuf were killed. Some of their buffaloes were also killed. Mian Ahmed Din was shot but he survived.'

Lambardar Mian Muhammad Hanif

'I belong to the family of *lambardars* of this village. I was sixteen years old in 1947. My family of Muslim Arains were the most prominent in Rajgarh. My elders had been granted a *jagir* (estate) by Maharaja Ranjit Singh. The main road in Rajgarh, Pir Baksh Road, is named after my grandfather. Rajgarh was chosen for the raid because it was the only Muslim-majority locality in a region surrounded by Hindu–Sikh areas. Rajgarh was connected only on one side with another Muslim locality, that of Sandayan to the west.

'The attack had certainly been planned well. There were reports that Sikhs from some princely states and Hindus from Krishan Nagar took part. The attackers arrived in the dark, creating maximum effect by exploding several bombs. At that time only two Muslims, Bau Amin and Mehr Feroz, had guns but they preferred not to return fire and thus draw the superior force of the Hindus and Sikhs onto them. The people stayed indoors. Also at that time a curfew was in operation. Several gypsies and Gujjars were killed and their huts burnt.

'By that time fires had begun to be set in the old city. There was only one Muslim building in Krishan Nagar, the Chiragh Building. The Hindus tried to set it on fire but could not succeed. Some Muslims from Rajgarh took part in clashes with the Hindus of Krishan Nagar. After Partition most Hindus and Sikhs left although in Krishan Nagar they stayed until some time in 1948.'

The battle for Lahore intensifies

On 18 May the government, invoking the Public Safety Act, ordered a ban on reporting of communal disorders other than those based on accounts by the government. No news item or pictures collected by journalists were to be published directly. Despite the fear created among Muslims by the attack on Rajgarh, the overall balance of power had shifted in their favour by the middle of May. Jenkins reported that Muslims had been responsible for most of the burnings and for about two-thirds of the deaths. In a telegram to the viceroy dated 21 May he wrote: 'Moslems seem determined to burn Hindus and Sikhs out of greater Lahore and are concentrating on incendiarism. Hindus and Sikhs are retaliating in kind but are concentrating mainly on acquisition of arms with a view to personal vengeance' (Carter, 2007a: 207). He asserted that the government had employed the maximum available strength of police but that this was not enough to cope with the deteriorating situation. He requested more troops. In addition to the 4th Indian Division, whose drafting-in had already been arranged, an additional complete brigade was needed for greater Lahore alone (ibid.).

In an article entitled 'Some Suggestions to Punjab Governor', *The Tribune* pleaded for more troops to be posted in Lahore; for mixed police forces to be deployed in the city (most local policemen were Muslims); and for soldiers to accompany the fire brigades when they went to put out fires, because otherwise goondas and other miscreants would obstruct their work by pelting them with stones (*The Tribune,* 20 May).

End of May

The month of May ended with the overall question of the partition of India and the Punjab entering a critical phase. An announcement from the Viceroy was in the offing, awaited with impatience, in the main cities and towns, by the educated classes of India. As far as the law and order situation was concerned, the Punjab remained disturbed, with violence having become endemic in Lahore and Amritsar, and with spurts in other parts as well. Yuvraj Krishan, who lived in a Hindu locality of Purani Anarkali, recounted that fires raged in the Hindu localities at the end of May. He recalled:

'Trouble in Lahore started with Master Tara Singh's speech on 3 March at Kuri (Girls') Bagh near Purani Anarkali, near our house. It resulted in communal clashes and police firing in which mainly Hindus suffered loss of life. Thereafter, everyday there were reports of someone being waylaid and robbed or stabbed. In the evenings the situation worsened even more. Communal animosity began to be expressed in terms of belligerent slogans and war cries from the rooftops. The Muslims would shout "*Nahra-e-Takbir, Allah o Akbar*". This was followed by screams of "*Har, Har Mahdev*" by the Hindus and "*Jo Bole So Nihal, Sat Sri Akal*" by the Sikhs. Each chorus dragged on only to be followed by the other side prolonging its menacing recitation of the religious call to arms. All this generated deep fear and insecurity. In May, attacks started taking place on a more organised basis, Hindus and Sikhs were attacked in those areas where they were in a minority and Hindu–Sikh gangs attacked Muslims where the latter were in a minority.

'When the trouble started, my father left for Kulu where our ancestral home was located. My elder brother, a cousin of mine and I lived together in our Dhobi Mandi house. On the night of 27 May, the Muslims set fire to Papar Mandi, a Hindu locality in the walled city. When the Hindus tried to come out the police ordered them back since there was a curfew at that time. At two o'clock in the night we could see from the roof of our house flames leaping from the direction of the old city. All this deeply discouraged and frightened us. The police in Lahore was overwhelmingly Muslim. It played a very partisan role during that period. We lost confidence in the state machinery. If a Hindu or Sikh went to the police station to ask for help it was denied in practice, if not formally.'

Vimal Issar

While in the dining hall of the India International Centre in New Delhi, I was joined by a group of people. Among them was the former Chief Justice of Pakistan, Dr Nasim Hasan Shah, who had come to Delhi to attend a conference. With him were two other persons. One of them was Vimal Issar, a retired senior officer from All-India Radio. Mrs Issar turned out to be from Lahore. She later helped me with a number of very interesting interviews. When I interviewed her on 13 March 2004, she narrated the following:

'I was born in Kutcha Mela Ram in the walled city of Lahore. My father, Harbans Singh Suri, had a flourishing sports business. We supplied sporting material and equipment to many clubs all over Punjab. My father was a modern man who did not believe in observing the caste rules of pollution. Therefore, at our home, Muslims ate freely. There was never a problem. Some Hindu women were always more concerned than men about these matters. A narrow lane went from our residence to the red light area of Hira Mandi. We had a number of Muslim workers employed. A Muslim washerman called my mother *bhabi*. Our furniture was made by Gul Muhammad who was a very skilful artisan.

'From March onwards, Lahore was disturbed but we were never ever attacked by our neighbours. We heard about Hindus and Sikhs being forced to convert to Islam in Rawalpindi but we were not scared at that time. I used to study in a school near University Ground. Salma, a Muslim, was my class fellow. My brother was in Hailey College and younger brother was in Government College. The student agitation started when police fired upon Hindu students in early March in the Gol Bagh. My brother Tej Kumar was there. He was lucky to escape unhurt when the police opened fire. Despite all the troubles, we decided to stay put as our neighbours were very good people and we did not feel insecure.

'However, by May, fires were ablaze in many parts of the city including in the walled city. Our washerman warned us to move as he had heard that an attack had been planned on our house. My father decided that we should move to Mohni Road which was just across the main road. It was a Hindu locality. At Mohni Road we followed with unease news of trouble in other parts of Lahore. Then one day, a mob came to Mohni Road shouting "*Ya Ali, Ya Ali*". That scared my parents. From our roof one could see the fires. They were spreading. Our relatives from Sialkot had already left for UP. My father sent me and my elder brother to Mathura, UP, where we had relatives. My mother and younger brother came in July and told us that our house had been burnt. My father left Lahore just before mid-August. Nobody in our immediate family was hurt or killed.'

Amritsar

In Amritsar, arson, stabbing and incendiarism wrecked the lives of people all over the city. The situation continued to get out of control as more and more people were engulfed by the violence, perpetrated mainly by criminal gangs against each other. By that time, most people had fled from mixed areas and regrouped in localities where their co-religionists were in a majority. Between 5 March and 16 May the authorities in Amritsar counted 209 dead and 422 injured. Complaints of 2,062 cases of alleged arson, murder, looting and injury, involving losses of ₹42 million, had been recorded by the police. Altogether, two hundred persons had been arrested. There were as many as 319 accused offenders in Amritsar according to the authorities. Several of them had gone underground (*The Tribune,* 27 May).

Another part of the Punjab which remained disturbed during May was Gurgaon district in Ambala division. Thirty villages, mostly inhabited by Muslims, had been burnt down (*Tribune*, 31 May). The *Pakistan Times* also highlighted the sad plight of Muslims in that easternmost district of the Punjab.

June

Sporadic violence continued in the first week of June. *The Tribune* of 2 June reported mob clashes in Amritsar on the previous day. Cases of arson, stabbing and other brutal attacks were reported from different parts of the city. There was a visible increase in hostilities from 8 June, when Governor Jenkins, in a telegram to the viceroy, reported a number of deaths from Lahore, Amritsar and Gurgaon (Carter, 2007b: 61-2). The second week of June witnessed a recrudescence of bomb-throwing, arson and stabbings, deaths and injuries in several parts of the province. Gujranwala had been disturbed since the beginning of June. Violent incidents were also reported from Gujrat, Gurdaspur, Jullundur, Ludhiana and Ambala. In Montgomery, six Muslims were murdered by Sikhs, according to a telegram from Jenkins dated 10 June (Carter, 2007b: 67-8).

The *Pakistan Times*, which had not been published during the period 19 May to 11 June, came out again on 12 June. It reported on the sixty-hour curfew that had been imposed in Mochi Gate inside the walled city of Lahore, where arson, stabbings and bomb-throwing continued unabated. The situation in Amritsar improved somewhat but on 17 June once again, incendiaries, hand-grenades and crude bombs were being used by rival gangs. Sheikh Sadiq Hasan, MLA and the

President of the Muslim League in Amritsar, sent a telegram to the governor informing him that about 14,000 unemployed Muslims, including those whose houses had been destroyed, were on the verge of starvation and needed immediate relief from the government (*Pakistan Times*, 17 June 1947).

The 16 June bomb attack on Luchman Das Hospital, Shahalmi, Lahore

On 16 June, as Jenkins reported in a telegram to the viceroy:

'The worst bomb explosion occurred when police party went to investigate earlier explosion [15 June] in [a] hospital outside Shahalmi gate of the city. Bomb was thrown at party causing 44 casualties, including one killed and several serious casualties including 3 policemen one of whom dangerously wounded. Remainder were members of the public (Carter, 2007b: 88).

Haji Abdul Rehman Gill, whose evidence has already been referred to in connection with violence at Shahalmi Gate on 3 March was a witness to the 16 June incident. He recalled:

'The Lahore Congress leader, Bhim Sen Sachar, addressed a public meeting in the compound of the Lala Luchman Das hospital, which was just outside Shahalmi Gate. I was at that time sitting at our milk shop in the *deira*. Three Muslim boys came from the direction of Mochi Gate. They openly discussed a plan to throw incendiary devices on the people in the public meeting. One of them was to go from the front via the bazaar, the other was to proceed from the park and the third was to go from behind the hospital and cast the bombs. I saw one of them cast the explosive device, which could be grenades. The wall of the compound was only eight feet from him. The bomb exploded and caused many casualties. District Magistrate Muhammad Ghani Cheema, who was in the neighbourhood, blamed the Hindus instead for possessing explosive material and even for throwing a grenade at him. He filed a case against the Hindus.'

The situation in the Punjab was rapidly getting out of control. The Punjab Police Abstracts continued to report a constant movement of Hindus and Sikhs from the western districts towards safety in the east, while Muslims from Gurgaon and also some from Amritsar and Lahore were moving westwards (*Disturbances in the Punjab, 1947: 234*). At the same time, Sikh mobilisation was reported from all over the central and eastern districts and in the Sikh states.

Lahore, Amritsar, Gujranwala, Gujrat, Jullundur and Ambala continued to figure among the disturbed areas, with ever-increasing violence. *The Tribune* of 21 June reported hundred bombs exchanged by rival mobs in Amritsar and twenty bombs seized in Mozang Lahore from Muslim miscreants. But the most dramatic change occurred in Lahore, which broke the will of the Hindus and Sikhs to hold on to the city. This was the notorious fire in the Hindu locality of Shahalmi Gate. Up to this point, whereas Sikhs had borne the brunt of Muslim-inspired atrocities (in the Rawalpindi division, in March) the Hindus of Lahore had remained confident that they would retain their presence in the walled city, at whatever cost.

The Sabzi Mandi bomb attack

The *Pakistan Times* and *The Tribune* of 22 June reported the explosion of two bombs in the Sabzi Mandi (vegetable market) on the previous day, which killed eighteen and wounded fifty-five. That market was essentially a Muslim business area and therefore, most of those killed and injured were Muslims. A Muslim witness to the bomb blasts, Mian Muhammad Sharif, gave the following account:

'I was helping my uncle, Khuda Bakhsh, with some purchases when suddenly there were loud noises in the Sabzi Mandi. I have a feeling that more than one bomb exploded. It was during the morning hours when it happened and many people were present in the market. I remember seeing charred bodies, completely unrecognisable. There were some limbs also lying around. People ran around in complete panic and horror. Nobody knew what to do. More than a dozen people died and many more were injured. It was a horrible scene. The bombs were surely exploded by the Hindus. They lived in large numbers around the market and therefore must have come from Gawalmandi or Nisbet Road which were close by.'

Dina Nath Malhotra

Malhotra's impressions of Hindu–Muslim relations before Partition have already been given in an earlier chapter. He refers to the bomb blast in the Meva Mandi (fruit market) but the newspapers and the government records mention the Sabzi Mandi. There is no record of a bomb blast in the fruit market. He gave me the following account:

'From late May onwards, fires were raging all the time in some part of Lahore. We lived in the Hindu stronghold of Nisbet Road. One could see smoke rising from the walled city and Hindus were on the losing side. I got involved in the 'Relief Committee for the victims of riots' under the Hindu leadership of Dr Gokul Chand Narang. On one Sunday morning we learned that five Hindu youth had been badly injured by bullet wounds inside the Shahalmi Gate in Haveli Nakain in the vicinity of Wachchowali. They needed to be taken to hospital urgently. It must be sometime in July, if I am not mistaken. I drove the big ambulance that we had purchased. I and my friend Vidya Ratan started that journey when the roads were deserted, as curfew was in force (we had the permission to travel), fires were raging all over, the police, mainly Muslim, were openly siding with the Muslim criminals and there was great insecurity. It was with very great difficulty that we were able to get to those injured men. One had died. We took the other four onto the ambulance. The mother of one of the men was crying hysterically. She also boarded the ambulance. With great difficulty were we able to exit from the Shahalmi Gate but then the shrieks of the mother made us stop. Her son had expired. We tried our best to console the unfortunate woman. Then Ft. Lt. Roop Chand, who belonged to the leading Diwan family, appeared on the scene in a station wagon. He then took the other three boys to the Sir Ganga Ram Hospital.

'Two days later, a meeting of the Relief Committee was held and it was decided to acquire firearms. Mr N.D. Kapur was in charge of that operation. He had arranged for the purchase of some guns from the Rawalpindi Ordinance Depot. I and a friend, Mahinder, went to Rawalpindi and brought back twelve revolvers which were hidden in the seat covers of the front row of a bus and stitched properly. That is how we were able to deliver those guns to Mr Kapur.

'One day I had to go to the Gawalmandi police station in connection with getting permission to acquire a shop of ours that our tenant, a Muslim tailor, was not using as he had not been coming to Nisbet Road for months. The reader at the police station was busy with some paperwork so I took a seat to wait for my turn to talk to him. The police had rounded up some Hindu youths after the bomb in the Meva Mandi had killed eight persons and over twenty had been injured. On such occasions the police use great brutality to obtain confessions and information. The SHO shouted the name Prakash loudly as he interrogated one of the young men. I knew Prakash had been picked up by the police near the bombing site. Prakash's voice was trembling and he blurted out my name among those who were involved in the bomb blast.

'I was scared to death when I heard my name. The reader was still busy with paperwork. I got up quietly and walked out of the police station calmly and then when I entered our lane, ran like mad to reach home. At home, my mother and brother decided that it was too dangerous for me to remain in Lahore. My brother drove me to our Arya Press and then in the evening took me to the Moghulpura railway station instead of the main Lahore station, from where I boarded the Punjab Mail and left Lahore. It must be some time in the end of June, but I don't remember the exact date.'

Dr Jagdish Chander Sarin

Dr Jagish Chander Sarin, earlier referred to with regard to the attacks in northern Punjab on Hindus and Sikhs, shared his recollection of the fires that raged on the same day in some Hindu localities inside the walled city:

'On 21 June fire was set to the Hindu area of Papar Mandi in Lahore. After that, Machi Hata and then Shahalmi were put on fire. There was a magistrate, Cheema, who personally directed the attacks on the non-Muslims. He would not allow the fire-brigade people to do their duty and if Hindus and Sikhs tried to flee from the place they were sent back. During those days I used to go to work from my house in Montgomery Park to the Plaza Cinema and then to the Balak Ram

Medical College on Queens Road. We heard daily that someone had been killed or seriously injured. If one day, seven Hindus were killed then next day, seven or eight Muslims were reported dead. In our own area, to the best of my knowledge, the local Muslims did not attack us. One day, two badly-burnt persons arrived in the hospital. They were most likely RSS cadres who had been trying to make a bomb. It had exploded and caused them severe injuries.

'A friend of mine came and told me that the Hindu locality of Mohalla Sareen in the walled city had been attacked the previous night and seventeen young men had been killed. They had no weapons to defend themselves with. A doctor was needed to help the wounded. I offered to go and help those people. I went to the head office of the Sarswati Insurance Company owned by the leading Hindu Mahasabha leader, Sir Gokul Chand Narang. It was also the headquarters of the Lahore Relief Society, which was actually a cover name for the Hindu militants. There we got the basic equipment for first-aid and also a .303 rifle and some cartridges. I had never used any weapon before and got very scared of the idea of carrying it. A Maharashtrian who had played a part in the socialist movement in the 1940s gave me bottles of ammonia and bromine capsules. He told me that if you are attacked and want to disperse the crowd you should throw them on the ground. Fumes will come up and the crowd will disperse. We concealed the rifle in a stretcher and other such things in bundles of cotton and drove to the Mohalla Sareen in Sir Gokul's big Buick car.

'We entered Shahalmi Gate, then Rang Mahal. Many people were assembled there. They were shouting, "Don't go further. A fire is raging ahead." We kept going, however, and entered Kashmiri Bazaar. We parked the car in front of Mohalla Sareen. We went in and stayed for some time, gave them the things we had taken with us and then left via Shahi *mohalla*. What we learned was that Muslim boys had been trying to enter the *mohalla* through a narrow gate with the intention of setting that locality on fire while the Hindu boys inside had been trying to stop them with the help of sticks and stones. Both sides seemed not to possess any other weapons. The next day seven members of the Lahore Relief Society, which were actually the RSS, went there to give them bullets. They were arrested by the police and later tortured.

'Afterwards the great fires in the walled city began and whole Hindu areas were burnt down. This continued unabated, but it was still by no means certain that Lahore would go to Pakistan. One day I said to Dr Gopi Chand Bhargava, who was a Congress leader, "Doctor Sahib, you should leave Lahore. There is a danger to your life here". He replied "No, I am a follower of Gandhi. If someone comes and kills me I shall die quietly". Another person, Mohan Lal, said jokingly, "Doctor Sahib, everybody is selling his property. Have you any to sell? I will buy it". Actually, the Hindu leaders of Lahore were very confident that Lahore would remain a part of India. Dr Gopi Chand Bhargava was convinced that Lahore would never go to Pakistan'.

Earlier, on a visit to Mumbai, I had met on 3 January 1997 the renowned Indian filmmaker B.R. Chopra at his office in Mumbai and talked to him at length about his Lahore days. He told me that his family lived on Chamberlain Road in Gawalmandi, a locality not far from Shahalmi. This was a predominantly Hindu area. Later they moved to an area behind the Punjab Legislative Assembly. During the conversation, I wondered if he had ever wanted to revisit Lahore. He told me he often thought that his days at Government College Lahore were the most unforgettable of his life and indeed he had maintained contact with some old friends. His old friend Sheikh Abdul Rashid had died but the Sheikh's children wrote once in a while. He admitted to having a very strong longing to go to Lahore, but his wife would not contemplate it because of the Shahalmi fire, which had played havoc with the Hindu community of that locality. She was too deeply traumatised by that experience. Even though she herself had escaped unhurt, many of her relatives had perished in that fire.

Even among Muslim old-timers, when the subject of the year 1947 and Partition comes up, the fire at Shahalmi is always mentioned as the turning-point at which the Hindus and Sikhs lost the will to fight and stay on in Lahore. In my own conversations over the years with Lahore Hindus, two subjects have been mentioned again and again – the Shahalmi fire and the allegation that City Magistrate Muhammad Ghani Cheema played a pivotal role in its eruption. Consequently, I particularly wanted to find out what exactly happened in Lahore on that occasion.

Haji Abdul Rehman was able to provide first-hand information on the fire at Shahalmi Gate as well, since he was involved in the plot. The details that he gave corresponded very closely to the report of the incident published in the *Pakistan Times* of 24 June 1947. In the interview that I conducted with him on 30 December 2004, I was particularly keen to know the exact date, but he could not recall it, beyond saying that it was an extremely hot night. Let me begin by quoting verbatim and in the actual format the report from the *Pakistan Times* of 24 June 1947.

> About 100 HOUSES, BESIDES 100 SHOPS WERE COMPLETELY DESTROYED IN A CONFLAGRATION WHICH FLARED UP INSIDE SHAHALMI GATE, PAPAR MANDI AND KUCHA HAWAGARAN IN LAHORE ON SUNDAY MORNING [June 22]. BUILDINGS ON BOTH SIDES OR [sic] THE BAZAR HAVE BEEN ENTIRELY GUTTED AND HAVE COLLAPSED. THE FALLING DEBRIS HAVE BLOCKED THE BAZAR. THE LOSS IS ESTIMATED AT SEVERAL LAKHS [000,000] OF RUPEES. THE LOCAL BULLION EXCHANGE, KARIANA MARKET AND WAREHOUSES ARE LOCATED IN THESE AREAS.

The fire was set during the small hours of Sunday morning inside Shahalmi Gate and later it spread up to Papar Mandi, Jore Mori and Bal Mata Steet.

A Corporation fire-brigade and two military fire engines which arrived on the scene remained idle for a considerable amount of time, owing to breakdown in the water supply. Gunshot fires repeatedly rang through early morning on Sunday and about 100 rounds were reported to have been fired by the troops and police on curfew-breakers, during the tumult and confusion caused by the spreading fire.

Three bombs exploded inside Shahalmi Gate on Sunday morning when a party of police officers led by the local magistrate was touring the affected localities. One military officer and two police officers were reported to have received injuries.

The police and military cordoned off the locality and took into custody about 150 persons including one woman.

At the bottom of the same page, another news item is given: In the evening Sir Evan Jenkins, accompanied by Sir J.M.T. Bennett, Inspector-

General of Police, visited the blitzed parts of Shahalmi Gate, Papar Mandi and Kucha Hawagaran, and also the Mozang area.

Haji Abdul Rehman Gill

'Magistrate Cheema used to come to our *deira* and talk to my father. He was a Jatt like us and knew my father very well. I was always with father because he used to have some fits and needed immediate attention; therefore I am privy to all that happened in those days. They would sit outside the potters' shops and talk. One day some Hindus tried to pull down the minaret of the Lal Masjid inside Shahalmi. My father wanted to go in and punish the miscreants. A lorry patrol led by a British sergeant was in this area. Cheema stopped the lorry and showed his identification papers to the sergeant, who saluted him. Upon Cheema's instructions the sergeant ordered his troops off the lorry and to fire at the desecraters. Total pandemonium broke out, people ran for cover in all directions. Some Hindus hid themselves in the wide sewerage lanes while others ran away.

'Immediately behind our house was another Hindu locality, Kucha Bal Mata. Hindus of that *mohalla* set fire to the upper storey of my grandfather's house, but the fire began to spread in the direction of Hindu homes rather than downwards. Anyhow, this provocation from the Hindus further infuriated my father. Since 3 March Muslim police from Mianwali was posted outside Shahalmi gate. The Assistant Sub-Inspector in charge was Karam Din. The men from Mianwali were tall and imposing and kept big moustaches. They also played a role in the first incendiary attack on Shahalmi. My guess is that Cheema sensed that since our houses had been set on fire and Father was infuriated, he could easily be persuaded to take part in an all-out assault on the Hindus. Thus one very hot late evening, while we were all sitting at the *deira*, Cheema said to my father "Billey give me some men, I want to put Shahalmi ablaze". This was the origin of the great Shahalmi fire.

'My father was hesitant, because we were a big family and except for me, the children were small. He said to Cheema, "I cannot take part in such an activity because I have many responsibilities now. 1927, 1935 and 1937 were different times, now I must think about the interests of my children*." Cheema said he understood, but was determined to set Shahalmi on fire. In order to make it safe for my father to take part in the plot, he ordered ASI Karam Din to take him to the police post and show in the police records that Magistrate Cheema had put Billa in the lockup under sections 107 and 151. He then said, "So, now, give me the men I need." Upon hearing this Father said, "Okay, Chaudhri" (Cheema, being also a Jatt, could be addressed as Chaudhri according to Punjabi convention).

'Father said to Cheema, "Give me a police constable and I will get you help." I, my father, and a constable then left for Sirianwalli Bazaar in Mochi Gate where my cousin Muhammad Shafi, also known as Shafi Itti or Shafi Nainanwala, lived. Sirianwala Bazaar is the same *mohalla* where Ilamuddin Shaheed lived. Father spoke to Latif and told him he needed material to set Shahalmi ablaze. He said, "Okay, *Pajee* (elder brother) come back after two hours". We returned after two hours. He had arranged two *pippas* (drums) of an oil-based chemical substance called "solution". Such a substance is used in shoemaking and a variety of other objects. When it is applied to an object it sticks to it and not only catches fire easily but once the fire is lit it is very difficult to put it out.

'Two of his close friends, Abdul Latif, or Tiffa Tarkhan and Laava Kankatta Kashmiri, accompanied him. It was around 10 p.m. and totally quiet in the streets because of the curfew. Soon we reached the place where Cheema and father were waiting for them. A Sikh in the police force, that the Hindus always wanted posted on night duty in Shahalmi, was sleeping on a charpoy near the Shahalmi Gate. That day Cheema had ordered Karam Din not to put him on duty. Cheema posted a policeman with a gun loaded with orders to shoot him if he got up and made a noise. After a while Cheema ordered us to begin our work. Father and Cheema remained outside. Two groups of two each were formed. The two groups went off in opposite directions to the farthest

*In 1927 there were disturbances against the lenient sentence awarded to Rajpal; in 1935, there were disturbances because of the Masjid/Gurdwara Shahidganj controversy and in 1937, the provincial elections were held under Government of India Act 1935.

end of Shahalmi and then began to apply the "solution" to the shop doors and *tharas* (shop-fronts), which in those days were always made of wood. At one end, near Haveli Lala Lachman Ram, the Hindus had built a *chaubacha* (small water tank) and filled it with water, and also drums were filled to the brim with water. This had been done as a precaution in case of a fire breaking out. The *haveli* was like a fortress. It was widely believed that Hindus had collected considerable amounts of weapons and ammunition inside.

'The other party went towards Mohalla Pari Mal. Both parties now began to smear the doors and *tharas* with the substance and also put it in the *chaubacha* and water-filled drums. When the big clock at Government College struck one o'clock Cheema ordered the fire to be lit. We started from the farthest end moving towards the Shahalmi Gate. In a matter of minutes the fire turned into a veritable inferno.

'To talk about the fire now after fifty-seven years and to see it with your own eyes when the conflagration took place are very different things. The cries and screams that accompanied that scene can never be forgotten. There is nothing more excruciatingly painful than to be burnt. The heat was unbearable even from a distance. While everything around was dark, Shahalmi seemed to be bathing in light. The atmosphere was unreal even while it was spectacular. Until recently, the Moti Mandir built by Jawaharlal Nehru's father Motilal Nehru stood here. It has now been destroyed. The *mandir* was near the canal that once encircled the whole walled city. The canal had been built by the British for the purpose of supplying water to the garden around the walled city.

'The fire brigade arrived immediately and positioned itself beneath the Moti Mandir. The engines started to suck water from the canal for splashing it on the burning buildings, but Cheema ordered the fire fighters to turn the nozzle of the hoses back into the canal. The result was that while it sounded as if the fire brigade was working full-throttle, the water was flowing back into the canal. The fire fighters were Muslims and in any case they could not have defied the orders of a city magistrate. When the fire reached full blaze Cheema said to my father, "Billey, now I want to eat *gurr waley choul* (sweet rice cooked in unrefined sugar) and *massar choul* (rice and linser)." These dishes were cooked immediately and we sat in a house in Kucha Dogran and ate them.

'I remember the fire was raging and many shops which sold spices were burnt. Burning spices emit peculiar smells. Some smelled good but when red chillies burnt people started sneezing. I saw a miracle take place that night. Whenever the fire reached the house of a Muslim it would take another direction. A Muslim prostitute lived next to the Lal Masjid. The fire left her house untouched. When it reached Pappar Mandi it stopped at the house of Muslim sheikhs. They had, in any case, thoroughly soaked their house in water. A Hindu *thanedar* (officer in charge of a police station), Pandit Devi Das and two of his Muslim constables whom we called Sajja and Khabba (Right and Left), came to Kucha Dogran, which was a Muslim locality. These Muslim constables were real rogues and acted as spies of Devi Das. He said to the Muslims of Kucha Dogran, "In my area there is no curfew, so go and put out the fire". Instead of obeying him, the Muslims of that *mohalla* decided to finish off all three. Consequently, they were lured to walk up the stairs of the sheikhs and watch from there what was happening around. The plan was that when they came to the top floor they should be thrown down. Devi Das went up a few steps, then sensed that something was wrong. So, he and the two constables ran away and did not even return to the police station.

'The fire lasted exactly twelve hours. It started at one o'clock in the night and died out at one o'clock in the afternoon next day. I have no idea of how many people were killed; they were probably less than a hundred because most ran away. They came out from Moti Bazaar via Lohari Mandi and then reached Lahori Bagh, where it looked as if a huge fair was taking place, but it was full of disturbed people rather than those seeking fun and joy. The *tongawallas* charged ₹100 per person to take them to the railway station. It was an exorbitant price at that time; the normal charge in those days was less than one rupee per passenger. Not all of Shahalmi was burnt in that fire; many buildings remained unaffected and the Hindus and Sikhs stayed on in parts of Shahalmi. Those buildings were later burnt in July and other people were involved.

'In the First Investigation Report registered with the police by the Hindus, only my father's name was mentioned. The senior police were still British. They began a manhunt for my father. He first took refuge with a relative in Topkhana Bazaar, who hid him in a shop. Then he moved to Chung, a forest outside Lahore. It has down the ages served as safe haven for people on the run from authorities. A relative of ours was already based in Chung and had considerable influence. He provided my father with protection during his stay in Chung.

'I and my father's younger brother were taken to Lohari Gate Police Station for interrogation. However, the Muslim League leader and member of Punjab Assembly from Lahore, the notable Khalifa Shujauddin, whom father used to help during elections and who was very fond of him, exercised his influence and we were released from police custody. But one of my brothers became very ill and Father, who loved him a lot, could not resist coming to see him. Someone informed the authorities about his arrival and the police immediately came to arrest him. Father escaped arrest by concealing himself in the *khurli* (manger) at the Tonga stand outside Nawan Bazaar where a *ganda nala* (dirty stream) used to flow. Thus, while the horses were eating the grass, Father was hiding underneath the pile. The police went away. My father visited us again in July but someone again informed the police and there was a raid, but my father managed to escape by hiding among the cowdung cakes in a Gujjar's house. A relative of ours, Dulla, a Jatt, who was also *billa* (with light-coloured eyes), was taken away instead of him. My father's eyes had been entered since 1927 in police records as his distinguishing characteristic. They also took another *billa*, Billa Karigarh. They released him but kept Dulla Billa, who was notorious for rarely speaking and could keep quiet for hours. They sent him to the Lahore mental hospital.

'We felt very concerned because Dulla was innocent and was also a Jatt. So we approached Chaudhri Kalim-ud-Din Ahmed, who too was a Jatt and a prominent Muslim League leader of Lahore. As a result Nawab Mamdot, Daultana, Shaukat Hayat, Abdul Hameed Dasti and Chaudhri Kalim-ud-din visited all the police stations and jails looking for him but they could not find him. Then a Muslim policeman told us that he had been sent to the mental hospital. They went to the hospital and found him standing chained to a charpoy; for some reason he had been forced to dig a big hole in the earth. They got him released.

'The fires in the Hindu localities of the city which followed later in Mohalla Sareen, Mohalla Wanwattan, and parts of Shahalmi were the work of other Muslim young men. These included boys from Bhati, Lohari, Mochi gates and refugees who had arrived from East Punjab. They broke open the locks and plundered the things inside. But the fire started by us was the one which turned the tide in Lahore. It was masterminded by Cheema and my father provided the necessary help with incendiary material and men who lit the fire.

'Father stayed in Chung until Pakistan came into being. After that, British control ended and Pakistani officers took over. Even then, Father was unsure how the authorities would treat him. He wanted to obtain clearance and proper permission before returning to our house in Shahalmi which had been lying vacant since 5 March when we left it to live with our relatives in Nawan Bazaar. Therefore on 22 August 1947, an application was submitted which read:

> To the duty Magistrate
> Lahore.
>
> Sir,
>
> With due respect I wish to submit that we the undersigned used to live in Suchian quarter in Shahalmi before we were forced to vacate our homes during the communal riots because the Hindus of that area used to threaten us. Now we wish to return to our homes, but while Hindu homes are still intact and under lock and key ours have been destroyed and plundered. We have already submitted several applications about the damage and loss of our property.
> We wish to inform you that from today, 22 August, we are returning to our homes.
>
> Yours obediently,
>
> Pir Baksh s/o Fazal Din (caste, Jatt),
> resident of Katra Susian, Lahore.
> Bahag Din s/o Umar Din (caste, Jatt),
> resident of Katra Susian, Lahore.
> Muhammad Buta s/o Maula Baksh (caste, Jatt),

resident of Katra Susian, Lahore.
Khuda Baksh s/o Ilahi Baksh (caste, Jatt),
resident of Katra Susian, Lahore.
Nur Muhammad s/o Karim Baksh (caste, Jatt),
resident of Katra Susian, Lahore.
Ghulam Hussain s/o Fazal Din (caste, Jatt),
resident of Katra Susian, Lahore.
Rahim Baksh s/of Saudagar (caste, Jatt),
resident of Katra Susian, Lahore.
Din Muhammad s/o Ghulam Muhammad (caste, Jatt),
resident of Katra Susian, Lahore.'

Ahmad Salim interviewed a veteran Lahore lawyer, Mr Hukum Qureshi, with regard to the situation in Lahore in 1947. His testimony confirmed the general picture that Lahore remained disturbed after March 1947 despite temporary decline in the overall incidents of violence. About the role of M.G. Cheema he had the following to say:

'Magistrate M.G. Cheema used to wear a steel helmet. He had decided to expel all Hindus from Lahore. Before the actual fire took place Muslims would fill bottles with soda-water gas. These were hurled into Shahalmi. They would explode and cause death and injury. In return the Hindus would fire from their housetops. There were no *badmashes* among Hindus. All the *badmashes* were Muslims. Some days before the Shahalmi fire, the sewerage lanes from Chowk Rangmahal to Shahalmi were blocked. Instead, kerosene oil and petrol were mixed and thrown into those lanes. The Hindus inside their stronghold of Shahalmi were fully fortified, but were helpless when their homes and shops were set ablaze. All this was masterminded by Cheema.'

Suleman Cheema

After interviewing Haji Abdul Rehman we started searching for material on Magistrate Cheema. He was long deceased but we learnt that his son Suleman Cheema lived in Lahore, though he was away in the United

States at the time. In more than twenty interviews with Hindus and Sikhs in India and elsewhere, the name of Cheema always came up. After several months I finally succeeded in contacting Suleman Cheema on 13 October 2005, on the telephone. He told me that he had been born after Partition and therefore had no personal recollection of those days. He confirmed, however, that Hindus and Sikhs had offered a prize of ₹125,000 to anyone who killed his father. His father had never mentioned that he had been involved in setting Shahalmi Gate on fire. By contrast, said Suleman Cheema, someone had come from India some time previously to meet his elder cousin and thank him for the help which Magistrate Cheema had rendered to his family to help them escape safely to India.

A Cheema Sikh still waiting for his father

Sometime in 2006 (the email was lost but its message deeply moved me) I received an email from a Sikh gentleman who had read a weekly column of mine in the Lahore-based *Daily Times* about the Indian filmmaker Ramanand Sagar. In it, I had mentioned that both Sagar and I belonged to the locality of Mozang. I present a transcript of the original email according to what I remember:

> Can you help me trace my father? You see, we tried to leave Lahore where we had a small firm that produced medicines. We tried to leave by the Wagah route but it was too dangerous. So we came back. My father went to Mozang to seek the help of a Muslim magistrate who, like us, was a Cheema Jatt. He never returned. I was eleven at that time and now I am nearly seventy, still waiting for him to come back. I just want to know what happened to him. Can you help me?

I wrote back that he must learn to accept that if his father had not come back home in all these years then in all probability, he was killed on his way to meet Magistrate Cheema. I have always wondered if the magistrate that the Cheema Sikh was referring to was M.G. Cheema.

Sikandar Lal Bagga

On 3 December 2005 I interviewed an elderly gentleman, Sikander Lal Bagga, in Delhi. He gave me the following explanation as to why Magistrate Cheema had turned against the Hindus:

'M.G. Cheema was a city magistrate in Lahore. During May 1947, he was prevented by the Hindus of Krishan Nagar to carry out investigations in Krishan Nagar. They even threatened to kill him if he came there. I have heard that there was also an attempt on his life but he was not hurt. Later, after the 3 June 1947 announcement when rioting, incendiarism and other forms of violence escalated and the Hindu resistance began to collapse, Magistrate Cheema took his revenge.'

In any event, the interview with Gill about the conspiracy to set Shahalmi Gate ablaze vividly brings out the nexus between local strongmen, the police and other officials and politicians. I interviewed the well-known Urdu writer Ahmad Bashir, who was a witness to the Lahore riots, in April 2003. He recalled a number of incidents and mentioned that he had also described in his novel, *Dil Bhatkay Ga*, how the Muslim *badmashes* of Lahore had murdered and looted in connivance with the police and Muslim League leaders (2003: 313). Indeed, without such connections, it would have been very difficult to carry out the ethnic cleansing which took place.

While the Punjab was burning and people were finding their lives gravely menaced or even threatened by wanton attacks on them and their property, the members of the Punjab Legislative Assembly, organised into a western and an eastern bloc, voted on 23 June. Reuters issued the following comment:

> 'With large sections of Lahore and scores of villages throughout the Province fire-blacked ruins, the 168 members of the Punjab Legislative Assembly laughed and joked as they shook hands in the lobbies of the Assembly building on their way to record their votes to decide whether the Punjab should be partitioned.
>
> 'Approaches to the Assembly building were blocked by barbed-wire barriers and the vicinity was under heavy police guard. The public was not admitted, but foreign and local pressmen filled the press gallery'.

The Tribune of 25 June gave government figures of 3,749 killed in the Punjab since 4 March 1947. It also reported that a bomb had been thrown at a police patrol accompanied by a magistrate near Sitla Mandir, outside Lohari Gate, but nobody had been hurt. In Delhi, in 2004, I talked to Mr Hari Dev Shourie, who had been duty magistrate in Lahore and the object of the attack. He told me:

'I and a police force were coming out of the Lohari Gate inside the walled city when somebody threw a bomb at us near the Sitla Mandir. Fortunately it exploded at some distance and nobody was hurt. When we came out in the park outside Lohari Gate a sea of humanity was assembled, desperately looking for protection against attacks. These were Hindus and Sikhs. They were trying to find transport to get to the Lahore railway station. The *tongawallas* were charging exorbitant rates. I tried to restore order but then Magistrate Muhammad Ghani Cheema arrived with his police force and told me to leave. It was a heart-rending situation as frightened men and women and children sought help but nobody was there to help them. Later, I was told that some Dogra troops arrived and things were brought under control. Many Hindus and Sikhs had left Lahore already by the end of June, but some stayed on in areas where they were in a majority. In the upper-class areas such as Model Town, things remained pretty calm until mid-August 1947. Then even there, raids on Hindus and Sikhs proliferated and we all had to leave Lahore'.

The Punjab leaders of the Muslim League, Congress and Akali Party met in Lahore on Monday, 23 June, to devise ways to bring the fast-deteriorating communal situation under control (*Pakistan Times*, 25 June). Later, they met in the Town Hall on Thursday 26 June (*Pakistan Times*, 27 June) to take active steps to restore the peace. *The Tribune* of 27 June reported that 75,000 refugees had arrived in Delhi from Gurgaon, western Punjab and the North-West Frontier Province. The next day *The Tribune* reported that twenty-six gangsters had been arrested in Lahore and that the appeal of the leaders of all the communities had had a positive effect. Thus, the Lahore streets and roads were calm but the Shahalmi fire had created a feeling of desertion in that part of the town. The officiating District Magistrate, Mr Williams, observed that the 'situation in the city was quiet' (*The Tribune,* 28 June). *The Tribune* of June 30 reported that the Chief Minister of the United Provinces,

Pandit Govind Ballabh Pant, had disclosed that as many as 100,000 refugees (Hindus and Sikhs) were living in his province. On 30 June, a couple of explosions took place in the village of Mandali near Jullundur. Although no deaths occurred, more than a hundred persons were injured. The explosion took place near a Muslim shrine when people were taking part in the annual fair (*The Tribune*, 2 July).

In a special report sent by Jenkins on 25 June to Mountbatten, the governor gave a detailed breakdown of the situation in the Punjab. As in all other reports, much of the focus is on Lahore and Amritsar. He asserted that Muslims were behind most cases of incendiarism thus far. The Hindus and Sikhs had, until the beginning of June, been quite ineffective at throwing bombs, though this was changing. He made an interesting connection between the bomb thrown at the Muslim-majority Sabzi Mandi on 21 June and the burning of Shahalmi in the early hours of 22 June, assertive that the latter was an act of retaliation (Carter, 2007b: 100).

In addition, Jenkins conceded that many of the officials in charge of maintaining law and order were no longer working impartially. Those who tried to do so were accused of partiality by the hostile groups and their leaders. Moreover, the political organisations were themselves involved in some of the outrages. Paid raiders and assailants were being used to carry out criminal acts. Thus an Indian Christian, and Purbia Hindus (Hindu labourers from northern India), had been paid money to set fire to Hindu property. On the other hand, the RSS was behind the bomb attacks carried out by Hindus and had highly respectable Hindu gentlemen at the head of the organisation. However, upon the governor's advice, the main Punjab leaders had issued an appeal for peace and a decline in violence had been noticeable in Lahore in the last week of June (ibid.: 98-101). But in Amritsar, the feeling was growing among Muslims that they were 'doomed and may as well do as much damage as they can before they migrate or perish' (ibid.: 100).

In the FR dated 30 June, Jenkins noted that the month ended with the violence abating to some extent, although the situation was still seriously disturbed. Apart from Lahore and Amritsar, Gurgaon was also the location of most of the violence. Communal attacks had occurred in Jullundur and Hoshiarpur districts, too (ibid.: 110-11).

References

Bashir, Ahmad. *Dil Bhatkay Ga* (The Heart Will Falter), Lahore: Ferozson, 2003

Iftikhar, K. *Jabb Amritsar Jall Raha Tha* (When Amritsar was Burning), Lahore: Khawaja Publishers, 1991.

Khosla, G.D. *Stern Reckoning,* Delhi: Oxford University Press, 1989.

Talib, S.G.S. *Muslim League Attack on Sikhs and Hindus in the Punjab 1947,* New Delhi: Voice of India, 1991.

Newspapers

Pakistan Times, Lahore, 1947.

The Tribune, Lahore, 1947

Official documents

Carter, Lionel, (ed), *Punjab Politics, 1 June–14 August 1947, Tragedy, Governors' Fortnightly Reports and other Key Documents,* New Delhi: Manohar, 2007a.

Carter, Lionel, (ed), *Punjab Politics, 3 March–31 May 1947, At the Abyss, Governors' Fortnightly Reports and other Key Documents,* New Delhi: Manohar, 2007b.

FR of Punjab Chief Secretary: IOR L/P & J/5/250.

Interviews

B.R. Chopra, Mumbai, 4 January 1997.

Yuvraj Krishan, Delhi. 21 October 1999.

Dr Jagdish Chander Sarin, Delhi, 24 October 1999.

Mushtaq Ahmad, Stockholm, 12 April 2002.

Vimal Issar, New Delhi, 13 March 2004.

Dina Nath Malhotra, Delhi, 15 March 2004

Hari Dev Shourie, New Delhi, 16 March 2004

Mustansar Husain Tarrar, Lahore, 17 December 2004.

Kaleb Ali Sheikh, Lahore, 25 December 2004.

Haji Abdul Rahman Gill, Lahore, 30 December 2004; 29 September 2005; 15 October 2005.

Ghulam Haider, Lahore, 13 January 2005.

Muhammad Munir, Lahore, 13 January 2005.
Muhammad Hanif, Lahore, 13 January 2005.
Mian Muhammad Sharif, 14 January 2005.
Hukum Qureshi, Lahore, 30 October 2005.
Suleman Cheema, Lahore (via telephone at 15.35 Stockholm time), 13 October 2005.
Sikander Lal Bagga, Delhi, 3 December 2005.
Dr Hafeez Ahmad Mughal, Lahore, interview via email 16 January 2006.

12

PARTITION MACHINERY AND PROCEEDINGS 1 JULY–14 AUGUST 1947

THE PUNJAB PARTITION COMMITTEE MET ON 1 JULY WITH THE PUNJAB governor as president and four members: two representatives of West Punjab, Mumtaz Daultana and Zahid Hussain, and two representatives of East Punjab, Dr Gopi Chand Bhargava and Sardar Swaran Singh. The main function of the committee was to organise the machinery for the implementation of the Partition. A Steering Committee consisting of one Muslim, Syed Yaqub Shah, and one Hindu, M.R. Sachdeva, was set up to liaise between the committee and various government departments. Likewise, in each department a senior Muslim and a non-Muslim officer were selected to constitute the departmental committees. Some expert committees were also established (Mansergh and Moon, 1982: 454-55).

Jinnah's announcement about becoming Governor-General of Pakistan

In the last stages of the Partition episode, there is perhaps no other event at the level of high politics that deserves to be noted more than Jinnah's rejection of Mountbatten as Governor-General of Pakistan. The details are given in Viceroy's Personal Report No. 11 dated 4 July 1947. The general understanding was that Mountbatten would be the governor-general for both India and Pakistan. Mountbatten was taken aback when Jinnah told him that while he wanted to retain British governors in all the Pakistani provinces except Sindh, and British heads of the defence forces, he himself would be the Governor-General of Pakistan. Mountbatten tried unsuccessfully to persuade Jinnah to appreciate the advantages of having one governor-general for both dominions in the Commonwealth, among them, having a strictly fair partition (ibid.: 839-42). Jinnah remained unmoved. In exasperation, Mountbatten said to him, 'Do you realise what this will cost you?' Jinnah replied, 'It may cost me several crores [10 million is one crore] in rupees in assets'. Mountbatten retorted, 'It may well cost you the whole of your assets and the future of Pakistan' (ibid.: 899-900).

Jinnah's rejection of Mountbatten as the Governor-General of Pakistan has been surrounded by much controversy. It is possible that he decided not to give the governor-general post to Mountbatten simply because he did not trust him. Mountbatten himself gave another explanation:

'I pointed out to him that if he went as a Constitutional Governor General his powers will be restricted but as Prime Minister he really could run Pakistan, he made no bones about the fact that his Prime Minister would do what he said. "In my position it is I who will give the advice, and others will act on it"' (ibid.: 898-99).

The noted Pakistani journalist, Hameed Akhtar, was of the opinion that Jinnah made a bad decision when he denied Mountbatten the governor-generalship. Much of the Partition riots, he suspected, were the result of a lack of common leadership supervising the transfer of population between the two countries, and indeed, between the partitioned Punjab. I have heard many other people in Pakistan express a similar view, albeit privately, as nobody dares to say it openly. The usual line taken in Pakistan is that Mountbatten was pro-India and therefore, by not letting him become the all-powerful head of state as the 1935 Act was laid down, Jinnah outmanoeuvred Mountbatten. However, the fact is that when a meeting was held on 1 August 1947 between Mountbatten, the Congress and Muslim League representatives to negotiate the division of the Indian military services, Viceroy Mountbatten presented a formula for distribution of troops and military units, as well as armament, equipment, and other facilities. The formula was not liked by the Congress, as it gave a disproportionate share of the common assets (roughly 70: 30) to Pakistan (Mansergh and Moon, 1983: 446-7).

Meanwhile, Sir Cyril Radcliffe, Chairman of the Boundary Commission, arrived in Delhi on 8 July. He had never been to India before. He left Delhi on 10 July to visit Calcutta and Lahore. In an interview dated 11 July, with Sikh leaders Jathedar Mohan Singh and Sardar Harnam Singh (later to plead the Sikh case before the Punjab Boundary Commission) Governor Jenkins noted that the Sikhs wanted a transfer of population:

> The only solution was a very substantial exchange of population. If this did not occur, the Sikhs would be driven to facilitate it by a massacre of Muslims in the Eastern Punjab. The Muslims had already got rid of Sikhs in the Rawalpindi Division and much land and property there could be made available to Muslims from East Punjab. Conversely the Sikhs could get rid of Muslims in the East in the same way and invite Sikhs from the West to take their places (ibid.: 103).

Equally interesting in that interview was that the Sikhs harboured a strong distrust of the Congress and the Hindus. They feared that the Hindus would try to eliminate their influence in the Punjab. Therefore they were planning to go all-out, and in a big way, to eliminate Muslims from East Punjab and in their place bring in Sikhs, with a view to creating a compact Sikh concentration in the eastern regions of the Punjab that could be used to thwart Congress and Hindu machinations against them (ibid). On 16 July, Sir Evan Jenkins requested early information about the date and content of the boundary award. He added, 'It will be necessary to take precautions, especially in those districts which are likely to be affected, particularly in the Central Punjab' (ibid.: 191). The final constitutional necessity leading to the transfer of power was the bill announcing the independence of India and Pakistan as two dominions within the British Commonwealth.

India Independence Act, 18 July 1947

Mountbatten had been conducting parleys on the Independence Bill with Indians of both national and provincial statures and had received letters and written statements from them. The bill's various drafts were also discussed in the British Parliament. Winston Churchill, then Leader of the Opposition, had asserted in Parliament on 1 July that he had agreed to support the transfer of power to Indian hands on the condition that two dominions, rather than independent states, would come into being. Therefore, in his view the appropriate title for the bill would be 'The Indian Dominions Bill, 1947' or the 'The India Self-Government Bill' (Mansergh and Moon, 1982: 812-3). The Labour government, however, decided to call it the India Independence Act, 1947, and as such it was adopted on 18 July. The bill stated: 'As from the fifteenth day of August, nineteen hundred and forty-seven, two independent Dominions shall be set up in India, to be known respectively as India and Pakistan' (Mansergh and Moon, 1983: 234).

With regard to the Punjab, the following provisions were made:

1) As from the appointed day –
   (a) the Province of the Punjab, as constituted under the Government of India Act, 1935, shall cease to exist; and
   (b) there shall be constituted two new Provinces, to be known respectively as West Punjab and East Punjab.
2) The boundaries of the said new Provinces shall be such as may be determined, whether before or after the appointed day, by the award of a boundary commission appointed or to be appointed by the Governor-General in that behalf, but until the boundaries are so determined –
   (a) the Districts specified in the Second Schedule to this Act shall be treated as the territories which are to be comprised in the new Province of West Punjab; and
   (b) the remainder of the territories comprised at the date of the passing of this Act in the Province of the Punjab shall be treated as the territories which are to be comprised in the new Province of East Punjab.
3) In this section, the expression "award" means, in relation to a boundary commission, the decisions of the chairman of that commission contained in his report to the Governor-General at the conclusion of the commission's proceedings (ibid.: 236).

The districts provisionally included in the new province of West Punjab in the second schedule were identical to those notionally included in the

3 June Partition Plan. All districts of the Rawalpindi and Multan divisions and all districts of the Lahore division, including Gurdaspur but minus Amritsar, were included in West Punjab. But more important was the fact that the chairman of the Boundary Commission alone enjoyed the prerogative of giving the Boundary Award.

The Punjab Boundary Force

As has been noted earlier, the Punjab government had several times requested more troops to deal with the persistent lawlessness. The Delhi government, however, replied that additional troops were simply not available. Yet, given that the Punjab was set to be partitioned, Mountbatten realised that armed troops were needed to deal with the anticipated volatile situation. It was decided that Bengal did not need any special armed troops but the Punjab did. On 17 July the decision to form the Punjab Boundary Force was taken by the Partition Council. Major General Rees, commander of the 4th Division, was to be the officer responsible for the PBF and his troops were to be operational in the disturbed districts of the Punjab by about 7 or 8 August. There was to be no change in the law governing the use of troops in aid of civil powers after 15 August (ibid.: 206-7).

Initially, the districts considered disturbed were Sialkot, Gujranwala, Sheikhupura, Lyallpur, Montgomery, Lahore, Amritsar, Gurdaspur, Hoshiarpur, Jullundur, and Ferozepore. Rees had a total of five infantry brigades and an armoured brigade. The tanks of the latter were to be spread over the whole area demarcated as troubled (ibid.: 272). Later, after discussion in the Partition Council, Ludhiana was also added to the disturbed list. General Rees was to be advised by Brigadier Digamber Singh Brar (India) and Colonel Ayub Khan (Pakistan) (ibid.: 326-7). Thus altogether twelve districts, considered to constitute the 'central Punjab' and belonging to the Lahore and Jullundur divisions, were to be monitored by the PBF. The date for the PBF to be in position was changed from the earlier 7–8 August to 1 August. Other British troops after 14 August were not to have any operational responsibility. British officers were to be present with practically every unit of each unit of the Punjab Boundary Force (ibid.: 404).

The area of the disturbed districts was greater than the area of Britain's Scotland and Wales combined. It included twenty-six towns and 17,000 villages, with an area of about 37,500 sq. miles [97,125 sq. km]. Jenkins wrote to Mountbatten on 8 August that the PBF had only five brigade groups with an average of 1,500 effective rifles. Thus, in addition to the police, it had some 7,500 men. Another 1,500 could be raised by using training centres and static troops. Thus, at the most 9,000 troops could be available to control twelve districts with a population of no less than twelve million. The governor supported Rees's request for more troops and if possible, a tactical reconnaissance squadron or at least some aircraft to monitor the Punjab (Carter, 2007b: 219).

During the Viceroy's 69th staff meeting on 9 August, the requests for more troops and a reconnaissance squadron were taken up and the Commander-in-Chief, Field Marshal Auchinleck, undertook to look into the matter. Since all the units of the PBF were mixed some doubts were expressed about the loyalty of the Sikh troops (Mansergh and Moon, 1983: 611-2). In his telegram dated 12 August, Jenkins stated, 'Strength of Punjab Boundary Force is not adequate to present and future tasks. I have already reported this' (Carter, 2007b: 226). The next day Jenkins gave more details of the impossible task assigned to the PBF. He calculated that the population of the twelve districts was in fact 14.5 million, spread over 17,932 towns and villages while the men at the disposal of General Rees were only 9,000 (ibid.: 230-1). On 14 August, the Chief of the General Staff, Sir Arthur Smith, wrote to Sir George Abell, Private Secretary to the Viceroy, that both India and Pakistan would provide three battalions each in a week's time (Mansergh and Moon, 2007b: 721). Auchinleck wrote on 15 August that 'Two more brigades (one from India and one from Pakistan) and one mixed armoured squadron are being sent to reinforce Punjab Boundary Force, but no amount of troops can stop the indiscriminate butchery which appears to be going on both sides' (ibid.: 736).

Although General Rees is generally seen to have acted impartially, the troops of the PBF under his command were infected with communalism. Kirpal Singh asserts that the Baluch Regiment, an entirely Muslim force, took part in the massacre of Hindus and Sikhs in Sheikhupura district in West Punjab (ibid.). Robin Jeffrey has written on the subject and his findings corroborated that. A number of first-person accounts from Sheikhupura as well as of Hindu and Sikh troops killing Muslims in eastern Punjab will be presented later. Suffice it to say that the PBF was disbanded from midnight of 31 August 1947, as a result of a decision of the Joint Defence Council, comprising representatives of the Indian and Pakistani governments who met in Delhi. Thereafter, India and Pakistan formed joint units that operated on both sides of the Punjab border trying to save lives and escort refugee caravans across the border.

Proceedings of the Punjab Boundary Commission

Of all the committees and councils established to supervise the partition of the Punjab, none was of such critical importance as the Punjab Boundary Commission. As soon as it was announced, all sides became engaged in feverish activity to marshal arguments and evidence to support their cases. Both sides had agreed that the Boundary Award would be accepted by them. Mountbatten declared that he would not interfere in the proceedings or the outcome of the award.

The compilation of official documents and transcripts of the proceedings of the Commission constitute a fascinating body of source material. The four-volume *The Partition of the Punjab 1947* (published in 1993) includes letters, telegrams, petitions, and statements of political parties, their local leaders and spokespersons, government functionaries, rulers and ministers of princely states, written memorandums and oral presentations of the counsels who represented the disputing parties as well as the statements and remarks of the members of the Punjab Boundary Commission.

My own exhaustive study, titled 'The 1947 Partition of the Punjab: Arguments put forth before the Punjab Boundary Commission by the Parties Involved', based on the above-mentioned publication is presented below in an abridged version.

The Punjab Boundary Commission, as already noted, comprised the chairman, Sir Cyril Radcliffe, and four members: two, Justice Din Muhammad and Justice Muhammad Munir, nominated by the Muslim League, and Justice Mehr Chand Mahajan and Justice Teja Singh, nominated by Congress. The Commission met in Lahore for ten days between 21 July and 31 July 1947, except on one Sunday between. The chairman did not attend any session. Arrangements were made to have the record of the proceedings flown to his office in Delhi for his perusal.

The controversy over 'other factors'

> Although the major consideration in the demarcation of the boundaries was to be contiguous Muslim and non-Muslim areas, the inclusion of 'other factors' in the commission's terms of reference considerably broadened the scope of the debate. Thus inevitably historical, religious, geographical, social and economic aspects were brought into the discussions'. That the Muslim-majority Rawalpindi Division should go to Pakistan and the non-Muslim majority Ambala Division be allotted to India was not disputed by the concerned parties. On the other hand, conflicting claims were staked by both sides to parts and portions of Lahore, Multan and Jullundur divisions (Ahmed, 1999: 123).

The counsels submitted written memorandums as well as oral presentations before the Commission.

The Congress case

M.C. Setalvad opened his brief by emphasising that the terms of reference upon which the Punjab Boundary Commission was to ascertain the claims of the various parties appearing before it consisted of two sets of instructions: to demarcate boundaries according to the principle of contiguous majority areas, and 'to take into account other factors'. He asserted that the term 'contiguous areas' should be interpreted as a substantial unit. It could not mean an infinitesimally small unit. As regards 'other factors', these could not be ascertained in a general manner; they could differ from area to area and between parts of the boundary. Further, there was 'no warrant for stating that "other factors" had a subsidiary place, nor any for stating that the "other factors" were such as might result in what was being termed as "local deviations only"' (ibid.: 124). He remarked:

> It stands very much to reason that if it is a matter merely of ascertaining the contiguous majority areas, the work need not have been assigned to a Commission of this weight and importance; in that case a map could have been drawn by having the census figures on the one hand and any Deputy Commissioner could have drawn the line on the basis of contiguous majority areas (ibid.).

Regarding the reliability of the 1941 census figures, Setalvad asserted that as early as the census of 1911, when separate electorates were introduced, each community had begun to exaggerate its numbers in order to secure more seats; by 1941 such a trend had turned into a complete farce. Putting great emphasis on 'other factors', he asserted that the former desert areas in western Punjab, the canal colonies of Lyallpur and Montgomery, had been developed mainly by the people of the eastern and central parts of the province who were allotted land in these areas. The Sikh Jats were the most prominent group that was allotted land. They owned the bulk of landed property, as well as business and commerce. Thus if the colonies in the Lyallpur–Sargodha and Montgomery districts were awarded to West Punjab, many of the Sikhs and Hindus would emigrate to India, as anti-Hindu and Sikh riots in NWFP and northern Punjab had already created great insecurity among them (ibid.).

Lahore

The Congress counsel very strongly emphasised that non-Muslims had deep cultural roots in Lahore. They had built colleges and libraries and also had outstanding economic interests in the district. Although the 1941 census figures (disputed by Congress) showed a 60.62 per cent Muslim and 39.38 per cent non-Muslim population strength, the Muslims paid only ₹5,81,235 as land revenue, while non-Muslims paid ₹12,63,830. Moreover, Muslims owned only 5,11,867 acres, while non-Muslims owned 11,50,450 acres (ibid.: 127). Thus, economic aspects of the division of Punjab must also be taken into consideration. As to the city of Lahore, he remarked:

> You will remember that so far as this city is concerned, the population ratio of Muslims and non-Muslims according to the census of 1941

> is higher still; not 61 and 39 as in the district but 64 and 36. But... you will find that definitely a larger proportion of the land is in the hands of the non-Muslims.... Another factor, which is an allied factor, is in regard to urban areas and also in some districts rural areas. Here again you will find that in certain areas which are Muslim majority areas, the position is that the trade, industry, and the factories and so on and so forth are almost entirely in the hands of non-Muslims (ibid.).

Another thing to consider would be the transport and road system, he asserted. No division could be acceptable which cut up the railway and the road transport into unworkable portions. Moreover, the facilities for repairs and maintenance of the railway line for the eastern part of Punjab required that the Mughalpura Workshops (located on the outskirts of Lahore) should be available to the eastern part in order that the railway in that part should be able to function (ibid.).

Special rights of the Sikh community and Nankana Sahib

Commenting on the Sikh community, Setalvad emphasised that their rights in the province should be evaluated in terms of their historical services to Punjab. They were a martial race who, prior to British conquest, had been the ruling community in the province. Later, after British annexation, the Sikhs supplied large numbers of soldiers to the Indian Army and contributed outstandingly to the development of the province.... More importantly, according to the notional principle, Nankana Sahib, the birthplace of the founder of the Sikh faith, fell within West Punjab. This was unacceptable. Therefore, necessary adjustments should be made in the demarcation of boundaries so that Sikh history and culture was not split and divided between two separate states (ibid.: 127-8).

Gurdaspur district

Coming to the crucial Gurdaspur district comprising the four *tahsils* (a *tahsil* is an administrative subunit of a district) of Gurdaspur, Shakargarh, Batala and Pathankot, Setalvad stated that up until 1921, Gurdaspur district had retained a non-Muslim majority. In 1931, however, Muslims were reported to be in a majority of 15,534, while in 1941 that majority was recorded at 26,435. Thus, according to the 1941 census, there were 589,923 Muslims and 563,588 non-Muslims in the district as a whole, representing a ratio of 50.6 Muslims to 49.4 non-Muslims. The Muslim majority was therefore very narrow. The religious composition of the four *tahsils* was as follows: Gurdaspur, 50.5 per cent Muslims; Shakargarh, 51.3 per cent Muslims; Batala, 53 per cent Muslims; and Pathankot, 65 per cent non-Muslims. At any rate, Gurdaspur district had been placed in western Punjab on the basis of notional division.

Setalvad argued that Gurdaspur was inextricably integrated into the Amritsar district because of trade and communication networks between them. After all, Amritsar was the clearing house for exports and imports of Gurdaspur. Moreover, the rail and road connection was such that it came up from Lahore to Amritsar and then went on to Gurdaspur and linked Kangra Valley and district with Amritsar and Lahore. Therefore, Amritsar and Gurdaspur should be taken as one unit. Together, they formed a non-Muslim majority and therefore should be awarded to eastern Punjab. Another major consideration for placing Gurdaspur in the eastern part was its intimate relationship with Sikh history, being the location of many famous Sikh shrines (ibid.: 129).

Proceeding on the assumption that partition of the Punjab would involve massive population movement, the Congress memorandum claimed the following areas for eastern Punjab:

1) The whole of Ambala division;
2) The whole of Jullundur division;
3) The whole of Lahore division;
4) Lyallpur district;
5) Montgomery district;
6) Such other adjoining areas as may be necessary from considerations of canal and colony needs. Such a division of the Punjab, argued Setalvad, would consolidate some 34 lakh [3.4 million] Sikhs out of their total population of 37,57,401 in East Punjab (ibid.: 130)

The Sikh case

The Sikh counsel, Sardar Harnam Singh, agreed with Setalvad's interpretation of the terms of reference. He asserted that the importance of 'other factors' was admitted even by the Muslim League, even when its main emphasis was on contiguous Muslim majority. Thus, it had claimed portions of the non-Muslim majority Pathankot *tahsil* where the Madhopur barrage on the Ravi was located and from where the Upper Bari Doab Canal originated (ibid.: 131).

Harnam Singh argued that the Sikhs were mainly peasant-proprietors who were rooted in the soil of the Punjab in both religious and economic terms. It was virtually impossible to transfer such people to another location. On the other hand, according to the 1931 census in the Lahore district, out of the total Muslim population of 1,49,29,896 some 46,95,957 consisted of *fakirs*, beggars, weavers, herdsmen, cobblers, *kumhars* or potters, *musallis* (untouchable converts to Islam), carpenters, oilmen, bards, barbers, blacksmiths, washermen, butchers and *mirasis* (a low caste associated with entertainment) – people who are described in the settlement reports as landless people and menials. These were a 'floating people' and could therefore be transferred easily (ibid.: 132).

The special religio-cultural claims of the Sikh community over Punjab

Coming to the theme of the special position of the Sikh community in the Punjab, Harnam Singh asserted that even the Muslim League in its memorandum had admitted that Sikhs deserved special consideration. He then said: 'I submit that the central divisions of Punjab from time immemorial constitute the national home of the Sikhs. The question whether they are fewer in number or very numerous is quite irrelevant from the point of view whether a particular region or a particular tract is their homeland' (ibid.: 133).

Now, if India was the homeland of the Hindus and Pakistan was the homeland of the Muslims then, Singh insisted, the area between the rivers Chenab and Beas was the homeland of the Sikhs (here he referred to several books and official documents in which the Majha region of Punjab, with Amritsar as its centre, was described as Sikh country). Thus, when a certain territory was recognised as the homeland of a community, its rights to it could not be denied merely on the basis of another community being in greater numbers in it. For instance, the Balfour Declaration described Palestine as the homeland of the Jews even when they were a minority in it in 1917 (ibid.: 133). Harnam Singh remarked:

> Therefore I submit that when you are considering this question, the special features of the Sikh community should be taken into account. I have the greatest possible respect for all religious denominations and for everybody's sentiments. But for the past two decades I have several times heard Muslim boys singing "*Ya Rab Mecca Madina le chal mujhe*". They have been looking westwards. They say, we are living in a strange country, in an alien country, we have no national home. Our national home is in Arabia. I am not hurting the feelings of my Hindu brethren when I say that they look to Hardwar and Benaras for their pilgrimage and the Muslims look to Mecca and Madina. But for the Sikhs, the city of Amritsar, the city of Nankana Sahib in Sheikhupura district, the city of Kartarpur in Shakargarh *tahsil* of Gurdaspur district, are their Mecca and Madina and their Hardwar and Benaras (ibid.).

He asserted that Sikh fears of again being persecuted by Muslims were based on historical experience. The core of his argument was that Muslim rulers generally had followed an intolerant policy towards the Sikhs (ibid.: 134). He stressed that Sikhs had clearly expressed a desire not to live in Pakistan. These facts had been set forth in detail in the Sikh Memorandum, signed by 32 out of 33 members of the Punjab Assembly, with the 33rd also joining eventually (ibid.).

The question of language

The Sikh counsel asserted that the whole of Punjab province did not speak Punjabi. Among them were included the people of Karnal, Rothak, Hissar, Dera Ghazi Khan, Isakhel and Mianwali. Even in Multan they did not speak Punjabi but Multani (today called Saraiki). Similarly, in Kangra, a different language was spoken. Punjabi was spoken in the central regions of the province – that is, in Lahore and Jullundur divisions and in the colony areas (ibid.).

The tract consisting of the Jhang and Multan districts and the trans-Jhelum area were acquired through conquest by Maharaja Ranjit Singh and retained by the British for the sake of administrative convenience. Thus, from the boundary of Delhi to the banks of the Jhelum, excluding the districts of Jhang and Multan, the population was as follows:

Muslims	10,761,560
Sikhs and others	11,184,886

From the boundary of Delhi to the banks of Chenab river, excluding Multan and Jhang districts, the population was as follows:

Muslims	9,191,618
Sikhs and others	11,885,834 (ibid.: 134-5)).

Protection of Punjabi in East Punjab

He argued further that the census reports pointed out that Muslims had increasingly been recording Urdu as their mother tongue while Hindus had been recording Hindi; only Sikhs had remained steadfast to Punjabi. In the eastern Punjab, the predominantly Hindu areas may be amalgamated with Hindustani-speaking areas. A division and a further division will be my argument.

> Therefore I say that if you are going to protect the language and culture of the people, you cannot do that by incorporating them in Pakistan where people are out to destroy that culture. It is not a matter of recent happenings in March, 1947. This thing has been going on for the past two decades. This again is a special feature which entitles the Sikhs to special protection (ibid.: 135).

Lahore and Nankana Sahib

Harnam Singh made a special effort to claim Lahore for the Sikhs. He pointed out that not only did the districts of Amritsar and Gurdaspur have many sacred shrines of the Sikhs, but Lahore district was also intrinsic to Sikh religious and cultural history. 'The fourth Guru, Ramdas, the ancestor of all the succeeding Gurus, was born and brought up in

Lahore' (ibid.: 136). The memorial to the fifth guru, Arjan, stood in Lahore on the spot where he was martyred. The city was famous as the 'Gurus' Cradle'. As regards Nankana Sahib in Sheikhupura district, the Sikh counsel insisted that it should go to the eastern part of Punjab, because here the founder of the Sikh faith had been born and it was the holiest Sikh shrine. The only solution, therefore, in order to maintain their communal unity and cultural continuity, would be to amass the Sikhs in eastern Punjab (ibid.).

Basing his calculations on the *zail* (a revenue unit comprising a cluster of villages) as the principal territorial unit, Harnam Singh asserted that a contiguous non-Muslim majority area extended from the Shaheedi Bar, beginning from the canal areas of Lyallpur and connecting to portions of Sheikhupura and Gujranwala districts, portions of Chunian *tahsil* in Lahore district to the eastern districts (ibid.: 137). Furthermore, trade and commerce in Montgomery district and the *tahsils* of Khanewal and Mailsi in Multan were entirely in the hands of Sikhs, claimed the Sikh counsel (ibid.). He also claimed Sialkot district because according to him it was part of Sikh sacred history (ibid.). It was claimed that 'the boundary of Eastern Punjab must extend up to the Chenab' (ibid.).

Extent of areas claimed by the Sikhs for eastern Punjab

The Sikh memorandum also stressed the inevitability of population movement and the need to consolidate the Sikh community in East Punjab. It claimed the following areas for eastern Punjab.

1) Ambala division;
2) Jullundur division;
3) Lahore division;
4) Lyallpur district of Multan division;
5) Montgomery district and Khanewal, Vihari and Mailsi *tahsils* of Multan division.

Such a division would have meant the consolidation of 34 lakh (3.4 million) Sikhs out of a total population of 37,57,401 in eastern Punjab (ibid.: 137-8).

The Muslim League case

Sir Muhammad Zafrulla Khan took issue with the Congress–Sikh position on equating 'other factors' with the principle of contiguous Muslim and non-Muslim majority areas. He argued that if the arguments of religious sentiments, vested interests, ownership of acres, ownership of banking and insurance companies, and of capital invested in factories, were used for dividing India, then it would not have succeeded. Moreover, while there were Muslim shrines all over India, it was impossible to measure how much sentiment Muslims attached to them in the same manner as gauging the religious sentiments of non-Muslims with their own. The Muslim League demanded the division of India on the sole basis of a Muslim majority in some regions of the subcontinent (ibid.: 138).

Khan asserted that the operative part of the statement of the British government which defined the functions of the Boundary Commission referred to ascertaining contiguous Muslim and majority non-Muslims majority areas. As for the 'other factors' it referred only to local factors. In some exceptional cases, the majority principle could be bent so as to accommodate local peculiarities. (ibid.: 139).

The Sikh demand for partition of the Punjab

Responding to the Sikh demand for special treatment, the counsel for the Muslim League asserted that two main reasons had been submitted by them for it. One, the allegation that during the Mughal period Sikhs and their religious leaders had been tortured and persecuted by the Muslims, and that if they were again subjected to Muslim rule, they feared that history might be repeated. The second reason was the more recent killings of Sikhs at the hands of Muslims in Rawalpindi and Multan districts (ibid.: 140).

Khan refuted both charges. Referring to several authoritative publications by Sikh authors and others, Khan asserted that the Mughals had actually been benefactors of the Sikh gurus. Muslim rulers had bestowed grants in land and respected and protected the Sikh religion. Many holy Sikh shrines, including Darbar Sahib and Nankana Sahib, were built upon endowments made by Muslims (ibid.). He went on to say that the reason why Guru Arjan was punished by Emperor Jahangir was the former's help to his son Prince Khusro who had rebelled against him. In some other cases, when Sikh gurus were persecuted by the Mughals, it was the Hindus who instigated the rulers to mete out severe punishment to them. On the other hand, during the time of Guru Gobind Singh, the Sikhs had preached hatred against Muslims and fomented rebellions against them (ibid.: 141).

Regarding the recent killings, the Muslim League counsel asserted that they could not be blamed on the Muslims. The Muslim League's civil disobedience movement, which had started at the end of January 1947 and lasted five weeks, was a largely orderly agitation which came to an end on 28 February. The ministry had resigned on 2 March, but it became known publicly only the following day. Master Tara Singh had incited Sikhs to violence when he came out of the Punjab Assembly with an unsheathed *kirpan* and shouted, '*Pakistan Murdabad, Sat Sri Akal*'. He and the Hindu leaders later that day had made more inflammatory speeches. In such communally-charged circumstances riots, it was asserted, violence and bloodshed had broken out in Lahore and the rest of Punjab (ibid.: 142).

In order to strengthen his assertion that the Sikh leaders had only lately changed their perceptions of Muslim–Sikh relations, Khan quoted a number of statements of Master Tara Singh. In the Gurmukhi magazine, *Sant Sipahi* of August 1946, the Sikh leader wrote:

> In respect of religious principles Sikhs are nearer to Muslims than to Hindus but their social connections are stronger with the Hindus. Among the Hindus there is a section which wants to put an end to our separate identity. Our ties with the Muslims are not strong but for that reason we have less to fear from them. I am in favour of an understanding with the Muslims and of promoting better relations with them. There are Hindus who through intrigue and diplomacy want to devour Sikhs. Our policy with regard to Hindus should be this: we should not be so far from them that we should be permanently estranged and we should not be so near to them that we should lose our entity. The Hindus should realise this position. If they give up the desire and attempt to absorb us we shall not be afraid to strengthen our bonds. But the past record and past history inspires no confidence in us. We shall have to remain alert.

> Congress is bound to seek our sympathy and assistance but has also been trying in the past to scatter our organisation and shall do so in future. It does not accept our separate political existence because we are opposed to it on principle. It should thus be borne in mind that the Congress and Hindus will try to destroy our separate political existence. During the last election utmost effort was made to this end but we saved ourselves. If the Sikhs who got elected to the Punjab Legislative Assembly had all been elected on the Congress ticket, we should have died as a community (ibid.: 141-2).

The economic basis of Partition

Zafrulla Khan presented the Muslim League's standpoint that the real reason for the partition of India, and by implication of the Punjab, was the economic disparity and inequality prevailing between, on the one hand, rich Hindus and Sikhs, and on the other hand, destitute Muslims. Economic exploitation during the British period by Hindus and Sikhs of Muslims had caused widespread poverty among the latter. Even though the 1900 Punjab Land Alienation Act had slowed down the acquisition of Muslim agricultural property by Hindu and Sikh moneylenders there were various other devices available through which debt-ridden Muslims continued to be alienated from their holdings by the non-Muslims (ibid.: 143).

As to the question of 'land to the tiller' and 'attachment to the soil', Zafrulla Khan argued that Muslim peasant-proprietors and tenant farmers far exceeded non-Muslims and were as much rooted in the land, even though Sikhs who undoubtedly had made valuable contribution to development in the Punjab, owned agricultural property in much greater proportion to their percentage in the total population of the Punjab. Muslims were generally owners of smaller holdings as compared to the Sikhs, but they were more numerous in absolute numbers (ibid.: 143-4).

The canal colonies

Commenting on the canal colonies, the Muslim League's counsel asserted that those properties were originally the homeland of Muslim nomadic and pastoral peoples. More importantly, the area allotted by the Crown in the canal colonies also showed that Muslims constituted a majority. Thus, in the Lyallpur, Montgomery, Multan, Sheikhupura, Jhang, Shahpur and Gujrat colony areas altogether 42,99,663 acres had been allotted. Out of these, Muslims cultivated 27,40,814 acres; Hindus, 3,79,001; Sikhs, 11,46,432; Christians, 22,786; and others, 10,635 acres. They represented proportions of: Muslims, 64 per cent; Hindus, 9 per cent; Sikhs, 26 per cent; and Christians and others, 1 per cent (ibid.: 144).

Regarding the crucial Lyallpur district to whose development the contribution of Sikhs had been emphasised so much by the opposite side, Khan noted that in Lyallpur Muslims were 62.8 per cent of the population; they owned 62 per cent of the area; paid 57 per cent of the land revenue and formed 69 per cent of the owners in the district. Further, Muslim Arains had also made contributions to agricultural production and not just the Sikh Jats (ibid.).

Claims should be based on contiguous tahsils

Zafrulla Khan argued that the unit for determining Muslim and non-Muslim areas should be the *tahsil* because it had existed consistently as the fundamental administrative and revenue unit in the Punjab's history. On the other hand, new districts had been created and old ones dissolved. Anything smaller than a *tahsil* such as a village or cluster of villages called the *zail*, or police *thana* would not be useful, because they tended to overlap and were also more prone to periodic adjustments (ibid.: 139). Thus if the *tahsil* were adopted as the unit for ascertaining contiguity, it would be found that in the Gurdaspur district, only Pathankot *tahsil* had a non-Muslim majority.

On the other hand, in the other three *tahsils* of Shakargarh, Gurdaspur and Batala, Muslims were in majority. Similarly, in the Ajnala *tahsil* of Amritsar district Muslims constituted the majority. In the Jullundur district, Muslims were in a majority in Jullundur and Nakodar *tahsils*. In Ferozepore district, Ferozepore and Zira *tahsils* were Muslim majority *tahsils*. Together, these *tahsils* formed a contiguous area connecting them to western Punjab (ibid.). Khan observed that the cut-off point of the international boundary between India and Pakistan proposed by Congress and the Sikhs at the Chenab would make Pakistan easily vulnerable to Indian aggression. Pakistan's defence required that its main communication lines and cities were protected from easy attack by the other side. For the protection of the Muslim-majority areas of western Punjab, it was essential that the boundary be fixed at the Sutlej (ibid.: 140).

Amritsar should remain in Pakistan

Although Lahore and Gurdaspur were Muslim-majority districts and had been placed notionally in western Punjab, the non-Muslim-majority Amritsar district of the Lahore division was not. Khan advanced two arguments for keeping Amritsar in Pakistan. First, that Lahore, Amritsar and Gurdaspur districts were contiguous and together had a population of 42,62,762. Of these, Muslims were 22,75,390, which meant a Muslim majority of 2,88,018. Therefore, they should be awarded to Pakistan (ibid.: 145).

The second justification was that although Amritsar and Taran Taran *tahsils* of the Amritsar district had a non-Muslim majority, they were surrounded by Muslim-majority *tahsils* (in the west by Ajnala *tahsil* of Amritsar district, Zira and Ferozepore *tahsils* of Ferozepore district in the south, the Muslim-majority princely state of Kapurthala in the east and by Batala and Gurdaspur *tahsils* of Gurdaspur district in the north). They were therefore not contiguous with eastern Punjab. Similarly, Ferozepore, Jhirka and Nuh *tahsils* were Muslim-majority *tahsils* in the non-Muslim-majority Gurgaon district of Ambala, but they were blocked from joining western Punjab because they were not contiguous to Muslim-majority areas. The Muslims must therefore reconcile themselves to Ferozepore, Jhirka and Nuh *tahsils* being left in eastern Punjab and non-Muslims must reconcile themselves to Amritsar and Taran Taran *tahsils* being left in western Punjab (ibid.).

Claim to portions of Pathankot tahsil on the basis of 'other factors'

A deviation from the Muslim League's stand, that the *tahsil* be the unit of territory on which claims should be based, was made when Khan argued on the basis of so-called 'other factors' for the inclusion of the non-Muslim-majority *tahsil* of Pathankot in western Punjab:

> The Canal Head Works of the Upper Bari Doab system are situated at Madhopur in the [non-Muslim-majority] Pathankot Tahsil of the Gurdaspur District... The whole of the Irrigation system of the Upper Bari Doab serves areas which would be comprised within West Punjab, the Head Works and a stretch of a few miles of the canal alone being within East Punjab... It is submitted therefore... to include within West Punjab the portion of the Pathankot Tahsil of the Gurdaspur District which lies to the West of a line drawn from a point two miles above Madhopur and running to the East of the Upper Bari Doab Canal up to the point where the Pathankot Tahsil joins the Gurdaspur Tahsil (ibid.).

Areas claimed by the Muslim League for western Punjab

Unlike the claims of the Congress and the Sikhs, which had been clearly stated at the end of their respective memorandums in the form of a list, the Muslim League, neither in the memorandum nor in the oral presentation, followed such an approach. Instead, several paragraphs were devoted to present its claim. Zafrulla Khan contended that of the seventeen districts of western Punjab, based on the notional division of the province into two parts, the Muslims had a majority in all the *tahsils* except Pathankot. They should therefore come to Pakistan, he said. He also claimed Pathankot *tahsil* under 'other factors' vital for the supply of water to western Punjab. Furthermore, the Muslim-majority parts of Fazilka and Muktsar, Hoshiarpur, Jagraon, Ludhiana, Samrala, Rupar, Una, Moga, Garh Shankar, Nawan Sahr and Philaur were claimed from the non-Muslim districts of eastern Punjab because they were contiguous to the Muslim-majority areas of Gurdaspur, Lahore and Montgomery. Dasuya *tahsil* in the Hoshiarpur district was claimed on the basis of a Muslim–Christian majority. Zafrulla Khan submitted that the Christians (*Ahl-e-Kitab* or 'People of the Book') would prefer to live in Pakistan rather than in India. Proceeding thus the Muslim League claim came up to the valley of the Sutlej river (ibid.: 146).

Zafrulla Khan rejected the Congress–Sikh thesis that partition would necessarily involve large-scale movement of populations across the Punjab borders. Even if that were to happen, there would be more Muslims leaving the eastern part than Hindus and Sikhs moving over to eastern Punjab (ibid.: 472-3). In the memorandum it was asserted that a division of Punjab on the lines suggested by the Muslim League would mean that in West Punjab, out of a total population of 20,427,946, there would be: 69.86 per cent Muslims; 12.75 per cent Sikhs; 12.24 per cent caste Hindus; 2.68 per cent scheduled caste and Ad-Dharmis; and 2.47 per cent Christians and others (ibid.). Hence the Muslim League's contention that the Sutlej be the line of demarcation was fully justified.

Arguments of the minor groups

Mr Bannerji, representing the National Christian Association, argued that according to the notional division, most Christians would be placed in West Punjab. But since Christians were organised on an all-India level, they would like such areas to be included in India. His credentials were challenged by S.G. Dutta, who claimed to be the leader of the Punjab Christian League. Badri Dass (representing the scheduled castes), claiming to have the support of all the eight scheduled-caste members of the Punjab Assembly and two members of the Constituent Assembly, asserted that the scheduled castes considered themselves part of Hindu society and would like to express their support for union with India. Darbara Singh argued that the Mazhabi and Ramdasia Sikhs – designations of Sikhs belonging to the so-called untouchable castes – were integral parts of Sikh society. Therefore, such areas should be included in eastern Punjab (ibid.: 147). The well-known Christian leader of the Punjab, S.P. Singha (representing the Joint Christian Board), asserted that there was no such thing as the National Christian Association and therefore Bannerji had no right to represent Christians. Naming a long list of Christian notable individuals and claiming to represent what he called the 'real' Christian organisations, he argued that Christians would rather have a united country according to the Cabinet Mission Plan. If the Punjab were to be divided, however, he said that they could expect better treatment in Pakistan than in a Hindu-dominated, caste-ridden India. Representing the

Anglo-Indians, Mr Gibbon informed the Commission that the Anglo-Indians were happy to be in Pakistan, as they regarded Lahore and West Punjab as their homeland (ibid.).

Bashir Ahmad, meanwhile, represented the Ahmadiyya community and argued that Qadian in Batala *tahsil* of the Gurdaspur district be included in Pakistan, as it was contiguous with the Muslim-majority *tahsils* of Ajnala and Narowal. The Sikhs, he said, were making a great case about their holy shrines at Amritsar and Nankana Sahib. By the same token, it could be asserted that the founder of the Ahmadiyya community was buried at Qadian in Batala *tahsil*, and that holy shrine should thus be in Pakistan (ibid.: 147-8). Further, it was not only the Sikhs who had rendered meritorious services to the British empire but the Ahmadiyya community as well, having served in the army in both First and Second World Wars. Thus '... even in the last Great War about 199 members of this community held the King's Commission and they held very high and responsible positions.' (ibid.: 148). It is to be noted that the total population of Gurdaspur district was 11,53,511. Hindus and Sikhs together made up 504,453 and Muslims 589,923 of the district population. The rest were Ad Dharmis, Christians, Jains and other miniscule minorities. That meant 85,470 or a bare one per cent Muslim majority. That majority was presumbably made possible by the inclusion of the Ahmadiyya sect among the Muslim population. The Ahmadis were to be found in sizeable numbers in that district, especially in Qadian in Batala *tahsil* where the founder of their movement was buried; in 1974 Ahmadis were declared non-Muslims by the Pakistan National Assembly.

Salig Ram, for his part, spoke out on behalf of the scheduled castes and Mazhabi Sikhs of the Pakistan Scheduled Castes Federation. (His credentials, however, were challenged by other members of those communities on the grounds that he himself did not belong to them.) He argued that the eight MLAs who voted that scheduled castes go to India, did not represent the interests of those depressed classes and castes. Moreover, because untouchability was not recognised in Islam, the scheduled castes have had experience of better treatment in the Muslim villages. Therefore, he said, their interests lay in being allied with the Muslims (ibid.). Further: 'So far as Mazhabi Sikh Untouchables are concerned they have separate temples, if they have any; they get a different kind of *amrit* and they have nothing in common with the rest of the Sikhs' (ibid.). R.C. Soni, representing Bikaner state, and Zafrulla Khan, who also represented Bahawalpur state, disputed the sharing of the river and canal waters passing through those states and the waterworks connected to them.

Reports of the Members of the Commission

The four nominated members of the Punjab Boundary Commission could not reach a unanimous decision and therefore submitted separate reports.

Justice Din Muhammad

Din Muhammad described the Sikh demand for special rights as 'most ridiculous, most unjustifiable and most unreasoned' (ibid.: 149). He declared the maps produced by the Hindu–Sikh side as misleading. He accepted numerical majority and contiguity as the main criteria for allocation of territory, but dismissed ownership of property as a valid basis for such a claim. On the other hand, security and economic stability, including allocation of canal head works, were considered by him as important 'other factors' (ibid.). However, in contrast to the Hindu–Sikh demand, he found the Muslim demand, 'to have been framed reasonably and moderately and not with a view to bargaining. It was properly related to the population factor' (ibid.).

Justice Muhammad Munir

According to Munir, the Sikh claim to special rights by virtue of their shrines had no direct relevance. Muslims also had shrines all over Punjab. Nor was the stand on language a valid one because *Lehnda* was only a dialect of Punjabi. He also sought to refute the accusation that Muslim rulers had persecuted Sikhs and quoted instead several Sikh sources urging hatred and strife against Muslims (ibid.: 149). The claim to hard work and exclusive contribution to the development of the canal colonies by the Sikhs was also dismissed as incorrect. In Lyallpur, not only the Sikh Jats but also Muslim Arains had played a great role in development (ibid.). The economic exploitation of Muslims by Hindus and Sikhs was the real reason for demanding a separate Muslim state. Therefore, invoking greater property ownership in Punjab could not be an admissible factor for the allocation of areas (ibid.: 149-150).

Examining the question of security, Munir opined that the Muslim League's proposal was the correct one. As the true measure of contiguity only the *tahsil* could be justly employed. Therefore, he concluded: '... the frontier between the two States should be that suggested by the Muslim League' (ibid.: 150). He assured the non-Muslims that they had nothing to fear in Pakistan because Islam treated all citizens alike (ibid.).

Justice Teja Singh

Teja Singh laid great emphasis on the fears of the Sikhs about living under a Muslim government. While reiterating the Sikh counsel's version of the Muslim–Sikh animosity during the Mughal period, he went on to discuss in detail more contemporary events. Commenting on the Muslim League's agitation against the Unionist ministry, Singh described it as violent. He quoted what he called 'patently hostile' slogans against non-Muslims, such as:

> *Aise lengey Pakistan* (We will take Pakistan)
> *Jaise liya tha Hindustan* (The same way we took India) (ibid.).

Singh noted that while the authorities did not lift a finger upon the outbreak of the Muslim League agitation, Sikh and Hindu students who marched in a procession on 4 March 1947, were hit with batons. Trouble then spread from Lahore to other parts of the Punjab. There were serious communal riots in the districts of Campbellpur, Rawalpindi, Jhelum, Amritsar, Multan and later on in Gurgaon. In the rural areas of Rawalpindi, Jhelum and to a lesser extent in Multan, Sikhs were pillaged by Muslim mobs (ibid.). Further, 'In some places the rioters numbered five to ten thousand, and almost the entire Sikh population including the old and infirm, women and children were either killed or burnt alive. A large number of people were forcibly converted, children were kidnapped and young women were abducted and openly raped' (ibid.: 150-51).

Singh pointed out that the Ahmadiyya community, who supported the stand taken by the Muslim League, and to which community Sir Muhammad Zafrulla Khan belonged, had also stressed the necessity of preserving the solidarity of their community (ibid.). Further, he reiterated that because many holy shrines and historical sites of the Sikhs were located in Lahore, Amritsar, Gurdaspur, Gujranwala and Sheikhupura districts, these should belong to eastern Punjab. In conclusion, he recommended a division of Punjab which largely, though not entirely, followed the position of the Sikhs. He observed, 'I have not calculated the figures but I believe that it would raise the number of the Sikhs in the Eastern Punjab to about 31 lakhs out of their total population of about 37 lakhs in the whole of the British Punjab' (ibid.: 152). The Congress and Sikh plans placed 34 lakhs in eastern Punjab.

Justice Mehr Chand Mahajan

Mahajan acknowledged that contiguous Muslim and non-Muslim areas should be separated and allocated to Pakistan and India, respectively. At the same time, he observed that 'other factors' were left to the discretion of the Commission. He made this interesting observation:

> I am convinced that it is possible for an ingenious Muslim to make the whole Punjab a contiguous Muslim-majority area by adopting a certain line and, similarly, it is possible for an ingenious non-Muslim to make the province of the Punjab right up to the River Jhelum a non-Muslim area by adopting another line. He may go up even to the city of Rawalpindi' (ibid.).

Proceeding in a relatively neutral and independent vein, Mahajan rejected the suggestion made by both the Congress and Sikh community that the Chenab river be the frontier between India and Pakistan. He said:

> This suggestion would seriously prejudice the claim of the Muslim League on the basis of the population factor and would also clash with the main principle of partition as it would include within the Eastern Punjab a huge majority of Muslims residing in areas which are predominantly Muslim. There are no such factors in this area which can override the population factor' (ibid.).

Regarding the Muslim League's contention to fix the border on the Sutlej river, Mahajan found that it had been worked out on the basis of the *tahsil* as the unit for demarcation of contiguous areas. It could easily be reversed and then non-Muslim parts of *tahsils* could be put together to create non-Muslim-majority contiguous areas and this could extend well into western Punjab (ibid.: 153). On the other hand, in the distribution of the two major canal systems and the canal colonies of Lyallpur and Montgomery, Mahajan sought to compensate both sides. Therefore, while most of Lyallpur including substantial portions of the Shahidi Bar should be awarded to western Punjab, Montgomery should go to eastern Punjab (ibid.). As for Lahore, Mahajan acknowledged the common claims of all the communities and preferred an arrangement under which it could be made a 'free city' jointly supervised by India and Pakistan (ibid.). On the other hand, he felt that Nankana Sahib ought to go to India.

He said in conclusion:

'In my view the frontier of India and Pakistan should be demarcated on the west of the Ravi and in the neighbourhood of that river, as strategically speaking this is the only workable frontier that can be laid down between these two states which are being divided on a religious basis' (ibid.).

Given the total disagreement between the members of the Punjab Boundary Commission, the prerogative of the chairman alone to determine the content of the Award became even more important. The Punjab leaders were informed of the Radcliffe Award on 16 August, although Pakistan and India had achieved independence on 14 and 15 August, respectively. The Award was published on 17 August 1947.

Remembering the proceedings of the Punjab Boundary Commission

I was very keen to track down some of the witnesses to the sittings of the Commission. Fortunately, we found two of them, whose accounts are excerpted below:

Syed Afzal Haider

'The Muslim League had made virtually no preparation for pleading its case before a Boundary Commission. The reason is that nobody believed that Pakistan would come into being. Thus, when the government declared that a commission will hear the arguments about the boundaries between Pakistan and India the only man of erudite learning and legal skills that could plead the case of Pakistan was Sir Zafrulla Khan. Zafrulla Khan, assisted by my father, Syed Muhammad Shah, Sahibzada Nawazish Ali, Sheikh Nisar Ahmed, Mian Abdul Bari, Sheikh Karamat Ali and Ahmed Saeed Kirmani, prepared the case. Khwaja Abdur Rahim as a senior civil servant had been appointed by the government to assist the Muslim League during the proceedings. He brought a sackload of statistics on the population, property and other factors and gave it to Sir Zafrulla. His collection proved very useful. A Hindu civil servant had been assigned to the Congress to assist it.

'Syed Maratib Ali arranged a stenographer and writing material, and also provided us with meals during the day. Sir Zafrulla told us that Jinnah had assured him that everything was ready and all he had to do was to go and present the case, but except for the papers supplied by my father and Khwaja Abdur Rahim and the food and other facilities by Syed Maratib Ali there was absolutely no preparation by the Muslim League or the lawyers associated with the Muslim League.

'Once in a while, the editor of the pro-Pakistan Urdu newspaper, *Nawa-i-Waqt*, Hameed Nizami, used to come. Otherwise, nobody from the leadership of the Muslim League ever attended the proceedings of the Punjab Boundary Commission. I used to carry the books and papers, my father and Sir Zafrulla would walk in front and that is how we used to reach the premises of the Lahore High Court where the commission heard the arguments. If I remember correctly, Daultana came once or twice, Mian Iftikharuddin once, Shaukat Hayat never. Ghazanfar Ali also came once. They all would say to Sir Zafrulla that he was more learned and they could not help him.

'Sir Zafrulla used to say, "Please help me prepare the case as solidly as possible. I don't want to hear that a Qadiani [Ahmadi] presented the Muslim League case and did not do it well". The arguments were prepared by my father and other team members, but Zafrulla presented the case. He left no stone unturned to plead the Muslim League claim. When the briefs had been presented Setalvad asked Zafrulla, "Sir Muhammad I must say you have won. How much did you charge?" Sir Zafrulla said, "Not a penny". Setalvad remarked, "Then, I must return the 7 lakh rupees [700,000] which I have charged the Congress".'

Syed Ahmed Saeed Kirmani

'I was the youngest member of the team that prepared the Muslim League case. Attendance was by special passes – that is why not many people attended the proceedings. At that time, Lahore was under curfew. I got the curfew card to go to the Punjab Library for books and this I did. Were it not for Khawaja Abdul Rahim and Sahibzada Nawazish Ali, we would have had great difficulty in finding official papers. The proceedings were very spirited. The Qadiani leader, Mirza Bashiruddin Mahmud, also used to come to hear. He could be seen talking to Zafrulla who was his ardent follower. On one occasion, Mirza was reprimanded by Justice Din Muhammad, but Zafrulla threatened to withdraw. He claimed it his right to consult anyone. The Christian leaders Singha and Gibbon also spoke passionately in favour of Pakistan. Hamid Nizami used to come. I don't remember any Muslim League leader who came. Setalvad and Tek Chand were not a patch on Zafrulla. He pleaded the Pakistani claims on the Punjab with great competence. I say this in all honestly although I am not a Qadiani.'

No comment from Governor Jenkins

It is interesting to note that Jenkins made no reference to the deliberations of the Punjab Boundary Commission. In his last FR, dated 13 August, he did mention the meeting of the Punjab Partition Committee on 11 August but said nothing about the Punjab Boundary Commission. The newspapers also refrained from making critical comments.

The Radcliffe Award

In his report containing the territorial award, Radcliffe wrote that the divergence of opinion 'between my colleagues was so wide that an agreed solution of the boundary problem was not to be obtained' (Mansergh and Moon, 1983: 745). He said further:

9. The task of delimiting a boundary in the Punjab is a difficult one. The claims of the respective parties ranged over a wide field, but in my judgment the truly debatable ground in the end proved to lie in and around the area between the Beas and Sutlej rivers on the one hand, and the river Ravi on the other. The fixing of a boundary in this area was further complicated by the existence of canal systems, so vital to the life of the Punjab but developed only under the conception of a single administration, and of systems of road and rail communication, which have been planned in the same way.
10. I have hesitated long over those not inconsiderable areas east of the Sutlej River and in the angle of the Beas and Sutlej Rivers in which Muslim majorities are found. But on the whole I have come to the conclusion that it would be in the true interests of neither State to extend the territories of the West Punjab to a strip on the far side of the Sutlej and that there are factors such as the disruption of railway communications and water systems that ought in this instance to displace the primary claims of contiguous majorities....
11. I have not found it possible to preserve undivided the irrigation system of the Upper Bari Doab Canal, which extends from Madhopur in the Pathankot Tahsil to the western border of the district of Lahore, although I have made small adjustments of the Lahore–Amritsar district boundary to mitigate some of the consequences of this severance... (ibid.: 746-47).

The Award ready on 13 August (announced 16–17August)

Although the Radcliffe Award was ready on 13 August, it was revealed to the political leaders on 16 August and made public on 17 August – two days after India and Pakistan had celebrated their independence. People in general got to know about it only on 17 August. The most controversial aspect of the boundary award was that three of the four *tahsils* of Gurdaspur district on the eastern bank of the Ujh river (which joined the Ravi a little further down) – the *tahsils* of Gurdaspur, Batala and Pathankot – were awarded to India and only one, Shakargarh, was assigned to Pakistan. Curiously enough, however, instead of choosing the

Ujh-Ravi rivers as the cut-off point for the border, 'The *tahsil* boundary and not the actual course of the Ujh river shall constitute the boundary between the East and West Punjab' (ibid.: 747). Such an arrangement gave both India and Pakistan some foothold on the other side thus making the border quite erratic.

The border then followed the boundary that already existed between the *tahsils* of Ajnala of Amritsar district and Lahore and *tahsil* Taran Taran of Amritsar and Lahore. This was to continue till the *tahsils* of Kasur of Lahore district, Lahore *tahsil* and Taran Taran *tahsil* meet. Thereafter, the border went southwards but portions of Kasur *tahsil* were taken away and given to India. Thereafter it went southwards, following the Sutlej largely till it reached Bahawalpur State (ibid.: 748-9).

The Radcliffe Award: An analysis

Huge controversy has surrounded the Radcliffe Award. The reason often given for its belated announcement is that Mountbatten expected fierce reactions from the various parties involved – the Muslim League, Congress and the Sikhs – in the conflict over the international boundary. Since he had to participate in the Independence Day celebrations of the two countries, he deemed it proper that the award should be made public after the official ceremonies were over (Tan and Kudaisya, 2000: 96). There is considerable literature available alleging that Mountbatten had the original text altered so that the whole of Gurdaspur, in which Muslims formed a very slim majority, would not be awarded to Pakistan. Three of the four *tahsils* of Gurdaspur district were awarded to East Punjab. The reason he did so, it is alleged, was to provide a land route for India into Kashmir through Pathankot. On the other hand, the counter-argument is that Pathankot was a Hindu–Sikh majority *tahsil* and would have gone to India in any case if the *tahsil* had been adopted as the unit for marking contiguous Muslim and non-Muslim areas. That would have effectively blocked Pakistan's access to Kashmir (Ahmed, 1999: 156).

According to Pakistani sources, Zira and Ferozepur *tahsils* in Ferozepore district had been awarded originally to Pakistan. In the final award, however, these were included in the Indian Punjab. Justice Muhammad Munir, who was a member of the Punjab Boundary Commission, has claimed that Radcliffe had agreed that Ferozepore and Zira *tahsils* – and portions of Fazilka and Muktsar *tahsils,* as well as the Ferozepore headworks – would be allocated to Pakistan (Munir, 1973: 55). He even claims that the non-Muslims had tried to bribe him to let Montgomery go to India and that Radcliffe had toyed with the idea of giving Lahore to India but that his (Munir's) vehement protest had made Radcliffe change his mind (ibid.: 50-55). Similarly Chaudhri Muhammad Ali, later Prime Minister of Pakistan, who was the Muslim member of the two-man Steering Committee of the Partition Council headed by Mountbatten, asserted that the British were clearly biased in favour of the Sikhs. Hence, the Muslim-majority Gurdaspur district as well as the Muslim-majority *tahsils* in Ferozepur, Amritsar and Jullundur districts were awarded to India (Ali, 1998: 210-21).

Kirpal Singh agreed that there is evidence to suggest that the *tahsils* of Ferozepore and Zira were included in a map drawn by Mountbatten's secretary, Sir George Abel, and sent to Jenkins. However, Singh asserts that it was merely an informal map which reflected the ongoing negotiations, rather than the final outcome (Singh, 1972: 99-103). He also asserts that the Muslim nominees on the Punjab Boundary Commission, Justice Din Muhammad and Justice Munir, were aware of the fact that Gurdaspur would go to India. He quotes from a statement of Munir in *The Tribune* of 26 April 1960 (then published from Ambala Cantonment):

> Today I have no hesitation in disclosing.... It was clear to both Mr. Din Mohammed and myself from the very beginning of the discussions with Radcliffe that Gurdaspur was going to go to India and our apprehensions were communicated at a very early stage to those who been deputed by the Muslim League to help us (ibid.: 99).

Alastair Lamb, however, asserts that the map in question was a printed one and was therefore official till 8 August. Some British officers then tampered with it under instructions from Mountbatten and changed it in accordance with the Wavell Plan, which had been drafted by the pro-Congress V.P. Menon. The changes were meant to placate the Sikhs who had escalated violence from 8 August, the day they got hold of the map (1997: 61-72).

After a careful perusal of the discussions of the Punjab Boundary Commission, another hypothesis can be proffered: The Radcliffe Award relied upon the principle of Muslim and non-Muslim majority contiguity and did not recognise claims to property as a valid basis for awarding territory. In particular, the Congress–Sikh claim to Lyallpur and Montgomery, other canal colonies and to Lahore, which was based on the ownership of overwhelming property rights in these places, was not considered legitimate to override the population factor. Therefore, these areas in which Sikhs in particular owned much of the land, and Hindus and Sikhs together owned most of the urban property, went to Pakistan. In this sense, then, the Radcliffe Award was more sympathetic to the claims of the Muslim League than to those of Congress and the Sikhs.

On the other hand, it can be argued that awarding the seven Muslim-majority *tahsils* to East Punjab was Radcliffe's idea of fair play in meeting, in some substantial measure, the Sikh demand to be consolidated in East Punjab. Such an inference is plausible as the various public statements of the British government mention a consideration of the special status of the Sikhs. Had Radcliffe openly admitted this, perhaps the controversy which has surrounded his decision would not have given birth to so many conspiracy theories.

Radcliffe Award almost identical to Wavell's Boundary Demarcation Plan

The most interesting point to note is that the Radcliffe Award was almost identical to the Boundary–Demarcation Plan of 7 February 1946 that Viceroy Wavell had prepared as a part of his top-secret breakdown plan of 27 December 1945. Wavell had argued that Amritsar must go to India as it was the holiest city for the Sikhs. Also, Gurdaspur district must be awarded to India, otherwise Amritsar would be surrounded by Pakistan in the north and west, which could jeopardise its security. The Ferozepore district in the south had a non-Muslim majority even when its Zira and Ferozepore *tahsils* had a Muslim majority. Wavell was at that time most certainly thinking in terms of contiguous districts and *tahsils* as the unit for demarcation of the boundary. Radcliffe added portions of Kasur *tahsil* to the Indian East Punjab though Muslims were

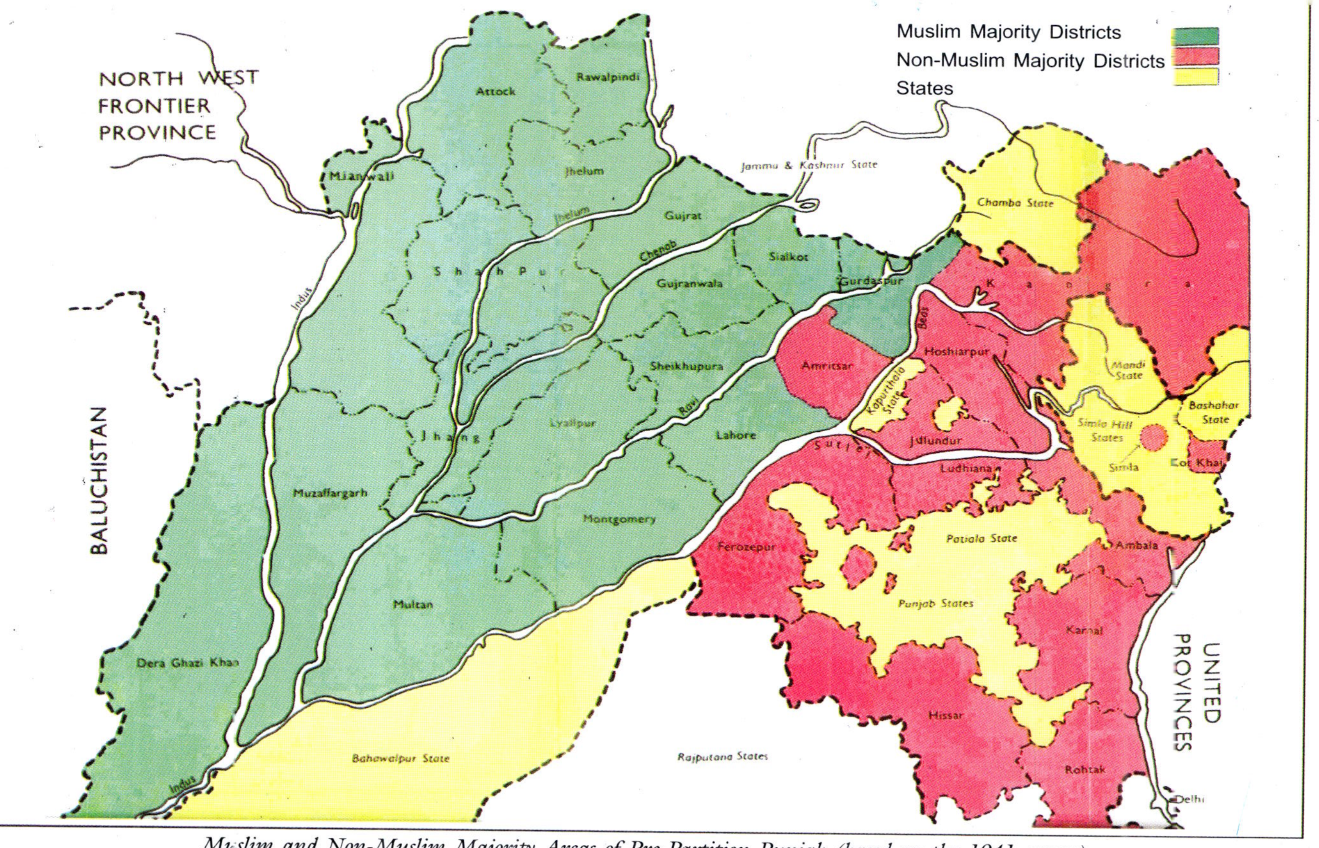

Muslim and Non-Muslim Majority Areas of Pre-Partition Punjab (based on the 1941 census)

Source: Ishtiaq Ahmed, 'Ethnic Cleansing and Genocidal Massacres 65 years Ago', Asia Portal, 14 September 2012, https://bit.ly/3GiXIG7.

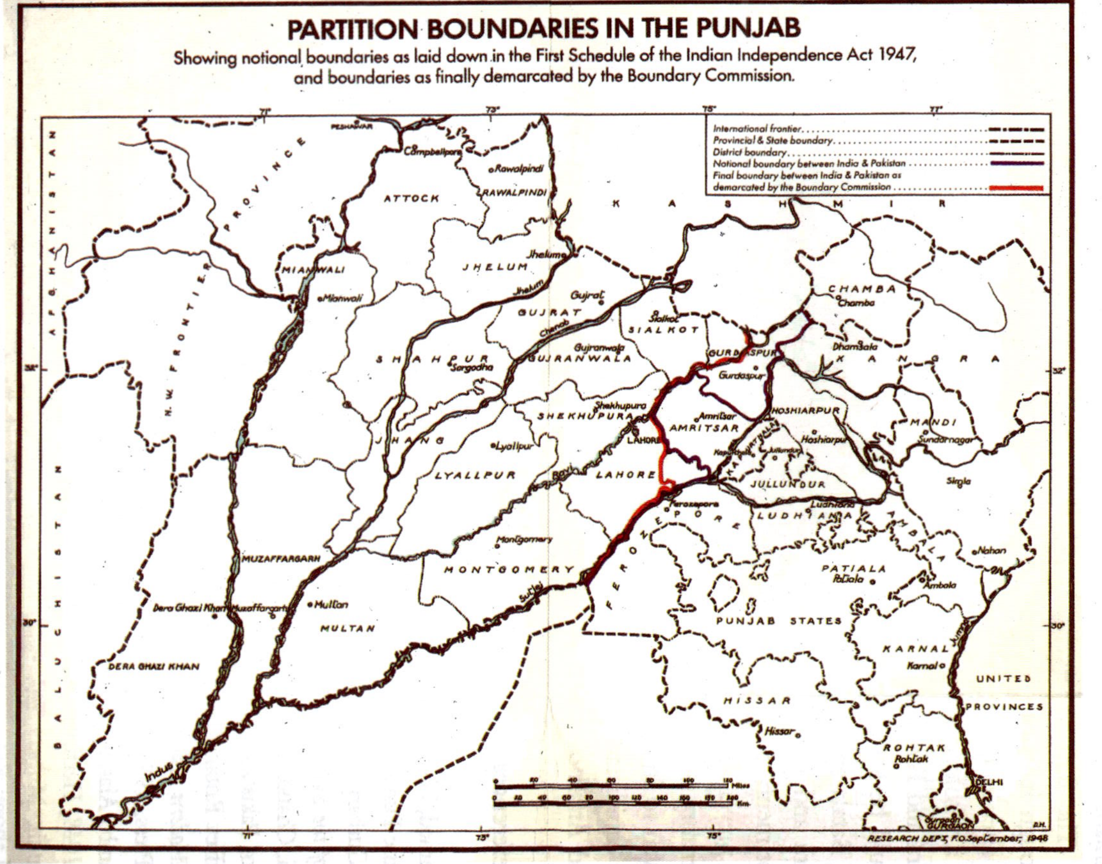

Source: Mansergh, Nicholas and Penderel Moon (eds), *The Transfer of Power, 1942–47, Volume XII: The Mountbatten Viceroyalty: Princes, Partition, and Independence, 8 July–15 August 1947*, Her Majesty's Stationery Office, London, 1983.

in majority in that *tahsil*. In Kasur *tahsil* there were 34,591 Hindus, including scheduled castes; 237,036 Muslims; and 123,446 Sikhs (Census Punjab, 1941: 61).

The Radcliffe Award apparently accepted Wavell's reasoning, even though it is possible that Mountbatten exercised pressure on Radcliffe to alter an earlier version of the award. One can argue that Ferozepore as a whole was a non-Muslim-majority district even if, at some stage, Zira and Ferozepore *tahsils* had been included in Pakistan. This perhaps could be a way of balancing the award of the Muslim-majority *tahsils* of Batala and Gurdaspur in the Gurdaspur district to India. However, Zira and Ferozepore *tahsils* were not given to Pakistan. Radcliffe did not mention it explicitly but the main consideration seems to have been to prevent Amritsar from being surrounded on three sides by Pakistani territory – north, west and south. Portions of the Kasur *tahsil* were given to India so that the border between Lahore and Amritsar should be equidistant. Thus it was drawn between Wagah on the Pakistani side and Attari on the Indian side.

References

Ahmed, Ishtiaq. 'The 1947 Partition of the Punjab: Arguments put forth before the Punjab Boundary Commission by the Parties Involved' in Ian Talbot and Gurharpal Singh (eds). *Region and Partition: Bengal, Punjab and the Partition of the Subcontinent,* Karachi: Oxford University Press, 1999.

Ali, Chaudhri Muhammad, *The Emergence of Pakistan,* Lahore: Research Society of Pakistan, 1998.

Jeffrey, Robin. *'The Punjab Boundary Force and the Problem of Order, August 1947'*, *Modern Asian Studies*, Vol. VIII, No. 4, Cambridge: Cambridge University Press, 1974.

Lamb, Alastair. *Incomplete Partition: The Genesis of the Kashmir Dispute 1947-1948*, Hertingfordburg, Hertfordshire: Roxford Books, 1997.

Munir, Muhammad. *Chief Justice Munir: His Life, Writings and Judgments,* Lahore: Research Society of Pakistan, 1973.

Singh, Kirpal. *The Partition of the Punjab,* Patiala: Punjab University Patiala, 1989.

Singh, K., *Select Documentation on Partition of Punjab – 1947,* Delhi: National Book Shop, 1991.

Tan, T. Y., and Kudaisya, G. *The Aftermath of Partition in South Asia,* London: Routledge, 2000.

Official documents

Carter, Lionel, (ed). *Punjab Politics, 3 March–31 May 1947, At the Abyss, Governors' Fortnightly Reports and other Key Documents,* New Delhi: Manohar, (2007b).

Census of India, 1941, Volume VI, Punjab, Simla: Government of India Press, 1941.

Mansergh, Nicholas and Penderel Moon, (eds.), *The Transfer of Power 1942-47, vol. XI, The Mountbatten Viceroyalty, Announcement and Reception of the 3 June Plan, May 31 to July 7, 1947*, London: Her Majesty's Stationery Office, 1982.

Mansergh, Nicholas and Penderel Moon, (eds.), *The Transfer of Power 1942-47, vol. XII, The Mountbatten Viceroyalty, Princes, Partition and Independence, July 8 to August 15, 1947*, London: Her Majesty's Stationery Office, 1983.

Sadullah, Mian Muhammad, *The Partition of the Punjab 1947,* volumes I, II and III, Lahore: Sang-e-Meel Publications, 1993.

Newspapers

Pakistan Times, Lahore, 1947.

The Tribune, Lahore, 1947

Interviews

Hameed Akhtar, London, 19 May 2002

Syed Afzal Haider, Lahore, 13 April 2003

Syed Ahmed Saeed Kirmani, Lahore, 31 Oactober 2005

13

THE PUNJAB DISINTEGRATES 1 JULY–14 AUGUST 1947

JULY 1947 BEGAN ON A DECEPTIVE NOTE OF CALM, AS THE PEACE initiative launched in the last week of June in Lahore was echoed elsewhere and peace committees were set up. On 1 July, a Central Peace Committee was formed in Amritsar. Kala Kesho Ram Sekhri, Muhamad Ismail Isa and Mian Ghulam Mahmud delivered speeches emphasising the need to maintain communal peace and harmony. It was also decided that peace committees should be formed at the *mohalla* level (*Pakistan Times*, 3 July 1947). On 4 July, two lawyers of the Rawalpindi Bar Association, T.R. Bhasin and A.R. Changez, issued a statement saying that it was senseless to continue with the killing orgy after HMG's 3 June pronouncement. They observed: 'There is no reason why the rights of minority communities will not be protected and duly safeguarded in both the [sic] Hindustan and Pakistan' (*Pakistan Times*, 5 July 1947).

The curfew from the previous month continued to be enforced in Lahore, Amritsar, Rawalpindi, and Gujranwala and was extended to new trouble spots. Intelligence reports noted that Sikhs were organising in the eastern districts and arming themselves for civil war in the event that the boundary in the Punjab did not match their expectations. Beginning in the second week of July, Sikh gangs in the Amritsar, Gurdaspur and Hoshiarpur districts began to roam the countryside and create serious menace in the lives of Muslims. Hoshiarpur district had been reporting skirmishes in the town and in some villages but the situation deteriorated rapidly when Sikhs armed with rifles, grenades and *kirpans* assaulted Pathan workers, killing many of them. This was repeated in many places in that district. Meanwhile, in Gujranwala, Muslims were blamed for starting fires and killing Sikhs and Hindus.

Sikh resolve to create trouble

The wire agency, Reuters, reported on 8 July that the Sikh community throughout the Punjab and in Delhi were wearing black armbands in protest of Partition. A gurdwara congregation approved a resolution declaring, 'Any partition that did not secure the integrity and solidarity of the Sikhs would be unacceptable and create a difficult situation'. It was further reported that Sardar Baldev Singh, Defence Member of the Interim Government, had said, 'Sikhs should be prepared to make all sacrifices if the verdict or the Boundary Commission went against them' (Mansergh and Moon, 1983: 17-18).

In the FR dated 7 July the chief secretary noted that the Hindu press, including *The Tribune*, was inciting Sikhs to resort to violence to get their demands accepted from the Boundary Commission. On the other hand, pro-Muslim League papers continued to oppose the division of the Punjab and especially Amritsar being awarded to India. Moreover, Mamdot and Noon had been ridiculing the Sikh demand that Gurdaspur be included in India. They advised them to seek a settlement with the Muslims and keep the Punjab united (IOR L/P & J/5/250).

Railway workers clash in Lahore

Thus far, communal violence had not affected the railway workers of Lahore, largely because the Communist-led trade union movement had a strong presence among them. But on 10 July, this bastion of proletarian solidarity succumbed to the madness of communalism (*Pakistan Times*, 11 July). Jenkins' FR of 14 July provided details of that incident. In his report, Jenkins said a bomb or cracker had exploded outside a canteen in the workshop area owned by a Sikh. Nobody was hurt in the explosion, but a brawl between Muslims and Sikhs quickly took the form of a hand-to-hand fight, in which *kirpans* and knives were used. As a result eight persons, all of them Sikhs, were killed; thirty-five were injured, of which thirty-two were Sikhs, two Hindus, and one Muslim.

The FR alleged that Muslims had most probably instigated the incident, reportedly stabbing the Sikhs with their own *kirpans*. In the same FR, Jenkins reported several murders and a couple of organised village raids that had occurred in the Amritsar district. In most of these cases the Sikhs were the aggressors (ibid.). The *Pakistan Times* of 16 July reported that the Sikhs were building their hopes on 'other factors' and Swaran Singh wanted the boundary to be fixed at the Chenab – a position the Sikh leadership had maintained consistently ever since they floated the idea of the partition of the Punjab in the early 1940s. Meanwhile, the government began bracing itself for the inevitable chaos and anarchy, which they anticipated would follow the division of the province.

During this period, the *Pakistan Times* and *The Tribune* reported daily cases of stabbing and burning from Lahore and Amritsar, although the first three weeks of July in these towns were relatively less ferocious. The Muslim month of fasting, Ramadan, started in the third week of July. To ease the life of the pious, curfew hours were shortened from a duration of the whole night to four hours, 11 p.m. to 3 a.m. (*Pakistan Times*, 19 July). On the overall Punjab level, too, the administration noted that the situation had 'stabilised'. Thus the Punjab Home Secretary A.A. MacDonald noted that Rawalpindi, Jhelum, Gujrat, Multan, Jullundur and even Amritsar were returning to 'normal'. Only in Mianwali was trouble brewing as '8,000 armed Pathans had collected' (ibid.).

Such optimism proved to be chimerical. In Lahore, the RSS embarked on a concerted bombing campaign, though police intelligence suggested that the bombs were supplied by top-ranking Akali Sikhs (*RSS in the Punjab*, 1948: 18-19). On 18 July some of its hardcore cadres threw an incendiary device at Muslim workers leaving a factory on Sanda Road, not far from the Hindu stronghold of Krishan Nagar; twelve workers were injured (*Pakistan Times*, 19 July). It was followed by a bomb explosion in a cinema in the predominantly Muslim locality of Bhati Gate on 20 July which killed three and injured twenty-four. The next day, bombs were thrown at a train compartment at the Mughalpura Railway Station outside Lahore, as well as onto platform No. 9 at the main Lahore Railway Station (*Pakistan Times*, 22 and 23 July). In Amritsar also, bomb blasts proliferated; the malefactors were mostly Hindus and Sikhs. In the FR dated 21 July the chief secretary observed that the

Sikhs were beginning to realise that by insisting upon partition of the province, they had seriously damaged the unity and solidarity of the Sikh Panth. He warned that a serious situation could arise if the canal colonies were to be included in East Punjab (IOR L/P & J/5/250).

Voices of concern and despair about the Punjab partition

Amidst such chaotic circumstances, voices of concern and despair began to be heard about the implications of the partition of the province. The Sikhs had been the first to demand the division of the Punjab, but after the notional division had placed seventeen districts in West Punjab and only twelve in the East, they began to fear that their community would be divided into two, with roughly equal numbers ending up in the two successor states. On 26 July the Sikh leader Giani Kartar Singh, Member Legislative, declared that his co-religionists would not accept an unjust award. He demanded: 'We must get our shrines like Nankana Sahib'. Repeating the refrain of Sikh grievances, he insisted that 'other factors' were equally important as contiguous Muslim and non-Muslim majorities for determining the international boundary in the Punjab (*The Tribune,* 28 July). On the other hand, the Muslims had been campaigning for the unity of the province and during July a campaign was launched to get Muslim League town committees all over the Punjab to send petitions to the government not to partition the province.

An interesting letter appeared in the *Pakistan Times* of 23 July, expressing fears about the plight of Muslims left in East Punjab after the Partition. In it, Barrister Mahmud Ali feared that if Muslim officers did not remain in the twelve non-Muslim majority districts of East Punjab, the Muslims would be entirely at the mercy of a non-Muslim administration from top to bottom. He went on to say:

> Migration of Muslim officers to Pakistan is neither good sense nor good politics and it does not appear to be even good patriotism. I know some Muslim officers are nervous about their future in Hindustan but can they not muster strength to serve millions of brethren who will need their assistance to a much greater degree than they do today (*Pakistan Times*, 23 July).

In July 2002, in Washington DC, I interviewed Abul Fazl Mahmud, formerly of Jagraon, district of Ludhiana, East Punjab. He told me that Jinnah had issued an appeal to Muslims to stay put in East Punjab to help the Muslim minority that would be left behind in India. Being a humble follower, he said, he obeyed his leader. Yet it proved impossible as non-Muslims went on a rampage to kill every Muslim they could get their hands on. (I have been unable to trace Jinnah's appeal, either in the multi-volume *Jinnah Papers* or in any collection of his speeches for the period 1946–48. Neither did the *Pakistan Times* nor *The Tribune* carry any such appeal.)

Needless to say, the administration was getting extremely concerned on how the Punjab partition was to be managed. Jenkins wrote in his FR of 14 July:

> The boundary problem is uppermost in everybody's mind. ... There is no doubt that non-Muslims are extremely nervous about serving in West Punjab and Muslims in East Punjab. In the Indian Civil Service not a single Hindu or Sikh has agreed to serve in the West, and only one Muslim (who has reason to think that the Muslim League would victimise him) has agreed to serve in the East. I am told the position is the same in the other services. With feelings as they are, it is not surprising that the boundary is a very live issue – it may even be a *casus belli* between the two Dominions. The Chairman of the Boundary Commission arrived in Lahore today, and I understand he believes it will be possible to give the Commission's award before 15th August. If an award is given, it seems to me that under section 4 of the Indian Independence Bill the award boundary will prevail over the "notional" boundary and must be adopted for the transfer of power on 15th August. If this view is correct, there may be considerable confusion, since we have necessarily planned on the basis of the "notional" boundary and the adjustments necessitated by any important change in it might well take some little time.... It is highly probable that the transfer of power will be attended by disorders, but whether they will break before or after 15th August and how serious they will be it is impossible to say. The Sikhs certainly intend to make a nuisance

of themselves; they are unlikely to approve any boundary, and now seem to me almost as suspicious of the Congress as they are of the Muslims (Carter, 2007b : 160).

East Punjab Secretariat instructed to move to Simla

On 22 July, Mountbatten was in Lahore. He instructed the East Punjab Secretariat to move to Simla by 10 August and 'the western section ... to be prepared to move to any place in Western Punjab in case the Boundary Commission cedes Lahore to Eastern Punjab' (*The Tribune*, 23 July). Although the statement was neutral on the future of Lahore, the Hindus and Sikhs took it as a cue to understand that since the East Punjab Secretariat had been advised to move to a town away from Lahore while the West Punjab Secretariat was not, Lahore was obviously going to be given to Pakistan. However, despite a clear Muslim majority in both Lahore city and district, many non-Muslims continued to believe till the very end that on the basis of 'other factors' it would be awarded to India.

Many of my Hindu–Sikh interviewees felt that Mountbatten's 22 July statement accelerated their community's exodus to the east. From some 300,000 in January 1947, their numbers had been constantly declining. The exodus began at the end of February, intensifying along with the increasing incidence of rioting and arson between March and June. After 22 July, many more left the provincial capital for safer havens eastward.

Towards the end of July, the writ of the colonial government began to be flouted extensively and escalating violence rapidly enveloped other parts of the province, but most of the fury was still confined to the urban areas; only in Amritsar district did a display of organised Sikh power begin to emerge as Muslim villages raided by *jathas*, forced terrified Muslims to seek refuge in the Muslim strongholds of Amritsar. The *Pakistan Times* and *The Tribune* of Lahore reported a new spate of stabbings, arson, and bomb-throwing. As in the past, the trend was set by events in Lahore and Amritsar. On Sunday, 26 July, a loud explosion was heard in Dharampura, near Lahore Cantonment. There were a number of injuries but no deaths, but revolver shots were heard and pandemonium broke loose. The Inspector-General of Police-Designate for West Pakistan, Qurban Ali Khan, District Magistrate Eustace, Senior Superintendent of Police Rice and Cantonment Magistrate Sheikh Ghulam Ahmed arrived at the trouble spot and some arrests were made (*Pakistan Times*, 29 July).

In Amritsar, the tables had begun to turn in favour of the Hindus and Sikhs. Muslims were now on the receiving end of violence, particularly in the rural areas, as Sikh *jathas* went about burning and killing. Women began to be abducted in almost all village raids. A loud explosion was heard in Taran Taran. District Magistrate G.M. Brander, Brigadier Stuart, Superintendent of Police L.V. Dean and Additional Deputy Commissioner J.D. Fraser and a police party raided the *tahsil* headquarters and unearthed a miniature bomb factory. Apparently, the bomb had gone off accidentally. The *Pakistan Times* of 31 July noted that the Amritsar administration described the district once again as seriously disturbed and fast getting out of control.

July ended rather dramatically, with Hindu anger coming out in the open against the Congress party in Amritsar. The RSS had been carrying out propaganda for a long time against the Congress leadership, especially Gandhi and Nehru. In meetings reported by the intelligence agencies, not only Jinnah, the Muslim League and Muslims in general were vilified, but the two Congress leaders were blamed for letting down the Hindus of the Punjab by agreeing to the partition of India. On 31 July, Mahatma Gandhi, who was on his way to Kashmir on a train, was greeted with black flags by a crowd of Hindu students and other activists when his train stopped at Amritsar station. They shouted slogans of 'Gandhi go back', 'Gandhi *murdabad*' (death to Gandhi), and 'Congress *murdabad*' (death to Congress). Magistrate Riaz Kureshi ordered the railway police to push back the agitators (*Pakistan Times*, 1 August).

In the 30 July FR, Jenkins mentions the incident at the Mughalpura Railway workshop and provides extensive coverage to the spread and escalation of violence outside the Lahore–Amritsar region into the Gurdaspur district, and beyond to the Jullundur–Hoshiarpur border. Bomb explosions had started taking place almost daily from 19 July, with the culprits being Hindus and Sikhs. The villages around Lahore and Amritsar had begun to be raided on a recurring basis. Sikh leaders had given a call to their community to gather at Nankana Sahib in the Sheikhupura district on 27 July. With at least 1,500 in attendance, the meeting heard speeches calling for a civil disobedience movement. The deputy commissioner persuaded them to disperse peacefully (Carter 2007b : 177-9). On the overall situation in the Punjab, Jenkins noted:

> Generally there is no enthusiasm for partition – the Muslims are naturally pleased at the establishment of Pakistan; but as Punjabis they wanted the whole of the Punjab; the Hindus and Sikhs on the other hand are apprehensive and most reluctant to leave Lahore. It would be difficult enough to partition within six weeks a country of 30 million people which has been governed as a unit for 98 years, even if all concerned were friendly and anxious to make progress (ibid.: 179).

First-person accounts of exits from Lahore in July

Dr Jagdish Chander Sarin

Dr Sarin's accounts of the March 1947 riots and the events in Lahore in June have been given earlier. In July, he left Lahore. He reminisced about his move:

'I left Lahore on 9 or 10 July for Jullundur because some friends had warned us that our house would be attacked. They told me to come back when normality was restored. The rest of my family members had gone already. It was many weeks later that we could trace each other. I actually started my return journey for Lahore on 11 August because on the next day I had to report for work. However, on the way I met fleeing Hindus and Sikhs in their thousands. It became clear to me that returning to Lahore was out of the question. I therefore gave up.

'An uncle and a cousin of mine were stabbed and taken to Mayo Hospital. They mentioned my name to a colleague of mine, Dr Muhammad Nazir, who was on duty. He looked after them as if they were his own uncle and cousin.'

Ramanand Sagar

The famous Bollywood writer, director, film and television producer Ramanand Sagar gave a detailed sketch of his life in Lahore to me. (Incidentally, he grew up less than a kilometre away from my ancestral home on Temple Road, where I was born on 24 February 1947):

'I was born on 29 December 1917 in Asal-Guru-Ki, a small village on the outskirts of Lahore. My father had business interests in Kashmir, but I grew up with my grandparents who lived in Cha Pichwara, Lytton Road, Mozang, Lahore. My childhood was spent in Mozang. In those times, children from all communities played together and the elders were respectful to each other's beliefs and traditions. As a youngster, I would sometimes go to the mosque along with my Muslim friends and join them in their prayers. I can't recall any tension between the different families in our locality.

'Later we moved to a house on Nisbet Road. I studied in the DAV High School, Lahore. After the Muslim League gave the call for a separate Muslim state in its Lahore secession of March 1940, some communal tension could be sensed in the otherwise very harmonious atmosphere of Lahore, but at that time nobody could imagine that Hindus will have to abandon Lahore. We were convinced that Lahore would remain a part of India. There was so much material and cultural contribution of Hindus and Sikhs to the development of Lahore that it never occurred to us that one day it would be taken away from us.

'The Congress leaders told us not to vacate Lahore. However, violent attacks against Hindus and Sikhs became a daily occurrence. We had to flee Lahore in the end of July when things went from bad to worse. We travelled to Sialkot and from there to Jammu and continued to Srinagar. The great Urdu poet Faiz Ahmed Faiz, who was a close friend of mine, visited Gulmarg in Kashmir in August and narrated the events which had taken place in Lahore after we left.

'We managed to board the plane from Srinagar to Delhi after the Pathans invaded Kashmir at the end of August. I worked for a while in Delhi but then came to Bombay. I have been in that city for some fifty-two years now. I have achieved outstanding success in the film industry, but still feel like a refugee. The feeling of being a refugee never lets go of you. It is a constant part of one's existence. Lahore is always in my heart, but I don't think I would ever visit it. I am told that it has changed considerably. I want to preserve the memory of the pre-Partition Lahore. It was indeed a city of love and harmony. Now, when I look back upon those events, which led to Partition, I am even more convinced than ever before that the real masterminds behind the division of India were the British. In some deeply evil way they wanted to punish us for demanding freedom. What could be more satisfying than to bleed those who had challenged their supremacy? I have written down my version of Partition in my novel, *Aur Insaan Mar Gaya* (And Humanity Died).'

It is to be noted that in the late 1980s, Ramanand Sagar began to cultivate Hindu religious themes in his work. The *Ramayana* epic was produced as a serial and shown on Indian television channels. He went on to produce other similar serials. When I asked him if his transformation from a secular humanist to a Hindu bothered him, he told me that the struggle between good and bad was eternal and he now used Hindu themes to transmit his message that doing good was better.

August: violence permeates through rural areas

And then came the critical month of August. It was only a few days before the Punjab would be divided. The Punjab Boundary Force began its work of maintaining law and order from 1 August, but by then, rioting had spread in all directions. On 1 August, a thirty-six-hour continuous curfew from 6 p.m. onwards was clamped on most of Amritsar's inner areas. Sikh *jathas* intensified their raids on villages, but in some places the Muslims offered stiff resistance. Troops of the Punjab Boundary Force were rushed to some of these villages to disperse the raiders.

In a detailed memorandum to Mountbatten dated 4 August, Jenkins questioned the charge that his government had failed to control the Punjab disturbances. In particular, he rebutted allegations that the British officers were callous and incompetent. However, he agreed partly that the fire services, particularly in Lahore and Amritsar, were inefficient to the point of being useless. Jenkins also asserted that imposing martial law would not have helped (Carter 2007b : 194-211). He also presented the total casualties up to 2 August 1947 as follows:

A. **Urban**	**Killed**	**Seriously Injured**
Lahore	382	823
Amritsar	315	666
Multan	131	230
Rawalpindi	99	171
	1044	2023
B. **Rural**	**Killed**	**Seriously Injured**
Rawalpindi	2164	167
Attock	620	30
Jhelum	210	2
Multan	58	50
Gurgaon	284	125
Amritsar	110	70
Hoshiarpur	51	19
Jullundur	47	51
Other districts	44	36
	3588	550
C. **Total**		
Urban and Rural	4632	2573

Jenkins conceded that the figures were incomplete, especially for Gurgaon, where the dead and wounded were usually removed by their own families or party members. Therefore, in his opinion, not less than 5,000 (and probably not more than 5,200) people had been killed in all, and not more than 3,000 seriously injured (ibid.: 200-201). Regarding community-wide casualties, Jenkins estimated that nearly all of those in the rural areas of Rawalpindi, Attock, Jhelum and Multan had been non-Muslims. In other areas, two-thirds of the casualties 'could have been' Muslim. Thus, the communal breakdown of casualties was as follows:

A. **Rural**	**Killed**	**Seriously Injured**
Muslim	522	1011
Non-Muslim	522	1012
	1,044	2,023

B. **Rural**	**Killed**	**Seriously Injured**
Muslim	357	201
Non-Muslim	3231	349
	3,588	550

Total		
Muslim	879	1212
Non-Muslim	3753	1361
	4632	2573

On this basis, Jenkins argued that since most of the casualties in Gurgaon were Muslim, of the 5,000 persons probably killed, 1,200 were Muslims and 3,800 non-Muslims, while of the 3,000 persons believed seriously injured, 1,500 belonged to each community (ibid.: 202). Whatever the exact figures, the situation rapidly worsened from that point onwards. The curfew in Lahore was extended to 15 August by the governor, but stray cases of bomb-throwing and arson were reported from many parts of the city on both 1 August and the next day. In Ferozepore district an armed attack on a village, Kokri Arayan, on 4 August resulted in nineteen deaths. The assailants used firearms and most deaths resulted from gunshot wounds (*Pakistan Times*, 6 August 1947). Bomb-throwing was reported even from Lyallpur and Jullundur. In all cases, some deaths and injuries occurred.

With regard to incendiarism between 14 April and 14 July, specifically in Lahore, Jenkins provided the following figures:

Nature of Fire	Muslim Property	Non-Muslim Property
Attempts	58	112
"Small"	38	149
"Large"	20	112
Total incidents	116	495

Overall total: 611 (ibid.: 208).

He observed:

> During these three months there were 611 incidents (during the worst period sometimes 20 or 30 incidents a day) of which 357 were controlled and 254 were not controlled. The proportion of fires controlled in Muslim buildings is much higher than that of fires controlled in Hindu buildings. The Muslims did not leave Lahore, and were extremely active in protecting their own property. The Hindus abandoned a very large number of buildings, and fires in Hindu property thus tended to become uncontrollable before they were detected (ibid.).

Muslim editors complain about attacks in East Punjab

While the Muslims had an upper hand in Lahore and western Punjab, the situation in the Hindu–Sikh majority districts began to turn against them. The pro-Muslim League newspaper editors in Lahore, poet Faiz Ahmed Faiz (*Pakistan Times*), Hamid Nizami (*Nawa-i-Waqt*), Nur Elahi (*Ahsan*), Inayatullah (*Shahbaz*) and Maulana Akhtar Ali (*Zamindar*) signed and sent a telegram to Mountbatten in which they reported:

'Organised attacks by highly armed gangs continue in Muslim villages in the districts of Eastern Punjab. The Government Machinery is incapable of giving protection to the Muslim minority. Pray Intervene personally and ensure drastic measures to stop massacre of innocent people' (*Pakistan Times*, 10 August).

The editors requested Muslim League leaders to help stop the outrages. They appealed especially to Sardar Shaukat Hayat Khan, who had been elected from eastern Punjab (though he belonged to Attock in north-western Punjab), to tour the eastern districts and do something to save the Muslims. Additionally they wanted Nawab Mamdot, as leader of the Muslims, to warn Dr Gopi Chand Bhargava and Sardar Swaran Singh that if the organised hooliganism continued, there would be repercussions for their co-religionists in the western districts (ibid.).

Salim Tahir's account of events in August

A detailed account of a Muslim youth from Lahore, Salim Tahir, who twice carried out daredevil missions of bringing five boxes loaded with rifles and ammunition in train carriages from the distant Mianwali district to Lahore, has been described by Hamid Hamdani. Salim Tahir told him that the money for purchasing the armaments was given to him by Mamdot, and they were to be sent to East Punjab, where the Muslim League felt that the Muslims were beleaguered as Hindu and Sikh gangs had begun to organise themselves. The last mission was undertaken on 11 August, when he left Lahore for Mianwali, but the return journey on 13 August took much longer than normal.

The chances of being apprehended were very high as Hindu and Sikh officers and soldiers leaving for India were travelling in those very trains and railway officials were checking each compartment. With the help of Muslim police and railway functionaries, he was able to return with his consignment to Lahore on the evening of 13 August. The boxes were handed over to Colonel Tajamul of the Muslim League National Guard on 14 August (Hamdani, 2003: 146-54). Salim Tahir described a shooting incident on Lahore Railway Station:

> This shooting was being carried out by the soldiers of the Baluch regiment. This regiment had been given to Pakistan. All its officers and soldiers were Muslims. On the way to Pakistan they had seen the genocide [of Muslims in East Punjab]. They had even tried to save Muslims and had won great acclaim for that. Those soldiers who had seen small Muslim children being butchered with spears and *kirpans* or women being raped and then killed, for them no law or military

code could have restrained their anger. The Baluch soldiers were no longer the employees of the British but soldiers of Allah.

When the Baluch regiment reached Lahore thousands of Hindus and Sikhs and Indian army personnel had gathered to leave for India. And some were sitting in the train carriages. The police was present to protect them. But for the soldiers of the Baluch regiment the slaughter of their mothers and sisters [a symbolic expression] and children had taken place before their eyes. They had also seen thousands of hungry and thirsty Muslims leaving on the way to Pakistan. When the Muslim soldiers saw all the Hindus and Sikhs they lost control over their senses and their officers could not restrain them. They had rifles and ammunition. They spread all over the station and started shooting intensely. They neither showed mercy to the Hindu railway staff nor any other Hindu or Sikh, military or civilian (ibid.: 151).

The more likely date of Salim Tahir's return to Lahore should be 14 August not 13, because the shooting by the Baluch regiment of Hindus and Sikhs took place in the evening, and we have a detailed account of Yuvraj Krishan who left Lahore on 13 August at 8.30 p.m., in which he does not mention a massacre of Hindus and Sikhs at the railway station. On the other hand, he vividly described the arrival of a train from Amritsar, carrying petrified Muslim women and children; the men had most certainly been butchered on the way. The Khosla report also suggests that the shooting by the Baluch regiment took place on 14 August (Khosla, 1989:122).

Ashwini Kumar was Assistant Superintendent of Police in Lahore, awaiting his transfer orders to Jullundur. He told me the following story:

'In those days the Muslim League National Guard had begun to loot Hindu and Sikh refugees at the Lahore railway station. On one occasion I saw the famous hockey player Ali Iqtidar Shah Dara leading one such team of looters. I said to him, "Shah Sahib, what are you doing? This is below your dignity". He looked embarrassed and said that he was with them to restrain them and to keep the loss of life to the minimum'.

Some incidents from Mozang

The Mozang locality, where I was born, saw considerable bloodshed in August. Two incidents have left an indelible impression on the memory of many people from that time; the brutal murder of an old Sikh carpenter and an organised attack on a Sikh *gurdwara*. The two stories have been told again and again and are likely to be repeated as long as those elders are alive. The massacre at the *gurdwara* is described in the interview with Mujahid Taj Din, a participant in that infamous assault. It appears later in the interviews section. My mother, Sitara Bano, narrated the second incident to me. She died in 1990. I have subsequently checked its details with my father and other elders who confirmed her story. The following is my mother, Sitara Bano's statement:

'Lahore was seriously disturbed by the second week of August but Mozang, being a Muslim majority locality, was considered secure. On 12 August I, just by chance, happened to be looking out of the window of our house on Temple Road. Some loafers and criminal types were standing at the crossing between Temple Road and Bhoondpura Street. It seemed they were on the lookout for some trouble. I noticed a big, hefty Sikh coming on his motorcycle. As he approached Chowk Bhoondpura the *goondas* tried to attack him. He pulled out a gun and they quickly dispersed. Half an hour later, another Sikh, this time an aged, emaciated carpenter, came down the same route on a rickety old bicycle.

'Like most daily workers, he was carrying his afternoon meal wrapped up in a dirty cloth, called *potli* in Punjabi parlance, which was tied to the handle of his bike. He seemed to be on his way to work as usual, oblivious of the big political game going on at that time. This time the roughnecks pounced upon him. One of them stabbed him. He screamed and tried to run away. Seeing a *tonga* nearby, he tried to climb on to it. The *tonga*-driver kicked him and he fell to the ground. His assailants now caught up with him and dealt him some more blows. He died screaming for help and mercy.'

Mujahid Taj Din

One of the most notorious attacks against non-Muslims took place some three hundred metres away from our Temple Road house. It was an organised assault on a historic Sikh *gurdwara*, built by the fifth guru of the orthodox Sikhs, Guru Arjan Dev. The man who led the attack gave us the following insight into what happened on that occasion:

'At the time of the Partition of India, I was living in Mozang. Being inquisitive by nature I used to visit Hindu temples, Sikh *gurdwaras*, Christian churches, besides praying five times a day in the mosque. I wanted to know how people, belonging to other religions, live and preach their faiths in their religious places. Now when I look upon those years I can say that the *Angrez* (English) have done more service to mankind than any other people.

'I was a very devout and active member of the Khaksar movement. When the call to create an Islamic state, to be called Pakistan, was given, many of us were fascinated by that idea. I took active part in that struggle against Hindus and Sikhs. I killed four Sikhs near Atchison College and took part in the killing, looting and burning of Hindus and Sikhs when fire was set to Shahalmi Gate and other Hindu–Sikh localities.

'The attack on the Sikh *gurdwara*, Chhaveen Padshahi, was masterminded by *thanedar* Malik Maqsood (sub-inspector or Station House Officer) of Mozang Police Station. He trained some of us for four days. We were to take possession of important Hindu and Sikh places when Partition was to be announced. He told us that if we died fighting against non-Muslims we would be *shaheeds* (martyrs) and if we survived we would be *ghazis* (soldiers of Allah). He told us that our Muslim brothers and sisters were being killed in India, and the main objective of the training was to protect Muslims and to take revenge.

'We were given a security plan to protect Mozang from Hindu and Sikh assault. Thus we established our *morchas* (defence posts) at Mozang Adda, Safan Wala Chowk, Mozang Chungi and Kanak Mandi. Those of us who took part in the training besides me were Zahoor Din Khaksar, Naseer, Bau Amanat, Hussain Ganja (*kabaddi* player), Bashir, Rasheed, Alamgir Baloch and Shah Din.

It was the twenty-sixth day of Ramzan (13 August) when we stormed the Sikh temple. I, along with five others, formed the advance party. Altogether we must have been 25 or 30. We entered the temple by climbing its high wall. We gave a *lalkar* (battle call) to the Sikhs to come out. Nobody responded. It was pitch dark at that time. We broke open the front door and entered the temple. The Sikhs had splashed hot *kora tel* (mustard oil) on the floor, with the result that our feet slipped as we walked on it. Then we struck a match and the oil started burning.

'I took *kabza* (possession) of the main *takht* (a long bench). We were shouting "*Pakistan Zindabad*" (Long live Pakistan) and challenging the Sikhs to come out. Suddenly one of them appeared from under the *takht* with a *talwar* (sword) in his hand. He delivered a blow at me, which struck my hand and I received a deep gash on my wrist. I succeeded in snatching the sword from his hand and killed him. Meanwhile, many other people had entered the *gurdwara*. Now, the Sikhs came out of hiding and a hand-to-hand combat began in the darkness. *Talwars*, *churras* (big knives) and *dandas* were used. Some pistol shots were also fired. Someone started a fire by spraying petrol. I suspect *thanedar* Malik Maqsood had provided the petrol to someone in our group. I myself was not informed about it. A few days earlier there were more than 200 Sikhs, but most had left. When we attacked there were not more than 20 to 30 Sikh men and women in the temple. All of them perished in the inferno. From our side, we lost Naseer.

'We were told that Pakistan would be an Islamic state where the *nizam* (system) established by Allah and his Prophet would again be revived. For doing that, Hindus and Sikhs, who were *kafirs* (infidels), had to be killed or kicked out of Pakistan. Only then could it be a successful Islamic state. Once Pakistan came into being, I, like many others, began anxiously to await the revival of the true and just Islamic state and society. During the period of General Ayub Khan, I was particularly hopeful that things would change. I wrote to him and to the governor of Punjab, Nawab Amir Mohammad Khan of Kalabagh, and became very close to them. Later, I pinned my hopes on General Zia-ul-Haq. I even corresponded with the Shah of Iran and many other Muslim rulers of the world in the hope that they will do something for the glory of Islam and the uplift of Muslims. [Many certificates from such dignitaries and the bloodstained sword that he wrested from the Sikh in the temple were displayed on the walls of the room in which the interview took place]. However, we never got our Islamic state. Every ruler looted us.

Pakistan is a very corrupt society. If all this were to happen, then why were we asked to do what we did?

'In 1968 I went with a delegation from Pakistan to attend the *Urs* (annual religious festival) of Hazrat Nizamuddin Aulia at Delhi. At the border, Sikhs welcomed us. They gave each of us two oranges and an apple. In Delhi, I was recognised by a Hindu who used to live in Anarkali, Lahore. He was very kind and offered his help and services for anything that I might need. It happens quite so often that I pray to God to give me *mafi* (pardon) for the murder of those Sikhs and Hindus. I have a feeling that Allah understands me and has forgiven me. We were misguided and used by our politicians.'

Mujahid Taj Din was involved in another carnage which he never mentioned. Another veteran from Mozang, the poet Saleem Shahid, told me that the police used him and some others to kill in cold blood a busload of Hindu and Sikh prisoners, who were ostensibly being driven from the Lahore Jail towards the district courts. But the bus was stopped on Lytton Road on the pretence of engine failure. The prisoners were taken out and slaughtered and thrown into the fields of Gulu di Palley.

Amritsar

Although the balance of power had begun to tilt in favour of Hindus and Sikhs since at least the middle of July, the Muslims of Amritsar held on to the belief that Amritsar would be given to Pakistan. The fact that the notional division of the 3 June Partition Plan had placed Amritsar district in the East did not seem to have registered with the Muslims of that city. Their leaders seemed to have gone into a trance. The first explicitly partisan act by a senior officer of the administration was that of the new Superintendent of Police, Pandit Autar Kishen Kaul, a Kashmiri Brahmin. Through verbal instructions and without the approval of his British superior, Kaul ordered the Muslim policemen of Amritsar to disarm (Mansergh and Moon, 1983: 667; 826). This order resulted in mass desertions. On 10 August, the first Pakistan Special train from Delhi to Karachi was derailed by a mine planted near Bathinda in East Punjab (ibid.: 648). One woman and one child died. The news spread quickly and attacks on trains proliferated. Apparently, Master Tara Singh headed the conspiracy to blow up trains carrying Muslims to Pakistan (*Note on the Sikh Plan,* 1948: i-iii).

On 13 August, the Punjab Boundary Force carried out a major operation in the Majitha area of Amritsar district. It shot dead sixty-one armed men who were carrying mortars, Bren guns, Sten guns, and other modern weapons. Within Amritsar city, a veritable battle for survival was going on. While the Sikh leaders, Master Tara Singh and Sardar Isar Singh Majhail, went on a tour of the rural areas, apparently to help restore peace and order, the main Muslim League leader of Amritsar and Vice-President of the Punjab Muslim League, Sheikh Sadiq Hasan and his wife, left for Lahore to use their influence to stop the violence in Amritsar (*Pakistan Times*, 15 August).

Telegrams of Sir Evan Jenkins

The telegrams between 1 and 14 August sent by Jenkins to Mountbatten, with copies furnished to the Secretary of State for India, graphically depicted how the Punjab was degenerating into total anarchy. The telegrams between 1 and 11 August speak of increasing violence against Hindus and Sikhs in Lahore and the western districts, and against Muslims in Amritsar, Gurdaspur, Ferozepore, and other eastern districts. The first telegram of 12 August, sent at 9.10 a.m., mentions widespread mayhem in Lahore, noting that the outrages were doubtless in retaliation for the derailment of the Pakistan Special, for Sikh excesses in Amritsar district, and the disarmament of Muslim policemen in Amritsar. Jenkins went on: 'Feeling in Lahore City is now unbelievably bad and the Inspector General tells me that Muslim League National Guards are appearing in uniform and that police are most unsteady' (Carter, 2007b: 226).

A second telegram despatched at 11.00 p.m. mentioned that a second attack on a train had occurred on the night of 11–12 August near Kahna Kacha, south-east of Lahore. Sikh passengers had pulled the communication cord, killed five Muslims, and injured another five. The same day in Amritsar district, twenty-five Muslims and seven Sikhs were reported killed. Gurdaspur district reported several persons killed near Batala. Deaths were also reported from Sialkot, Gujranwala and Lyallpur in the west, and Ferozepore and Ambala in the east. In the same telegram the governor reported, 'Several districts report mass migration of Moslem' (ibid.: 227). A third telegram, also sent at 11 p.m., declared:

> Police in Lahore and Amritsar now unreliable. There was serious (omission) indiscipline at Recruitment Training Centre Lahore today and men concerned numbering 300 and 500 cannot be used for emergency duty. I am still awaiting news of state and rural police stations in Amritsar some of which are said to have ceased functioning. We have no strength of troops and police required to restore order and railways will not be safe unless Army can take over [on] "War Department" lines with full railway security. Moslem League National Guard now very active in Lahore city and exceedingly truculent to non-Muslims (ibid.: 227–8).

On 13 August, at 10.40 p.m. Jenkins reported that Lahore was gravely disturbed. Forty casualties, mainly from stabbing, had taken place on 12 August and of these, thirty-four were non-Muslims. 'In addition Moslem [sic] attacked Sind express near Cantonment killing 9 and injuring about 30 non-Muslim passengers'. With regard to Amritsar, the Muslims were under attack from all directions: 'Party of Pathan labourers attacked on Grand Trunk Road near Chheharta and 30 killed. Commander of Punjab Boundary Force informs me 200 Moslems killed by Sikhs in village near Jandiala. One of his detachments with tanks encountered [Sikhs] Jatha near Lajith and opened fire killing 61 and wounding 9'. Casualties were also reported from Sialkot, Gurdaspur, Ludhiana and Ferozepore. Simultaneously, another telegram reported: 'Lahore urban area and Amritsar district out of control'. Further that he had ordered a search of Dera Sahib *gurdwara* as 'Sikhs had been firing from it'. Moreover, 'Severe punishment inflicted on Majitha Jatha may have deterrent effect in Amritsar. Commander of Punjab Boundary Force informs me he hopes to be reinforced by two brigades' (ibid.: 233).

Last governor FR

In his last fortnightly report, Sir Evan Jenkins provided details about the various incidents briefly covered in the telegrams sent during 1–13 August. He frankly admitted:

> I have submitted daily reports on the situation. They are almost certainly incomplete because raids and murders are now so frequent that it is difficult to keep track of them all, and the regrouping of the services as a preliminary to the transfer of power has not improved our organization or the collection and analysis of reports (ibid.: 228).

He reiterated his earlier stand that the Punjab Boundary Force needed at least 20,000 effective fighting men and not the 7,500 it had at its disposal (which could go up to 9,000 if static troops and those at training centres were included). He shared some general reflections as well:

> Until 1946 I do not think that we had ever experienced in India any large communal upheaval outside the cities – the Moplah rebellion is perhaps an exception to this general statement. The lesson of the 1947 disturbances in the Punjab is that once the interlocked communities begin to fight all over the country-side, the only remedy is to employ a very large number of troops. I should say that the Amritsar district could at the moment do with two full-strength Brigades in addition to the old Police force. It has in fact one weak Brigade, and a Police force which has largely disintegrated.
>
> It is impossible to say anything definite about the future. The Sikhs probably have two objectives in mind – they wish to take revenge for the Rawalpindi massacre, and they wish to assert themselves on the boundary question. It is impossible to defend their conduct in any way, but the Muslims have failed to understand the horror caused by the Rawalpindi affair and seem to think that by reprisals they can bring the Sikhs to a less violent frame of mind. I very much doubt this – I believe that reprisals in Lahore will lead only to further outrage by the Sikhs, and so on.
>
> The Hindus are terrified and the Muslim movement from the East is balanced by a similar movement of Hindus from the West. We seem to have for the moment scotched the main Hindu–Sikh bombing conspiracy, and the Hindus are more concerned to get out of Lahore than with anything else.
>
> Many of the Muslims are remarkably smug. They say that as soon as the British leave peace will be restored. It has long been rumoured

> that Daultana and his like intend to make as much trouble during the last few weeks before the transfer of power so as to discredit the British regime. If this is so, it does not seem to have been appreciated that if all Muslims outrages stop in Lahore on the morning of the 15th, it will for practical purposes be clear that the local butchery was organised by the leaders themselves…Some Muslims are most uneasy, and one very good Muslim police officer has just resigned. I am told he felt unable to serve in a completely communal regime (ibid.: 231).

The FR ends rather sentimentally: 'This is, I suppose, the last letter to be sent by a British governor of the Punjab to a British Viceroy. It takes with it my very best wishes to Your Excellency' (ibid.: 232).

Last telegram

On his last day in office, Jenkins was to witness the Punjab descending into total anarchy and chaos. In the last telegram sent on August 14 at 9–10 p.m., Jenkins described the situation in Lahore city and Amritsar district as 'most unsatisfactory'. Two trains had been attacked, presumably by Muslims, in Rawalpindi as reprisals for Sikh activities in central Punjab. The last sentence read: 'Situation will now be for new Government to deal with' (ibid.: 234).

Forced migration before 15 August 1947

Neither Jenkins nor Akhtar Husain have given an estimate of the number of Hindus, Muslims, and Sikhs who fled their homes before India or Pakistan became independent. Organised attacks on Muslims in eastern Punjab did not start till July. Jenkins noted that the first large-scale movement of Muslims towards the western districts did not occur till 12 August. On the other hand, Hindus and Sikhs had started moving to safety from the time when the 1945 election campaign took off in real earnest and extremist slogans were raised against Hindus and Sikhs by the Muslim League. Following the riots in Hazara district of NWFP and after the March riots, Sikhs from Multan and especially some districts of Rawalpindi division left in large numbers for safe havens in central and eastern Punjab. Major General Fazal Muqeem Khan has given the following estimate for the March riots:

> After the troubles during the spring of 1947 in a few places in the Punjab, some two to three hundred thousand Sikhs and Hindus had voluntarily migrated from the West Punjab, and Frontier Province and Baluchistan, expecting these areas to be included in Pakistan. These emigrants were cleverly used to inculcate hatred against the Muslims. False stories were spread, Passion plays were [sic] purporting to represent actual happenings were enacted regularly (Khan, 1963: 62).

Another 200,000, if not more, had most certainly fled after the spring riots. That means that at least 500,000 Hindus and Sikhs were already in East Punjab and other parts of what became India at the time of Independence.

People leaving Lahore

The famous Indian painter, Satish Gujral, lived near Nishat Cinema on Abbot Road, an apparently safe area with many Hindu localities in the neighbourhood. But in August, no place was safe for Hindus and Sikhs. He writes:

> I had just enough time to escape before hooligans came to loot whatever little I had. The only safe haven I could think of was Lajpat Rai Bhavan where my father's friend Lala Achint Ram and others associated with the *Servants of the People Society* were staying. I covered the distance of five kilometres at a run. There were many other fleeing Muslim mobs who were venting their fury on Hindus and Sikh life and property (Gujral, 1997: 73).

Satish Gujral blames the Punjab Hindus for practising untouchability against Muslims. He mentions that in Jhelum his father tried his best to bring the two communities together but, 'Hindus who had joined the Congress were very enthused by its call for national independence, but were unwilling to befriend Muslims or change their attitude towards untouchables' (ibid.: 77). He mentions tribal Pathans attacking Hindus and Sikhs in Jhelum. On the Indian side he was witness to atrocities committed on Muslims. He writes:

> The worst among them was the attack on a Muslim girls' hostel in Amritsar (this happened on 15 August 1947). The inmates were stripped and forced to march in procession through the Hall Bazar, the town's main market. There the girls were gangraped and subjected to the most perverse treatment that any sadistic imagination could devise, before being murdered (ibid.: 80).

Kumar Chand

Professor Anjali Gera-Roy, herself from a Hindu Arora family originally from Lyallpur, and I had been discussing the Partition issue in Singapore for quite some time. One day in 2010, she took me to meet Kumar and Meera Chand at their residence in Singapore. I heard his story but before publication, reconfirmed it on the phone. Kumar Chand had the following story to tell about his escape from Lahore in 1947:

'We, a Sindhi trading family, had settled in Lahore in the 1940s. After living in different places we settled in Qila Gujjar Singh, which had a mixed population of Hindus, Muslims and Sikhs. Rioting had been going on for several weeks in Lahore. My mother and sisters had already been sent to a hill station for safety. One day in August, towards the evening, a mob arrived in our area. They began to kill and pillage. It struck panic in our hearts. We ran out from the back door into the street. That saved us because the raiders became busy in looting the house. Soon, however, some came in hot pursuit after us, but we managed to come out on the main road and then found refuge in a camp that had been set up near the Lahore Railway Station. That was the brush with death I can never forget.'

Pran Nevile

'I joined government service in Delhi in 1946, but my parents were in Lahore when the riots started. One day in June, my father was coming back on a *tonga* from a visit to Mughalpura. A Muslim mob recognised that he was a Hindu from the way he wore his turban. They were about to attack him when one of them, for whom my father had once done some favour, stopped the others. In fact, he accompanied him all the way to Beadon Road, where it was safe. Although my immediate family members could leave Lahore safely, many of my schoolteachers and professors were killed.

'My father was in the postal department. He actually opted for Pakistan. When things became really bad his Muslim friends persuaded him to leave Lahore for the time being. They said, "Panditji, you can leave for the time being and return when law and order are restored." On 14 August he boarded the train for Amritsar. His friends accompanied him to the railway station and found him and my mother seats in a compartment where many Europeans were sitting. They arrived in Amritsar safely, but for some three weeks we did not know anything about their whereabouts. My father could never recover from the shock of leaving Lahore. He was posted to Ambala Cantonment, where he died in 1954, a heart-broken man at the age of fifty-eight.'

Nirmal Tej Singh Chopra

'It is very agonising to recall our life and events which took place during the pre-Partition days in 1947 in Lahore, the capital of Punjab in India which became the hotbed of killing, raping, arson, looting and all other hideous crimes.

'We lived in Kucha Mota Singh, a very narrow street, located in an inner part of the central walled city, inside Shahalmi Darwaza (Gate), the part of the city which was predominantly a Hindu area. The street was off the main bazaar (market) and was named after my great-grandfather. Our ancestral home was a five-storey-high, fairly large building spread over two streets, with eighteen rooms (most of them with high ceilings), in which I, my three elder brothers, and my two elder sisters were born and grew up. From the top of our house, we could see most of the city.

'My father, who had retired as the Deputy Controller of Military Accounts, was highly respected by all the families who lived in our *mohalla*. There were ten other houses and a fairly large *haveli*, occupied by mainly Hindu families, with the exception of three houses in which Muslim families lived. Ours was the only Sikh family, not only in our street but also in the neighbouring streets. But all of us, Hindus, Sikhs and Muslims, were living in perfect harmony celebrating all festivals, such as Diwali, and Eid and Holi together. Exchange of gifts, festival foods and other goodies used to take place on festive occasions as well as at other functions such as weddings. All the houses, big and small, were adjoining each other in our *mohalla* as those were in other parts of the inner city throughout the walled city.

'My three elder brothers were army officers in the Indian Defence Forces and the elder two brothers were married and had children. My unmarried brother was serving in Singapore with the British Indian Army. In 1947, I was seventeen years old, studying BA at the FC College (Forman Christian College), Lahore and was living with my parents and sister in our house in Lahore.

'The events took an ugly turn from March/April 1947. Communal riots between Hindus and Muslims became rampant in Lahore. We all started storing essential commodities which were not easily perishable. After the announcement that the British were giving independence to India and that the country would be divided into two countries, India and Pakistan, and Punjab would be partitioned into two parts, East Punjab to go to India and West Punjab to Pakistan, tensions rose very high. In the absence of any actual demarcation line in the Punjab of the international boundary, demonstrations, protests, *hartals* (strikes), and the like, started to take place in Lahore and in many surrounding cities and areas.

'However, we still had to buy fresh vegetables, fruits, milk and other perishable goods from the bazaar at very high prices, during non-curfew hours. Curfew was imposed mostly at night. At the entrance to our street, we had a very old, strong, thick and tall gate. In those days we used to keep it closed and bolted from inside, particularly at night and sometimes during the day, whenever we heard of some mob activity near our street. Adjoining streets were also quite narrow and the street outside our street was a kind of thoroughfare which would lead you to many other parts of the walled city. I feel afraid and a little nervous, even now, to mention some of the incidents which we used to see almost every day from the windows of the second and third floor of our house, during the months of June, July and August 1947.

'I have seen men, women and children being killed mercilessly by heartless mobs, outside the gate of our street. Sometimes the killers would remove the dead bodies to an open space nearby but some dead bodies were thrown in a small well which was situated outside our street. Occasionally we would see Hindus killing the Muslim passerbys but most of the time, it was the Muslim *goondas*, torturing and killing innocent people.

'I have also witnessed Muslim youths shamelessly raping young girls in the presence of their crying parents, held firmly by the members of the gang, before killing all of their victims. In some incidents, the breasts of the women were cut brutally before they were killed. We used to hear news from passersby that such incidents were happening all over the city.

'I believe that no Muslim or Hindu, in his right senses, would take part in such cruel and brutal atrocities. It was an extreme madness which drove some Hindus and Muslims to indulge in such communal riots in the name of religion, coloured by political designs.

'During June and July 1947, the mobs increased their activities to burn the buildings, here and there in the city. At night, the fireballs, made of old clothes and rags dipped in petrol or kerosene oil, could be seen flying around from the top of the houses in the city, falling on targeted houses and engulfing those in fire.

'Many of us became convinced in our minds that these *badmashes* and *goondas* were being encouraged and protected by certain Muslim police officers in our area, to drive the Hindu population away. I do not now remember the names but some names were being mentioned openly. Yet no action was taken against those officers by the higher authorities.

'One of the Muslim families in our street had a young man by the name of Rafique. He was a rough-and-tough kind of man. I think that it was because of him that no fireball was thrown in any of the houses in our street, which seemed to be enjoying a kind of protection. Yes, Rafique even in those days protected us because we were neighbours. On the other hand, my father used to safeguard the Muslim families in our street. But by the end of June, the Muslim families started feeling unsafe in our predominantly Hindu *mohalla* and left to live in the Muslim areas. Some of the Hindu families also left our street to live in safer areas.

'Our family started feeling very unsafe and isolated in our *mohalla*. We had no telephone in our street or nearby. Our lives were in danger but we could not do anything. We could only pray to God, wishing and waiting to be rescued to safety.

'My brother, Colonel Gurcharan Singh Chopra, who was working in the headquarters of the defence forces in New Delhi, officially arranged with the help of his British officers, for a military station wagon, with armed British soldiers as security staff to fetch us from Lahore. Facing all kinds of dangers and risks, my brother came to rescue us on the second of August 1947. Stopping the vehicle on the main road, outside our street, escorted by armed British soldiers, he came to the house and told us to leave with him immediately. He said that the time was very short and it was very unsafe even to wait for a minute. With a very heavy heart, my parents, my sister and I left the house in just the clothes we were wearing, carrying absolutely nothing with us.

'While we were travelling in the well-protected station wagon, escorted by British out-riders carrying Tommy guns, we saw unruly mobs on the road and on both sides of the road. The Shahalmi Darwaza buildings were burning here and there. The only people the rioters were still afraid of were the armed military personnel, specially the British officers carrying Tommy guns. Our British driver drove the vehicle very fast through mobs gathered here and there, and eventually we arrived safely in Delhi.

'We lost all our moveable and immoveable property in Lahore. Suddenly my father became penniless and homeless and we all became refugees. Still we were thankful to God because we were all alive and together. We were lucky that my brother, Colonel Chopra, rescued us almost at the eleventh hour and gave us refuge in his bungalow in New Delhi, India.'

Harkishen Singh Surjeet

'I was in Lahore in August 1947. To us who were politically aware, it was clear that Lahore would be given to Pakistan because after Amritsar and from Wagah onwards, Muslims were in a majority and Lahore had a clear Muslim majority. I left Lahore on 12 August and returned to my native Jullundur. Other comrades such as Sohan Singh Josh had left a few days earlier. Teja Singh Swatantar came a few days after Partition. When I recall my stay in different parts of western Punjab before 1946, I can't remember any trace of animosity between the three communities. However, things quickly changed. The way people looked at each other was so different. Nobody was safe. I did not want to leave Lahore, but my friends advised me to go for the time being. Many times in recent years I have wanted to visit Lahore but the threat from the extremist Khalistani Sikhs (who have had bases in Lahore since the 1980s) has deterred me from doing so.'

Surjeet did visit Pakistan in March 2005 along with some other Communists. He not only met some of his communist friends from pre-Partition days, most notably C.R. Aslam, but the delegation was received by President Pervez Musharraf, who sent a message via them to the Indian government for the need to normalise relations between India and Pakistan.

Giani Mahinder Singh

'I was the head of the General Local Gurudwara Committee, near Maharaja Ranjit Singh's samadhi in Lahore. I had been given a station wagon to rescue Sikhs from places in Lahore where they were being attacked. By 12 August Hindus and Sikhs were a beleaguered lot in Lahore. On 12 [13] August the famous, historic Sikh *gurdwara*, Chhaveen Padshahi, was set on fire. The attack was in the morning. Sardar Swaran Singh, Sardar Kapur Singh, Sardar Sampuran Singh and Gopi Chand Bhargava were in Lahore at that time. I pleaded with them to go to the military for help. We talked to General Rees of the Punjab Boundary Force. He told us frankly that nobody listened to him anymore.

'When we arrived at the *gurdwara* in Mozang, no Sikh had been left alive. The Lahore Sikhs despatched me to Delhi for help. It was decided that I should go to Delhi to ask Sardar Baldev Singh for help. Giani Kartar Singh was also in Delhi. Sardar Baldev Singh took us to Sardar Patel. Patel was lying on a sofa. I told him the story of Lahore.

He retorted, "*Qatal kar do.*" (Murder them). I replied, "Sardarji what advice is this? It is we who will be wiped out if no help is sent and not the Muslims. Lahore is a lost case". My impression is that Patel had no comprehension of the Lahore situation and was speaking in a state of delirium.

'I could never return to Lahore because Pakistan had come into being. My children had already been sent to Amritsar. The Sikhs wanted no partition, but if it happened then they wanted their rights fully safeguarded. The Maharaja of Patiala wanted to reach an understanding with Jinnah but Master Tara Singh was opposed to it. If the Punjab were partitioned, they wanted a separate province. We were the main losers but the Muslims leaders were not really keen on having Sikhs in Pakistan.'

Yuvraj Krishan

'By early August many Hindus and Sikhs had left for the eastern part, perhaps not with the intention of going away forever. It must be pointed out that the political leaders of all parties, including Jinnah, had assured the minorities that they need not leave, but since the division of the country also envisaged that the services will be divided, the administration had been split notionally and no longer owed allegiance to a unified state. Thus, the officials and functionaries began openly to favour their own co-religionists. The Hindus and Sikhs in Lahore felt that they had no protection against the criminal elements of the Muslim community.

'Since I had opted for India, I was required to leave for Jullundur and take charge of the office there on 14 August. The Radcliffe Award had not been announced yet, but the notional boundary had become the effective line of demarcation between western and eastern Punjab. Most of us knew which areas were Muslim majority areas and which were Hindu–Sikh majority areas. Lahore, we felt, would go to Pakistan and Jullundur to India. Also, Amritsar was going to go to India. Non-Muslims, especially the Sikhs, however, were hoping to win Lahore on the basis of "other factors".

'On 13 August I got to Lahore railway station at 6 p.m., just before the curfew commenced, to catch the train to Jullundur. At that time the curfew began at six in the evening. Our train was to leave at 8.30 p.m. My boss, a South Indian Christian, accompanied me. He was entitled to travel in a separate saloon and wanted me to accompany him. The train, however, got delayed. An hour later, at 9.30, the saloon carriage arrived, although the train, which was to take us, had not arrived yet. My *chaprasi* (orderly), a Hindu who was an ex-armyman, was also with us. He told me that we should not sit in the saloon because it was dangerous to be alone. The fellows who had brought the saloon carriage pulled it back into the yard when they realised that we did not intend to occupy it. I think this saved us. Murders at the railway station before 14 August did not take place on the main platforms, but in the various yards and sidings where the railway carriages were stabled.

'I remember that while we were waiting, a trainload of Muslim refugees arrived from Amritsar. Most of them were women. Many were carrying children in their arms. My guess is that the men had been killed but the womenfolk spared. It is fifty-two years now and my memory perhaps betrays me but what I remember distinctly from that evening of 13 August are the horror-struck faces of those women. I realised that more retaliatory violence will now follow in Lahore as the reports of the various riots and attacks reach different parts of western Punjab. A train finally left late in the night. I arrived in Jullundur city early in the morning of the 14th.'

Khushwant Singh

On the fiftieth anniversary of Partition, Sikh writer, journalist and historian Khushwant Singh wrote an article, 'Last Days in Lahore: From the brittle security of an elite rooftop, a view of a city burning'. According to him, the escalation in rioting occurred in mid-June. He records:

> The score was invariably in favour of the Muslims, the chief reason for Muslims having the upper hand was that the umpires were Muslims. Eighty per cent of the Punjab Police was Muslim; the state government was Muslim-dominated. It was the same story all over western Punjab. Hindus and Sikhs had begun pulling out of Muslim-dominated towns to Lahore. And finding Lahore equally

unsafe, trudged on to Amritsar and towns of eastern Punjab where Hindus and Sikhs outnumbered Muslims.

That June afternoon of 1947 remains etched in my mind. I had returned from the high court when I heard the uproar. I ran up to the roof of my apartment. The sun burnt down fiercely over the city. From the centre billowed out a huge cloud of dense, black smoke. I did not have to make guesses; the Hindu–Sikh *mohalla* of Shahalmi was going up in flames. Muslim *goondas* had broken the back of non-Muslim resistance. After Shahalmi, the fight went out of the Hindus and Sikhs of Lahore. We remained mute spectators to Muslim League supporters marching in disciplined phalanxes chanting: *Pakistan Ka Naara Kya? La-Ilaha-Illilah* ['What is the Slogan of Pakistan? It is that there is no God but Allah' – author's note] .

The turmoil had little impact on the well to do that lived around Lawrence Gardens (today's Bagh-e-Jinnah), and on either side of the canal, which ran on the eastern end of Lahore. We went about in our cars to our offices, spent evenings playing tennis at the Cosmopolitan or the Gymkhana Club, had dinner parties where Scotch which cost Rs.11 per bottle flowed like the waters of the Ravi. In elite residential areas, the old bonhomie of *Hindu–Muslim bhai-bhaiism* ['Hindus and Muslims are brothers' – author's note] continued....

The juggernaut gathered speed. Hindus and Sikhs began to sell properties and slip out towards eastern Punjab. One day I found my neighbour on one side had painted in large Urdu calligraphy *Parsee Ka Makan* ['Parsee's house' – author's note]. One on the other side had a huge cross painted in white. Unmarked Hindu–Sikh houses were thus marked out. We were within walking distance from Mozang, a centre of Muslim *goondas*....

By July 1947, stories of violence against Muslims in east Punjab circulated in Lahore, and a trickle of refugees flew westwards. This further roused Muslim fury....A week before Independence, Chris Everett, head of the CID in Punjab ... advised me to get out of Lahore. Escorted by six Baluch constables, my wife and I took the train to Kalka to join our two children who had been sent ahead to their grand-parents in Kasauli.... I arrived in Delhi on August 13, 1947.

Muslims leaving Amritsar

The following excerpts about events of early August made by an eyewitness, whose account of prior events since March 1947 has been referred to earlier, are quite revealing:

Chaudhri Mohammad Said (or Saeed)

The morale of the Muslims remained high till the 10th August and there were no signs of weakness anywhere, though the Muslims had lost the courage of offensive after the announcement of Lord Mountbatten regarding constitutional changes and notion division of the Punjab [which had placed Amritsar district in East Punjab because it had a Hindu–Sikh majority]. On the 10th of August, Muslim police constables were ordered to appear before Mr. Kaul, Superintendent of Police, Amritsar, and to state if they wished to serve Hindustan or Pakistan. Even those reserve forces which had been drawn from other districts were called upon to do the same. Those who appeared and declared for Pakistan were ordered to surrender their arms and remain in the Police Lines. Some refused.... In place of the Muslim Constables, new hands were recruited and were said to be I.N.A. members. In reality, they were members of the Rashtriya Swayam Sewak Singh and Panthic Party.... These people created havoc in the city on the very first night by indiscriminate firing at the Muslims and they led the Sikh and other non-Muslim mobs which raided Muslim areas systematically.

Simultaneously police pickets stationed in Muslim areas were withdrawn on the pretext of paucity of men... The military posted in the city conspired with the rioters and even "bogus military" was used to terrorise Muslims. This completely broke the morale of the Muslim masses. They ran in terror from several Muslim pockets to Sharifpura or to the Railway Station and a large number were killed *en route*.... Great shelter was afforded by the Mission Hospital for Women,

> Mahan Singh Gate premises, through the good offices of Miss Atkinson. About 5,000 people took refuge there and ultimately shifted to Amritsar Cantt....
>
> On 14th [August], people flocked to Sharifpura from all pockets in the city and suburb areas. The population immediately swelled to about one lakh [100,000].... People coming from the villages related stories of abducted young women carried away by the Sikhs with assistance of the State Military of Kapurthala and Patiala on vehicles brought especially from these States. About 600 such cases from different villages were brought to our notice in Sharifpura.... Cases of abduction even took place in the city. Some women coming from Mahan Singh Gate to Sharifpura were forcibly kidnapped on the road in broad day-light and taken to Burj Bhai Phoola Singh. This was brought to the notice of Rai Bahadur Badari Dass, Superintendent, C.I.D., who visited Sharifpura on the 15th and in spite of promises he did nothing to save those girls (Said, 1993: 143-8).

Sheikh Arshad Habib

'My family was among the prominent business families of Amritsar. All the communities lived peacefully and except for some miscreants, the rest of the people were very friendly and co-operative. Moreover, unlike elsewhere in the Punjab, the Muslims were not economically less advanced than the Hindus and Sikhs. We owned eighteen houses and three hosiery factories. My father was a staunch supporter of the Congress party. But the propaganda of the Muslim League that Amritsar would be given to Pakistan was so effective that even he believed that it would be so. From March onwards, there was a constant shuttling between Lahore and Amritsar of the Muslim League leaders. Among them I remember Sardar Shaukat Hayat in particular because he used to come frequently. The Muslims of Amritsar were told that they had to play their historical role in winning Amritsar for Pakistan. In practice, it meant that already from an early date a network between the criminal element with their stronghold in Chowk Farid, the Amritsar Muslim League leadership and some people based in Lahore existed. The Muslim League exploited religion to mobilise the poor masses who were told that once Pakistan came into being they would be the owners of the shops and houses owned by the Hindu *Lalas* and Sikhs.

'Once violence broke out in March, it never ever left Amritsar in peace. Almost daily some case of stabbing was reported. There was a British deputy commissioner and chief of police in Amritsar. It is absolutely wrong that they sided with the Hindus. In fact most of the police in Amritsar were Muslim. As long as the British officers were in charge they arrested all those who committed crimes. Not surprisingly, the police was always patrolling Muslim areas in search of criminals. This they did in the Hindu and Sikh *mohallas* as well.

'We left on 10 August for Lahore because by that time the change in administration had taken place and now a predominantly non-Muslim administration began to side with their co-religionists. That is when Muslim families began to move towards Lahore. My father first brought us to Lahore then returned but finally on 22 August he came back to Lahore. By that time the balance of power had changed radically and Muslims were like *gajar mooli* ['like carrots and radishes', a Punjabi expression conveying a sense of complete indifference in destroying life]. They were being killed by armed gangs of Sikhs and Hindus. We saw many dead bodies on the way to Lahore. All this was so unnecessary. The Punjab never regained its previous calm and peace.'

Chaudhri Muhammad Siddiq

'I was born in Amritsar's inner city in Waddi Galli Arainan Di. There was a Chotti Galli Arainan Di as well. There was never any problem between us and the Hindus and Sikhs. The street next to us, Galli Tiwarrian, was entirely Hindu. All the doors in those days were open and there was complete trust among the communities. The elders from the three communities saw to it that nobody was harmed or harassed. Everyone felt safe and secure. Even when rioting erupted in Amritsar and continued our neighbours never attacked us. The same way, we did not allow the criminals to harm our Hindu and Sikh neighbours. Outsiders or intruders spoiled the environment. There were completely unknown people who would come and throw fire bombs and then run away. After 10 August, it became difficult for Muslims to live in Amritsar as the administration changed hands and Hindus and Sikhs took over. Also, armed *jathas* began to raid Amritsar.

'We left on 13 August. My grandfather Mian Chanan Din stayed behind insisting that my father should first take the women and children to a safe place and then come back to fetch him. We came through Taranwala Bazaar to Hatti Darwaza. We were some 300 households. Then my father, Mian Abdul Ghani, turned back to fetch my grandfather, but alas somebody had killed him. Also, on the way to the railway station an aunt of mine, Khala Mariam, was shot dead. I used to be her special nephew and to this day I remember her and my grandfather. Both were saintly human beings.

'At the railway station there was a dramatic increase in firing. Surely Hindus and Sikhs were shooting at Muslims who were fleeing. I saw many people fall to the ground. The station was filled with distraught humanity. It was an utterly chaotic scene. There were so many people in the train we boarded that our family could not stay together and had to find space in different compartments. On the way to Lahore, one could see dead bodies lying near Khalsa College. At Lahore station the situation was equally chaotic. I remember, corpses were littered on the platforms and outside the station. In order to cross the road we were forced to walk on them. This was the situation in Lahore on 14 August.'

Omar Saeed

'Our family was originally from Gujjar Khan in northern Punjab but in the late 1920s, my grandfather settled in Amritsar. He was a government servant who was posted for a long time in Amritsar and decided to stay on. We lived close to the Jallianwala Bagh. Amritsar used to be politically very active. The Khaksars and Ahrar used to hold their marches and the Sikhs and Hindus were also organised. There was a strong Congress presence also. Many prominent Muslims were its members, including Dr Saifuddin Kitchlew. Our family was basically non-political, but sympathy for the Muslim League existed as my father believed that only in a Muslim state would justice prevail. Trouble had started already during the 1945 election campaign. I was then a first year student of MAO College. It was in early March that the Sikhs provoked the first clash. Thereafter things never returned to normal. I had Hindu and Sikh friends. Balraj Bawa, Premchand Vohra and Nikhal Singh lived in the same street as my family. Then there were Hassan Bakhsh and Muhammad Sarwar who lived near Hall Bazaar. We were a close group who enjoyed going to the movies together and we were also fond of music and songs. You won't believe it, but some gruesome acts of murder and grievous injury took place before our eyes, yet within our group there was no animosity.

'Our group kept on meeting even when the situation deteriorated but then in late May my Hindu and Sikh friends came and advised us to move because the RSS and some extremist Akalis were planning to raid Muslim localities. Still, my father was reluctant to leave because in our area lived one of his senior Hindu colleagues whom we called Mehta uncle. Both had worked together in the postal service and our families used to meet. I remember his daughter Parvathi getting married. She touched the feet of my mother and father as well when she was leaving her parents' home on the night of her wedding. This happened in early 1946.

'In early June we shifted to Sharifpura, where we put up with another Gujjar Khan family that had settled in Amritsar. By early August, Muslims were on the run. Muslim women from the villages outside Amritsar were being abducted in large numbers and everyday traumatised men, women and children would arrive in Sharifpura. I learnt that many of the elders had been abandoned in the villages because it was impossible for them to walk or run. I remember one young girl whose face had been smashed and her breasts were badly injured. She had resisted the Sikhs and was struck with *kirpans* when the troops led by British officers arrived. She died just before we left on 12 August. Her father had already been killed. There were many others who had taken refuge in Sharifpura. There were hundreds of others who wore bandages and some had lost an arm or hand. It was a very terrifying spectacle to see so many people in pain and fear. Living conditions in Sharifpura were awful but people helped each other. The women used to recite the Quran all the time while men took turns to guard Sharifpura from attacks. Several times Sikh *jathas* raided but were repulsed.

'On 12 August my maternal uncle arrived with a truck. His best friend was an ex-army man who had managed to get hold of a truck abandoned by some Hindus in Gujjar Khan. We left late in the night. Many people wanted to come with us but it was mainly the two Gujjar Khan families and another from Rawalpindi who could fit into the truck. On the way it was dark, so I had no clue when we arrived in Lahore. Fires were raging in Lahore and we stayed only a few hours and then drove to Gujjar Khan. My father and his friend used to write to each other till sometime in the 1950s. Many times in my life I have wanted to know where my Hindu and Sikh friends are but could never pursue that idea. Now I am too old and sick. So, Amritsar and those friends will have to remain in my thoughts till the day I leave this world.'

Ali Bakhsh

'I belong to the community of shoemakers. It was a young man from our caste who unfurled the Muslim League flag on the walls of the Amritsar Jail during Direct Action in February 1947. He was shot dead by the police. In our *mohalla* there was complete Muslim domination and our young men took part in many raids on Hindu and Sikh *mohallas*. Both sides were armed and willing to kill and did not show any mercy. The Muslim leaders of Amritsar used to assure all Muslims that Amritsar will not only be in Pakistan but would lead the struggle for liberation from British and Hindu rule.

'A month before Pakistan came into being, Sikh *jathas* became very active and began to raid Muslim areas on the outskirts of Amritsar. Each day, the pressure increased and Muslims from the neighbouring villages began to arrive in Amritsar with harrowing stories of cruelty against them. On 13 August, our whole *mohalla* decided that we should seek refuge in Lahore. Some young men carried weapons, but we were all armed with our occupational tools. Therefore we could keep the Sikhs at bay on the way to the railway station. However, we were fired upon and some people in our group of some 500 were killed. My friend Aslam was among them. It was a horrible murder. The gunshot struck him in the neck. The trauma he suffered could be seen on his dead face and his eyes. He used to be a good singer and we were close to each other.

'Some half a dozen people in our group died before we reached the railway station. Their bodies had to be abandoned without proper

Islamic burial. What could we do? At the railway station it was *kayamat* (doomsday). Shocked men, women and children were in pain as injuries, hunger and thirst were affecting them. The struggle to board the train for Lahore resulted in many brawls and ugly scenes. We managed to find place by brandishing our knives and other tools and warding off others. The journey to Lahore was slow and agonising. After several hours we arrived in Lahore. It was 14 August and at the Lahore station dead bodies of Hindus and Sikhs were strewn all over.

'We walked all the way to the inner city where we had some relatives. Shahalmi and other Hindu localities had been burnt down. Thick black soot was everywhere. Nobody in my immediate family died, though I am convinced thousands died for making Pakistan possible. I am not sure if this was the Pakistan we wanted. We were a poor working community in Amritsar and moving to Lahore did not change our fortunes in any sense, but we love Pakistan nevertheless.'

Ferozepore: Sheikh Hamid Ali

This interview was conducted by Faneez bint Asif in Lahore on 15 April 2017.

'I was born in Jullundur on 15 January 1927. My father was in the Indian Railways, and he died when I was in class three. I grew up in a lower middle-class family which had to work hard to get going in life. It taught me the importance of humility and honesty. I passed my matriculation exam in 1944 from Islamia High School, Jullundur, which was then affiliated with the Punjab University, Lahore. Soon after matriculation, I got a job in the Indian Postal Service and was posted in Ferozepore in 1945. My elder brother Shaukat Ali (now deceased) was already posted in the same post office and lived at Kot Muhammed Shafi, a Mohalla of Ferozepur, along with his family. We moved to Ferozepore along with my widowed mother and two younger sisters. We were happily living in that town and had cordial relations with our neighbours. Some of them were Hindus and Sikhs. We would mingle with them and discuss multifarious social issues. We used to participate in their weddings and festivals, and they would also happily join us in celebrating our festivals. Sending food to each other on religious festivals was a goodwill gesture we all observed. The staff of the post office in Ferozepore was a harmonious blend of Muslims, Sikhs and Hindus. Abdul Rasheed, Ghulam Muhammed and Ismat Ullah were Muslims. I distinctly remember the names of my Sikh and Hindu friends. They were Jagdeesh, Prem Nath, Dilip Singh, B.N. Chadha and Girdaari Lal, whom I cannot forget. We used to visit one another every weekend.

'In June 1947, the 3 June Partition Plan was announced. A few days later, my elder brother and I were transferred to Sialkot. We thought it to be a routine transfer. We were to report at our new station on 12 August 1947. My elder brother left for Jullundur with the entire family before he could join his duty in Sialkot. I, being the bachelor, was left in Ferozepore. I did not observe any change in the behaviour of my Hindu and Sikh friends after the announcement of the *Mountbatten Plan*. We were friends first and Hindu, Muslim or Sikh later. Meanwhile, news started coming from Amritsar and Jullundur of Hindu–Muslim riots. The communication system was badly damaged during the riots. I lost contact with my family, which was still in Jullundur, but I was safe in the company of my non-Muslim friends. When I left for Sialkot, they all came to the Ferozepore Railway Station to give me a warm send-off. They were all sad and we resolved to keep in touch. I left Ferozepore for Sialkot on the evening of 10 August 1947. Abdul Rasheed, Ghulam Muhammed and Ismat Ullah also accompanied me on the journey to Sialkot. When the train reached Lahore, there was pin-drop silence. Some people informed us that a bomb had been blasted an hour before the arrival of the train. At Gujranwala, I saw many burnt buildings around the railway station. The train reached Sialkot on the morning of 11 August 1947.

'I had no problem finding a place to live because *my paternal cousin's husband* was already living there. However, I was very perturbed because I had no contact with my mother, brother and sisters, who were still in Jullundur. I cannot explain how I spent those couple of months in Sialkot amid reports of massive killings of Muslims in Jullundur, particularly in Amritsar and adjoining areas. Luckily, the telegraph system was restored and I received a telegram from my brother that that they had locked up their house in Basti Nau, Jullundur, and shifted to a refugee camp established by the army. After a month, they all joined me safely in Sialkot.

'I would not boast about taking part in the Pakistan movement as many of my age did after reaching Pakistan. The harsh conditions of life had taught me not to make extravagant claims. Let me frankly say that to this day, I remember and miss my Hindu and Sikh friends. I kept in touch with them for quite some time, especially Jagdeesh, but then transfers from one place to another and other changes resulted in the exchange of letters gradually ceasing. I wonder sometimes if they are alive. One would really want to meet them again and find out how life had treated them.'

References

Said, Chaudhri Mohammad. 'A Brief Account of the Happenings in Amritsar by Ch. Mohammad Said M.A., L.L.B., ex-Terminal Tax Superintendent, Municipal Committee, Amritsar, Present Address:- 3/30, Nisbet Road, Lahore' in *The Journey to Pakistan: A Documentation on Refugees of 1947*, Islamabad: National Documentation Centre.

Singh, Khushwant. 'Last Days in Lahore: From the brittle security of an elite rooftop, a view of a city burning', *Outlook*, Delhi, 28 May 1997.

Talib, S.G.S. *Muslim League Attack on Sikhs and Hindus in the Punjab in 1947*, Delhi: Voice of India, 1991.

Hamdani, Hamid. '*Lahore Jall Raha Tha* (Lahore was Burning) in Chughtai, Hakim Muhammad Tariq Mehmood Abqary Mujadidi (compiler and editor), *1947 ke Muzalim ki Kahani khud Muzlumon ki Zabani* (The Story of the 1947 Atrocities from the Victims' Themselves), Lahore: Ilm-o-Irfan Publishers, 2003.

Documents

Carter, Lionel (ed). *Punjab Politics, I June 1947–14 August 1947: Tragedy, Governors' Fortnightly Reports and other Key Document,* New Delhi: Manohar, 2007b.

Fortnightly reports of Chief Secretary for 1947, IOR L/P & J/5/250, (on microfilm), London: British Library.

Khan, Fazal Muqeem (Maj-General). *The Story of the Pakistan Army*, Karachi: Oxford University Press, 1963.

Mansergh, N. and P. Moon, (eds.). *The Transfer of Power 1942-47,* vol. XII, 8 July to 15 August 1947, London: Her Majesty's Stationery Office, 1983.

Note on the Sikh Plan, Lahore: Government Printing Press, 1948.

Newspapers

Pakistan Times, Lahore, 1947
The Tribune, Lahore, 1947

Interviews

Pran Nevile, Delhi, 21 October 1999
Harkishen Singh Surjeet, Delhi, 21 October 1999
Yuvraj Krishan, Delhi, 21 October 1999
Dr Jagdish Chander Sarin, Delhi, 24 October 1999
Ramanand Sagar, Delhi, 25 October 1999 and Mumbai, 18 October 2001
Mujahid Taj Din, Lahore, 2 and 25 February 2000
Saleem Shahid, Lahore, 5 April 2003
Giani Mahinder Singh, Amritsar, 27 March 2004
Chaudhri Muhammad Siddiq, Lahore, 27 April 2003
Omar Saeed, Lahore, 27 December 2004
Sheikh Arshad Habib, Lahore, 27 December 2004
Ali Bakhsh, Lahore, 30 December 2004
Ashwini Kumar, Delhi, 2 December 2005
Kumar Chand, Singapore, 10 May 2010
Nirmal Tej Singh Chopra, Singapore (via email) 5 January 2011
Sheikh Hamid Ali, Lahore, 15 April, 2017

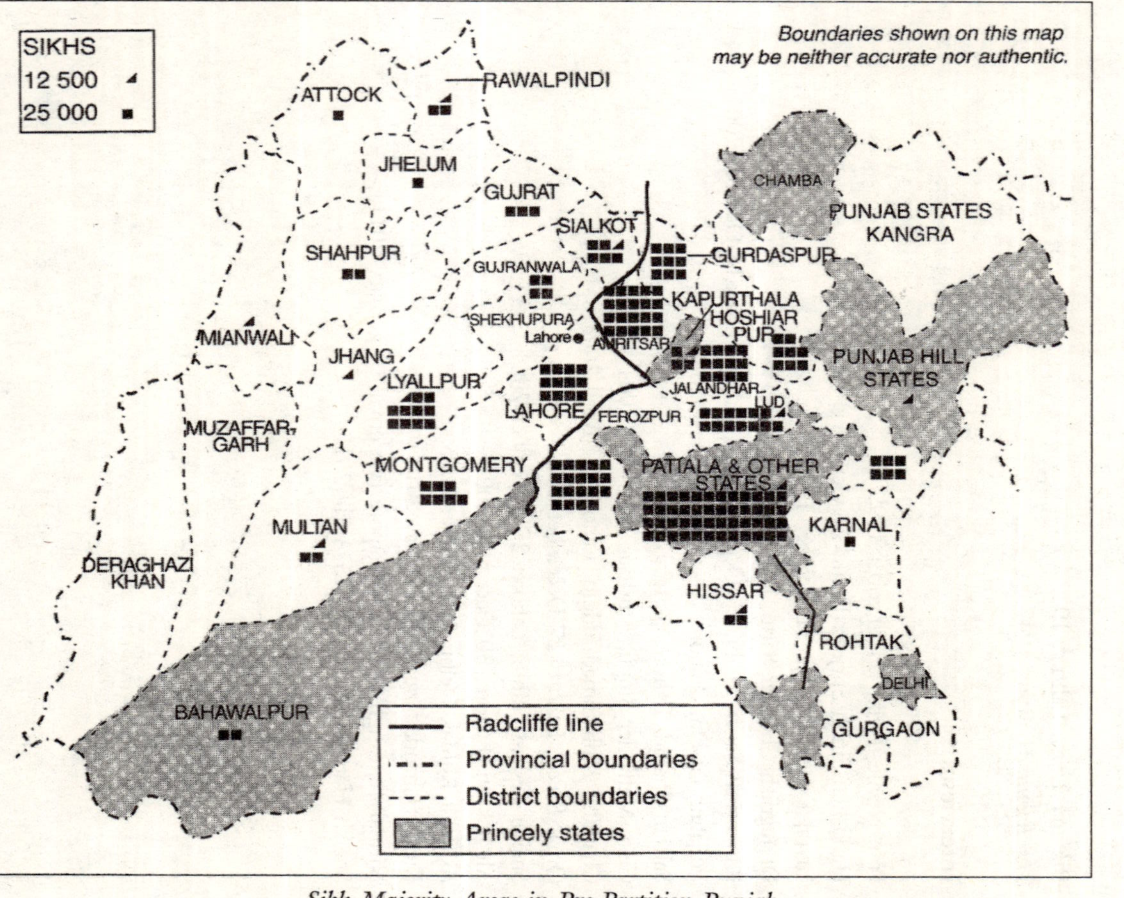

Sikh Majority Areas in Pre-Partition Punjab

STAGE 3

Ethnic Cleansing
15 August–31 December 1947

INTRODUCTION

On 15 August, power was transferred to the East and West Punjab governments. C.M. Trivedi became governor and Gopi Chand Bhargava, the previously Lahore-based Congress leader, became Chief Minister of East Punjab. In West Punjab, Sir Francis Mudie became governor (prior to that he was governor of Sindh), and Nawab Iftikhar Hussain Mamdot, the chief minister. The two administrations were obligated by legal undertakings and informal understanding to cooperate with each other to protect the minorities. With the British no longer the supreme authority, the two administrations were now answerable only to their national governments. As already noted, signs of siding with co-religionists had begun to appear from the time of the 1945 election campaign. Such a tendency only strengthened in the subsequent period. From 15 August the abuse of authority became the rule rather than the exception.

Not surprisingly, both administrations accused each other of failing in their duty to protect the minorities. Some of the joint committees that had been established to monitor the Partition met and exchanged not only information but incriminations as well. Mudie wrote on 5 September 1947 to Governor-General Jinnah about the need to push Hindus and Sikhs out of West Punjab:

'I am telling everyone that I do not care how the Sikhs get across the border, the great thing is to get rid of them as soon as possible. There is little sign of 3 lakh (300,000) Sikhs in Lyallpur moving, but in the end they too will have to go' (Singh 1989: 145).

This letter was originally published in the Khosla report (1989: 169) but Kirpal Singh, whose work on the Punjab partition has already been mentioned, contacted Justice Khosla to find out if it was authentic. Justice Khosla replied that he had been supplied with a photographic copy of the letter which the East Punjab intelligence agencies had intercepted. Later, Kirpal Singh confirmed the letter's contents from Sir Francis Mudie himself (ibid.: footnote pp. 145-6). I, in turn, confirmed this while interviewing him at his home in Chandigarh on 2 January 2005. The letter need not be treated as conspiratorial. It is merely a matter-of-fact assessment of the existing situation.

The *Pakistan Times* of 4 December reported that the Sikh leader, Tara Singh, opposed the return of Hindus and Sikhs to Pakistan and wanted Indian Muslims to migrate to Pakistan. He said:

> The irresponsible advice to them to return to Pakistan was fraught with dangers. My advice to Hindus and Sikhs of Pakistan is that they should leave that Dominion forthwith and those who do not do so immediately will certainly come to grief. No Sikh or Hindu can be loyal to Pakistan which means a Muslim country.... Similarly, Indian Muslims will have sympathy with Pakistan and to trust all of them will be unpardonable folly.

Influx of Muslims into West Punjab

On 13 August the *Pakistan Times* reported that at least 5,000 refugees had poured into Lahore from Gurdaspur district in the previous three days. On 24 August the paper reported an increase in that number to 150,000. On 8 September it was reported that 50,000 were reaching the city every single day. On 14 September the total number of refugees was reported at 1,200,000: Lahore received via Wagah 500,000; Kasur in Lahore district, another 400,000; and Narowal in Sialkot district, 200,000; while some 100,000 walked into Pakistan over the Sulemanki Bridge. About their settlement, it was reported that Montgomery and Multan districts had absorbed 350,000 and Lahore district, 100,000. The rest settled in the districts of Jhang, Sargodha, Gujrat, Gujranwala, and Sheikhupura. On 15 October the *Pakistan Times* gave figures of 5.4 million Muslim refugees from East Punjab who would be relocated to West Punjab. It also mentioned a figure of 495,000 Hindus and Sikhs who had crossed into India. At the Walton group of relief camps, 117,712 Muslim refugees were reported, according to the *Pakistan Times* of 7 November. On 6 November Jinnah had visited the Walton Camps and noticed that the morale of the people was high.

The *Pakistan Times* of 9 November reported that the Refugees and Rehabilitation Minister in the Punjab Government, Mian Iftikharuddin, had given a figure of 1,881,939 Muslims resettled in West Punjab. The Commander of the Pakistan Military Evacuation Organisation, Brigadier F.H. Stevens, said that 350,000 Muslims were still stranded in East Punjab awaiting evacuation (*Pakistan Times*, 22 December 1947). The *Pakistan Times* reported on 25 December that 4,680,000 refugees had been evacuated as of 10 December.

Influx of Hindus and Sikhs into East Punjab

The Tribune of 29 August spoke of thousands of Hindus and Sikhs fleeing West Punjab. On 1 October it was reported that the East Punjab government had decided to provide 1,500 trucks and two battalions of the army to evacuate refugees from West Punjab. On 4 October *The Tribune* reported that 1,431,600 Hindus and Sikhs still awaited evacuation. On the same date, it reported that as many as 115,000 refugees were marching to India. On 7 October, it took up the sad plight of 50,000 Hindus and Sikhs detained by the Pakistan government at Balloki. The East Punjab government was finding it difficult to relocate hundreds of thousands of refugees stranded in Amritsar. *The Tribune* of 8 October reported that Hindus and Sikhs in Lyallpur were being attacked by mobs, while East Punjab Minister Sardar Ishar Singh Majhail announced that molestation of Muslim conveys by armed *jathas* would not be allowed. Other Sikh leaders issued appeals not to attack Muslims leaving for Pakistan. On 10 October, *The Tribune* reported that more Indian troops had been despatched to Lyallpur and Sheikhupura to help Hindus and Sikhs still in those places to escape to India. Its 12 October issue gave a figure of 10,000 Hindus and Sikhs awaiting help in Jhelum city alone.

On 16 October *The Tribune* reported that the Indian government had chartered from the United Kingdom twelve Dakota aircraft, each capable of carrying fifty-seven passengers, to evacuate Hindus and Sikhs from isolated places in Pakistan. On 18 October it reported that two million Hindus and Sikhs still stranded in West Punjab and NWFP needed to be evacuated. Moreover, foot convoys had been crossing over from the Balloki headworks into India. Convoy numbers 16, 17, 18 and 19 had arrived: the average number of people in each was 40,000 to 50,000. On 29 October, it was reported that Pakistan troops had refused to evacuate Hindus and Sikhs from the interiors of Rawalpindi, Sargodha and Mianwali districts on the plea that the Hindus and Sikhs did not want to leave Pakistan. It was claimed that there were 80,000-100,000 Hindus and Sikhs still in those areas. *The Tribune* of 16 November reported that by 6 November, 3.2 million Hindus and Sikhs had arrived in India from West Pakistan. Of these, 2.9 million were from West Punjab and NWFP. One million still needed to be evacuated.

Disbandment of Punjab Boundary Force

It may be recalled that the Punjab Boundary Force (PBF) was formed in July and became functional on 1 August. It had been given the task of preserving peace in the central districts. After the partition of the Punjab, these were Lahore, Gujranwala, Sialkot, Sheikhupura, Lyallpur and Montgomery districts in West Punjab and Amritsar, Gurdaspur, Hoshiarpur, Jullundur, Ferozepore and Ludhiana in East Punjab. The PBF comprised some 9,000 to 15,000 troops. Major General Fazal Muqeem Khan argued (1964: 66) that the PBF was doomed from the beginning because it had been given a task too big to handle; moreover, the troops, and even in some cases their officers, were affected by the rioting which tended to compromise their impartiality. More importantly, the PBF had no jurisdiction in the Sikh princely states of East Punjab where the worst massacres of Muslims were taking place. After the Force was disbanded, the two governments agreed to manage the refugee problem through the coordinated efforts of their respective armies. Major General Fazal Muqeem Khan writes:

> After the abolition of the Punjab Boundary Force, units of the Pakistan Army were withdrawn to the home side of the border, and those of the Indian Army, to India. The units which were still mixed, being part of the PBF, were now split. It was also agreed that the Muslim troops would be used to protect Muslim refugees

> in East Punjab and vice versa. These troops would be lent by one Dominion to the other, and would be under the command of the military commanders of the areas in which they would be located... Those convoys who [sic] could be given an army escort seldom lost any refugees to the raiding gangs (ibid.: 67-73).

Asaf Ali Shah, with whom I had been corresponding in connection with my weekly column in the *Daily Times*, suggested that I get in touch with Lieutenant General Aftab Ahmad Khan, who had served both on the PBF and later in the coordinated army arrangement, and who could give me a first-person account. Accordingly, I wrote a letter to Lt General (Retd) Aftab Ahmad Khan, who was a major at the time. In a reply dated 2 February 2007, Aftab Khan emphasised that the PBF had been composed almost entirely of Indian and Pakistani soldiers, with only a few British as top commanders. He also confirmed that the Force had been hopelessly undermanned and given no clear plan for handling the complex and explosive situation it faced. Despite these handicaps, hundreds of thousands of lives had been saved, and it remained the rule that whenever an army escort was available, very few casualties were suffered. The convoys, according to Aftab Khan, were sometimes 20–30 miles long and included as many as 150,000 human beings: 'bullock carts, trucks, cattle, men, women, children, the sick and old'. He gives examples of his own efforts to save the lives of both Muslims and non-Muslims.

Neither Maj. Gen. Fazal Muqeem Khan in his book, nor Lt General Aftab Ahmad Khan in his testimony to me, remembered the active participation of the Muslim soldiers of the Baluch regiment in gunning down Hindus and Sikhs on 25 and 26 August in Sheikhupura – the action which precipitated the dissolution of the Punjab Boundary Force. Muslims who took part in the massacre afterwards argued that the non-Muslims had fired on them, but this was challenged by the Hindus in that unit. An inquiry into the soldiers' conduct was dropped by the Pakistan authorities after the force was disbanded (Jeffrey, 1974: 516). The problem was that they, too, were outnumbered by well-armed marauders roaming all over the Punjab. Moreover, by the end of August, PBF troops had started firing upon each other as the suffering of the co-religionists began to affect their relations as well (Marston, 2009: 496).

Subsequently the armies of India and Pakistan agreed to form joint rescue units. Lt General Aftab Ahmad Khan was among those who helped thousands of Hindus and Sikhs cross the border safely into India. He was active particularly in the Montgomery (Sahiwal area). Another officer of the Pakistan Army was Maj. General (Retd) Syed Wajahat Husain. He has given details of his efforts in Jullundur, Ludhiana and Kapurthala State. He writes that the evacuation of the Muslims of East Punjab began from the second half of September 1947 (Husain, 2010: 54-73).

Not all refugees had been evacuated from both sides by the end of 1947; the process continued into the early months of 1948. Violence peaked between 15 August and mid-November. According to the oral histories that we gathered, it was clear that, in general, people were neither willing nor prepared to leave their hearth and home. They were driven away by brute force. Many were hoping to return to their homes once law and order was restored. It seemed that they did not comprehend that two new states had come into being, both armed with standing armies, border police, and patrols. Henceforth the movement of people across the international border in the Punjab would be regulated in accordance with the interests of the governments in power. Any hope of a right to return to their pristine abodes, from which they had fled, were sealed finally on 8 April 1950. On that day, the agreement between the Governments of India and Pakistan regarding Security and Rights of Minorities, also known as the Liaqat–Nehru/Nehru–Liaqat Pact, was signed. With regard to Punjab, the agreement did not explicitly overrule the Right to Return, recognised as a human right in the Universal Declaration of Human Rights (1948). It, however, assumed that minorities will be accorded complete equality of citizenship irrespective of religion. It was mentioned that the two governments shall ensure that citizens enjoy, 'a full sense of security in respect of life, culture, property and personal honour, freedom of movement *within each* country (emphasis added) and freedom of occupation, speech and worship, subject to law and morality' (*Middle East Journal,* 1950: 344). This point was further reinforced by the following formulation: 'Both Governments wish to emphasise that the allegiance and loyalty of the minorities is to the State of which they are citizens, and that it is to the Government of their own State that they should look for the redress of their grievances' (ibid.). It was quite clear that the partition of the Punjab had become irreversible.

References

Husain, Syed Wajahat. *Memories of a Soldier: 1947 – Before During After*, Lahore: Ferozsons (Pvt) Ltd., 2010.

Jeffrey, Robin. 'The Punjab Boundary Force and the Problem of Order, August 1947', *Modern Asian Studies*, Vol. 8, No. 4, Cambridge: Cambridge University Press, 1974.

Marston, Daniel P. 'The Indian Army, Partition, and the Punjab Boundary Force, 1945-1947' *War in History, vol. 16. no. 4,* London: Sage Publications.

Singh, Kirpal. *The Partition of the Punjab*, Patiala: Punjabi University, 1989.

Khan, Fazal Muqeem Khan (Major-General), *The Story of the Pakistan Army,* Karachi, Lahore: Oxford University Press, 1963.

Khosla, Gopal Das (first published in 1949). *Stern Reckoning: A Survey of the Events Leading Up To and Following the Partition of India,* New Delhi: Oxford University Press, 1989.

Official documents

Agreement between India and Pakistan on Minorities: Jawaharlal Nehru and Liaqat Ali Khan, *Middle East Journal*, *Vol. 4, No. 3 , July,* Washington DC (1950).

Newspapers

Pakistan Times, 1947.

The Tribune, 1947.

Interviews

Kirpal Singh, Chandigarh, 2 January 2005.

Asaf Ali Shah, Lahore (via email) 3 January 2006.

Kumar Chand, Singapore, 2010

Lieutenant General Aftab Ahmad Khan, Lahore (via letter), 2 February 2007.

Exodus from West Punjab

14

LAHORE DIVISION

LAHORE DIVISION BELONGED TO CENTRAL PUNJAB AND CONSISTED of the districts of Lahore, Amritsar, Gurdaspur, Sialkot, Gujranwala, and Sheikhupura. All districts except Amritsar had a Muslim majority, but Hindus and Sikhs constituted a substantial minority of nearly thirty-seven per cent in the division. In the notional division of June 1947, Amritsar was part of East Punjab, as was confirmed by the Radcliffe Award. However, Gurdaspur district, which had a tiny Muslim majority, was split and its Shakargarh *tahsil*, on the western bank of the Ravi, was given to Pakistan. On 15 August 1947 the majority of Hindus and Sikhs of West Punjab were still living in their ancestral abodes, although refugees had been moving in droves towards the eastern districts since at least the March 1947 riots in northern Punjab. After 17 August, attacks intensified on Muslims in the areas that were awarded to East Punjab. As a result, hundreds of thousands of Muslims began to arrive in West Punjab. That, in turn, provoked a rise in retaliatory attacks on the Hindus and Sikhs who were still in West Punjab.

Shakargarh *tahsil* of Gurdaspur district

Shakargarh *tahsil*, on the western bank of the Ravi, extended to some minor areas on the other side of the river; these, too, were awarded to Pakistan. Thus the established administrative unit of the *tahsil* rather than the natural boundary formed by the river was made the international boundary. This odd arrangement applied in the other direction as well and, because of it, India got a foothold on the western bank. On 15 December 2006, I met Chaudhri Anwar Aziz, twice federal minister in

Pakistan, once in the cabinet of Z.A. Bhutto and later of Muhammad Khan Junejo. The following is an excerpt of his account.

Chaudhri Anwar Aziz

'In July 1947 we were in Hoshiarpur. In July, most of my family members went to Sialkot because some trouble had started taking place in Hoshiarpur, whereas I decided to go to our ancestral village Meripur in Shakargarh *tahsil.* We are from the Gujjar clan and had considerable influence in the villages around us. I think it was a Friday on 14 August [Friday was actually on 15 August] and it was the month of Ramazan and I went to offer prayers at the main mosque in a nearby village. People from several villages used to collect there. I was asked to make a speech to explain what was happening. I told them not to panic. An agreement had been reached between the three communities in our area not to resort to hostilities. There was a village of Hindu Brahmins called Rehal. The Brahmins from there were known for their erudition and piety. They provided many facilities to human beings as well as animals free of any charge and were very much respected for that by all communities. One of them, Ram Saran Sharma, wrote a textbook on Persian grammar which was used in schools and colleges. Later, when Pakistan came into being, some Muslim wrote his own name as the author and published the same book. I studied Persian from him. He was truly a man of knowledge.

'There was considerable confusion about where Gurdaspur district would end up: in Pakistan or India. The Radcliffe Award split Gurdaspur district even when it had a Muslim majority but Shakargarh was placed in Pakistan. At that time violence broke out on a massive scale. The Brahmins came to my father and pleaded for help. They started crying and so did our elders because they and we have had very good and close relations. The womenfolk from both sides also started crying. They offered ornaments as the reward for protecting them, but my father told them not to worry. So, they decided to leave seven of their young girls, all very beautiful, sophisticated and educated, in our protection while some 20 of us young men and some elders took the other women and men to the river to find a passage for them to the other side. The

Ravi was in high spate at that time but a brisk traffic of boats in both directions was going on. The boat owners were charging exorbitant price for taking the people across the river. At the bank on our side a boat brought over Muslims who were badly injured, two women had their breasts removed and were in great pain. When their men realised we were going to take the Hindus to the other side safely, they became very angry and tried to attack them, but we became a wall against any such outrage. We told them that the Hindus who were in our charge could not be blamed for what their co-religionists had done on the other side. Also we were better armed than them and so nothing happened and the Brahmins were safely taken to the other side.

'The Brahmin girls stayed with us for seven months. Although they were polite and respectful, they refused to eat our food or use our utensils. So, we had to arrange a separate kitchen and other facilities for them. They even built a mud temple in our courtyard for prayers and borrowed oil to light up small earthen pots called *diyas* as was their custom. One day the Indian Army came looking for them. Somebody had wrongly informed them that the girls were being kept by us against their will. So the army surrounded our house and took positions with Bren guns and other weapons pointing at us. There was a captain to whom I said, "What is your problem? Why are you pointing guns at us?" He replied "We have heard that you have Hindu girls detained in your house." So, I told him to talk to the girls themselves. Just at that time two Hindu men related to those girls came out of their hiding places and came to our door. They began to cry again when they met our elders and our elders were also moved to tears. The captain felt ashamed and apologised as the girls confirmed that they have been treated very well. We returned the ornaments that their elders had deposited with my father. Then they left. Those were bad times indeed.'

Lahore city and district

In his book *Lahore: A Sentimental Journey,* Pran Nevile reminisces in the best of spirits about the city of his birth and youth. He lavishly praises its joyous and boisterous citizenry and recounts many tales of fun and scandal involving Hindus, Muslims and Sikhs alike. He expressed the pathos and trauma of Hindus and Sikhs who left Lahore in 1947 in the following words:

> It was for us a heart-rending experience to leave our beloved Lahore for good and seek refuge across the border which was created to divide the subcontinent. In the city which had been the home of our near and dear ones for centuries, there was no one left now to look back to. Suddenly, Lahore had become a foreign land (1993: 18).

Som Anand

Another Lahore Hindu, Som Anand, also expresses the profound sense of loss felt when Hindus were forced to flee Lahore:

> Communal riots became more intense after March '47 and it seemed that the Muslim leadership was out to clear the city of its non-Muslim inhabitants. That is not to say that every Muslim in Lahore liked what was happening. There were some who dreaded the prospect of the Hindus and Sikhs leaving the city for good. But such people could not speak of their feelings (1998: 36).

He gives the following account of the fateful August days:

'We lived in Model Town, an upper-middle-class locality, comprising mostly Hindus and Sikhs. It was a Sunday. A friend of my father's, Mr B.P.L. Bedi (father of the internationally-known actor Kabir Bedi), who was a famous Communist leader in Lahore, called upon us and said to my father, "Lalaji I need some money." My father, who was a banker, replied, "'Bediji today is Sunday, the banks are closed." But he [Bedi] insisted that since he [Som Anand's father] had the keys they could go and fetch the money. My father agreed and they went away.

'A relative of ours was staying with us at that time. He was about four-five years older than me. We decided to call upon an acquaintance. During our absence, some Afridi Pathans raided our house. At that time many Pathan gangs had descended from the tribal areas upon Lahore. They would go around looting and plundering non-Muslims. Some ten, twelve of them came to our house in *tongas*. Just at that moment, our Muslim neighbour, Maulvi Sahib, who was a supporter of the Congress party, arrived. Our families shared the same porch at the entry. When he saw the Pathans he came over and admonished them, telling them to fear the wrath of God for their misdeeds. Instead they became angry and shouted at him for defending Hindus. In the commotion an elderly Sikh gentleman Kartar Singh, who lived right opposite our house, came towards our house to find out what the matter was. His whole family had left and he was waiting for a truck that would transport his buffalo away. When the Pathans saw him they shot him dead. People heard them regret that they had to waste a bullet; a stab with a knife would have done the job cheaply.

'My father stayed on in Lahore in spite of all the killings. He had married a Muslim lady. He was a managing director of a bank and the Pakistan government needed his services. When he died in 1957, I came over from India to attend the cremation ceremony. A Brahmin who continued to live in Lahore and was a government employee performed the funeral rites, although he was not a practising priest.'

Som Anand pays tribute especially to the editor of the Urdu literary magazine *Adabi Dunya,* Maulana Salahuddin Ahmed, and the popular Punjabi poet Ustad Daman, both of whom were deeply saddened when the non-Muslims left Lahore (ibid.). He observes that although Hindus and Sikhs had begun to realise that Lahore may go to Pakistan, it did not mean that they were willing to accept such a fate easily. Many of their leaders continued to believe that they would get Lahore on the basis of overwhelming economic claims to that city. Others, including his father, argued that whatever happens, non-Muslims could continue to live on in Pakistan. The communal violence, however, made such a choice virtually impossible. He admits that Hindus and Sikhs also carried out terrorism against Muslims. An attack on the Muslims of Rajgarh, a suburb of Lahore, made the situation explosive. The RSS and other militant Hindu organisations were behind such activities (1998: 29).

I talked to him over an evening in Delhi in October 1999 and besides many other stories, he narrated that of the tragic murder of Professor Brij Narain, a Professor of Economics at Punjab University. Despite being a Hindu, Narain had defended the demand for Pakistan and developed a sophisticated range of economic arguments to prove that it would be a viable state. Som Anand told me:

'Professor Brij Narain was an ardent supporter of the Pakistan idea. He used to write articles in the press proving, with his vast knowledge of economics, that Pakistan would be a successful and viable state. It is said that Jinnah had asked him to stay on and he had fully made up his mind to devote himself to serving Pakistan. He sincerely believed that Jinnah wanted to create a democratic state where non-Muslims would have equal rights. Hindus had been leaving in large numbers since at least May 1947 and by 15 August, only some 10,000 were still around, believing things would cool down and they would be able to continue living in Pakistan as it was where their roots were. But as soon as the Radcliffe Award became public, criminal elements went on a killing and looting spree. That completely shattered the hopes of those who believed in Jinnah's secularism. Professor Narain, however, stuck to his guns and said that Pakistan was his real homeland and therefore he had no reason to leave.

'A mob arrived in the area where he lived. They were burning and pillaging abandoned Hindu and Sikh houses. Narain went up to them and advised them not to do so as it was now Pakistani property. His arguments convinced the first lot, who moved away. Soon after that some more ruffians arrived and began pillaging and burning. Again he went up to them and presented the same arguments. But one of them shouted "He is a *kafir* (infidel), kill him." The mob fell upon him and Pakistan's most ardent Hindu champion was killed mercilessly. When that news spread, there was hardly any Hindu or Sikh who any longer believed that Jinnah's Pakistan would be safe for them. Almost all of them left Lahore immediately.'

I learnt from a relative of the professor that he used to live on Nicholson Road, Lahore. The same incident is reported in another famous book on Lahore, *Lahore Ka Jo Zikr Kiya: Aap Bitee* (Remembering Lahore: An Autobiography) by Gopal Mittal. Mittal was originally from Malerkotla in East Punjab. He was a journalist, writer and poet, who had made Lahore his home and spent most of his time with Muslim colleagues. He wanted to stay on, but Brij Narain's murder made him change his mind.

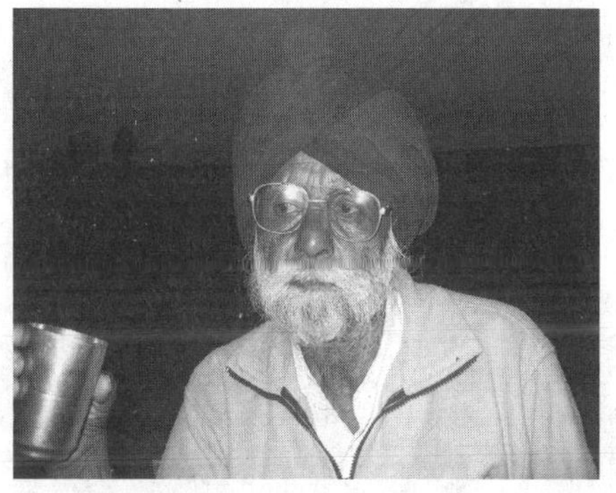

Amar Singh, 29 November 2005, village Dangoli, Rupnagar (Ropar) district

Ambassador Moni Chadha, formerly of Rawalpindi, 6 December 2005, New Delhi

Amrik Chand Ahluwalia, 7 January 2005, Patiala

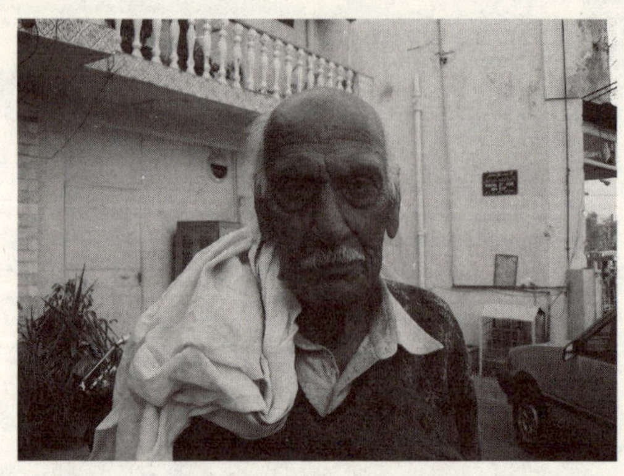

Ataullah Malik, 22 December 2004,
Multan, Pakistan

Author and B.R. Chopra, formerly of Lahore,
4 January 1997, Mumbai

Author with Ramanand Sagar, formerly of Lahore,
and his family, 18 October 2001, Mumbai

B.K. Bakshi, formerly of Rawalpindi, 21 February 2011, New Delhi

Babu Khan, formerly of village Kakra, Patiala State, 4 January 2005, Malerkotla

Chaudhri Muhammad Siddiq, formerly of Amritsar, 27 April 2003, Lahore

Chaudhri Roshan Din, formerly of Adampur, Patiala State, 15 December 2004

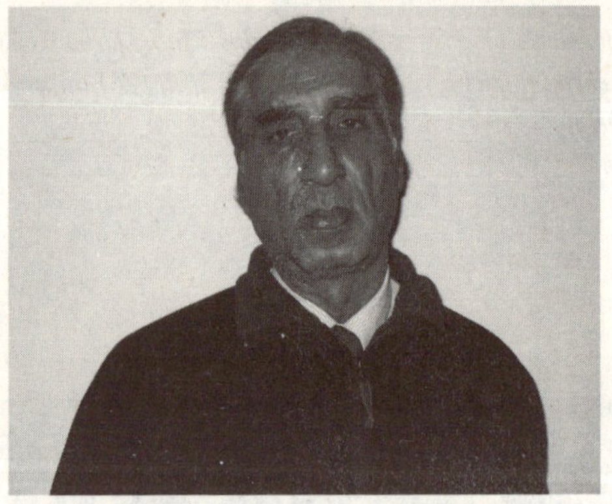

Chowdhry Abdul Wahid, formerly of Dangoli, Rupnagar (Ropar) district, 20 December 2004, Multan

Haji Abdul Rehman Gill, Lahore, 30 December 2004

Haji Sher Khan, Thamali, district Rawalpindi, Pakistan, 14 December 2004

Hitesh Gosain (left) and Teja Singh (right), village Boran, Patiala State, Fatehgarh Sahib district, India

Hitesh Gosain, Virender Singh and inhabitants of Adampur, Patiala State (currently Sirhind district)

Inside walled city Lahore, 28 December 2004

From the right: Ajaib Singh and Harmail Singh, names of others not known

Kaleb Ali Sheikh, 18 April 2011, Lahore

Karnail Singh and Des Raj

(Left to right) Mrs Kuldip Kaur Chopra, formerly of Dhariwal, Gujranwala district, and Nirmal Singh Chopra, formerly of Lahore, 20 April 2011, Singapore

(Left to right) Ahmad Salim, Rana Muhammad Rashid, formerly of Hoshiarpur district, and author, 18 April 2003, Lahore, Pakistan

(Left to right) Ahmad Salim, Zaman and Haji Sharif and Ali Safdar, Parayal, 13 December 2004

(Left to right) author and Chaudhry Muhammad Bashir, formerly of village Makhanpur, Gurdaspur district, 18 April 2003, Lahore

(Left to right) Colomel Raj Chopra, Pushpa Hans and author

(Left to right) Khawaja IkIftikhar, formerly of Amritsar, and the author, 17 April 2003, Lahore

(Left to right) Pran Nevile and Yuvraj Krishan,
both formerly of Lahore, 9 January 2005

(Left to right) Raj Babar and the author, 20 October 2001, Mumbai

(Left to right) Riaz Ahmed Cheema and Mushaq Ahmad, Stockholm

(Left to right) Seth, formerly of Multan, and Vimal Issar, formerly of Lahore, 10 January 2005

(Left to right) The author and Prof. Prem Kirpal, formerly of Lahore, 14 March 2004, New Delhi

(Left to right) Chaudhri, formerly of Kakra village, Patiala State, and Dr Nizam Din, Malerkotla, 4 January 2005

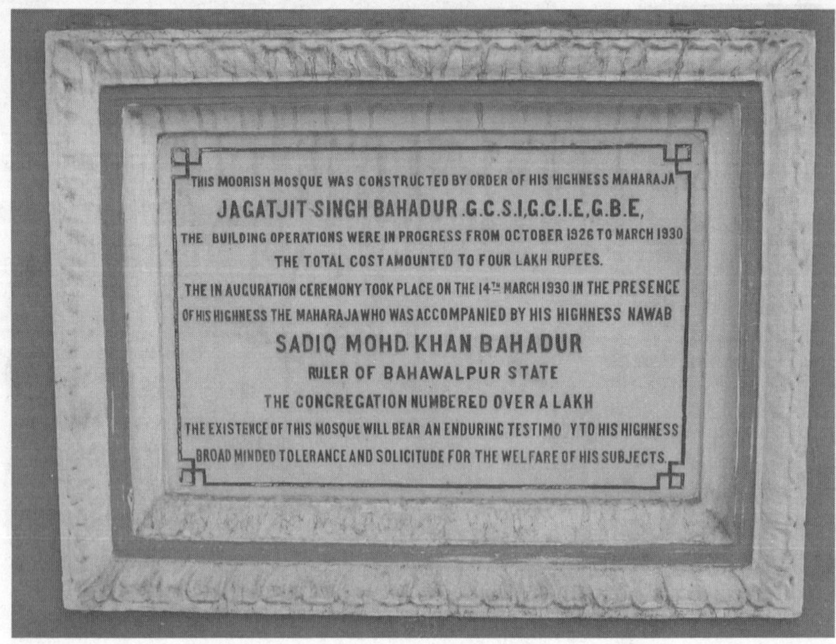

Marble plaque at the Moorish Mosque, 3 June 2005

Mujahid Al-Hussaini, formerly of Sutlanpur Lodhi, Kapurthala State, 19 December 2004

Mujahid Tajdin, Lahore, picture taken in the 1960s

Naseeb Kaur, born Azmat Bibi, village Phul Khurd, Roopnagar district, India, 29 November 2005

Naseeb Kaur with her family, village Phul Khurd, Roopnagar district, India, 29 November 2005

Nasim Hassan, formerly of Simla, 12 April 2011, Baltimore, USA

Pandit Lala Harcharan Das

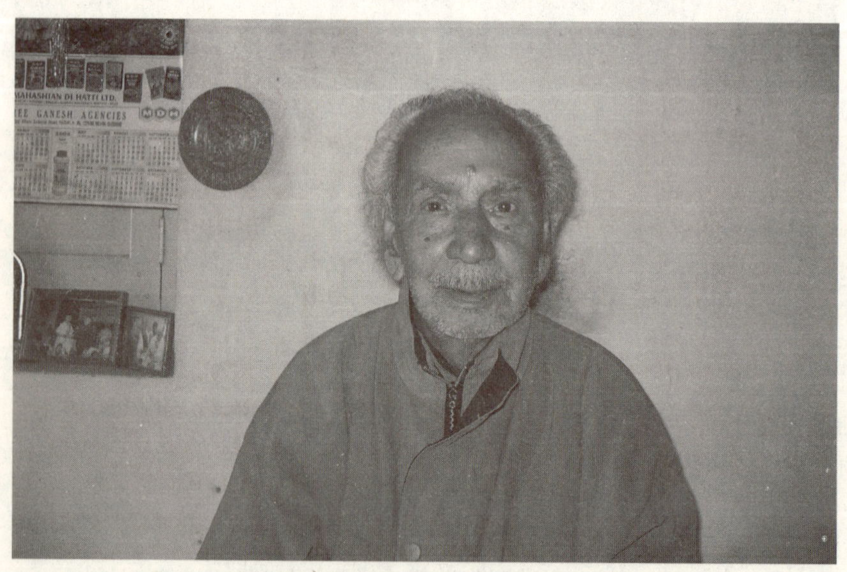

Pandit Mohan Lal Ballo, Patiala, India, 7 January 2005

Qamar Yurish, formely of Amritsar, 27 December 2004, Lahore

Raghbir Singh Sahni, formerly of village Gujjial, tahsil Chakwa, Jhelum district, 7 January 2005, Patiala

Raja Riasat, Choa Khalsa, 15 December 2004

Rana Muhammad Azhar Khan

Ranjit Singh Bhasin, Kapurthala, 3 January 2005

Ranjit Singh aka Ajit Singh, 4 January 2005, village Nathu Majra, near Malerkotla, India

Reginald Massey, Llanidloes, mid-Wales,
5 July 2006

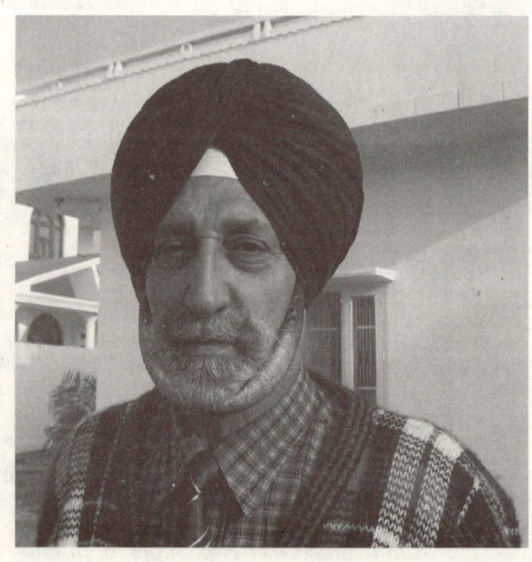

Shamsherjit Singh Virk

Sheikh Habib, Lahore (Amritsar), 26 December 2004

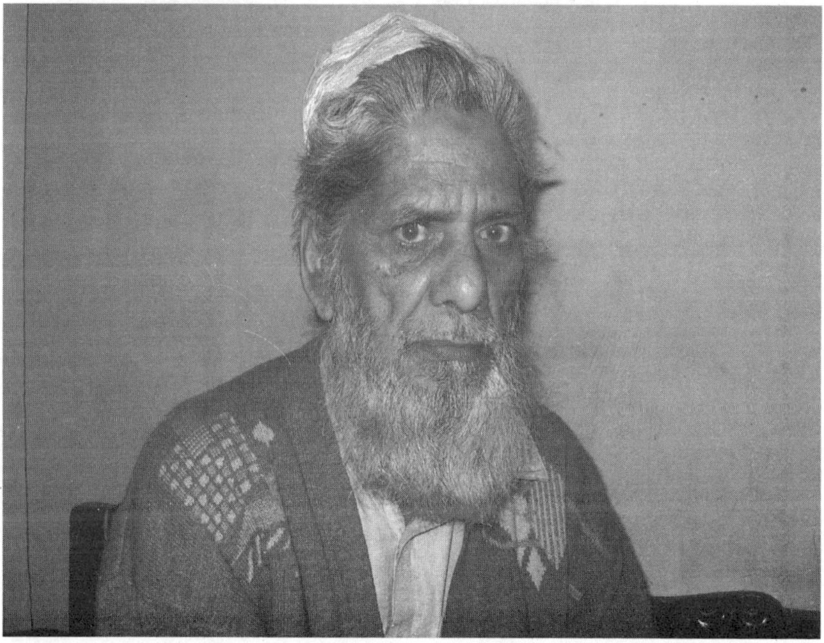

Smashad, Multan (Gujjarwal), 21 December 2004

(Standing left to right) Khawaja Waqas, author, Khawaja Tariq Masood. (Sitting left to right) Dr Hassan Amir Shah and Ali Haroon Shah, 29 November, Lahore, Pakistan

Sunil Dutt, formerly of village Khurd, Jhelum district, and author, 20 October 2001, Mumbai

Syed Khurshid Abbas Gardezi, Multan, Pakistan, 22 December 2004

The Moorish Mosque at Kapurthala, India, 3 January 2005

Uma Vasudev and author, 7 January 2005, New Delhi, India

Vimal Issar (left) and Vimla Virmani (centre), and author, 7 January 2005, New Delhi, India.

He wrote:

> Professor Brij Narain was an internationally acclaimed economist. While most economists were of the view that Pakistan would not be economically sustainable and therefore its existence will be unstable, Prof. Narain had written several articles in support of the view that Pakistan would be fully capable of being economically feasible and self-sufficient. He had decided to remain in Pakistan and even the most diehard Muslim Leaguers were convinced that he was a man without any prejudice [against Muslims and Pakistan]. His murder proved shattering for me. He was my teacher and had played a role in the formation of my personality. My family was already against my staying in Pakistan but now even my resolve to stay in Pakistan began to waver. When the last caravan of buses destined for Amritsar left Lahore, I boarded a bus and left (2003: 143-4).

Rattan Chand

On 19 October 1999, I met Rattan Chand at his home in Daryaganj, Delhi, and recorded this harrowing tale of survival:

'I lived with my family in a locality across the Lahore Railway Station but had my photography business near the Australia Building. By July 1947, communal attacks became more frequent. In early August, hell broke out all around us. Hindus and Sikhs living around the railway station were attacked by bloodthirsty mobs. Many of us took refuge in a Hindu hostel. I don't remember its name now, but it proved an easy target. Some fifty of us, men, women and children therefore sought refuge in the nearby Naulakha Church. However, we left our possessions in a cellar of the hostel. The Christian priest, who was a convert from Hinduism and bore a Hindu name, gave us all protection, sharing with us the meagre food at his disposal. He contacted the authorities and used his influence to procure help. A military truck manned by Gurkha troops arrived which took us to a safe place in the Lahore Cantonment.

'During this period a Sikh woman, whose husband had been killed some days earlier and who had lost her child, became very friendly with my wife and me. She always took our baby daughter in her lap. We both felt very sorry for her. She pleaded with me to go back to the cellar in the hostel and fetch her belongings. I also wanted to bring over our own trunk. On 15 August I came back to the hostel, but everything had been looted. Worse still, suddenly I found myself surrounded by a crowd. They wanted to kill me. The local butchers were among them. They were waving their knives in the air. I ran for my life. They followed me. I felt that death was imminent. Suddenly I found myself in front of a police station. I jumped over its low wall. In the compound, a British police officer was sitting on a chair surrounded by his Muslim staff.

'I threw myself at the feet of the Britisher and implored him to save my life. He remained unmoved and did nothing. I now pleaded with the other police officials to save my life. They scolded me, calling me bad names and hit me with their rifle butts. They said that nobody would kill me and therefore I need not make such a fuss. Outside the wall of the police station the crowd waited for me. I sensed that a violent and painful death would be my lot any moment, and made one more effort to escape. I ran out of the police station in a direction which seemed unguarded. The crowd followed in hot pursuit. I felt that my end had come. There is nothing that can be compared to the fear of death. I was now running in the middle of the road. Suddenly a fire brigade truck with Sikh staff appeared from somewhere. I cast myself on the ground in front of it. The crowd quickly dispersed when they saw the Sikhs in uniform. The Sikhs took me safely back to the cantonment where I was reunited with my family.

'We crossed over to India on 16 August. We had to go through many hardships. We had lost everything. There was nowhere to turn. Eventually I arrived in Delhi. Here I began to work in a camera shop owned by a Muslim. Mr Ahmed Hassan, the owner, decided to migrate to Pakistan in 1948. I have once again prospered through dint of hard work. I became the President of the Delhi Photographers Association. Some years ago I retired. I recall my Lahore days. All the communities lived in peace and concord. I still have Muslim friends in Lahore and Karachi. Some of them have visited me. They have invited me to the weddings of their children, but the memory of that mob chasing to kill me has traumatised me forever. I would like to go back and see Lahore, but probably will never do so.'

Ram Parkash Kapur

Another exit from Lahore, but in a very different manner for an upper-class Hindu family who had close connections with Muslim League leaders, was narrated to me by Ram Parkash Kapur:

'I was born in 1924 into a very well-known family of textbook publishers. The name of our firm was Attar Chand Kapur and Sons. My great-grandfather founded it. After my grandfather died in 1925, my father, Lala Ram Jawaya Kapur, and his brothers took over the business. We had a very big printing press behind Nishat Cinema, which we also owned. The press was built in 1927, and the cinema in 1928. My father worked indefatigably day and night and he brought the firm to the same level and standard as British publishers. In 1927 he was nominated as municipal commissioner of Lahore. He was so close to the British that the governor would call him and seek advice on which Hindu to nominate as a minister. At that time, elections had not been introduced.

'My father had very good relations with Muslim leaders too. Sir Sikandar Hayat, Sir Abdul Qadir, Sir Shahabuddin, Mumtaz Daultana and so many others used to often visit our house. Firoz Khan Noon, Nawab Mamdot and Shaukat Hayat were very close friends of my father. Not only at the elite level but also on the popular level there was no tension between Hindus and Muslims.

'In the morning of 14 August, Shaukat Hayat and Nawab Mamdot came to my father. Shaukat was a minister and Mamdot, chief minister of the new Muslim League government in Punjab. They told my father not to leave Lahore. He was to stay in Pakistan and continue his business and maintain business relations with India. They were to provide him full protection. When my father heard that the leaders of the new Pakistan would give him complete protection he decided not to leave. We had a house on 10 Egerton Road. It was built on two and half acres of land. We had a very successful and established business in Lahore. So, he saw no reason to leave and go to India.

'But after 16 August communal frenzy flared up in Lahore, especially in the inner city. In our own area, nothing untoward happened until then. My father was an honorary magistrate. The Deputy Commissioner

[Additional District Magistrate] of Lahore, Mr Williams, asked him to inspect the situation in the trouble spots. And so my father went as instructed. At that time there was a city magistrate, Mr Cheema. He said to my father: "What business do you have to come here? Pakistan has been created and I am in charge." My father replied: "No, I have been instructed by the deputy commissioner to come and look at the situation. If he says, then I will not come again." Now, this man Cheema was rabidly anti-Hindu. He managed to dissuade Williams and next day my father received a phone call from the deputy commissioner to the effect that he should not go on any such rounds any more, because that would endanger his life. My father rang up Nawab Mamdot and explained the whole situation. Mamdot replied that there was nothing to worry about as there was no danger to his life.

'In the meantime, riots in eastern Punjab broke out on a big scale. Actually in western Punjab riots had begun already after 3 March. My feeling is that the people had been incited to believe that an Islamic state was going to be created in Pakistan, and therefore non-Muslims had to be expelled from such a state. Otherwise a proper Islamic state could not be established. When the Muslim leaders gave the call, "Islam is in danger", the people got carried away. In any case, we stayed on some more days in Lahore.

'On 5 September, Mamdot and Shaukat Hayat again visited my father. They expressed great regret that things had gone out of control and hence they could not protect us anymore. My father said: "How can I leave now? Until 14 August I could get help from others who were leaving. Now, I have no truck or anything else to carry my belongings." They said: "Your business assets will have to remain in Pakistan. However, your personal belongings and household articles can go along with you. We will arrange the transport for you and also proper police protection so that you can cross the border into India safely."

'They gave us three trucks. We knew somebody in the army. He promised to lend us another one or two trucks. Our family and my uncles' families left our Egerton Road House on 7 September. While driving through Baghbanpura on our way towards the border, a police inspector stopped us. He said: "You cannot carry so many things with you. All this is now the property of Pakistan. Leave everything here."

However, Mamdot had ordered a police superintendent to help us cross the border safely and with our belongings. He asked the police inspector: "Why have you stopped these people? The chief minister has ordered that they can go to India with their belongings". The inspector retorted: "Who are you? All these things belong to the people of Pakistan." The SP tried to explain to the inspector that he was implementing the decision of the chief minister and if he obstructed him, he had the authority to suspend him. The inspector remained defiant. Finally, the SP ordered him to take off his belt and badge and hand it over to him. The SP now came to our car and said: "When you cross over from Pakistan to India, please unload the government trucks and send them back." My father did exactly that and when we reached Amritsar, the trucks were sent back to Pakistan. The responsibility for the Partition riots was that of Jinnah. He wanted Pakistan at all costs. Our Congress leaders were such fools, they played into his hands.

'Nobody in our family saw the violence with their own eyes because we never went to the old city or other trouble spots. Ours was an upper-class area. In Lohari and Shahalmi gates, Anarkali, Ichra, Chauburji, and even Kila Gujjar Singh, which was very close to our house, riots did take place. In our factory, most of the workforce was Muslim. All the machine-men and bookbinders were Muslims. They were completely devoted to my father. None of them created any disturbance or trouble for us.

'We left our property in the charge of the son of Sheikh Nur Elahi, inspector of schools of Lahore division. He and my father were like brothers. We had a paint factory, called the Crescent Paint and Varnish Factory, on the canal-bank. My father entrusted that factory to him and said: "Please keep it under your control. If we return, then we can get it back. If we don't, then it does not matter whether you keep it or someone else takes it."

'The press and other properties remained with my youngest uncle who stayed behind with a friend of his, Mir Hussain Sani, who lived on Temple Road. My uncle had severe diabetes. His family had crossed over to India, but he was hoping to retain our property in Lahore because everything was jointly owned by my father and his brothers. Two years later he crossed over to India, but the day he arrived in Amritsar he died. My father came over to Delhi from Amritsar. He was bitter with the Congress leaders for accepting the division of India.

'I tell you what happened during those days. Nehru was in Lahore just before 14 August. He met with a number of Hindu notables at the residence of Bhim Sen Sachar. In the meeting, he was told by all those who were present that circumstances were such that no Hindu will be able to stay on in Pakistan. Panditji replied that Hindus had lived under the Mughals in the past; they could do it now under the Muslim rulers of Pakistan. My father said: "Panditji at that time, Hindus lived in an undivided India and the Mughals ruled in an undivided India. They could not have thrown out all Hindus from such a state. Now the situation is completely different. You are completely cutting off a part of India and giving it to Pakistan. Here, they want to establish an Islamic state and not simply a Muslim kingdom. In such a state Hindus will never be safe and they will not be wanted. You should not have agreed to the division of India." Panditji showed visible signs of irritation and replied: "You people don't understand anything. You do not want the British to leave."

'The problem with Nehru was that he never wanted to go into the details. Moreover, he wanted to become the prime minister. He therefore accepted the idea of Pakistan and made Gandhi also concede to such a demand. I sometimes think that although Mamdot and Shaukat were good friends of my father, the riots in Lahore would not have taken place had they really opposed them. At some point they must have connived at the attacks on Hindus. They wanted to rule in Pakistan unchallenged by non-Muslims.'

Dr Prem Sobti

Dr Prem Sobti, personal physician to the President of India, narrated to me his experiences of the fateful Partition days. He confirmed that many Hindus had believed that Lahore will remain in India. He said:

'Lahore was a paragon of communal peace and harmony. Even when politicians were busy with their divisive tactics and gradually things were beginning to change, nobody could ever imagine Punjabis murdering each other but I saw it happen with my own eyes. Some two weeks before Partition I went to Bombay to study gynaecology, because in Lahore very little research was done on it as women did not come for such problems to the hospitals. I had worked after college and started my medical education a few years later than normal. The Hindus were convinced that Lahore stood a very good chance of being included in India, therefore I was not particularly worried that my parents were in Lahore while I went to Bombay. However, when it was announced that Lahore had been given to Pakistan and rioting had started, I left everything and came to Delhi in the hope of catching a train to Lahore. Two of my brothers were also in Pakistan. I had only ₹50 on me at that time. It was probably 19 August when we left for Lahore. It took twenty-two hours to reach Amritsar. Then I went to the medical college at Amritsar looking for help. There I learnt that I could go to Lahore safely only if I could get help. A friend who worked for the government advised me to go to Ferozepur as it was easier to reach Lahore from there.

'At Ferozepur I volunteered to bandage and give injections to refugees who had come from West Punjab. Then I crossed into Pakistan under a Muslim name, Pervez. A very beautiful young Muslim girl from Hoshiarpur, perhaps only twenty, begged me to take her with me to Lahore because her parents had been killed and her brother had abandoned her. She complained that the men in the refugee camp had already begun to molest her and she feared the worst. I said that I was a Christian and no Muslim would allow a Muslim girl to be with me. So, I advised her to get into the women's section of the camp and seek help there.

'I met some Muslim students from the medical college who recognised me. I was frightened but one of them told me to go and talk to the Sikh military officer who was sharing the job of supervising the flow of refugees along with a Muslim officer. He turned out to be the elder brother of a friend of mine. He was kind enough to send me in a military vehicle to Lahore along with an armed guard. When I reached our home nobody was there. Upon making enquiries from our Muslim neighbours I learnt that they had shifted to the DAV College refugee camp. They [the neighbours] had sent them in their own *tonga* to the DAV College. At the refugee camp I learnt that three trucks full of Hindus and Sikhs had left early in the morning for Amritsar, but two were returning because they had been attacked and there had been a heavy loss of life. The third had crossed the border because police arrived in time to protect it. I began to cry. The two trucks came back. It was a shocking sight. Nobody had been spared. Women, children, old – their mutilated dead bodies could be seen. My parents were not among them. So I with the help of the same Sikh officer reached Wagah from where I managed to get to Amritsar.

'There I saw a train pull up at the station, full of dead Muslims. That was an even more horrible sight. Almost everyone had been slaughtered. An old man who was alive told me that Sikhs had attacked the train and killed without mercy. The next day I saw a train full of Hindus and Sikhs arrive at Amritsar station from somewhere in the Pakistani Punjab. People were writhing in pain. Almost half the passengers had been killed and the rest were badly injured. Then my friend who had advised me earlier to go to Ferozepur helped me get to Ambala. I wanted to get to Delhi because we had relatives there and I was sure that my parents, if they were still alive, would have gone to Delhi. Luckily, in Ambala I got help from Arjan Singh, later India's famous air marshal. He was two years junior to me at Government College, Lahore. He very kindly arranged for me to travel to Delhi in a vehicle at his disposal. In Delhi I found my parents. Later my brothers also came to India.

'After a few days, I paid a second visit to Lahore when some of us with some medical training volunteered to help badly injured Hindus and Sikhs who were being treated in the famous Sir Ganga Ram Hospital. That too was an awful sight. Legs, arms, and hands had been cut off. Women had been violated by gangs of rapists. It was a sight which I cannot describe. We then paid a visit to King Edward Medical College where our teachers tried to persuade us to stay on and complete our studies. While we were at the college, somebody came and said that a fellow student of ours, Shanti, who had decided to stay on in Lahore and complete her medical degree, had been murdered. Then we left the college quickly. Finally, with the help of a professor of medicine, Dr Shah and his daughter, who was like a sister to me, I went and collected some jewellery from a bank vault on behalf of a relative. After that I returned to Delhi. It must have been the end of August. I saw all hell break loose on both sides.'

In July 2002, I visited the US and used that opportunity to record a number of interviews with Lahorites settled in the States. Two interviews are excerpted below; the second confirms a particular murder that took place as well as a description of the culprit.

Kanta Singh Luthra

'I was born in 1935. My mother was a poor woman from Mianwali and my father died when I was very young. My uncle, Madan Gopal Singh whom I regarded as my father, was the registrar of Punjab University, Lahore. We lived in the residence provided by the university. I used to go to the Sir Ganga Ram School for Hindu girls. My father had several Muslim friends. I remember Abdul Rahman, who used to visit us from Multan. Then there was this girl Mumtaz who was a very dear friend of mine. We children never cared for the religious taboos of those times. Those were good days.

'Madan Gopal Singh [her father] was a renowned scholar, not only of literature, but also of religion. He taught us to respect all faiths and to believe in one God. He had sent my mother and the children to Jullundur but stayed on to complete the transfer of records and wrap up other formalities as Punjab University was also going to be divided and re-established in East Punjab. I can still remember that fateful day, 31 August 1947. A day before, we had arrived in Jullundur and were staying at the government rest house. It was evening when a military truck drove up. An officer, Capt. Verma, informed us that Father had been killed that morning in his office at the university.

'We went back to Lahore, although Mother was not willing to take me with her, but I cried and cried to have a last glimpse of Father. We went to Sir Ganga Ram Hospital and saw his dead body. He had been stabbed fourteen times. We were told that before he died, my father had recited the *kalima* (formula for conversion to Islam). Back in Jullundur, I saw the same hatred, the same madness. The scene is indelibly etched on my mind. One day I saw a gang of Hindus and Sikhs shouting "*Har, Har, Mahadev*" and "*Wah Guru Ji Di Fateh*". They were menacing two young, half-naked Muslim women with spears and *lathis*. The bleeding girls fell on their knees and begged for mercy. What happened to them is anybody's guess. That day I wondered if God had died or taken a sedative while His children had rebelled against Him and joined hands with the devil.'

Satyendra Kumar

This interview was conducted at Satyendra Kumar's residence in Gurgaon, Haryana, on 17 March 2013.

'We are Kashmiri Pandits. My forebears moved to Delhi the same year when the French Revolution took place (1789). They took up service with the feudatories of the Mughals. Being well-versed in Persian, Arabic and Urdu, their services were readily sought by the princes of those times who were always in conflict with one another and needed experts to formulate treaties and other agreements. One of them, Ganga Ram, moved to Punjab on the invitation of Ranjit Singh. He was given a haveli (mansion) near the famous Wazir Khan Mosque in the walled city of Lahore. His son Diwan Ajodya Parshad took up service in the Sikh army and was a colleague of Mian Ilahi Bakhsh from the famous Arain family of Baghbanpur, Lahore. Mian Ilahi Bakhsh was an artillery commander and that branch of the Mian family carries the title of 'topchees'. My grandfather, Raja Narendra Nath, was educated in the madrasa of Wazir Khan Mosque. He was fully conversant with the Quran and could recite it. When he died, the Muslims wanted to bury him as a Muslim insisting that he was a *hafiz* (one who can recite the complete Quran from memory). However, others said that he was a Brahmin and should, therefore, be cremated. The family cremated him according to our ancestral rites.

'Our family is related to the Nehrus as all Kashmiri Pandits are to each other, being a small community. Jawaharlal Nehru's mother was from a Lahore Kashmiri Pandit family. My father's sister Rameshwari was married to Jawaharlal's first cousin Brijlal (father of B.K. Nehru, ex ambassador to the US). Sir Tej Bahadur Sapru, another famous Kashmiri Pandit from UP, used to say that my uncle, that is, Raja Sahib, may be the leader of the Hindu Mahasabha but when he is angry he uses Arabic abuses!

'Raja Narendra Nath was the all-India leader of the Hindu Mahasabha.

Did that make him a communalist? Well, not really. The reason was that he was a very wealthy man and the Hindu Mahasabha, rather than the Congress, represented his class interests. He had very close Muslim friends and many Punjabi Muslim leaders were among them. Among his close Muslim family friends in Lahore were the Mian family of Baghbanpura, Sir Sikander Hayat and Khizr Hayat Tiwana's father, Malik Omar Hayat Tiwana. Rajaji helped Khizr Hayat in becoming premier of Punjab after Sikander's death in December 1942.

'Narendra Nath died in 1943. There is an interesting anecdote about him that I would like to share with you. Once the Punjab governor asked him what he was doing. He told him he was translating John Stuart Mill's *On Liberty* into Urdu. That must have worried the governor quite a bit who quickly made him a member of his advisory council to placate him. My father, Diwan Anand Kumar, was an educationist. He did not take part in politics. He lived in Fair Field on Waris Road (the present author was born only some 400 metres away on Temple Road and remembers Fair Field as a grand mansion in that area).

'At the time of Partition, I was 17. We arrived safely in India first in Dehradun in UP. Sir Tej Bahadur Sapru asked me if we had come over safely. I said we had and everything we could carry with us has come safely. Everything meant for me the furniture, including two marble cockatoos and my guns, because I was fond of hunting. The women in the family had in fact left Lahore in May 1947. I left after Shahalmi was set ablaze but before the new borders between India and Pakistan came into being. The truth is that we were never threatened. Our tenants came and protected us during the riots. The only time we felt any danger was when a friend of my father Maulvi Muhammad Shafi, who lived on nearby Mason Road, sent a message that the hoodlums of Bhoondpura, a Muslim majority area nearby our house, were about to launch a raid. Our servant Yusaf's son lived in Bhoondpura and although he took part in attacks elsewhere, he made sure that we remained safe. Therefore, no attack took place on our residence.

'My father left after Partition and only after the mother of a friend of his, also a maulvi from the walled city, saw a Hindu being beaten to death, his bones mercilessly broken, she said to him, "Tell Satyendra to leave forthwith." In India, things were as bad. While driving down from

Solan, at a railway crossing near Kalka, he found a Muslim survivor, who had managed to alight from a train that had been attacked and most Muslim refugees on the way to Pakistan butchered. He took him to the hospital at Kalka where some Hindus objected to his help to a Muslim. He responded, "*Mareez kaa koi mazhab nahin hota* (A patient has no religion)." That settled the issue and the doctors helped that lone survivor.

'As a young boy, I often used to ride on horseback to the village Bir, near the lands of Nawab Qizilbash, called Illaqa Nawab Sahib. Bir belonged to us. We had rented out our land to mainly Muslim but also some Sikh tenant-cultivators. Many boys from the village used to be part of my hunting team. My family never treated the tenants badly. It was said that while Nawab Qizilbash always needed bodyguards to protect himself, we Hindu Brahmins never felt any such need. I believe common folk are loyal and kind when they are treated well.

'I had always wanted to visit Lahore, where the happiest years of my life were spent. I had many friends at Aitchison College, Lahore. The first occasion arrived in 1998: the same year both India and Pakistan exploded their nuclear devices. People warned me not to go but I was not worried. Setting foot on Lahore soil was something I cannot describe, even though we had had to flee from it so many years ago. My memory of Lahore was only of very happy days. I went and saw our old house in the walled city. I also saw Fair Field but from a distance. It had become the Fatimah Jinnah Hostel for girls studying to be lady doctors. Their college was only a few minutes away, built by Sir Ganga Ram. The second time I went was at the time of Basant in 1999. The old kite-flying memories came back with a lot of emotions. Lahore was the same in many ways. I visited Bir with Azhar, my Pakistani host's 8-year-old son, an old Aitchisonian like me. I found some elderly people sitting and talking in the village square, quite like old times. I joined them and began to ask them where the old banyan tree was and where the 80-acre mango grove had gone (Bir in total was about 1,500 acres). The old men remembered that the mango grove originally belonged to our Rajas family but in 1947 when they left for India, someone who had come from India was granted the land. He cut the mango grove and built a colony and the new posh locality of Johar Town had sprung up on it on the outskirts of Lahore. One of them told me that he used to accompany Raja Sahib's grandson Chicku Sahib (my nickname) on his hunting trips. At that point I asked Azhar what my name was and when he called me Chicku Uncle, they realized who I was. Suddenly, many old men were embracing and blessing me (a 71-year-old), welcoming me back. We reminisced about old times and suddenly were back in the past as young men who had played together and had had a great time. That evening, hundreds of people gathered to talk with me. It was a deeply emotional occasion.

'In 2001, my daughter Gargi went to Lahore. She went to see our walled city. An old woman, originally from Amritsar, embraced her and started crying loudly. Her daughter had been killed in Amritsar and I suppose she wanted to lift a heavy weight off her chest, and Gargi's presence provided her with the opportunity to express her grief and deep sorrow. Gargi went to Bir as well, where she was treated as a daughter and given many presents. She could even go into Fair Field and see our old house from inside and take pictures. This was the first time my family had seen Fair Field and even the room I was born in. For us, Lahore will always be part of our lives.'

Visharda Hoon

This interview, dated 13 May 2013, was conducted via email from Chennai. It also includes an adaptation of an article by A.J. Philip titled 'From Lahore to Chennai' in the *Herald of India*, December 2009.

'Although we are a Lahori family, I was born on 20 June 1926, at Sheikhupura, about 150 kilometre from Lahore, where my father Raisahib Swamidas was posted as an executive engineer with the Public Works Department. He was transferred back to Lahore in 1927, where he built a spacious house in suburban Model Town. It was named "Vidya Niwas" after my mother. My mother was his second wife. I had two older stepbrothers, Lachman Das and Roshan Das. Lachman was 20 years older than me and was another father figure for me. My mother gave birth to four children. She was well-versed in Punjabi, Hindi, Urdu and English. She could even read and write in them although she did not have any formal degree.

'Life was leisurely. We had a lot of freedom. We were fond of swimming, sports, yoga and dance. There was a floodlit badminton court in our backyard. Whenever a new product such as a radio, record player or refrigerator came into the market, we were sure to get it. We often went to Lahore in my father's old vintage Essex car to see movies and attend fairs. I joined Punjab College for Women in 1941. It was run by my aunt Amar Kumari Verma. Those were crucial years in Indian history. Some of its famous students include former Prime Minister I.S. Gujral's wife Sushila, actor I.S. Johar's wife Rama Hoon and Congress Socialist Party (CSP) leader Prem Bhasin's wife Kamla Ahuja.

'On 9 December 1942, I participated in a strike and procession in Lahore and Anarkali market. We were lathi-charged, rounded up and sent to Lahore Central Jail. It was a new experience for me. I was only 16 years old. Those four days in prison taught me a lot. My mentors were CSP leaders including Tilak Raj Chadha, Prem Bhasin, Achyut Patwardhan, Ashok Mehta, Ram Manohar Lohia, Jayaprakash Narayan and Ramnandan Mishra. Jayaprakash Narayan and Ramnandan Mishra had escaped from Hazaribagh Jail. They were our heroes. The CSP attracted more youngsters than the Congress did. I started participating in rallies, college strikes and soon became the women students' wing secretary. Communal propaganda did not influence me much. Some of my close friends were Muslims. I specifically remember Aziz from the Frontier Province. Model Town was a heterogeneous colony and I had several close Muslim friends. In fact, our Muslim friends helped us during the riots. We did not want Partition to take place. We were not prepared to leave. No one anticipated that the Hindus would have no place in Pakistan.

'Meanwhile, after completing my BA, I joined Government College, Lahore, and took psychology for my master's. When things became intense and displaced persons started arriving in Lahore from interior West Punjab, my parents panicked. It was decided that we would go to Dehradun for a while. My uncle worked at Doon School as a housemaster, my aunt also worked in the same school as a matron. We arrived in Dehradun in May 1947 in the hope that we would return home once the riots stopped. I carried only my books and clothes.

'On 14 August 1947, one of our relatives was shot dead by Muslims at the Lahore station. So my brothers, who had gone back to take care of the house, took the car and crossed the border, leaving everything behind. There was utter chaos and large-scale massacres had started on both sides of the newly defined border. From Dehradun, my parents shifted to Delhi as all the refugee rehabilitation work was being done there. I was worried about my studies and MA examinations. Punjab University partly shifted to Solan near Simla and a camp college opened in Delhi. In April 1948, I finally wrote the examination and passed with a first division.

'Meanwhile, my marriage was fixed to Ranjit Singh Hoon, my aunt's stepson. We had grown up together. You could call it a love marriage, as I had known that I would marry him. He had an MA in history and ran an interior decoration business in Lahore. We got married at a friend's house on 30 January 1948, the day Mahatma Gandhi was assassinated. About 100 guests attended the function. At 5.05 p.m., Mahatma Gandhi was shot dead. Within five minutes, the news reached us.

'After marriage, my political activities stopped as we were looking for livelihood. My father-in-law was rather conservative and did not like my mingling with young men. I was also expecting my first child. We moved to Calcutta in 1949. Ranjit started a scrap iron business there. I took up a teaching job at the Birla School for Girls as a Hindi teacher in 1952. By now I had two children. Soon, there was a need to start a branch of the family business in Chennai. So we left Calcutta and moved to Chennai in 1953. My third child, Vineeta, was six months old. I have lived in Chennai ever since and been involved in the Punjab Association in this city. I have great satisfaction of having served society as a teacher and educationist for most of my life.

'I could never visit Pakistan again. I made friends with some Pakistani ladies whom I met at international conferences. A few years ago, I saw photos of my old home, with my father's name and "Vidya Niwas" still inscribed on a marble slab. I would love to visit Model Town, just to see how it has changed, but would not like to live there, as I have become a stranger to the place.'

Adieu Lahore: Upendra Kumar Pandit

This interview is dated 12 July 2014 and was conducted via email from Amsterdam, Netherlands.

'The lottery of birth placed me in a family of the Kashmiri Pandit community of Lahore. My father was professor of Chemistry at the Government Dyal Singh Graduate College, Lahore. My mother's education had ended at the High School level. Perhaps for this reason, she wanted her children (two boys and two girls) to attain the highest level of education. Her hard work and effort led to the accomplishment of this ambition. The motto of Dyal Singh College was: "Gather Ye the Wisdom of East and West". My father identified himself with secular principles and placed great importance on good education. Against this background, the girls were sent to The Convent of Sacred Heart and the boys to the St. Anthony's High School, in Lahore. We lived in a house on Beadon Road and enjoyed trips to the old city, especially to Anarkali Bazaar. The walks along the Mall to the Lawrence Gardens and the boating excursions on the Ravi were favourite activities. Life in Lahore was comfortable, highly stimulating in all manner of ways and full of hope for the future.

'As 1947 began, dark clouds started gathering on the horizon of these youthful dreams. Communal disturbances in Lahore started in May. I do not recall the date, but starting from the first fateful day, we could see a glow of light in the sky from the fire in the old city. In the passing weeks and months, this glow expanded and I never saw it extinguished. We also frequently heard the chants of "Allahu Akbar" in varying decibels, emanating from the general direction of the city.

'My father maintained that the situation would settle down once the approaching partition of the country was formalized. Muslims, Sikhs and Hindus had lived together as neighbours and there was no reason that that could not continue even after Partition. The first shocking news for us came in the middle of July, when we learnt about the murder of my mother's cousin (Shammi). He was a role model for me and I particularly remember the rides on his motorcycle. A short time later, we heard that the first cousin of my father [Kumar] had been killed. His multi-stabbed corpse was found in an open water tank near where he lived. By then, the fear of staying on in Lahore had crept in. One learnt of the fires started in various parts of the walled city: the Shah Alami Bazaar, Chunna Mandi, Akbari Mandi and other areas. (Photographs: "LAHORE NAMA" by Santosh Kumar (*Vibha Publications,* New Delhi,

2002). Street after street was burnt and destroyed, while the police stood by and did nothing—we were told. By the end of July, we understood that the old city had been ethnically cleansed of Hindus and Sikhs. At that stage, my mother and three children left for Delhi to stay with some relatives.

'One incident that shook me and my father was the scene of the murder of a man, literally hacked with knives. We saw—and could hear—the complete incident through the window of the bank where we had gone to draw money. A second personal event which has remained engraved in my memory is my attempt to send a telegram to the family in Delhi—to inform them that my father and I were alright (i.e. alive). The procedure at the time required that a message drafted on paper be presented at the Telegraph Office for telegraphic transmission. I promised my father that I would carry out this task. Accordingly, I went with the written message to the main Telegraph Office, which as per my memory was just off Mall Road—not very far from where we lived. The choice of that office was also based on the assumed security of the selected walking route. At the Telegraph Office I joined one of the several lines of people involved in a similar task. While standing in the line (or que, as it was called), I could hear the loud conversations that were in progress between persons within my own line and the general exchange between those standing in different lines. The essence of the conversation—in a group composed totally of Muslim men—made me feel very threatened. There were some who were so enraged that they openly expressed their intention to search for Hindus and Sikhs to kill. While I knew that I would not be taken for a Sikh boy—without the identifying turban—I felt very worried that the Hindu name would be revealed as I would hand over the telegram to the clerk at the desk. As the line advanced, the mental conflict whether to send or not to send the telegram assumed an ominous character. The knife-edge on which I found myself was constituted by the life-threatening atmosphere on one side and the advancement of my position within the que towards the counter, on the other. After all these years, I cannot recall the exact number of persons ahead of me when I felt that it was extremely dangerous for me to present the telegram. Consequently, in a cowardly act, very quietly and in a manner not to arouse attention, I detached myself from the que and walked out of the Telegraph Office, to return home. I felt deeply embarrassed to tell my father that the telegram had not been sent. However, when I explained the circumstances to him, he understood why I had acted the way I had. In the days that followed, there were further unhappy incidents which created a general gloomy picture of the prospects of a "normal life" in the new circumstances.

'The owner of a dairy, in our mohalla, had contacts with the police. He relayed information to the neighbours on the security issue. On 25 August, he told us that the police could no longer protect us and that we should prepare to leave. On 27 August, together with six Hindu and Sikh families from our mohalla, my father and I—carrying one small suitcase and a sack of rice and dal—left in a caravan of tongas for Lahore Cantonment Station. This was in the hope of finding a train going to Amritsar.

'At the Cantonment Railway Station one encountered a scene of total confusion and chaos. There were men, women and children wandering about amongst piles of bags, bundles, half-made beds, pots and pans and even some charcoal braziers. Presumably, some had been there for a long time. There was no question of any railway authority or a train timetable.

'Whenever someone shouted that the train on Platform X was going to Amritsar, the cry would be picked up and a whole horde would move in the direction of Platform X. Upon one such announcement, my father and I decided to enter the indicated train. The Wagah border was only 15 miles (24 kilometres) away. Little did we know then how *far* those 15 miles would seem to be as the unfolding events revealed. Joining the stream of people, we reached the train. If I recall correctly, my father pushed me through a carriage window and entered it via the door himself. It was a third-class compartment with bare wooden seats. Only a few could sit, as for the available space, too many had entered. The train started late in the afternoon, very slowly—one could easily walk alongside it and keep pace. Every so often it would stop for no apparent reason. At one time, when we stopped, we heard gunshots. Some of these appeared to pass by the carriage windows. People tried to find protection by moving away from the windows or ducking down. As the train moved again, we could hear distant screams of *humans* as I had never heard before or have since. No one dared to look out of the windows to see what was happening. From my vantage point, I saw a man, half-naked and covered with blood, shouting and waving his arms in a fruitless gesture to convey his plight. Those screams, though now muffled by the passage of time, I can never forget. Their memory, once triggered, especially at night, can plunge me into a sleepless void.

'Just when we thought that we were close to Wagah, we stopped once again; we then saw the engine uncouple itself and a few moments later pass us going in the opposite direction. So there we sat in an "engine-less" train in the approaching darkness. It was noticeable that people did not talk much. Each one was trying to fight their personal fear of the unknown before us. Soon it became dark and one could not see whatever was happening in the menacing world outside. At some point in time, the day's accumulated exhaustion took over me and I fell asleep. For how long, I do not know, though it must have been for some hours. Because, when I woke up, the train was moving and in the pale early light I could see ghostly trees through the window frame of the train carriage. The train moved further, ever so slowly, till we saw a mass of people gathered close to the train track. My first reaction was one of intense apprehension. However, it soon became obvious that the people were waving and shouting happily at the train and its human cargo. I heard my father say, with what I recognized as a sense of intense relief—"We have reached India."

I have not returned to Lahore since that day.'

Professor Shaukat Ali

A few days later, on 29 July, I visited Professor Emeritus Shaukat Ali, a veteran Pakistani educationist, at his son Dr Saleem Ali's house in Mansfield, Massachusetts. His description of pre-Partition Lahore and his Hindu teachers has already been presented in Chapter Four. The later part of the interview was about what happened in 1947. To my surprise he confirmed the murder of Madan Gopal Singh and also identified the man who killed him. This is what he told me:

'From May onwards the walled city was always disturbed. The old, relaxed life style had been drastically altered and people lived in fear of random attacks. Bhati Gate remained peaceful even when fires in the typical Hindu localities of Papar Mandi and Shahalmi had been raging for quite some time. Most of the demonstrations and group agitations were confined to the Mall and other modern parts of the city. I remember slogans like "*Pakistan ka matlab kya, La Ilaha Il-lilah*" and vulgar cat-calls against the Khizr government being recited in the demonstrations by the Muslim Leaguers. A few days before, on 14 August Mohalla Jallotian, where we Muslims were in a minority, and mostly Hindus households lived, was marked by plotters. Suddenly there were signs painted on Hindu houses but ours and other Muslims homes had been skipped. It created panic and some of the Hindus left their homes, but since most were from ordinary, lower-middle-class backgrounds they did not have anywhere to go. One evening fire was set to their homes and suddenly, the worst type of screams could be heard. Burning skin exuded a foul odour. I am even now disturbed in my sleep and the desperate voices haunt me.

'You referred to the story of Kanta Luthra. What she told you is very true. Madan Gopal Singh was a highly respected scholar and a most dedicated registrar at the university. He was murdered by his stenographer, who used to sit next door to him. I can't remember his name now. The partition of India was most unnecessary. A thousand years of integrative processes were brought to naught in a matter of weeks and days. Nobody could foresee that the Punjab holocaust was on the way. I am glad that my venerable teacher Prem Kirpal safely left for India but I don't know what happened to Professor Nayyar. I hope he too was saved. Both were great men and I will always remember them as my true benefactors.'

Kaleb Ali Sheikh

Earlier, with Kaleb Ali Sheikh's help, the background to the bangles and henna incident of May 1947 has been presented. He had more to tell of what happened in Lahore from the second half of August 1947:

'In August 1947, Lahore was a burning inferno. Most Hindus and Sikhs had fled; their will to stay on in Lahore had been broken. But some were not leaving. They were behaving as if nothing had happened.

I saw three men with my own eyes being killed. A young, handsome, well-dressed Sikh was confidently riding his bicycle near our house behind the Lahore railway station. It seems he was familiar with the place and was riding at a leisurely pace. Suddenly a pack of *goondas* pounced upon him. They hit him from behind with a long stick. He fell to the ground and then they thrust long knives into his body. He died writhing in pain. The second case was that of a Hindu shopkeeper in our neighbourhood. He used to sell cooking oil. He was probably going to fetch oil and had tied drums to his bicycle. He too was stabbed to death. The killers were after his money. They snatched his wallet and ran away. The third person was some stranger who was lying dead in a pool of blood. I do not know whether he was a Muslim or a Hindu. All the three murders took place when the curfew was in force. Obviously it was professional criminals who took the risk of breaking the law and committing such serious crimes. The real killings in Lahore started after 17 August when Amritsaris came in their thousands to Lahore. Among them were those who had been among the top law breakers of Amritsar. They were definitely connected to the administration. Some were part of the group that Sardar Shaukat Hayat had established in Amritsar during his regular visits to that city. Many of them were later allotted shops and houses in Anarkali left behind by the Hindus and Sikhs.

'One day my father, who was a constable in the railway police, came back home and told my mother that although trains had been pulling in daily at Lahore railway station from both the eastern and western districts full of dead bodies, he had learnt that a train coming from northern Punjab had been attacked in Kamoke and not a single Hindu or Sikh had survived. [This event is presented in more detail later in this chapter – author.]. Therefore the train was sent to a washing shed to be cleaned. It is, however, important to emphasise that in Lahore the administration was still feared by those who broke the law during the early days after the partition. One reason was that many officers in the police were still British. Also, the new Inspector General of Police Qurban Ali Khan was an officer of exceptional integrity.'

Lahore District

Sardar Shaukat Ali

While I have collected stories from Lahore city in abundance, it was not easy to meet people who could recount what had happened in the rural areas. However, I talked on 3 May 2003 to the veteran Communist leader, Sardar Shaukat Ali, at his home in New Garden Town. He narrated the events which unfolded around his village in the Lahore district:

'After the Radcliffe Award, gangs of raiders and looters were seen roaming all over. Comrade Ghulam Nabi Bhullar was deputed by the Communist Party to bring over Muslims from across the Sutlej and Beas to Pakistan and to escort Hindus and Sikhs to the other side. I myself helped many Hindus and Sikhs cross from our side of the river. I had a Sikh comrade, Joginder Singh. One day he and his brother arrived in our village with a sackful of Qurans which fleeing Muslims had left behind.

'Now Sikhs from a village only 8–10 miles from the Sutlej were trying to cross it. Rains had fallen and everywhere water was on the rise, in the river, the streams and the canals. It was a big caravan and most of them did not know how to swim and there were few boats that could be brought to help them. They were attacked viciously by Muslim marauders. Many were killed. The women had tied their jewellery to their bodies. The raiders would snatch the jewellery and sometimes ears and necks were torn away from the bodies. There is a place called Mandi Usmanwala. The Wahabbi *maulvis* from there took an active part in looting jewellery. They also killed many Sikhs.

'In Lahore city attacks took place because the *goondas* and *badmashes* were being backed by politicians. There were two factions. Muslim League leaders were involved in the sense that they had close contacts with *goondas*. Mian Amiruddin's place was the centre of such activity. But there were very decent Muslim Leaguers too. Sheikh Muhammad Rafiq was a member of the Communist Party but had joined the Muslim League on the party's instructions. He and Ahmed Saeed Kirmani, who was a Muslim League student leader, discouraged attacks on Hindus and Sikhs. Mian Iftikharuddin, Daniyal Latifi, Sohan Singh Josh, Tikka Ram Sohan were senior comrades who used their influence on their communities not to indulge in killing and looting. Shamim Ashraf Malik and I were the younger Muslim cadres of the party who tried to help people in need as much as we could. The violence and insanity I saw during those days continues to haunt me even now. The idea of breaking up India on a religious basis was a very bad one. It gave recognition and importance to religious fanatics who used that opportunity to propagate religious hatred.'

On 18 March 2004, Vicky and I visited a rather large village, Kishanpura Kalan, district Moga, East Punjab. We had been tipped off that refugees from Lahore district had settled in it and adjoining villages.

Pyara Singh Naulakh

'My name is Pyara Singh, son of Kundan Singh Naulakh. Our village was known as Naulakha Bunga, *tahsil* Chunian, district Lahore. It was a mixed village of Muslims, Sikhs, Hindus. We lived in peace and there was a lot of *prem* (love and affection) among all communities. It was only in 1947 that activists from the Muslim League visited our village. They won over a tailor called Faqiria. They came and stayed with him but there was no untoward incident. The Sikh leader Baldev Singh had sent a message to us that he would send troops to help us in case we were attacked or forced to leave. We were told that there was a dispute over Chunnian *tahsil* which was in Lahore district and Zira *tahsil* on the opposite side of the Sutlej in Ferozepur district. In Zira, Muslims were in a majority while in Chunnian, Hindus and Sikhs were in a majority. We were told that if Jinnah wanted to take Chunian then we will have to go and if he wanted Zira then we could stay on. We think that Jinnah gave up Zira because there was no way of connecting it to Pakistan since the Sutlej became the boundary in that part of the Punjab.

'One day we learnt that Pakistan had come into being. Our Muslim neighbours promised to provide us protection against any intimidation or violence. It must have been a few days after 15 August that loud noises and gunfire rudely woke us up while we were fast asleep on the roofs of our houses. We were told that the village had been attacked by a large group of armed men. So within minutes we assembled at a central point and started walking towards the Sutlej. They wanted to frighten us so that we should leave. We were ambushed on the way and some people were killed. It was nighttime and nobody knew who ran where for protection. But the army arrived just in time to prevent any great loss of life. I think the deaths from our village were not more than fifty. Near our village there were the purely Muslim villages of Satoki and Mir Mamda. The raiders were not from these villages either. They had come on a rampage from outside and were mostly criminals who wanted to loot people.

'Other, mainly Hindu–Sikh caravans, were less fortunate. One behind us was attacked by Muslim soldiers and police. Some 200–250 people were machine-gunned and women and children were taken away by the looters who were with them. Some of them managed to join our caravan and tell us what had happened. Troops of the Indian Army who were escorting us panicked when they realised they were too few and poorly armed to fight trained combatants and troops. It is we who gave them moral support and lifted their spirits. There were very good horse riders from our village who helped the army to escort the caravan which had by that time swelled to many thousands; perhaps as many as 50,000.

'We finally reached the camp at Jambar. Then, in early September, we crossed the border. We did not abandon anyone. The elders who could not walk were put on carts, women with small children and pregnant women were also put on carts. We first went to Amritsar and then came to Zira and then someone told us to go to Kishanpura. There were five *pattis* (areas of specific clans and castes) in the village: four comprising Hindus and Sikhs and one of Muslims. We settled in the Muslim *patti* from where the Arains had gone to Pakistan.'

Sheikhupura

Sheikhupura was undoubtedly the most important district in religious terms for the Sikhs in West Punjab. They wanted it to be included in East Punjab more than any other place because the founder of their religion, Guru Nanak, was born in Talwandi village in that district. It later became known as Nanakana Sahib. But the population factor favoured the Muslims. Of the total population of 825,508, Muslims were in a majority with 641,448 (63.62 per cent) but Sikhs formed a significant minority of 106,706 (18.85 per cent) while Hindus, including the scheduled castes, were 77,740 (9.12 per cent). Initially, the Sikhs tried to stay put even after the Radcliffe Award had given Sheikhupura to Pakistan. Also, there was no immediate attempt by the Muslims to expel them and the Hindus. But when Muslim refugees started arriving from East Punjab, the situation changed very rapidly.

One of the biggest carnages in the western districts took place in Sheikhupura. The SGPC report captures that pithily:

'Sheikhupura's Hindus and Sikhs were perhaps, after Rawalpindi and Multan, the worst sufferers at the hands of Pakistani fanaticism and cold-blooded murderous frenzy. The blow fell on them suddenly and swiftly – leaving between 10,000 and 20,000 of them dead in two days' (1991: 167).

The Khosla report has given many details of some of the worst acts of slaughter. Khosla blames the whole Muslim administration as party to the massacres, alluding to even the English Deputy Commissioner C.H. Disney, who had decided to stay on in Pakistan, as party to the conspiracy. According to the report, it began with him imposing curfew on 24 August from 6 p.m. to 6 a.m. although Sheikhupura till then had been free of any violent conflict. The only thing that had started happening were the stabbings in the trains between Lahore and Lyallpur from 21 August onwards, and Hindus and Sikhs were being killed that way. Open trouble broke out on 25 August when Hindu and Sikh houses were set ablaze. The military and police that arrived began to shoot people who came out of their homes. The trouble peaked on 26 August (Khosla 1989: 126-9).

I managed to track down people who I hoped could tell us about the events in Sheikhupura on those two days. A gentleman whom I met in Delhi on 8 March 2004, gave me the following account of what happened in that town at the time of Partition. I later sought further clarification from him via telephone on 30 January 2006.

Kevel Krishan Tulli

'I was born on 6 December 1936 in Sheikhupura. We lived in the street, Awana di Galli, in Sheikhupura town. It was a *cul-de-sac*. Our house was next to that of a Muslim advocate whose name I can't remember now. Things were very peaceful and friendly. We played in the street and *mohallas* and nobody really thought much about religious differences. My father, Lala Ram Rakha Mal, was an *arrti* (wholesale merchant). Our business was fairly good. The trouble started suddenly. It was the Baluch regiment of the Punjab Boundary Force, which goaded on the Muslims to do something to avenge the crimes committed by Hindus and Sikhs in East Punjab. Suddenly, panic broke out as gangs of men went around looting and stabbing Hindus and Sikhs. It was really a very terrifying experience as men and women were chased by mobs and killed mercilessly.

'We quickly left our home next morning seeking refuge in a safe place. We saw Hindus and Sikhs running towards the railway station or to Sardar Atma Singh's rice mill. It was a big place with a large compound. I have a feeling that thousands of people had taken refuge in it. The military surrounded the mill and mounted machine guns facing the mill. They ordered the Hindus and Sikhs to surrender their weapons. They also carried out a check to see that nobody was concealing anything. They then ordered us to surrender all gold, silver and cash. We were told that if we cooperated they would take us to a camp, which had been set up for Hindus and Sikhs. A high pile of gold and silver jewellery which was collected was taken away.

'Then some of the criminal elements began to molest young women. A soldier tried to drag away a Sikh girl, whereupon her brothers pounced upon him and killed him. That resulted in the machine guns coming into action. People fell in the places where they were standing. The panic was total. People ran in all directions. I and my mother ran in one direction while my father, who was carrying my six-month-old sister, ran towards the railway station. He was killed, along with hundreds of other people. The hordes were not sparing anyone. However, nobody tried to kill my infant sister. She lay on the ground and licked the blood around and survived! Somebody picked her up and brought her to Amritsar where we found her again. She now serves in the Indian Air Force.

'My mother and I were being chased by some men when a Muslim gentleman who was himself a refugee from East Punjab intervened and saved us. He would not let anyone kill us. Later, he took us to the refugee camp. At least 15,000 people were killed in those raids. I still remember seeing dead bodies all around in the compound of Sardar Atma Singh's mill and outside. The machine gunfire caused blood to flow like water. We were in the refugee camp when Pandit Jawaharlal Nehru came to Sheikhupura. He saw with his own eyes the utter devastation that had taken place. Later, we were put in a train in which hundreds of people, many of them seriously injured, were sitting. It was a slow journey. We arrived first at Lahore and then finally after many hours the train reached Amritsar.

'In Amritsar we went around looking for my father. Somebody said that he had seen him running towards the railway station. Others said they had seen him lying dead. There was complete disorder in Amritsar. We never saw him again. I still think about him a lot. He loved me very much. He was a kind man and was respected by Muslims as well. But we found my sister, so there is some consolation. From what I heard the people who organised the assaults in our area were Muslim Arains. I can never forget that slaughter.'

Chaudhri Nazir Ahmed Virk

Since the outrage against Hindus and Sikhs in Sheikhupura was a notorious case of mass slaughter, we searched for a Muslim witness who could give their own account of what happened. One of them, Chaudhri Nazir Ahmed Virk, was interviewed in Sheikhupura on 30 December 2005 by Ahmad Salim. Here is his account:

'I was born in Sheikhupura on 18 January 1935 in the old town. In 1947 I was in the seventh class in the Government High School. It was a small town. There was never any conflict here. No communal agitation. One of the elders of our Virk clan of Jats, Chaudhri Ibrahim Virk, was the Chairman of the Municipal Committee of Sheikhupura. Swami Nand Singh, a Sikh, was a member of the Committee. When Lahore and Amritsar were ablaze they both went around on a *tonga* announcing "O Brothers. Sheikhupura is a small town. We have been living peacefully together. Please try to save our town from the virus of communal conflict. If somebody is keen to fight he should go to

Lahore or Amritsar. We will pay the fare, but for God's sake don't spoil the harmonious relations in Sheikhupura".

'One day we were playing behind a mosque when a man called Imam Din, a cobbler who worked near the railway station, came and said, "A train has come from East Punjab filled with dead bodies. There are women whose breasts have been cut off and children have been cut to pieces. The whole train is full of blood. There is no one alive". We ran to see the train. It was 25 or 26 August. The boys from Ahmedpura *mohalla* brought hatchets and *balams* (long bladed weapons) and some Sikhs who were shopping in the bazaar were hacked to pieces. The next day, at about 12 or 1 p.m. in the afternoon, a military jeep came with a *subedar* (non-commissioned officer) and three other soldiers. They shouted, "Are you people asleep? Don't you know what has happened to your brethren in East Punjab? Join us and we will avenge the wrong done to our co-religionists". One of my relatives, Chaudhri Muhammad Shafi, and his tenant Muhammad Baloch ran along with the jeep. The *subedar* told them to bring any gun they had. There was only one gun available at that time in the *mohalla*.

'Ata Muhammad Awan, who was the cook of the deputy commissioner, had a single-barrel gun. He brought it. The soldiers also told the crowd to bring kerosene oil. One drum full of kerosene was collected. Near the Lunda Gate in front of Ramgarh, a Hindu–Sikh neighbourhood, the soldiers laid themselves on the ground and took positions near the railway line. They ordered the people to set fire to the factory of Bagra Singh. This was done. The Sikhs inside the factory went to the roof from where they started firing because they had guns. The soldiers then fired back, killing them one by one.

'Then the fire spread to the old town. They also set fire to the house of Santokh Singh. Then the Tundhpurian *mohalla* was also set on fire. Everyone felt scared that evening. The next day in the morning, it was announced that a camp had been set up so all Hindus and Sikhs should go there. So they came out of their homes and went to the camp near Atma Singh's factory on Jandaya Road. There they collected in their thousands. Then tanks were brought with machine guns fitted on them. They gunned them down.

'Even Nehru got news of the genocidal attack. He decided to visit Sheikhupura. When the police got to know of the visit they arranged for some untouchables to take away the bodies and burn them or conceal them. Some were thrown in wells or in ditches and some were taken away and thrown away in the fields. But so much killing had taken place that dead bodies were lying around the railway line and the Lahore – Sheikhupura Road when Nehru arrived and saw them. He got out of the car and said to the public, "You people are heartless and cruel." A man, probably a cleric who wore a beard, replied, "No, you are more prejudiced because the carnage started first from your side. Why are you shouting now?"

'Many Sikhs and Hindus even converted to Islam. There was Kaka Singh who was close to Muslims. He stayed for a few days but then when the refugees were going to India he also left. Two policemen and some *goondas* came along with two girls to our door and told us to keep them. They said they'd take them later when they returned. Those men were going around looting. About 10 minutes later, a Sikh and his wife and small children came to our door and implored us for help. The man said, "We are your brothers and sisters. We belong to this same town and have always lived here. Please help us." We took them in too. The girls belonged to the same family. They embraced each other and were very happy to be united. But they were all greatly frightened. Then the policemen and the roughnecks came and demanded that the girls be handed over to them. We refused. So, they left. The Sikh became a Muslim and the girls also started learning the Quran but when they realised that people looked at them with suspicion, then after a month they too left for India when the Indian Army came to fetch survivors.

'People from good, respectable families did not take part in the killing and looting. When the caravans of East Punjab Muslims reached Sheikhupura, they would prostrate themselves on the ground and start chanting, "*Pakistan ka matlab kiya, La Ilaha Il lillah*". Some Hindus and Sikhs did come back after the trouble had subsided. Even now Sikhs come every year. There is no doubt those killings were a holocaust. But people acted spontaneously and there was no pre-planned slaughter of non-Muslims. Some Sikhs also killed Muslims here in Sheikhupura. At that time man had become a wild beast. Some 20,000 people may have died in Sheikhupura.'

Jawaharlal Nehru's visit to Sheikhupura

The Chronicle of Pakistan, compiled by Khurram Ali Shafique for the month of September, reported that the Indian and Pakistani prime ministers, Jawarharlal Nehru and Liaqat Ali Khan had, under an agreement, been touring different parts of divided Punjab to see for themselves the effects of communal violence. On Wednesday, 3 September 1947, the two held a press conference in Lahore in which they reiterated, 'the determination of the two Central and the two Provincial Governments that law and order should be immediately established and all lawlessness suppressed and punished.' It was also stated: 'Illegal seizure of property will not be recognized and both Governments will take steps to look after the property of refugees and restore it to its rightful owners.'

They visited Amritsar, Batala, Hoshiarpur, Lahore, and Sheikhupura and were deeply moved by the suffering in the refugee camps, where thousands of people from both sides were awaiting either exodus or rehabilitation. In Sheikhupura, an old peasant had said: 'This country has seen many changes of rulers. They have come and gone. But this is the first time that with a change of rulers the *riyaya* (subjects) is also being forced to change.' An elderly Hindu woman said to Nehru, 'Partitions take place in all families. Property changes hands, but it is all arranged peacefully. Why this butchery, loot and abductions? Could you not do it the sensible way families divide?' (*Chronicle,* September 1947).

Sheikhupura massacre and dissolution of Punjab Boundary Force

According to Robin Jeffrey, the active participation of the Baluch regiment in gunning down Hindus and Sikhs on 25 and 26 August precipitated the dissolution of the Punjab Boundary Force. It failed to stem the violence despite several sincere attempts, but when the events in Sheikhupura exposed the partisan behaviour of some of its members, both sides agreed to dissolve it. The plea taken by the Muslims who took part in it was that the non-Muslims had fired upon them but the Hindus who were in the PBF challenged that. An inquiry that had been ordered into the conduct of the Baluch soldiers was allowed to be dropped by the Pakistan authorities after the force was disbanded (1974: 516).

Sikhs' honour killing

One day in January 2004, when Vicky and I were in Ludhiana, we met a Sikh police inspector who told us that his own family had killed all the women in the family before leaving their village in Sheikhupura, so that they would not fall into the hands of Muslim men. When I visited India again in January of the following year we went to their village in Haryana. A wedding was about to be held in the family, so in one sense it was rather awkward that we arrived to talk about death and killings from the past. But it was the only chance of hearing about this phenomenon directly and the elders kindly gave us an interview. We reached the village of Lakhmari, district Kurukshestra, in Haryana state in the afternoon. The family were Virk Jats, formerly of village Kathiala Virkan (also called Kathiala Virk), Muridke *tahsil*, district Sheikhupura. We were met by Shamsherjit Singh Virk, a strikingly handsome man. His cousin had informed him about our visit. He introduced us to his uncles who gave the following accounts of what happened:

Sardul Singh Virk

'My name is Sardul Singh, I was born in 1928. I passed my matric in 1944 and then joined Forman Christian College in Lahore and studied until 1947. Ours was a big village of some 400 Sikhs and 6,000 Muslims but almost all the land belonged to us Virks. The Muslims worked as tenant-cultivators for us. Life was easy and peaceful until about early March 1947. Then the first batch of Sikh and some Hindu refugees from Rawalpindi and the NWFP arrived in our area and one became aware of the growing tension in the Punjab. But our village remained completely peaceful until the announcement of the Radcliffe Award. We had been watching fires as far away as Lahore, Gujranwala and Sheikhupura with the help of a telescope. But we remained convinced that Nanakana Sahib will be awarded to East Punjab and were determined to stay on at all costs.

'On 22 August, Station House Officer Muhammad Ghauri, a god-fearing person, called a meeting of all – Hindus, Muslims and Sikhs. He told us that he could no longer guarantee our safety so we should make preparations to leave. Muslims had been arriving from Gurdaspur district and they had many tales of woe to tell. Things would soon get out of control, so non-Muslims should leave as early as possible. Indeed violence was increasing even in our area and thousands of Sikhs and Hindus from neighbouring villages had come to our village or were sleeping in the fields around. On 25 August, thousands of people had collected. We had firearms with us. The caravan began to move and we had probably gone 3–4 kilometres when we were surrounded by Pathans. When night fell some people ran away and others returned to the village. We spent the night in fear. Some of our people went back to the village. Some became Muslims but we Virks were not willing to surrender. Rather then let our women fall into the hands of Muslims, we decided to kill them. They too wanted to die that way rather than be desecrated by raiders. We killed thirty-three of our women. They were beheaded. Some were only children.'

Faqir Singh Virk

While the interview was going on, another senior member of the family, Faqir Singh Virk, joined us. The following is his account:

'Our family had the leading position in Kathiala Virkan. We were the *zaildars*. Most of the land belonged to us. There was a primary school in the village. There was one Hindu and one Muslim teacher. Both were very good men. The most respected man among the Muslims was Maulvi Mahboob Alam, who led the prayers in the village mosque. He was a saintly man. Pir Maqbool Shah lived in the nearby village of Junianwala. He too was a very good man. He used to visit our village riding his horse. Somebody from our family would hold the stirrup and then he would dismount from the horse. That was the tradition and we showed great respect to the elders and spiritual people of all the communities.

'I think it was 25 August when hundreds, and perhaps thousands of armed men started surrounding our village. Some of us ran away and hid ourselves in the fields. I and some others were saved by Piran Ditta Arain who took us home and kept us there. It was raining heavily in those days but for a week we could not step out even to drink water.

I stayed with him for three months. He used to cultivate our land and was a very good man. Most of the attackers were from outside but some from the village also joined them. We heard that many of them had come from Batala. Many Hindus had also taken refuge in our village. We were overwhelmed by the attackers. Some 300–400 people were killed. The Sikhs killed their own women. In our family thirty-three women, old, young and just small girls were killed with *kirpans* by the family men. We heard that the Pakistan Army was going to raid the village and against them we had no chance of defending our women. So, our elder, Gurbaksh Singh, decided that all women and female children will be killed. Some of them were frightened and crying but most accepted that decision and quietly offered themselves for a noble end to their lives.

'In 1995, after nearly 50 years, I visited the village again and the locals welcomed us with open arms. They wanted to know about what happened to those of us who safely crossed the border into India. I went to the grave of Piran Ditta Arain and Maulvi Mahboob Alam to pay my respects. I also met a man whom I saw killing a Hindu. I saw him pursue the Hindu and hack him down with an axe. This time he was very friendly towards me. One old lady whom we used to call Bua Phhuppi wanted to know if Shamsher Singh, who was only four then, was saved or not. She said, "He was such a beautiful little boy".'

At that point Faqir Singh Virk began to weep, and we thought it best to pause the interview. I asked Faqir Singh if he would be willing to name the man who killed the Hindu, but he refused, saying that bygones are bygones. Those were times, he said, when men became beasts. Another younger member of the family, Surat Singh, told us that he was injured but a family of *khumars* (clay potters) saved him and his family. They were taken to the mosque and invited to convert to Islam. Some did but then when the Indian Army came they left for India. A Hindu who was staying in the same house was killed; his wife jumped into the well but was saved. Sub-Inspector Ghauri had saved many Sikhs. 'May God bless him,' said Faqir Singh.

Shamsherjit Singh, who had met us first and had arranged for the meeting, was present at that time. His mother was among those killed on that day. I looked at him, wondering how he felt being orphaned at the age of four. He told me that he visited the village in 1998 and asked for Bua Phhuppi, but she was visiting someone and was not there at the time. He therefore left some gifts for her to thank her for remembering him. Before we left, we asked the senior members what happened when the soldiers arrived. It turned out that it was a unit of Indian troops and not the Baluch regiment that had come to the village. Had the Sikhs not killed their women, some of them perhaps would be alive even today.

Chaudhri Tawwakullah Virk

The killing of women and children by the Sikhs of Kathiala Virkan has continued to be a topic of discussion for people from that area in Pakistan. We talked to a prominent parliamentarian in Sheikhupura on the same day when evidence given earlier was collected, Chaudhri Tawwakullah Virk, that is, on 30 December 2005:

'My name is Chaudhri Tawwakullah Virk. I was born on 5 July 1937, in Chandikot our ancestral village, previously *tahsil* Nanakana Sahib, then part of district Sheikhupura but now of district Nankana Sahib. I joined the Pakistan People's Party in 1970 and have always remained a member of the PPP. I was elected member of the Punjab Legislative Assembly once, and twice to the Pakistan National Assembly. Sheikupura district had the biggest concentration of Virk Jats of which 10 per cent were Muslims and 90 per cent Sikhs. The Sikhs were a martial people. My family owned 15,000 acres and among the Virks we were highly respected. The Sikh Virks and we felt that we were one *biradari*. We did not make any distinction when eating together. Barbarism started first in East Punjab and then when refugees came to Pakistan a reaction was triggered.

'We also had very good relations with Hindus in this area. Most Sikhs and Hindus left safely at least from this place. Our *munshi* (accountant) Sohan Singh crossed the border and kept in contact. His son has a bookshop in Amritsar. He writes to us. Virk Sikhs from our *biradari* visit us and we still have contacts with them. When they come to Nankana Sahib they always visit us.

'In 1947 the Sikhs came to our place. My father Chaudhri Khushi Muhammad invited them to embrace Islam. We did not want them to leave. They were impressed by the invitation, but declined the offer saying that it would be a betrayal of Sikhism. About Kathiala Virkan, the story is like this. The Sikhs of that village were a very proud people. They killed their own women fearing that they will fall into the hands of wicked men. The dead bodies were put in boxes. Perhaps some were cremated. When refugees came, they saw the dead bodies of women in the houses. Some had been put in boxes. For a long time people in this area talked about the harrowing scenes of Kathiala Virkan.'

Gurbachan Singh Tandon

The story of Gurbachan Singh Tandon stands out as one of the strangest and saddest among the events of 1947. I learned about him from Professor Gurnam Singh of the Political Science Department, Guru Nanak Dev University, Amritsar. The interview was tape-recorded on 29 March 2004, at the Tandons' residence in Noida, outside Delhi:

'I was born on 25 July 1934, in the village Tapiala Dost Muhammad, *tahsil* Shahdara, district Sheikhupura. It is located along the railway line between Lahore and Gujranwala. My parents were Hindus, belonging to the Tandon sub-caste of Khatris, but I was raised as a Sikh. Among Hindu Khatris of western Punjab, it was quite common for one son to be brought up as a Sikh. In my case, the decision to make me a Sikh had a special significance. It so happened that my parents had only daughters, but they longed for a son. They took a holy vow that if God gave them a son they would give him up to Sikhi; hence my Sikh identity. My younger brother was also raised as a Sikh.

'Our village represented communal amity. Elders of all communities were respected and their word really mattered. Tapiala Dost Muhammad comprised two-thirds Muslim and one-third Hindu households. There were only two Sikh families in the village. We were known as the Lalas, a generic term used for Hindu traders in the Punjab. However, the Khatri families of the village were also landowners. We owned a big orchard and also 25–30 acres of land. The Muslim landowning families were known as the Chaudhris.

'In 1947, I was in the 8th class. The village school had children from all communities. Our religious affiliations did not stand in the way of our friendships. Similarly, the village activities were usually jointly organised. There were also the regular sittings of card players and wrestling bouts in the *akharas* (wrestling areas).

'News of the rising communal tension and riots did reach our village. There were one or two battery radios in the village and the newspapers *Nawa-i-Waqt, Vir Bharat* and *Milap* were also received by some people, but after 15 August, when the Pakistan independence celebrations were held in Lahore, things began to change in our idyllic rural surroundings. Some people organised meetings in the village under the Muslim League banner. I believe most of them were outsiders. They were carrying spears, axes and long-bladed weapons. The Muslim elders immediately intervened and told them not to create trouble. The Chaudhris in particular made it clear that they would not allow any non-Muslim to come to harm. A peace committee was formed. I remember two names now – Chaudhri Mu'af Ali and Sheikh Muhammad Bashir who were members of that committee.

'However, after mid-August the fires raging in Lahore could now be seen from our village which was only 25 kilometres from that city. At night time we observed the skyline in the direction of Lahore. It was like an unending twilight. Reports of the killings and fires in Amritsar and other parts of the Punjab also began to circulate in our village. However, life continued as usual. The card-players continued to have their sessions under the tree in the village square and the wrestlers continued to practise their prowess in the *akharas*. Soon afterwards, however, our area began to receive refugees in large numbers from Gurdaspur district. That is when the peace in the village began to be challenged. They would say that while we have lost our family members and homes and been forced to flee, how come the Khatris were still living in Pakistan?

'They mobilised activists in some twelve to thirteen villages around Tapiala Dost Muhammad with the intention of raiding our village. The news somehow reached the members of the peace committee. They told the plotters to kill them first if they wanted to kill the Hindus or Sikhs, because otherwise they would not allow them to harm the non-Muslims. Anyhow, on 25–26 August a large crowd of at least 1,500, carrying weapons, launched a surprise attack on our village. As the news spread all the Khatris headed towards the two big multi-storeyed brick houses belonging to prominent Hindus. I, my younger brother, two sisters and my mother took refuge in the house of Manohar Lal. The members of the peace committee put up a resistance, but were overpowered and the raiders surrounded the two houses in which some 60 Hindu families had taken refuge. The raiders told Manohar Lal that he and his family would be spared if he surrendered his rifle. He agreed and told us to go to the other house, which we did.

'The crowd was trying to break into the house. Someone from our side threw a brick at them. One of them was killed. This incited them even more as they cried for revenge. They set fire to the house in which we were hiding. I remember the house began to shake because of the intense heat and rising flames. It was decided to kill the women instead of letting them fall into the hands of the mob. One young girl was beheaded in front of my eyes. By that time complete commotion prevailed. There was an exit at the back of the house and someone from among the crowd told us to give up our possessions and escape through it. Some ten-twelve of us tried that. I and my brother followed them. But the killers were lying in wait for us. I saw my brother being struck down, then I received a blow with an axe. [Mr Tandon then showed me a deep gash on his head. He also showed ugly marks of wounds on his elbow and shoulder inflicted by a spear].

'I fainted upon receiving the blow on my head. It must have been 11 o'clock in the morning when this happened. Many Hindus were killed. At about 4 o'clock the Muslims of our village began to drag the dead bodies away to drop them into the Dake *nala* (stream). When someone pulled my leg I opened my eyes. That man said, "He is the boy of the Lalas." I said, "Water." He took me home and gave me sweetened milk to drink and then some water. He then took us to the village mosque where other Hindus were also being kept. I found my mother and sisters among the survivors. Later my father, Hari Ram, and my grandfather, who had hidden themselves in the fields, also joined us but my younger brother had died.

'We spent the night in the mosque. Later we were moved to a house where we stayed for ten-twelve days. Three more attacks against us took place but our Muslim brethren from the village were now well-prepared and we remained unharmed. Later the military arrived. We were taken to Lahore around 10 September where we stayed for four days at the camp set up in Government College. Attacks on that camp also took place.

'We arrived in Amritsar on 14 September. My sister's husband was already there. We learnt that a brother-in-law of ours who lived in a nearby village, Gopa Rai, near Khalsa College, outside Amritsar was planning to go next day to our village to find out what had happened to us. He was a *subedar* in the army and was going to bring us in a military truck. My mother and father wanted to stop him since we were already in Amritsar. They left on foot early morning at around 4 o'clock. On the way they met a Baman (Brahmin) who ran a medical clinic. He asked them, "Who are you and where are you going?" My father told him that they had come from Pakistan and were on the way to the house of Lal Shah [Shahs are Hindu moneylenders]. He advised my parents not to walk on the Grand Trunk Road because the Pakistan military were patrolling it. They should take a path going through the fields. They followed his advice. It was a trap. It led them to a place where four Sikh Jats were waiting for them. They ordered them to hand over whatever was in their possession. They had only seven rupees with them. They took the money but realising that their crime would be detected because Lal Shah was a well-known man, they killed them.'

At this point Mr Tandon burst into tears. His wife and daughters also began to cry. I decided to stop the interview.

Gujranwala

Gujranwala town and district were overwhelmingly populated by Muslims, who made up 70.40 per cent of the population; Hindus and Sikhs together formed 22.70 per cent. Gujranwala was an important town from the Sikh historical point of view, as it was the birthplace of the last indigenous ruler of the Punjab, Maharaja Ranjit Singh. In more contemporary terms, Gujranwala represented the same socio-economic pattern as prevailed elsewhere in the Punjab. Entrepreneurial interests and trade in general were in the hands of the non-Muslims.

Hafiz Taqi-ud-din, who was a resident of Gujranwala, saw spurts of communal violence throughout the period beginning from March 1947. In July, the town was declared disturbed, and after 15 August arson and killing escalated quickly and Hindus and Sikhs were forced to flee. The Khosla and SGPC reports mention the murder of Dr Tej Bhan and his family by the police. Taqi-ud-din provided the details of that murder in which the key person, Chaudhri Ilam Din, who was then *thanedar*, described the chain of events that led to the murder of the Bhan family. According to Ilam Din, he along with a constable had gone to investigate if weapons had been stored in the house. They did not find any. However, a number of misunderstandings occurred, including the emergence of a rumour that he and the constable had been killed. It resulted in a police force attacking the house. All twelve members of the family present there on 27 August were killed (1999: 285-6). Hindus and Sikhs had no choice but flee Gujranwala.

According to Hafiz Taqi-ud-din, the trouble started when one day to a rumour spread that a mosque in Dal Bazaar, a predominantly non-Muslim area, had been set ablaze. The Hindus and Sikhs immediately announced that they had nothing to do with the fire. They made a pledge to restore the mosque completely with their own funds. Later it was discovered that a Muslim artisan, who used to dye clothes near the entrance of the mosque, had left quickly before curfew time and had failed to put out the fire in the stove after he boiled some water. It had resulted in the fire spreading to the mosque. Miscreants were active in Gujranwala, however, and they insisted that the fire was a result of a deliberate act of arson by the Hindus. Also, knives and long blades and other such weapons began to circulate in Gujranwala. Then one day a young Muslim supporter of the Ahrar, Sardar Shah, was found dead in a Muslim-majority area. That murder was also blamed on the non-Muslims, although no proof was provided. It resulted in a further deterioration of communal relations. The Hindus and Sikhs began to fear for their safety.

A peace committee with the Ahrar leader Pir Syed Faiz-ul-Hassan as president, and the Congress leader, Narinjan Das Bagga was set up. The Muslim League, the Akali Sikhs and the Khaksars were also members of the peace committee. One day, the body of a Muslim labourer who was an outsider, was found in Mohalla Reitanwala. The rumour quickly spread that a Muslim had been killed by the Hindus. Bagga came barefoot to the *mohalla* with his head uncovered in solemn fashion to express his grief. But people from the housetops threw bricks at him, and he died, bleeding profusely. Pir Faiz-ul-Hassan then came. He picked up the body and personally brought it back to the family of Niranjan Das Bagga. That murder broke the hearts of all decent people in Gujranwala. Pir Faiz-ul-Hassan and other nationalist Muslims took part in the cremation ceremony but from that time onwards, things got out of control. The deputy commissioner of Gujranwala at the time was Sunder Das Midha. He was later posted to Jullundur where he instigated attacks on Muslims (ibid.: 289-92).

Kidar Nath Malhotra

I met Kidar Nath Malhotra in Delhi on 14 March 2004. He had fled from Gujranwala in late August 1947 and recalled his escape in the following words:

'The police and National Guard began to roam Gujranwala after 17 August and carried out many attacks on Hindus and Sikhs. In particular, the murder of Dr Tej Bhan made the Hindus and Sikhs panic. He was a god-fearing man and used to help all communities. I think there were more than ten people in that family. Not even the old were spared. That is what broke my father's resolve to stay put. We owned a general merchant's shop in Gujranwala town. My father believed that Pakistan would not create any special problems for non-Muslims because Jinnah was an enlightened leader. Moreover, he had very good Muslim friends. They had assured him that no harm will come to us. But as a precaution he let my mother, sister and younger brother move to Jullundur where my grandparents lived. I was twenty at that time and was a student in Lahore. In August I was in Gujranwala. I too did not want to leave Gujranwala.

'I believe it was either 27 August or a day earlier or later that Dr Bhan and his family were murdered. We had shifted to a *gurdwara* where both Sikhs and Hindus had assembled in the hope of being escorted to India. It was late in the afternoon that the police, national guards and others carrying spears, axes and hatchets attacked the *gurdwara*. Some of the men inside the *gurdwara* were armed with guns but most people had either *kirpans* or nothing. Engineer Vijay Sharma, Lala Kishorilal Khanna and many other Hindus were also in the building. Everybody was praying.

'The water supply had already been cut off and the children and sick were in great distress. The women began to wail and cry loudly when the first raid took place. It was repulsed by some of the men who went out to confront the assailants. I remember a young Sikh who fought bravely but fell fighting. His dead body was brought into the *gurdwara*. Some people suggested that the women and children should be killed instead of falling into the hands of Muslims. However, nothing could be decided as others argued that we should hold on until help arrived. Some of the elders had gone to seek help from the authorities. The problem was that the Hindu and Sikh policemen had either gone to India or had been killed.

In the evening, some people managed to escape into the streets nearby. What happened to them? I have no clue, but my father was not wiling to leave the *gurdwara*. He sent a message to his friend Ramzan for help. Ramzan Chacha had gone to Kamoke some days earlier in connection with some bereavement in his family. He sent his son Javed to the *gurdwara* to fetch us, but my father insisted that I should go while he would remain in the *gurdwara*. This way, at least one of us had a 50-50 chance to live. I cried and told him that I will not leave him but he insisted that I should go. At about 7 o'clock I left the *gurdwara*. I believe only half an hour later the *gurdwara* was set ablaze and most of the people, around 150, were slain or were burnt to death. Ramzan Chacha was very angry with me and Javed why we left Manoharlal [my father] in the *gurdwara*. But nothing could be done. It was too late to save him.

'I stayed with Ramzan Chacha and his family for a few days. They were very kind in every way. I was given only vegetarian food and could drink water directly from the water pump they had at home. Being an orthodox Hindu, this was my first experience of living and eating in a Muslim home. Javed and I became very close. He was a few years younger than me. In early September, Indian military came to Gujranwala and I could accompany other refugees to Amritsar. On the way I saw many dead bodies. The road between Wagah and Amritsar was littered with dead bodies. They must have been Muslims, I suppose. I came to Jullundur where the rest of the family was already living. There were still Muslims living in Jullundur at that time, but most of the Muslim *mohallas* were deserted. It was clear that they had also suffered greatly. We had to struggle very hard to make a living. I gave up my studies and opened a general merchant's shop in Jullundur. My mother could not recover from the shock of losing her husband. She died in 1950. My brother and sister live in Jullundur, but I moved to Delhi where my son and daughter now live. Often times I think of Gujranwala, our house and the neighbourhood where Ramzan Chacha lived. I am eighty-one now but Javed should be seventy-nine or seventy-eight. I always remember that family in my prayers.'

Sudharshan Kumar Kapur

'I was born on 31 July 1931. My family is originally from Jalalpur Jattan in district Gujrat. On 14 March 1947 we left our hometown which had a population of 17,000, one-third of which were Hindus and the rest were Muslims. My father was informed by a Muslim friend, Muhammad Husain Dar, that an attack on Jalalpur Jattan was imminent. That attack never took place in March; it did in August. I was then preparing for my matriculation examinations but we had to abandon our home and flee for safety. We left for Akalgarh in Gujranwala district where my maternal grandparents lived. We lived there for five months. In the first week of August, Muslims attacked the Hindus. They burnt and looted and also attacked the neighbouring hamlet of Ram Nagar, forcing the entire Hindu population to flee. The Hindus sought refuge in the Akalgarh Arya Samaj Mandir. The local Hindus and Sikhs offered all the help they could. The prominent Muslims of the town assured them full security of life and urged them not to leave under any circumstances. The Hindus and Sikhs of Akalgarh gathered at the Sikh temple and made a pledge that they would not leave the place. However, they gave us the liberty and exempted us from the pledge as we did not belong to the place. We were allowed to go anywhere we liked.

'On 14 August I was present at the function organised in the Akalgarh Municipal Committee compound, when the Pakistan flag was unfurled atop the building to celebrate the creation of Pakistan. On 18 August we learnt that rioting had started in Gujranwala and in my hometown, Jalalpur Jattan. More than 100 Hindus were killed. I am grateful to Dar Chacha whose warning saved us and we had left Jalalpur Jattan in time. He was a fine singer of *naats* (Islamic sacred songs). On 22 August we boarded a truck escorted by Dogra troops, and thus began a long and arduous journey to the Indian border. We stayed in Lahore for a few days and then crossed the border into India. I later learnt from Badri Nath Kapur, the famous lexicographer of Hindi whose family was from Akalgarh, that the Hindus and Sikhs in that town were attacked and killed almost to the last man on 7 September 1947. In East Punjab we saw thousands of Muslims killed with the same degree of brutality.'

Massacre on train at Kamoke

Attacks on trains had already started in March 1947, killing dozens of people. The attacks escalated from the beginning of August, and by 14 August, the outrages had already claimed thousands of lives. I was told by a retired senior Pakistani army officer that he saw dead bodies on a train bound for India in early 1948, but mostly, towards the end of November 1947, such attacks had come down drastically. One of the worst massacres of Hindus and Muslims took place at Kamoke on 25 and 26 September. Earlier in this chapter, Kaleb Ali Sheikh was quoted as mentioning that his father, who served in the railway police came home and talked about the massacres at Kamoke. *The Tribune*, which had moved to East Punjab from Lahore, reported that outrage on 1 October 1947 and gave the date of the event as 30 September, which is incorrect. Both the Khosla and SGPC reports mention it. Anyhow, that train had started from Pind Dadan Khan, a hamlet in the Jhelum district for India. It was attacked at Kamoke in the Gujranwala district. Out of 3,500 Hindus and Sikhs on the train, only 150 survived the carnage, according to *The Tribune*. *The Tribune* of 2 October quotes survivors as saying that the train was taken to the shed for washing rather than continuing on to Lahore. I met Mrs Savitri Dutt-Chibber in Noida, outside Delhi on 29 March 2004. She told me that she had relatives in Pind Dadan Khan. Many of them, including her aunt and her husband, were on that train; none survived the attack.

The Khosla report takes up the Kamoke massacre, too. It gives an estimate of the number of casualties that is lower than that provided by *The Tribune*. According to the report, six hundred women and girls were abducted by the marauders (1989: 151-2). The Punjab police abstract of intelligence dated 27 September 1947, meanwhile, notes: 'At Kamoke, near Gujranwala, 408 Hindus and Sikhs were killed; 50 seriously injured and 537 slightly injured. ... A large number of women are reported to have been abducted also'(*Disturbances in the Punjab* 1995: 384). The same report mentions that Sikhs crossed the border and attacked Muslims in Kasur and other places. News had also been received of Muslim women being abducted by *jathas* from across the border while the Officer Commanding Major Daljit Singh, did nothing to prevent it (ibid.: 384-5).

An eyewitness account

A senior Pakistani official, who requested anonymity, gave the following account of the massacre at Kamoke:

'My father stayed behind in Delhi as he was involved in the negotiations of the Partition Council headed by Mountbatten. We and some six other Pakistani families lived near the Palam Airport. The Baluch Regiment had been assigned the task of guarding that area, but one day my father noticed that Dogra and Gurkha troops had replaced them. That made him apprehensive. In the evening a mob shouting angry slogans descended upon our area. We had no firearms with us. My father and my elder brother, who was 14, went out armed only with sticks. The rest of the family was told to hide under the beds. Fortunately, the mob decided not to attack but next day, my father met Viceroy Mountbatten and told him that while he would stay on, his family must be sent to Pakistan.

'So we were put in a chartered plane. When the pilot, an Englishman, learnt that our family was originally from Jullundur he brought the plane quite low and said, "Look, what you people are doing to each other."

Down below the scene was horrific. Dead bodies were lying all over. Houses were burning. It was a shocking sight. Anyhow, we landed in Lahore, where we stayed for a few days. Then we were sent by train to Rawalpindi.

'We were in a compartment all by ourselves. The doors had been locked from inside so that intruders could be kept away. On the way, the train stopped at Kamoke, some 50 kilometres north of Lahore. My mother lifted the blinds of one of the windows and out there was another ghastly scene. I particularly remember a young woman in pink clothes lying just outside the train. She looked like a new bride. She had been murdered mercilessly. Hindu and Sikh passengers of a train coming from upper Punjab had been slaughtered. Dead bodies were lying all round. My father got down and by chance met his cousin who was a police superintendent and posted there. His cousin told him that the central cabinet had issued orders that the train had to be stopped and the non-Muslims killed because that was the only way to stop the bloodbath of Muslims that was taking place in East Punjab. From what I have heard, after that, trains coming from East Punjab to Pakistan were not attacked by Hindus and Sikhs.'

'Later, at Jhelum I saw with my own eyes a massacre going on. Hindu and Sikh men, women and children were being pursued by men armed with long knives, spears and other metal objects. The victims were crying and shrieking loudly. It was a horrible sight.'

An email about Wazirabad

Wazirabad is a town in Gujranwala district. It was famous before Partition for the manufacture of different types of knives. The factory owners were mainly Hindus. At the time of Partition, the Hindu and Sikh minority of Wazirabad came under heavy attack. The notorious slaughter of the Hindu and Sikh passengers on the train that left Wazirabad for Sialkot demonstrated that, as everywhere, there were instances when friendship and close ties helped save innocent lives. I was contacted by an email dated 14 December 2004 by Davender Bhardwaj, who gave me an account of how his grandfather escaped from that town:

'My *nanaji* (maternal grandfather) Pandit Basant Ram was a leading personality of Wazirabad. He was active in the municipality and was one of the wealthiest men in Wazirabad. His life was saved by a loyal Muslim friend. He had to take a circuitous route through Jammu and Kashmir state and his feet were swollen and ulcerated when he arrived in Jammu. The same friend who saved him from the murderous mobs sent all the things to him from Wazirabad that had not been burnt when his house and the whole *galli* (street) where Hindus lived was set on fire. My grandfather continued to write to his friends in Wazirabad. This continued until he died. He would almost everyday talk about Wazirabad. In some sense, time had stopped moving for him and mentally and emotionally he was always in his old town.'

Davender Bhardwaj then put me in contact with a Pakistani in Lahore who knew about that story and even knew the family that had helped Pandit Basant Ram escape safely to India. The person in question turned out to be an old acquaintance that I had met in Stockholm many years ago. Akram Warraich had returned to Pakistan and was active in Punjabi cultural and literary activities. He sent me the following information dated 22 December 2004:

'There are thousands of Partition stories. Mistri Naseer saved the life of Panditji. Mistri Sahib died some years ago but his son, who is blind, knows about the friendship between Pandit Basant Ram and his father. Although blind he is famous in Wazirabad as a diehard activist of the Pakistan People's Party. He takes part in demonstrations against dictatorship and army rule. He is not afraid of getting beaten by the police. You will have to interview him for getting the details about how his father helped save the life of Panditji.'

Sialkot

The ancient town of Sialkot had a clear Muslim majority, although Hindus and Sikhs were prominent in the economic activity of the town, especially in the manufacture of sports goods. According to the 1941 census, the district as a whole had a total population slightly less than 1.2 millon, with Muslims comprising 62.90 per cent of the population; Hindus, 19.41 per cent; and Sikhs, 11.71 per cent. As elsewhere, relations between Muslims and non-Muslims were cordial in the district but from mid-August onwards, rioting broke out and several deaths took place, mainly of Hindus and Sikhs (Khosla, 1989: 142-6; SGPC, 1991). Sialkot is on the border with Jammu and received a very large number of refugees from Jammu and Kashmir state during the partition rioting. I met an elderly Sikh named Sampuran Singh, once a resident of Sialkot city, in Delhi on 9 March 2004. He gave me the following story about what happened in Sialkot:

'I was born in 1921 in Sialkot into a Sikh family belonging to the Khatri subcaste of Sachdev. I and my family took refuge in Gurdwara Baoli Sahib where many Sikhs had assembled when the trouble began. The attack took place after Pakistan had come into being. We had decided to stay on in Sialkot. My father was a postman and was highly respected by all communities. He also had a traditional medicine that he gave free to everyone who had toothache. So, he was a much-sought-after person. The attack was led by the police and some of the participants were wearing uniforms of the Muslim League National Guard. They chanted slogans such as "*Allah-ho-Akbar*" (God is great) and "*Ya, Ali madad*" [O saint of warriors, Ali, help us]. The Sikhs also shouted slogans in return but we were heavily outnumbered and surrounded from all sides. We resisted but the fire and gunshots proved too overwhelming. Some people started to run out of the *gurdwara*. My father and I managed to come out; we were holding hands as my father was old and could not run fast and neither could my mother and sisters. Some of the men came charging towards us but then one of the *badmashes*, whose name was probably Bashira, shouted, "Don't kill them. They are under my protection". The crowd stopped. He happened to be from our area and once my father had provided him with medicine to ease his toothache. That saved our lives, but my mother and sisters were burnt to death. I still think of my mother. She loved me very much. She was very pious and had many Muslim friends too. My youngest sister was going to be married in the winter while the younger one was going to school. They all died. At least fifty people died in that attack.

'We stayed in a camp for several months. Finally the military came and escorted us to Jammu in the beginning of November. My father was too heartbroken and could never overcome the grief of losing his wife and daughters. He lived for another ten years. I married rather late and then moved to Delhi. Now we have Muslims as neighbours in Delhi. They are good people and we have polite relations, but the scar on my heart will never be healed. I try not to tell my children what happened; I believe they are not even interested in knowing about the past.'

Colonel (Retd) Hans Raj Chopra

The Khosla and SGPC reports describe several incidents of harrowing attacks on Hindus and Sikhs fleeing from Sialkot. In particular, attacks on trains figure prominently among their accounts. I was able to track down an eyewitness to one such attack, where the train from Wazirabad arrived in Sialkot drenched in blood, and packed with mutilated bodies. Colonel Chopra described to me in an interview recorded at his residence in Defence Colony, Delhi, on 31 March 2004, what happened. He also told me of his escape from Sialkot:

'I belong to the 16th Punjab Regiment [the troops were Punjabi Mussalmans]. We served in Burma during the Second World War. In March 1947 I was posted in Rawalpindi. The rioting there was the first indication that things were not all right. Then I was sent to Sialkot where in August things got out of hand. Hundreds of deaths took place, mostly of Hindus and Sikhs but there were counter-attacks on Muslims too and naturally, some of them died. Even in the cantonment area some incidents took place. My superior officer, an Englishman, summoned me at about twelve in the night and told me that he had appointed me camp commander for the Hindu and Sikh refugees that were collecting in the refugee camps. I saw with my own eyes [on 14 August] a train derailed some two or three kilometres from Sialkot. It had left Wazirabad with hundreds of Hindus and Sikhs who were hoping to reach Jammu via Sialkot. It was a horrible sight. Blood was oozing out of all the carriages which were packed with dead bodies. I must say the shock I received seeing such a slaughter was very different from the killings that took place in Burma during the war. My uncle Chet Ram Chopra was governor of Jammu. I told him that I was sending him refugees.

'My wife Pushpa Hans (famous Punjabi folk singer) wanted me to opt for Pakistan because her roots were in Lahore and she believed that things would return to normal as soon as both governments took full charge; but a Muslim friend warned me that some gangsters had planned to kill me and I could not be sure that my life would be safe in the cantonment area. I took up this issue with my superior officer who said that instead of opting for either India or Pakistan I should quietly cross the border into Jammu in order to save my life. He provided me escort to the Sialkot–Jammu border and then I had to make my way to Jammu. I reported for duty at the Indian military base there. They had no papers about my opting for India, but I was able to persuade them to accept me and thus I rejoined the army in India. The British did not play any dirty game. They tried their best to maintain order but by the middle of August the situation was out of control and nothing could be done to prevent the criminals from looting and killing hapless, unarmed ordinary people.'

Sialkot rural areas

In early January 2005, I met several displaced families from the Sialkot rural areas settled in Batala and Gurdaspur. Some had crossed the border into India and reached Jammu without any loss of life; others were not as fortunate. Here is an account dated 5 January 2005 by Bhagwan Das, office secretary of the Congress party, Batala:

'I was born in Mian Harpal village, *tahsil* Pasrur, *thana* Kila Soba Singh, district Sialkot. It was a big village where all communities had very good relations with one another. There were Brahmins, Khatris and Sikh Jats as well as and Muslims and Christians. Most Muslims from our village were *lohars* (blacksmiths) who worked in Lahore. The *zamindars* were Sikh Jats. We are Ramdasias. My father, Chaudhri Jagat Ram, was in the Congress and took part in its activities. This was unusual in villages, but political awareness had started making an impact on villagers too. I used to go to school, which was some five kilometres from our village. It was up to the fourth class. The teachers were either Brahmins or *maulvis*. Both were very good and treated us with affection and care. When the trouble started the Hindus and Sikhs of the village took a pledge that if the attackers were from their community they would face them first and the Muslims said that if the attackers were Muslims they would face them first. First the rumour spread that Sikh *jathas* were heading towards our village. So, Hindus and Sikhs from our village went forward to meet them but it proved to be false rumour. On the contrary they were ambushed at Pahgowal, a village nearby, and many were killed. Some ran away into the fields. Then the Sikhs also went out to attack, but the Muslims were strong and they returned to the village. One day a large group of people attacked our village. Some of the bad characters from our village had actually invited the raiders. One of them was Abdul, the *teli* (oil presser).

'The leader of the raiders was Mehdi Shah of Alipur Syedan, a big and prominent Muslim village in that area. He killed many Hindus and Sikhs. The other Shahs of Alipur Syedan were good people. Another *badmash* who took part in the raid was Kaim Barwala of Chak Qureshian. The attackers came riding horses. The Muslims from our village tried to prevent the attack but were overwhelmed. Many Hindus and Sikhs were killed. Mehdi Shah killed most of the people. Two Sikhs managed to escape and contacted the Indian military stationed at Krawale. It is on the canal on the Pakistan side. The Indian military then came and brought us to Krawale. Then women, the old and the children came in trucks. Mostly Sikhs were killed, some 150 from our village. A few women and children were also killed.'

Richpal Singh

I visited Adampur, a village near Sirhind, Fatehgarh Sahib district (formerly in Patiala state) to find out how the people on the other side remembered a notorious carnage of Muslims in that village which I had recorded with Chaudhri Roshan Din in Kallar Syedan, Rawalpindi district, in December 2004. Hitesh Gosain and Virender Singh were with me. Many Sikhs from Sialkot had settled in large numbers in the village although the locals were still around. The *sarpanch* (headman) of the village, Richpal Singh, told us the following story:

'I was born in a village near Sialkot. While disturbances elsewhere had taken a great toll of life, in our area things remained peaceful until the middle of September. There was an attack from outside, but young Muslim men from our village came and formed a wall and told the raiders that first they should kill them before the Sikhs and Hindus could be harmed. That warded off the danger and nobody dared come back. They then took us to the refugee camp at Daska *tahsil*. We left the camp in early October. The Sikh and Hindu population of some 80 85 villages formed the caravan, which trekked all the way towards the border near Jammu. People from our village and some other friendly Muslims accompanied us till we safely crossed the border. Among them I remember the names of Chaudhri Fateh Dad and his son Sadiq, Ghulam Hassan Cheema and Fateh Din Maitla. They were brave men who protected us like brothers. Many of them were Jats like us and that must have played some role, but this was not true everywhere. From what I remember, nobody was killed. We must have been more than 20,000 people who crossed the border into India. We were first sent to Kapurthala and then allotted land here in Adampur. What I saw on this side, I cannot narrate. It was a slaughter.'

References

Anand, S. *Lahore: Portrait of a Lost City,* Lahore: Vanguard Books, 1998.

Jeffrey, Robin. 'The Punjab Boundary Force and the Problem of Order: August 1947', *Modern Asian Studies, vol. VIII, No. 4*, 1974.

Khosla, Gopal Das. *Stern Reckoning: A Survey of the Events Leading Up To and Following the Partition of India,* New Delhi: Oxford University Press, 1989.

Mittal, G. *Lahore ka jo Zikr kiya: Aap Biti* (Remembering Lahore: An Autobiography), Lahore: Book Home, 2003.

Nevile, Pran. *Lahore A Sentimental Journey*, Delhi and Karachi: Allied Publishers Ltd, 1993.

Taqi-ud-din, H. *Tarikh ki Adalat Mein, (In the Court Room of History),* Gujranwala: Jeenay Do Publications, 1999.

Singh, Kirpal. *The Partition of the Punjab*, Patiala: Punjabi University, 1989

Talib, S. Gurbachan, *Muslim League Attack on Sikhs and Hindus in the Punjab 1947,* New Delhi: Voice of India 1991.

Shafique, Khurram Ali (compiler). *The Chronicle of Pakistan,* Available online at: http://www.therepublicofrumi.com/chronicle 1947_09.htm, 13 December 2010.

Khan, Fazal Muqeem Khan (Major-General). *The Story of the Pakistan Army,* Karachi, Lahore: Oxford University Press, 1964.

Official documents

Disturbances in the Punjab, Islamabad: National Documentation Centre, 1995.

Interviews

Som Anand, Delhi, 18 October 1999
Rattan Chand, Delhi, 19 October 1999
Ram Parkash Kapur, Delhi, 20 October 1999
Dr Prem Sobti, Personal Physician to the President of India, Delhi, 31 October 2001
Mrs Kanta Singh Luthra, Salem, Oregon, 15 July 2002
Professor Emeritus Shaukat Ali, Mansfield, Massachusetts, 29 July 2002
Sardar Shaukat Ali, Lahore, 3 May 2003
Kevel Krishan Tulli, New Delhi, 8 March 2004; clarifications via telephone on 30 January 2006
Sampuran Singh Sachdev, Delhi, 9 March 2004
Kidar Nath Malhohtra, Delhi, 10 March 2004
Pyara Singh Naulakh, Kishanpura Kalan, district Moga, East Punjab, 18 March 2004
Gurbachan Singh Tandon, Noida, 29 March 2004
Mrs Savitri Dutt-Chibber, Noida, 29 March 2004
Colonel Hans Raj Chopra, Delhi, 31 March 2004
Bhagwan Das, Batala, 3 December 2004
Davender Bhardwaj, email from USA, 14 December 2004
Kaleb Ali Sheikh, Lahore, 25 December 2004
Akram Warraich, email from Lahore, 22 December 2004
Sardul Singh Virk, Lakhmari, district Kurukshestra, Haryana, 8 January 2005
Faqir Singh Virk, Lakhmari, district Kurukshestra January 8, 2005
Shamsherjit Singh Virk, Lakhmari, district Kurukshestra, 8 January 2005
Kirpal Singh, Chandigarh 2 January 2005
Richpal Singh, Adampur, 28 November 2005
Chaudhri Nazir Ahmed Virk, Sheikhupura, 30 December 2005
Sudharshan Kumar Kapur, Old Gargaon, outside Delhi Delhi, 1 December 2005
Chaudhri Tawwakullah Virk, Sheikhupura, 30 December 2005
Chaudhri Anwar Aziz, Lahore, 15 December 2006

Satyendra Kumar, New Delhi, 17 March 2013
Visharda Hoon, Chennai, 13 May 2013
Upendra Kumar Pandit, Amsterdam, 12 July 2014

15

RAWALPINDI DIVISION

RAWALPINDI DIVISION INCLUDED THE NORTHERN AND NORTH-western districts of Gujrat, Shahpur, Jhelum, Rawalpindi, Attock (Campbellpur) and Mianwali districts. It was overwhelmingly Muslim; Hindus and Sikhs together made up only fourteen per cent of its population. It was awarded to Pakistan. I could collect stories from some of its districts.

Rawalpindi city

Although Rawalpindi city and the surrounding rural areas witnessed some of the most vicious communal clashes in March 1947, which in the case of the villages were essentially one-sided attacks on Sikh villages, the situation eventually stabilised. In August, however, the situation again deteriorated although, as noted by the Khosla report, the Deputy Commissioner Sheikh Anwar-ul-Haq 'made a gallant attempt to control the situation'. Unfortunately, noted the report, he received no assistance from his subordinates or the police (1989: 196). Muhammad Feroz Dar, whose story about the situation in Rawalpindi was quoted in earlier chapters, remembered the period of July to September 1947 as particularly traumatic for a boy of eleven.

Muhammad Feroz Dar

'It was either late July or early August that unbridled killing and looting escalated again in Rawalpindi. We had shifted from the officer colony into the railway workers' quarters where the majority were Muslims. One day, in the morning, I went to buy milk. Some boys had gathered and told me that a number of people had been gruesomely murdered and the dead bodies were lying some 200 metres from the mosque in the Railway Colony. It was a most shocking sight, something I had never seen before and never again afterwards. The skulls of small infants had been smashed against the walls. The bodies of the grown-ups had been torn open or hacked to pieces.

'Then on the way back I saw that a house in the officers' colony belonging to two Hindu brothers, Om and Parkash, who were prominent railway athletes, had been set ablaze. They and their families were being escorted away by a British police officer. Their Muslim friends, Hanif, Raza and Bau Rafi, who were also athletes, were standing and watching that sad situation. They said that they had tried to prevent the *goondas* from carrying out that outrage. It was also another shock for me.

'Thousands of Muslim refugees began to arrive in Rawalpindi from India. They had been treated most brutally. The loss of life among them was also very high, we were told. The railway department arranged for Hindus and Sikhs to leave for India and special trains were arranged for the massive flight from Rawalpindi for the non-Muslims. I don't remember if anyone that we knew from among the Hindus and Sikhs ever visited Rawalpindi again. But then I have been away from Pakistan for more than forty years.'

Kamla Sethi

'My father Sir Gokul Chand Narang was the Hindu Mahasabha leader of the Punjab. I was married to an army officer in 1937. We were posted in different places. He was posted to Rawalpindi in 1945, where we lived till 3 October 1947. During those two years, one could sense that there was some tension in the air but in the military bungalows, hardly anything unusual was ever noticed. The servants used to come back with stories of angry agitations and, occasionally, of communal violence. I remember, in March, for a while Rawalpindi was disturbed and Hindus and Sikhs were subjected to extreme violence by Muslim mobs, especially in the villages but we never felt threatened in the cantonment area. Then Partition happened and my husband who had opted for India was posted to Delhi, but the actual transfers took place much later.

'There was so much camaraderie. An officer, Gulsher Ali Noon had already moved to Pakistan from some posting in India. He and his family and we shared the same house for several months. They had half the portion and we the other half. The British were also here in large numbers. A lot of killing took place in Rawalpindi again in August and later. One of our British friends, Bill Graham, with whom we played bridge at the club, knocked vigorously at our door late one evening. Some miscreants had attacked houses in the neighbourhood, he reported, and asked if we needed help. That was the only time when we felt insecure. The partition of the Punjab was such a huge tragedy for all Punjabis. It was only traditional lower-middle-class Hindus who practised untouchability against Muslims. Among the educated classes such ideas had been abandoned for a long time. My father had warned in a speech in 1932 that a partition of India would result in heavy loss of life for all communities. That is exactly what happened.'

Bhisham Kumar Bakshi

'We lived in Rawalpindi on Saidpur Road. I was eleven in August 1947. The March riots were intense. In the city the population of Muslims and Hindu–Sikhs was 50–50. I was in school in Lal Kurti on that day. A mob from the villages around came towards us but our *mohalla* was not attacked. Those riots lasted for some ten days. Then we went to Jammu where my maternal grandparents lived, and stayed there for a couple of months. The Sikhs left first while Hindus stayed on. Then, Muslims from Delhi and other areas started coming to Rawalpindi. My father Radha Krishan Bakhshi opted for Pakistan. He believed we would stay on. My *dadi* (paternal grandmother) was in our ancestral village, Mattor. Our Muslim neighbours in the village did not allow any attackers to touch her. Then after Pakistan came into being, she was put into a bus and sent to Rawalpindi. In 1986 when I visited our village, the old people asked if she had arrived in Rawalpindi safely. Nobody from our family was killed. The Khaksars of Rawalpindi played a very glorious role in saving Hindus and Sikhs during the riots.

'Dr Budh Singh, a doctor, had chartered a plane on 29 August. My father first sent me to Delhi in that plane. Next my sister came in a train along with Sikh soldiers. It took them some ten–twelve days to reach Ambala. My father came in October. I and my mother and my sister were in Meerut. We did not know who was where. It was a very rainy year. Then we heard about each other on the radio and met in the middle of October.

'My father was a very secular and enlightened person. He began having a well dug in our village. His Brahmin relatives came and said that only Brahmins should draw water from it. When my father heard that he ordered the digging to be stopped and had the well filled with earth. That made them change their minds, and later the well was used by everyone in the village – Hindus, Muslims and Sikhs. That well is still there. I went in 1992 to Rawalpindi with my wife. Our *tonga*-driver Khan Bahadur was a very good man. We made enquiries about him but he had died many years earlier. His younger brother Ramzan was still alive. He was my very close friend from childhood. Ramzan collected all his relatives and arranged a big feast for us. Then he told all his relatives:

"These people who are our guests are from a very high class Hindu family. One day I was waiting outside in the verandah for this gentleman who is my friend. His father came and took me in and we both drank tea together. This shows that they were very good people."

'I told my wife, "Look, these people must have felt very bad when Hindus practised untouchability against them". Hindu attitudes played a very big role in embittering relations. The Muslims accepted untouchability gracefully. In 1986 we went to the village, but not in 1991–92 because we did not have a visa to go to the village. General Shah Nawaz Khan of the Indian National Army was from our village and was our neighbour.'

Rawalpindi rural areas

Following the Punjab riots, huge numbers of Sikhs from Campbellpur, Rawalpindi, and Jhelum divisions shifted to central and eastern Punjab. Those who were still around in small pockets began to leave quietly, and by August 1947, most of them had been evacuated. Those who remained were attacked again. The survivors fled, though the journey was full of hazards on the way to East Punjab.

Gujrat

Gujrat had an overwhelming Muslim majority of 85.58 per cent while Hindus and Sikhs made up 14 per cent of its population. In Gujrat town, most shops and businesses were owned by Hindus though some Sikhs also were shopkeepers and businessmen. The March killings of Sikhs and Hindus had affected mainly the Rawalpindi district, and to some extent Jhelum too. From mid-August 1947, however, there was a sharp escalation in the attacks on non-Muslims in Gujrat as well. Several elderly men admitted that they took part in those attacks. The following account provides a vivid picture of the events:

Colonel (Retd) Nadir Ali

'Our family was always a supporter of the Congress party in Gujrat. It is a misconception that Muslims were averse to joining the Congress party. Those who believed in the freedom of India were either in the Congress party or some Islamic movement such as the Ahrar or Khaksars. Some were, of course, influenced by Communism. The Congress party in Gujrat had built quite a network in which Hindus, Muslims and even some Sikhs were active. My father was an active member of the Congress. The Muslim League was from the very beginning prone to extreme slogan-mongering and people who in the past were loyal to the British Raj became Muslim Leaguers and wanted a separate state for Muslims. The first round of mass mobilisation that took place in Gujrat was in January 1947. It resulted in the communal poison spreading in all sections of society. But violent activities against non-Muslims started only a few days before Partition. I remember the main shopping bazaar in the town being attacked by hoodlums. It was almost entirely owned by Hindus. They were honest and very civilised people. Among those who led the attacks was Thurre Shah a Syed from Moinuddinpur. He stabbed a number of Hindus and looted their shops. They formed gangs and waylaid innocent non-Muslims fleeing from Gujrat. They even raided the town of Jalalpur Jattan where Hindus were killed in large numbers. None of the criminals involved in those crimes was ever put to trial.'

Mahinder Nath Khanna

I met an elderly Hindu gentleman in the lobby of the Mohan Hotel in Amritsar on 3 January 2005. He happened to hail from Gujrat. What he narrated to me was a most shocking account of the massacre of Hindus and Sikhs in Gujrat in August 1947:

'I was born in Gujrat on 30 May 1926. My father had a shop in the main bazaar. We sold cloth but also had a side-business in moneylending. Most of the shops were owned by Hindu Khatris. My father suffered from asthma. We were a large family. My paternal grandparents lived with us. We were six children; three boys and three girls. My mother's sister had been widowed and she also lived with us. We were, however, a fairly prosperous family. We had relatives living in the villages close to Gujrat and my *mama* worked in the revenue department in Gujrat but his house was in another part of town. Our relations with the Muslims were very good. In fact, our main customers were Muslims and there was never a problem in dealing with them. I went to the local government school. Children from all the communities studied together. The first time any tension was felt was when the Muslim League held its meeting in Lahore in 1940. I remember it was discussed in the bazaar and some people were apprehensive that if a Muslim state came into being their businesses and lives would not be safe. But nobody panicked and life went on as usual.

'A young Muslim girl used to go past our shop. Although she wore a *burqa*, occasionally she would let her face be visible. She was very beautiful and she too noticed that I always looked at her. I still think of her sometimes. I think her parents were not in good health because her mother limped while her father walked with the help of a cane. They could not be very well-off, I thought. But in those days there was no question of communicating with a girl who was not a close relative. One could not even talk to a Hindu girl, so there was no question of a Hindu and a Muslim of the opposite sex talking to each other.

'In late January 1947, the Muslims began a mass agitation in Gujrat. Although no violence was involved, the agitators shouted angry slogans and threatened to impose Islamic laws on Hindus and Sikhs. I remember that caused great concern among the Hindus. It was even decided that the main Hindu temple should be guarded against any attack. In the bazaar we were in the majority, but a feeling of insecurity began to grow. Some people even sold their shops and left to live with relatives elsewhere but we had all our relatives in Gujrat. My father used to worry a lot since I was the eldest child. My youngest sister was actually only seven in 1947. However, we had nowhere to go and that option was not discussed at home.

'In July some acts of violence took place and a rumour went round that Muslims were about to attack us. Then in August, a few days before Independence, it was announced that an assault had occurred in the bazaar. Some shopkeepers were killed. That created real panic. But my father suffered from asthma and my grandmother was too old and sick. That made it difficult for us to go anywhere else. Most Hindus started leaving after the first attack. Then two days after Eid [Wednesday, 20 August] our house was attacked. It was a Hindu area but most people had left and few able-bodied men were there to protect us. The attackers were *goondas* from the area. They were all known to us but on that day they were in a nasty mood.

'My father went out to talk to them. They wanted us to surrender all our gold and silver and the money we had. My father agreed to hand over everything provided they did not harm us. They told us to leave immediately. We started walking towards the railway station which was quite some distance. The *goondas* accompanied us for a while but then turned back to loot other properties. On the way some other Hindus and Sikhs joined us. Gujrat was burning and there were dead bodies lying all around. My grandmother could not walk and therefore decided to stay at the temple. My grandfather also refused to leave but told us to go on. My father cried and pleaded with them to try to walk but they simply could not.

'Just before we reached the railway station a mob carrying spears and swords and shouting "*Ya Ali, Ya Ali*" pounced upon the Hindus and Sikhs, who were a group of at least 500. We had nothing to protect ourselves with. I saw my father being struck with a spear. My mother went to help him but someone hit her on the head with a hammer. I saw her skull burst open as she fell. I ran towards the railway station. Some others also succeeded but my brothers and sisters and most other children, women and the old could not make it. There was real butchery that took place that day in Gujrat.

'Some of us, mostly young men, got together and occupied a carriage of a train that had pulled in from the north. It was going to Lahore. Fortunately, some Englishmen were also on that train. Therefore it could safely get to Lahore without being attacked. At Lahore railway station things were in bad shape but we met some Gurkha soldiers who escorted us to the DAV College where a camp had been set up to help refugees. The conditions in the camp were appalling. Almost everyone had lost a close relative and it seemed we were all gathered at a funeral. We stayed in Lahore until the first week of September. Everyday I would go around asking if someone from Gujrat had arrived. Some families did arrive but nobody from my immediate family was among them. I later learnt that the Hindu temple where my grandparents had taken refuge was burnt down and all the people inside were killed.

'We arrived in Amritsar where the Muslims were on the receiving end. There was great pain inside all of us. Most of us had lost our near and dear ones. Then someone told us that it was our duty to take revenge on the Muslims. I must admit that I and many others from the Gujrat group took part in attacks on Muslims. How many did we kill? I think I stopped counting after I had struck the first victim with an axe. It is now a long time since all that happened. It was quite unnecessary but it happened. I never married because I could never overcome my grief and sorrow. My life was shattered in August 1947.'

Gujrat rural areas

Jagan Nath

'I was born in 1926 in a village called Keerowal which was located west of Gujrat town. Our father had a cloth shop in the main bazaar. There were 30 Hindu families; the rest were Syed Muslims. We had excellent relations with them. The whole village was one big family in which all communities celebrated each others' festive occasions and took part in each others' joys and sorrows. Although we heard of trouble in Gujrat there was no trace of any tension in the village. But suddenly on the occasion of Eid, which was on Monday, 18 August it was announced that Sikh *jathas* were coming to attack the Muslims. This was an excuse to attack us. We had the shops on rent but the owners were Muslims. When the attack took place the Hindus ran away and left their shops unlocked. Those who attacked our village were outsiders. The people from the village did not attack us. The Syeds did not attack us. When it became bad, they asked us to become Muslims. We did so for a few days but then when the military came we were taken to the camp in Gujrat town. Nobody in my immediate family was killed. We left Gujrat on 25 September. The journey was slow and very tiring. We spent a night in Gujranwala. Then another by the canal. An army captain was with us.

'He brought us to Nanakana Sahib were we stayed for two nights. Then for a few days we stayed in the Lahore DAV College. The RSS was present in the camp and provided us with food and other help. We finally arrived in Amritsar on 2 October. The *lambardar* of our village was Ghulam Qadir. Muzammil Shah and Ghaus Shah were my good friends. They were Sunnis. Ours was a Sunni village. I still remember the streets of the village. I had a friend Bashir Ahmed who was from the *nai* (barber) *biradari*. He used to write to me. The attack on the Hindus was instigated by the *maulvis* but those who took part in the raid were outsiders. We faced great difficulties in India but our immediate family was safe. It took a long time before we found our feet and could earn a reasonable livelihood. Keerowal is always in my thoughts. I have no grudge against Muslims. They cannot be blamed for what happened in 1947. There were bad and cruel people on both sides.'

Professor Muhammad Sharif Kunjahi

I talked to the famous Punjabi writer and poet, Professor Muhammad Sharif Kunjahi, in Gujrat on 20 April 2003 about the 1947 events in Gujrat. He provided an interesting historical sketch which provides insights into the tensions that preceded the actual Partition rioting:

'I was born on 13 October 1915 in Kunjah, which was an important marketplace in Gujrat district. People from the surrounding villages came to buy and sell goods there. We had a high school and a post office since 1903. Boys from all communities studied together in that school. Our teachers, both Hindus and Muslims, were very kind and saintly people. Kunjah was a well-knit small town. Communal influence in Kunjah started when a Sikh leader, Kharak Singh, in 1927–28 issued a statement that Sikhs should not buy meat from Muslims because it was slaughtered according to the Islamic ritual. He performed the opening ceremony of a *jhatka* meat shop where the animals were killed in one blow. It had a bad impact on communal relations. Maulvi Abdullah then opened a separate Muslim school in 1930. Hindus and Sikhs could study in this school and some did.

'After passing class twelve I searched for work but could not find any. That turned me against the British. I was attracted to the Congress party which had a presence in Gujrat as well as in Kunjah. I was also a member of the Majlis-e-Ahrar. Although mostly Hindus were in the Congress, anti-imperialist Muslims were also its members. We were instructed to go to the villages and preach liberation from colonial rule. The Congress party was opposed to untouchability but Hindus in Kunjah adhered to the pollution code. For example, there was a Hindu *halvai* (sweetmeat seller) in Kunjah and sometimes we'd go to his shop to drink *lassi* (drink made from curd). The *halvai* had separate mugs for Muslims and would wash them thoroughly after we finished drinking. I don't know how the ordinary peasants felt about it, but I resented that treatment. The Muslims were also envious of the fact that Hindus and even Sikhs were economically more advanced. They lived in brick houses while Muslims lived in mud houses.

'But deep friendships were also possible. I had a friend called Jai Chand Nayyar, who was getting married. We were to go to Wazirabad for his wedding. I said to him it is better I don't go because there I will be served food separately. He went and told his mother. She said, "Never mind about these foolish Hindu practices. Both of you will sit together and eat together and we will see what happens." That is exactly what we did. Nobody minded and so it went off well. Had the Hindus changed their habits in time, things would have been different. Now in India there is no difference. Such differences were exploited by the politicians. The British also exploited this and used such contradictions.

'Baba Sunder Das was the only doctor in Kunjah. He would himself go to patients and treat them. His charges were very nominal and the poor, he treated for free. But then collective madness took over at the time of partition. There were still some Hindus and Sikhs in this area when Pakistan came into being. Hordes of criminals and some from the Muslim League National Guard took part in the assaults on non-Muslims. The attack in Kunjah took place on Eid, 18 August. It was a massive attack and included burning, pillaging and killing. The *badmashes* were roaming all over here. Some women were abducted and taken away. Even Pathans from the Frontier Province came looking for booty. They committed the most heinous crimes. I can still remember totally innocent human beings being killed like cattle before my eyes. More than 500 Hindus and Sikhs must have died in Kunjah alone. Elsewhere things were as bad.

'A Brahmin, Beli Ram, gave me his keys before he left for India. He had three houses. His son came later, accompanied by the police. They had buried their gold and jewellery in those houses. He collected the gold and jewellery and left. The government agencies were responsible for sowing communal discord. They would use agents to create mischief. The Ahrar were never corrupt. It is also true that the Unionist Party helped Muslims. Partition was not inevitable.'

Professor Kunjahi died on 20 January 2007.

Syed Aftab Hassan

Another vivid account was provided by Syed Aftab Hassan, whom I interviewed in Gujrat after recording Professor Kunjahi's interview. The following are excerpts of his narration:

'I was born on 1 March 1939 in a village called Jamna near Gujrat. But by the time of Partition my father, who was a postman, had been posted in a *kasbah* (small town) called Shadiwal. It had both Hindu and Muslim inhabitants who lived in peace and amity. The Hindus also owned small businesses, which prepared *achaar* (pickles), and ghee (clarified butter) which were sold far and wide. We also had a cloth market. My father, Syed Fazal Hussain Shah, was also a Shia *imam* (prayer leader in a mosque). He was respected by all communities. He preferred to live in a Hindu-majority area and never felt threatened. The Hindus were generally very civilised, educated and peace-loving people. We lived in a rented house in the Hindu area. Among our neighbours, uncle Diwan Chand and his wife Channan Bai were very close to us. If she bought something for her son she would buy the same for me, too.

Pakistan had come into being and it was Eid day. My father had gone to lead the Eid prayers. A rumour spread that Sikhs had attacked the congregation and my father had been killed. In reaction, Muslims came out and a clash took place near the bridge of the canal nearby. Three Sikhs were killed. That night, criminals among the Muslims organised a major attack on Shadiwal. Some sixty Hindus were killed. They tried to dump the dead bodies in the canal but the animals carrying the bodies could not move because of the great weight put on them.

'My father then took charge of the situation the next day and invited the Hindus to come and stay in our house. A Muslim mob arrived and wanted all of them handed over to them. My father told them that they would have to kill him and his wife and children first. "I have given them refuge. Those we give refuge to, we never let down". Some of the attackers had covered their faces with scarves. They were actually from Shadiwal and had joined the *badmashes* just to loot. They uncovered their faces and left the mob. This resulted in the rest also leaving the village. After three days, the Hindus went back to their houses. Then the Indian Army came and they left.

'A Hindu *sadhu*, Ram Asra, who used to live near the Hindu crematorium, declared that he wanted to become a Muslim. He was accordingly named Allah Asra. One day, he was walking in the street and happened to have a ten-rupee note in his pocket. My father was distributing post at that time. Somebody killed him. We believe it was only to get the money. He was not buried. They threw him in a well that the Hindus previously used to draw water from. A Hindu, who had survived the attack when 60 of them had been killed, later wrote his story in an Indian newspaper. My father read about it and told it to us.

'Some Muslims from Haryana came and settled in Shadiwal. They brought stories of their own suffering at the hands of Hindu Jats and Sikhs. One boy told me that he was sexually assaulted at the Walton Refugee Centre by Muslims. He was more traumatised by that experience than what he had gone through while escaping from East Punjab.'

The Khosla report mentions a Muslim officer, Major Aslam, who did his duty with the utmost integrity and saved the lives of hundreds of Hindus and Sikhs in Mandi Bahuddin, which was another important trade centre in Gujrat (1989: 156).

Jhelum

This western district had an overwhelmingly Muslim majority of eighty-nine per cent. Hindus and Sikhs made up nearly eleven per cent of the population. Acts of savagery had already been perpetrated in the villages of Jhelum district in March 1947 and a refugee camp had been set up in Jhelum town at that time. Many Hindus and Sikhs had left their villages in March for safer places eastwards or had moved to Jhelum town, where a military contingent had been posted permanently. August passed somewhat peacefully but at the beginning of September violence erupted again.

Sunil Dutt

The famous Indian filmstar, Sunil Dutt, who belonged originally to the village of Khurd, some twenty kilometres from Jhelum town, told me the following on 20 October 2001 when I met him at his residence in Mumbai:

'I was born on 6 June 1929 in a small village called Khurd which was not far from Jhelum town. It had both Hindu – mainly our caste of Dutt Brahmins – as well as Muslim inhabitants and also some Sikhs. Dutts are part of the large Mujhail caste of Brahmins who believe their ancestor Rahab Sidhu Dutt was in Arabia during the tragedy of Karbala in which the Prophet's grandson Imam Hussain and his small band of followers were massacred. Rahab Dutt and his seven sons fought on the side of Imam Hussain and died fighting. Therefore, our elders throughout the ages have commemorated the Karbala tragedy and observed the rituals connected with that event even though we have remained Hindus.

'My father died when I was only five and my younger brother Som was only a baby. We were brought up by my *tayaji* (father's elder brother). Our social standing and economic conditions were otherwise good as our family were the main landowners. At the time of Partition, I was on the Indian side of the Punjab border, but the rest of my family were in the village. An army truck arrived to take Hindus from that area to the main refugee camp in Jhelum. This must have been sometime in the beginning of September or perhaps in the second week. All my family members boarded the truck, but *tayaji* remained behind as the feeling was that things might return to normal. Just before they left my mother informed him that she had left her gold ornaments in the house as she did not have time to collect everything. She explained where those were kept.

'Now, *tayaji* was the only Hindu left in the village. As was his practice he went to the village well where the men traditionally met and smoked the *hookah* (hubble-bubble). Things appeared to be all right. But then on Friday the *maulvi* in his Friday sermon wondered why a Hindu had remained in the village. Some of his friends therefore advised him to leave. He pretended not to be worried and went to the well the next evening too. But then he came home, collected the ornaments and went to another village, Nawan Kot, to seek help of my father's old classmate, Yaqub. He told him that his life was in danger and that he carried with him my mother's ornaments. Yaqub told him not to worry: "If someone wants to kill you he will have to kill me and my brothers before he can even lay a finger on you".

'His escape from the village was detected soon after he left. They had a good idea that he must have gone to Yaqub for help because there was no other way he could escape on foot from that area. Some of them came to Yaqub and demanded that he should be surrendered to them. But Yaqub and his brothers pulled out their guns saying that their guest was dearer to them than their own life. So, they went back. However, a *pir* then sent a message to Yaqub saying that he was on his way to him to find out why he was protecting a non-believer. At that point Yaqub told my uncle to leave immediately and provided him with a horse to ride to Jhelum. He left in the middle of the night and reached the refugee camp at Jhelum. Two days later Yaqub visited the camp to find out if *tayaji* had got there safely. That is how my family escaped unhurt from Khurd.'

Sunil Dutt died on 25 May 2005. His wife was the iconic actress Nargis, a Muslim.

Raghbir Singh Sahni

'I was born in 1926, in village Gujjial, *tahsil* Chakwal, district Jhelum, police station Duman. In our village, all the Sikhs were from the Sahni sub-caste. The rest were Muslims. We were moneylenders and also owned shops. India's Prime Minister Manmohan Singh is from our district. We had good relations with Muslims. They gave us a lot of respect. When we were attacked from outside the Muslims of our village saved our lives. We had a shop in Fitaki village which was nearby. Shah Muhammad took my father from the shop and safely brought him to our village. From our village, many had joined the army. My *chachaji* (father's younger brother) was in the army. There were seven brothers from a Muslim family in our village. During the war they had been captured by the Germans. We used to manage their salaries and properties, and when they returned they found that we had taken good care of their interests. We had bought property for them.

The raiders who attacked us were repulsed by those seven young men. Their mother said to them, "*Mein dudh tadd bakshan gi jey tusi annadey kum aoy*." (For the milk you have sucked from my breasts, go forward and save these Sikhs). One of them was called Bostan Khan. They all climbed onto our roof. There were about nine–ten Sikh families in our house at that time, about sixty to seventy people. The brothers said that they would shoot and the raiders ran away. The military was summoned and we all left. My brother was only forty days old. We then came to Chakwal. We stayed in Kalekey. Then we went to Patiala some fifteen days after Pakistan came into being. My father and my grandfather and uncles went back and brought back everything. We only lost the debts that the Muslims owed us. We charged very little. *Chuwani* (four annas) or *athiani* (eight annas) were charged for ₹100.'

Tilak Raj Oberoi

'I belong to Hasil, a large village in Chakwal *tahsil* of the Jhelum district. We had very good relations with the Muslims. There was a window opening into the main street from our house. It served as the medium for contact with people all the time. In March 1947 I was in Rawalpindi where I worked in the Imperial Bank. There was an attack on the village but our family and other Hindus were protected by our Muslim neighbours. So, Hasil escaped any major untoward incident. However, in August, things were no longer under control. The local people could not have helped even if they wanted to. It was clear that Hindus and Sikhs had no place in what was to become Pakistan. My parents and siblings went to Attock and stayed there for several months. It was a big refugee camp with some 200,000 people. They were subsequently transported to India with army escort. I was in Rawalpindi but did not know that my family was not far from there. I came to India in October. Our train, too, had army escort and therefore no attack took place on us.'

Shahpur district

Shahpur district, which included the modern city of Sargodha, was very much a part of the western overwhelming Muslim-majority areas of the Rawalpindi division. The Hindus and Sikhs together made up nearly fifteen per cent of Shahpur district's population. While visiting Panipat on 30 November 2005, Hitesh Gosain drove me to Panipat, where we spent the afternoon with Professor Narendra Mohan Vaid, who not only talked about his father's exit from Burewala in Multan division, but also took me to meet Chaman Lal Ahuja, who cried when he learnt that I was from Pakistan. He was a freedom fighter in Sargodha and had been in jail together with Mian Iftikharuddin, whom he considered a great leader and human being. Mr Ahuja told me that most of the people in Sargodha were friendly and trouble started only in August 1947. Later, I interviewed Hitesh Gosain's mother who belonged originally to Shahpur district, but who in 1947 was living in Bhera, a small town with a large Hindu presence.

Raj Rani Gosain

'We are Punjabi Brahmins. I was born in Sargodha, Shahpur district, in January 1918. We used to live in Block Two. I was married on 9 May 1930 to Gosain Krishan Lal of Miani. The Gosain family had their ancestral home in Jhikki Galli, Miani, and owned agricultural land in Malakwal. My husband was a dispenser. After my marriage I lived in various places like Sargodha, Phularwan etc, wherever my husband was posted. In 1947, we were in Bhera. My husband was working there in the Civil Hospital. Relations between Hindus and Musalmans (Muslims) were perfectly normal prior to the talk of partition. On festivals like Diwali, we used to send sweets to known Muslim families of the town and *mohalla*. Similarly, Muslims used to send sweets, etc. on Eid through some Hindus or Hindu shops.

'But prior to Partition, the situation started worsening. There were rumours of Muslims attacking and looting Hindus and murdering Hindu men, women and children. Towards the end of July, the situation became very tense. We womenfolk kept chilli powder, stones, and water buckets and drums always ready in the house. Water was kept on the rooftop so that if the Muslim mobs set our houses on fire, we could put it out. Men kept daggers ready. Women were also given poison packets to swallow if the men went down fighting. It was better to die than lose our *izzat* (honour). While there was no attack in our locality, there were two instances which were frightening.

'Once all the women of the *mohalla* had gone to one of the houses to make rotis in the *tandoor*. Suddenly, there were shouts of "*Aa gaye, Aa Gaye*" and we ran helter-skelter. The utensils, the dough and rotis were littered all around. We all rushed to our respective houses, bolted the doors and went to the roof ready with all the material that I have narrated before. Fortunately, no mobs came to our *mohalla*.

'From July onwards, my husband used to go to the hospital under escort of two policemen. Similarly, two policemen would drop him back. These policemen were Muslims but were protective and trustworthy. However, in August, a police sub-inspector at the hospital asked my husband to fill-up and light his hookah. My husband told him that the ward servant would come and do that for him. The sub-inspector became angry and said, "Let the riots begin, I will pump the first bullet into your chest.' My husband replied, "We will see".

'Rumours of a lot of bloodshed in Malakwal began to circulate. Therefore, my husband's elder brother (Gosain Baij Nath) and his family as well as my sister (Lajwanti) and her family shifted with us in Bhera.

At the time of Partition there were nineteen family members in our house. However, my husband's younger brother, Gosain Shaligram was in Miani at that time in our Jhikki Galli house. One day, around two weeks prior to the Partition date, news came in that many Hindus had been killed in Miani and the survivors had got to Bhera. My husband and his elder brother immediately went to the railway station and came back a little later crying. The survivors told them that Shaligram had been murdered by Muslims. He tried to escape from our house to a nearby house which was known as *Suthrayan da Dharamshala* (inn of an ascetic group). This house was unoccupied but always remained open and there was a well there from where people used to draw water. There was a large tree beside the well. Shaligram was wearing rubber-soled shoes and as he tried to climb the tree to cross over to next house, his foot slipped. By that time the attackers caught him and killed him. There were ten or twelve murders reported on that day. The survivors said that later they mass-cremated all the corpses in the wood-stockyard (*taal*) of one Chuni Lal Wasan.

'There was another incident in Miani of which we learnt later. There was one Diwan Jagdish, a lean and thin person of our *biradari*. He owned a lot of land and was very much respected. His house was just behind our house in Miani. Both houses were double-storeyed. Diwan Jagdish had four daughters but no son. He used to treat the Muslim agricultural labourers working on his land with a lot of affection. At the height of the tense period, the *muhajirs* (Muslim refugees from East Punjab) came to his house and knocked the door. On enquiry from Diwan Jagdish, they politely replied from outside the shut door of the house, "*Bauji, assi tuhade wastey aaye haan*" (Sir we have come to see you). The trusting Diwan Jagdish opened the door and he was killed on the spot. His body was found with his head inside a *chaati,* a big earthern pot. Fortunately, at the time, his wife and daughters were in another nearby house belonging to one of our relatives. They survived to tell the tale.

'There was an influential gentleman of Bhera called Diwan Sahib. He had married an English lady and was in Delhi at the time of Partition. It is said that someone told him that while he was living peacefully in Delhi, his beloved Bhera was in trouble. It is said that he organised a Maratha battalion to evacuate people from Bhera to Mandi Bahuddin from where nineteen trucks were organised to evacuate people to Amritsar. A few days after 14 August, we moved in groups to Bhera railway station with very little luggage that we could personally carry. Luckily, we could carry cash and ornaments. We locked our house and gave the bunch of keys to Baba Rehmani, the ward-servant at the hospital. We told him that we will take back the keys if we come back, otherwise all the household goods belonged to him. Baba Rehmani and the other Muslim families of the *mohalla* wished that we all would come back soon, once the anarchy was over. But that was never to be.

'We got to Bhera station and boarded the train. The train pulled out but stopped a little later. It was brought back to Bhera station. Everyone was tense. Maratha troops trained their machine guns. A little later, the train started again. We reached Mandi Bahuddin. We all walked to a fort-like structure through a huge gate. We had brought a lot of home-made snacks to eat. Next day there were rumours that eatables and water outside the compound had been poisoned by local Muslim goons. None of us ate anything from outside. Families shared the home-made food. Water was arranged inside the compound. The trucks arrived on the third day. We moved out single file. We were allowed to take only what we could carry. Most people left some of their luggage behind. The local policemen charged ₹100 per person as a bribe. There were negotiations also. The trucks were escorted by the Maratha battalion again, who told us to keep our heads low during the journey. We reached Attari without any incident. A little later, the trucks stopped and formed a circle in an open field. Everyone stayed in the middle. We were told to lie down if an attack took place. The Army stood guard the whole night. Next day, the train arrived. Those days all trains were running for free. We all reached Amritsar safely and went to the Golden Temple. There were many refugees in Amritsar. We saw some people with cholera symptoms. We learnt that my sister's husband never reached Amritsar as he had been killed in Lahore. We immediately boarded another train and came to Jullundur. An acquaintance gave us food. We slept at the railway station and finally boarded a train to Kurukhetra via Ludhiana where many of our relatives had also managed to come.

'Yes, there were many Muslim families with whom we had very cordial relations. One of them in Bhera was the Mirza family. Mr Mirza was also a dispenser at the hospital along with my husband. His wife was a very good woman and we were friends. Her grandfather was a Hindu and many of her customs were similar to ours. She had two lovely daughters – Mumtaz and Suraiya. They were in the same age group as my own daughters – Swaraj, Savinder and Daya. The girls used to play together and freely ate in each other's homes. Though we adults refrained from eating in Muslim households, the children were tacitly allowed that liberty. In fact, the Muslim households never took it amiss that we do not eat food or drink water in their houses as we respected each other's customs.'

Mianwali

Mianwali had a Hindu–Sikh minority of nearly fourteen per cent, mainly Hindus. The Khosla report mentions that in Mianwali no major assault on non-Muslims took place until 26 August, when a Sikh army officer, Captain Grewal, was murdered at Paikhel railway station. The deputy commissioner then announced on 30 August a plan to evacuate the non-Muslims from the district, which apparently encouraged the Muslims to attack the non-Muslims. The first attack took place on 2 September and thence onwards the attacks gained momentum (1989: 204-8). The SGPC report, however, claims that 3,500 Hindus and Sikhs were killed in Mianwali (1991: 197).

On 8 June 2006, in London, I was standing outside the Ealing Broadway Underground station after having mistakenly taken the wrong tube. I approached an elderly Sikh who turned out to be quite friendly and helpful. We went to have some tea and, upon my request, he let me take notes of his tales about his family's ordeal in Mianwali, a remote part of the old Punjab.

Jaspal Singh Kohli

'We are originally from village Dina in Jhelum district. My father, who was a police sub-inspector, was posted in Mianwali in 1947. I was in the sixth class at that time. My grandparents from both sides were in Dina. My mother's parents had moved there from their village, Gah, in

Chakwal after it had been attacked and a massacre took place in March 1947. My married sister who lived in Jhelum was also in the village in connection with some religious occasion. My father had opted for Pakistan and his colleagues welcomed that idea. But towards the end of September, Muslim refugees from East Punjab began to arrive in Mianwali. They along with retired servicemen began to organise attacks on the non-Muslims. We as a Sikh family were easily identified.

'I think it was a Sunday when everybody was at home, and a gang accompanied by Muslim League National Guards attacked our house. The local Sikhs in the area had also assembled in our house because it was considered a safe haven as my father was in the police force. My father had his revolver at home. Therefore the attackers would not come close to the house. But in a short while, the mob swelled into several thousands and some of them were definitely soldiers armed with guns. My father, and our neighbour Santokh Singh and his two sons were guarding the house from different positions outside the house, though only my father had a revolver. When darkness came, the marauders attacked again and all the men, including my father, were killed. The mobsters took away the young girls but, for some reason, the children and elderly women were spared. My mother hid me behind her. In the morning some elderly Muslims from our locality came to our house and told us to accompany them to the refugee camp. I believe it is because of them that we were saved.

'We arrived in a camp from where we were later taken in trucks to Amritsar. It took many days. We reached Amritsar in the beginning of October. My grandparents and my sister's family were not so lucky. They were killed in Dina. I moved to England in 1959. Sometimes I meet Muslims from Dina and Jhelum but seldom people from Mianwali. It is a strange feeling to hear all those accents of Punjabi. I have never forgotten my father. He was a tall and handsome man. He died fighting. So did many other men. I think some ten or twelve men were killed and some five young girls were taken away. Life has been cruel to us in many ways but then, life must go on.'

References

Khosla, Gopal Das. *Stern Reckoning: A Survey of the Events Leading up to and Following the Partition of India*, New Delhi: Oxford University Press, 1989.

Talib, S. Gurbachan. *Muslim League Attack on Sikhs and Hindus in the Punjab 1947,* New Delhi: Voice of India, 1991.

Interviews

Sunil Dutt, Mumbai, 20 October 2001
Professor Muhammad Sharif Kunjahi, Gujrat, 20 April 2003
Syed Aftab Hassan, Gujrat, 20 April 2003
Colonel (Retd) Nadir Ali, Lahore, 5 April 2003
Tilak Raj Oberoi, Chandigarh, 2 January 2005
Mahinder Nath Khanna, Amritsar, 3 January 2005
Kamla Sethi, Delhi, 7 March 2004
Jagan Nath, Delhi, 8 March 2004
Raghbir Singh Sahni, Patiala, 7 January 2005
Chaman Lal Ahuja, Panipat, 30 November
Raj Rani Gosain, Noida, 2 December 2005
Jaspal Singh Kohli, London, 8 June 2006
Bhisham Kumar Bakshi, via email from Delhi, 5 March 2007
Muhammad Feroz Dar, Stockholm, 18 February 2007

16

MULTAN DIVISION AND BAHWALPUR STATE

PRE-PARTITION PUNJAB'S SOUTHERN-MOST DIVISION WAS MULTAN. IT comprised Montgomery (Sahiwal), Lyallpur, Jhang, Multan, Muzaffargarh, Dera Ghazi Khan districts, as well as the Baloch Trans-Frontier Tract. It also included the most significant canal colonies of Lyallpur and Montgomery. Hindus and Sikhs made up twenty-two per cent of its population. Most of the Sikhs were from villages in the eastern districts and had been allotted land there when the canal colonies were developed. Both the Khosla and SGPC reports provide details of attacks on Hindus and Sikhs.

Multan city

Rioting in March 1947 had already exposed the vulnerable position of the Hindu community of Multan district. Sikhs were even less in number. An exodus of Hindus had taken place in March, though on a smaller scale; the majority were still around when the boundary award was announced. They were hoping that once law and order was restored, they would have the opportunity to continue living in the city and the villages. That proved to be wishful thinking, however, as incoming refugees from East Punjab incited revenge attacks that led to loss of lives and property amongst the Hindu and Sikh minorities. Forced conversions also took place but, as elsewhere, the non-Muslims left for India once military assistance arrived. The Khosla report provides data on the scenes in Multan where thousands were stranded when the trains stopped running on time or the tracks got damaged. Killings in the villages were also reported.

Lajpat Rai Seth

'I was born in Mohalla Pipal Thala near Hanu Chajja in the centre of Multan. My family was in the grain business which we supplied to all the jails in the Punjab. Our ancestors were originally from Multan who retained their religion despite Muslim rule here for centuries. The Hindus lived in the centre of town while most Muslims were settled in the outer areas of the city. Scheduled caste Hindus also lived outside the main city centre. Our washerman, Khuda Baksh, and my mother had become brother and sister by tying the *rakhi* (the thread that united a brother with his sister). One of our most trusted business associates was Ziauddin. He visited us frequently in the shop. He had business interests and brought customers and got his commission. We ate meat and even ate together with Muslims. The relations between the communities were very close and friendly.

'The March riots had already made the Hindus nervous. Burning of Hindu properties and several cases of murder had taken place, but then violence subsided and not until the second half of August did it erupt again. But everyone was hoping that things would settle down once Pakistan came into being. On 14 August I took part in the flag-raising ceremony at Chowk Bazaar to celebrate the creation of Pakistan. Soon afterwards, Hindus from the villages began to pour into Multan. Muslim refugees were also arriving in large numbers. I remember my father and other elders discussing the incidents that had taken place in various parts of Multan. The attacks on Hindus and Sikhs in the villages escalated. Suddenly thousands of distraught and bewildered human beings were in Multan. Many had lost family and cases of forced conversion were being reported all the time. I was only 13 at that time. I did not see any violence myself but a Muslim friend of my father, Daya *mochhi* (cobbler) who used to smoke the hookah with my father, was killed by Hindus and his body thrown into a well. Even Hindus took part in murderous attacks. Muslims who entered Hindu localities were not spared, but undoubtedly, the Muslims had the upper hand. By the end of August it was quite clear that we could not stay anymore in Multan.

'In our *mohalla* there used to live a young Hindu man, Sadanand, who in spite of the grave situation in those days returned to duty in the railway department in Quetta. Everybody tried to dissuade him but he would not listen, even taking his wife and children with him. In Quetta, his home was attacked. He locked his wife and children in a room. The raiders killed him and left quickly. But his wife and children were saved and evacuated to Delhi.

'We had decided not to travel by train because it was very unsafe. Thrice we tried to reach Multan airport but had to return because the road to the airport was controlled by armed Muslim gangs. Then Ziauddin helped us get to the airport and we took the flight to Ambala. It must have been sometime in early September but I can't remember the exact date. Nobody in our immediate family was killed. In Ambala we were helped by the station master Mr Kapur. He was originally from Multan. He allowed us to occupy some rooms. We saw dead bodies of Muslims lying all over and they were rotting. Caravans of Muslim refugees would also walk past the railway quarters where we had been put up. After a few weeks Ziauddin came over from Multan with two suitcases which we had left behind. He was so kind and bold to take the risk to come to Delhi in October and deliver the suitcases to us.

'Life in India was a big struggle. We were a rich family but were reduced to penury by the Partition. I had to rely on scholarships and other help to get an education. God has been kind and we are doing well now, but my greatest desire is to visit Multan at least once before I die.'

He then broke down in tears and I ended the interview.

Multan rural areas

I had gone to do some shopping for Shireen, my bosom friend Haroon Shah's wife, in a Delhi supermarket, from where I made a telephone call to Lahore to check if I had the right directions to go to a particular shop. The owner of the shop from where I made the call was a Mr Gulati. He and I struck up a conversation since he judged that I was a Punjabi from Pakistan. He related a story about a village in Multan where a major genocide of Hindus took place in 1947.

Trilok Kumar Gulati

'I was born on 10 October 1946 in the village Khan Bela, *tahsil* Shujabad, Multan district. My mother told me this story about our ordeal in early September when people from our and other neighbouring villages were massacred in hundreds, perhaps thousands. Nobody knows exactly how many. Our family had the main retail shop and my father Lala Naresh Kumar was a well-respected man. The majority of the population was Muslim but there was a sizeable number of Hindus too. When the attack took place, people ran in all directions. My mother, who was carrying me, was given protection by the daughter of the village *maulvi*. My mother and she were very close friends and were inseparable. She kept us in the backyard of the mosque while the men, many of them outsiders, went around committing unspeakable atrocities against Hindus. Nobody survived except me and my mother. Later in the evening we were taken to some army people who were in the area. My mother was wearing a *burqa* and the *maulvi* sahib's daughter and her brother, who was also a very good man, was with her so we could go past the criminals all along the way.

'My mother told me she saw villages burning all around and dead bodies lying in the fields all over. She was put in a truck and taken along with some other survivors from the neighbouring villages. For hours along the road devastation could be seen. She arrived in Multan after a twelve-hour journey. My mother did not get food for three days. Then some relief arrived. We were put on a train which had military escort. They brought us to Lahore and from there we crossed the border into India. My father was only thirty at that time. He and my grandfather were killed. Only my mother's elder brother who lived in another village was saved. All our relatives were killed. We lived in the Punjab for a while but then my mother moved to Delhi where my *mamaji* had settled. Life has been very difficult for us.'

✧

In the Khosla report, the carnage in Khan Bela, Khaji Wala, Jalalpur Pirwala, Budhe and several other villages in Multan district is described in some detail (1989: 184-9).

Lyallpur

Lyallpur district was a 'canal colony' named after Lyall, a British governor, during Raj times. Thirty per cent of its population comprised Hindus and Sikhs. On the other hand, in the town itself out of a total population of 69,930, the Hindu–Sikhs made up a majority of sixty-two per cent. The town was settled by people brought from all over the Punjab. It was well-planned and well-maintained. Several industries, especially cotton ginning and weaving factories, had been set up. As elsewhere, the owners were either Hindus or Sikhs. The Hindu–Sikh counsels made an aggressive but unsuccessful case before the Punjab Boundary Commission for the inclusion of the district in the Indian Punjab, although it was overwhelmingly Muslim in population. Very few incidents of communal violence took place before August. On the other hand, some Hindus and Sikhs had already started migrating from the town from May onwards. Mrs Vimla Virmani, daughter of the Punjab Hindu Mahasabha leader Sir Gokul Chand Narang, lived there with her husband.

Vimla Virmani

'I was born in Lahore and studied at Kinnaird College. My father, Sir Gokul Chand Narang, was the Punjab leader of the Hindu Mahasabha. Those were beautiful days. Young girls from good families of all communities would meet and nobody bothered much about religious dogma. My husband belonged to a leading Khatri family of Abbotabad but we had lots of property in Lyallpur. We first lived in Karachi but then came to Lyallpur. Our house was in the upper-class Civil Lines area, very close to the office of the deputy commissioner. Lyallpur was a very nice town. Everything functioned well. We met Muslim families and the whole crowd in that upper-class area socialised with each other. I played the piano and sometimes the Muslim ladies came and listened to me when I was playing it. Things were very good indeed. Sometimes the Muslim deputy commissioner, whose name I cannot remember now, would come to our place and would jokingly say that he would change his residence for ours when Pakistan came into being. But then things were getting bad everywhere in the Punjab. Lahore was going through rioting everyday and cases of stabbing and arson became more and more frequent. In either the end of May or early June, we left Lyallpur and went to Mussourie hill station. We left a lot of property in Lyallpur, but nobody believed at that time, especially in June, that a permanent movement of populations would occur. But that is exactly what happened. I did not see any violence with my own eyes but when the Punjabi Hindus arrived in India they had harrowing stories of rape, murder and injury to tell. In September attacks against Hindus and Sikhs in Lyallpur began to take place in real earnest. I learnt this from several families that relocated to India. Partition destroyed a happy and peaceful Punjab. My father was never happy in Delhi and always longed for Lahore. So did my father-in-law and other elders.'

Naqsh Lyallpuri

I met the noted Bollywood lyricist, Naqsh Lyallpuri, in Mumbai on 2 January 1997. His nostalgia for the old Punjab and especially his hometown, Lyallpur, was very obvious as he reminisced about his childhood and early youth. He said:

'I was working as a journalist in Lahore when Partition took place. So, I had to rush back to Lyallpur. We joined a long caravan comprising Hindus and Sikhs. As in many other cases, the Partition brought out the evil nature of mob violence that was let loose on us, as well as some magnificent examples of human mercy and solidarity. We were so terribly hungry that I took the risk and went into one of the villages in search of food. I met a farmer and pleaded with him for some food. He took me home. I was too frightened as to what might happen now that I was all alone. That fear proved to be misplaced. He brought vegetables and wheat flour and also milk, as I had told him that we had infants with us. His name was Inayat Ali. On the way, we were attacked many times but there were armed Sikhs in our convoy. They warded off the worst raids. We saw thousands of corpses on the way. It [the area around] smelled bad. On the Indian side, the scenes were no less harrowing. I don't think any one community can be blamed for what happened in 1947.'

Ghulam Rasul Tanveer

'I was born in Lyallpur in 1924. I studied at the Islamia High School and then at the Khalsa College, Lyallpur, during 1942–46. It was a Sikh educational institution but Hindus and some Muslims also studied there. Later I did my MA from Government College, Lahore and then started teaching English. I retired from the Faisalabad Agricultural University as a professor of English.

'Lyallpur, as Faisalabad was known then, was not an old town at all. Rather, it was one of the canal colonies. Consequently, almost all residents were newcomers who had come from several other areas. My own family originated from Ludhiana district in East Punjab. In the *chaks* (villages) of Lyallpur district, whole villages from east Punjab were transplanted in the settler colonies. Therefore, while the inhabitants of Lyallpur town had to build new connections and relationships, in the villages things remained more or less the same as before.

'Consequently the town had an open and progressive social ethos. The Pakistan movement was in full swing at that time when I was in college. The atmosphere was friendly and congenial but communal sensibilities had sharpened considerably, with the result that even a slight indiscretion by members of one community against the other would inflame feelings. Even trivial things were given importance. But Muslims were poor and only Munshi *mohalla* was predominantly Muslim. The rest were Hindu and Sikh neighbourhoods. They did not allow Muslims to enter into business. There were only five or six Muslim shops. Therefore the Hindus and Sikhs enjoyed complete economic monopoly. The Hindus had started buying even Munshi *mohalla*. Then the Muslims began to move to another part of Lyallpur. It was a new colony that Mian Ghulam Bari, elder brother of Mian Abdul Bari the Muslim League leader, had started developing.

'In one area only the communities were mixed. It was *mohalla* Vakilan where I was born. The people who lived here were educated. There were some very decent and gentle Hindus too. Dr Dodi, the main dentist in Lyallpur, and his wife, were very broadminded. They were originally from Kunjah, Gujrat. We could even walk into their kitchen and there was no pollution code practised when eating at their house. They also came and ate at our place. So much so, when Dr Dodi and his wife went to see a film they would leave their children, a young boy and a little girl, at our place. They were truly liberal but their relatives resented their open-mindedness.

'At the time of Partition, there was hardly any serious rioting in Lyallpur town. The deputy commissioner, Mr Abdul Hamid, exercised strict impartiality and therefore the non-Muslims left this town safely. There were Hindus and Sikhs in Lyallpur in large numbers even in the end of September. I remember one incident, however. One day soon after Pakistan had come into being the deputy commissioner was addressing a public meeting of all communities at the famous landmark of Ghanta Ghar (Clock Tower) in which he emphasised his commitment to make sure Hindus and Sikhs could remain in Pakistan if they wanted to. While he was speaking there was a hue and cry as someone had been stabbed. Some non-Muslims had been injured and probably also died. It was a huge gathering but after that incident people dispersed quickly and it ended on a bad note.'

The Khosla report acknowledges that Deputy Commissioner Agha Abdul Hamid did his duty impartially and thus saved thousands of non-Muslim lives. It alleges, however, that in the end, the deputy commissioner's writ began to be flouted, and the situation got out of control. The Sikhs in particular were singled out and subjected to savage reprisals for what their co-religionists were doing in East Punjab to Muslims (Khosla 1989: 166). The worst incidents took place in the rural areas.

Lyallpur rural areas

The villages in the Lyallpur district had a significant Sikh presence as they were one of the major beneficiaries in agricultural land allotment schemes that were introduced in the canal colonies. Although violence hit those villages, on the whole the Sikh and Hindu population of the rural areas as well as of Lyallpur town suffered less loss of lives as compared to other districts. While this is only my general impression, some of the interviews excerpted below indicate that this is probably true.

Abdul Bari

'We are Arains. Our family shifted to a village of Toba Tek Singh *tahsil* from Hoshiarpur in 1898. Ours was a Muslim village but Hindu Khatris who belonged originally to Bodhowala owned the few shops. The Hindus were educated. We had good contacts with them but they did not allow us in their kitchen and did not eat our cooked food. There were many Sikh villages in our area. Pakistan had already come into being and the Hindus and Sikhs were not leaving. So, the Muslims started attacking them. In those raids many Sikhs were killed. The young among them hid in fields, some of them remained in hiding till the military came and rescued them. The Muslims who took part in the attacks had come from Jhang. The Sikhs like us were settlers from East Punjab.

'I had a Sikh friend, Gurbachan Singh, who studied with me. He lived in a nearby village. His father Hakim Singh had retired as colonel. He had just retired some two months earlier and shifted to India. However, Gurbachan Singh refused to leave despite his parents' pleas. I am told he came to see me but I was away on an errand in Jhang at that time. So, the people in our village said to him, "You are a friend of Abdul Bari so we will not harm you. Please go." He went away but was killed in Toba Tek Singh. I sometimes remember him and tears come to my eyes. He was a very decent person. In the Toba Tek Singh area Hindus were oftentimes not harmed but thousands of Sikhs were killed. The reason was that stories of great atrocities committed against Muslims in East Punjab were circulating all around. Sikh women were also abducted; some were recovered but not all.'

One fact emerges clearly: when a refugee caravan was escorted by the military, the number of casualties from attacks by Muslim gangs was small, compared to when the refugees left without military escort. An example below of a caravan that left on 15 August without military escort, and of another which left in September with military escort following the same route before reaching India, indicates the huge difference. Vicky, our driver Nanak Singh and I visited a number of villages in the Ludhiana district in March 2004. We found that many Sikhs from villages in Lyallpur had come to Ludhiana. Some of the first-person accounts follow.

Nashatar Singh

'I was born in *chak* 275, Lyallpur *tahsil* and district. We were all settlers. There were only some Muslim *telis* in our village but no landowning families. We had very good relations with the Muslims from the neighbouring villages. They were Virk and Gill Jats while we were Garewals. Ours were the first caravan which left Lyallpur for India on 15 August. The reason for leaving quickly was that some of the Virks and Gills had warned us that attacks on the Sikhs were being planned by Muslims from Jhang and other neighbouring districts. Many people from the adjoining villages decided to leave with us but there were many who mocked us for panicking so quickly. On the way more and more people from the Sikh villages joined us. The caravan was so long that nobody knew what was happening in different places. I learnt later that the caravan was thirty-two miles long. It must have included more than 50,000 people. We left without any military escort. At Jaranwala, we had to cross a wide and deep canal. There we met some units of the Pakistan army. They ordered us to surrender the weapons we had with us. There were many retired soldiers and officers in the caravan. Our pensioned captains came forward and said that they would not give away their arms. The Pakistani soldiers tried to take the ammunition that we were carrying with us and also took away some rifles by force. This resulted in a shootout between them and us. Two women, one man and two children were shot dead. The return fire from our side resulted in the deaths of six Muslims and a seventh was captured. We recovered 3,000 rounds of bullets that had been taken from us.

'The caravan had to break journey and armed men from both sides took up positions along the canal. The police or army shot at us if we went to the canal to get water. They had Bren guns and other automatic weapons. We waited for eighteen days on the canal. We ate anything we could find. It began to rain and cholera and malaria broke out. That resulted in more deaths than from firing by the Pakistani soldiers. Then one day Dogra soldiers from the Indian Army appeared from somewhere. They took us to the Balloki head works. Many people were seriously ill. Some people who were leading the caravan believed that more than 1,000 people perished during that journey. While crossing to the Indian side, we saw some Muslim caravans from East Punjab crossing the canal. We were kept away from each other. After another seven days we arrived at Khem Karan in East Punjab.

'Don't ask me what I saw on that side. Bodies of men, women and children were lying all around. Dogs and vultures were eating the dead bodies. There were human carcasses lying all over. Thousands had died but most were killed by the heavy rain and diseases that spread during that terrible monsoon.'

Gurdev Singh

'I was born in 1922 in *chak* (village) number 68, in Lyallpur district. We were *lambardars* and *zaildars*. Buddh Singh was our elder who was one of the two *lambardars*. Bhishen Singh was the *zaildar*. We had Muslims of artisan castes also living in our village. There were *telis*, *julahas* (weavers) and a *lohar* (blacksmith). Our village was on the Jhang branch. Giani Kartar Singh, the Akali leader, was from our area. He did not favour us leaving Lyallpur but we were forced to do so. Actually there was not much killing after 15 August. But then Hindus and Sikhs in Sargodha were attacked and they had to flee. They had to cross from this area but were attacked by the Muslims of Tariqabad in Lyallpur town. Many people were killed. Then Giani Kartar Singh came and told us to prepare for the worst. We bought guns from Muslims of the Frontier (NWFP) but we also had our own licensed guns. The Muslim *thanedar* (police sub-inspector) told us that he had been instructed to confiscate our arms and that we should hide our guns. Bahadur Sher was his name. He was a good man who knew that we were defenceless against an attack by armed groups that were preparing to attack. We went to *chak* 40 and met Giani Kartar Singh's father, Bhagwan Singh, who told us that we were to get our horses ready. But Giani Kartar Singh told us not to move until the military escort arrived. The Gills from *chak* 9 also joined our caravan.

'We left on 31 September accompanied by Gurkha and Dogra soldiers who had been sent to help us. We had to keep to the road. People from some ninety to hundred villages had joined the caravan. I think it was from *chak* 1 to 100 who joined that mammoth column of people on the move. The most difficult problem was that many old people had to be carried and there were sick and handicapped people as well as pregnant women and scores of children. It was a sea of distressed and scared humanity that were leaving villages where they had put in so much hard work and effort. There were several ambushes and sniper shootings. Some deaths did take place but not many because our Gurkha and Dogra soldiers were very vigilant. That discouraged any major raid on us. I think that less than a hundred lost their lives.

'We were taken to Khalsa College in Lyallpur. [At this point in the interview, he started to weep – author.] There we waited for two days. Then, near Balloki head works, we had to cross over to India. The Pakistan Army was also present in strength. They took away our cattle. They even prevented us from getting water. A British officer was with them. He was supervising the Pakistani soldiers rounding up our cattle. A Gurkha who was accompanying us then pulled out his gun and protested: "Do you want to fight or do you want justice to prevail?" Thus our animals were returned to us. Then a Sikh officer went and talked to the British officer, told him that he was drunk and didn't care what was happening to the people. After that we came to Kasur and then entered India from Khem Karan. From there we were taken to Kapurthala and later were sent here.

'Many of us went on pilgrimage some eight or nine years ago to visit Nankana Sahib in Sheikhupura district. The police announced on the loudspeaker that some Muslims from our village had come to see us. Some messages had been coming and going over the years between us and the Muslims from our villages. These included an occasional letter and visits to holy shrines from both sides. Through such channels contact had been maintained. When we met them after such a long time, they cried and told us that life was much better when we were living there. Muslims who settled in our village and those around were after all outsiders and they could never develop the same close contacts and relationships as existed between them and us. They were still poor, the same as they were in the past. We gave them woollen clothing and other gifts. They cried and so did all of us. I always think of the very peaceful and friendly relations we once had in those villages left behind in Pakistan.'

Gobind Thukral

'Sometimes vague memories are more impassioned than the vivid ones. This is what has happened to a whole generation of youngsters who were forced to migrate along with their parents and relatives because of the political partition of the Indian subcontinent and a traumatic mass migration that followed in 1947. Violence that they saw, by most accounts of hundreds and thousands killed, maimed or humiliated in a variety of ways by their own neighbours and friends, left a haunting indelible mark on their collective conscience. Those who survived would sit back and talk to each other about their lost homes, lands, meadows and rivers for years till they died. They would miss their dear friends and relations and the blood and gore to which they were helpless witnesses would haunt them. It would sometimes be cathartic too.

'I remember, as I said, a bit vaguely in our village Jakhar, *tahsil* Toba Tek Singh, district Lyallpur, how one day our youngest *chacha*, a tall handsome man, rode on horseback from our ancestral village, Kasowal in Sahiwal or Montgomery district, to meet us. He sat with Father, my maternal uncle and our eldest cousins and explained to them with the help of some Urdu papers and maps how the country was being partitioned and we may have to leave this land and go beyond Amritsar. No one would agree with him, although he read out reports from the papers. My father would not agree and even rebuked him, but somewhere he was feeling very lonely and sad. What if this happens? After that the usual hustle and bustle, joyrides on horseback each day to the farm – it all looked distant. In school where I was then in class second, one of our teachers, who was a Muslim, would joke with his long knife that he had started keeping, by making signs how he could cut our necks. Maulvi Ghulam Mohammad, our class teacher (a dear friend of my father) would rebuke him in his chaste Lehndi.

We were not very frightened and went our way counting numbers and reciting poems till we told our elders about it. In any case, school days were soon cut short. Freedom and Partition both were announced simultaneously. Common folks would not know why a good tide had turned into a bad one. But it must have been clear to our elders that they have to protect themselves and maybe they will have to move out where they could be safer. Hindus and Sikhs, most of them related to each other by blood, formed a committee to protect and negotiate with their Muslim friends and neighbours with whom except blood they had age-old ties; visiting each other's places of worship. We had several mosques, *dargahs*, a Shiva temple and one large *gurdwara* in the village. We shared each others' joys and sorrows and were part of festivals and farming. Some had common trade relations, too.

'Soon our area was a small fortress and each able-bodied person had a *gandasa* (sharp blade mounted on a wooden handle), a strong *lathi* or a sword and some even had guns. One could hear war cries from the other at the outskirts of our small village. Interestingly, the local Muslims would often visit their friends and neighbours, offer hopeful advice and moral support. Some even brought fresh vegetables and promised to look after the cattle and the farms. A tranquil village, nevertheless, was turned into two hostile armed camps, each fearful of the other. Suddenly we children found our games changed from *kabbadi* and football to war games. We, too, had our small arms and we feigned some fighting. I would not know about the negotiations that were going around us, but at times it looked fearful. There were fires in the distance and, at night, we could hear cries and wailing.

'Some family had been wiped out. A few days later it was decided – I have no idea why, but safety must have guided the elders – to shift in a caravan to the nearby town of Kamalia. Local administration might have told them that they have to leave for Hindustan as this area was now Pakistan where only Muslims could live. We were to hear later about the word 'partition' more often. But it made no sense then except that we would not be able to play with our Muslim friends. We called each other by our nicknames and differed in no way, except our clothes during festivals. It mattered little.

'Everything was packed; my mother even took her *charkha*, the spinning wheel. How hopeful she must have been, not knowing that she would never return to see her village again, her home and hearth. We had to leave behind our cattle. At Kamalia, we were lodged in some relatives' house, a three-storey fortess-like place with a big basement. All the steel trunks and other luggage were squarely placed and as women got busy in cooking and other daily chores, men guarded the house and the streets, too. Some improvised weaponry and some guns were always handy. But what struck us, the children, was that we were given new clothes to wear and even money, more than normal pocket allowance of a paisa or half an anna [sixteen annas made one rupee] daily to buy *ladoos* (a sweet made out of Bengal gram and sugar) or *burfi* (a mixture of milk and sugar). We loved this and played around in the street. We had never lived long enough in a city. So this was pleasure. Soon it would be cut short.

'One day some military trucks came and everybody, men, women and children, rushed out to be part of a caravan for a distant land called Hindustan. We heard the word *kafla* (caravan) for the first time. But it turned into a catastrophe. Those two or three trucks were sent by some Hindu officer from Jullundur to pick up his relatives. But whoever could board it, went away. The rest who were left behind became fodder for waiting marauders and looting gangs. There were cries; women wailed and children shrieked. I would not understand the fires and gunshots and people lying dead in pools of blood. We were all terrified. For the next few days we were in a school building, separated from dear and near ones and guarded by able-bodied people with guns. I have never before heard people pray so fervently. There was not much to eat or drink. Children got something from an improvised open kitchen. One hand pump supplied water. Doctors got busy dressing the gunshot or sword wounds. We could hear firing close by and some hand grenades falling in the compound of the school.

'After a few days, a caravan was formed as the military had arrived and we were shifted to the grain market of a once bustling town. Life was hell here. Only limited food and no utensils. Fearful people just sat huddled and talked in whispers. They counted who has not been able to make to this camp. When it became unbearable, my father and his friend went with swords in their hands to the town two kilometres away to pick up utensils and buy some food. The women protested and asked them not to take such a risk. But they went their way and returned with big load of utensils. Some food later came from Muslim *chachas* and *phuphis* (uncles and aunts). I missed my favourite *phuphi*, a sister of our uncle, that tall handsome man, Kalu Jakhar. I missed her sweet hugs. She was tall and a charming, spirited lady. I still cherish her teasing. For my father, she was as dear a sister as his own and both seemed to be fond of each other.

'After a month or so, some army trucks came and we were again part of a caravan that moved to Lahore. Some boarded trains and moved on to Lahore. On the way, we could see massacred bodies and ruined fields. Dead men, women and children were strewn along the highways and in the farms. No one was sure of the next breath. Our first night and the last in the city of Lahore, the capital of then Punjab, about which we had heard beautiful stories and were also told that one day we would go there to study, was a harrowing one. Dysentery had struck and people were vomiting and defecating all around. Luckily, as mother would tell us later, we survived that nightmare with the help of simple onions she had packed in her *jhola* (pouch).

'The next morning we left Lahore. We crossed Wagah border and reached Hindustan, the land no one had any idea about and no one was sure about his or her destiny either. Still, there were shouts of joy and everyone kissed the ground beneath their feet and blessed those who had survived and wept for those whom they had lost. I still remember the way people jumped from the packed trucks to the fields amidst joy, perhaps feeling that at least, they were sure of not being killed.'

Professor Prem Singh Kahlon

I contacted Professsor Kahlon via the Internet because of our common interest in Punjabi culture and the way Punjabis were coping with life in the diaspora. I asked him to write an account of how his family left their ancestral abode and came to India in 1947. This is what he wrote:

'I was 11 years old in 1947 and was brought up in a village, Lyallpur, near the border with Jhang district. Most of the population in that area was Muslim. In August we moved from our village to my *nanke* (maternal grandparents) that was close to Kot Nihal Singh (the name of that railway station is changed now – it is just before you get to Gojra station near Toba Tek Singh). Along that railway track, going from Lyallpur to Gojra, there was a cluster of Sikh villages. We were not in any danger because there was a sizeable population of Sikhs in those villages who were heavily armed with locally made firearms. I heard that trains used to stop near the villages and Muslim hoodlums would jump on to kill and loot. After they had done their job the conductor would then whistle and the train to go on to the next village. However, these people were not successful in our area because of the armed Sikh population. But after some time we had to vacate some villages and move away from the railway lines. We all congregated at Theekri Wala Bangla, some ten miles from Lyallpur town on the Lyallpur–Jhang road.

'One day a policeman came and told my father that the *thanedar* had asked him to come to the police post at Theekri Wala. My father went to see him and as he entered, the young man said, "*Chacha, eh topan-shopan band karo, nahin te military avegee.*" (Uncle, stop firing the cannons otherwise the military will come). This man was from Jhang district and his father knew our family. In those days, a police officer could pick up anybody and just kill them. He was trying to be helpful because a small Muslim population in this area had complained that they were in danger on account of many armed Sikhs who had camped there. My father told the Sikhs to stop target practice otherwise the military might attack us. We stayed there until 15 October. We started our 20-mile-long caravan of bullock carts under heavy Indian military escort and headed towards the border. After eight days we crossed the border at Khem Karan. I am not aware of any loss of property or life in that area. Many years later I learnt about people who were in Gojra and some along the railway lines near Lyallpur. The local Muslim population in general was supportive of the Sikhs.'

Burewala

Hitesh Gosain and I visited Professor Narendra Mohan Vaid (orginally from Burewala) at his residence in Panipat, Haryana, on 30 November 2005. Burewala, a small town of Multan district in 1947, was known as Mandi Burewala at that time. It is now part of Vihari district. The interview I conducted on that occasion was lost so I requested Hitesh to kindly help me get the story of Professor Vaid's exit from Burewala. The interview was conducted by Arvind Vaid, his brother, and sent to me by email on 14 April 2010. The professor's words are quoted below:

'Our father Late Dr Ramji Lal Vaid was born at Ahmedpur Sial in Jhang district, but after getting his graduation and medicine degrees from Lahore he started his clinic at Mandi Burewala, where he settled with his family. He was a devotee to social work and to the teachings of Mahatama Gandhi. He was also an active member of the Congress party. He never wanted to migrate even when he realised that Pakistan was going to be created. He and many other Hindus remained in their homes when Pakistan came into being, but then tension began to mount quickly. An *Aman* (peace) Committee was formed and father was made a member.

'However, things did not remain peaceful and attacks on Hindus and Sikhs began to take place. One of father's Muslim friends, Mr Alla Yaar who was Deputy Superintendent of Police, warned him that some people were after his life and it was best to leave for India. He helped our family board the train which had Gurkha troops on it as well. The decision to leave was so sudden that we left without taking any belongings with us. We left Mandi Burewala in early September 1947.

'The Gurkha Jawans became the saviours as they used to stand guard, armed with rifles, whenever the train stopped at the stations or elsewhere. Gangs of armed Muslims did try to approach the train, shouting slogans and wanting to attack, but the presence of the Gurkhas kept them away. At Pattoki they changed the train and took another one going to Ferozepore.

'My younger brother Chander was born Ferozepore on 5 September 1947. I was only two and half years old at that time. A cholera epidemic broke out in Ferozepore. So we shifted to Ludhiana, where once again, cholera broke out. That made us shift again and we reached Kurukshetra. From there we shifted to Panipat and settled here. Our parents always remembered their places in Pakistan and the many good friends they had. They always believed that those places they left behind were far better, but life must go on and now Panipat is our home. They also told us that atrocities were committed on both sides. Human beings had lost their humanity in those days.'

Montgomery (now Sahiwal)

The second most important canal colony was Montgomery, also named after a British governor who was the grandfather of the Second World War's Field Marshal Lord Montgomery. Here Sikhs (Bedis and Sodhis) had been allotted vast agricultural tracts, while Hindus were prominent in trade and also owned a number of mills and factories. The Hindus and Sikhs made up nearly twenty-eight per cent of its population. According to the Khosla report, peace prevailed until 10 August because Mr Said Zaman, the Deputy Commissioner of Montgomery, was a good man. The situation changed, however, beginning 11 August, when Raja Hassan Akhtar took over. Violence broke out and Sikhs in particular were made the target of vicious attacks. Between 11 and 25 August, the Sikhs were targeted by gangs that were operating in Montgomery town and the surrounding villages (ibid.: 161).

Some accounts are presented below. The first was sent to me on 1 August 2005 by Mrs Inderjeet Kaur, headmistress of the Montgomery Girls' High School, Kapurthala, in the Indian Punjab. We had been corresponding about Lahore, which she had visited in connection with a pilgrimage to West Punjab. The school of which she was head had been established by Sardar Jarnail Singh Pasricha when he relocated to Kapurthala after Partition. The interview was conducted on my behalf by Mrs Inderjeet Kaur.

Sardar Jarnail Singh Pasricha

'I was just ten years old when the Partition tragedy took place. My father had many Muslim family friends as Montgomery had a mixed population. We lived in a very congenial atmosphere. But in August, Montgomery was rocked by communal frenzy. Strict curfew was imposed and no one was allowed to venture out at night or even during the day. Mass killings and stabbings went unabated. Montgomery began to burn with hatred and communal tension. A Baluch unit of the army was trying to control the atrocities. I recall one Muslim who did not obey the curfew rules and went out shouting on the street. The soldiers told him to go back, and when he refused they shot him dead as they had orders to shoot-on-sight. This resulted in violent repercussions because the Muslims thought that their Muslim brother was killed at the instigation of Sardar Hukam Singh, a Sikh leader of Montgomery. He was on the wanted list of the Muslim rioters; the list was soon expanded to include all Hindus and Sikhs in the area. Some Hindus and Sikhs left by train but the Muslims stopped the trains and committed murders, rapes, and looting. The train that was stopped at Raiwind resulted in mass butchery.

'The military smuggled Sardar Hukam Singh to Lahore disguised in military uniform, where he met Pandit Nehru and provided a first-hand account of violent upheavals and Sikh women jumping into wells to save their honour. Sardar Hukam Singh brought Pandit Nehru and Mr Liaqat Ali Khan to Montgomery in order to show the aftermath of the mass murders of Hindus and Sikhs. Pandit Nehru then ordered special trains with military guards to bring the Hindus and Sikhs to Ferozepur in East Punjab. My father, Bhai Gobind Singh Pasricha, and his family, along with other Hindus and Sikhs, were on those trains. Refugees scrambled on to train roofs in order to save their lives. It was a horrible experience. As refugees in East Punjab, we camped for fifteen days at Ferozepur. Later, one of our relatives reserved a burnt house of a Muslim who had fled. It was allotted to us by the government. We lived in that house until 1994.

'While living in East Punjab, my father never spoke of his past happy days in Montgomery nor the upheavals of 1947. He was optimistic and with enterprising zeal set forth to open colleges and schools. In 1983 we paid a visit to Pakistan, accompanied by my wife and daughter with twenty other ex-Montgomery residents. Unfortunately we did not possess the appropriate visas to have a *darshan* (offer devotion) of our holy *gurdwaras*.'

Professor Vinay Kumar

Professor Vinay Kumar and I had been emailing each other for a long time. He was eager to tell me his story about what had happened to his family in Okara. On 3 February 2005, he visited the famous medical centre, the Karolinska Institute in Solna, a suburb of Stockholm, to attend a conference. We met in a Chinese restaurant in Stockholm and recorded the following interview:

'I was born in December 1944 in Okara. My maternal grandfather, Dr Uttam Chand Ahuja was originally from Lahore. He was in the Punjab Civil Medical Service and served in several places in the Punjab. When he retired some fifteen years before Partition he decided to settle in Okara town, in Montgomery district, where he owned a large house. He took no payment from his patients. The compounder (medical technician) Harbans Lal had a box in which the patients could, if they wished, put some money, in lieu of a fee. He was a very large-hearted and pious person who never discriminated against anyone on the basis of religion or caste. People would travel fifty to sixty kilometres in the night to ask him for his company in seeing their sick or pregnant wife or child. He would do so immediately, riding on his horse. The people would show their gratitude by sometimes bringing a cow or a horse or some other animal and leave it as a gift.

'He was an integral part of that society. To have expelled him from there was like cutting his hand or leg off. He had two *tongas*. I remember he used to take me on *tonga* rides in the evenings. Although I was only a very small child, I remember even now him asking me, "Which tree is that?" I would reply, "Lalaji, it is a *tali*". Sometimes I would say, "I don't know". One day my cousin, who was a teenager at that time, took me to the grounds where he played volleyball. Somehow I got lost. People asked me who I was and where I lived. When I gave my grandfather's name, within minutes I was brought back; everyone knew Dr Ahuja.

When the Partition process started, fear and anxiety began to bother Hindus and Sikhs who were a minority in Okara. When the trouble started, the *tahsildar* and *lambardar* came to our house along with other important people. They said to him, "Doctor Sahib, you are not to go from here. You are ours, don't be afraid". Grandfather said, "Of course I belong here and have not even thought of leaving". But then the situation worsened as Muslim refugees began to pour into Okara. Then the same men came with tears in their eyes. They placed their turbans on the ground [a mark of respect] and said, "Doctor Sahib we are very ashamed, and we ask your forgiveness: we can't protect you any longer. The people of Okara will not touch you but we can't control those thousands that have arrived from East Punjab. They have seen blood and cannot be controlled. But we guarantee that we will escort you to the border safely." This is exactly what they did. They took him to the border and made sure that he had crossed safely. Which month it was I don't know, but it must have been either October or November.

'This shattered him. He settled in Khanna, in Ludhiana district, where he was given land. He continued the same practice of never asking for any fee. Whatever people could give was accepted. He wore a *kullaywali paggri* (style of turban used mainly by Muslims) with a suit. All this I have heard from Lalaji, my father, and my *mamaji*. My father was posted in Agra in 1947. He was in the army Ordinance Corps and was therefore not affected.'

Old Mr Arora

I met an extremely elderly Hindu gentleman in Kishanpura, district Moga, East Punjab. I could record only 'old Arora Sahib' for his name. Asking the name of elderly people, after all, is not generally practised in the Punjab unless they themselves mention it. He had settled there after moving to other places from district Okara, Multan division. This is his account:

'I was born in Mitha Bhatti, *thana* Chuchak, *tahsil* Okara, district Montgomery, 1957 *bikrami*, or in 1898. I am 106 years old. I lived in a Muslim village. It was not a village of settlers but of locals. There was one Hindu and one Sikh family. There was a village, Kaluwal, nearby where the moneylenders were Lashman Das, Ram Das and Ganda Ram. They belonged to the Swani sub-caste of the Ororas like us.

'I was a hardworking but poor shopkeeper. I have also seen abject poverty but worked hard. I had three Muslim employees. They were very loyal to me because I treated them well. I had excellent relations with the village, never charging them exorbitantly or selling bad or poor quality stuff. They considered me their son, but the Swanis were moneylenders and rather greedy and were badly treated by them when Partition took place. They were made to eat beef. I and my family were not humiliated that way. On the contrary we were protected till the military came to fetch us. Also I paid my employees well.

'Meghanas, Malanays, Chandurs were the Muslim castes in the village. I, my wife and four sons left nine days after the Radcliffe Award. When we were leaving, one of the villagers came and gave me five seers of ghee, others came and gave money to my sons. When I came over the old connections remained. They wrote to me and I wrote to them. It stopped after a few years, however. Now I do not get any more letters. I settled in Kishanpura.

'We had Dogra Army with us when we left. The caravan was nine miles long. The villagers of Mian Khan Wattoo sent a message that we should leave all the cattle and take only enough for three days, but the Dogra military that was accompanying us said that they would never allow an attack so we need not abandon our cattle. So, no attack took place. We first lived in Fazilka and then were sent to Saharanpur and then to Ambala. We lived in a camp, people would send us weets. My sons were with me. My older son was in the sixth class at that time. Later, I moved to Shabazpura, a nearby village where some of our relatives lived. After three years I came to Kishanpura. Here, I used to sell vegetables on a cart and then again established a small shop in 1954 I began my business here. I competed with the two local shopkeepers but was more successful. We now own agriculture land and are quite prosperous.'

Pakpattan

Pakpattan is famous because one of the most venerated Sufis, Baba Fariduddin Ganjshakar, is buried there. The Khosla report mentions that Pakpattan was looted on 23 and 24 August, and the next day, a Hindu and Sikh convoy left the town. They were stopped at *chak* Daula Bala where the Muslim *zaildar* announced that he had received orders from the deputy commissioner and Superintendent of Police to finish off the Sikhs. The Hindus could save their lives by embracing Islam. The Sikhs had to pay the price for what their co-religionists were doing to the Muslims in the eastern districts. The Hindus converted but when the Indian military came they decided to go to India. This happened on 29 September (1989: 163). On the whole, the loss of life in Pakpattan was not extensive. Syed Afzal Haider, whose testimony has already been presented in connection with the proceedings of the Punjab Boundary Commission, provided the following sketch of the events in Pakpattan:

Syed Afzal Haider

'My father, Syed Muhammad Shah, played a major role in the awakening of Muslims. He was one of the pioneers of the Muslim League in the Punjab. Although we are Shias, my father would lecture after the Friday prayers in the main mosque on the need to support the Muslim League, and my mother mobilised women, many from the villages to come to hear him. The dominant family in Pakpattan was that of Diwan Sahib, the custodian of the shrine of Hazrat Baba Fariduddin Ganjshakar. Hindus had lots of property in Pakpattan. All the developed areas were owned by Hindus. They had their own bank and completely dominated the commerce of Pakpattan. They had very good relations with Diwan Sahib. The Muslims were poor. In 1910 the landlords, all Muslims, of Pakpattan opposed the opening of a school in Pakpattan. In reaction, my father started the movement for educating Muslims. He established a cooperative bank. My grandfather owned eighty-one *murabbas* (squares of land, each of twenty-five acres) but at that time the income from land was negligible. It was difficult even to pay the land revenue tax from the income. The big money was in business and commerce.

'The truth is that Pakistan came into being on 15 August and not 14 August. On 15 August my father's *munshi* (clerk) Allah Ditta, told him that a communal clash was about to occur in Pakpattan. He was performing his *zohar* (noon) prayers at the time. He left without completing his prayers and ran barefoot. He reached just in time to prevent an ugly clash from occurring. Hindus were ready with their weapons on one side and Muslims were rallied on the other side. The Hindus left Pakpattan some days later for India via the Sulemanki head works. Very few deaths occurred in Pakpattan. Hindu property was looted after they left.

'A Hindu and his three young daughters were walking along the bank of the canal. When they reached Baseerpur someone killed him and his girls were taken away. This stirred a local uproar. A sufi of Baseerpur intervened and brought the girls home. He told their abductors that he would decide next day who would marry which girl. But early next morning he sent the girls with an escort to Sulemanki and got them across the border safely.

'On the other side, the Sikhs were preparing to attack a caravan of Muslims who were about to cross over to Pakistan. The three girls came forward and said that they had been saved by kindly Muslims, and that if any Muslim woman were harmed they would commit suicide. That deterred the Sikhs and the Muslims crossed safely over to Pakistan. This story was told to us by the Muslims who came from the Indian side to Pakpattan.'

Batool Begum

Brigadier (Retd) Yasub Ali Dogar's mother, Batool Begum, narrated the following story of how her father, Chaudari Maula Baksh Dogar, saved Sikh women from being killed by their own families. She recalled:

'During the 1947 holocaust, my father who was the *lambardar* of his area, learnt that the Sikhs of a *chaki* (small village) near his village (Chak 68/EB-Arifwala) were determined to burn their womenfolk. He at once mounted his horse and came at full gallop to the *chaki,* jumping over the mud walls. He shouted at the Sikh *sardar* to desist from burning any women. Their leader, who was a friend of his, told him that he could not afford to leave them or take them as he feared being assaulted on the way to India. They would rather burn their women than risk them being kidnapped, raped or killed. They would not bear such an ignominy or insult, being the *chaudhris* (honourable people) of their area.

'However, my father's persuasion prevailed and the Sikh ladies were saved. He provided them security up to the Sulaimanki border with India. Similarly, our family provided security to the Sikhs of Chak 9 and 10 12/L near Chichawatni. The family of of Lt Col. Hargurjit Singh Sandhu who was the classmate of my uncle Chaudari Nur Karim, also belonged to these villages. They too, were provided security till they crossed the border into India.'

Jhang, Mianwali, Dera Ghazi Khan and Bahawalpur State

The outlying districts of western Punjab, Jhang, Mianwali, Shahpur, Muzaffargarh and Dera Ghazi Khan were overwhelmingly Muslim. The

Hindu–Sikh population was seventeen per cent, overwhelmingly Hindus and a very small Sikh community. The Khosla and SGPS reports provide considerable data depicting events after 15 August. The loss of life and property in them was also considerable. According to the Khosla report, Raja Sultan Lal Hussain was the Deputy Commissioner of Muzaffargarh until 20 August. After he left, the non-Muslims were attacked savagely (1989: 191-6).

Jhang

The Khosla report blames the Muslim League Member of the Punjab Muslim League, Pir Mubarak Ali Shah, District Magistrate Zafar-ul-Haq Khan, Additional District Magistrate Mohammad Akbar and City Magistrate Hasnat Ahmad for fomenting riots against Hindus and Sikhs with the help of the *goondas*. The rioting began, according to the report, on 25 August (1989: 179-84). The following are some of the accounts that I recorded about those events.

Gurdev Singh

'I was standing at my fruit stall in the main bazaar when Muslim *goondas* ransacked the bazaar where mainly Hindus had their shops. There were a few Sikh vendors. I don't remember the date because I am not educated. But Pakistan had come into being. The Sikhs and Hindus had decided to stay on because we had good relations with the Muslims. But Shahji (Pir Mubarak Ali Shah) had incited the *goondas* to attack us. Earlier at the time of Muharram, the Sikhs and Hindus used to take part in the Ashura procession. He used to bless us all, but now he turned into a monster. Guns and spears and long knives were used. We had *kirpans* and therefore succeeded in escaping but the Hindus were unarmed. They were easily overpowered. Some converted to Islam and others were killed.

'I and my cousin, Buta Singh, hid in the fields for days. We could see fires all around and people crying for mercy but the *goondas* showed no pity. Even children were killed raised on spears. We used to come out in the evening and get some food or ate grass and survived for more than two weeks. Then many Hindus and Sikhs who were hiding in the fields began to collect and waited for help. A British officer then came with the police and collected people who had survived in the attacks. Some had taken refuge with Muslims. Not all Muslims were bad. We were loaded in trucks and brought to Sulemanki where we crossed into India. I had no family myself and was brought up by my uncle. He died a few months before Pakistan came into being. His wife had died long ago. So, it was only I and my cousin who were left.

'I must confess we later joined the Sikh *jathas* and took part in many attacks on Muslims on the other side. Don't ask me if I killed anyone. Killing is a sin but those were bad times. Yes, I saw dead bodies strewn all over in Fazilka and later in Muktsar.'

B.R. Lal

'I was born on 15 May 1925 in Ahmedpur Sial, a hamlet in Jhang district in a family of Arora Hindus. Aroras and Khatris were the main Hindu trading community in the western Punjab. We had a small business in Ahmedpur Sial where ninety per cent of the population was Muslim. I studied in the Islamia Primary School and then won a scholarship to study in the DAV School and did my matriculation from Khanewal. Before the trouble started there was never any tension, although in March some rioting did take place in Jhang town. However, trouble did take place in late August in Ahmedpur Sial, too. My father was murdered, then my brother, when a mob surrounded our house and attacked. The rest of the family was brought by escort to Lahore where we stayed for some time at the DAV College refugee camp. Then we crossed the border into India. There, my younger brother was stabbed to death. Nobody knows who did that. Thus my father and two brothers were lost during the Partition. It dealt us a severe blow but now things have improved for us. I have many Muslim friends here in Delhi.'

Dera Ghazi Khan

The Khosla report tells us that the idea of Pakistan was almost unknown in Dera Ghazi Khan. The Hindu–Sikh population was nearly twelve per cent, almost all of them Hindus with only a few Sikhs. There was no mass killing of non-Muslims; looting took place after they had left. In one village, Dajal, forty non-Muslims were killed on 13 September, and earlier also in September, at Ghajaniyan, twenty-seven were killed. Then Dogra soldiers arrived and the non-Muslims were taken to safety. But even in October some non-Muslims were still in Dera Ghazi Khan district. On 6 October, a bus from Vahowa to Dera Ghazi Khan was attacked and nine non-Muslims were killed (1989: 208-12).

Professor J.M. Manchanda, who teaches English Literature at Delhi University, contacted me after reading one of my weekly columns in *The News*, an English language paper published in Pakistan. He told me that his family was originally from Dera Ghazi Khan. I met him when I visited Delhi briefly in March 2007. On my behalf, he interviewed two elderly gentlemen originally from Dera Ghazi Khan, and sent the following summary on 11 and 12 March 2007, written in his own words.

Professor Manchanda's account of Manmohan Taneja

'I was able to speak to Mr Manmohan Taneja, seventy-seven years old, on 7 March and again on 10 March 2004. He informed me that when the Partition was announced, he was in Lahore where trouble had broken out. Sikhs carried out reprisals against Muslim rioters, and some Hindu activists also shot at them in Rawalpindi with homemade guns. He then moved back to Dera Ghazi Khan where he rented a house. Originally a resident of Rojhan village, he preferred the security of the city. Rojhan remained quiet in those times and the Hindus even got assurances of safety from some powerful Muslims there, but they were apprehensive due to reports appearing in the local Urdu press about rioting elsewhere. Some of them, belonging to Umarkot in Rajanpura *tahsil*, hired a truck to get away but were robbed of their belongings on the way. Therefore, Mr Taneja and other members of his family chose to stay on till a Gurkha unit of the army arrived and escorted them to Amritsar. From his account, I did not gather any information about rioting in Dera Ghazi Khan, although there were reports of sporadic incidents of violence by poor Muslims in the countryside.

'Though he could not give me the exact dates, it seems he stayed on for several weeks in Dera Ghazi Khan partly on account of the area being peaceful, and partly due to caution. He told me that the journey from Dera Ghazi Khan to Amritsar had to be completed in several stages, and the family arrived in India months after Partition. By then, the governments in both India and Pakistan had controlled the situation and rioting and reprisals had ended.'

Professor Manchanda's account of Dr Satya Pal 'Bedar'

'I met Dr Satya Pal "Bedar" today (11 March 2007). He retired from our Hindi department about ten years ago. He is a distinguished poet and has broadcast programmes in Saraiki for All-India Radio's External Services. Dr Bedar belonged to a village called Jhokotra, about 18 miles from Dera Ghazi Khan *tahsil,* which had a record of communal peace. He told me that the rural areas in that district saw a lot of trouble from late August 1947 onwards, forcing him to move to Dera Ghazi Khan in October in order to save himself. He reported that 25 Hindus were killed in his village where 80 per cent of the population was Muslim though the Hindus dominated prior to Partition. The trouble started through Urdu papers (he mentioned *Zamindar, Milap,* and *Pratap* among them) and propaganda unleashed through Nawab Jamal Khan and other local Muslim League leaders. According to him, the choice given to them was to convert to Islam and to give away their daughters to Muslim young men. He also reported abduction of some Hindu women among the reasons why Hindus in surrounding villages moved to Dera Ghazi Khan, which had a British deputy commissioner who kept the troublemakers under control. He stayed there for about a month and half and was escorted across the Indus and beyond in November by Gurkha soldiers who made the rioters lie down and threatened to shoot any one raising his head. He reported about 7,000 Muslims surrounding the city at one time. The refugees travelled initially in military trucks and later by train and heaved a sigh of relief on crossing the Wagah border.'

Dr Teja Singh

Dr Teja Singh and I had also begun emailing each other sometime in 2006. Upon my request he noted down the story about his family's ordeal during the Punjab partition. He wrote:

'My grandfather, Sardar Bahadur Lehna Singh, OBI, was a resident of *chak* No. 134/9L, in the Montgomery district. He had settled there after a land grant for his military services in the First World War. Gian Singh, my father, was his younger son and a graduate of Dyal Singh College, Lahore. He served as a revenue officer, with magisterial powers, in the Multan Civil Division of the united Punjab. He was posted in Lyallpur where I and my brother went to college. In 1946, he was posted to Taunsa Sharif in Dera Ghazi Khan but we continued to study in Lyallpur.

'It was soon becoming clear that India was ultimately to be partitioned. Being a loyal and optimistic person and having many Muslim friends, Father sincerely believed that the change in government would not imply a shift in residence. He opted to stay and serve the Government of Pakistan. When Pakistan was formally created on 14 August 1947, he as a local officer dutifully hoisted the new flag on the court building.

'Shortly before the Partition, my mother was invited to the wedding of her younger brother in their village, Ghost Poker, about three miles from Gurdaspur city. As it was a special occasion all of us, with the exception of father who was in Taunsa Sharif, left Lyallpur to attend the wedding. We were advised to prolong our stay there because the law and order situation had deteriorated rapidly in some parts of the Punjab. Full-scale rioting broke out while we were there. So we stayed where we were.

'Father was advised by friends to migrate soon to the eastern Punjab for safety. The summer torrents had blocked the direct road traffic to Dera Gazi Khan, the district headquarter. The only choice left for him was to travel across the Indus river to catch a train to Multan and onwards. This was sometime in the beginning of September. The river was in full spate because of the summer melting of the Himalayan snows and the monsoon rains. Four peons (office orderlies), three Muslims and one Hindu, Bhanjan, dressed as a Muslim with a fez cap, escorted him to the site where he could take a boat to cross the dangerously flooded river. The Muslim peons bade him farewell to return to Taunsa, and Bhanjan accompanied him all the way to India. They got safely to the railway station on the other side and caught the next train. My father was in an upper-class compartment, with hardly any other passenger in it. When the train arrived at the next station, a Muslim officer whom he knew joined him. Surprised at seeing my father travelling alone, he sat next to him and narrated horrible stories of violence that had been trickling from the other sides of the border. It was from him that Father learned for the first time how the law and order situation had worsened in the Punjab. He cautioned Father to take care of himself as some gangsters dressed in the uniform of the Muslim League National Guard were seeking revenge and he could be a soft target because of being easily identified as a Sikh because of his beard and turban.

'Arriving in Multan, where he had served for three years prior to his transfer to Lyallpur, Father was to catch another train for the journey to Lahore, the capital city of the Punjab, now in Pakistan. He learned to his great disappointment that the train had been cancelled. Thinking that some waiting period was involved, he headed for the official waiting room, accompanied by Bhanjan, to rest, as he was totally exhausted after a tiring day.

Bhanjan went to see the station staff to find out the trains' departure timings. He was told that there would be no transfer train available for the next few days and that non-Muslims were advised to go to the area within the city walls and join others who were similarly waiting for the next train for Lahore. It was getting dark so they decided that it would be safer for them to leave the waiting room and go and spend the night with a Muslim landlord known to my father since the time he was posted in Multan.

Bhanjan picked up the luggage and came outside the railway station to hire a *tonga* to travel to the landlord's mansion nearby. On their way, the driver had to stop at the revenue post for an official check-up on taxable items of passengers entering the city. The clerk on duty immediately recognised my father and said in utter surprise, "What are you doing here Sardar Sahib, travelling at this hour of the night? There is a complete breakdown of law and order, and you could be attacked at any time." Hearing this, Father felt danger to his life for the first time since he had left Tanusa. How different the situation now was in the city where he had served earlier as a magistrate to maintain law and order during the Muharram period. They quickly headed for his friend's mansion and were welcomed by the servants guarding the gates.

'The next morning, after breakfast, the landlord personally greeted my father. He had made enquiries and told him that it would not be safe for him to stay outside the city walls. He offered to take him inside the city to join others in a similar condition, as they were officially protected while waiting to be escorted away. Arriving there, he felt safe in joining others who had been promised to be taken to the next available train as soon as possible. It turned out to be a long wait over many days, probably as long as three weeks.

'When they were finally informed that a train was available for their journey, they were escorted and transported to the railway station. The district deputy commissioner was already there. His orderly saluted my father, having recognised him from his previous posting in Multan, and introduced him to his new boss, who greeted him with a warm handshake. In a brief exchange of views on the current situation in the Punjab, he asked my father to do everything possible to strengthen law and order in East Punjab when he got there. The orderly took him to the compartment which had been reserved for him. After acknowledging the kind gesture, my father asked the orderly that other passengers be allowed to enter as well since there was over–crowding in the other compartments.

'The train made a slow start for the long journey to Lahore. A small contingent, probably three Gurkha soldiers, provided security under the command of a British officer. All went smoothly up to Montgomery, the half-way point of the trip. Father told me that he looked towards the landscape of the *chak* he belonged to, and thought of Wary Singh, the *lambardar*, who might be on his routine daily trip to the city on numerous chores as a part of his official duties. He was totally unaware that the Sikh inhabitants of his *chak* had already left on foot as a caravan migrating to East Punjab. As the elders were the veterans of the First World War, they were guiding their progeny during the long march.

'The stop at Montgomery turned out to be a long one. Some passengers went out on the platform to look for food and drinks, but could not find any vendor nor an open stall. Instead, they heard the shouts and slogans from a hostile Muslim group, soon followed by the bang of a gunshot. The Gurkhas and their officer were patrolling the platform and doing their best to maintain order and to ensure that everyone was safely back on the train. The unpleasant episode had caused considerable delay. Having witnessed what had transpired, the train engine driver expressed his reluctance to proceed any further. A soldier had to be assigned for his protection before he agreed to continue on the perilous journey. The passengers who had some food to spare shared it with the hungry children.

'They were now being driven slowly in the darkness of the night. In the early hours of the next morning, they heard the locomotive whistling incessantly as the train slowed down almost to a halt. Father could see from his window a group of gangsters, armed with spears, running towards the railway track from a nearby village. Fearing the potential slaughter of innocent passengers, the soldiers were seen pointing their guns in the direction from which they had emerged. The soldier assigned to the driver was persuading him to accelerate and keep the train moving. A similar incident occurred once more, repeating the same pattern: the locomotive whistles in quick succession, the train slowing down suddenly in the vicinity of a big village, some adults with spears emerging to attack the train, and Gurkha soldiers at the ready to shoot if the mob advanced any further.

'The train finally approached the outer boundaries of Lahore district which showed many damaged and burnt houses. Evidently the region had experienced carnage and looting on a much bigger scale than the areas they had left behind. Within the next hour they were in the outskirts of the capital city. The journey that normally took eight hours had already taken them more than two days. They had been without any food beyond what little they had brought with them. Arriving in Lahore was a great relief; much of the killings of train passengers had occurred in the previous days in the adjoining areas. They had to wait for another day to take them out of the city and finally across the border.

'Soon after Independence and the creation of Pakistan, I came to Amritsar from Gurdaspur. I stayed in the precincts of the Golden Temple, looking for any clue about my father. I also walked every day to the military-controlled main check-point on the Grand Trunk Road where all incoming caravans of migrants were identified and allowed to proceed further. Spending my day talking and enquiring from anybody who might have seen my father as a co-passenger in trains arriving at Amritsar railway station, I returned every evening to the Golden Temple for prayers, and for sleeping overnight on the marble floors. Gurus (communal free food) provided me ample sustenance during a greatly depressing period of my youth. It gave me a chance to see and meet devotees and visitors, and get first-hand information on the killings and carnage that took place in the name of religion. Most of them lamented such independence that had turned them into refugees in their own province.

'I was sad listening to the constant reply, "We have no news about your father". Suddenly somebody spotted me one day to tell that he had seen him in a train moving beyond Amritsar. The news hit me as a big surprise, as if it was too good to be true. I had to check it once more to believe it. He assured me that he had spotted the right person, my father, even though he had seen from a distance. He was right.'

Bahawalpur state

Bahawalpur state connected to Multan division. In 1941, it had a total population of 1,341,209 living in an area of 45,911 km² (17,494 sq miles). The Muslim nawab acceded to Pakistan. The Muslim component of the population was eighty-three per cent and the rest were mainly Hindus and some Sikhs and Christians. The irrigation canals and other facilities had resulted in canal colonies being established in some northern parts of the state. Most of the settlers were Muslims but some Sikhs had also been granted agricultural land in them. Rioting broke out in Bahawalpur state too in the month of August. According to Penderel Moon, who in 1947 was serving as the Revenue and Public Works Minister in the state, the nawab was in England at the time of Partition. He did not return till October. He was not in favour of his Hindu and Sikh subjects leaving. However, because disturbances in the rest of the Punjab and in the Hindu princely states in Rajputhana on the other side of the new international border took place, Bahawalpur also experienced rioting. Most Hindus and Sikhs, though, were helped to cross the border safely to the other side through police and military escort, for foot convoys as well as special trains. In a few cases the men escorting the convoys joined in looting the non-Muslims, but on the whole, the transfer of population was orderly (1998: 232-35).'

Notes

Moon, Penderel. *Divide and Quit: An Eyewitness Account of the Partition of India*, New Delhi: Oxford University Press, 1998.

Interviews

Naqsh Lyallpuri, Mumbai, 2 January 1997
Syed Afzal Haider, Lahore, 11 April 2003
B.R. Lal, Delhi, 12 March 2004
Mrs Vimla Virmani, Delhi, 13 March 2004
Gurdev Singh (formerly of Jhang), Delhi, 16 March 2004
Old Mr Arora, Kishanpura, Moga district, East Punjab, 17 March 2004
Gurdev Singh, (originally from Lyallpur rural areas) village Galib Kalan, Ludhiana district, 18 March 2004
Nashatar Singh, village Galib Kalan, Ludhiana district 18 March 2004
Ghulam Rasul Tanveer, Faisalabad (Lyallpur) 19 December 2004
Abdul Bari, Multan, 20 December 2004
Lajpat Rai Seth, Delhi, 10 January 2005
Trilok Kumar Gulati, Delhi, 11 January 2005
Professor Vinay Kumar, Stockholm, 3 February 2005
Professor Prem Singh Kahlon, Nashville, Tennesse via email, 15 June 2005
S. Jarnail Singh Pasricha interviewed by Mrs Inderjeet Kaur, headmistress Montgomery Girls' High School, Kapurthala and sent by email on 1 August 2005
Manmohan Taneja, interviewed by Professor Manchanda in New Delhi 7 and 10 March sent on 10 March 2007

Dr. Satya Pal 'Bedar', interviewed by Professor Manchanda in New Delhi 11 March 2007, sent on 11 March 2007

Dr Teja Singh, Edmonton, Canada, 17 March 2007, via email

Gobind Thukral, Chandigarh, via email, 21 July 2007

Professor Narendra Mohan Vaid, Panipat, interviewed by Arvind Vaid, who sent it by email on 14 April 2010

Batool Begum, interviewed by her son, Brigadier (Retd) Yasub Ali Dogar, sent from Lahore, 3 March 2011

Exodus from East Punjab and Princely States

17

AMRITSAR AND THE THREE *TAHSILS* OF GURDASPUR

THE HINDU–SIKH MAJORITY AMRITSAR DISTRICT WAS PLACED IN East Punjab in the notional division of 3 June 1947. The Radcliffe Award upheld that placement. In the case of Gurdaspur district, the 3 June Partition Plan placed it in Pakistan, but the Radcliffe Award gave three of its *tahsils* – Batala, Gurdaspur and Pathankot – to East Punjab. Not surprisingly, such outcomes generated quite peculiar situations and responses.

Amritsar city

The longest running battle between the criminal underworlds of Muslim and Hindu–Sikh *badmashes* and *goondas* of Amritsar continued till the announcement of the Radcliffe Award. They were aided and abetted by their sympathisers in the administration and political parties. The Lahore Hindus and Sikhs had convinced themselves that Amritsar would be given to India, notwithstanding the clear Muslim majority in both Lahore city and district. In the same way, Muslims of Amritsar believed that despite it being home to the holiest Sikh shrine, and even though they were in a minority, the city would be given to Pakistan.

In *The Emergence of Pakistan*, Chaudhri Muhammad Ali quoted a British officer's profoundly shocking description of what he saw in Amritsar: 'On 15 August the day of liberation was strangely celebrated in the Punjab. During the afternoon a Sikh mob paraded a number of Muslim women naked through the streets of Amritsar, raped them and hacked some of them to pieces with *kirpans* and burned the others alive' (Ali 1973: 256). The incident of Muslim women being paraded naked appears also in Iftikhar's *Jabb Amritsar Jall Raha Tha*, though he places such an incident in March. Most other writers record this date as 15 August.

Iftikhar, as noted earlier, has the tendency to depict with unmitigated gusto Muslim excesses in violence as if he relished them; when Muslims were the victims, his heart bled. His is no doubt an unusually partisan account of the same crime. At any rate, by the middle of August, the Muslims of Amritsar were totally defeated. What happened in those days is portrayed in graphic detail. We learn that the Muslims who remained trapped in the city and had not shifted to Sharifpura were butchered. The crimes committed against Muslims who had taken refuge inside a famous mosque called Masjid Rangrezan in the city, are described in full and harrowing detail by Iftikhar. The savagery that was let loose did not spare even milk-suckling infants, while women and young girls were lying dead naked in pools of blood. (1991: 212-14). Iftikhar wrote:

> The Muslims of Amritsar wrote about that tragedy to the prime minister of Pakistan, Liaqat Ali Khan. Khawaja Ghulam Nabi Leader, Advocate Khawaja Ghulam Hassan and Sufi Ghulam Muhammad Turk, collected pieces of the bodies of the naked women lying inside the mosque and in the bazaars and put them on white sheets of cloth and with tears of blood in their eyes began to wait for the late Liaqat to visit Amritsar.
>
> In accordance with the programme, Liaqat landed at the Amritsar military airport and met the Muslim refugees in the relief camp there. He heard directly from the survivors of that terrible ordeal and began to cry. He was so badly shaken that he did not have the courage to go and see for himself the scene at *Masjid Rangrezan*, and went back. Upon returning, he sent military trucks and special trains to fetch the Muslims safely from Amritsar. That proved to be a great help in transporting the Amritsar Muslims to Lahore (ibid.: 214-15).

Chaudhri Muhammad Said

Chaudhri Muhammad Said, whose account of the events in Amritsar extending from March 1947 onwards is quoted in earlier chapters, said the following about the period from 14 August onwards:

> Early on the 15th morning a meeting was conveyed to form a Managing Committee of the Camp at [Sharifpura] and it was also decided to hoist Indian Flag and pay homage to it in the presence of local officials and in return to ask them to ensure our safety.
> The local officials were contacted. At about 11 a.m. R.E. Badri Dass, Superintendent C.I.D., S. Ujagar Singh, D.S.P., C.I.D., and Seth Sant Ram, M.L.A., came to Sharifpura. Indian Flag was hoisted in their presence and the people assured them of their loyalty to the State and the Flag and in return demanded protection of their lives, honour and property. All persons mentioned above addressed the crowd and assured them of safety measures to be adopted forthwith. This put heart into the people and there was a wave of satisfaction... but nothing was done.
> Next day [August 16] we were bold enough to leave Sharifpura premises and to take a deputation to the Deputy Commissioner (Mr. Nukul Sen) [Sen did not take over till 23 August though]. He promised everything, but did nothing....
> Next day, I went to the Brigade Headquarters and asked for assistance to transport rations. With the assistance of a Muslim Major I was able to get two military lorries and by evening brought 200 bags into Sharifpura. This allayed our fears regarding the ration shortage. ... Thereafter, Rationing Controller was able to send a small number of bags when required by us.
> The camp was gratified to learn that Mr. A.K. Malik, I.C.S., had been appointed as Liaison Officer by Pakistan Government.... Perhaps through his exertions we were able to get special trains which ran twice a day and evacuated refugees from Sharifpura Siding. About 5,000 people were cleared off in each trip.
> With the announcement of Boundary Commission Award, our last hope of remaining in Amritsar disappeared.... Panic was created in

> Sharifpura but with the posting of Military pickets the situation did not deteriorate seriously and people remained intact....
>
> On his first visit to Amritsar after 15th, I was called by Pandit Jawahar Lal Nehru to see him as a representative of Sharifpura Camp. I was escorted to his place at night by a military guard. I narrated to him all the incidents which had taken place, especially after the 10th August. He gave a patient hearing but a very excited reply. He said that the same and similar things were happening on the Western side and there was only retaliation on the Eastern side. I was amazed to hear such a reply from such a high and responsible personality. He said evacuation was necessary and no security could be assured to those Muslims who wished to remain in Amritsar. The incident of Kucha Rangrezan was verified by him in my presence.
>
> On the 27th, I was informed by the Brigade Headquarters that the Sharifpura convoy would be despatched on the 28th... but on the 28th I was informed that the convoy could not be despatched as there had been some incident near Ravi in Lahore District and the entire convoy would have been killed if sent on that date....
>
> On the 30th evening, the Honourable Mr. Liaquat Ali Khan passed through Sharifpura along with the Honourable Shaukat Hayat Khan and S. Swarn [Swaran] Singh, East Punjab Minister. I narrated to them the situation of the camp and with their assistance the convoy started on 31 August, at 7 a.m....
>
> In the Cantonment Camp it was heard that about 1,100 persons had been murdered in Nowshehra Punuan, Taran Taran Tahsil, and some persons were still hiding there. I went to the spot with some military escort and brought 59 persons from there being the only remnants of the aforesaid number. It was alleged by them that the Dogra Troops stationed there took active part in the massacre.
>
> I reached Lahore on 4th September, 1947, at 8-30 p.m. with a Military Convoy (*The Journey to Pakistan* 1993: 148-53).

Said provides many other details, narrating how difficult it was to survive in the Sharifpura camp for several days before he arranged the supply of flour and other items. Sanitary conditions were appalling, water and electricity supply were deficient, and there were much worse conditions. He was also detained in police custody on 1 September for a few days without food and water, for resisting a Sikh police constable who wanted to take away a *tonga*. He was released on 4 September the same day he left for Lahore (ibid.: 153).

A. Hameed

In Lahore, I met the well-known Urdu writer, A. Hameed, on 24 April 2003, at his residence in Samanabad. He was not keen to be interviewed and kept evading me but eventually gave in to my sheer obstinacy. I was curious to talk to him because he was a bonafide Amritsari of Kashmiri descent and, down the years, his love for his hometown had only grown. I was thus quite intrigued why he would not be willing to be interviewed. I was to discover during the interview why.

'I was born in 1928, in Mohalla Kataiala Singh. Most were Kashmiris. There was a Hindu locality close to us. We played with Muslims. There were Hindus and Sikhs too, but most of my friends were Muslims. Amritsar was a stronghold of the Ahrar and nationalist Muslims but when the Muslim League gave the call for Pakistan, it transformed the politics of Amritsar. It was clear that the Muslims wanted Pakistan and wanted it passionately. Quaid-i-Azam was easily accepted as the real leader of the Muslims while the Ahraris and Khaksars were relegated to the periphery. As long as Master Tara Singh had not said that he would not let Pakistan come into being there was no clash in Amritsar, although polarisation had already taken place. Thereafter, things got out of hand but the provocation was clearly that of the Sikhs who, on 4 March went around beating drums to call Hindus and Sikhs to come out and oppose the Muslim League from coming into power. Hindus were not involved in the Chowk Pragdas massacre. It began with Sikhs attacking Muslims praying in the main mosque.

'We were sure that Amritsar would be a part of Pakistan. That is why till the end the Muslims did not emigrate though they had been forced to seek protection in Sharifpura. It is true that the Muslim leaders came from Lahore and encouraged us to stay put and insist on Amritsar being given to Pakistan.

'Amritsar would not be part of Pakistan. Muslims had no idea that they would not be able to return to Amritsar. Nobody in our family was killed. Only those Muslims were killed who were in Hindu and Sikh *mohallas*. It is true that during the worst of times some Sikh Communists came to our locality to return copies of the Quran *Sharif*. They also brought some Muslim girls and handed them over to us. The Pakistan military evacuated the Amritsar Muslims. I have no idea of what happened in the rural areas though Muslim refugees began to arrive in Amritsar in August. I don't think many Muslims were killed in Amritsar city. Perhaps the number of casualties on both sides was the same.

'Had Pakistan not come into being, the Hindus would have kept us tied down by poverty and the caste system. They had been dominated by Muslims for a thousand years. In a united India, they would have taken their revenge from the Muslims. It was imperative to create Pakistan. That Pakistan could not develop into a true Islamic welfare state is a tragedy but the ideal that inspired us was to create a society free of all forms of exploitation.

'Yes, I had some Hindu and Sikh friends. Some of them were Communists but they still went to the temples and *gurdwaras*. Jawaharlal Nehru was a secular intellectual, but not the main Congress leadership. Patel hated the Muslims. Jinnah was right to insist on Pakistan and get it for us. Without Pakistan we would have no identity of our own.

'You ask me about the Muslims that were left behind in India. Don't you see how they are persecuted and killed? You cannot understand the Hindu mind. It is too devious. Muslims are not like that. Especially Sunni Muslims are egalitarian and have always been attracted to justice for all.'

I asked A. Hameed if he ever regretted using harsh words for fellow writers such as Upinder Kumar Ashq, whom he described in his stories as a 'deeply prejudiced Hindu'. He said he did not, because Hindus were 'by their very nature full of prejudice against Muslims and Islam'. He told me that although he had many friends in the Progressive Writers' Movement, he was always opposed to their Marxism. Islam already had a philosophy of social justice so why must Muslims borrow anything from others, he wondered.

In an unguarded moment during our long discussion, Hameed deviated from the script he had prepared and began to brood about the censorship laws that applied to Pakistan television plays. He told me that for years he wrote plays for Karachi television. The standing directions for writers to follow were that a man and a woman could not declare that they were in love with each other unless the audience was already informed that both were going to marry. As time passed, I noticed Hameed implicitly admitting that India, as a secular state, provided much more freedom to writers than was possible in Pakistan. At one stage, he was almost waxing lyrical about Jawaharlal Nehru, telling me that he had been reading his book, *The Discovery of India,* and was amazed to discover what an enlightened person he was.

I spent a number of days in Amritsar in March 2004 and talked to a wide range of old residents of that city. Some interviews are presented below.

Gurcharan Das Arora

'What happened in Amritsar was inevitable. It was a very political city since the beginning of the twentieth century. After the Jallianwala Bagh carnage of 13 April 1919, Amritsar never ceased to buzz with political activity. The Muslims had a large presence through the Majlis-e-Ahrar and the Khaksars. The Muslim League was a late arrival and the Amritsar Muslims remained lukewarm about the election campaign of 1945–46. That is when Muslim Leaguers from Lahore started visiting Amritsar on a regular basis. I suspect that what they could not do in Lahore – because of the presence of the British governor and other high officials – they were able to do in Amritsar. The main political party of Amritsar was always the Congress; Satya Pal and Dr Saifuddin Kitchlew were its leaders. Amritsar was the finest example of Hindu–Muslim–Sikh cooperation. There were many Muslim poets in Amritsar who could move the masses with their radical socialist ideas. There were communal riots once in a while, but largely because of misunderstandings and not at all for any deep reasons. Indeed, the Amritsar that existed before 1945 was a citadel of secular, anti-colonial forces that seemed determined to win freedom for all Indians.

'I will not deny that the RSS and the Sikhs had begun to prepare for the worst, but so had the Muslim National Guard. I am an old man now, but then I was young and very active in Hindu religious activities. My father Lala Gian Chand was the head of a *mandir* committee. Such activities did not hamper our commitment to the freedom struggle. It was equally true of very pious and good Muslims. The Hindus did not eat with Muslims. That must be admitted. It was something which should have been abolished earlier but in those days people really never made a big issue of it.

'All this changed in March 1947. The goodwill that existed between the communities day by day turned into fear and suspicion. It was not safe to go out, and Hindus and Sikhs confined themselves to their own localities and Muslims to theirs. Sometimes I think that all this was being orchestrated from somewhere. Perhaps the British were behind it. Anyhow, from June onwards, the Muslims had been put on the defensive though earlier on their *goondas* could commit many crimes and get away with them.

'I remember Muslims from the neighbouring villages arriving in the city with their stories of mainly Sikh atrocities. This began to happen on an expanding and cumulative basis from the beginning of August. By that time the Muslims had been driven away and most of them were hiding in Sharifpura and some other localities outside the city.

'You want to know what the total loss of life in Amritsar was by the end of 1947. Well I would not hesitate to admit that thousands, not hundreds, were killed. I have seen bodies cut up into pieces, even of children. One woman had a spear pierced into her vagina. It was a ghastly sight. This happened on the main road that entered Amritsar from Batala. She must have been fleeing from some village because she was dressed up as a villager. She was a Muslim. There was no doubt a very huge increase in the raids after the announcement of the Radcliffe Award. I think the people in Sharifpura were able to leave without too much loss of life because the military came and escorted them to Pakistan. After August, the Muslims who were killed were from the rural areas.

'It is true that some Muslim women were paraded naked in Amritsar. It was a hideous spectacle. I can't remember the date, but it was in

August. I don't know if it happened earlier as well in March, as you suggest. The August parade of Muslim women is too well-known. God will never forgive those who were behind such crimes but the responsibility must be that of the Muslim League who wanted to divide our common homeland. Once in a while some Amritsari Muslims come from Lahore. Since I am an elderly person whose family has had a shop in these areas, some of them are sent to me by other Amritsaris. Often they want to visit the streets where they lived. I have seen many of them crying. It is not uncommon that they jokingly say that they want to come back but I think that is a sentiment that will die out soon when the generation that knew another Amritsar – one of love and joy – is gone. I will be gone soon, so who will help them find their homes? All this was so unnecessary. Done is done and now Amritsar is a very different place.

'Some Kashmiri artisans and traders have settled in Amrtisar. If you go into the streets behind Hall Bazaar you will find them working and selling their products. If you go to the town centre you will find that the mosques are again being revived. Not only the Kashmiri Muslims but lots of Muslim *bhaiyyas* (Urdu-speakers) work in Amritsar. They are mainly from eastern UP and Bihar. Therefore, slowly, Muslims are returning to Amritsar. I really don't know if it is a good idea to mix people again, but India is a democracy and the rules allow people to work and settle anywhere. Therefore Muslims are bound to come back, but they would be aliens. The Muslim poets and writers who were once so much a part and parcel of Amritsar life are a memory from a bygone era which will always haunt my generation.'

The past had left indelible marks on Mr Arora's personality. He spoke with conviction, combining nostalgia with a belief that the Muslim League was responsible for the tragedy that befell the Amritsar Muslims. Vicky and I went into some streets and found several Kashmiri Muslims busy at work as tailors and shawl merchants. Apparently they lived in the same place where they worked, but I could be mistaken. Also, the freshly painted green minarets of some mosques suggested that they were in use.

Amritsar district

From 18 August onwards, the Muslims of Amritsar and Taran Taran *tahsil* were for quite some time at the mercy of the Sikh *jathas*. The PBF was operating in it as elsewhere but it seriously lacked troops committed to stopping the killings. In Muslim and Pakistani accounts, the rural areas of Amritsar, and the road from Amritsar to the Wagah border post from where West Punjab began, have been described as the killing fields. That is of course true. Whatever restraint on abuse of power remained in Amritsar city, as soon as one moved away from it the situation, was one of total abandon and Muslims were cut down mercilessly.

Legendary singer Mohammad Rafi's village

Kotla Sultan Singh (*tahsil* and district Amritsar) is the third village on a metalled road which branches off perpendicularly on the opposite side of a *shaadi ghar* (wedding hall), located on the left side of the main road as one exits from the tiny town of Majitha, some 25 kilometres northeast of Amritsar. To many readers Kotla Sultan Singh probably does not ring any bell. But for those of us who grew up listening to film music from the 1950s, this village is truly a major pilgrimage site. The greatest male singer of Urdu/Hindi/Punjabi films, the late Mohammad Rafi (died July 1980), was born here. On 27 March 2004, Vicky, Nanak Singh and I arrived at Kotla Sultan Singh after completing an eleven-day whirlwind tour of East Punjab, travelling some 2,200 kilometres during which I conducted interviews with witnesses to the Partition. Winding up such a tour with a visit to the place of birth of a man whose popularity cuts across all religions and state boundaries of south Asia was for me a very appropriate way to end my sojourn. We learned that the village received a regular traffic of Rafi devotees. Some came and prostrated at the spot where Rafi's house was located. Others consecrated that spot by taking some soil from there with them. We were taken to an elderly Sikh gentleman who was sitting on the traditional charpoy.

Sardar Kundan Singh Samra

'We belong to the landowning section of the village. Before Partition, half the population of the village consisted of Muslims. It was a very well-knit community in which people shared each other's joys and sorrows and took part in each other's religious festivals. Although Rafi and his family and most other Muslim villagers were Sunnis, there were some Shias, too. They would borrow our horse to take out the Muharram procession.

'The Muslims of our village belonged mainly to the non-agricultural professions. In 1945, Rafi was married to his cousin Bashiran here in the village. We all took part in the wedding ceremony. He told me about his efforts to get a break as a playback singer in the Lahore film industry. Soon his songs began to be played on the radio and we learned that he had gone to Bombay to try his luck there. In 1947, the Muslims of our village had to go to Pakistan. Miscreants from other villages attacked them and some were killed. Rafi was in Bombay at the time. In 1956, Rafi came to Amritsar for a concert. Some of us went there and met him before the show began. He met us with a lot of warmth. He promised to come to the village on another occasion. Whenever someone from our village went to Bombay, Rafi would help him in whatever way he could. They could stay at his place and enjoy his hospitality. Unfortunately, he never could visit Kotla Sultan Singh before his death.'

In Delhi, I told the Rafi story to Nirupama Dutt, a leading Indian journalist. She explained why Rafi may have hesitated to visit Kotla Sultan Singh. She said, 'The women of the Kotla Sultan Singh once told another interviewer that when the Muslims of their village were attacked in 1947, some women from Rafi's *biradari* were abducted by the raiders. He possibly felt uncomfortable coming again to Kotla Sultan Singh.' That made a lot of sense to me.

A Muslim refugee from another rural part of Amritsar district, from Taran Taran *tahsil*, had the following story to tell about his ordeal in those days:

Haji Muhammad Akram

'We lived on the outskirts of Taran Taran, district Amritsar. It was a Jatt village, mostly Sikhs, but some generations ago our ancestors had converted to Islam when a holy man came there and began to preach Islamic ideas. Since July or even earlier, Sikh *jathas* had been observed riding past our village. The Sikhs and Hindus in our village were good people. In fact the elders of all the communities had made a pledge to stand by one another. After we learnt that our village had been placed in India, a discussion took place between the elders. We were told that the Sikhs from the surrounding villages were going to raid all the Muslim villages and they will be in such big numbers that whatever our village did we will be overpowered. That created panic.

'Next day was Eid [18 August], but it was decided that we should leave before the sun came up. My paternal grandfather was too old and too ill. There were also other old people and one or two who were not mentally sound. We had only a few carts at our disposal. The elders decided to stay on, saying that if God willed they would be saved, otherwise their time had come. I remember my father crying when they had to leave the elderly and infirm behind, but what could we do. That night nobody slept. Very late in the night my grandfather said to my father, '*Sajjay [Siraj] ikk daffa Akram nu kavvo key ucchi, ucchi Rasulpak di shan wich o na'at sunaway jerri o gaanda honda hai*' (Siraj, tell Akram to sing the sacred poem that he usually sings about the Holy Prophet). I was only thirteen at that time. I had a melodious voice and used to sing sacred songs at the time of Islamic festivals. Everybody started crying when I began singing. I myself had no real idea of what was about to happen though it was clear that we were parting and our lives were in danger. Even the Sikhs and Lalaji [the village Hindu shopkeeper] were moved to tears as I sang '*Ya Nabi salaam-o-laika, Ya Rasul salaam-o-laika*' (Peace be upon you O Prophet, peace be upon you O Messenger of God). He touched me on the head and said, '*Puttar mennu bhull na jaween*' (My boy, don't forget me). I was his only grandson, as my elder uncle had only daughters and my aunt had recently been married and gone to a village in Kapurthala state.

'Soon we were on the road; some people from our village had relatives in Lahore so we followed them. We must have been at least 800 people. Old women, pregnant women, and small children were put on the carts while the rest began to walk. Some elderly men also decided to come but they had to walk. The idea was to keep to the main road. Soon Muslims from adjoining villages joined us. It seems many people had taken the same decision – to leave before the sun rose. Soon it must have been thousands who were walking. The women were murmuring Quranic verses while the men kept guard. As the day became brighter, the first Sikh *jathas* came and attacked from all directions. They had all sorts of weapons, including rifles and revolvers, but most of them carried spears and *kirpans*. We had not even managed to offer Eid prayers and suddenly Karbala had broken loose on us [symbolically used to signify the carnage of Prophet Muhammad's grandson, Imam Hussain and his family in present-day Iraq, in AD 680].

'My mother had died the previous summer, so my father had only me. He was holding my hand and we began to run into the fields. Of course, many from our village were with us, but when the attack came everybody ran away to save themselves. A gunshot hit my father and he fell. I kept running till I could hide myself in the fields. Around us the shrieks and groans of people could be heard while the Sikhs were shouting slogans and abusing in coarse Punjabi.

'Soon, I found others hidden in the fields. Our village cleric, Pir Abdus Samad Shah, was one of them. I used to learn the Quran from him and he also trained me to sing *na'ats*. He very kindly took care of me and soon some other people from our village also joined us. Shahji [the cleric] consoled all of us as we were crying. His wife had died and he had only a daughter who was pregnant. Her husband had gone to Calcutta where he worked. She had been placed on the cart with other women. After the attack took place, Shahji did not know what had happened to her. He kept chanting Quranic verses, reminding us that God was testing us and we must continue to believe in His mercy and kindness. Meanwhile, Sikh *jathas* kept riding past us. Once in a while they would even come into the fields to find out if someone was hiding. Some people were found and killed. I believe they took the young women with them.

'When night fell, we came out and some people who knew the way began to lead us towards Lahore. We must be several hundred, mostly men, though some women had also escaped into the fields. Several thousand must have died. We saw many dead bodies. Our village *lohar* (blacksmith) Karam Din's body was found with a spear thrust into his neck. Everywhere, body parts were scattered. It was a ghastly scene. I wanted to go and look at my father again but was dissuaded by all others from doing that.

'The next day more Muslims joined us. We continued to avoid the main roads and two days later reached Wagah. Many were badly injured. Some died on the way. As we crossed into Pakistan, people began to cry again, remembering their dead and lost relatives. On the other side, Hindu and Sikh corpses were littered. The angel of death had a wide embrace.

'The fact is that before 1947 there was no problem at all between the different communities. I used to go to school in a Hindu village. That meant walking some distance. Normally many of us would go together, including Hindu and Sikh boys from the neighbouring villages. In our village, Muslims were in a majority but Sikhs and Hindus also lived there. They showed great respect for Islam while we also returned the same respect to their beliefs. In our village there was no problem as most of us used the same wells and other facilities.

'Life has never been the same for me, though I have done well in life. My son, Manzur, went to Saudi Arabia and earned a good income. My grandchildren have done well in studies. One is an engineer. He, too, works in Saudi Arabia. Pakistan is our homeland but I always think of my mother who is buried in our village and my grandfather and father. I was too young to try finding out what happened to my grandfather. Some people later told me that all were killed by raiders and nobody was spared.'

Batala, Gurdaspur and Pathankot *tahsils*

From the Muslim point of view, the most dramatic climax–anti-climax that attended the Partition of the Punjab was what transpired between 15–17 August in the three *tahsils* of Gurdaspur district that were awarded to East Punjab. It may be recalled that Gurdaspur had a very narrow fifty-one per cent Muslim majority. On 14 August, the Pakistan flag was hoisted in those *tahsils* by Muslims who believed that Gurdaspur district as a whole would be given to Pakistan because of its Muslim majority, however narrow. In fact, the Pakistan government appointed Mushtaq Ahmed Cheema as Deputy Commissioner of Gurdaspur. He 'served' in that role from 14 to 17 August. Hindu–Sikh accounts mention that the Muslims began to take over Hindu properties and businesses using considerable violence. This is admitted by some people I interviewed, though they play down the extent of violence that took place in those two or three days. The announcement, on 17 August, that those three *tahsils* were awarded to India brought forth fierce reprisals by Hindus and Sikhs.

Syed Zia Mohiuddin

'Our family enjoyed great respect in Batala as we belonged to the leading *pir* family. Since my father was a *pir*, Hindus and Muslims respected us. Some Hindus had family relations with us. Rai Bahadur Bhawani Singh, a Hindu, was very close to us. They were Rajputs. They were like brothers to my family. We used to exchange sweets with Hindus. My father's name was Syed Nazar Mohiuddin. He was always elected unopposed to the Batala Munipality. Batala had some industry. C.M. Latif, who later became a major industrialist in Pakistan, was from Batala.

'We believed that Batala would come to Pakistan. Batala was the biggest town in Gurdaspur district. On 14 August the rumour spread that Batala had been awarded to Pakistan. For three days the Pakistan flag was hoisted in Batala. We started giving protection to our Hindu friends. On 17 August things changed. We did not feel any impact. Hindus did not harass us. We had no confrontation. We did not suffer directly.

'In the rural areas, there was massacre of Muslims by Sikhs. The fight was between Sikhs and Muslims. In Gurdaspur rural areas the Sikhs were very militant. Hundreds of thousands of Muslims started coming to our house for protection. Sometime during 17–20 August most of our family was sent to Pakistan. Eight of us stayed to help the Muslims.

We saw Muslims being killed on the outskirts of Batala. We came to Lahore then on 10 September. The Hindus came to us and said, you should not go. There was a Sikh doctor and a senior Hindu doctor, Luddar Maini, they came to us saying, don't go. We said we will look after ourselves. Then they said, okay, go for a while but then come back. My father was of the same opinion. We were used to going to Lahore. Batala was only 60 miles from Lahore. We lost all our property. Our family then settled in Sialkot where we had many disciples. My father was elected. Then we were allotted the house of a colonel at 49 Jail Road, Lahore.'

Ayaz Khan

'Batala is my ancestral town where several generations of us Kakezai Pathans were born. My mother was from Pathankot. I was born in my maternal grandparents' home in Pathankot. In 1947 I was in the fifth class at M.B. High School, Batala, situated near Bansaan Walla bazaar. There was no riot in Batala in March. Some trouble took place in June or July. It was summer vacation, so my younger brother Ejaz and I were in Lahore. Sikhs from Majitha in the Amritsar district raided Batala and created havoc. They attacked our house as well but luckily my mother and younger brother Izhar, along with other women, managed to leave safe and sound. They reached Lahore by truck. My father was wearing a bowler's hat and was part of a caravan consisting of thousands of men and women. The president of the Muslim League, Batala, Syed Bahawaldin, was shot dead in the police station where he had gone to ask for protection for the Muslims. [According to a Hindu witness, he was beheaded – author.]

'My maternal uncle, Sheikh Muhammed Riaz, was president of the Muslim League, Gurdaspur *tahsil*. He reached Lahore station and was waiting for the train to Gujrat where a close relative of ours was posted. Someone tried to snatch the gold bangle of my *nani* (maternal grandmother). She shouted to her son, "Riaz, Riaz this man is trying to take off my *karra* (bangle)". He replied, "Mother, he probably needs it more than us. Let him take it". Some of our relatives were killed but most managed to cross over to Pakistan soon after 18 August, and therefore escaped the slaughter that took place in the days and weeks that followed.

Nehru helped in Batala

One of the leaders of the Punjab Muslim League, Begum Shahnawaz, whose father, Sir Muhammad Shafi, was once considered a leader of Jinnah's stature, had many relatives in the villages around Batala. She recorded the following events that took place. Although she did not mention any dates, it must be after 15 August.

Begum Shahnawaz

> Nawab Mamdot rang me at 10 p.m. one evening and said that he had learnt from a reliable source that Batala city was to be attacked by the Sikhs that very night. The place was full of our tribesmen [Arains to which Begum Shahnawaz belonged] and the whole family of my aunt, Lady Rashid (wife of Pakistan's first chief justice, Mian Abdur Rashid) was there. He said me to do whatever I could to save a huge massacre ... I was very upset and I rang up Miss Maqueen, niece of Sir Francis Mudie, the Governor. She told me that the Governor had not been well and had gone to sleep. I requested her to ask him to talk to me, as it was very urgent. He spoke to me on the telephone and I appealed to him to ring up the Governor-General of India, Lord Louis Mountbatten, and try to save Batala. I had sent my car to fetch Uncle Rashid and on his arrival I made him telephone Pundit Jawahar Lal Nehru, to ask him to prevent the massacre of Muslims of Batala. Uncle talked to Punditji and he promised to do his best. My mother was in New Delhi at the time, staying with my brother, Mian Muhammad Rafi, Secretary of the Central Assembly. I telephoned her and asked her to see Punditji early next morning and request him to help the Muslims of Batala. She saw Pundit Jawahar Lal Nehru, who respected her a lot, and he promised to help in the matter. Tazi and I could not sleep the whole night but, thank God, Batala was saved (2002: 210-11).

Chaudhri Muhammad Bashir

'For three days Gurdaspur was included in Pakistan. Then the news came that it was given to India. So we hurriedly left our Makhanpur village, *tahsil* Pathankot, distict Gurdaspur. The population was half Hindu, half Muslim. No Hindu in our village attacked us; we did not attack them either. When we left, Charan Singh and Dalip Singh from an adjoining village accompanied us to the border. If they had not helped, things would have been very different. We went towards Kashmir. Then we crossed the river and entered Shakargarh *tahsil*. We had no weapons. My parents were already dead so I and four of my brothers and *dadi* came to Pakistan.

Then I came to Lahore, prepared a claim for property left behind, but the Pakistan government did not help us. The Hindus of our village were good people. Next to our house in Makhanpur lived a Brahmin, Bua Ditta. He was a moneylender. He charged very nominal interest. One day I was crying because my eyes were swollen. He came and put some medicine in my eyes. I recovered very soon. The Quran says never tell a lie. So I speak the whole truth. They were very good people. There we felt secure. We were part of that soil. I have always wanted to go back. I have seen criminals do well in Pakistan. Two of my sons are lawyers. So, we have done well despite all the difficulties, but things were much better in our idyllic village setting.'

A visit to Batala in March 2004 proved very useful as we met an eyewitness and participant in the rioting that took place in Batala.

Riaz A. Khan

This interview was sent to me via email from London on 28 October 2012. It bore the title 'My Memory of the Journey to Pakistan at the Time of Partition' and described Riaz Khan's experiences in Talwandi village, district Gurdaspur:

'My family hails from village Talwandi, Gurdaspur district. It was during the summer of my sixth year. I was an independent, gregarious young boy and remember a prolonged period of commotion and many people coming to and from our house. Something of great significance seemed to be happening though I did not understand what. Suddenly, one early morning, my parent's voices echoed through our home: "*Jaldi jaldi challo challo niklo* (Get out quickly and move)'. My father instructed my whole family (parents, youngest sister and my widowed aunt) to immediately vacate our home. We could not take any of our belongings. I was told that we were going to Pakistan. I did not know what this meant or why we had to go. My grandfather, Baba Moula Bakhsh, was a hakim (one who practises traditional medicine) and a landowner. He had many Hindu and Sikh friends and felt comfortable in his surroundings. Hakims were respected by all communities as they helped people in distress. He believed he would see us in a couple of days because everything would return to normal and we would return. He had no idea of the mass exodus taking place at that time across both sides of the border that had been created between the new states of India and Pakistan. My aunt and my four-year-old sister remained with him. They were hidden by the Hindu and Sikh friends of my grandfather. They were evacuated three days later by Muslim soldiers (from the Indian Army I believe). Even at this stage, my grandfather refused to leave. I never saw him again.

'I remember seeing a stream of people moving out of the village. We joined them and started walking towards somewhere. To me it seemed a very long way. I have those visual recollections etched on my mind. It was a mass movement of people and the noises were disorientating and startling. We walked through fields to avoid travelling on main roads. More and more folks joined our caravan. I saw a pool of muddy bloody water with a hand sticking out of it. It was the body of a dead man. My father hurriedly pulled me away. I also remember passing a corn field. Suddenly the crowd started running as there was some movement in the field. It transpired that there were some farm labourers weeding the field who jumped up with their sickles and scared the whole crowd. We believed they were lying in wait to attack us. In fact, my parents told me later that the labourers were frightened to see such a huge group of men, women and children and felt that their lives were in danger. They meant no harm. Yet fear was on the minds of all, and the air was thick with treachery.

'The journey seemed endless. I remember being carried by my father for some of the journey. We arrived at a place where many more people had assembled. It was a river bank, almost like a beach. I saw boats come and go, each leaving and then returning with lots of people on each vessel. This was the river crossing between India and the newly formed Pakistan. Muslims were crossing over to Pakistan and Hindus and Sikhs were leaving for India. I remember there was some talk of collecting money for the boatman and my mother taking off her earrings and bangles and giving them to my father (apparently for the fare). Many women did this. By the time a boat arrived for us, it was quite dark. My father carried me first to the boat walking in the water which reached his waist, amongst what seemed like dozens of other people shoving and pushing. He almost threw me in the boat and tried to walk back a few steps to help my mother and my aunt when the boat suddenly started to move and my family could not get in. I was alone. I became very confused and started crying. People were asking each other and shouting out to ask if anyone knew whose child I was. Someone recognized me and took care of me until we reached the other side. More boats came and went, and I guess that the people who looked after me probably knew that they would at some point be able to hand me over to my family.

'I cried myself to sleep. My guardian went to look for my parents at first light. When I was thankfully reunited with them and saw my father and mother, I was frightened. I thought it was my fault that I had lost them and was relieved to know that they were not angry with me! My mother later told me that she had fought with my father and had cried all night blaming him for deliberately "throwing me away—the only precious thing they could retrieve from India"! I remember that experience as being a profoundly harrowing event.

'My father never spoke of this journey or what he had left behind in India. He wanted to forget the trauma and I believe he felt incredibly guilty for leaving his father behind and not insisting on his joining our exodus. The borders closed soon after we left. We had no opportunity to travel back to see what had happened to our village. I believe my father never forgave himself for this.

'We came to Pakistan penniless but managed to get to my mother's relatives near Narowal from where my father contacted a friend in Chakwal.

He invited my father to come to settle in Chakwal and welcomed us with open arms. That's where I grew up and that's where my mother and brother and sister still live. And that's what I still call "home" after having lived in England over 50 years.'

Inderjeet

'I am Batala-born. Here Hindus, Muslims and Sikhs used to live in perfect peace. We used to exchange sweets during festivals. Hindus used to receive raw meat, mutton, from Muslims. I had two close Muslim friends, Sattar and Yusuf. Chakri Bazaar was a Hindu stronghold. The Hindus were in the middle of the town and Muslims all around. For two and a half days, district Gurdaspur was believed to be in Pakistan, then it was announced that it would be in India minus Shakargarh *tahsil*. At that time there was a Muslim SHO, Shaikh Ghulam Rabani, posted in Batala. Curfew had been imposed. He sent the police to arrest my brother because the Muslims had given an application that they were afraid of Hindu young men. Baloch, Sikh, Gurkha – all such military units were in Batala.

'The Muslims had planned to take over Hindu–Sikh houses and women. Bahawaldin, local president of the Muslim League, was one of them. He used to boast that openly. He belonged to Achli Drawaza. Another Muslim who entertained similar nefarious designs was Hameed Tiddi Muchan (twisted moustaches). In those two and a half days, when Batala was deemed as part of Pakistan, village Chuawal was attacked. Muslims came to kill and loot, even from as far as Sharifpura, outside Amritsar.

'However, on 17–18 August the tables turned completely when we learned that Batala belongs to India. Bahawaldin's head was chopped off. Hameed escaped wearing a *burqa* (fully veiled dress). Then Hindus burnt a busload of Muslims. It had run out of steam. DSP Sapuran Singh saved all Hindus. I myself went with a knife to kill but did not find any. I had a big *churra*, but our military had taken bribe and let seven busloads of Muslims pass. Then for twenty-four hours Muslims were in a camp on Bearing Road. There firing took place. On the whole, Hindus lost a lot of property but Muslims lost many lives. I remember military people coming to sell jewellery seeping in blood at my father's shop. He was a jeweller. Thousands of Muslims died in Batala and Gurdaspur districts. Dogra *fauj* [Kashmir Army] was involved in the killings of Muslims.

'Six or seven years later there was a hockey or cricket game in Lahore. I don't exactly remember because there were a number of such events. Many of us young men went to Pakistan. I met Yusuf who gave me excellent hospitality. We stayed in Yakki Gate.'

Notes

Ali, Chaudhri Muhammad. *The Emergence of Pakistan,* Lahore; Research Society of Pakistan, 1973.

Iftikhar, Khawaja. *Jabb Amritsar Jall Raha Tha* (When Amritsar was Burning), Lahore: Khawaja Publishers, 1991.

Said, Chaudhri Mohammad. 'A Brief Account of the Happenings in Amritsar by Ch. Mohammad Said M.A., L.L.B., ex-Terminal Tax Superintendent, Municipal Committee, Amritsar, Present Address:- 3/30, Nisbet Road, Lahore', *The Journey to Pakistan: A Documentation on Refugees of 1947,* Islamabad: National Documentation Centre.

Shahnawaz, Begum Jahan Ara. *Father and Daughter: A Political Biography,* Karachi: Oxford University Press, 2002.

Interviews

Syed Zia Mohiyuddin, Stockholm, 24 June 2002

Chaudhri Muhammad Bashir, Lahore, 18 April 2003

Haji Muhammad Akram, Lahore, 23 April 2003

A.Hameed, Lahore, 19 April 2003

Gurcharan Das Arora, Amritsar, 24 March 2004

Sardar Kundan Singh Samra, 27 March 2004

Inderjeet, Batala, 3 January 2005

Ayaz Khan, Linkoping, Sweden (via email),14 January 2007

Riaz A. Khan, London, 28 October 2012

18

JULLUNDUR DIVISION

JULLUNDUR DIVISION COMPRISED KANGRA, HOSHIARPUR, JULLUNDUR, Ludhiana and Ferozepore districts of central Punjab. Muslims constituted a substantial minority of thirty-four per cent of its population in 1947. In none of its districts were Muslims in a majority, but in several of its key towns they were in a majority. In the notional division of 3 June 1947 Jullundur division was part of East Punjab. The Radcliffe Award gave it without any alteration to India.

Ferozepore (Firozpur)

To the south of Amritsar district began Jullundur division, with its Ferozepore district touching portions of the Lahore district. Muslims made up forty-five per cent of the population of Ferozepore district. There is bitter controversy about two of its Muslim-majority *tahsils*, Ferozepore and Zira (altogether there were five *tahsils*), being first included in Pakistan and then eventually being awarded to India under pressure from Mountbatten. As a result, an army arsenal located in Ferozepore cantonment remained in India (Roberts 1995:94).

Ferozepore city

In Ferozepore city, including the cantonment area, Muslims were nearly forty-seven per cent of the total population. Both the Muslim League and the Congress had their supporters. Before August 1947, very few serious violent incidents took place in the city.

Malik Muhammad Aslam

'On 17 August, the Muslims of Ferozepur were shocked when it was announced over the radio that their district had been placed in India. Among the Muslims, such an outcome had not been contemplated. Nawab Mamdot, who was the chief leader of the Punjab Muslim League, used to visit Ferozepore, and he and his associates never indicated that Ferozepore would not become part of Pakistan. I used to study in Lahore in those days. An uncle of mine lived in a street off Nisbet Road. We had very good relations with our Hindu neighbours in Ferozepore. One of them, Lala Dhuni Chand, came and talked to my father in the afternoon of 17 August warning him that he had information that the Sikhs and RSS were planning an attack on Muslims.

'That shattered all our dreams of staying put. My father was actually a great supporter of Mahatma Gandhi. He was a government servant and had many friends in the Congress party. He was in two minds about what to do when, soon after the sun set, the Sikhs went around on horses firing at Muslims. That created panic. Fortunately, my maternal grandparents were already in Lahore with my uncle, so my parents, my three sisters and I were at home. The Muslims living around us came crying to my father. He was educated and the people wanted him to give them directions as to what to do.

'At about 10 p.m. there was another raid. Some people came running and told us that the RSS were attacking Muslims. It was decided that we should all assemble in the Friday mosque rather than be hunted down one by one. Most of the women had never entered the mosque and there were no particular rooms for them. So, about 300 of us sought refuge there. It was close to the police station; the idea was that the police would not allow an attack in a place close to it. My father, and some other elders, Syed Safdar Hussain Shah, Pir Fazal Haq and Mian Ahmed Hassan, went to the police station and met the officer-in-charge. He was a Hindu from Sirsa who had been posted there in March. There were some Muslim policemen, too, who were serving there. He told them that he could post some policemen outside the mosque, but it was advisable that we should leave early next morning because he could not guarantee what would happen the next day.

'That night seemed never to end. Gunshots could be heard all around. We also heard men and women, even children, shrieking in pain and horror. Some of them managed to reach the mosque. We had hardly any arms except *dandas,* and some people had brought knives with them. A hockey player carried his hockey stick with him. We were thus easy targets, but the *jathas* and RSS cadres kept away from the mosque because it seemed that the Hindu SHO, probably his name was Trilok Nath, had warned them to keep away.

'At about three in the night Lala Dhuni Chand's son, Amarnath, came to the mosque to find out if everything was all right. Curfew had been imposed but somehow he had managed to make his way to the mosque. My father was severely diabetic but he had forgotten to bring his insulin syringe with him. By that time he was feeling ill. My mother began to cry and so did my sisters. Others offered sympathy but it was important that he got his insulin injection. Amarnath offered to go to the shop and Lalaji had a medicine shop in town. He never returned. Later I learned that he was shot dead by the RSS, who were against any Hindu who showed sympathy for Muslims. It was confirmed by many people that we later met in Kasur and Lahore.

'By early morning my father was in a very bad shape. He could hardly talk. He told us to leave him at the mosque and go with the others who were leaving. My mother would not agree and said, "Malik Sahib I would prefer to die by your side rather than leave you". We children also said the same but father just managed to tell her, "Zeenat, you should think of your three daughters and your son. They should have one parent at least". He told me that I am the man who shall have to take responsibility. Other elders intervened and finally we agreed to leave him in the mosque. I think some other elders also stayed back. My father was only fifty-one at that time, but because of his illness he had become very weak.

'Outside the mosque the two Muslim policemen had stood guard but when the caravan began to leave they, too, joined us. Both had guns with them. It was decided that we should take the Husainiwala–Ganda Singh Wala route and try to reach Kasur. Just as we left the outskirts of Ferozepore, Sikhs fell upon us. My mother and sisters were with other women while we men would walk up and down, seeing to it that things were under control. Some people had taken their bicycles and there were also one or two motorbikes. The rest had to walk. The children were crying, some old women and men could not walk anymore and begged their families to walk on. It was a very tragic sight. Some of the people had weapons but they were no match for the heavily armed Sikh *jathas* who surrounded us from all sides. The attacks were swift and focussed. Nobody was spared.

'I was struck on the head and fainted. When I regained consciousness I discovered myself surrounded by corpses. I realised that it was almost evening and I had been lying there for nearly twelve hours. The dead bodies of my mother and three sisters and several of our neighbours were lying around. For a moment I thought I should return to the mosque, perhaps my father would still be alive. I wanted to have my family with me. I was only nineteen and everybody in my life was dead. Suddenly, a jeep of the PBF appeared on the scene. I did not know who they were so I just stood there. The officer-in-charge was an Englishman who took pity on me and drove me all the way to Kasur. On the Pakistani side Hindus and Sikhs too had been killed without mercy. We were given medical aid by Christian volunteers. Those volunteers were helping thousands of people in the camps.

'You ask me today after fifty-eight years how I feel? You tell me, what would you feel if you were in my situation? Thousands, perhaps thousands of families suffered because the politicians could not agree on how to share power. There is nothing more to it than the lust for power. I still remember the night when Amarnath volunteered to go to his shop to get the medicine my father needed but was killed by fanatics of his own community. His father and mother must have been devastated. I lost everything.'

Ferozepore rural areas

Begum Shahnawaz

A story about events in Ferozepore's rural areas is also mentioned in Begum Shahnawaz's book. She wrote:

Early [the] next morning, we were having our breakfast when we heard someone crying and shrieking. The servants came and told us that a gentleman named Chaudhri Shafqat Rasool, a very influential tribesman from the Ferozepur district, had arrived and was weeping like a child and asking for me. When I met him, I found him in such a terrible state of collapse that he could hardly relate his woe.... Slowly, when he had calmed down, he told us harrowing tales of what had happened in the Ferozepur district. He said that he had come by a circuitous route and had, by the Grace of God, reached Lahore, somehow. Over 70,000 Muslims, including his family with two grown-up daughters, were taking refuge in a small island between the canals, Sikhs from Faridkot State were practically surrounding them, and they might all be massacred any moment. He said he would rather see his family dead than have his daughters fall into the hands of the ferocious Sikhs. The tales received from different places were that they were killing the elder members of families and taking the girls away. He was sobbing and beseeching me to save the honour of his family.

For two days I tried to pull every string possible, but without any success. Shafqat Rasul was frantic and practically going mad with grief. On the third day, I decided to seek the help of Brigadier Muhammad Ayub Khan, who was Second-in-Command of the Boundary Force.... I rang up Ayub asking him to come to my house, and when he arrived Chaudhri Shafqat Rasul explained everything to him. Ayub thought for a while and then said that the only help he could give was to send Shafqat Rasul in one of their weapon-carriers and he advised me to send a letter to the British Brigadier in charge of the force in Ferozepur. When he gave me the name, I was glad I knew him well.... Shafqat was sent that very evening with an escort to Ferozepur and my letter to the Brigadier. Ayub was very helpful and sent a unit of soldiers with Shafqat Rasul to the trouble spot. They arrived in time, just when the main attack of the Faridkot Sikhs had started. The lives of all the innocent besieged Muslims were saved (2002: 211-12).

Jullundur

In Jullundur district, Muslims formed a very large minority, of forty-five per cent. It was a stronghold of the Muslim League, but the Congress also had a large following besides the RSS.

Jullundur city

Jullundur city and cantonment had a fifty-nine per cent Muslim majority. It was a stronghold of the Muslim League, though both the Congress and the RSS were also well-organised and active. The Sikhs were not a prominent group in Jullundur.

Mian Jalal Din

'Jullundur should have been awarded to Pakistan. There was a contiguous Muslim majority that connected Jullundur to Lahore via the *tahsils* on the way. Radcliffe was influenced by Mountbatten not to accept the Muslim claims. We were devoted to the idea of Pakistan as Islam was a very strong force in our lives. My family was well-placed as my grandfather was a rich landowner and had built several houses in the city. It is true that the Hindus of Jullundur were good people, but the RSS had a strong presence here. The Muslim League National Guard and the RSS were often in tension.

'The Radcliffe Award was received in Jullundur with great consternation. For a while, our elders decided to stay put, but then Hindus and Sikhs started coming in large numbers with stories of Muslim atrocities in West Punjab. That set in motion Sikh *jathas* and RSS terrorism. The Muslims still believed that they would be able to manage the situation but the Hindu deputy commissioner was thoroughly partisan. He had been shifted from Gujranwala where probably Muslims had committed atrocities against his community. Attacks on Muslims began to mount by the day, I would even say by the hour. The criminals used all types of weapons. I have a strong feeling they used to come in from Kapurthala state on horses and even vehicles, shoot around and set fire to the buildings. No mercy was shown to anyone.

'I had a Hindu friend, Arvind Sharma. They were Brahmins. His father was in government service posted in Delhi. One day he came and informed me that he had heard that a decision to drive all Muslims out of East Punjab had been taken and therefore it was best that we leave. Most other people had shifted to the camps but ours was a powerful and influential family, so we left only in October. My father had arranged for three trucks on which our immediate family and essential things were loaded. We were escorted by Muslim troops all the way to Wagah. On the way, I saw corpses all over. Pakistan was the only solution for the Muslims of India. Sometimes I do think of Jullundur and the old Jullundur families maintain contacts. Mostly marriages are also arranged within them, but the younger generation no longer feels anything for Jullundur. I once visited Jullundur in the 1960s, the old buildings were there. Some Hindu Khatri family from Hafizabad had been allotted our house. They were kind enough to let me go in and see my room where I used to sleep and study. They even offered tea and we had a long talk. Their story was very similar to ours. I am told the old buildings still stand but Jullundur cannot be the same.'

Some events in Jullundur have already been presented in an earlier chapter from Muhammad Ayub Khan's *Tarikh-i-Pakistan Aur Jullundur* (The Pakistan Movement and Jullundur). About the events that transpired after 15 August, the following are some significant incidents.

Muhammad Ayub Khan

In early September [probably around 15 August] the All-India Congress Party sent their party president Dr Zakir Hussain (later president of India) to Jullundur to examine the situation [Dr Zakir Hussain was not party president. He was a professor at the Jamia Millia, a pro-Congress Muslim seat of education – author.] When the news spread that Dr Zakir Hussain was coming, Muslims in large numbers who were living in fear in the adjoining areas began to arrive in the city with their families in the hope that their security and safety of life would now improve. Instead they became easy bait for Sikh *jathas* who carried out an orgy of killing.... Magistrate Khan Tariq Ismail Khan arrived there with his wife and children from Karnal. Since he looked like a European and was dressed in Western clothes he was able to ward off the attackers. The platforms at Jullundur were littered with dead bodies. Some seven to eight thousand Muslims had taken refuge in the waiting rooms.... Dr Zakir Hussain was donning Muslim clothes and some people tried to attack him but Congress workers gathered around him and no harm could be done to him.... When Tariq Ismail Khan learnt that Dr Zakir Hussain was at the station he and some other Muslims went and met him and informed him about the thousands of Muslims who were hiding in the waiting rooms and asked for his intervention. Dr Zakir Hussain urged the Congress workers and the government officials who were present to help the thousands of Muslims reach the refugee camps safely or else he would sit down in protest. This galvanized the Congress workers who arranged trucks and other means of transport for the awe-stricken Muslims who were taken to the camps (2002: 271-3).

On September 24 [This would be 24 August or even earlier – author.] Prime Minister Jawaharlal Nehru visited Jullundur... Nehru was accompanied by two *maulvis* from Ludhiana who belonged to the Majlis-e-Ahrar and were nationalists. [One of them was Maulana Habibur Rahman. This I learnt in Ludhiana when I interviewed his grandson who is based there and is head of the main mosque – author.] A public meeting was held in Committee Bagh. It was attended by a large number of people. From the Muslim side the Muslim League worker Shamsul Haque Shaheed spoke and gave details of the atrocities committed by Hindus and Sikhs against Muslims.

Nehru said in his speech that such conduct could not be that of good and decent people. It was the behaviour of criminals and *goondas*. A Sikh Communist then said, 'Whether these people are criminals or *goondas* they are all around you'. Upon hearing that Nehru said, 'I have come to establish peace and amity. Those people who have left their homes and gone away I will bring them back'. He then sternly instructed the Hindus, Sikhs and

> the administrative officers to maintain law and order. The result was that afterwards the attacks on Muslims reduced considerably (ibid.: 273).
>
> A week after Pandit Jawaharlal Nehru's visit, the Home Minister of India Sardar Vallabbhai Patel visited Jullundur. Instead of meeting the people he confined his meeting with the administrative staff and Congress workers. What was the mission of this visit? This was kept a secret but after he left the intensity of attacks on Muslims increased considerably. From this one can infer that the main reason of his visit was to defeat and make ineffective the mission and purpose of Nehru's visit. As soon as he left a curfew was imposed. In practice it applied only to the movement of Muslims. Hindus and Sikhs went around without any worry or fear. They would roam about freely waving their swords and *kirpans*. Gurkha soldiers who were on duty to patrol the area were taken off because they prevented Hindus and Sikhs from carrying out attacks. Instead Dogras were put on patrol duty. Unlike the Gurkhas they were very prejudiced. The Dogras under the direction of the Hindus began to assassinate leading Muslims of Jullundur (2002: 273-4).

With regard to this narrative, it is to be noted that the dates given are incorrect, but the events described have been verified by other sources. The book gives specific details of attacks on Muslim localities and names some of the prominent Muslims who were killed by the collaboration of the Dogra troops and Hindu–Sikh gangs. Some of the instances quoted are truly shattering; for example, Muslims who were brought to the civil hospital were not given treatment, and some were even hanged (ibid.: 275).

He writes that the Muslim League workers and leaders kept resisting in the face of heavy odds against them. Three Muslims kept them provided with intelligence about Hindu–Sikh designs, including a plot to attack all Muslim localities and kill their leaders. Among the three was Abdul Ghani who worked in a Hindu owned printing press. He could read Hindi and Gurmukhi and could therefore follow the messages that were being sent from there. Another was Havaldar Abdul Hamid, who was employed in the secret branch of the CID. Another was Assistant

Sub-Inspector Sheikh Abdul Rahim. However, a notorious Muslim who sided with the Hindus and Sikhs was Khushi Muhammad, who was also an assistant sub-inspector in the police. He would appease his non-Muslim superiors by raiding the homes of Muslim League activists. He became known as Khushi Ram among the Muslims. Among the incidents is mentioned the jailbreak by Muslim prisoners who overpowered the jail staff. Some died but others escaped (ibid.: 317-20).

When the refugee camp at Nurpur was attacked 150 Muslim girls jumped into wells and killed themselves rather than fall into the hands of non-Muslims. In an estimate of deaths caused during combat between Muslim League youths (National Guards) and Hindu–Sikh attackers in a number of villages and other areas around Jullundur, he mentions some 60,000–70,000 Muslims killed, whereas only some 10,000–12,000 Hindus and Sikhs were killed. He also mentions that some 700 to 800 women in the camps in the Ludhiana district drowned themselves in the river Sutlej because the camps were poorly protected and the men folk had fallen fighting the Hindu–Sikh gangs (ibid.: 320-25).

Report of the Communist Party of India

A detailed report prepared by the Communist Party of India, dated 21 September 1947, describes raids on Muslims in several parts of East Punjab. One of the reports from Jullundur city dated 24 August 1947 mentions two visits of Jawaharlal Nehru to the city. One would presume that both visits took place before 25 August, and that certainly is correct. Muhammad Ayub Khan asserts that Col. Ayub Khan, who represented Pakistan on the Punjab Boundary Force, visited Jullundur after Nehru's visits. The Punjab Boundary Force, which included Indian and Pakistani military personnel under the command of Major General Rees, was disbanded on 1 September. The two armies, however, continued to cooperate in the transferring of refugees till much later.

The CPI report mentions that the Muslims of Jullundur were confident that Jullundur division would go to Pakistan. They had therefore made no preparation to leave but were prepared for rioting. On the other hand, the RSS and the city administration, including many magistrates, had prepared a detailed scheme for an attack against the

Muslims. On 17 August that scheme was put into action in Jullundur city. In fact, after 15 August, the RSS had already begun spreading rumours of Muslims having burnt down all Hindu localities and businesses in Lahore. An additional district magistrate, Mr Vaisisth, gave lurid accounts on the strength of what had been said by officials who had come from Lahore. Similar reports of Hindu suffering in Sialkot and Gujranwala were also spread. Copies of photos of Hindu women alleged to have been raped by Muslims who stood proudly near Muslim League flags were shown to people. Bomb blasts that took place were blamed on Muslims even when Muslims were among those who had been killed or hurt. Another photograph showed naked Hindu women being paraded in the streets of Dera Ismail Khan or Dera Ghazi Khan (1993: 170-71).

Even prominent, decent Hindus took part in such propaganda. The result was that anger soon reached fever-pitch. From 17 August onwards, Muslim houses were systematically burnt down. Some Muslim women were raped, including Shamim, a women's leader in their community. Lootings, killings, and other outrages were committed with abandon, often using rifles, revolvers, and Sten guns. The control of the railway station passed into the hands of Sikhs and RSS activists masquerading as Punjab relief workers. The respected Congressman Dr Zakir Hussain could be saved only with great difficulty. After Nehru's visit, a Muslim refugee camp was set up at Jullundur. Others went to the Pathan settlements around the city or other places where Muslims had gathered. The Muslim refugees who were armed, attacked the electric power house and other targets. By 24 August 1947, about one-third of the Muslim population was still in their homes and localities in the city.

The report tells us that Nehru paid a second visit and the conflicts sobered thereafter. The situation, however, continued to be tense in the villages. Horrible atrocities were committed. It is stated: 'The Additional District Magistrate (Bhalla) openly told us that he knew about the plans chalked out for burning Muslim localities and that if Nehru had not come, Krar Khum *mohalla* (the biggest Muslim locality) would have been burnt on the 22nd and others after that' (ibid.: 172).

Another despatch dated 30 August 1947, dealing with the rural areas of Jullundur district, gives extensive data of assaults against Muslims.

On 15 August, Muslims took part in the Independence celebrations but Akali propaganda had poisoned the atmosphere beyond repair. The report states further:

> On the 15th the Jullundur District Magistrate, one Mr. Midha (whose son is known to have been stabbed in Gujranwala) gave the people a clearance by telling them to "do whatever they liked for three days". He is alleged to have asked people to avenge the stabbing of his son. Police and military officials distributed ammunition and joined in the murder, arson, and loot. Some Congress leaders joined in. Darbara Singh, the District Congress Committee President took a leading part and has collected heaps of booty (ibid.: 174-5).

Such coordinated violence in which the government officials, civilian and military, and RSS, Akali and Congress leaders took part, convinced the Muslims that they could not be protected by the Indian government. An Akali leader who became known for terrorising Muslims was Sant Hari Singh Kahanpuri, a prominent religious leader. His gangs were supported by men of the Faridkot state forces. Some 2,500 men of his militia were trained in centres in Faridkot state in the use of guns, rifles, Tommy guns and Bren guns. It is stated:

> Sant Hari Singh has become a terror name for the Muslims. With his mounted gang he goes form village to village. He holds a mass meeting in a victim [sic] village usually 3000-4000 strong. There the Sant delivers a harangue about the glory that was the Sikh Empire, the atrocities committed by the Muslims in West Punjab, [and] the duty of the Khalsa to finish them. In the end, he exhorts them to indulge in conversions or loot or murder them all. After this the Muslims are liquidated (ibid.: 175).

Major General (Retd) Syed Wajahat Husain served in the PBF. He writes that he arrived via train in Jullundur at midday on 23 August with a small mixed force, thirty tanks and some vehicles, and quickly headed to the cantonment suburbs where the Muslim Pathan *mohallas bastis* (settlements) were located. Many well-to-do Muslims lived in these areas. They were saved and taken to refugee camps, from where they later moved to Pakistan (Husain, 2010: 58).

Jullundur rural areas

Muhammad Ashiq Raheel

On 29 December 2004, Ahmad Salim and I interviewed the Punjabi writer Muhammad Ashiq Raheel at his home in Outfall Road, Santnagar, Lahore. This is what he told us:

'I was born in Qasbah Nur Mahal, in my mother's parents' home. Otherwise our village is Pindhor in Patiala state. We are Bhatti Rajputs. I grew up in Jullundur because there was no school in our area in Patiala, therefore my *mamas* brought me over so that I could go to school. I was in the seventh class when Partition took place. Nur Mahal had mainly Hindus and Muslims. There was no attack on our town. We were all here in Nur Mahal. We came to Nakodar camp and stayed there for months. Then a train in mid-October came and took us to Pakistan. We had to sit on top of a train compartment. My mother died in Lahore one month later. I was still a small boy and had a younger brother just a year old. Our elder sister brought us up. My father was killed at the border of Nabha and Patiala.

'I kept contact with a Sikh class fellow who later moved to Calcutta and died there. Some years ago I visited Nur Mahal. Many people remembered my *nana* and *mamas.* They treated me like a prodigal son. Going back was a very emotional experience. I have written about it in my stories.'

I came into contact with Dr Muhammad Afzal through Asaf Ali Shah, mentioned in an earlier chapter in connection with the communication with Lt Gen. Aftab Ahmad Khan, who served in the PBF and later in the joint India–Pakistan military operations to escort refugees. Dr Afzal held many important positions in the Punjab government in Pakistan, retiring as Deputy Secretary, Local Government and Rural Development. Dr Afzal sent me his book, *Dastan-e-Sandham (The Story of Sandham)* with his autograph, dated 31 October 2007. It contains a heart-wrenching account of another round of slaughter of Muslims after 15 August.

Dr Muhammad Afzal

I was born in Sandham village, *tahsil* and district Jullundur, in July 1938. In 1947 it was located on the border between Jullundur and Hoshiarpur districts. Its population consisted almost entirely of small farmers of the Arain caste. Sandham had been razed many times in the past but always managed to rise from the ashes. In the 19th century the spread of Sikh rule was particularly bad for its people.

On July 23, 1947 the people of Sandham were as usual busy with their chores when the first attack by the Sikhs of a nearby village, Sos, on a Muslim family took place. A young woman, her brother and her child who were walking past this area were attacked and killed. The infant was flung in the air and the body landed on a spear, the young man fought back but was mercilessly killed. The young woman was first raped and then killed. Rana Muhammad Hanif, ASP, investigated that outrage and that is how we learnt about the horrendous details.

On July 25, a Sikh *jatha* killed a Muslim farmer Maulvi Allah Baksh who was attending to his farm on the outskirts of village Dhoboli. The people of Dhoboli went out to confront the Sikhs. From Sandham too the men left under the leadership of Pir Shah Muhammad and Chaudhri Muhammad Ismail to help the people of Dhoboli. There was a fierce battle. The leader of the Sikhs was killed but Chaudhri Muhammad Ismail was also stabbed. He was taken to the hamlet of Sham Churasi where the Hindu doctor carried out an operation but he could not save his life....

[The following are descriptions of other murders of Muslims from the village.]

From early morning of August 26 Sikh *jathas* began to congregate southwest of Sandham at Khera. Some people thought that we should offer resistance.... But the Sikhs using the cover of the growing crops entered the village while the people of Sandham the same and left. The raiders burnt the houses. ... In the beginning of September some 15 thousand Muslims had assembled in Sham

Churasi and began to organize themselves for their defence. They began to prepare to go to the refugee camp at Jullundur cantonment. The problem was that because of the Hindus in Sham Churasi it was not easy to conceal the plans that were being made. Dogra troops that had been posted to protect the Muslims had been to the Sikh villages around Sham Churasi. It was rumoured that they were going to participate in an assault on the Muslims along with the Sikhs and Hindus.

On September 13 Sikh *jathas* attacked, from all sides. The hamlet was surrounded from all sides and there was no way to escape. Because the attack took place just before dawn the Muslims were unprepared to fight the attackers. Earlier in the attacks that had taken place spears, swords and axes had been used. In this attack on Sham Churasi guns and rifles were used and their sound reverberated in the air. The massacre began with the help of the soldiers. Some 300 Muslim men, women and children were killed.

There is only one gate of the Sham Churasi Middle School. The compound of the school was filled with Muslim refugees. They were all butchered before the sun had risen. The streets and the areas around the hamlet were littered with dead bodies. There was a mosque, Masjid Shorgaran some 200 metres from the school. Muslims were offering the early morning prayers. Maulvi Sultan Ai of Kotli was leading the prayers. The mosque was surrounded and all worshippers were killed. It was raining lightly. The hall and the compound of the mosque became red because of the blood spilled. Chaudhri Ali Bakhsh [the paternal grandfather of Dr Afzal] and his nephew Chaudhri Fazal Muhammad were martyred in that raid. In the history of Islam their names were added to those killed while offering prayers…

The hapless refugees were then attacked while walking past Hamira, Dhalwan and Beas railway stations… Hungry, thirsty and dead tired refugees were facing the assaults of the merciless Sikhs when suddenly the rising waters of river Beas engulfed them. By that time it was late night. While the flood water was rising the trees around were infested with snakes. … The Sikhs were waiting at the railway station. Where could such powerless people turn? … thousands of them drowned in the waters of the Beas…Those who survived were ravaged by cholera… many perished (Afzal, n.d: 48-57).

Ludhiana district

The Muslim percentage of the population of the Ludhiana district was thirty-seven per cent. The Sikhs were the biggest community in Ludhiana district, making up nearly forty-two per cent of its population. The most ferocious killings of Muslims took place in some of the Sikh princely states as well as in the rural areas of Ludhiana district.

Ludhiana city

Ludhiana city, including the cantonment area, had nearly sixty-three per cent Muslim majority. It was located further east and south of the Sutlej river, yet because of its Muslim majority, the people there believed that Ludhiana district would be placed in Pakistan. The SGPC report mentions that the Muslim League was very active in Ludhiana and some clashes also took place, but the situation remained largely peaceful till about the beginning of August. Mohan Lal Jhanji, advocate and *sarpanch* of village Virk, district Ludhiana, told us that before the riots, Ludhiana thrived on great goodwill. Two famous Muslim poets, Sahir Ludhianvi and Tufail Hoshiarpuri, were his close friends. Baldev Verma told me that his father was a leading member of the Ghadar Party that in the early twentieth century attempted to foment an uprising against the British. His father served a fourteen-year prison sentence. He confirmed that Ludhiana was a radical city, but after the 1946 election, communal relations began to sour and soon made a turn for the worse.

Syed Muhammad Islam Shah

'Our family is originally from Simla [now Shimla] but my father had settled in Ludhiana. He was a *hakim* (medical practioner using the Yunani or Greek–Islamic system). He was a god-fearing man who treated all human beings with love and sympathy. He was also a Sufi, belonging to the Chishtia order. Hindus, Muslims, Sikhs, Christians – all could come to him for treatment, which was very cheap. He did not charge the poor.

'Some trouble had been taking place in Ludhiana but all the communities were agreed that peace and good relations should be maintained. In August, however, the situation began to deteriorate rapidly. Attacks on Muslims began to take place all over the town. People really had no clue where the border between India and Pakistan would be drawn. The Muslims of Ludhiana had made no preparation to leave their homes. Eid was celebrated in a half-hearted manner. Mostly people met at the prayer grounds and mosques. It proved to be an opportunity to discuss what course we needed to take. The intensity of atttacks kept increasing. People began to leave their homes and gather in the *havelis* of important and influential people. All Muslims were now equal. Everybody needed somebody else. In a few days, the Muslim *mohallas* began to be attacked. The authorities had become totally biased and partisan. Nobody was willing to help. Some Hindus and Sikhs did give protection to their friends and neighbours, but on the whole, nobody wanted to confront the Sikh *jathas*. The RSS was also active in Ludhiana.

'Soon, a long procession began moving towards the camp which had been set up for Muslims. On the way, suddenly we were surrounded by armed Sikhs. They were about to attack when one of them recognised my father. I believe his name was Milkha Singh. He shouted to the raiders not to commit sin by attacking such a saintly man who had always helped people in distress without ever making any distinction or exception. His words had a magic effect. They gave way and we safely got away from that dreadful situation. God saved us. Milkha Singh proved to be an angel. This happened in early September though I am not sure. I was only a little boy at that time.'

Maulana Habibur Rahman Sanvi Ludhianvi

While in Ludhiana, to my huge surprise I learned from Baldev Verma that the grandson of a leading anti-imperialist cleric, who belonged to the Ahrar, was still in Ludhiana. He headed a major mosque in the city where on Fridays, thousands of people came to pray, requiring the main roads being closed to the traffic. I met Maulana Habibur Rahman Sanvi Ludhianvi the same day, on 4 January 2005. He narrated the following story:

'My great-great grandfather, Shah Abdul Qadir Ludhianvi, was the first in Punjab to take up arms against the English East India Company in 1857. He collected a large fighting force, which included Muslims, Hindus and Sikhs, that drove the English out of both Ludhiana and Panipat. He then headed to Delhi with his men to support Bahadur Shah Zafar. He fell fighting along with thousands of others at Chandni Chowk in 1857.

'However, his descendants continued to support revolutionary struggles and both the Ghadar Party, and later, Bhagat Singh's associates were aided by them. They also helped Subhash Chandra Bose cross Punjab safely into the North-West Frontier Province. *The Tribune*, Chandigarh, of 7 January 2001, carried a story on the anti-imperialist services of my family.

'My grandfather Maulana Habibur Rahman Ludhianvi was a founder member of the Majlis-e-Ahrar. In September 1947, we were forced to leave Ludhiana because the attacks by the Sikhs were too intense and overpowering. With great difficulty our family managed to get to Ludhiana railway station. Thousands of Muslims were on the station waiting for trains to transport them to Pakistan. We managed to board one of the trains. It had military escort and although it was delayed for many hours on the way, it reached Lahore without suffering any major attack.

'Grandfather stayed for a day in Lahore. We had some relatives and therefore the family could be taken care of. He returned to Delhi because getting off in Ludhiana was impossible. He was received with great respect by Nehru who wanted to make him the Vice President of India but the Deoband ulema got jealous and secretly opposed that idea. He remained in Delhi for quite some time but then gradually we were given back the possession of the main mosque in Ludhiana. Grandfather felt it was his duty to be in East Punjab because of the Muslims who had been left behind. Here and there, all over the Punjab, some Muslims survived. Mostly they were from poor backgrounds. Now of course there are thousands of Muslims again in Ludhiana. They are mostly textile workers from UP and Bihar.'

Maj. Gen. (Retd) Syed Wajahat Husain, who was earlier stationed in Jullundur, was ordered to move to Ludhiana towards the end of August. In his book, he described horrific scenes that he witnessed in that city: Muslim men, women, and children whose bodies he saw lying all over He also mentioned a case of insubordination by a non-commissioned Hindu Jat who wanted to obstruct a train from leaving for Pakistan, alleging that in it were Hindu Jat women who were being taken to Pakistan. He was arrested and taken away. In other words, the mixed PBF was also getting affected by the communal poison that had spread in other sectors of the society (2010: 58-9). There is some confusion in his account because he claims to have heard the Radcliffe Award being announced over All-India Radio while in Ludhiana (it was already announced on 17 August) and upon hearing that Colonel James Bell, the British Commander of the Ludhiana Force, reportedly remarked, 'Well chaps, get ready for more serious trouble' (ibid.: 59).

Sheikh Anwar Ali

The celebrated Pakistani cartoonist and fiction writer Anwar Ali (creator of the character 'Nanna' who used to appear in the *Pakistan Times* of Lahore) was a student at the Mayo School of Arts in Lahore in 1947, when the Partition riots broke out. This is what he told me:

'Lahore was burning when I left for Ludhiana in the first week of August. For some reason, the Ludhiana Muslims kept on believing that their city will remain in Pakistan. The Radciffe Award created panic. I was able to bring my family and relatives safely to Pakistan but saw with my own eyes the hell that broke loose in those days. The biggest losers in the Partition were ordinary people, those who were never consulted as to what they wanted. It is true that in Ludhiana, most of the hosiery mills were owned by Hindus and Sikhs and most Muslims were labourers. The economic disparity that resulted from such an unbalanced development in the Punjab created an untenable situation. It exploded into genodical attacks on both sides.'

Now, whereas after mid-August, the Muslims of Ludhiana began to be attacked in ever-increasing measure, some horrible incidents of Muslim aggression also took place. I met Selja Saini at Professor Bhupinder

Brar's home on 20 March 2004 on my visit to East Punjab. She told me her story:

Selja Saini

'I was four at the time of Partition. It was either in April or May 1947 that my *mama*, Bhagat Singh, who was in the Indian National Army, was released and came home. He was 35 at that time; he had first served in the Indian Army and then as a prisoner-of-war in Japanese custody, he joined the INA. He and many other such people were put on trial but were gradually released before the British left.

'My *nana* (maternal grandfather) was the *lambardar* of our village. Next to our village was a Muslim village. In August, Muslims from four other villages had gathered in our neighbouring village. My *mama* was tall and handsome and my mother loved him a lot. He and some other Sikhs went to the Muslims to assure them that no harm would come to them. He had come back after serving with Muslims in the army for a long time and had no animosity towards them. He and his friends wanted to help them in their hour of need. However, when they reached the village, someone shouted, "Kill them." He and his friends had to start running. He was attacked with a hatchet and killed mercilessly. His body was never found. Since that day, my mother is always in mourning. He left behind two daughters. The younger one was born after his death. A long time has now passed but not for my mother. She is still traumatised and it seems she is still waiting for him to come back somehow. What happened to the Muslims of Ludhiana you can yourself find out but I know that those who fled left everything behind. It must have been a real slaughter from what I have heard, but I was too young at that time. In fact, I was in Khushab in western Punjab where my father was then posted.'

Ludhiana rural areas

Ludhiana's rural areas were predominantly Hindu–Sikh. The attacks on Muslims in the villages around Ludhiana were most vicious. It seems that the stories from Rawalpindi district had been circulating and the

Sikhs were determined to repeat on a much grander scale the savagery that was reported from northern Punjab and Hazara.

Amar Singh

Amar Singh is quoted in an earlier part of this book in connection with the March riots in Rawalpindi. He was one of those who fled to the eastern districts and became a militant Sikh committed to revenge. This is what he said:

'*Assi ikk nyeen jan ditta* (Not a single Muslim escaped). In Moga, we wiped out all those we could get hold of. At Khanna station, Muslims were killed to the last man. Even in Kapurthala and Patiala nobody survived. These attacks took place in September and continued till the end of October. Although the Sikhs from Rawalpindi were among those who used to tell their stories when Sikh congregations took place, it was overwhelmingly Jats of the rural areas all over eastern Punjab who were the mainstay of the raids. However, the real assaults began only after trains with dead bodies of Hindus and Sikhs began to arrive in India. That news ignited the campaign that had taken months of preparation. It is true no mercy was shown, but do you remember what the Muslims did to our brethren? So, our retaliation was bound to take place.'

During a visit to Nathu Majra, now in Sangrur district, but in 1947, a part of Ludhiana district, I met the father of Vicky's classmate. Unfortunately, I forgot to ask his name as we met among other guests and the discussion started without me realising that I had not recorded his name. This is what he told me:

Father of Vicky's classmate

'I attended a meeting in Amritsar in April 1947, where the Sikh leaders took the decision that if the Punjab was partitioned along lines unacceptable to the community we should ensure that no Muslim remained in East Punjab. Later, after the Partition had been decided, a man came from Takht Hazara in western Punjab. His name was Arjan Singh and he met the Maharaja of Patiala to persuade him that Muslims from Malerkotla should also be expelled.

'Killing in these areas started at Bahadargarh and spread quickly to the adjoining villages, but nobody pursued fleeing Muslims if they entered the territories of Malerkotla. So, the maharaja must have refused to accede to Arjan Singh's demand. Deference for Guru Gobind Singh's ruling that the Muslims of Malerkotla should not be harmed in any future conflict meant that even those who entered Malerkotla and did not belong to that state were spared. Thousands of lives were saved that way. My father, Sardar Kundan Singh, was in the Congress party. He helped save many Muslims. One Muslim woman was found alive a month after the attacks had begun. How she managed without proper food only shows that human beings can survive in the worst of conditions. Most of the Muslims from the villages in the English territory [that is, outside Malerkotla] who survived, left for Pakistan in October, and even later, while some settled in Malerkotla.'

Ranjit Singh [Ajit Singh]

Before I arrived in India on my first tour of East Punjab in March 2004, Vicky, upon the instructions of Professor Bhupinder Brar, had toured many villages. While at Nathu Majra, he was introduced to Ranjit Singh, who told him about his participation in the attacks on Muslims. (He was also known as Ajit Singh; his real name remains a mystery.) He claimed to have killed thousands of Muslims. We visited Nathu Majra in March 2004, but on that occasion, we were told that he was away. On my second visit in January 2005, we again visited Nathu Majra. This time he agreed to be interviewed. He even allowed me to photograph him. He narrated the following story:

'We learned about the suffering of the Sikhs first in December 1946 when hundreds of families from Hazara took refuge in Patiala. Young women had been molested; some had arrived with their breasts torn off. We were told many had died. Then again in March a large number of Sikhs brutalised and traumatised by Muslim hordes in the villages from Rawalpindi took refuge here. From that time onwards, we young men and those from amongst the refugees had taken a vow that no Muslim will be spared if an occasion arose and we had to act. The stories of rapes and murder of Sikhs were told by individuals who had escaped from those areas. When a train from Lyallpur came with dead bodies, we decided that the time to act had come.

'The camp at Payal was the one that we particularly butchered. All women and children were killed in five hours. We were thirty-five and we killed 20,000. We had two revolvers and one rifle. By the time 400 people more joined us. We killed young men, not women and children. Some women were also abducted.

'The attack on Muslims started here on 2 September and continued intensely for four days. The Sikh *jathas* were mobile and we could move quickly from one place to another on our horses. One large group of Muslims, some 25,000–35,000, was attacked by us. I believe most were killed; some may have escaped into the fields. My guess is that some 500,000 Muslims were killed in East Punjab. I was in contact with the leaders who were organising the raids. Their estimate was that some 500,000–700,000 Muslims perished.'

'We did not kill anyone who crossed into Malerkotla.' Ranjit Singh expressed himself in Punjabi in the following words, '*Bauji, jerra Mussalman Malerkotla jaan wali sarrak dey dusrey passey Angrezi illaqay wich si unnu assi chadeya nai tey jerra ess passey aa gaya si unnu assi hath nahin laya*' (Sir, those Muslims who were on the other side of the road belonging to English territory were cut down without any exception but those who crossed over into Malerkolta were not touched). 'Those caught on the road were also not spared. They had to be in Malerkotla state territory not to be attacked.'

'We also attacked the Muslims who were heading for the camps that had been set up in Sirhind and Raikot. Those Muslims who reached there were saved. Those who could not were killed. The worst killing was in August–September. I was a young man and belonged to the gang of Niranjan Singh. Jageer Singh and Kirtar Singh were also members of our *jatha*.

'I think it was wrong what happened. To kill a human being is *paap* (sin). We considered it *dharma yudh* (religious war). We did not kill Muslims from our own village. I killed at least 3,000, mostly young Muslim men. Gujjars, Arains, Jats, *faqirs, telis* – all sorts of Muslims – were legitimate targets.'

Hans Raj Khatri

On 17 March 2004, I interviewed Hans Raj Khatri (born 1920) of Sidhwan Bet, the twin village of Saleempura, in Jagraon *tahsil* of Ludhiana district, East Punjab. He told me this heart-rending story of two Muslim sisters:

'Before Partition, these villages were populated by Muslim Arains who had a large presence throughout the Jagraon *tahsil* as well as the rest of the district. After the Radcliffe Award, Sikh *jathas* became very active. The Muslims in our area started preparing to migrate to Pakistan. Bhaisakha Singh, a Sikh from the neighbouring village of Kishanpura, told them they did not need to worry. The communities had long lived together in peace and now that the Muslims were leaving, they would be escorted safely to the nearby refugee camp.

'They trusted him and next day the caravan began the short journey towards the camp. Suddenly, two gunshots were fired at them. Baisakha Singh told the men to walk to the camp on their own and leave the women and children in his protection. So, leaving the women and children behind, the able-bodied men walked away. However, some scoundrels raided the women in Baisakha Singh's custody and were able to take away some of them. Among them were two married sisters, Ramzan Bibi and Zainab Bibi. Kidnapped women were selling at the time for as little as ₹300. The sisters pleaded with their captors to first let their families pay for their freedom. They agreed and approached Inder Singh, also of Kishanpura, who was in the Indian Army, to find out if the families were willing to pay the ransom. Inder Singh asked me to talk to them. The goons demanded ₹1,000 for each sister. Ramzan Bibi's husband was in England at that time. Her father-in-law, Ata Muhammad Mehr, said that if he did not try to get her freed, his son would never forgive him. After some wrangling, the deal was made at ₹700 and she was returned. Zainab Bibi's father-in-law offered only ₹300, saying he could not pay more. Her husband did not protest. The kidnappers said they would not charge less than ₹1,000. They argued that Zainab Bibi was younger than Ramzan Bibi and more attractive. Her in-laws, however, refused to raise their offer. She was never returned. I am not aware of what happened to her later.'

Hameed Akhtar

Veteran journalist Hameed Akhtar has been one of the best-known columnists in the Pakistani Urdu press. He was a leading light of the Progressive Writers' Movement. I met him in London in May 2002, when we both were attending the World Punjab Congress meeting. He narrated the following story of his escape from his village to Lahore:

'I was born in 1924 in village Tihara, *tahsil* Jagroan, Ludhiana. Jullundur and Ferozepur also touched our village. Kishanpura in the south was in Ferozepur district and in north was Nakodar. That is why it was called Tihara (three-sided). My father died when I was only three. I was the youngest and was made a Hafiz-e-Quran. We are descendants of Khawaja Bakhtiar Kaki, the famous Chishti Sufi buried in Delhi. The *khanqah* of Shah Diwan is still functioning in Tihara. People who don't have sons come there to pray and ask for a son. In 1947, it was a village of 1,800 inhabitants, mostly Muslims. I came to Ludhiana at the age of ten to join high school. We never even thought of each other as Hindus, Muslims or Sikhs. Those were days of great amity. Some clashes did take place but nobody paid much attention to them before 1947.

'In August 1947, Sahir Ludhianvi and I were in Bombay. We left Bombay on 9 August. My brother had opted for Pakistan and gone there, leaving the family in the village. Our family and other members of the Syed *biradari* decided to fight and not leave. However, by the end of August, Muslims from the villages around Tihara had started taking refuge in Tihara. There was no police. Muslim officers had been disarmed. But then slowly people began to leave. We came to Sidhwan Bet from where we could get *tongas*. I had seventy women and children with me. Some men were with us. We went to the camp in Nakodar as we believed that Jullundur would be awarded to Pakistan.

'An uncle of mine who had retired from the police used to take opium. After some days his stock finished, so I went out of the camp wearing a bush-shirt and trousers to buy it. I bought it and was going back when a Nihang approached me with his sword. A Sikh officer at that moment came and embraced me. It was Narinder Singh, a very dear Sikh class fellow from school days. The Nihang quickly disappeared. Narinder was at that time military secretary of a minister. My sister

Fatima was very ill in those days. She used to say that she would die. "Do not bury me without washing me." When she died the people in the camp were not willing to help. So, I had to perform the washing ritual. Finally, we were transported to Pakistan. All our relatives who had stayed behind were killed. Very few Hindus took part in the attacks. The RSS was not as strong as is believed. It was the Sikhs who organised the attacks on Muslims. The Akalis and Sikh maharajas were the main patrons of the *jathas*.

'On this side, I learnt that Sardar Shaukat Hayat and others were involved in setting ablaze Amritsar and Shahalmi. The common man had nothing to do with it. *Goondas* mainly took part in such activities. I do not think Jinnah did the right thing by not letting Mountbatten become Governor-General of Pakistan as well. After he was rejected by Jinnah he was probably no longer interested in a peaceful transfer of power.'

Chaudhri Riasat Ali

'I was born in Halwara, East Punjab, on 29 Novmeber 1933. It was a large village close to a famous air base. We had lived in the village for 800 years. We were converted by Makhdoom Jahaniyan to Islam. The land was owned mainly by my *biradari* of Muslim Rajputs. There were other castes as well, Muslim Arains and Jats, Sikh tailors, Hindu Brahmins and Khatris. I was in the seventh class when Partition took place.

'Our village was peaceful until the very end. In fact, we protected non-Muslims. We even encouraged them to go to their relatives in nearby villages. We had many serving and retired military and police officers as Muslim Rajputs were always welcome into such services. Many had come back after the Second World War. We had collected a lot of weapons. So, there was complete preparation to ward off any attack. We had no idea if the village would go to India. We used to shout slogans against Hitler. We believed that the British would remain forever. Many of our relatives had become prisoners in Hong Kong and Singapore. The Japanese were brutal to them. Some of our relatives were members of the INA. Capt. Zafrullah Khan was one of them.

'Our village was 99 per cent in favour of the Muslim League but some old people were followers of Bukhari [Ahrar leader] and Azad

[Congress leader], but most were for the Muslim League. The young men used to shout, "*Le ke rahange Pakistan, Batt ke rahe ga Hindustan*" (We will get Pakistan, India will be divided). Some of our boys in Lahore were very active in the Muslim Student Federation.

'Now, we know that our village would not have come to Pakistan. Our village was on the east side of the Sutlej. Even during the time of Maharaja Ranjit Singh this part of east Punjab was not in the Lahore kingdom. Anyhow, the news that Halwara and Ludhiana district would go to India came, and it created a serious crisis for us. Before that many Muslim families had taken refuge in our villages. *Badmashes* [criminal] from among the Sikhs started terrorist attacks. Then we made our own groups. So we established our own *jathas*. I was only fourteen at that time. Our blacksmiths could produce weapons of all sorts. We had gunsmiths, too.

'When we realised that the army of Patiala state was being mobilised it became clear that we could not hold on for too long. A village near Raikot was declared a refugee camp. We moved to that village. It was a very difficult decision for our elders to leave the village because our ancestors were buried there. We discussed this in great depth. When we were on the road one of our elders said he would not go. Captain Zafrullah gave him the inducement that we should leave now but come back when things settled down. We stayed there for a week then a cousin of mine brought trucks and took us to Lahore.

'We suffered the most because our social structure was destroyed. The village could not be restored. Only in *chak* 40 in Lyallpur there is a mini Halwara. Halwara had seven *pattis* [sub-units of a large village].'

Gujjarwal

During my visit to Multan, I recorded on 21 December 2004 a detailed interview with Muhammad Abdullah Shamshad, a leading journalist. He had this story to tell:

'I was born on 20 September 1937 in a rather large village named Gujjarwal, in the Ludhiana district. It was almost a small town and proper sanitation arrangements existed for 1,000 or more houses. It had a civil hospital, a veterinary hospital, a post office, and government schools for girls and boys. Originally it was populated by Hindu Rajputs belonging to the Suhuta sub-caste. Some of them converted to Islam, as did our family, many generations ago. This turned the Hindu Rajputs against us. They always nurtured ill-will against us. Therefore we invited Muslim Arains to come and settle in the village. They were offered land free of cost and encouraged to settle down. In the 1940s the communal balance was the following: 400 Muslim households, including the biggest group of 300 Arain families, 20 Sikh families and the rest, Hindus.

'My family was the leading Muslim family in Gujjarwal. Many of my relatives were highly educated and included medical doctors, scientists, and educationists. They were posted in different parts of the Punjab but would always come to the village when they were on holiday. This way, the bond with the village and the family was maintained. The reason we had taken to education was that as a minority Rajput community, we felt that education was necessary to safeguard our interests against the Hindu Raputs. When the Pakistan movement started, the Muslims were attracted to it while the Hindus were supporters of the Congress.

'Among Muslims we were the leading family and were considered the *chaudhris*. The tradition was that at the time of marriage, a Muslim girl from our village would always depart to her in-laws' home from our house. It was to indicate that our family stood behind her and she should not be treated badly.

'At the time of election in 1945–46, the divisions that were already present in the village became deeper. Ludhiana was a stronghold of Congress Muslims. The Ahrars were also strong in Ludhiana city. Maulana Habibullah contested a general seat on a Congress ticket but lost to a Sikh. The Hindus did not vote for him. This was a major setback for Muslims. It resulted in them becoming pro-Muslim League. Things in the village were quiet during the election campaign, but Hindus and Sikhs would congregate in the *dharamsalas* while Muslims met in a *pandal* (shamiana) separately to discuss political matters. I studied in the Gujjarwal Government High School. Our teachers were very good and considerate and helped all students with an open heart. From 1945, however, Hindu and Sikh teachers started becoming resentful towards Muslims. They would make a point of harassing us. They would say "*O Muslay,* stand up." ["*Muslay*" is a derogatory term for Muslims]. I was twice beaten by Sikhs when on my way to school. Hindu boys played with us, but if we ever came near their kitchens they became hysterical. This made us feel that we were not one of them. This attitude hurt the young generation of Muslims and we started shouting slogans such as "*Quaid-i-Azam Zindabad, Pakistan Zindabad*" (Long live Quaid-i-Azam, Long live Pakistan). This made the Hindus and Sikhs truly agitated. In those days Pathans were a big scare. They used to roam around East Punjab and occasionally came to Gujjarwal. I remember, if ten–twelve of them came to Gujjarwal the Hindus would panic. They would approach my father to tell him that they did not want any trouble.

'Sikhs were different. They were tough. A notorious troublemaker, Jagga Daku, of this area was killed in an encounter with the police. One of his lieutenants, a Sikh from our village who had been wounded during the encounter, lost one leg. That made him change his way of life and he returned to Gujjarwal to settle down. He was very well read in Hindu, Sikh and Islamic religions. He believed that he had done great harm to human beings. Now he wanted to serve mankind. He became known as the Baba. All Hindus, Sikhs and Muslims were expected to respect him. He would tell us boys to recite Quranic verses and for doing that he gave us some sweets. His name was Jagjit Singh. But when the political campaign for Pakistan started in 1945–6 even he changed and stopped asking us to recite the *kalima* and other Islamic texts. So, you can understand that the social order was changing.

'My family had a radio and all Muslims were welcome to listen to the news. I still remember hearing that an atom bomb had been dropped on Hiroshima. We were aware that the English would leave, because World War II had exhausted them completely. The Muslims felt that Hindus would not be just to them. We had no idea that our village would go to India. Moreover, we believed that since Congress had given a ticket to a Muslim from our area we would not be harmed if we continued to live in India. But I must say that most Muslims believed that Ludhiana would be given to Pakistan, even when they knew that Muslims were in a minority in the district. The Muslim League also gave us assurances that we would be included in Pakistan. Another problem was that the Deobandi ulema and the Ahrars were confident that Hindus will not harm us.

'14 August was the 27th [day] of Ramazan. We had gone to offer the *tarawiyaan* prayers (special prayers during the fasting month) in the evening. Outside, Hindus and Sikhs were in a festive mood. We were going to stay the whole night in the mosque but the shouting outside scared us and we dispersed and went home. That year, the month of Ramazan was of thirty days. On Eid-ul-Fitr [18 August] the Muslims assembled in the main mosque. That was the last time we were all together in one place. The elders could sense that trouble was on the way and decided that families who were living in Hindu and Sikh *mohallas* should collect at our place. It was a big house made of bricks and had strong, sturdy gates. The Arain *mohalla* was compact and they were advised to stay there because they were in sufficiently large numbers.

'I remember it was 23 August when the attack took place We were aware of the fact that Sikhs have put the village under siege. My father had told my mother to make *parathas* (flat bread fried in clarified butter) and give them to all the children. Many were from poor families and had eaten *parathas* for the first time. This made one of the women ask my father, "*Chachaji*, what date is it today?" He said that it was the sixth day of Eid or 23 August. This way she wanted to emphasise that it was a special day for them. Father was killed the same day.

'Firing started before the *parathas* had been cooked. Some shots were fired at our house. My father went to the roof and saw that the Arain *mohalla* was burning. This was early morning. We had no arms at home because the police had come and taken away all our weapons. They had raided our homes some four or five times in the last two months and thus the Muslims were entirely unarmed. The police were mainly Sikh. They did not leave us with even a big knife. Even long sticks were impounded.

'When the firing became intense the women and children were sent out of the house by making them climb down ladders from one side of the house. They were advised to run into the fields or disperse to other houses. My father was supervising everything. There was no other man in the house. The Sikhs were shouting that women were escaping from the house of the *chaudhris* (headmen). The raiders were Sikhs from outside but our village Sikhs were watching everything and giving directions. The Nihangs (a special group of armed Sikhs) threw sharp objects and metal rings into our house. Anybody struck by them would be badly hurt. Some children and women were killed. We spent the whole night inside the house. I believe they thought we had ammunition and therefore did not launch a direct assault.

'My father had gone to another house of ours which was next door to us to find out if people who were hiding there were all right. He was shot dead while there. It was 4 o'clock in the afternoon. My mother, my two sisters and my *khala* (mother's sister), some other women who had taken refuge and I, then a small boy, were in the house. We must have been around forty people altogether. When night approached, they tried to set fire by throwing kerosene oil on our house but since it was made of bricks, it did not catch fire completely and only some wooden doors were destroyed.

'The Sikhs now mounted the roof of our house and came in by jumping into the veranda. They were interested in looting. My mother, my two sisters and I were sitting on one of the staircases. I ran up to the roof. Three Sikhs were standing there. One of them said, "This is Noor Din's son. We killed his father earlier." One of them attacked me with a *gandasa* (spear). I managed to avoid the blow. I jumped from the roof and escaped. A Muslim woman living next door helped me with her dupatta to climb the wall and enter her house. They did not kill my mother and sisters or the other women. My sisters were younger than me. One was two years younger and the other, only two. Early in the morning I, my mother, two sisters and *khala* left the village.

'A *jatha* of some 150 Nihangs suddenly surrounded us. My *khala* begged an old Sikh not to kill me because I was the only male member of the family left alive. The Nihangs however kept coming close to us. They were marching in a state of triumph. Someone said, "This is Noor Din's son". The man who said this was the grandson or son of the old Sikh to whom my aunt had pleaded for mercy. The old Sikh could barely walk. He said, "*Dafa ho jao* (Get lost). First kill me before you kill him. Leave him alone". The old Sikh was from our village. The Nihangs, who were at least 150 in number, then dispersed and we were spared.

'We came out of the village and sought refuge in the fields. There we met other Muslims. My *khala's* husband who was my *chacha* was already sleeping in the fields. We spent the night and next day in the fields. On the third day we went to another village where the Muslims had a *chowpal* (gathering place). We stayed there for three or four days. Then we learnt that Muslims from the villages around were getting together to form a caravan and go to Pakistan. Our first stop was to be Malerkotla state which was only twenty miles (thirty-six kilometres). On the way we met others from our village too. We learnt that only three persons survived in the Arain *mohalla*. The rest were killed. My uncle and his children also joined us. We were in the thousands now. Our immediate aim was to get to a place called Mandi in Malerkotla. On the way we met some soldiers of the Baloch regiment. They gave us protection. We were attacked twice, but both attacks were repulsed. Finally we reached Mandi where food was given to us. In Malerkotla town we met the family of my teacher Muhammad Yaqub. We celebrated Eid-ul-Zuha (festival of sacrifice) in Malerkotla. My youngest sister died in Malerkotla because of illness. The other one became very sick.

'A train then left Malerkotla for Pakistan. My *khala* and *chacha* had already left. At Ferozepur our train stopped, because the track had been uprooted. Hundreds of people were killed. My mother told me to run away. My sister could not walk and was in the train compartment. We met some more people from our village. The raiders were looking for jewellery and cash. They would kill or ignore people and then left. Then the train started again and we reached the bridge on the river Sutlej that would have taken us into Pakistan, but Gurkha soldiers were patrolling it and they openly sided with the Sikhs and Hindus. They were killing people before they could cross the bridge.

'We dispersed once again. I, my sick sister, my mother and some other people waited along the bank of the river waiting for an opportunity to cross the bridge. We spent many days in the fields, hiding from the Sikh *jathas* that were on the loose in that area. One day some Baloch regiment soldiers could be seen on the bridge. They announced that all Muslims who wanted to cross the bridge and go to Pakistan could do so.

'I remember seeing babies being carried on spears and their fathers being told to repeat "Pakistan *Zindabad*". Women's breasts and vaginas were violated. We were forced to drink urine. Poison was put in wells and ponds. Many people died through drinking poisoned water. My sister drank poisoned water. She died as soon as we reached Kasur on the Pakistani side. We buried her in the camp. Then my mother and I boarded a goods train in the hope of reaching Multan, where my uncle lived. Instead, the train went to Sheikhupura.

'At the station we had nothing to eat. My mother began to cry because now we had to beg. I also wept. A railway employee came out. He gave us a postcard to write to my uncle, who was in the animal husbandry college in Multan. He also gave us food. We stayed there for a few days but no reply came. He told us that next day a train would be going to Multan. He asked the guard to let us travel without ticket. And so we were put on the train to Multan.

'We got off at Multan city instead of the cantonment station. It was 4 o'clock in the afternoon. It was the tenth day of Muharram and the Ashura procession was marching through the town centre. We spent the night on the *phatta* of a shop. My mother believed that her brother-in-law was a regular doctor so next day we went to the main hospital and waited for my uncle. When the chief doctor arrived and was told that some people were waiting for him, he came to see us. He was the district health officer. Incidentally, his house was next to my uncle's. He knew that my uncle had received the postcard and had sent his son to fetch us from Sheikhupura. He gave us the directions and we reached my uncle's villa. He was sitting in the veranda. That way we finally found security.

'However, my tragedy did not end there. My mother died in 1949. I lived with my uncle. It was kind of him to accept me in the family but I always felt like an outsider. On festival days I was treated differently from their own children. This left a deep scar in my life. When I was sick I was neglected. But God has been kind. I got education and became a journalist. I have served as editor of *Imroze,* then of *Nawa-i-Wakt*. Now I am retired but write in the *Khabrain*.'

Visit to Gujjarwal

Mr Shamshad's story had profoundly affected me. In one sense, I had heard it before. His detailed descriptions, however, were different and made me curious enough to visit his native village. Mr Shamshad had told us that the village of his birth was a big one; indeed, it had continued to grow. This time I had with me two young men from Delhi, Hitesh Gosain and Virender Singh. Hitesh and I had been corresponding for quite some time after he read my weekly columns in the Pakistani newspaper, *The Daily Times*, of Lahore. The three of us arrived in Gujjarwal on 29 November 2005.

We were told that 9,000 people currently lived in Gujjarwal, which is twenty kilometres from Ludhiana city. We visited Mr Shamshad's old school and took pictures of the register in which his name and other details were recorded. It was a big, historical school. Right in front of it a technical college has been built. We were put in contact with the *sarpanch's* family who quickly summoned some elders. They had heard of Shamshad's father, Noor Din, but since they belonged to the part of the village where the Arain *mohalla* was located they were not able to witness the atrocities committed on Shamshad's family. Still, they provided us harrowing accounts of what happened in Arain *mohalla*.

Ajaib Singh

'I was born in Gujjarwal in 1932 and went to school here. The school was established in 1882. It was the second oldest school after the high school in Ludhiana. Here, my father did his matric and so did I. We belong to the Chandel branch of Rajputs. The Garewal *gotra* of Jats also originated from Gujjarwal. Muslims, mostly Arains, lived in large numbers here. The main shopping bazaar was owned by Hindus. Sikhs were also present in significant numbers in the village. Even a sizeable Jain community lived in Gujjarwal. We lived in peace and shared each others' joys and sorrows. The Arains were prosperous agriculturists and owned significant land. I remember my class fellows, Sardar Khan and Habibullah. The Muslims of our village were extremely decent and god-fearing people. None of them was a fanatic.

'I don't know if some of the Hindu Rajputs had converted to Islam. I was too young at that time to take interest in such things. We had very good and kind Muslim teachers such as Master Afzal, who came from a nearby village and Master Ismail too. Master Ismail was the kindest man I knew. He was a tall, impressive person. He used to pray five times a day and was most helpful to pupils. He could walk into any house and was received with a lot of respect. I was a student of class eight.

'On 15 August, when India became independent, a band in the village which was mainly Muslim went around playing happy tunes and songs. Such festivities lasted only a day or two because as soon as the Radcliffe Award became known, Sikh *jathas* comprising criminal elements from the nearby villages began surrounding the village. Very few people from this village took part in the attacks on Muslims.

'The most tragic part of that episode was that some of them agreed to embrace Sikhism. They were brought to a house where they were baptised. However, the next day, the slaughter began. Just a day earlier a rumour was spread that the Muslims of Jarahoan village had attacked Hindus and Sikhs. They were alleged to have used guns and rifles. We later found out that the story was entirely false. Some of the elders of our village resisted the raiders. Among them was my father Ranjit Singh. But they had just two 12-bore guns, whereas the criminal gangs carried many .303 rifles and other powerful firearms. The ringleader of the attackers was Haakim Singh, a notorious character from Kila Raipur. They came in the thousands.

'When the attack took place, some very poor Muslims of the *mirasi* caste took refuge in our house. They were scared to death and some urinated and defecated in their pants. My mother Basant Kaur gave them food and also took care of them. They were saved. A small boy, Dilshad, whose parents had been killed, was found roaming aimlessly and without any clothes on him. My father took all of them to Malerkotla and left them there.

'As I told you, the origin of the Garewal *gotra* of Jatts is from this village. A few families had become Muslims but most of them were Sikhs. Khairu was an old Muslim man of that *gotra*. His house was also surrounded. He kept resisting for a long time as he had a gun with him. He was shouting from the roof of his house, "O Garewals I am one of you. Why do you want to kill me?" His pleas fell on deaf ears because the criminals wanted his blood. Finally, he succumbed to the injuries he had received and died.

'Master Ismail, whom I have mentioned before, was our drawing master. His wife was pregnant when his house was attacked. They killed him and her without any pity. One of his sons, Abdul Aziz, perhaps ten years old at that time, ran into another house to save his life but was caught by a criminal from our village. He picked up the boy by one leg and with a long knife stabbed him several times. The boy's screams still haunt me. His sister Sardaraan was only fifteen. In her arms she was carrying her younger sister who was a small baby. They were caught and for two months Sardaraan was raped by the criminals. Her face became pale and she was in a terrible state. Then one day her brother, who was in the navy, came looking for her. He had police with him. She was recovered. I can still see her face in my mind. It was a terrible outrage against a young girl. Hundreds of girls and women were taken to the canal and raped and made to walk naked.

'However, *dai* (wet nurse) Amanat Bibi and her family were spared. She was needed by the village for helping with delivery of babies so nobody hurt her. She died some fifteen years ago. Her son Riyasat Ali later became a compounder and worked here. He died in an accident. His daughter became a teacher and worked in a school some distance from here. She too died in an accident. Amanat Bibi's family now consists of a number of households.

'Now, once again the mosque in Gujjarwal is being used. We are all very glad that it is so. We have Muslims from Bihar and UP living here. There has never been any communal incident in Gujjarwal since those dark days of Partition. Religion should never be mixed with politics.'

Harmail Singh

'We are originally from Gujjarwal but our family was allotted land in West Punjab a long time ago so I grew up in Arifwala in western Punjab. In 1946, I returned to Gujjarwal. I did my B.Sc and then M.Sc degrees and have been teaching in our school here. Yes, there was a prominent Muslim called Noor Din, but that family lived in another part of the village. The village was large even then and spread out. At the time of Partition my elder brother and others came to India safely from Arifwala. Muslims came with them to the border and they parted after embracing each other. There was not a single attack on them, but one bad character among the Sikhs, Sukhminder, cut the throat of a Muslim policeman on the way and then an attack took place, but otherwise they came over very safely.

'I have seen the holocaust of Muslims in this village and around this region. There can be no comparison with the situation in West Punjab. Here the level of violence was infinitely greater. Hordes of gangsters, criminals and drug and alcohol addicts took part in the raids. They were looking for an opportunity to loot and pillage and let loose their evil lust on women. They committed heinous crimes.

'The Muslims who had converted to Sikhism were hiding in our house, but then a *goonda* from Gujjarwal called Bind brought people from Raipur who overpowered my father and Ajaib Singh's father. They entered our house and ordered all the Muslim men, women and children to line up against the wall on the roof. They were then attacked with spears and hatchets and thrown down. Below, other criminals were standing with their spears ready to pierce the falling bodies. Those of infants were raised in the air and some of them danced around with their bodies up in the air. One boy, Siddique, whom I knew, was cut into many pieces. The motivation was not religious. It was only a desire to loot and the lust to violate women.'

Hoshiarpur

On 4 January 2005, Vicky and I visited Hoshiarpur, where Muslims were in a minority, both in the city and in the rural areas, in 1947. We called on the Congress Party Office, where the General Secretary District Congress Committee, Mr Rajnish Tandon, invited us to his home. His father, whose name I failed to ask, narrated the following stories about his town:

'Hoshiarpur remained peaceful till about the end of July. Hafeez Hoshiarpuri and Tufail Hoshiarpuri were famous poets from this town. They did not live far from our house. There was never a problem here. Then Sikh *jathas* began to roam in this area. There were sizeable Muslim communities in the city and in the district. Till 18 August, very few serious raids took place here. Then, Muslims began to vacate their homes and those who could find help took it and moved to Pakistan. Most of the heinous crimes in this district took place in the early days after the

Radcliffe Award was announced because people had no armed escorts. Then things changed as both governments decided to cooperate and that meant that Pakistani military began to escort the Muslims to Pakistan.

'It was all so unnecessary. The politicians wanted power. Their ambitions buried an old Punjab, which is no more. It was so much more interesting when all the communities lived together. There is a grave of a Muslim holy man in our house. We light a candle every Thursday. Hindus believe that all holy persons should be respected.'

Captain Mohammad Shafi

Captain Mohammad Shafi has written down a detailed account of how Muslim notables who owned property in Hoshiarpur district and were unwilling to vacate their villages were summoned to Makerian Police Station on 23 August to do so by Hindu–Sikh police in Hoshiarpur district. They were threatened to leave. The conspiracy included DSP Chaudhri Dalip Singh and Sub-Inspector Parmanand. When Shafi and other prominent Muslims resisted the pressure, they were put under detention. The police then forced them to pay a ransom of thousands of rupees in order to be released. He also learned from a disgruntled foot constable who had been excluded from a share in the loot that the plan was to kill them if they did not pay the ransom (Shafi 1993: 162-5). The story ends there, but the fact remains that all Muslims were forced to leave Hoshiarpur and go to Pakistan.

Hoshiarpur rural areas

Ahmad Salim recorded an interview on 30 December 2005, in Sheikhupura with a 1947 refugee, Haji Mukhtar Ahmed Khan, from a village in Hoshiarpur district.

Haji Mukhtar Ahmed Khan

'I was born on 8 January 1929 to a Rajput family in a village called Pandori Bhawa, district Hoshiarpur. It was founded by our ancestor some nine generations earlier. Nobody had ever thought that we would be forced to leave our homes. Before Pakistan came into being, we did not have close relations with Hindu Khatris. As children, when sometimes we went to a Hindu classmate's home, their mothers would expressly forbid us from entering their kitchens. They would say it would become polluted and they would need to clean it with cowdung! On the other hand, our relations with Sikhs were all right. After doing my matric I joined the police. I was admitted because of my talent in hockey. The police officer Mr Lincoln recruited me. I was posted in Jullundur when the Muslim processions during the election campaign took place. We were given *dandas* to hit Muslims who were fighting for our rights. So, I resigned and came back to my village. My father got me employed as a sub-inspector in the cooperative department. It took some time before I was discharged in November 1946. The situation was tense. Attacks on Muslims started already in July and from then continued on a small scale. Sikh *jathas* carried out raids in our area.

'18 August was Eid. The first attack on our village took place on the night of 19–20 August. Ours was a small village. I was struck with hatchets. My right-hand fingers were cut off and I received deep wounds on my shoulder and my ear was also injured. Altogether I sustained four wounds. Two of the stabs took place when I was on the ground. I fell unconscious. Somehow, the rumour spread that the military has come. So the Sikhs ran away. Next day I saw dead bodies lying all over. From our side, too, someone fired a homemade gun and two Sikhs were killed. My father hid himself in the fields. Then the police came. They wanted to take the corpses for post-mortem. There was a Muslim constable with them who was disarmed; the rest were armed. He found a chance and told me not to give the dead bodies to the police because then they would take some of us to Hoshiarpur and arrest us on charges of killing the Sikhs. So, we had to just tell them we didn't want to file any complaint. Just then my father returned home. It was 10 a.m. He was a well-known man. He told the police that he did not want to file a complaint and would not want the dead bodies to be taken for post-mortem.

'Then we dug up graves and buried our dead. We stayed in the village on 21 and 22 August. Then the Baluch regiment came and told us that we could not stay here anymore and must go to Pakistan. Then we were taken to a civil hospital in Hoshiarpur. There were scores of injured people in the hospital. After the bandaging we were still in the hospital. Someone said, "Don't get any injection because you might be poisoned". So my cousin, nephew and I left for the camp at Islamia school which was only a kilometre from there. The whole town was ablaze and curfew was also in place, but people were risking everything in search of safety.

'In the camp, Shafi Salar of the Khaksars was in charge. He served all the injured and sick with such devotion that I am convinced he had been granted a place in paradise at that very time. He would make soup from meat and bring it for us. On 26 August, an Omni bus convoy was brought from Lahore to take us there. The injured were given place to go first in the bus. The military was with us. That night we reached Jullundur. On 27 August it rained cats and dogs. We saw people walking on foot. When we reached Wagah, we finally heaved a sigh of relief. We stayed in Lahore for a few weeks. We had a relative living in Purani Anarkali. We stayed for some time with him. In those days the whole of Anarkali and the shopping area on the Mall was burnt down. Hindu and Sikh dead bodies were lying all over. We used to see people loot the buildings and shops at Tollington Market. After a few weeks I got a job in Sheikhupura in the cooperative department. Life has been tough but it must go on.'

Colonel (Retd) Ata Muhammad Dogar

'I was born on 1 January 1930 in village Banial, *tahsil* Dasuya, distict Hoshiarpur. It was a big village populated mainly by the Dogars. Its total population must have been some 3,000 people. The Dogars were a dominant tribe in that region. There were some 44 Dogar villages in the same area. The Dogars have been described in the British records as a fearless and independent tribe engaged mainly in agriculture. Even during the time of Maharaja Ranjit Singh, when the Sikhs were the ruling power in the Punjab, they could not harass our people. We were surrounded by Sikhs on all sides except the east, where there were some Hindus too, but they were few. The other main Muslim tribe in our neighbourhood was that of the Awans. Our relations with the Sikhs were excellent. They held my father, Chaudhry Fazal Karim (Ilahi), in deep respect and used to bring before him their disputes for arbitration, including conflicts about property. He was known for his impartiality and integrity. There was a Sikh family of five brothers. One of them had become a brother of my father through the custom of exchanging turbans. A dispute arose between them with regard to property. They brought it to my father. He gave a verdict which did not favour any of them. They accepted his verdict.

'Things were all right in Dasuya *tahsil* even after the Partition had been announced. But then Sikh *jathas* began to attack Muslim villages. They raided our village the first time but were repulsed. Then they came back a second time. Our people were caught by surprise and in that raid some twenty to twenty-five people, mostly old men and women and children, were killed.

'Consequently, it was decided to vacate the village. I think we left on Eid Day, 18 August, and went to Bhagran village where all the Dogars were assembling from the villages around. It was the village of my maternal grandparents. Then four–five days later we came back to our village because the Sikhs assured us that they will not attack us. But all our houses had been burnt and looted. We managed to stay on even in those difficult circumstances for a few days but one afternoon at about half-past three, Sikh *jathas* converged again on our village Banial and attacked. This time again our people ran away and took refuge in the fields and in other places around. This must have been sometime in early September. My mother and father were going in one direction when some Sikhs on horses surrounded them. They were about to attack my mother but my father shouted at them to stop. When they looked around they recognised my father. They were actually from a family that had very good relations with my father. They got off their horses and fell at his and my mother's feet, begging them for forgiveness. That is how both my parents were saved.

'But our people were not willing to take this sitting down. Consequently we also armed ourselves and began to raid Sikh and Hindu villages in the neighbourhood. Some seventy Sikhs and Hindus were killed in raids carried out by our men. Such conflict continued for quite some time but then it was decided to leave the village and migrate to Pakistan. First we came to the village Haryana, where Rajput Muslims joined us. Then the caravan went to Dasuya and finally to the camp in Hoshiarpur. There several trucks were arranged to take the people to Pakistan. Women, children and the elderly were put in them. Many other Muslims also jumped onto those trucks. There was overcrowding, no food and no water. But we had the Baluch regiment escorting us. The convoy left for Jullundur where we stayed for one night and then left for Amritsar. I remember it was the middle of September when we arrived on the bridge on Beas river. It had rained heavily and people who had been waiting along the banks of the river were swept away by the strong currents. Hundreds of dead bodies of people and animals were floating in the river. It was a terrible sight. In Amritsar, a child who was on the truck with us was slowly dying of thirst, but the Sikhs who were waiting along the road would not give him any water for free and his father had to give ₹300 for a glass of water.

'My father, my elder brothers and maternal and paternal grandfathers, uncles and other grown-up men stayed in the camp at Hoshiarpur till about the beginning of November. Then they began the journey to Pakistan. On the way, some of the Dogars would get out of the column and attack and kill Sikhs and Hindus. But then the Indian Army arrived and began to shoot. Then our men joined the convoy and entered Pakistan. It is true we lost some 100 of our people but until the very end no Sikh or Hindu was spared. So we also killed an equal number among them.'

Rana Muhammad Azhar Khan

On 16 March 2016, I recorded an interview with veteran socialist, painter-artist and sculptor, Rana Muhammad Azhar Khan, at the Government College Faculty Guest House in Lahore. My friend Zakria Khan and his brother, Yahya Khan, drove all the way from Sahiwal, on the way picking up Rana Azhar from Okara and bringing him to Lahore. Rana Azhar's story is one of the most fascinating accounts from the time of the partition of the Punjab.

'I was born on 14 December 1934 in a Rajput family belonging to the Naru clan of the Rajputs, who converted to Islam some centuries earlier and were settled mostly in the Hoshiarpur district and the areas around it. My elders were the chiefs of the Naru Rajputs. We belonged to Hariana, a *kasbah* (hamlet) nine miles north of Hoshiarpur district. Hariana is at the foot of the Shivalik mountain range. In those days, it would rain a lot, sometimes for a whole week. The rain water used to gush rapidly through the streams, some of which would become quite deep, thus disrupting communications and transport. Those powerful currents of water were known locally as choas. Apart from Muslim Rajputs, the other main religious community in our area were Hindus. The Rajputs owned most of the land while the shops were owned by Hindus. There were very few Sikhs. The Rajputs held important positions in the traditional social order and were granted administrative and honorific titles such as honorary magistrate, *zaildar*, *lamberdar*, *sufedposh*, and so on, by the government.

'Hariana was a paragon of communal harmony, peace and solidarity. Our idyllic community could pride over a school called Hindu-Muslim High School. The name of the school and the idea of building it was that of Pandit Lala Harcharan Das, a local Brahmin. He approached our elders for a grant of land, which my uncle Rana Muhammad Ali gave happily. Lalaji was childless. He donated all his property and savings to the school. The school building was built with his money. Unfortunately, he died before the building was completed. However, Panditji's contribution was always remembered with gratitude by the people of Hariana.

'The novel name of the school attracted idealistic people from all over the Punjab of those days. Lala Madanlal Chadha, who belonged originally to Bhaati Gate, Lahore, joined the school as headmaster. He was an amazing personality. I have yet to come across someone more charismatic. He devoted his life to the school, always maintaining the best standards and providing good education. Once in a while he would visit my uncle who was the head of our clan. Uncle would get up to welcome him, notwithstanding the fact that he himself commanded the highest social standing in Harianvi society. Our teachers were saintly people. Maulana Rahimuddin belonged to Meerut. He used to teach Persian. He also led prayers on important occasions. During the daily hour reserved for *deeniyat* (religious) studies, Pandit Mastram used to teach Hindus and Sikhs their scriptures while Maulvi Fateh Mohammad taught Muslim students about Islam. He was from Lyiah, a small town in southern Punjab. He was such a simple man that when Partition took place he was in Lyiah. However, he did not realize the big change that had taken place and started his journey from Lyiah after the summer holidays to return to Hariana. Someone from Hariana saw him at the Lahore Railway Station and informed him that he could no longer return to his work because Hariana was now in India.

'Then, there was our Sikh teacher, Master Attar Singh. A Kashmiri Muslim family lived in Hariana. The head of the family was in the British Indian Army. They had a tiny little boy. His grandmother brought him to school. He used to wear a shalwar while the rest of us wore pants or narrow churidar pyjamas. He would cry all the time. Master Attar Singh took him under his care and gave him a lot of affection. Thereafter, he would always sit beside Masterji and eventually started taking interest in his studies.

'Our school used to get donations from the maharajas of Kapurthala. The tradition was that the maharaja of Kapurthala would come in a motorcade of fancy cars and jeeps. The students would dress up smartly wearing turbans to welcome him. Once, I was also among the welcoming party. Master Madanlal Chadha never went to receive him. He kept away from such pomp and show. It was Maulana Rahimuddin who would offer tribute (symbolically) to the maharaja on behalf of the school and in return receive donation to the school.

'All the religious festivals were celebrated with great joy and with all communities taking part in it. Especially the Dussehra festival was celebrated for 10 days and thousands of people came to attend the festivities. Dussehra was a Hindu festival but Rana Mohammad Hussain Khan zaildar (Hariana) presided over the organizing body of the function. On that occasion, Hariana girls married outside that area would come to visit their parents. It was a great occasion every year as mangoes were still available in our part of the Punjab. They were grown in abundance, and both rich and poor could enjoy them. The cool winds from the mountains, plenty of mangoes and festivities created an ecstatic environment in those days.

'Hariana remained free from the confrontational politics of the 1940s. Once, Mahatma Gandhi, Pandit Nehru, Maulana Azad, and some other

Congress leaders came to our remote community. They had heard about the Hindu-Muslim High School and wanted to express their support for such an initiative. A *pehlwan*-type fellow of Hariana raised up Gandhiji on his shoulders so that everyone could see him. There was a lot of clapping because such national-level leaders were not expected to come to such a faraway hamlet in a remote corner of the Punjab.

'Rana Nasrullah Khan, an independent candidate, was the MPA from Hariana in the 1937 Punjab Assembly. He was supported by us. In 1946, he contested on the Muslim League ticket. Our elders, however, were supporters of the Punjab Unionist Party. My uncle, who contested the seat on the Unionist ticket, lost the election and Rana Nasrullah won.

'In any event, our area remained peaceful till the very end when Partition was announced. Our elders did not want to leave at all. However, there were people from Hariana and adjoining villages who worked in Lahore and in the western districts of the Punjab. They wanted to leave because they had jobs in what was going to become Pakistan.

'My father had died but my mother was alive. My elder cousin Anwar Khan had just completed his first examination of the law exam at Lahore. We were determined not to migrate to Pakistan. Nevertheless, it was decided that two of my cousin sisters should be sent to Lahore, where we had some close relatives. They wanted me to come along. I started crying as I did not want to leave Hariana. So they left by car but it got stuck in one of the choas. We learnt later that two Sikh strangers had helped pull the car out while the women stood aside. Thereafter, they travelled to Lahore without a problem.

'One of my uncles, Mahmood Khan, was employed in the revenue department. He was appointed in charge of the Walton Refugee Camp. My cousin sisters were staying with him. They used to come daily with him to the camp with a view to finding out if we had arrived from Hariana. There was not much killing in our part of Hoshiarpur, but by that time the Punjab was seriously disturbed and communal killing was going on around us. The first attack which took place in the neighbourhood was on a Muslim Gujjar village, Mastiwal, by Sikhs. The Gujjars were employed in the army and so they fought back while their women escaped on foot. We offered them refuge but they only needed milk and some food and preferred to stay in the refugee camp which had been set up when attacks began to take place. I remember our Hindu neighbour Prem Sagar and another Hindu came to the refugee camp and expressed great sorrow. Prem Sagar was a very good football player. In fact, the Hariana football team was one of the best in the Punjab and included Hindus, Muslims and Sikhs. There were other good Hindus and Sikhs too who remained loyal to their Muslim neighbours. Rameek, Mohinder and their brother Jatinder were close friends of my cousins. Another was Susheel Kumar.

'I was in the eighth class at the time of Partition. After August 1947, the Muslims of Hoshiarpur began to leave for Pakistan as it became clear that they would not be safe in India anymore. We left about two months later. Our relatives sent a military convoy consisting of soldiers of the Baloch regiment from Pakistan to fetch us. There were four trucks in which all of us had to find a place. Women sat separately in one truck. Chacha Aslam Khan sat with them. Each truck had one respected elder in it at least. A Pathan family had joined us. The head of the family, a doctor, was in Africa at that time. The rest came with us. It was October and it was raining heavily. There were nine choas or streams that we had to cross. We started early in the morning but it took us 12 hours to cross the gorges spread over a distance of nine miles. We saw people in the thousands on their roofs when we reached Hoshiarpur. After crossing Hoshiarpur, we encountered another choa called Nasralla choa. It was so deep that the trucks could be bogged down completely. We spent the whole night there because it was raining. We did not get any food until about one o'clock the next day. However, we children started playing and collected wood and stones to stop the flow of water. This idea appealed to the elders and they began to collect wooden logs to obstruct the flow of water and thus enabled the trucks to cross the choa. I remember an abandoned house was pulled down and the logs in it were used to fill the gaps created by the strong water currents. A Sikh military captain came in our direction. He let us cross first. So we crossed the choa. Many dead bodies were lying around. I saw dogs eating dead corpses. Those were horrifying scenes.

'Then we reached Jullundur. After Jullundur, we crossed river Beas. Dead bodies were no longer floating in it although we heard that some weeks earlier it was full of them. Then we reached Amritsar. We were warned that an attack will take place near the Khalsa College (now called Guru Nanak Dev University). Everyone was scared. The soldiers were ready with their Sten guns and other firearms to meet any attack but fortunately nothing happened. Then we crossed Amritsar and people began to shout "Pakistan Zindabad" as we saw the Wagah signposts.

'Then Chacha Mahmood brought us to 19 C Model Town, Lahore. My cousins were already living there. It was a big bungalow. It had many books and pictures. For two months we ate very simple food made from radishes. Local Lahorias would come with empty trunks. They would bribe the constables, who would let them fill the trunks with goods left behind by the Hindus and Sikhs. They would ask us where goods were to be found. We told them and then they would fill the trunks. Our sisters told us that Pathans had killed a Hindu. My bua (father's sister) lived on 47 Poonch Road, near Chauburji, Lahore. Sometimes we would assemble there. That became the centre where all relatives from different parts would gather.

'Now, when we were leaving Hariana my taya (father's elder brother) was left behind. Nobody noticed his absence until we had gone far away from Hariana. A local trader, Seth Pyarelal, took tayajee home. Seth Pyarelal told him, "Rana Feroz Din, during the day you can go around here, but now uprooted Hindus and Sikh from West Punjab have arrived in this area. It is no longer safe for you to be out in the evening. You come here and sleep here in the same room as me."

'Then someone came from Pakistan with a truck looking for his family. They had been killed. So, tayaji came to Lahore with him. One day, I saw tayaji walking on Poonch Road. He knew buaji was living there. So, finally we were all united. Nobody in our immediate family was killed.

'There was a Sikh whose surname was Sharna who was a very close friend of the Muslims. He gave his pistol to them when Sikh jathas began to roam and hunt down Muslims in the villages and localities of Hoshiarpur. He would inform us about Sikh plans to attack. When we were leaving, he helped lift goods to the trucks the whole day. Later, Sharna became the custodian of a shrine of a Muslim holy man, Shami sahib, in the town of Sham Chaurasi, a famous centre of classical music. The Khalistani terrorists killed him in the 1980s.

'Some of my cousins have been to Hariana and met their old friends and class fellows. They were received very well. Our immediate relatives never accepted Partition and always longed for Hariana. Once, when Prime Minister Nehru visited Pakistan, he met one of our elders, Lt. Col. Aziz Ahmad Khan who belonged to the INA. Nehru invited him to return to India and promised him that his and the property of others who wanted to return would be returned to them. However, things had changed so much by then that it was too late to return and we have been here since then. Our clan is now dispersed over West Punjab. We settled in Okara, some of our relatives went to Arifwala and Chechawatni, others to Lyallpur, Sheikhupura (Manawal) and Lahore. My heart, however, belongs to Hariana and I will always be the son-of-the-soil of Hariana.'

Kangra

Muslims were in a small minority in district Kangra – only 4.8 per cent of the total population. It was a predominantly Hindu district comprising mainly hilly terrain. An interview that I conducted in October 1999, when I first began to collect material on Lahore, contained the following information on Kangra from a veteran artist and poet, Amar Nath Sehgal.

Amar Nath Sehgal

'I am originally from Campbellpur, northern Punjab. In 1939 I arrived in Lahore to study at the Government College and graduated from there in 1941. In May 1947 I left Lahore because stabbing, looting and burning had become a daily routine. It was a shattering exit from a place I had learnt to love dearly. However, when I arrived in eastern Punjab, things were no better. In the Kangra–Kulu Valley a wholesale slaughter of the Muslim minority took place between August and September. Out of 35,000, only 9,000 managed to escape alive to Pakistan. The Beas was filled with dead bodies and a foul odour was in the air for weeks after the mass killings. I remember feeling sick for many days and would frequently have nightmares. Especially the images of dead children fixed on spears and young women with their legs torn apart continued to haunt me for a long time. I still have such bouts.'

References

Afzal, Muhammad. *Dastan-e-Sandham,* Islamabad: Chaudhry Muhammad Ajmal (no date given).

Husain, Syed Wajahat. *Memories of a Soldier: 1947 Before, During, After*, Lahore: Ferozsons (Pvt) Ltd, 2010.

Khan, Muhammad Ayub. *Tarikh-i-Pakistan Aur Jullundur* (The Pakistan Movement and Jullundur), Lahore: Asatair, 2002.

Roberts. *Eminent Churchillians*, London: Phoenix Books, 1995.

Shafi, Mohammad. 'Statement of Capt. Mohd. Shafi, Resident of Mansurpur, Police Station Makerian, Distt. Hoshiarpur' in *The Journey to Pakistan: A Documentation on Refugees of 1947,* Islamabad: National Documentation Centre, 1993.

Interviews

Amar Nath Sehgal, New Delhi, 2 October 1999
Chaudhri Riasat Ali, London, 18 May 2002
Hameed Akhtar, London, 19 May 2002
Syed Muhammad Islam (fomerely of Radio Pakistan, Lahore), London, 19 May 2002
Sheikh Anwar Ali, Islamabad, 15 April 2003
Mian Jalal Din, Lahore, 22 April 2003
Amar Singh (formerly of Rawalpindi), Delhi, 15 March 2004
Hans Raj Khatri, 17 March 2004
Selja Saini, Chandigarh, 20 March 2004
Malik Muhammad Aslam, Lahore, 17 December 2004
Muhammad Abdullah Shamshad, Multan, 21 December 2004
Muhammad Ashiq Raheel, Lahore, 29 December 2004
Vicky's classmate's father, village Nathu Majra, Ludhiana district, 4 January 2005
Ranjit Singh (Ajit Singh), village Nathu Majra, Ludhiana district, 4 January 2005.
Mohan Lal Jhanji, 4 January 2005, Ludhiana
Baldev Verma, 4 January 2005, Ludhiana

Maulana Habibur Rahman Sanvi Ludhianvi, Ludhiana, 4 January 2005
Father of Rajnish Tandon, Hoshiarpur, 6 January 2005
Ajaib Singh, Gujjarwal, Ludhiana district, 29 November 2005
Harmail Singh, Gujjarwal, Ludhiana district, 29 November 2005
Haji Mukhtar Ahmed Khan, Sheikhupura, 30 December 2005
Colonel (Retd.) Ata Muhammad Dogar, Lahore, 10 May 2007
Rana Muhammad Azhar Khan, Lahore, 16 March 2016

19

AMBALA DIVISION AND DELHI

AMBALA DIVISION WAS THE EASTERN-MOST HIGHEST ADMINISTRATIVE unit of the old Punjab. It consisted of the districts of Ambala, Hissar, Rohtak, Karnal, Gurgaon, and Simla. The Muslim minority made up fifteen per cent of its population. Although most districts were Hindi-speaking (in its several local dialects) there were substantial Punjabi-speaking communities in Ambala and Simla districts.

Khan Bahadur Malik Khuda Baksh wrote a long report dated 4 October 1947 on the situation in Ambala division as well as on Jullundur and Ludhiana. He had been visiting these areas and had collected information on the local Muslims. It is not clear in what official capacity he was there but it seems he must have held a senior position in either the pre-Partition Punjab administration or was representing Pakistan. It is, however, quite clear that the Muslims were hoping to stay on but were forced to leave. He mentions mainly the raids conducted by armed Sikhs from Patiala state on the Muslim communities in the Ambala division. Here are excerpts pertaining to the areas he visited in the Ambala district:

Ambala district

The Muslim population of Ambala district was nearly thirty-two per cent. In the environs of Rupar *tahsil* there were many Muslim villages. The following are some of Malik Khuda Baksh's observations:

1. Looting of Muslim shops in Ambala Cantonment has been going on systematically. The police, mainly non-Muslim, have

throughout participated in such incidents. Although the orders are that the looters should be shot at sight, these orders are being carried out only by the Deputy Commissioner Mr. Grewal, while other subordinate staff are observing these orders only in breach [rather] than in observance.

2. In village Seeswan, Rupar *tahsil,* people clad in military uniforms told the villagers that they had come to take them to Kurali camp. Under this pretext they brought them out but killed most of them. In one small area one army captain found 300 dead bodies of Muslims.
3. Near the Ghaggar Bridge, a convoy of Muslims coming from Patiala State was attacked by an armed Sikh gang and Muslim girls had to save their honour by jumping into the river.
4. The Muslims of Bheraily, Kharar *tahsil*, a village mostly populated by Syed Muslims, was attacked by armed Sikh gangs (it is said from Patiala State) and they are reported to have killed several people. Young Syed girls threw themselves into wells to save their honour but they were taken out and it is reported that they were dishonoured [raped] (1993: 2003).

Syed Qamurruzaman Shah

'My family belonged to the Ahrars and had a strong presence in Ambala. Our position had always been that dividing India would divide the Muslim community. The Ahrars enjoyed considerable goodwill in Ambala city. In mid-October my father and his friends realised that it would be impossible to continue living in Ambala because of the thousands of Hindus and Sikhs who were arriving from western Punjab. Some of the young men among them were looking for revenge and Muslims were being targeted in increasing measure. The local Congress leaders were close friends of the Ahrars. They also advised us that we should leave but return when peace was established again. Muslims from the rural areas who had managed to come to Ambala were in a very bad shape. Because of rains and attacks on the way many were injured and sick. Many died in the camps and at the railway station. We were not attacked on the way because we had a military escort.'

Ambala rural areas

I met Chowdhry Abdul Wahid in Stockholm in the mid-1970s. He was a student at the International Graduate School of Stockholm University, while I was in the Department of Political Science. He shared with me the harrowing details of the calamity which hit his family and other Muslims in October 1947 in the villages of Rupar *tahsil.* On 20 December 2004 we met again, after many years in Multan in Pakistan, and I recorded an interview with him on that subject.

Chowdhry Abdul Wahid

'In 1947 I was about six years old. We lived in a small village called Dangoli. It was in Rupar *tahsil*, district Ambala [Rupar district is now in India's Punjab state, whereas Ambala city is in India's Haryana state]. Ours was a village of Muslim Gujjars to which my family also belonged. The surrounding villages were also populated by our *biradari.* Some Hindus, mostly from the untouchable castes, also lived in Dangoli. There was no shop in our village, but there was one in Kinoli owned by a Hindu. We went to school in Kinoli. I don't know when we became Muslims but three generations before my father we had certainly been Muslims.

'At the time of Partition, my father was working in Simla. I, my mother and my brothers and sisters were in the village. From what I have learnt later, our elders believed that Rupar and Hoshiarpur would be given to Pakistan. But then the attacks began and we had to vacate Dangoli and move to a large open space at the graveyard just outside Dangoli. Thousands of Muslims from the neighbouring villages had also taken refuge there. The total number could be more than a hundred thousand. We stayed there a long time. Our cattle would not leave us; they surrounded us from all sides. We felt insecure because it was not an organised camp with any security or protection of the police or any other government agency. We did not have any firearms. Some knives, hatchets and spears were quickly prepared by the artisans amongst us.

'One day the Sikh military and the Hindu assistant commissioner arrived at the graveyard and ordered us to surrender all weapons. In return we were promised safe passage to Kurali where the main camp had been established. Our leaders were reluctant to comply but ultimately they agreed. This was a trick. Sikh *jathas* were hiding in the fields.

'We began to walk towards Kurali which was some distance from our village. We walked through the thickly wooded forest, small hillocks and streams. When we left the rainy season had started. I was carried by my maternal uncle. My mother, paternal aunt, two brothers and one sister and other members of the family all walked together. We were ordered to enter the stream. At some places it was deep and women and children began to drown. We had no food with us except *channey* (roasted gram) and *makai danay* (maize). On the way we were again checked for weapons and were told to surrender all gold and other precious metals and stones. They would be returned to us when we reached Kurali, the assistant commissioner told us. In some cases, women wearing jewellery were attacked and their ornaments were snatched with such brute force that ears were torn and hands and necks would start bleeding. For example, my paternal aunt who was wearing gold was treated so badly that her arm got dislocated.

'After a while we were ordered to get out of the stream and start walking on land. It was raining heavily. My paternal uncle could not bear the pressure and panicked. He ran away towards the high grass and bushes. We have never seen him again. My maternal uncle's son also ran away into the fields. He later managed to get to Pakistan.

'During this period we were constantly being attacked by bands of Sikhs. Women and girls were abducted. The caravan was many kilometres long and therefore the attacks took place at different places. The firing was indiscriminate and people just fell when hit. We finally arrived at the camp in Kurali. It was still raining. By that time, thousands of deaths had already occurred. Many women and children drowned. Only a quarter of our caravan got to Kurali.

'The camp at Kurali was not in the records of the Pakistan administration. For some three months we stayed there. There was no supply of food. People had to fend for themselves. The only thing we could buy outside the camp from the villages around was peanuts. The hygienic conditions were appalling. Clean water was not available, the toilets were full of excrement and insects crept all over the place. No medical help was at hand. Thousands of people died of cholera, malaria, typhoid, pneumonia and other such diseases. Among them was my mother. I remember her lying on the ground and not responding to me. I began to cry. I was told she was sleeping.

'Finally, someone learnt about Kurali and the Pakistan government sent trucks to fetch us. We arrived at Walton outside Lahore some three months after we fled our village. Of those hundred thousand or more, only one-fourth survived and reached Pakistan safely. My father had gone directly from Simla to Lahore when he learnt that Dangoli and other villages had been burnt down. He, too, had expected our villages to be included in Pakistan and was therefore completely unprepared for the upheaval that took place. He used to visit the Walton camp everyday and one day he met someone from our *biradari* who told him that we were also in the camp. He took us to Faletti's Hotel in Lahore where he had some connections. He was later posted in Sahiwal where we then set up home.

Just before the partition of the Punjab, my father had purchased some land but the registration had not been completed. We got some compensation for the losses incurred but most of our possessions were lost. My maternal uncle saved my life by carrying me in his arms most of the way. I always bless his memory. He retired from the army and then died in Multan.'

Chowdhry Abdul Saeed

The next day, 21 December 2004, we went to Bahawalpur where Chowdhry Abdul Wahid's elder brother, Chowdhry Abdul Saeed, practised law. Chowdhry Abdul Saeed was a few years older, born on 1 January 1937. This is his story:

'There was tension in the school at Ghanoli between Muslim and Hindu–Sikh boys because the Muslims were supporters of the Muslim League and wanted Pakistan, and the non-Muslims were opposed to the creation of Pakistan. Even the Hindu and Sikh teachers became unfriendly when the idea of Pakistan gained currency. Most of the pupils were Sikhs. That region was dominated by Sikhs. We could not enter the homes of Hindus and Sikhs because we were considered *mleccha* (foreigners; unclean persons). For example, at school we could not drink water from the same tap. When we protested, a separate section was built for Muslims. Later my elder brother started a school in Rupar and I also went there. There, too, the situation was tense.

'The reasons for the Muslim–Sikh enmity are rooted deep in history. At Chamkor, near Sirhind, there is a sacred Sikh *gurdwara*. It was built at a place where the Sikhs believe the sons of Guru Gobind Singh had been buried in the walls on the orders of the Mughals. Therefore Sikh fury against Muslims in the region had always existed. In 1905, the Sikhs and Muslim Gujjars had a violent confrontation over the slaughter of a cow. The Muslim leader among the Muslim Gujjars, Maulvi Abdullah Rupari [his son-in-law, Hafiz Saeed, became the main leader of the Lashkar-e-Taiyyiba, which later gained notoriety as a terrorist organisation], was a strict follower of the Ahl-e-Hadith school of Islam.

'Consequently, one day when the Juma prayers were being offered the Sikhs attacked the worshippers. The Muslims retaliated and some thirty to forty Sikhs were slain. The memory of that clash continued to persist and constantly affected relations between Muslims and Sikhs. In 1947, the Sikhs were looking for revenge not only for what was happening in West Punjab but also the humiliation and the wrongs allegedly done to the sons of Guru Gobind Singh.

'After the Radcliffe Award was announced attacks on Muslims began immediately. The Muslims of Dangoli, Dogoli, Ganoli, Chandial, Marsali, and other villages assembled at the Mian ka Qabristan, a graveyard around the mausoleum of a holy man who had come from Dera Ghazi Khan and settled outside Dangoli. We lived there for two–three months. It was already the beginning of winter. It started raining and in those areas the rains are very violent. We learnt that Sikhs from Ludhiana, Patiala and Jullundur had collected in *jathas*. We were not willing to leave our villages and several times when Sikhs attacked, our people fought back and repulsed them. Maulana Abdullah Rupari organised bands of fighters who fought the Sikhs in the hills, streams and everywhere. Gunfire was also exchanged.

'Sometime in October, the decision to move to the camp at Karoli was taken. The Muslim caravan was spread in several miles. The military and the assistant commissioner who were accompanying us used loudspeakers to announce that all weapons should be surrendered. Further, they made the caravan split into smaller groups. Some were in front, some in the middle and some behind. Then they began the search for weapons and even long sticks were impounded. Then Sikhs who were hiding in the fields attacked unarmed people and a slaughter took place. Thousands were killed. The water of the streams and canals became red. Children and women were not spared. My paternal uncle, my aunt's husband and many of my close relatives were killed.

'The Sikhs wanted to cut off the legs of Abdul Hamid, brother of my uncle's wife, and they did it. She would not abandon him but he insisted that she should leave because he was dying. She then put a cloth on him and went and joined the caravan. We were saved because we were at the front of the caravan. Those behind were almost all wiped out.

'The camp at Kurali was a living hell. There was no place to bury the dead. So one simply dug a hole and put the dead body in it. That is what we did with the dead body of our mother. The Sikhs took young girls and most of them were never recovered. Thousands were killed. Some Sikhs, however, were kind to us. Mangal Singh, who belonged to the Saini caste, was from our village. He had a general merchandise shop. He used to come to our camp in Kurali and would give sugar and other food items to my brother. Similarly, other Sikhs who had friends among Muslims would come to help. We had good relations with Hindus too. Some of them visited the camp and provided help of different kinds.'

Visit to Dangoli

Late in the afternoon of 29 November 2005, Hitesh Gosain, Virender Singh and I arrived in Dangoli. It is some ten kilometres from Rupar town. This part of East Punjab is very green as the rains come early and last longer. Small hills, streams and ravines, and a new canal built after Independence, have all made it a very productive place. Just to the north-east is Himachal Pradesh, where the hills become visible, rising gradually as they join the Shivalik mountain range.

Chhittru

'I am the village *chowkidar* (watchman). We were here even in 1947. The new people of Dangoli are Sikh Jats who came from Pakistan and settled here. Before Partition, the village was inhabited by Muslims of the Gujjar caste. The headman was Umra Gujjar [Umar Din according to Chaudhri Abdul Wahid]. When the attacks took place all the villages across the Sutlej river were surrounded by the military and the Sikh *jathas*. They would set the Muslim villages ablaze and force people to flee. They crossed the river and gathered in the graveyard. A Muslim holy man, Gauhar Shah, is buried a little farther. At least 80,000 to 100,000 had assembled here. *Lambardar* Umra told us to leave the village because the Muslims who had been uprooted would take their revenge. So we left and went to Khanoli. The Muslims were not leaving. They were determined to stay in their villages but the military coerced them to leave. On the way, many attacks took place and people were killed in the thousands. Here all the houses were burnt, including ours. Later, when we returned, we rebuilt our homes with material from the houses of the Muslims. If you want the full story you should talk to *lambardar* Amar Singh. He is now in his eighties.'

We drove to the village and after some enquiries, were helped by a young girl who led us to his house. It was a big brick house. As we learnt from the *lambardar* himself, he belonged to the formerly untouchable caste. The family had obviously prospered and Amar Singh was an important man, but the house was located just outside the old village – it was difficult to say if this was because of the continuation of the caste oppression or simply that more land was available outside the village. In the compound, we sat for our interiews.

Amar Singh

'I was born in Dangoli in 1922 in a Harijan [Dalit] family. This was a village of Muslim Gujjars and a few Harijan households. I had many friends among Muslims. We all lived in peace. *Lambardar* Umra was a very good and just man. Others who I remember by name were Khair Din, Shah Muhammad, and Sher Muhammad.

'This area had many Muslim villages. Up until 1947, relations were peaceful but then some notorious characters and *goondas* amongst the Sikhs, the local administration and the Sikh military attacked the Muslims. There was panic all over. Muslims from the surrounding villages and as far as Nalagarh state and Nurpur Bedi collected in the graveyard near the tomb of a Muslim Sufi, Gauhar Shah. There must be nearly 100,000 of them. Many of them were related to one another, probably belonging to the Gujjar *biradari*. It rained a lot in those days.

'*Lambardar* Umra told us to leave as our lives were in danger from the Muslims who believed that Harijans were involved in the attacks. We moved to a nearby village, but were well aware of what was going on. The Sikhs were organised in *jathas* and armed with guns, axes and hatchets. The military was initially brought here by the Sikhs of Khanoli, who feared that the growing Muslim presence in the neighbourhood might put their lives in jeopardy. The Muslims were ordered to leave Dangoli for the camp at Kurali. They resisted the orders and some clashes took place. But they were compelled to proceed towards the camp. Then they moved farther on from here to high ground, onto mounts and hillocks near a place called Shahzada Pir. They stayed there for almost a month. Then the Sikh military and Pandit Lakshmi Chand, sub divisional magistrate [whom Chaudhri Abdul Saeed described as assistant deputy commissioner] ordered the Muslims to surrender all their weapons and also gold and silver objects and money. Most people complied with the orders but some of them resisted and then the military opened fire with Sten guns. This resulted in lots of casualties.

'A massacre took place. Thousands of people were killed. We found corpses all over in a radius of many kilometres. Bloated corpses floated in the streams and ponds and some wells were filled with women, who had either jumped into them and killed themselves, or were thrown in by the Sikhs and the military. I don't know how many died altogether but it must be thousands. The caravan then went to Kurali where I believed it stayed for some time before the Muslims were taken to Pakistan. Everybody knows this story. The Muslims of this area were very peaceful people. Some of them have visited their villages but I don't remember if anyone came to Dangoli.'

Naseeb Kaur or Azmat Bibi?

On the way to Dangoli, we learnt about a woman who was born a Muslim but was saved by a Sikh and brought up as a Sikh. After talking to Amar Singh, we went to her village, Phul Khurd. We arrived at about 7 p.m. Meeting her was not a problem. We walked into a traditional peasant home with cows, buffaloes and goats in the compound. Naseeb Kaur turned out to be a kind and sweet woman. The following account might strike some as stranger than fiction:

'I was only four at the time of Partition. Our village was set on fire and I was separated from my mother, who was holding my hand when the Sikhs raided our village. My father died soon after I was born, so she and I were the only immediate family. A woman found me and brought me to a Sikh overseer who worked in the canal department. That woman later left for Pakistan.

'My *chachaji* [referring with respect to the Sikh overseer] saw me and liked me immediately He had himself participated in the raids on Muslims many times but to me, he was like a father. He had a daughter already but after I joined the family, two sons were born and he prospered in business. He believed that I had brought good luck to him and his family and whenever he went out he would say that I was the source of all the happiness in his life.

'I was named Naseeb Kaur [meaning 'Princess of Destiny']. I did not know my real name at that time. When I grew up, I married a Sikh and now I have children and grandchildren. But all those years I could not forget my *bibi* (mother) who loved me greatly. I used to think about her everyday.

'She had survived the slaughter and reached Pakistan safely. She had married again but never stopped thinking about me. Then she met the woman who had given me to the Sikh gentleman. In 1990, she came to my door and told me she was my mother. Of course I recognised her and she recognised me. She told me that my Muslim name was Azmat Bibi.

'We met after forty-three years. I was now a Sikh and had a family. My mother was a devout Muslim who prayed five times a day. I told her that my adoptive parents and their children had treated me very well and the whole village had been kind to me. I also told her that I had become an orthodox Sikh and was very attached to my faith and family.

'She went back satisfied that I was happy. Then I visited Pakistan and met my relatives there. My mother had two sons. Then my uncles and aunts also met me. I have visited Pakistan three more times. They have all accepted me and always send gifts to my family. Nobody has tried to persuade me to return to Islam. We are all happy with the way life has gone on since the partition of the Punjab in 1947.'

I felt greatly moved by this amazing account of human endurance and how people approach life in practical rather than doctrinal terms. The millions of lives shattered in 1947 were a great tragedy, no matter what line one takes on the partition of India, Bengal and the Punjab.

Hissar

The Muslim minority of Hissar district in 1947 was 28 per cent. Khan Bahadur Malik Khuda Baksh notes the following in his report about Sirsa *tahsil* of Hissar:

> The Muslims of Sirsa Sub-Division are reported to have organized themselves into a defensive corps and seeing this, the Jats did not molest them. They fought their way through Sirsa and it was estimated that about sixty thousand Muslims had already reached Bahawalpur. It was first reported that the Bikaner state authorities were not allowing a passage but eventually they became more helpful with the result that the Muslims got through. Captain Ranjit Singh, Minister for Development, East Punjab Government, told me that he would be able to evacuate Muslims to Bahawalpur from 17 localities in this district (1993: 208).

Pushpa Goel

During my visit to Delhi and East Punjab in March 2004, Vimal Issar, whose interview on Lahore was given earlier, took me to meet a Hindu family that had protected the family of the famous Pakistani cricketer Inzamam-ul-Huq in Hansi, district Hissar. Mrs Goel told me the following:

'During the last Pakistani tour of India, Inzamam had expressed a desire to visit his parents' original home in Hansi. This had not been allowed by the Indian government, but my son contacted Inzamam at his hotel and met him. Back home, Inzamam told the story to his parents and his father immediately remembered me and my parents. We had saved their family during the riots. A mob had come looking for them, but my father was able to send them away. A telephone call came from Multan. Inzamam's father talked to me. He asked: *"Arre Pushpa kaisi ho tum?"* (Pushpa, how are you?) I said, "*Bhai Sahib mein teekh hun*." (I am well, Brother'). And so, the conversation continued. He invited me to attend Inzamam's wedding in Multan in 1999. Prime Minister Atal Bihari Vajpayee at that time paid a visit to Lahore so it was easy to get a visa.

'I was overwhelmed by the hospitality they gave me. It was like coming back to one's own family. Our elders had always had very close relations. Everybody took care of the fact that I was a strict vegetarian. The women in the family were so warm and kind. I can never forget my visit to Multan.'

Rohtak

In district Rohtak, the Muslims made up 17.4 per cent of the population. What follows is Khan Bahadur Malik Allah Baksh's recollection of the situation in September 1947:

> Although wild rumours have been afloat that the Muslims of Rohtak district had been wiped out yet the situation was not so bad. I was told that the residents of Sonepat, Bahadurgarh, Gohana and other Muslim villages had been slaughtered but I got it from several Muslim soldiers who had gone there to evacuate their families that Muslims at all places, with the exception of Bahadurgarh, had concentrated in various villages and were fighting back both the Jats and the military. Kalanaur was said to be impregnable from any attack by any number of Jats. Rohtak town was also safe although the people were living in a state of terror and want of food (1993: 207-8).

Mohammad Farid Mirza

'I belong to an influential Mughal family of Rohtak. Our immediate family were staunch Muslim Leaguers. My *mamuji* was a supporter of the Congress party. We had a good understanding with the local Congress leaders. Nobody wanted us to leave. However, other Muslims were not in such a good situation. In some rundown *mohallas* attacks had begun to take place soon after the Radcliffe Award was announced. Till then nobody believed that we would be forced to flee. Our own family had decided to stay in Rohtak because we owned a lot of property and had deep roots in the town.

'RSS and Sikh *jathas* began to raid Rohtak and the villages around it in late August and early September. They first came in the dead of night but then the raids started taking place in broad daylight. It became clear that we would not be able to stay any longer. Some of our relatives went to Delhi in the hope that once things calmed down they would return to their homes. Since we were known for our Muslim League links, my father decided that it was imperative that we shift to Sahiwal [called Montgomery in 1947] where we had some relatives.

'One day the raiders actually attacked our house and set it on fire. So, we had to leave empty-handed immediately. Others also joined the stream of Muslims running away. We learnt later that some people abandoned their old parents; others left behind mentally and physically challenged children. Some women were carried away by the raiders. In one case a street was littered with dead bodies, in many cases with the head severed from the body. Women whose breasts had been cut off just lay there dead and abandoned. I continue to have nightmares about those days. The attackers were outsiders, but there is no doubt that the police and administration helped them.

'In the camp, the situation was pitiable. The monsoon rains wreaked havoc. Many people died. I still remember a traumatised woman holding on to her dead baby, not letting anyone take it from her. We stayed there for more than a month but finally were transported on a train that had Pakistan Army soldiers on it. Most ordinary people had to join the foot convoys that were leaving for Pakistan.

'On the way, Sikh *jathas* fired upon our train and some people were killed and injured but the soldiers kept the Sikhs away. We arrived in Pakistan in November. Most of our relatives who shifted to Delhi were killed, only some could join us in Pakistan. I believe they arrived in late December. I do hope to visit Rohtak before I die. I am now eighty-two, so this must happen quickly, but this wish will be fulfilled only if Allah grants it.'

Brigadier Sarjit Singh Chowdhary

I had been corresponding for quite some time with a young Sikh writer, Tridivesh Singh Maini, who promotes amity between the two Punjabs. I met his maternal grandfather during a visit to Delhi in 2005 and learned that he had escorted Muslims from different villages in Haryana to Pakistan. Brigadier Chowdhary had the following to narrate about his association with the Partition process.

'I am from Kahuta, district Rawalpindi. I was a captain in the 8th Punjab regiment and had just returned from Iraq in 1947. I did not join the boundary force but my services had been loaned to the Punjab police. I was posted in Rohtak. During 1 September and 31 January 1948, I escorted Muslim Rangars [Muslim Rajputs] of eleven villages to Hussainiwala, on the Kasur border. This was done in the face of tough opposition from Hindus and Sikhs who had fled from West Punjab and wanted revenge for the crimes committed against their kith and kin in Pakistan. People from both sides behaved like beasts. No description is needed to depict what they did to each other. It was truly shameful. I did my duty and safely escorted the Rangars to the Pakistan border.'

Karnal

District Karnal also had a substantial Muslim minority of nearly thirty-one per cent. Liaqat Ali Khan, who would later become Pakistan's first prime minister, hailed from Karnal. On 28 November 2005, Hitesh Gosain, Virender Singh and I drove into Karnal city and stayed for the evening at Virender's parents' home. I was able to speak to an old

Brahmin gentleman whose full name I failed to record, but everybody was referring to him as Panditji. He told us that there was a massacre of Muslims in Karnal, in which several hundred died. It took place not far from where we were sitting. The fleeing Muslims were attacked by Hindu Jats. Some 200–300 could have been slaughtered. He confirmed that prior to 1945–46 all communities lived in peace. Sir Chhotu Ram (d. 1945), leader of the Punjab Unionist Party, was from Karnal. With his demise, the old type of pluralism quickly dissipated and instead communal tensions began to rise.

Khan Bahadur Malik Allah Baksh

> The situation in Karnal district had been deteriorating and there was considerable loss of life and property in the villages. Muslims of various localities were reported to have concentrated in big villages and till 20 September they were able to withstand the attacks; but everybody believed they would not be able to survive for long. Adequate protection was not available and immediate evacuation was, therefore, the only solution. I was told that the deputy commissioner told the Muslims to arrange their own evacuation as he was not responsible for their safety any longer. I was told that Mian Muhammad Shaffi, PCS [Provincial Civil Service] who was still in Karnal, would be willing to work as Liaison Officer so as to arrange for the evacuation of Muslims from the district. A riot took place in Karnal on 20 September and it was reported to have resulted in a considerable number of casualties [probably the same riot that Panditji had mentioned above] (1993: 2007).

Simla

The Muslim population of Simla district was eighteen per cent in 1947. Being the summer capital of British India, this picturesque hill station enjoyed considerable prestige and importance. However, after the partition of India, the Muslims in that district had to face the same threat to their lives as applied elsewhere for them in the pre-colonial Punjab.

Khan Bahadur Malik Allah Baksh

> Alarming reports came from Simla in the second week of September. Three special trains were run from Simla to Kalka and the two trains leaving Kalka brought most of the refugees. There were a number of respectable Muslim families stranded in Simla, Solan and Kasauli. Their evacuation was a job that only the military could do because of the influx of Sikh refugees into Simla and adjoining areas and the type of territory through which these refugees had to pass (1993: 208).

Nasim Hassan

I came into contact with Nasim Hassan, a US-based engineer, because of my weekly columns where I sometimes wrote on the Partition theme. Upon my insistence, he wrote down his memories of those days. He was very young at that time but remembered the journey with great clarity. He reminisced:

'Around 1912, my grandfather Ibrahim and his younger brother Ismael left their village in Gurdaspur district and came to Simla in search of better opportunities. My grandfather made good money and returned to his village. His younger brother became a successful businessman specialising in European-style tailoring. He made good money by the standards of that time. He had about ten people working in his shop which was located on the famous Mall Road.

'My father, Khadim Hussain, became a civil servant in Simla. A large number of our relatives used to come to work during summer and returned home in winter. Our home was located quite near the Mall Road. A small road passed in front of our home leading to the Reading Hospital. I can close my eyes today and visualise distant hills of various colours – gray, green and white. On the road there was a fence on one side and a row of houses on the other side. This fence acted as a safeguard as there was a steep incline and deep gorges on the downhill side. The hills were lush green and the valley down below was full of wild flowers. The partition of India was a defining moment for millions of people. At that time everyone looked for himself and his family. Before Partition, Hindus and Muslims lived in peace without any problem. I still remember a number of names like Mukand Lall Sood, Dr Pamrey and Gurbir Kohli, who were friends of my father.

'In June, sporadic incidents began. In July, the Muslims started leaving Simla for Pakistan. The rich were the first to leave. I remember very vividly that our house was locked from outside. The time-frame has to be July–August. Another Muslim family moved into the upper storey of the house. We had a servant named Mukhtar who was worldly-wise and could get along with people of all religions. He was our lifeline and would bring food and other items that were needed, while the family was locked in.

'During this time, we lost all contacts with grandpa Ismael and his family. He was attacked in his shop and had to flee to a nearby hotel. He was caught, and then killed by a mob that included his Sikh business rivals in the same area. My father learned of his death in Simla but kept the news to himself till we arrived in Pakistan.

'In August 1947, we moved to Ripon Hospital with the help of Dr Pamrey, a Hindu doctor, and stayed there till we could catch a train for Pakistan. Narrow gauge trains from Simla wind down into Kalka. I recall a refugee camp that was like a tent city. One night there was an attack on the camp. My parents physically covered my two sisters and me so that we could be saved.

'After three days' stay in Kalka, we, along with other relatives, boarded the train to Pakistan during the night. The passengers locked their compartments from inside so that no one could board the train. Sometimes people tried to hang on to the windows but were pushed away by people inside the train. The train slowly made its way through the plains of Punjab. I recall the bright sunshine when the train arrived at a station. I saw a huge crowd of Sikhs brandishing swords and violently raising slogans like "*Sat Sri Akal*." The train was about to stop as the crowd was getting closer when all of a sudden it started moving in the reverse direction.

'After this episode, the train crossed over to Pakistan in the middle of the night using an alternate route. We and other refugees were placed in a camp in the Walton Refugee Camp outside Lahore. Everyday people would go around looking for their lost relatives. My father told us about his uncle Ismael's death only after we settled down in Lahore.

'In the 1980s, long after Partition, I went to India on a business trip. After completing my work I took two weeks' vacation and went to Simla by train. The train passed through hills and valleys. The first scene that rattled me was the denuded hills and a multitude of small houses. The Simla of my dreams lay in shambles. While walking up the hill I did not notice any tall trees or the lush green hills of yesteryears.

'Outside the railway station there were a large number of hotel agents and coolies. The latter were mostly from Kashmir. Even when carrying my luggage they seemed to walk faster than me. After checking in at a hotel, I walked around looking for something that would look familiar. I could not find anything that resembled the Simla I had first known. The next day, I got up early and went to Jakhu Hill. I remembered I used to visit the Hanuman Temple with my mother on the top of the hill with monkeys jumping around everywhere.

'As I started climbing up the hill slowly, I noticed tall deodar and pine trees. This place looked exactly the same as I had seen more than thirty years ago. Gradually I moved up the hill and I saw a group of monkeys walking leisurely at a distance. Other groups of monkeys of all sizes and ages later appeared in the vicinity of Hanuman Temple.

'It seemed like time had stopped and the place had the same everlasting beauty. I was alone on Jakhu Hill that morning for about two hours. The first to appear was a small vendor selling fried snacks. I was his first customer so he gave me more than my money's worth. While taking photographs of the surrounding area, I heard someone calling me. Behind me there was a family consisting of a couple and three kids. The man asked me to take pictures of his family. I did, without any hesitation, and took photographs from various locations. The man thought that I was a local photographer from Simla and could give them the photographs the next day. They had come from Jullundur. He became very friendly after I told him about myself. I promised to send him their pictures from the US.

'As the afternoon approached, the weather became pleasant and I started walking down. Coming down took half the time compared to the uphill track. In the afternoon, I sat in front of the old church built by the British. People were sitting on a small ridge facing the sun. I also sat down to enjoy the warm sunshine. The person next to me introduced himself as Sukhbir, who worked for the state of Himachal Pradesh. As soon as I told him that I was visiting my birthplace after thirty years, Sukhbir transformed into a long-lost friend and called me *Vatni* (from the same place). He introduced me to many people including the local Ayurvedic *vaid*, a restaurant owner, and his colleagues. All of them treated me like a part of the larger Simla family. For the first time during my visit to India, I felt I had come home.'

Gurgaon

The Muslim minority of Gurgaon district was nearly thirty-seven per cent. It was on the border with Delhi and is now an up-and-coming suburb of Delhi. The distinguished Pakistani journalist and human rights champion, I.A. Rehman, narrated the following story about what happened in Gurgaon.

I.A. Rehman

'I was born in a village on the Yamuna river, some thirty miles south of Delhi in Hassanpur, district Gurgaon. Hassanpur was a mixed village, nearly half-Muslim and half-non-Muslim. The landowners were Muslims. They were from the Baloch tribe called Rind. The Rinds were settled during the reign of Humayun [sixteenth century] in a number of villages in an outer arch of Delhi to defend it from attacks by Hindu Jats.

'Our relations with the Hindus of Hassanpur were very friendly. We studied with Hindus and our teachers were also Hindus. We never felt any animosity towards them. We had close family friends among the Hindus. In the beginning of World War II, there was not much income so our elders laid emphasis on education and even girls in our village were sent to school. My grandfather Abdur Razzaq Sahib established a school for girls in our house.

'The political atmosphere was anti-British in our village. Nobody joined the colonial Indian Army. My elders were attracted to the Khaksar movement. Then some joined the Muslim League but not very keenly. My father, who was a lawyer, had established his practice in Kalwal, a town close to Gurgaon. He was not a member of the Muslim League. On 14 August 1947 the prominent people, including my father, went around in a truck to the villages telling them not to leave. They told the people that they had been living there for centuries and therefore there was no reason to abandon their homes.

'Already in February 1947 rioting had taken place, but the reason was not political. It was local enmity between the Hindu Jats and Muslim Meos. It is interesting to note that the Meos were not fully Islamicised at that time. They followed both Hindu and Islamic rituals. They used to settle their disputes on the basis of *gotra* (clan). For some reason someone introduced a communal dimension and that resulted in rioting.

'On 10 September, our village was attacked. The raiders were in the thousands. People from the village next to ours took part but some had come even from as far away as 150 kilometres. There were no Sikhs. They were Jats. Many people were killed. This was the first attack. Two of my cousins, strong and well-built, were killed by a Hindu friend whom they had known for twenty years. He was a Bania (trader caste). What motivated him to commit such a heinous crime remains a mystery to me. Many of our family and *biradari* were slain in the raids that came in waves.

'Mountbatten saw what was happening and sent a message to the army unit in Mathura. As a result, some lives were saved. This is mentioned in the diary of Campbell.

'Then our people shifted to Kalwal. Gandhiji sent Maulana Habibur-Rehman and Pandit Sunder Lal who was Gandhiji's secretary. They told us not to go. My father said to them, "I don't want to, but now the two governments have reached an agreement. What should I say to the men and women who have become refugees? Can you guarantee our security?" They said, "We can't".

'We then left Gurgaon for Bhatinda and then on to Fazilka. We had a military escort. My father left the keys of our house and his office with his friend, Rao Bahal Singh, saying that when peace was restored he would come back.'

Delhi

Delhi was not part of the Punjab province, but many civil servants from the Punjab used to serve in Delhi. Also, because of a very large number of Sikh and Hindu refugees from West Punjab, the Muslims from Punjab were under great pressure and threat to flee to Pakistan. The Khosla report mention ferocious attacks on the Muslims of Delhi. It asserts that the Muslims had instigated riots as early as November 1946 but then in September–October when the attacks on Muslims took place, at least a thousand were slain (1989: 283). The late Dr Ishtiaq Hussain Qureshi, former Pakistan Federal Minister for Education and Vice-Chancellor of Karachi University, has written an account of what happened during those days when the Delhi Muslims were being attacked all over the city and in the suburbs.

Ishtiaq Hussain Qureshi

'The following day, I sent my family into the Old Fort, where the Muslim refugees from the city had congregated and plunged into rescue work. There were many memorable incidents, but the most significant of these was that I brought Dr Zakir Husain, later President of India, from his house at Jamia near Okhla, at that time several miles out of Delhi, and both of us went and saw Gandhi. We did not have to tell him much because his workers were reporting events fully and truly. There was no effort to hide the truth from him. I said to him that only he could stop the carnage. For a moment he grew thoughtful and promised simply, "I will put my best into the effort." And I think he did keep his promise. Otherwise he would not have been assassinated' (Qureshi 1995: 192).

Riaz Ahmed Cheema

My oldest friend in Stockholm, Riaz Ahmed Cheema, belonged to one of the Punjabi families who were in Delhi because his father was posted there. He narrated the following:

'I was born on 5 February 1937. We are originally from Sialkot but at the time of Partition my father, M. Abdulla Cheema, was posted as a civil judge in Delhi. He belonged to the Punjab Provincial Services. It was common for officers from the Punjab to be posted in Delhi even though Delhi was not a part of the Punjab Province. My parents and we, their eight children, lived in the civil lines area in Ataur Rahman Lane. He had many Hindu, Sikh and Muslim friends, but the closest among them was a businessman by the name of Ram Krishan. He owned a printing press in old Delhi. Another was Chaudhry Ghulam Abbas who was city magistrate of New Delhi. He hailed from Chakwal, West Punjab.

'Delhi did not experience any communal tension in the beginning of 1947 but strikes and demonstrations did take place. However, after the rioting of March 1947 in Rawalpindi many Sikhs came to Delhi where they had relatives. At that time there was already a sizeable Sikh community from the Punjab settled in Delhi. They were engaged in business and trade and a whole range of miscellaneous jobs. Some of the Sikhs from Rawalpindi went back but others from the villages stayed on. The atmosphere began to turn tense as the Sikhs narrated their tales of Muslim atrocities to their relatives and in *gurdwara* congregations. Thus, on several occasions our parents did not send us to school fearing that revenge attacks might occur. In any case, we were not allowed to go out after dark.

'After 3 June, when the Partition Plan was announced, things began to move very fast. My father opted for Pakistan and received orders to join duty as senior civil judge in Jhelum. We left Delhi on 16 August. We were given a second-class compartment. My father had a rifle and a revolver with him. Stories were circulating that trains were being stopped and Muslims were being killed by Sikh hordes near Amritsar, but our train reached Lahore safely. Before we left Delhi, a Sikh colleague of my father requested him to look after his peon who was also a Sikh, as he was travelling on the same train to fetch his family from Rawalpindi.

'At Lahore railway station my father went to the compartment in which the peon was travelling. He was there. But when the train pulled out of Lahore he noticed some *goonda*-type characters jumping on to the running train. At Gujranwala he went back to check if the peon was all right, but did not find him there. Some people in that compartment told my father that the *goondas* attacked him and he jumped out of the window into the river when the train was passing the bridge over the

Ravi. What happened to him then, could he swim or not, did he survive or got killed, nobody could say anything. When we arrived in Jhelum it was either Eid day or a day before. In Jhelum, Sikhs and Hindus were still there. I remember Sikhs sitting in their sweetmeat shops selling their delicacies.

'I remember even now the local Delhi Muslims did not seem to have been preparing to leave for Pakistan. One of our neighbours in Ataur Rahman Lane was the family of Sultan Ahmed Japanwala. He was a very rich businessman and a native of Delhi. The Japanwalas had three sons and a daughter of almost the same age as us children and we were close friends with them. One of the boys later became the Finance Minister in the Sindh Province of Pakistan. But in August 1947, it seems that the Japanwalas had no intention of migrating to Pakistan. On the eve of our departure for Pakistan they gave a party for all those who were leaving for Pakistan from that area. They distributed sweets to children and beautiful tiny insignias with "*Khuda Hafiz*" (may God protect you) written in the middle.

'It is a huge irony that the Muslim League got its greatest support from the Muslims of the Hindu-majority provinces. In the Muslim-majority provinces, the Muslim League gained support very late. Jinnah never spelled out the ideological basis or geographical boundaries of his Pakistan scheme. I read in a recent book that in 1942, the Muslim League floated the idea of Pakistan that would include not only all the Muslim majority provinces but also Delhi where the Muslims were not in a majority. On what basis such a plan was made remains a mystery.

'In 1964, I paid a visit to Delhi and went to see my father's colleagues and friends. It so happened that on one such occasion I met their guest from Bombay who turned out to be originally from Lahore. When he learnt that my surname was Cheema and that my father was a civil judge he asked if we were related to Magistrate M.G. Cheema of Lahore. I assured him that M.G. Cheema was no relative of ours. I had heard about his reputation as the mastermind in the fires that were started in the Hindu localities of Lahore. Many years later, I had the opportunity to meet M.G. Cheema in Lahore. I did not broach the issue of the 1947 fires with him because he was a senior person and would have minded my prying into his past that he did not want to be known.'

References

Qureshi, Ishtiaq Husain. 'Hindu Muslim Social Relations 1935-47' in Hasan Mushirul (ed). *India Partitioned: the Other Face of Freedom*, Volume II. New Delhi: Lotus Collection, Roli Books, 1995.

Malik, Khuda Baksh (Khan Bahadur), 'A brief report made by K.B. Malik Khuda Baksh regarding the districts of Ambala, Karnal, Rothak, Hissar, Simla, Ludhiana and Jullundur', in *The Journey to Pakistan: A Documentation on Refugees of 1947,* 1993, Islamabad: National Documentation Centre, 1993.

Interviews

Mohammad Farid Mirza, 7 April 2003

Pushpa Goel, Delhi, 29 March 2004

Chowdhry Abdul Wahid, Multan, 20 December 2004

Chowdhry Abdul Saeed, Bahawalpur, 21 December 2004

Syed Qamurruzaman Shah, Lahore, 28 December 2004

Panditji, Karnal, Haryana, 28 November 2005

Amar Singh (*Sarpanch* Dangoli), Dangoli, 29 November 2005

Chhittru, village Dangoli, district Rupnagar, 29 November 2005

Naseeb Kaur (Azmat Bibi), Phul Khurd, district Rupnagar, 29 November 2005

Brigadier Sarjit Singh Chowdhary, Delhi, 1 December 2005

I.A. Rehman, 14 January 2005

Riaz Ahmed Cheema, 16 May 2006

Nasim Hassan, Delaware, USA (by email), 1 January 2007

20

EASTERN PUNJAB PRINCELY STATES

THE CONTROVERSY ABOUT THE FUTURE OF THE PUNJAB WAS originally about the twenty-nine districts that were directly British-administered, otherwise known as the British territories. The future of the princely states was a different matter altogether, as they had formally accepted British paramountcy through a treaty. Upon the termination of British rule they were, therefore, technically entitled to freely work out their relationship with India and Pakistan. However, allegedly as early as March 1947, soldiers from the Sikh princely states participated incognito in the rioting in Amritsar. Later in May, soldiers from Faridkot and Nabha states took part in a raid on the Muslim locality of Rajgarh in the outskirts of Lahore. Moreover, Mountbatten facilitated talks between the Maharaja of Patiala and Jinnah in the same month to probe the possibility of a deal between the Sikhs and the Muslim League on keeping the Punjab united. It failed famously. Perhaps even more crucial was the fact that from December 1946, Sikh refugees from Hazara and in March from the rural areas of Rawalpindi, Attock and Jhelum districts, fleeing from slaughter and looting at the hands of Muslim mobs, sought safe haven in the princely states. They had been narrating their woes in gatherings of their community about the cruelties of the Muslims. Therefore, the Sikh princely states were already integrated with the events taking place in the British territories since at least December 1946.

However, the involvement of the princely states with the future of the Punjab pre-dated the rioting of the previous months. The Akalis had been campaigning in the princely states since the 1930s for greater compliance with orthodox Sikhism and had gradually been gaining ground. At least from 1945 onwards, Master Tara Singh and his clique and Maharaja Yadavindra Singh of Patiala had been in regular contact to discuss strategy to meet the challenge posed by a Muslim state coming into being as a result of the partition of India. Ian Coupland notes that because of the growing Akali influence in the princely states, the royal families and other nobles had begun to adhere to orthodox Khalsa identity. A religious revival in cultural and symbolic terms was therefore underway through royal example. By early 1947, such changes carried important communal implications. Thus, for example, faithful Muslim and Hindu retainers were replaced by Sikhs – Liaqat Hayat Khan and D.K. Sen of Patiala, Abdul Hamid of Kapurthala and Mohammad Sadiq of Jind were some of the scapegoats (Coupland 2002: 675-77). Liaqat Hayat Khan (brother of Sir Sikander Hayat Khan), Abdul Hamid and Mohammad Sadiq were until then serving as chief ministers or *diwans* and were thus an intimate part of the traditional order representing a pluralist council of ministers and administrators.

Robin Jeffrey points out that the villain of the piece with regard to organising the *jathas* and training them was an ex-INA Lt Col. Niranjan Singh Gill (1974: 50 7). It is ironic that the INA failed to take root, given its reputation for being a patriotic army constituted by Indian soldiers captured by the Japanese, and having been groomed by Subhash Chandra Bose, into becoming a fraternity that shuns religious and caste prejudices, by eating together and accepting each other as brothers irrespective of their religious affiliations. I remember hearing from some elderly people of Rawalpindi that ex-INA Muslim soldiers had participated in the savage attacks on the Sikhs.

Coupland, however, attributes the initial mobilisation of *jathas* to Gyani Harbans Singh, whom he describes as follows:

> Gyani Harbans Singh, an escaped criminal under the overall direction of a Council of Action in Amrtisar whose members included ex-Indian National Army officer Narinjan Singh, Sardar Baldev Singh, Giani Kartar Singh, Master Tara Singh and Raghbir Singh, the former Patiala minister. The Committee also took on the job of raising money to buy arms and equipment for the *jathas*, eventually amassing a war-chest of between 10 and 12 *lakhs* (Coupland, 2002: 680).

Such preparations were augmented with political inputs as well. The RSS and Hindu Mahasabha were approached to join ranks to prevent the Punjab from coming under Muslim domination. Contacts with the Maharaja of Patiala were already in place. Master Tara Singh invited the ruler of Faridkot in early April 1947 to undertake military operations in his part of the Punjab. According to one version, the district of Ferozepore was offered to him by way of payment. The rulers of Patiala, Nabha, Kapurthala and Kalsia, in different ways took part in preparing the Sikhs for a major confrontation with the Muslims in case the Punjab was partitioned in a way unacceptable to them. The *jathas* thus formed were highly motivated and adequately armed. Some of them even carried heavy machine guns, but in most cases lighter automatic guns were at their disposal, such as Bren guns and Tommy guns, grenades, petrol bombs, and other firearms such as rifles, pistols, revolvers besides *kirpans* and spears. They had at their disposal jeeps, trucks, and some were proper motorised units. Coupland notes that such belligerent moves were not approved by all Sikhs, including those belonging to Master Tara Singh's Akali party (ibid.: 680-2).

The Sikhs wanted to conduct raids into towns given to Pakistan, but as long as Nehru was prime minister such activity could not be permitted by the Indian government (ibid.: 683). They, therefore, confined their campaign to eradicate all Muslim presence in their territories, across the Sutlej and especially in the Sikh princely states. According to a report of the British High Commission in New Delhi, between 800,000 to a million people were organised in *jathas*. Other reports have suggested as few as 1,000 hardcore killers, while Coupland estimates that the strength of the *jathas* was around 200,000 (Coupland, 2002: 687).

The selection of targets was made with great care: large concentrations of Muslims were not attacked. Those convoys that were accompanied by armed military escorts were also not targeted. Once the target was selected, the raid was carried out with military efficiency as many of the cadres were ex-servicemen. Attacks on trains were planned in accordance with the railway timetables. The initial attack was usually in the form of strafing by machine guns or light machine guns followed by assaults at close range with *kirpans*, spears and other traditional weapons. The attacks on villages were also planned in military fashion. Women and children were carried away in the final stage, as spoils of war (ibid.: 688). Looting was a major attraction during the raids. In light of such overall context, some events that transpired in the princely states of eastern Punjab are examined below.

Patiala

The biggest and most powerful princely state in eastern Punjab was Patiala, ruled by a Sikh Maharaja, Yadavindra Singh. It had a total population of 19,36,259. His Muslim subjects made up 436,539 or nearly twenty-four per cent of the population. The massacres of Muslims in the Sikh states, particularly Patiala, are proverbially mentioned as proof of a Sikh conspiracy hatched much before the partition of the Punjab was on the cards. The West Punjab Minister for Refugees and Rehabilitation, Mian Iftikharuddin, in a note dated 9 November 1947 asserted that only some 200,000 Muslims from the state had moved to Pakistan by 16 September, and 236,600 were unaccounted for. The reports published by the Pakistan government suggest that the ruler of Patiala was at the head of a plot, which included the participation of the rulers of Nabha, Kapurthala and other minor states, to eliminate Muslims from eastern and central districts. (I discovered that it was the crown prince of Nabha state, known as Tikka Sahib, and not the maharaja, who was involved in the anti-Muslim rioting.) A report prepared by the Communist Party of India also mentions a similar conspiracy. The senior Communist leader and former Secretary-General of the Communist Party (Marxist) Harkishen Singh Surjeet also took this up in my recorded interview.

It is, however, important to reiterate that whatever plans the Sikhs had for eliminating Muslims from East Punjab were subject to the partition of India. Had the partition of India not happened, there would have been no reason to drive the Muslims out of the princely states of East Punjab. A partition of India would always entail a partition of the Punjab – this harsh reality was repeatedly emphasised by the Punjab governors. Moreover, the Sikhs were not going to accept a partition of the Punjab which would leave their religious locations, the canal colonies and Lahore in Pakistan. The Punjab administration had been warning about private communal armies, and the fact that the Sikhs wore *kirpans* made them an armed community even in the time of peace. Since at least March 1947 (though some point out the riots in Hazara in December

1946) a narrative full of graphic imagery of Muslim atrocities against Sikhs had been circulating. Stories of harrowing Muslim atrocities against Sikhs – women being raped, their breasts slashed with knives, their vaginas pierced by spears, infants being flung into the air and as they fell their bodies being torn apart with swords – were repeated over and over again in Sikh congregations and in local village gatherings.

The Sikh sense of honour was always invoked and seeking revenge for the crimes against their community and religion was declared to be the sacred duty of all self-respecting Sikhs. All the hallmarks of a violent confrontation were in place because the Sikhs were bound to find their ambitions on the Punjab frustrated by the fact that in no central and western districts were they in a majority; even together with the Hindus, they were still in a minority. As far as the safety of Muslims is concerned, it was already in jeopardy because the Punjab Boundary Force had no jurisdiction in the Sikh states. Therefore, after the Radcliffe Award the Muslims were at the mercy of the Sikh *jathas* in the princely states. However, not all rulers were involved in the attacks on the Muslims.

Sardar Abdul Aziz, retired Superintendent of Police, Patiala state, gave a detailed picture of the conspiracy as it unfolded in Patiala. Aziz retired at the end of 1944, but according to him, much before that the maharaja had been attracted to the idea of establishing a great Panthic (Sikh) state with him as its leader. While still serving as a police officer, Sardar Abdul Aziz learned that a *Raj Jyotshi* (royal astrologer) had made the prediction based on a Sikh text called *Sau Sikhi* in which the suzerainty of the Sikhs over the Punjab had been foreseen. The description of the Sikh leader who would become the ruler tallied with that of Maharaja Yadavindra Singh of Patiala. When the maharaja heard about the prediction he summoned the astrologer and, after listening to him, made him part of his personal staff.

The maharaja thereafter began to prepare for the Panthic state. Mr Hutton, a British employee of the ruler, and several Sikh officers were instructed to start producing rifles and other weapons. The maharaja also sought close contact with the Akalis – something which had been avoided by previous rulers of Patiala. Baldev Singh, Master Tara Singh, Giani Kartar Singh and others began to visit the state. Muslim and Hindu officers in the state services began to be replaced by Sikhs. Sikh *jathas* were organised and a large fighting force was put together. Sardar Abdul Aziz mentions several cases of butchery committed by the Patiala forces against Muslims (1993: 195-200).

In the two Government of Pakistan publications, *The Sikhs in Action* and *Note on the Sikh Plan,* prepared by the police during the Unionist regime or from when the governor assumed power on March 5, under Section 193, deals with the activities of the Akali leaders and the Akal *Fauj* (the 'Sikh Army'). No firm date is given as to when the Sikh Plan was formulated; the data is from 1947 onwards. The reports stress that many former Indian National Army Sikh soldiers were involved in preparing the Sikhs and Hindus for a showdown with the Muslims. The following is stated in the *Note on the Sikh Plan*:

> It is clear from this evidence that as part of the more ambitious irredentist dream of Sikh sovereignty, the immediate objectives of the plan were (a) extensive sabotage and destruction of Muslim life and property and (b) the elimination, if possible, of Muslims from the Sikh belt along with the eastern border of West Pakistan... The central figures of the conspiracy were Master Tara Singh, Giani Kartar Singh, Udham Singh Nagoke and other leaders of the Akali party... All sections of the Sikh community – the intelligentsia, religious and political leaders, ex-INA men, peasants, teachers and students – were mobilised to perfect the plan and extensive, and in some cases elaborate, arrangements were taken in hand to train men both for staff work and for murder, looting and arson. ... It also makes it clear that the Sikhs States no less than the Sikh leaders of British Punjab were active members of the conspiracy and the militant sections of Hindus (in some cases inspired, guided and trained by Hindu apostles of violence in other provinces of India) helped their designs throughout, by carrying on underground terrorist activity and by organising useful information and intelligence' (1948: 28-29).

The Sikhs in Action, meanwhile, describes the Maharaja of Patiala's plans to become the ruler of a consolidated Sikh state covering the whole of East Punjab. The account is based on the evidence of Sardar Abdul Aziz which is provided above. I was therefore very keen to probe into the events that transpired in Patiala at that time.

A number of stories are given in a collection of first-person accounts titled, *1947 key Muzlumon ki Kahani, khud Mazlumon ki Zabani* (The Story of the Atrocities of 1947 in the Words of the Victims Themselves) compiled by Hakim Muhammad Tariq Mahmud Abqari Majzubi Chughtai. We look at two of them. They are given under the heading, '*Patiala key Musalmanon per Tootney Waali Qiamat-e-Sughra*' (Mini Day of Judgment that Broke out on the Muslims of Patiala). After that are given some of our own findings.

Muhammad Afzaal Sharif

> Peace, law and order were exemplary in Patiala. People used to sleep with their doors open. Muslims, Hindus and Sikhs lived peacefully together. They shared each other's joys and sorrows.... In 1945 slogans in favour of Pakistan began to be shouted even in Patiala. The Muslims started pinning badges on their chests with the picture of Jinnah on it. They would shout, 'Quaid-i-Azam Zindabad' (Long live Quaid-i-Azam) and 'Bann key rahey ga Pakistan' (Pakistan will be established), but the environment in the State remained peaceful.... My father was a painter of cinema decoration boards and posters.... My father and Seth Charan Das were sworn brothers. Seth Charan Das and Chaudhri Eid Muhammad built a new cinema and my father was decorating it around June 1947. He was climbing a wooden ladder when a pole supporting the wooden plank on which he and his assistant were standing broke and they fell down. My father fell and badly hurt his skull. He was immediately taken to the hospital where Seth Charan Das's father-in-law Ragunath tried his best to save his life. The rule was that anybody who died in the state hospital was not allowed to be taken to the city. He was taken directly to the graveyard. But since the families were on very close relations the surgeon told my paternal uncle Ghaus Muhammad to take him home as he would expire in a few hours. Thus father was brought home where he breathed his last. Thus we three small brothers and my infant sister became orphans and my mother a widow (ibid.: 24-25).

The rest of the testimony gives details of how the situation got from bad to worse. It includes harrowing details of how his aunt and her son and daughter were murdered by Sikhs when they were travelling from Ambala to Patiala. The Muslims had come to realise that Patiala would not be included in Pakistan and had raised black flags on their housetops to express their sorrow. Before the trouble started Sikhs, who had been uprooted from West Punjab, had settled in Patiala. They would visit Muslim localities ostensibly with small items to sell, but actually to spy around about who owned what (ibid.).

Continuing with the story, Sharif says that after the fasting month of Ramazan started, the situation deteriorated quickly. Some Muslims were murdered at the Patiala Railway Station. The maharaja ordered the police to raid Muslim residences and confiscate all weapons. Eid (18 August), however, came and went peacefully. Some five days later, however, curfew was enforced on Patiala. The Muslims began to move to places where other Muslims were present. Thereafter the Sikhs lured the Muslims into various traps and would kill them. Sharif lost some more relatives. Then they moved to the house of another relative. Within an hour after they had arrived, gunshots were fired against them. As a result, another aunt and her husband and their young son and his small children were killed. After a few days they realised that a massacre of Muslims was inevitable.

The rest of the article gives several examples of heart-rending savagery against Muslims. Although the number of deaths is not given, it must have been in the thousands. Sharif lost many of his relatives. Two doctors, named 'Dr Hakim' and the other 'Dr Karim', are specially mentioned. They had collected thousands of cartridges and would fire gunshots in the air every now and then to stop the Sikh–Hindu marauders from attacking Muslims. According to Sharif, 'Dr Hakim himself killed all the women in his own family. He thought that all of us men would be killed and why should his wife and daughters fall into the hands of Sikhs' (ibid.: 27).

In any event, the killings continued for some time and the survivors were taken to a camp at Bahadurgarh where they lived for some three months. The living conditions in the camp were appalling. Many died. The dead were not even given a proper burial. They were dumped into a huge hole in the ground. Later, the dead bodies began to be burnt. The narrative continues to give more shocking details. Many able-bodied men were taken from the camp to work on the farm of the maharaja. Sharif's maternal grandfather was among them.

Then Pakistani soldiers from the Baloch regiment arrived and they were escorted safely to Pakistan. Many girls were abducted and raped; some were recovered while others were never returned. Many decent families were reduced to abject poverty including begging. This was the price the Muslims of East Punjab paid for the creation of Pakistan. He stresses that this fact should not be forgotten. In the end he mentions that Seth Charan Das kept writing to them after partition to visit Patiala but nobody in the family wanted to go back (ibid.: 27-33).

Interviews in Patiala

The popular story in Patiala is that anti-Muslim riots started in Patiala town after Dr Hafiz, a leading Muslim doctor in the town, first shot at the maharaja, which resulted in him turning against Muslims and giving a free hand to Sikh *jathas* and his army to exterminate Muslims. This story I heard from a number of people we met in Patiala on 7 January 2005. It sounded rather incredible that some Muslim would dare commit such a blunder in a Sikh state where the Muslims were in a minority and far removed from the border with Pakistan. I wanted to check it with some reliable witnesses.

Vicky, Nanak Singh, and I looked around the streets in Patiala for some educated and responsible people to interview. We had no particular local reference or contact so it had to be a random affair. We talked to elderly people in the streets. Many of them were refugees from West Punjab but we met some locals, too. One name that kept being mentioned in connection with the rioting in the town was that of Dr Hafiz. Nobody could remember Dr Karim and Dr Hakim. We were told that Dr Hafiz was indeed a leading Muslim of Patiala. Amrik Chand Ahluwalia (born 1925), a native of Patiala town whose recollection of the pre-Partition Punjab is presented in Chapter Two, was present in the town in 1947.

Amrik Chand Ahluwalia

'The trouble in Patiala was started by the RSS and Akali workers. Previously there was no scope for political activity in the state. But in August 1947 the situation became volatile. Dr Hafiz was a Muslim leader and a very well-respected medical practitioner. It is true that the troubles started in the town when gunfire was exchanged between Dr Hafiz and the Sikh police. It is not true that he fired at the maharaja. It was another police officer who had come to his place to collect weapons when the shootout took place.

'The police spread the rumour that Dr Hafiz had shot at the maharaja. That resulted in mayhem. Dr Hafiz was arrested and killed. In the Sabzi Mandi at least fifty Muslims were killed. In the Thakk Bazaar, here where we are sitting and in Akal Mandi also Muslims were killed. Patiala was then a town of 25,000. At least a thousand Muslims lost their lives here. I saw in village Sufera, some ten kilometres from here, dead bodies of 200–300 Muslims. Nobody survived. The Muslims in Patiala were helpless just as Hindus and Sikhs were in West Punjab.

'One of our neighbours, Muhammad Sattar, came in from Pakistan in 1950. He had hidden five *tolas* of gold in the wall of his house. He found it and then returned to Pakistan. Some Muslims did remain in Patiala and never left.'

Pandit Mohan Lal Balo

'I was born in Patiala in 1923. In early 1947 I was in Lahore, where I worked as a music director in the film industry; along with another colleague, I composed the music of the famous Punjabi film *Yamla Jutt*. Shamshad Begum and Noorjehan have sung for me. I learnt music from Ustad Ashiq Ali Khan. In March 1947, my sister's wedding was to take place so I had returned to Patiala where my family lived and then stayed on. Dr Hafiz had a big clinic in the town. There was a scuffle between him and the police at his clinic during which Dr Hafiz fired some shots, but it was not at the maharaja. The police officer belonged to the royal family. That signalled the beginning of an all-out attack. Dr Hafiz was killed brutally. Some Hindus and Sikhs were also killed but most of the casualties were among the Muslims. The ringleaders were Sikh refugees from West Punjab, particularly those from Rawalpindi and Peshawar. They wanted revenge and made full use of the opportunity. The local people did not take part in those strikes against Muslims.

'My friends Wali Muhammad, Zakir Hussain and many of our neighbours took refuge with us in the Hindu temple. My father had retired from the police department and therefore we had some weapons at home. This kept the raiders away. When the situation improved, my father told me and my brother Brij Lal to take them to the Bahadurgarh Fort where a camp had been established for Muslims. We used to provide food and other items to our friends in the camp.'

Chaudhri Ghulam Rabbani

Chaudhri Ghulam Rabbani, President of the Muslim League of Nabha state, wrote a detailed report of events in several Sikh states. With regard to Patiala, he noted that Dr Hafiz bravely faced the onslaught of the Patiala forces:

> The Muslims who dared to use firearms in self-defence had incurred the greatest warth [sic] of the Maharaja. One such person was Dr. Hafiz of Patiala who had manfully fought for the lives and honour of his family. The Maharaja razed his house to the ground with a tank. All the members of his family were buried under the falling debris. Dr. Hafiz was caught alive, hanged to a tree upside down, and flayed alive. I have taken great pains to verify details of this tragedy and was satisfied that they were perfectly true (1993: 223).

Dr Hafiz or Dr Hakim?

Barring the possibility that the narrator, Muhammad Afzaal Sharif, forgot the correct name of the Patiala doctor, or he or the compiler of the stories, Hakim Chughtai, deliberately invented the names 'Dr Hakim' and 'Dr Karim', even perhaps creating a fictitious second brother, the person in question has to be Dr Hafiz. In the other accounts, only Dr Hafiz is mentioned and there is only one key person – that is, Dr Hafiz himself. Since Dr Hafiz reportedly killed the women in his family, this deception may have been invented to evade any legal complications for Dr Hafiz [Dr Hakim]. Ahmad Salim and I tried repeatedly to contact Hakim Chughtai and even visited his clinic located in a row of houses inside a locality at Mozang Chungi, but he was not available. Ahmad Salim had talked to him on the telephone and informed him about my visit to Pakistan and that I would like to talk to him, but unfortunately we could not contact him.

Mian Noor Muhammad

The second testimony in Hakim Chughtai's book is provided by Mian Noor Muhammad, advocate. According to Mian Noor Muhammad, after completing his education at the Muslim University at Aligarh, he returned to Patiala and set up practice at Bhatinda. He was the only Muslim lawyer in that town. By dint of hard work he soon established a flourishing practice. He writes:

> Among the judicial officers, Sardar Ranjit Singh Sarkaria is particularly praiseworthy. Inspite of the fact that he was a Sikh he was a particularly fair and just person without any prejudice against any community. Therefore the public held him in great respect. Also, the ruler of Patiala, Maharaja Bhupinder Singh, previously did not discriminate at all against his subjects. Many times the chief ministers of Patiala were Muslims. After the death of Maharaja Bhupinder Singh, his son became the ruler. He continued with the same policy (p. 34).

Mian Noor Muhammad tells us that when on 23 March 1940, the resolution in favour of Pakistan was adopted in Lahore, ripples were felt even in Patiala state. The Muslims of Patiala felt drawn to the idea of a Muslim state. Despite the ban on political parties in the state, the atmosphere began to be politicised. The 1946 elections returned the Muslim League as the main party of Muslims with a heavy majority, but the provocative statements of Master Tara Singh on 3 March 1947 created tension in Patiala. He further narrates:

> It was Eid on 18 August. The Sikhs began the carnage of Muslims in Bhatinda, which was a part of Patiala State. I was told that

marauders were on the way to my house. I lived in a Hindu *mohalla*. I was the only Muslim lawyer in that *mohalla*. We sought refuge in a Muslim *mohalla* and were safe with a kind Muslim family. Then shooting began. After five days we came out. My mother carrying my infant daughter went towards the railway station. I ran in the other direction with my wife and two small boys. But after going in a circle we also arrived at the railway station. There were too many people assembled at the station. The Sikhs were waving *kirpans* and shouting anti-Pakistan slogans. Suddenly a Sikh armed with a spear ran after me. I began to run like anything and entered the fields outside the town. I hid there for many days. When the situation improved somewhat I returned to the railway station. It was dead silent there and the earth was red with blood.

Suddenly I longed for my wife and mother and realized that I had been left all alone in the world. I could not resist crying loudly. I started walking and after some time arrived in a village. I knocked at a door. A woman came and upon seeing me started shouting 'Kill, kill, a Muslim is here'. I again ran and found refuge in the fields and stayed there for a few days. Finally I arrived at Dabwali, a hamlet [in present-day Sirsa district of Haryana]. I found myself in front of a police station and went in. A Hindu constable took pity on me and gave me a proper meal. After hearing my story he told me that a new *thanedar*, a Muslim, has been posted to the station. He was out investigating a case in the town but I should wait until he returned.

I was surprised at the unexpected news. Instead of waiting for him I found out where he had gone and went to him. When I introduced myself he turned his face away. Now what could I do in such a situation? I walked away to the side where he could see me. This time he said annoyingly, "Get into the car". Then he drove me to Sirsa....Then we were taken to a camp for Muslims in Hissar...From Hissar I sent a plea to the civil judge of Bhatinda, Sardar Ranjit Singh Sarkaria, to look for my mother, wife and children. After a while I received news from him that through his efforts my wife and children had been found alive.

Our train left on October 24 for Hissar via Bhatinda for Pakistan. Sardar Ranjit Singh Sarkaria was himself present on the station

> with my wife. The joy of finding my wife soon gave way to grief when I found that the children were not with her. I learnt they had been killed. Also my mother and my daughter were not found (1993: 34-36).

The story continues and we learn about the hard times he faced in getting started in Pakistan. Eventually, his infant daughter would be found.

Patiala rural areas

While collecting oral histories in December 2004 in the villages around Rawalpindi, Ahmad Salim and I were informed by some local people about Chaudhri Roshan Din at Kallar Syedan. We met him on 15 December 2004. His was one of the most shattering and gruesome accounts we ever heard in the course of our research. I later visited his village Adampur and neighbouring villages in November 2005 to get the perspective from the other side. We met two other survivors, Chaudhri Abdul Shakoor and his cousin Babu Khan, in Malerkotla, East Punjab.

Chaudhri Roshan Din

'I was born in June 1936 in an Arain family in village Adampur, near Sirhind Sharif [now in Fatehgarh Sahib district] in Patiala state. It was a big village populated mainly by Sikhs and some Hindus, both Brahmins and *chamars* (Harijans or untouchables) and only seven Muslim households. There were three Arain families and some Muslim Gujjars and *telis*. My family owned land and cultivated it. We had built a big brick house with many rooms and a large compound. Relations between the communities were friendly. There was never a problem. We had no intention of leaving our home. Life was peaceful and quiet until one day in *bhadon* (the monsoon season) thousands of Sikhs began to menace this area. They came suddenly and in large numbers. The mob was screaming, "Pakistan has come into being, what are Muslims doing here?" People from our village told us to leave. Some of the hooligans took advantage of our small numbers. Before we could flee, my cousin Jamal Din was killed at his *kho* (well) by Jaimal, son of Nagia Daku (Nagia the dacoit) and

Bageeru or Ghabeer Singh. Both were from our village. They abducted his wife and sister. Later they were recovered through the coordination of government agencies. The mob was accompanied by a military vehicle carrying men of the Patiala State Army.

'We ran as fast as we could and reached the nearby Muslim village of Mathi. Several thousand Muslims from around had also gathered there. Nobody amongst us had weapons and therefore we were helpless when the Sikhs struck. They first separated the men from the women and children. The men were taken away and killed at some distance. My father was among them. I and my younger brother, who was only six at that time, were with our mother. No mercy was shown to the women. Hundreds were carried away. My mother was hacked to pieces in front of me. Small infants were raised on the spears. At least a thousand people died. I and my younger brother (he died here in Kallar Syedan some years ago) and another thirty or so children were saved because we hid ourselves under the dead bodies.

'After the slaughter had been carried out a fire was lit up and the dead bodies were thrown into it. While throwing the bodies in the fire they would shout, "Your Pakistan is now made and completed. Here, you go to your Pakistan". It was late night by then and they left without collecting the bodies which were spread some distance away over a large area; we crawled away quietly and escaped detection. Soon afterwards some Harijans came to check the dead bodies and found us alive. A *chowkidar* (watchman) from among them gave us protection and we slept on the roof of one of the buildings. There was nothing to eat. We went to Boran, a Sikh village nearby. The Sikhs of that village kept some of the children and others were sent away. They probably wanted to use them to take care of their cattle and goats. Then two *chamar* Sikhs (untouchables) were sent with us as escorts to take us to Sirhind Sharif where a huge camp for Muslims had been set up. Our parents were dead; also our maternal and paternal grandparents and many other close relatives.

'Our sister who lived with her husband in a village in Ludhiana district and her son were killed but her husband survived because he was in Ludhiana at that time. A paternal uncle of mine and his son also survived. He could not help us in any way. Three of their daughters were abducted but later two were recovered. One of them lives in Faisalabad.

'In any case, at the camp we were provided one plate of porridge everyday. The conditions in the camp were wretched. That year it rained all the time. It was very dirty in the camp and a stench was always present. Many children died. We both decided to try going to our sister's village (not knowing she had been killed) but could not summon the courage to do so. After one and a half month a relative of ours whom we used to call *Tayaji* (father's elder brother), but whose exact relationship I did not know, said to us that peace had been restored and that if we wished to go to our sister, now was the time.

'We both started walking. We met a man who was cutting grass in a field. He took pity on us and gave us two *annas* (small coins). I believe he was a Hindu. As we were going we saw Sikhs coming in our direction, riding horses. They were pursuing a Muslim who probably had strayed away from the camp. Anyhow we reached Kumandgarh. First we met a young Sikh couple. The woman in particular showed great sympathy to us. She gave us food and a *chaddar* (long cloth) to sleep on. She wanted us to remain in the village but we decided to continue. We hid ourselves in the fields on the way and later reached the road that connects Ludhiana to Patiala. A *kumhar* (potter) was grazing his donkeys. He too was a Hindu. He too took pity on us and gave us four *annas*. We continued walking and reached Gobindgarh. There we asked a *tonga*-driver how much money he would charge to take us to Malaud. He said just sit and I will help you. He took us to a *gurdwara* and said, "Here you can get help. There are other Muslim children here too". We, however, quietly slipped away and continued walking towards Malaud.

'When it became dark we lost our way and turned back towards Gobindgarh. There we were surrounded by a couple of Sikhs. Both were drunk. One wanted to kill us but the other told him to let us go. It resulted in an altercation. It gave us a chance to flee. We saw bullock-carts going. We tried to get on to them but couldn't. Then we found a wooden log lying by the path. We slept there, resting our heads against it. Next day we started again. A Hindu met us and asked who we were. We told him that we were Muslims. I did not want to hide my identity. He said, "Okay I can take you to the *bania* (moneylender). You take care of his cattle and goats". But I said that we wanted to go on to our relatives. We continued and reached the town of Khanna. We were walking on the lane away from the main road. A Sikh wearing *kachha* (shorts) waving his *kirpan* in the air called us: "Come here you two!" We said that we were Muslims and had come from Roza Sirhind Sharif. Our family had been killed. He called a man and said, "Take these boys to my home and tell the Sardarni to take care of them and give them food". The *sardarni* [his wife] made us sit down and gave us *kheer* (sweet dish made of rice and milk) spread on *roti*. A man came and said he wanted to kill us. They locked him up in a room saying that he had lost some of his family and had gone mad.

'We asked the way to Chota Khanna [now called Khanna Khurd]. They showed us the way and we continued… When we reached Chota Khanna we enquired from a girl grazing cattle in the field the way to Reona where my cousin lived [This is possibly Reona Ucha. There are other Reona villages but they are in another direction.]. She showed us the way. It was some distance and the road was hot and dusty. My brother became thirsty. We came to a well but we could not pull up the bucket to get water. Then a young Sikh boy came along and he helped us draw the water. We quenched our thirst. Some boys were playing cards. We asked them for directions which they gave us.

'Then a man came running to us and said, "I am a Muslim. Don't be afraid of me. I am wearing a *kara* (bangle) and [have] converted to Sikhism but I will help you. You stay with me this evening". We stayed with his family. We changed our clothes. We took a bath. Many other people gathered. Suddenly a messenger came saying that two Sikh women were at the *lohar's* (blacksmith's) house. They would help take us further. We went with them and stayed in another village. We stayed three nights there. Then on the fourth day the brother of those two Sikh women took a sword with him and told us to come along with him. We had to cross the bridge over a canal. There the Sikh *jathas* confronted us. They said, "Sardarji where are you taking these boys? We will finish them". He took out his sword and said "Kill me first". Then they let us go. Finally we reached Malaud, a hamlet in Ludhiana district and near Malerkotla state.

'There we learnt that Sikh soldiers were in the neighbourhood. The Sikh then made us tie turbans on our heads. His sisters were coming slowly behind us. Then they took us to their village Chananwal. It is on the border of Malerkotla. We stayed for twenty days with them. They found out that all our relatives from our mother's side including our grandparents had been killed. We saw hatchets and spears with thick dried blood on them in their house. We realised that they had taken part in the raids and killed Muslims. But God bless the Sikh lady who cooked food for us and took very good care of us all those twenty days. She was truly god-fearing. I pray she gets a place in paradise.

'She would cook linseed and vegetables for us as we were not willing to eat the forbidden food that they ate. One day a *chamar* came to their house and told her that in the neighbouring village of Rohera in Malerkotla a man was sending Muslims to Pakistan by bus. If she wanted he could send us boys on that bus. She agreed on the assurance that we would not be harmed. He took us to the *lambardar* who was an Arain. His mother and sister also took good care of us. His wife said she had no brothers but God had sent her two brothers. The *lambardar* also wanted us to stay because he had no sons while he owned twenty-five *bigahs* of agricultural land. I refused.

'A *nai* (barber) came to Malerkotla and told the people that two boys had come from Sirhind Sharif, Patiala, and their names were Roshan Din and Taj Din. My *khala* who was married in Malerkotla heard our names and said we were her nephews. Our aunt and cousins recognised us. But after a few days her husband got tired of feeding us. He said that a train was coming to take people to Pakistan. He put us on that train. Thousands of people were in the camps in Malerkotla. Not everyone could climb on to the train and so many had to walk all the way. The train went and came back thrice. We got a chance to board on the third trip.

'When we arrived on the border the railway track connecting to Kasur on the Pakistani side had been dismantled. Truckloads of armed Sikhs were waiting on the banks of the river Sutlej on the opposite side. Gurkha troops that were accompanying the train sent a wireless message to Pakistan. Pakistan despatched all the soldiers and trucks that could be spared. They brought us over. The men walked, while the elderly, the women and children boarded the buses and then we all crossed over to Pakistan.

'We stayed in the camp for three days. Then we were taken to the camp at Hassan Abdal close to Rawalpindi. Then a school master came to the camp and promised to take care of me while another man, Ghaffur, decided to take care of my brother. I was employed in Rawalpindi with a *tahsildar*, Haji Safdar Ali. There was a clerk, Fazal Ahmed, also a refugee, who helped us with our claim to property left in Adampur. I requested him to write a letter to the *lambardar* of my village to confirm that we had land in that village. Additionally he filled a form for me to claim evacuee property in lieu of property left in East Punjab. Haji Sahib signed the application on my behalf as I was a minor. A few weeks later a letter confirming our claim duly signed by the *lambardar* of Adampur also arrived. Even then things did not work out so well and we went hungry for days. Our relatives did not help us in any way. Then finally we got land here. Since 1955 I've been settled here in Kallar Syedan. Sometimes I want to kill all the Sikhs. They committed so many atrocities against my family. Nearly all my close relatives were killed. Of course some of them were good, god-fearing people but still I can't forgive what the Sikhs did to us.

'Things are now good for us. I have been the chairman of the local Pakistan People's Party. I have never done anything wrong or illegal. Now I own two or three markets. My children are well-placed. We have five villas here. There are very few from our *biradari* in this region. This worries me a lot. We want to marry our children within the Arain *biradari* but it is difficult to find suitable matches in this area. I still love Bhutto Sahib. I have been in jail. Zia-ul-Haq put me in jail. Two hundred of us were put in jail and the high court released us. This was in 1986. The police came in the middle of night and arrested us. Our PPP MP, A. Qayyum Butt, was very supportive and always helped me. The assassination of Bhutto was a great crime.'

Interviews recorded in Adampur

Hitesh Gosain, Virender Singh, and I, along with their local contact – a Sikh gentleman who proudly wore a blazer showing that he had represented India in international matches in the sport of *kabbadi* – arrived at Adampur at about 11 o'clock in the morning. It had been settled in by refugees from Sialkot in West Punjab, but some locals were still around. We found them sitting at the entry to the village from the main road. They were initially reluctant to talk, but after we assured them that we were not from the police and were doing research on the events of 1947, they agreed to be interviewed.

Two elderly persons gave us the interview, namely, Basta Singh (seventy-five) and Naugurdial Singh (over eighty). We learned that they were Siddhu Jats. The following excerpt is a composite of both their narrations.

'Adampur was mainly populated by Sikhs. There were also some Brahmins and scheduled caste Hindus and some seven to eight Muslim families. Three households were Arains and maybe one or two Gujjars and some *telis*. The Arains had moved to Adampur from village Saliani near Gobindgarh. They bought land here and lived in a big house with many rooms and a thick wall all around. Before the trouble started we all lived peacefully and took part in village festivities. There was a common well for the whole village from which the people drew water, but the Muslims had a different access to it. One of the Arains was called Jamal Din. His father's name was Allah Baksh. Allah Baksh had two brothers, Barkat and Sondhi. Sondhi had no children. Barkat then married Sondhi's wife and children were born to them.

'It was in *bhadon* (a month during monsoons) that trouble started here. The Muslims left immediately heading towards Mathi, a Muslim-majority village. Among the raiders were retired Sikh soldiers of the British Indian Army and refugee Sikhs from West Punjab. They said they wanted to avenge the brutalities on the Sikhs in the western Punjab. Some bad characters from the village also took part in the assaults. Among them was Jaimal son of Nagia, who was a known criminal registered in the police records as *dus numberia* (a police list of local criminals). Both father and son are dead now. Criminals do not live long. Two Muslims, Maghi and his son Chamba who were *telis* were killed here in the village. We heard that Jamal Din Arain was also killed but it was not in the village.

'Some Muslims from the lower castes embraced Sikhism and stayed on. One of them lived here but died a few years ago. There was a massacre in the villages, especially in Mathi. Many Muslim women jumped into wells and men and children were pushed into them.

'We did not give protection to the Muslims because the attackers could punish us or the police would involve us in some case. We, however, did not kill anyone nor take their belongings. It rained everyday that year. It was the eighth month of the year.'

We then drove to Mathi which was close to Adampur. The current *lambardar* told us that he was born after Partition and therefore did not know much about what happened. He had, of course, heard that Muslims in large numbers had been slaughtered just outside Mathi but the crimes were committed by outsiders. He was unwilling to record an interview. He told us that nobody in the village would be able to help us because the majority were refugees from Pakistan. Upon our insistence to talk to some, he told us to go to village Boran which was only a kilometre away. There, we met Teja Singh, who knew all that happened in Mathi.

Teja Singh

We found Teja Singh (seventy-six) sitting on a *charpoy* outside his house. He was a tall, impressive-looking Sikh. This is what he told us:

'Mathi was a Muslim-majority village. It was the criminals from outside who raided it in 1947. We treated our Muslims like brothers. There were Jat Muslims too, one of them was called Ilalhi Baksh. There were also many Muslim *kumhars* (potters) who lived in Mathi. Mathi was bigger than Boran. The attack took place during day time. It was raining that day. I was out grazing the cattle. Some 800–1,000 Muslims were killed. I came to Mathi to find out what happened to the Jats. None of them had survived. Only a small boy of theirs was alive. His name was Jaamu, son of Chanan. I took Jaamu under my protection and he lived with me for about five years. Then his maternal uncle came from Pakistan. He said all his family was dead. If the boy went to Pakistan then they could claim the land which belonged to his father. I left him at the police station, asking him to write to me from Pakistan but no letter ever came.

'A Muslim *kumhar* woman also stayed on in Mathi. The *lambardar* of Mathi was Gajja Singh. He did not have children from his first wife. His wife consented to him taking the Muslim woman as his second wife. The *kumharni* was called Bachni. She was actually the daughter-in-law of the *kumhars*. Her husband and all her in-laws were killed in the carnage. But the police traced her and she was first taken to Jullundur, but Gajja Singh went there and spent a lot of money bribing the officials and brought her back. She, too, was willing to stay with him. They had three sons and two daughters. Gajja Singh and Bachni are now dead. Their son Baldev is now the *lambardar* of Mathi [the man we had met earlier but who did not want to give us an interview].

'When the Muslims from the adjoining villages began to collect in Mathi, the Sikh Jats fled and came to Boran. The man who masterminded the attack on Mathi was a bad character, Banta Singh from Boran. He had relatives in Dadheri. He brought Jathedar Baba from Dadheri, a village near Gobindgarh, who led the assault. He was accompanied by criminals from the surrounding villages.

'The raid was vicious. The Muslim men were forced out of their homes under the pretext that they would be baptised and made Sikhs. Then they were treacherously murdered in the fields. Elderly women were killed. The younger ones were raped or taken away. Some of them jumped into the wells and others were thrown in. Even children and the elderly were hacked to pieces and thrown into the wells and ponds. All this started when a train arrived at Sirhind, full of Sikh women with their breasts cut off and their bodies transfixed with spears and other sharp objects. The Maharaja of Patiala had decided that if Nankana Sahib was attacked by Muslims he would order an attack on the camp at Sirhind. Since it did not happen the Muslims in the camp at Sirhind were not attacked. Many died because of epidemics, malnutrition, and other illnesses borne by the filthy living conditions.

'The main reason for the assaults was to pillage and loot. Imam Din and Nizam Din were well-to-do *telis* who used to help people by extending them interest-free loans. They also helped people of all communities in times of need. Nobody was spared when the attacks took place.'

Teja Singh's son, Gurdeep Singh (forty-eight) helped his father during the conversation because Teja Singh spoke in a very low voice. Gurdeep Singh told us that *lambardar* Gajja Singh used to say that the Muslims here were very pious and good people.

The Malerkotla exception

I was aware that the tiny princely state of Malerkotla ruled by a Muslim nawab had been a safe haven for any Muslim who entered its territories in 1947. The 1941 census placed its total population at 88,109, where the three communities were evenly balanced: Hindus made up 23,479 or nearly 27 per cent of the population, almost evenly divided between caste and scheduled-caste Hindus; Muslims were the biggest community, 33,881 or 38.4 per cent; and Sikhs 30,320 or 34.4 per cent of the total population. As earlier noted, the Sikhs did not pursue the Muslims who entered Malerkotla. They explained it as part of their deference for Guru Gobind Singh's positive remarks about the Muslim nawab, who refused to bow to the pressure of the Mughals to arrest the sons of the Sikh Guru. He was also believed to have said that henceforth the Muslims of Malerkotla were not to be harmed.

Ian Coupland, however, lays emphasis on the fact that the Muslims inside the state territories were armed and that factor could have played an important role in deterring aggression. We learned that a Sikh from Takht Hazara tried to persuade the Maharaja of Patiala to allow the *jathas* to go after Muslims inside Maletkotla but he did not agree. In the event, while Muslims were being killed in the thousands around Malerkotla those inside it remained unharmed and that included refugees as well.

I was very keen to visit Malerkotla and find out what happened there. A friend of mine in Stockholm, Rizwan Dar, helped me arrange my visit to Malerkotla. His cousin is married to Dr Nizam Din of Malerkotla. Dr Nizam Din showered us with warmth as he received us at his residence on 6 January 2005.

Dr Nizam Din

'I can tell you about what happened in Malerkotla. Malerkotla escaped a bloodbath because Nawab Sahib maintained neutrality. One of his cousins was a leader of the Muslim League in Lahore and used to pressure the royal family to support the Pakistan demand. However, this was resisted by the notables. The Nawab of Malerkotla had good relations with the Sikh princes and the Hindus and Sikhs of Malerkotla remained loyal to him. There were some Muslim League supporters but, by and large, communal peace prevailed.

'It is true that some preparations had been made to resist an attack by Sikhs. The state police and the small army had weapons and would have put up resistance but that would have been inadequate in preventing a large contingent of armed Sikhs from entering Malerkotla. My understanding, though, is that Nawab Sahib had been given firm assurances by the Maharaja of Patiala that Malerkotla will be spared. I have also learnt that the British had been contacted and informed about a possible assault on Malerkotla. Therefore, at the highest levels, everybody was informed. Had the Sikhs invaded Malerkotla it would have become big news. The *jathas* did not want *that*; they wanted to pursue their agenda in utmost secrecy. In a village called Baras, some 300–400 Muslim women and girls threw themselves into wells to escape molestation by the Sikhs.

'Malerkotla took care of hundreds of thousands of Muslims who sought safe haven here. Thousands died just outside Malerkotla. Perhaps the Sikhs spared Malerkotla because of Guru Gobind Singh's instructions to them not to harm the Muslims of this place. Most Sikhs do revere Guru Gobind Singh and his word must have mattered as well.'

Refugees in Malerkotla

Dr Nizam Din helped us interview two cousins who escaped from the village Kakra and then settled down in Malerkotla.

Chaudhri Abdul Shakoor

'I was born in Kakra, Bhagwanigarh, Patiala, in a Muslim Kamboh family. It was a large village of some 1,200–1,300 households, mostly Muslims. The second group was Hindu, mostly Khatris and *kumhars*. The main Muslim *biradaris* were Rangar Rajputs, Kambohs, Gujjars, *telis*, *dhobis* (washermen) and some twenty-five to thirty *fakirs*. There were no Sikhs in our village. There were five mosques and one Hindu temple. The Rangar Rajputs known as Khan Sahibs were the leaders of the village.

'It was the third day of *bhadon* [corresponding to 3 September 1947] when suddenly the village was surrounded by thousands of Sikhs. It was raining that day. The *zohar* prayers had ended and the clock had just passed two in the afternoon when my cousin who was on the way to the well with the food, came back shouting, "Look, lots of people are coming towards our village from the direction of Toda". My uncle left everything and sat on the camel and put his son behind him. Someone shot at him and he was hit in the leg. He managed to get home. The attack had begun. Many Muslims, perhaps as many as 250–300 were killed, but also some raiders. People began to abandon the village.

'We left at around ten in the night. It was raining when we arrived at Chhitanwale. Many more villages had joined us. There was another attack at Chhitanwale, and some seven more people died. We left that village on *bhadon* 6 [6 September]. This time too, we started our journey in the night, hoping to escape detection. We entered an area called Tunga in Nabha state. It has *tibas* (hillocks). We stayed there for a few days and then continued our journey towards Malerkotla. We crossed a canal and found ourselves in a place that was completely barren. Salinity and water-logging had destroyed all vegetation. Thus a vast empty plain was full of Muslims with no protection. Then the real massacre started. Thousands of people died. There was complete chaos. Nobody knew what was happening. My father, all paternal uncles except one, my father's uncle, four of my brothers and four cousins – all were brutally killed. Some forty-five members of my family lost their lives. I and a brother of mine and our mother survived.

'I was injured. [He showed me a deep gash on the chest. – author.]. We hid in a sugarcane field. Then we crossed the bridge over the canal. We saw two sisters lying dead. Eid had recently been celebrated. They were wearing pretty clothes and their shoes were identical. One had a boy of four months and the other, a two-month-old girl. Both the infants were alive. My mother said, "We should take them." I and my brother picked up those infants. We came to Jainpur just outside Malerkotla. There we met some Sikh Jats armed with rifles. They told us to stop. Then more people collected there. We were twelve or fourteen altogether. The Sikhs would not let anyone kill us. We were taken to a place where we met some 200 to 250 Muslim girls. The Sikhs were disputing among themselves about how to share them. They were saying "I will take this one," and others said, "We'll take them". But some Sikhs forbade that and the criminals dispersed. Then we all walked on and reached Manak Majra. Here the Malerkotla soldiers were waiting. There were also doctors and vehicles. We gave them the infants and walked on to Malerkotla. We met our *dadi* who had arrived there on her own.

'We have since then been living in Malerkotla. Several thousand Muslims were killed in front of my eyes. *Kirpans*, *barchas* (spears) and rifles were used. The people were pleading for mercy and were willing to give up everything but they were cut down or taken away. Later some women were recovered. We have never felt afraid here in Malerkotla. Dr Nizam Din is like our family.'

Babu Khan

Babu Khan (born in 1940), cousin of Abdul Shakoor, joined later. Babu is the son of Abdul Shakoor's paternal uncle. He said:

'On the day of the attack, my uncle came home and said to us children who were playing, "Hurry up, we must leave immediately". We tried to leave but the village was surrounded from all sides. So we came back. The attackers were all outsiders. Thousands of armed men with spears, hatchets and long-bladed knives were coming towards the village. We had no weapons. The scene was most frightening.

'We decided to hide in the fields. So, my mother, father and my brothers and sisters went into the fields. The Sikhs attacked, shouting to us to come out but we did not do so. My mother was hit by a hatchet. My father was also hit. He kept moving back but the assailants continued to pursue him until finally he fell. I was standing there seeing everything. They said nothing to the children. My younger brother started crying. My mother said, "Don't cry". She showed him that her stomach had been cut open and the intestines were hanging out. We were petrified with shock. Then a Sikh said, "Burn the field." I started running. The Sikhs ignored me, saying, "He has nothing. Go for the grown-ups with money and jewellery". I sat in a bush. Thousands of people died in front of my eyes.

'Then I began shouting for my mother and my siblings, but she and two of my elder brothers and two younger brothers were lying dead. My father had also been killed. A Kamboh girl came along. She was a relative. She was slightly older than me. Only the two of us had survived. There was a well very close. We went there. It was raining. I felt very hungry. I decided to go to the village and look for food but it was burning. Then I returned to the well. The girl had gone, or somebody had taken her.

'I spent the night at the well and slept in the room nearby. There was no food to eat. On the third day, a boy from our village came to the well. He was slightly older than me. When he saw me he began to run. I shouted at him, "I am Babu, don't be frightened". He returned. We decided to go back to the village and look for food. When the Khatris saw us they started abusing us. Two Sikhs with *kirpans* ran after us. The other boy ran in another direction. They went after him.

'I came to Bhawanigarh where we owned land and had a well. There I spent the night looking for *makki challis* (corn on the cob) but found nothing. I returned to Kakra one more time. Nobody was at home. Only the animals were there. There I saw a Nihang (militant Sikh). He was taking away the animals. I started walking behind him. He saw me and said, "You look after the cows". I followed him. After a while I slipped away. I found myself in the same place where the girl had met me. The boy who had separated from me had also survived.

'We went to the house of my elder paternal uncle and slept there. Nobody was there of course. Then we decided to go to village Channa Nanakwalia. The boy said we should go even if it is a Sikh village. At most, they will kill us. I said, okay, that would put an end to our misery. We saw a Sikh coming our way. The boy started crying. I ran into the field. The Sikh said, "Don"t cry. Are you Majal?" "Yes," he said. "What happened to your father and mother?" "They have been killed," he replied. "Your sister?" "I don"t know."

'The Sikh said, "Come with me, I will say nothing". Then that boy shouted, "Babu, come out. He will not harm us". He was really a very good man. He touched our heads fondly. He took us to Harnam Singh and Prem Singh who were *lambardars*. He said to them, "We must keep these boys." They gave us food. Then they gave us beds to sleep. They locked the doors and said, "You stay here". That village had saved some seventy Muslims. We remained there for two months. We used to take their cattle to graze in the fields. The *lambardar* had instructed his nephew to always stay with us. We were not to be left alone. And that is exactly what he did.

'One day they sent me to fetch tobacco for his hookah. I met an old man from our village who turned out to be my *khala's* father-in-law. I told him that I was the son of Ismail. He started crying when I told him that my parents were dead. He told me that in four or five days he would be going to Malerkotla and offered to take me with him.

'Accordingly he sent a message to me to come but the *lambardars* sent him the message that I did not want to accompany him to Malerkotla. So, he went away. In Malerkotla he met my *chacha* and told him that I was with the *lambardars* in Channa Nanakwalia. My *mama* was also in Malerkotla. He sent a Sikh named Amar Singh to the *lambardars*. But I was scared and began to cry.

'Amar Singh told me he would take me to my *mama*. So, I decided to go along with him. At ten in the night, we reached village Pharee. There we stayed. Next day we came to Channa Bandarwalian. Amar Singh's cousin was there. She said, "Why are you taking this Turk [a way of demonising a Muslim] with you? Kill him". He replied, "I know his family". The next day we went to the village Sarburpur. It was his village. His wife told him that my uncles had come looking for me. Then we had a meal and came to Bhaini [known also as Bhaini Kamboa], where my uncles were waiting for me. When they saw me they began to cry. We live in Bhaini now. I got married there. My uncles arranged a match for me.'

Visit to Kakra village

The next stop after Malerkotla was village Kakra. Hitesh Gosain, Virender Singh, and I arrived the same day in Kakra after completing the round of interviews in Adampur, Mathi and Boran. It was very difficult to find pre-Partition people; most of the current inhabitants were Sikhs from West Punjab, especially from villages on the Gujranwala–Hafizabad route. Karnail Singh, an elderly Sikh originally from Uudowala Seikhon, directed us to a Hindu *mistri* (artisan) Des Raj (aged seventy) of the Mahant caste who was a native of the village.

Des Raj

'Kakra was a big village with some 900 Muslim families and around 300 Hindu households. Abdul Shakoor and I used to play together. It was a happy and cheerful village in which the various castes and the Hindu and Muslim communities lived peacefully. The Rangar Rajputs were the leaders although the Kambohs were the largest group. As a tradition, the Rajput Khan Sahibs served in the Patiala Army and were very influential.

'This area was disturbed when Pakistan came into being. Thousands of Sikhs and Hindus had been arriving from West Punjab in the villages around here. On *bhadon* 3, I remember at about 4 o'clock in the afternoon a large *jatha* mounted on horses and others on foot arrived from Moga and encircled the whole village. Many of them were known criminals.

'In Kakra, Muslims from the surrounding villages had been gathering for some time. The assault was massive and sudden, but some Muslims put up resistance. The odds were very uneven. In the initial fighting, eleven of the attackers were killed and some 300 Muslims. It was mostly those who had come from other villages to seek protection and were walking around in the fields that were killed. The police came and buried them the next day.

'We temporarily vacated Kakra because the Muslim *lambardar* had told us to take precautions. Although the village Muslims would not harm us, he was not sure of the attitude of the Muslims from the surrounding area. We moved out but remained in the neighbourhood and returned the next day to find that the village was burning. The police had arrived and was hurriedly burying the dead in mass graves. Looting and plundering of the vacated houses was still going on.

'Many of Shakoor's relatives were killed in the first attack. What we learned later was that those people from our villagers who went in the direction of Kotla were saved, while those that headed for Chhitanwale and crossed the canal were killed in large numbers. Babu Khan was the son of Ismail. He also lost most of his family. These incidents took place in the villages around here so we know what happened here.

'Abdul Shakoor visited the village after fifty-two years, accompanied by another man, Rafiq. I immediately recognised Rafiq who was my bosom friend. Also I remembered Shakoor's face but not his name. Babu Khan also visited Kakra subsequently, along with Abdul Shakoor.'

My own experience

While in Kakra, we were told that the village mosque had been rehabilitated and Muslims from Uttar Pradesh and Bihar who worked in Kakra had settled there. We were taken to the mosque where a young cleric was teaching the Quran. I was deeply moved by that experience and decided to make a donation, which the Maulvi Sahib accepted with some hesitation, saying that he lived a simple life and had few needs. I also made a donation to Des Raj because I was told that he had happily offered his expertise to restore the mosque and had not charged for his services. He, too, was a proud old Punjabi who would not take any money but I told him it was for any cost in the future for repairing other mosques. The young boys came to meet me and were very pleased to see a Muslim from Pakistan visit their village school. They showed me around, particularly across the strong and stout brick buildings of the Muslim Rajputs who lived there and which still stood proud as symbols of power and influence.

The evening became emotional as the elderly Sikh, Karnail Singh, who had brought me to Des Raj, turned out to be from a village of Gujranwala district. He spoke Punjabi in the same accent as my Lahori Punjabi. When he and other Sikhs arrived in Kakra the signs of violence were still visible. It seemed he wanted to talk more and more; we were from the same part of the old Punjab, after all. Did I make the monetary contributions because of some strong Islamic streak in me or was it simply a way of marking the deeply tragic nature of the Partition? I have never been able to figure out what particular feelings made me do that. However, Hitesh Gosain, Virender Singh, Des Raj, Karnail Singh, the Muslim cleric, the children, and I – all seemed to find those moments very touching. Some of us were even moved to tears.

Jagpal Singh Tiwana

I had been in contact with a number of Sikhs for years, largely because of our shared love for the Punjab. Some of their stories appear in other parts of this book. Here I have an account from Jagpal Singh Tiwana:

'My village, Chinarthal Kalan, is situated between Patiala and Sirhind in East Punjab. In 1947 it was in district Patiala of the Patiala princely state and had a population of about 1,000. It was inhabited mostly by Sikh Jats of the Tiwana sub-caste, but about a quarter of the villagers were Muslim Tiwanas [Muslim Tiwanas of West Punjab usually claim a Rajput origin but in East Punjab they are considered Jats]. There was a *gurdwara* for the Sikhs and a mosque for the Muslims. Relations between the communities were quite cordial. Muslim Tiwanas were originally Sikhs, but were converted to Islam by Aurengzeb, we were told.

'I was twelve years old in 1947. I distinctly remember when the riots broke out and the elders of our village, led by my grandfather, Sardar Sampuran Singh Tiwana, came to the rescue of our Muslim population. A meeting was held at Bangla, a central place in the village, to decide a course of action. The majority, especially seniors, were in favour of doing no harm to Muslims as they were our Tiwana brothers, but younger elements provoked by refugees from West Punjab were less sympathetic. They had eyes on their cattle and property. Then the pressure from neighbouring villages to attack "the enemy" was mounting day by day as stories of riots began circulating. One day, we saw a *jatha* of villagers appear, fully armed and led by Sardar Lal Singh of village Turkheri. They wanted to demolish the mosque. On the advice of our elders, they agreed to first allow the Muslims take out their religious books and other belongings. The miscreants could demolish only a couple of minarets of the solid cemented *masjid*. However, no physical harm was done to any Muslim.

'Loot and plunder of Muslim property was going on in the neighbouring villages. The outsiders had an eye on the Muslims of our village. We were expecting an attack on them any day. Realising the gravity of the situation, our people again met at the Bangla to decide what to do. The younger group wanted to kick out the Muslims and usurp their property, but the elders came out with a solution. They said they would advise the Muslims to embrace the Sikh religion, or else they would be helpless when the attack came from outside. *Mirasi* Muslims (singers and entertainers) readily agreed to become Sikhs. They said their ancestor, Mardana, was a companion of Guru Nanak. Seeing a danger to their lives, others too agreed to adopt the Sikh faith. The younger and the irresponsible elements among our people still had reservations. They alleged the Muslims would go back to their faith once the situation became normal. So they must be made to eat pork at the baptising ceremony, as that would make them leave their religion for good. A Muslim was asked to kill and cut up a pig, and the meat was cooked and served. When offered the pork, some of the Muslims vomited. I am not sure if any of them ate the pork. It was a most loathsome sight to see.

'As the news spread in the neighbourhood that at village Chinathal the Muslims were safe if they adopted Sikhism, several Muslims came out of their hiding places. One poor fellow had not eaten for three days, hiding in a sugarcane field. Our *gurdwara* became a small relief camp.

'Nobody was killed. Fateh Muhammad became Fateh Singh, and Fakiria became Fakir Singh. They wore blue turbans and carried a small *kirpan* slung from their shoulders. One day we heard that Fateh Singh was seen in a barber's shop getting his beard trimmed. Both Fateh Singh and the Hindu barber were summoned to a meeting at the *gurdwara*. They accepted their fault. The Sikh priest announced the punishment. They were to pay a small fine, clean shoes and dishes, and attend the *gurdwara* for seven mornings to listen to *Gurbani* (recitation of Sikh scriptures). We were told that it was a very mild punishment as the Sikh priest was a pious man.

'Then after a week we heard that some Muslims with loads of their valuable belongings had slipped out of the village at midnight and joined the Muslim camp at Rouza Sharif near the Sirhind shrine. [This was the same camp where Chaudhri Roshan Din sought refuge.] This incensed the young ruffians, who shouted at the elderly village folk: "Didn't we warn you not to trust them?" They hatched a plan to teach the Muslims a lesson. They advised the Muslims not to sneak out of the village but if they did not wish to stay on as true Sikhs, they would escort them to the camp. A few Muslims accepted the offer which they found to be too tempting. One night they left the village to join the camp at

Rouza Sharif under the protection of some young Sikhs. On the way near village Pandrali, there was a thick jungle where their bullock carts were stopped. The Muslims were told to surrender all their jewellery and cash. Then the daughters and daughters-in-law were pulled into the nearby bushes and mercilessly raped. This shameful story circulated in the village the next morning. A knot of old people sitting around my grandfather were heard lamenting: "*Salian ne moonh kala kar ditta, ohna noon camp vich miln joge ni chhadia*". (The scoundrels have blackened our faces. We are now not fit to even visit them in the refugee camp).

'My grandfather had given shelter to a Muslim family. The men in the family were given work at our *bhatta* (brick kiln). The family had two young unmarried girls. Now the young men had eyes on them. Before any harm could come to them, my grandfather one day quietly escorted the family to Rouza Sharif.

'We had a few unmarried men in our lane. They had little or no land and had a bad reputation. They had abducted some Muslim women from somewhere and were living with them. Bachan Singh, known as Khooni Bachna (he had committed a couple of murders) had two young girls in his house. It was, however, a short-lived honeymoon. All Muslim women were recovered by the police and sent to Pakistan.

'Sometimes we get our Tiwana brothers from Pakistan to visit us. A young man, Tanveer Tiwana from Lahore, discovered me on the Internet. His grandfather, Mr Abdul Rashid Tiwana, lived with his family in our village before 1947. He calls me *dadaji* (paternal grandfather) and stays in touch. According to him, nobody was hurt in his family. With the help of their Sikh neighbours they made it to the relief camp safely. According to Tanveer, the Tiwanas from our village are now settled in the districts of Sheikhupura, Sargodha, Kasur, and Lahore.'

Nabha State

The total population of Nabha state was 340,044, comprising a Muslim population of 50,972 or nearly fifteen per cent. Dr Khushi Muhammad Khan retired from the Hamburg Institute of Development Economics in 1991. He was my guest in Stockholm in June 2003. He narrated the following:

Dr Khushi Muhammad Khan

'I was born in Amlo district, Nabha state, on 12 October 1930. Its ruler was a Sikh. Muslims constituted about twenty per cent of the population of the state. All communities lived together in peace. The relationships were very congenial – we grew up in each other's homes. I used to eat with my friend, a Brahmin, in his kitchen. His mother treated me like her own son. She was, however, worried that orthodox Hindus might mind the fact that she allowed a Muslim to enter her kitchen and eat there.

'There were no newspapers in our area and so we had no idea that the Partition and its troubles were on the way. All sorts of people would come to my father for his services. He was a lawyer. Mostly Hindus and Sikhs would hire him to represent them in court. There was no Congress or Muslim League in Amlo district.

'Some people used to talk about Pakistan but nobody had any idea of what that would entail. My father was approached to become president of the local Muslim League but he declined, saying that his duty towards his children and wife were more important. Further he said that all communities were living happily together so why should he do something that would ruin that fine milieu.

'In the early 1940s, we moved to Nabha town. The news about the killings in Bengal in August 1946 and in Bihar of Muslims did begin to reach Nabha, but we did not feel at that time that the Punjab would be affected. In fact, the realisation that we might have to leave Nabha came only after 14 August. But it did not become necessary for us to leave until November 1947. There was only one public radio in Nabha town, at the shop of the *paanwala* (man who sold betelnut leaf). People used to listen to the news and reports of killings would figure prominently. Previously few Hindu and Sikh refugees came to Nabha state because it was removed from the main Grand Trunk Road and there was not much economic development. But by October and November the number of refugees began to increase and the Muslim minority began to feel that reprisals were being planned against them. Some of our relatives were also living in the same street, but other communities were also living there. However, by November, attacks on Muslims began.

'We left in November. The decision to leave was taken when my mother began to protest that reports were coming everyday about attacks on Muslims in the villages around Nabha town, and unless we left we would also fall victim to Hindu–Sikh violence. My father then contacted the *nazim* (mayor) of Nabha town, a Sikh who had been his class fellow. He advised my father to seek refuge in the Nabha Fort for the time being. He himself lived there, so did the head of the police and the district medical doctor. My father decided instead to go back to Amlo where our ancestral home was located.

'Another Sikh class fellow of my father, Partap Singh, who owned the local bus service, told him that an attack by the Akalis was planned so we should be ready to leave early in the morning next day. He promised to drive us safely to a refugee camp. My father accepted his offer and we left the next day without telling anyone in our area.

'We left early in the morning. We hardly had anything with us. On the road to Nabha town, Akali Sikhs armed with swords and lances tried to stop us, but Partap Singh evaded them and we reached the camp at Nabha. Many of our relatives were already there. My father went to the court and learned from Mian Abdul Latif, who started his career as a lawyer by assisting my father, that the ruler of Nabha had issued orders that nobody should be attacked in Nabha town. In the villages, however, attacks could be carried out.

'A caravan of refugees left Nabha town in early November and we walked for some ten days before reaching Pakistan. There must have been at least 100,000 people in the caravan. On the way we found corpses littered all over. Thousands had been slain. Our caravan was not attacked, although the alarm was raised many times. Nobody could sleep during the night. Some died on the way. Soldiers of the Pakistan Army from the Baloch regiment had come to escort us and that is the reason why the caravan was not attacked.

'We arrived via Kasur because the Wagah–Attari route was much too dangerous. We soon found ourselves in Gujranwala. My father, who had a thriving practice in Nabha, could not compete with the English-educated lawyers. He therefore decided to work as an application writer outside the district courts in Gujranwala. He often talked about his real home in Nabha and tearfully recited a Persian verse which meant: *The thorn of my home soil is better than all the roses in a foreign place.*

'I came to Germany in 1963 and from there began to contact my old school in Nabha town. The response from there was very warm, but it was not until 1979 that I got permission to visit Nabha again. The whole town seemed to have come to welcome me. I was invited for a meal in many homes. A family of Muslim butchers and cloth dyers had stayed on because the people needed their services. Now I go regularly and spend about a month each time. I stay with my friend Ashwini Kumar Sharma, a Brahmin. His wife and children treat me with great love.'

Kapurthala state

Vicky, Nanak Singh, the driver, and I arrived late in the afternoon of 3 January at Kapurthala. Once famous as the 'Paris of the Punjab states', it seemed to have retained some of its pre-Partition glory. Kapurthala city was not far from Jullundur. As we entered the centre of town a beautiful mosque stood there in quiet majesty. There is a marble plaque built into the wall of the main mosque in the centre of Kaputhala town which reads as follows:

> The Moorish Mosque was constructed on the order of his Highness Maharaja Jagatjit Singh Bahadur. The construction spanned the period October 1926 till March 1930. The total cost amounted to four lakh (400,000) rupees. The inauguration ceremony took place on 14 March 1930, in the presence of His Highness the Maharaja who was accompanied by His Highness the Nawab Sadiq Mohammad Khan Bahadur, Ruler of Bahawalpur State. The congregation numbered over 100,000. The existence of this mosque bears an enduring testimony to the Maharaja's broadminded tolerance and solicitude for the welfare of his subjects.

The 1941 census gives the total population of Kapurthala state as 378,389. It had a Hindu population of 61,546, which included 20,892 members of the scheduled castes. Although the ruler was a Sikh, the Sikhs numbered only 88,350. The Muslims were the largest group, constituting of a total of 213,557. That meant that the Muslims were in a majority of 56.4 percent. Now, of course, no local Muslim was to be found there. We also visited Sultanpur Lodhi, a town some thirty kilometres from Kapurthala, because of a promise I made to one of its former residents, Maulana Mujahid Al-Hussaini. He wanted me to take some pictures of the mosque in Kapurthala and of two Sikh temples in Sultanpur Lodhi. About what happened in his home town, he had the following story to tell:

Mujahid Al-Hussaini

'I was born in Sultanpur Lodhi, Kapurthala state in 1925. Ours was a very peaceful and friendly society. The maharaja, Jagatjit Singh, was a very enlightened, tolerant and just ruler. He was widely travelled and used to visit Morocco many times. In 1930, he built a majestic mosque in the centre of Kapurthala. Most of his subjects were Muslims and the mosque was a present from him to his people. Muslims served as his chief ministers and were also employed in the state services on a fair basis. In Sultanpur Lodhi, there were two famous, historical *gurdwaras*, Gurdwara Beir Sahib and Gurdwara Hatt Sahib. They continue to haunt me because I used to play in their vicinity. Children from different communities played together and the environment was friendly and secure. Respect for each other's religion was standard practice.

'The Majlis-e-Ahrar had a big following in Sultanpur Lodhi and other parts of Kapurthala state. My family was also closely associated with the Deobandi school of thought. My surname Al-Hussaini is based on my devotion to the ideas of Maulana Hussain Ahmed Madni, the chief thinker of the Jamiat-ul-Ulema-i-Hind. We were not in favour of the partition of India on a religious basis, but things began to turn tense when in March 1947 Sikh refugees from Rawalpindi arrived in our state. They went around telling horrifying stories of atrocities committed against them by Muslims.

'In August 1947 the maharaja was away in Europe when Partition took place. His son the Tikka Sahib (crown prince) was a different type of person. He was under the influence of the Akalis and gave the go-signal for an all-out assault on Muslims. This happened in Sultanpur Lodhi soon after Partition. In the initial attack the loss of life among the Muslims was in several hundreds; some of the assailants were also killed.

A decision was taken by the Muslim elders to leave Sultanpur Lodhi and we stared to trek towards Jullundur. The convoy was in the thousands. We were attacked a number of times. I saw the Tikka Sahib himself giving orders to shoot down Muslims. A Sikh from our town recognised me and saved me while thousands of people were massacred in the plains.

'Those of us who managed to escape finally arrived in the camp outside Jullundur. I saw thousands of dead bodies littered all over the fields and by the road. It was all so unnecessary. Kapurthala would not have gone through a bloodbath if the maharaja himself had been in India at that time.'

Sheikh Nur Muhammad

'I was born in Kapurthala, but during 1935–45 we lived in Lahore. I remember the 23 March 1940 meeting of the Muslim League. It was a very festive occasion but at that time people had no idea what the creation of Pakistan would entail for millions of ordinary people. In 1945 we went back to Kapurthala. Muslims were in a majority. The maharaja built the mosque near the railway station. The maharaja was such a good man. [Here he began to weep]. We had no hatred between the different communities. Only when Partition was announced did we realise that we were not in Pakistan. Suddenly, attacks on Muslims started in the villages. The maharaja was not there at that time. A train was sent to Pakistan. It was after August. My father was an old man. Three of my sisters were married in Lahore. They and their husbands had actually left Lahore because of the violence in the hope of peace and safety in Kapurthala. They were also now caught up in the new tragedy. I gave the keys of my house to our Hindu neighbour and asked him to keep an eye on our house until we came back.

'My brother-in-law overheard a Sikh, who happened to be General Jai Singh of Kapurthala state, tell another Sikh that there was a plan to attack the train once it left Kapurthala. When my elderly father heard that, he told us not to take the train. We did as we were told and came back to our house. We lived in the *nakeyband mohalla* (neighbourhood where hookah-makers lived). The tonga-driver charged us much more than the normal rate. We came back home. At nine that night, the whole town learned about the attack on the train and how the Muslims had been slaughtered.

'We stayed put in our house. Everyday we heard that Muslim convoys were being attacked. Finally we learned that trucks were going to take Muslims to Jullundur Cantonment, where a camp had been set up. In the town of Kapurthala there were no attacks. We left in nine trucks. Some half a mile before Jullundur, there was an Islamic High School, where Hindus and Sikhs from Pakistan were being kept in a camp. Our Sikh driver stopped the truck. Immediately we were surrounded by Sikhs and Hindus flashing swords and spears. Many of us jumped off the truck but some were cut down. My father and uncle were seriously hurt. Suddenly another truck came with Sikh soldiers. The officer was a good man. He fired on the assailants, who ran away, and we were saved.

'We walked to the main road through the fields. There we saw some tanks. The soldiers allowed us to climb onto the tanks. After two or three miles we met others from our convoy. A Muslim boy helped us stay in a hospital. He brought some rotis. The injured were taken care of. Then we met some Pathan soldiers who took us to the cantonment. We stayed for twelve days in the camp. We had carried some food with us.

'Then one day, a Hindu from Kapurthala came to our camp and told me that my father and uncle were safe but very hungry. I gave him the food. Then we came to Mian Meer Station outside Lahore. Some troops were there. I met my father in Mian Meer. We were under the impression that the troops were Muslims but they were actually Gurkhas. We alighted at Mian Mir Station and came to Mohani Road where my family has been settled since.'

In July 2007, Dr Muhammad Farooq contacted me after reading an account of my visit to Kapurthala which was published in the *News International* on 14 July 2007. He wrote a detailed account of his mother's ordeal when she and her family had to flee Kapurthala. Dr Farooq sent me, in an email dated 14 August 2007, the following from his mother:

Mrs B.A. Choudhary

'My maiden name is Manzoor Akhtar. I vividly remember that Kapurthala was a prosperous and flourishing state in East Punjab in undivided India during the second quarter of the twentieth century. It was ruled by a Sikh maharaja, His Highness Maharaja Jagatjit Singh Bahadur. He was deeply revered by his subjects as he was a just and kind-hearted ruler. One more quality which he possessed was that he had an open, secular and tolerant mind. He never showed discrimination against any ethnic or religious community among his pluralist realm. For this reason, not only Sikhs but people belonging to other factions also held important positions in the state's administrative setup. My father, who belonged to the Muslim community, held a high position in the Horticulture Department of the state and had as his status a legion of manual workers as his subordinate staff.

'I was born in Kapurthala in 1927, and there I lived my childhood and early adolescence. I did my matriculation at the Maharani Harbans Kaur Girls High School in Kapurthala, which was also popularly known as Jalau Khana. This school was housed in a section of a three-storey, old but graceful building, originally the abandoned palace of the maharani. Some sections of the building were being used for other useful social activities. For instance, a portion of the building was used for teaching sewing, knitting, and handicraft-making to widows, orphan girls, and destitute women, all under the guidance of an expert named Shirimati Koolan Devi. This lady used to come to her office in a horse-drawn chariot. The vastness of the school can be judged from the fact that during my ten years there, I never managed to see all the rooms. It was located in the vicinity of the old palace. It had a number of basements and tunnels, most of which were abandoned and dark. I still remember the names of my schoolmates, my Sikh class fellows such as Beero and Jeeto.

'There was a separate famous educational institution for boys named the Randheer Government School/College, Kapurthala. Students from far and wide used to come to this institution. As already noted, Kapurthala was a pluralist society in which Sikhs, Muslims, Hindus, and Christians, lived together in a friendly atmosphere, like members of one family.

'Our family lived a comfortable life with many domestic servants. There was a grand mosque in the centre of town. It was a novel piece of architecture. It was flanked with 30–40 living quarters which were primarily used as hostels for the students who had come to Kapurthala from far off places for Islamic studies. There were sprawling lush green lawns near the mosque. I, along with my parents and siblings, quite frequently visited the mosque. On these occasions my father used to go inside the mosque to offer his prayers, while we children along with our mother would stroll in the green lawns of the mosque.

'The railway station of Kapurthala was not a very big one but quite impressive for a visitor. Its tidiness and cleanliness were striking. At the railway station one could conspicuously see the parked sparkling-white private railway saloon of the maharaja, which was used by him whenever he travelled by rail.

'I still remember that fateful day when people were eagerly crowded around radios for the official announcement about the Partition. Our joy knew no bounds when in the preliminary announcement it was declared that Hoshiarpur, Gurdaspur, Jullundur and Ferozepur had been included in Pakistan. [This must have been a result of some misreading of the facts]. Upon hearing this, every one of us heaved a sigh of relief because it meant that we would not be dislodged from our homes. However, soon the news spread like wildfire that all the districts and the states of East Punjab had been given to India. We felt utterly dejected and dismayed. Within hours, this news led to a near civil war and anarchy in Kapurthala. The various ethnic and religious communities who had enjoyed cordial relations for decades turned hostile, particularly towards Muslims. Trustworthy friends became foes in no time.

'At this critical juncture, to our bad luck, Maharaja Jagatjit Singh was on a long foreign trip. He, therefore, could not come to the aid of his Muslim subjects at that crucial time.

'The acting ruler, Tikka Sahib, who was the eldest son of the maharaja, did not have a soft heart for his Muslim subjects. In fact, as later events unfolded, he did not make any sincere effort to protect his Muslim subjects and their families from the attacking Sikhs. Otherwise, much of the carnage and destruction which took place could have been avoided. He had no regard or appreciation for the loyal workers and their families who had given the best years of their lives to the service of Kapurthala. At this stage, some Muslim notables decided to approach Tikka Sahib for help and assistance for the safe exit of the affected Muslim families. The request was granted half-heartedly. A convoy consisting of some twenty-eight trucks protected by armed vehicles was sanctioned to take the Muslim families to their destination. As the convoy was to take the refugee families next day, because of anarchy and security reasons, groups of Muslim families assembled together at various suitable places, guarded by the male members, so that they may remain safe from the Sikh marauders. The next day at about evening time, the convoy of trucks arrived, though not accompanied by armed vehicles. The nervous and panic-stricken Muslim families thronged to the trucks to get into them. We were told that according to the chalked-out programme, the convoy would first report to the main boulevard of the city, where, in a solemn ceremony, the Tikka Sahib would salute the departing Muslim families in recognition of their services to the state. Maharaja Jagatjit Singh had desired this to be done. The convoy took us to the main boulevard where we were met by a salute by the Tikka Sahib. The farewell ceremony went well after which the crown prince and other dignitaries dispersed.

'After the ceremony, according to the scheduled programme, our convoy was supposed to move and take us to Pakistan. Instead, we were told that some changes had been made in the departure time because the armed vehicles were not ready to accompany the convoy. As a result of this decision, we were dropped back to our houses and the families returned back to their homes and had to wait till the convoy could pick them up the next day. When we got home, I was taken aback to see that our adjoining Sikh neighbours, who were our close friends, had broken into our house and had made vents in the boundary walls in order to loot our house. Many valuable goods had already been looted. The ceiling fans were also missing. It is odd that only hours earlier at the time of our departure with the convoy, the same looting Sikh neighbours, while giving us a warm send-off, and with tears rolling down their cheeks due to uncontrolled emotions, had assured us they would take good care of our house and that we would find our house perfectly safe and sound even if we returned decades later.

'At this sudden change in their attitude I couldn't keep control of my emotions and started crying loudly. My mother hushed me with a silent gesture and tried to make me understand with her gestures that the neighbours could kill us in order to avoid the embarrassment of being exposed for not keeping their word. It was a nightmarish sleepless night for us. The next day everyone was eagerly waiting for the arrival of the convoy of trucks. After an endless wait the convoy arrived in the evening. The nervous and scared Muslim families once again made their way to the trucks. The trucks were crammed with passengers. At this time, my father and my grandfather, who were carrying a briefcase containing gold ornaments and currency notes, were attacked by some Sikhs and made captives. They were therefore separated from us and could not accompany us in the convoy. The convoy staff covered the trucks with giant-size opaque plastic sheets so that Sikh marauders couldn't see young girls, women and children. We were on Truck No. 7 in the convoy. My mother hid me and my siblings in the truck. She also kept telling us to keep pin-drop silence.

'After having travelled some distance, the convoy was attacked by a Sikh mob and only the first eleven or twelve trucks escaped the assault. Most of the remaining convoy could not continue as bullets were fired into their tyres by the attackers. Hidden under the plastic sheets we could hear the helpless screams of women and children who were under attack. These screams faded gradually as our truck moved onwards. By then it was dark. The convoy stopped in a jungle-like place. We were told that Kapurthala state ended there and that from there onwards we would have to continue our journey on our own. We were told that there was a railhead some two miles away. It started raining heavily. We were ordered to get out of the trucks. We could see the gushing rainwater everywhere. Like other passengers of the convoy, we were wading through deep rainwater which was two or three-feet-deep at places. My mother was carrying our only brother, of five sisters, who was only six at the time. I was accompanied by my three sisters aged 16, 11 and 9 years, while I was 13. My elder sister was too timid and could not guide us. The responsibility, therefore, rested upon my shoulders. Our eldest sister had already been married at that time and was living with her husband in Pakistan. While wading through the deep rainwater, we lost our shoes, as a result of which our feet were bruised and cut by the sharp-edged stones. The razor-like wild weeds were also cutting into our feet. Like the other refugees, we too had to remove the leeches from our limbs. Some were bitten by snakes. We had to hide for about ten long days. It was a real testing time for all of us because there was neither food nor clean water to drink. We were forced to eat dry grains of wheat which some families had with them. Some men brought drinking water from distant wells but it was in very small quantities. There were no toilets and the men had to hold up pieces of cloth to provide privacy for their wives and daughters.

'During this stay, we learned that there was no nearby railhead as we had been told. However, a road that led to Pakistan lay some two miles ahead. We got to that road. After some time, a convoy of trucks stopped there. It was a convoy of the Pakistan Army and was escorting refugees from India. Everyone was scrambling to get into the trucks but there was hardly any room available. We felt ourselves greatly handicapped because of the absence of our father and grandfather. My mother begged the soldiers to take her children to Pakistan. She had decided not to go to Pakistan but wanted to search for our father and grandfather. She only wanted her children to get to Pakistan safely. She preferred to give her young children to Muslims rather than to Sikhs. One of the soldiers took pity on my mother and promised to take us to Pakistan but there was no place for us on any of the trucks. We were forced to stay on till the next day. Next day, at about noon, the convoy came and the soldier recognised my mother and asked her to get into the vehicle along with us. But my mother, while making us sit in the truck, explained to the soldier the reason for her not accompanying us. With tearful eyes she said goodbye to us and told the soldier, "I am leaving my children in your custody in a state of utter helplessness. Please take care of them. May Allah keep them in his protection".

'The truck moved away. We looked at our mother and were convinced that we'd never see her again. Soon she disappeared in the dim distance. Feeling unprotected at this tender age and in a strange environment, we were all sobbing. The convoy stopped after travelling some distance. Beside the road, a young Muslim woman was lying motionless. She had been attacked and the soldiers stopped to help her. They discovered that she was still alive although she had bled profusely. She was comatose. Her abdominal viscera were oozing out from her deep wounds. The soldiers wrapped a piece of cloth around her stomach as a bandage. She was carried onto our truck. We were asked to pick out the ants from her blood-drenched body. All this was a nightmarish experience for us. The convoy continued its journey. Finally we were told that we had reached the Wagah border.

'The refugees in the convoy kissed the earth of Pakistan with emotion and reverence. The wounded woman was shifted to an ambulance. I have no idea whether she was alive or dead by then. The families who had escaped with all their family members were particularly jubilant. However, our faces reflected gloom and despair as we had lost our parents and our grandfather. People brought food and utility items to help the refugees. After spending some time at Wagah, the trucks moved towards the Walton Station refugee camp. It was a very big refugee camp. We stayed at the camp for eleven days. There was an elaborate arrangement for loudspeakers to announce the names of all refugees. The names of the recently arrived refugees as well as those already there were repeatedly announced so that their friends and relatives in Pakistan could find them. Furthermore, the names of the Pakistani relatives were also announced so that they could be found and reunited by their relatives from India. Similarly, two-way announcements were also being continuously being made on Radio Pakistan.

'On the eleventh day, while we were listening to the announcements, I heard the name of one of our distant relatives who was living in a house at Beadon Road. It was a ray of hope which consoled us after a miserable journey full of ordeal and adversities. We at once decided to get to Beadon Road. We approached a *tonga*-driver and asked him if he would take us to Beadon Road though we had no money to pay him the fare. At that time nationalist and patriotic sentiments of Pakistani citizens were very high. He readily agreed. We got to the house and our relatives were shocked to see us clad in tatters and without shoes. Before Partition, whenever they visited us in Kapurthala, they found us living very well. They asked about our parents and when we told them the whole story they felt even more grieved.

'After a shower we were given clean clothes. We enjoyed a sumptuous and delicious lunch after a very long time. We stayed there for about ten days. Our relatives managed to get our names and addresss announced in Radio Pakistan. This announcement caught the attention of other relatives in Pakistan. In this way, our reunion with our near and dear ones became possible. My parents and my grandfather joined us after a lapse of over a month. This was because the bridge over the river Beas was damaged by floodwater and therefore the convoys of refugees could not cross over for many days.'

Sheikh Muhammad Farooq

I met Sheikh Muhammad Farooq during a visit to Rajgarh, Lahore, on 13 December 2004. He told me this story about their exit from Sultanpur Lodhi:

'My mother, sisters and I lived in Sultanpur Lodhi. My father had died, so there was no grown-up man in our family. When the rioting started a Sikh friend of my father, Santa Singh, came to our help. He carried me on his shoulders while my mother and sisters walked behind him on the way to a refugee camp. Suddenly we were surrounded by a Sikh mob. Those armed men wanted to kill me and my mother and take away my sisters. Santa Singh challenged them and said: "First you kill me and then can you touch this woman and the children. They are like my family. Is this what the gurus taught you?" An old Sikh who heard him rushed forward and stood next to Santa Singh. He said, "Let this Sikh keep his word. Do not molest this Muslim family." The mob dispersed upon hearing that.'

A letter from Pakistan to Kapurthala

During the trip to Hoshiarpur, already mentioned in another chapter, I wrote that we were taken home by Mr Rajnish Tandon, General Secretary of the District Congress Committee. His wife told me the following story about Kapurthala:

'I am originally from Kapurthala. My father had many Muslim friends. They all left in 1947. One day a letter and a money order arrived from Pakistan for my father. It was from an old Muslim friend of his. They were like brothers. When Partition took place, his friend had to leave for Pakistan. He had borrowed some money from my father, which he could not return before he left. In the letter he informed my father that he was lying on his deathbed and would be gone any moment.

'He had to face very hard times in Pakistan and could not save money to pay back his debt, but was now returning it. He hoped my father would forgive him for taking so long. My father began to cry and wrote back to him that the loan was not important at all and he did not even remember it. He was very pleased to hear from him after all those years, but his heart was weeping that he could not be by his bedside during his last moments.'

Faridkot state

Faridkot had a total population of 199,283. It had a large Sikh population of 115,070 (57.7 per cent) while Muslims were 61,352 (30.7 per cent), and caste Hindus and scheduled caste Hindus were only 21,789 (10.9 per cent). The maharaja of Faridkot had been won over to the Akali cause quite early and the Faridkot military had been involved in a raid on Rajgarh outside Lahore in May 1947. The military and the police raided both urban and rural localities and many Muslims were killed. The maharaja himself supervised the expulsion of the Muslims from Faridkot city. They were not allowed to take with them more than a small piece of luggage (*Disturbances in the Punjab,* 1995: 396). There are different versions about the exit of Muslims from Faridkot. One story, narrated by Haroon Saleem Bhatti's grandmother, is that the maharaja's mother dissuaded him from using force against Muslims, saying that since many of his own soldiers and palace guards had been Muslims he was morally bound not to harm their community. The maharaja, therefore, provided the Muslims safe escort till the Hussainiwalla head works, from where they crossed the border into Pakistan. Another story was told to me by Hassan Din.

Hassan Din

'We were small farmers, living in Faridkot city though we ploughed our fields just outside the city. The Sikhs had begun to menace Muslims from the beginning of August. Then we were told that the maharaja had ordered all Muslims to leave. We were accompanied by the Faridkot military up for some distance and then they turned back. We were several thousand people of all descriptions trudging along. The old were carried on carts and some were seated on bicycles. I remember, in some cases it became impossible to carry the old and weak and people began to abandon them. Often times the older people themselves insisted on being left behind, while they implored their families to try to reach Pakistan as soon as possible. There was no doubt they realised that the situation was hopeless, but as god-fearing Muslims they seemed resigned to their faith. In some cases the other family members would not leave. It was a long convoy so I don't remember what happened to the people who could not continue.

'Just after we reached English territory [He is likely referring to the vicinity of Ferozepore *tahsil*] we were attacked by *jathas* armed with all sorts of weapons. They were shouting and raising slogans. People ran in all directions. My father was holding my hand while my mother was carrying my little sister, who was only six months old. My elder brother and sister were also with us. When the attack took place, we got separated. I was only a small boy. A Sikh on horseback thrust a spear in my father's chest and he fell down with a cry. I started screaming so the Sikh on the horseback went away. Another one came towards me but when he saw me clinging to my father he hesitated and then moved away. Who knows what crossed his mind, but he did not want to kill me.

'There were dead bodies all around, only some children had been spared. Some old women were also spared but they carried away the young girls. My mother and sister were dead. Both had been hit by gunshots. I never found out what happened to my elder brother. Of the several thousand of us who had left Faridkot city, only a few hundred managed to save ourselves by hiding in the fields. In Ferozepore we luckily met some troops led by an English officer. Among them were Muslims who helped us. It took us several days to reach Kasur where we got medical aid from Christians.

'I lived in a camp in Kasur for a few days. The conditions were very bad but we were all in Pakistan and felt safe. Small children like me who had lost all their family and had nobody to take care of were helped by some god-fearing local Muslims who gave us food. The local *maulvis* also did all that they could to help us. Then one day my *mama* found me. He was working in the Civil Secretariat in Lahore. He and his wife were childless so they brought me up as their own son. Life has been a very painful and difficult struggle. I miss both my mother and father. Now I have my own children but the old wounds have never healed.'

Khan Bahadur Malik Khuda Baksh

The testimony of Khan Bahadur Malik Khuda Baksh has been presented with regard to some eastern districts of the pre-Partition British Punjab. He also visited some Sikh states during that period. He had the following to say about them:

Patiala

> A 48-hour curfew was imposed in Patiala town on September 1, 1947 and during this period the Sikhs began killing Muslims. The Muslim leaders are reported to have been called by His Highness and were told that Muslim refugee camps had been set up in the three wards of the town and they would be guarded by Muslim troops. The Muslims of Patiala, therefore, proceeded to these camps. A clash took place between the Muslim troops and the Sikh troops which resulted in the rout of the Muslims. After this the Muslims were ruthlessly murdered. Hundreds of young naked Muslim girls were made to march in a procession through the city and the Sikhs were asked to select whom they liked. I would not say anything about the way which Muslim women were raped in the open and their breasts removed....
>
> In Sirhind Sharif about thirty thousand Muslims had been collected from adjoining villages. I saw this concentration in and around the Khankah of Hazrat Mujadid-i-dul Alfsani. ... It is said that His Highness the Maharaja has declared that this Khankah sould [sic] not be touched till Nankana Sahib is safe. If anything untoward happened to Nankana [Sahib], the same would be done to Sirhind Sharif. .... In Patiala State, Muslims have lost heavily in life and property. In fact Patiala State people are responsible for what has happened in Ambala, Ludhiana and Karnal (1993: 210-12).

Nabha

I got in touch with the prime minister, Nabha, who was kind enough to assure me about the safety of fifteen thousand Muslims, but urged their early evacuation. This is what he wrote:

> I am sending Sardar Rajinder Singh, Deputy Superintendent of Police, to personally acquaint you with the whole situation. The political settlement, the communal madness, the geography of the State and the insufficiency of the Military and Police Force point towards the immediate evacuation of the minority population of Muslims in the State....
>
> The situation in Nabha was causing great anxiety when I left Ambala. I trust the Prime Minister would do all but I doubt if he would succeed in the long run. The evacuation of Nabha people to Bahawalpur seems the only solution (ibid.: 212).

Kalsia

Kalsia was a tiny state with a total population of only 67,393, of which Muslims constituted a large minority of 25,049 or thirty-seven per cent. Khan Bahadur Malik Khuda Baksh writes:

> Kalsia seems to be competing with Patiala in uprooting Muslims. Its geography, however, enables Muslims to escape to Ambala and I believe the loss of life and property has not been so much as in Patiala. I took the Muslims of Dera Bassi (Kalsia State) safely to Mubarikpur Camp (ibid.).

Nalagarh

Nalagarh, a hill state was even smaller. It had a total population of only 52,780. The miniscule Muslim minority was only 6,862 or thirteen per cent only. Khan Bahadur Malik Khuda Baksh writes:

> Frantic telegrams addressed to Syed Ghulam Bhik Narang, M.L.A. of Ambala, showed that the Muslims were being butchered. I wired

His Highness the Maharaja, whom I know personally, to safeguard the life and honour of Muslims. I received a wire from him that he will do his utmost but reports continued to come that the Muslims were being massacred in his State (ibid.: 213).

Khan Bahadur Abdul Aziz, Chief Justice, Jind state

Another detailed report by the former chief justice of Jind state is also available. Some excerpts from it are noted below:

'It cannot be denied for a moment that there was a manifest conspiracy between the Akali leaders, the rulers of Patiala, Nabha and Faridkot states supported by Mr. Patel, the Deputy Prime Minister of the Indian Union' (1993: 190).

He goes on to narrate a number of incidents, including attacks on a train heading towards Pakistan that was attacked at Bhatinda and Dhuri, both within the jurisdiction of Patiala state. Many personnel of the Pakistani dominion were in those trains. A number of fatalities took place. Therefore the Pakistan government had to ban traffic by that route. He thought that if the Pakistani government had taken 'appropriate action' the atrocities that were committed on the trains could have been avoided. He then writes:

> I am definitely of the opinion that Mian Iftikhar-ud-Din [Minister for Rehabilitation in the Pakistani Punjab government] can never succeed in his search to find out 250,000 Muslims missing from Patiala. They were certainly killed and so the search is absolutely futile on his part (ibid.: 192).
>
> As far as Jind State is concerned, where I had to serve for about 9 years, I unhesitatingly observe that this State is fortunate to have an unbiased ruler. He had absolutely no intention to injure his Muslim subjects. Whatever was done in that State was done under the pernicious influence of the rulers of Patiala, Nabha and Faridkot (ibid.).

References

Coupland, Ian. 'The Master and the Maharajas: The Sikh Princes and the East Punjab Massacres of 1947', *Modern Asian Studies*, Vol. 36, No. 3, Cambridge: Cambridge University Press, 2002.

Jeffrey, Robin. 'The Punjab Boundary Force and the Problem of Order, August 1947', *Modern Asian Studies*, Vol. 8, No. 4, Cambridge: Cambridge University Press, 1974.

Aziz, Abdul (Khan Bahadur). 'Report made by Khan Bahadur Abdul Aziz, Chief Judge, Jind State', *The Journey to Pakistan: A Documentation on Refugees of 1947,* 1993, Islamabad: National Documentation Centre, 1993.

Disturbances in the Punjab, Islamabad: National Documentation Centre, 1995.

Malik, Khuda Baksh (Khan Bahadur). 'A brief report made by K. B. Malik Khuda Baksh regarding the districts of Ambala, Karnal, Rothak, Hissar, Simla, Ludhiana and Jullundur', *The Journey to Pakistan: A Documentation on Refugees of 1947,* 1993, Islamabad: National Documentation Centre, 1993.

Muhammad, Mian Noor. 'Patiala ke Musalmanon par Tutne wali Qiamat-e-Sughra: Hissa Dom' (The Mini Day of Judgement that befell the Muslims of Patiala: Part Two) in Chughtai, Hakim Muhammad Tariq Mehmood Abqary Mujadidi (compiler and editor), *1947 ke Muzalim ki Kahani khud Muzlumon ki Zabani* (The Story of the 1947 Atrocities from the Victims' Themselves), Lahore: Ilm-o-Irfan Publishers, 2003.

Rabbani, Chaudhri Ghulam. 'Statement of Ch. Ghulam Rabbani S/0 Ch. Abdul Azia Caste Arain, Contractor, Mohalla Hakiman, Nabha', *The Journey to Pakistan: A Documentation on Refugees of 1947,* 1993, Islamabad: National Documentation Centre, 1993.

Sardar Abdul Aziz. 'Statement of Sardar Abdul Aziz: retired Superintendent of Police, Patiala State', *The Journey to Pakistan: A Documentation on Refugees of 1947,* 1993, Islamabad: National Documentation Centre, 1993.

Sharif, Muhammad Afzal. 'Patiala ke Musalmanon par Tutne wali Qiamat-e-Sughra: Hissa Awwal' (The Mini Day of Judgement that befell the Muslims of Patiala: Part One) in Chughtai, Hakim Muhammad Tariq Mehmood Abqary Mujadidi (compiler and editor), *1947 ke Muzalim ki Kahani khud Muzlumon ki Zabani* (The Story of the 1947 Atrocities from the Victims' Themselves), Lahore: Ilm-o-Irfan Publishers, 2003.

Government publications

The Sikhs in Action. Lahore: Government Prining Press, 1948.
Note on the Sikh Plan. Lahore: Government Prining Press, 1948.

Interviews

Harkishen Singh Surjeet, New Delhi, 21 October 1999
Hassan Din, Lahore, 13 April 2003
Dr Khushi Muhammad Khan, Stockholm, 16 June 2003
Chaudhri Roshan Din, Kallar Syedan, Rawalpindi district, 15 December 2004
Mujahid Al-Hussaini, Faisalabad (Lyallpur), 19 December 2004
Sheikh Nur Muhammad, Lahore, 27 December 2004
Mrs Rajnish Tandon, Hoshiarpur, 3 January 2005
Dr Nizam Din, Malerkotla, 6 January 2005
Chaudhri Abdul Shakoor, Malerkotla, 6 January 2005
Babu Khan, Malerkotla, 6 January 2005
Amrik Chand Ahluwalia, Patiala, 7 January 2005
Pandit Mohan Lal Balo, Patiala, 7 January 2005
Sheikh Muhammad Farooq, Rajgarh, Lahore, 13 January 2005
Basta Singh, Adampur, Fatehgarh district, East Punjab, 28 November 2005
Naugurdial Singh, Adampur, Fatehgarh district, East Punjab, 28 November 2005
Teja Singh, Boran, Fatehgarh district, East Punjab, 28 November 2005
Des Raj, Kakra, East Punjab, 28 November 2005
Jagpal Tiwana, Dartmouth, NS, Canada, via email, 11 April 2007
Mrs B.A. Choudhary, Lahore, (via email sent by her son Dr Muhammad Farooq) 22 July 2007

21

ANALYSIS AND CONCLUSIONS

THE EVENTS LEADING TO THE PARTITION OF THE PUNJAB IN MID-August 1947 have been presented in chronological order, beginning from the 1945 election campaign to the end of 1947, when unwanted minorities had more or less been eliminated from both sides of the divided Punjab. An analysis of those events is attempted in light of the theory of ethnic cleansing presented in Chapter One. On that basis, a conclusion is drawn as to whether the Muslims and/or Sikhs had a grand plan in hand to achieve ethnic cleansing. The study ends with a discussion on identity. It combines theoretical arguments and empirical facts to evaluate identity, in general, and Punjabi identity in particular.

The Punjab in transition: the predicaments of modernity

On a general theoretical level, one can note that after the British annexed the Punjab and decided to modernise and develop it in accordance with their overall colonial strategy, the changes that were wrought began to transform traditional society. As new economic opportunities arose within a capitalist framework, benefits were derived by the Hindus and Sikhs while the Muslims lagged behind. At the beginning of the twentieth century the first signs of Muslim resentment over Hindu and Sikh traders and moneylenders acquiring agricultural land of Muslim owners – big and small – were taken care of with the Punjab Land Alienation Act of 1901, which prohibited non-agricultural castes acquiring agricultural land. Informally, however, the moneylenders continued to do so through

Muslim front men though on a much smaller scale. In spite of such changes, when in July 1947, the Congress and Sikh counsels pleaded their cases before the Punjab Boundary Commission, their contention was that Hindus and Sikhs owned seventy-five to eighty per cent of the property in the Punjab.

On the political level, however, the predominantly Muslim, pro-British Punjab Unionist Party succeeded in establishing an inter-communal power-sharing formula that successfully served as the basis of stability and communal harmony. However, the religious revivals of the early twentieth century generated bad blood between Muslims, Hindus and Sikhs in the towns and cities where the revivals were taking place. They produced 'high cultures', representing standardised, so-called 'purer and authentic' versions of their respective religions. Unsurprisingly, the emphasis was on differences. Such a trend came into conflict with the popular traditions of the Punjab, based on live-and-let-live, that over the centuries had been produced as a result of the efforts of Sufis, *sants* and gurus. The cities and towns were affected most by the religious revivals, which, in political terms, were reflective of religious nationalism.

Consequently, clashes between the revivalist movements took place in urban contexts while in the rural areas the old order continued to be reproduced as it had in the past – people knew their place and largely accepted it. It was a type of composite society that maintained peaceful relations while simultaneously upholding social hierarchy and inequality *within* and *between* them. Traditional values and beliefs encouraged an attitude which made people accept the status quo as something given and unalterable: the long past confirmed the authenticity of the existing situation.

The publication of the *Rangeela Rasul* booklet and the murder of its publisher, Rajpal, at the hands of Ilam Din, followed by Ilam Din's hanging in 1929, were indicative of the problems that a modern society was going to face: freedom of speech upsetting age-old beliefs and relations. The Masjid/Gurdwara Shahidganj controversy followed a few years later in 1935, and exposed the potentiality of mass mobilisation in the name of religion and religious identity. Some communal riots were reported from Multan, Rawalpindi and other urban centres, but largely, the Punjab remained peaceful under the leadership of the Punjab Unionist Party.

Without a doubt, the March 1940 Lahore Resolution adopted by the Muslim League, that demanded separate states for Muslims in Muslim-majority areas, struck a huge blow to the traditional stability and communal harmony in the Punjab. The Hindu and Sikh press assailed it as the 'Pakistan Resolution'. The Sikhs reacted by demanding the partition of the Punjab on a religious basis. Thus, the basic logic of the partition with regard to the Punjab was encapsulated in a simple but explosive formula: if the Muslims get a separate state through the division of India, then the Sikhs should get the same. There is some evidence that the Akali leaders began to cultivate their lobbies in the Sikh princely states but as yet there was no grand Sikh plan in hand. Moreover, no one had a clue in the early 1940s about what exactly the partition would entail in reality.

It was clear that the Muslim League could not attain its objective without undermining the support that the Punjabi Muslim voters had previously given the Unionist Party. After the Lahore Resolution was passed, and more so after Sir Sikander died in December 1942, the leadership contest within the Unionist Party started. Sir Khizr Tiwana could not maintain the support of the landlords who one after the other, began to decamp and join the Muslim League. As yet the stage was not set for the partition of India and the Punjab because the British had not made any categorical announcement about their departure and transfer of power to Indians.

Nevertheless, the politics that gained momentum after the Second World War in India was based on the assumption that the British were prepared to quickly hand over power to the Indians. A change in government in London that brought the Labour Party into power was accompanied by an announcement from the colonial government about the holding of elections to the provincial assemblies and the Constituent Assembly. For all practical purposes, the outcome of the election began to be treated as a referendum on whether India should remain united or it should be partitioned. The partition of both Bengal and the Punjab did not figure as an important theme at that stage.

Stage one

The election campaign that took off in July 1947 in the Punjab did not have the partition of the Punjab on the agenda, although the Sikhs had been warning for a long time that if India was divided, so should the Punjab be. It was only natural that, given their small numbers, the Sikhs could attain such a goal only by aligning themselves with the Punjab Hindus. During the election campaign, the Muslim League targeted the Unionist Party as well the Congress and the Sikhs. While Sir Khizr was assailed as a traitor to Islam and abusive slogans were hurled against him, the discourse against Hindus and Sikhs was laced with demonisation and dehumanisation of those two communities as both 'infidels' and 'exploiters'. This has been recorded in ample measure in the FRs of the Punjab governor and chief secretary. The Unionist Party retaliated by deploying pro-Congress Ahrar orators who tried to question the Islamic credentials of the Muslim League and its leaders, especially Jinnah, but their campaign fell on deaf ears. In the critical period prior to the election campaign – August 1942 to June 1945 – the Congress party across India and in the Punjab was sitting in jail. That gave the Muslim League an opportunity to propagate its mission of achieving 'Pakistan' without a serious challenge.

The Muslim League election campaign in the Punjab was conducted with the help of ethnic activists such as Brelawi clerics, Muslim communists, and Muslim students of Aligarh University. The combined efforts to portray Pakistan as a future paradise on earth captivated the fancy of Muslims, whether or not they were voters. The election results proved to be a recipe for disaster. Fear and anxiety had begun to affect Hindus and Sikhs while the campaign was underway; the results only confirmed their worst fears. The Muslims of the Punjab had voted solidly and incontrovertibly for the Muslim League. The Unionist Party had been rejected. The Sikhs also voted for the Panthic parties – all of which were behind Master Tara Singh and other Akalis, who wanted the Punjab partitioned if Pakistan was created. Moreover, the crucial Hindu Jats of Ambala division had begun to shift loyalty from the Unionist Party to the Congress after Sir Chhotu Ram's death in early 1945. The Hindu Mahasabha, the Ahrar, and other minor parties were eliminated. The three religious communities were now electorally and politically aligned to three political parties. While the Muslim League was clearly the majority party its advantage was entirely representatives of the Muslims. Moreover, it fell short of attaining a parliamentary majority by ten seats.

The Congress and the Sikhs were determined to subvert the Muslim League's bid to form the government in the Punjab and decided to support Sir Khizr as prime minister. The coalition government that took office was formed in consonance with constitutional theory and practice, but it provoked the Muslim League to threaten direct action. Secret government reports had earlier warned that 'private armies' that began to take shape from the start of the election campaign had been growing in number and that the Muslim League National Guards, the RSS, and the Akal Fauj could be dangerous entities in case of a protracted political crisis in the Punjab. However, the actual acceleration towards confrontation was triggered by Sir Khizr when he ordered the police to raid the Muslim League head office in Lakshi Chowk, Lahore. The RSS office was also raided. It was, however, the drama that the raid on the Muslim League created that worsened the Punjab situation. The Muslim League leaders resisted police entry into the premises of the office. They were arrested and, for the first time in the history of the Muslim League, its senior leaders – albeit of a province – were put in prison for defying government orders.

By that time, Muslims in Lahore and in the main cities and town of the Punjab had begun to believe in the righteousness of the 'Pakistan' demand. The police lock-ups and the jails swelled with people volunteering to be arrested. Simultaneously, the damning propaganda barrage against Khizr increasingly turned vicious as the slogan-mongers concocted the filthiest Punjabi abuse to run him down. It is not absolutely clear if Khizr restrained the police and other officials from using the notorious high-handed tactics to quell the agitations that had enveloped the whole of the province or, as government reports suggested obliquely, the overwhelming Muslim administration already sympathised with the Pakistan demand. After all, more than seventy per cent of the police was Muslim. While the latter seems to be closer to the truth, neither does it rule out Khizr's desire to avoid confrontation with the Muslim League. Most of his associates had, by that time, abandoned him and joined the Muslim League. What most certainly demoralised Khizr was the statement issued on 20 February 1947 by the British government that it would transfer power to Indians by June 1948. He could not foresee a political future for himself without the continuation of the Raj.

From the Hindu–Sikh point of view, the election campaign of 1945 and direct action from 24 January to 26 February merely confirmed that they would be left at the mercy of a brute majority. Thus, when Khizr resigned on 2 March – after an agreement with the Muslim League to call off direct action had been reached – the Hindu and Sikh leaders were shocked. Master Tara Singh's histrionics outside the Punjab Legislative Assembly proved the next catalyst in accelerating a confrontation which was bound to get violent short of a miracle. Indeed, such miraculous intervention was in short supply. On the evening of 3 March, the speeches by Hindu Mahasabha and Sikh leaders calling for an all-out war ignited the spark that would set ablaze violent passions and eventually lead to unprecedented communal violence.

The clashes between Hindu–Sikh and Muslim activists on 4 March 1947 in Lahore, followed by similar outbursts in Amritsar, Jullundur, Multan, and Rawalpindi aggravated the volatility whose seeds had been sown for quite some time. The clashes began with unruly Sikh–Hindu agitators shouting anti-Pakistan slogans and Muslim activists challenging them. On 5 March 1947, the situation in the Punjab changed fundamentally when governor's rule was imposed; from that time onwards no elected government was in office. Subsequent efforts to bridge the gap between the Muslim League and its main rivals, the Sikh Panthic Parties and the Punjab Congress, proved unsuccessful.

It is interesting to note that at the outbreak of rioting in Rawalpindi the Sikhs enjoyed the upper hand for a couple of days until the tide turned on 6 March. That evening, Muslim raiders headed towards predominantly Sikh villages surrounded by a sea of Muslim villages and hamlets. Such villages were attacked by large mobs, sometimes running into several thousands, which easily overwhelmed the resistance that was offered. The pogroms and carnages that took place were undoubtedly genocidal – well-planned and executed with the intention of killing. That the Sikhs killed their own women only makes that episode more tragic; it is the code of honour of those times that dictated such behaviour, which outsiders might describe as 'bizarre'.

I sought to enquire from several people who have held senior positions in the civil administration in Pakistan as to why it took so long for the army to arrive in the troubled areas and intervene. The army did not move into such areas till 13 or 14 March, nearly a week after the initial outbreak of violence. The villages were not more than an hour or two's drive from the Northern Command's headquarters in Rawalpindi and it is impossible to believe that the British officers had no access to intelligence provided by their own agencies.

Not one of those I spoke with could come up with a convincing explanation. They agreed that a conspiracy of sorts to let blood spill, perhaps locally, could not be discounted. Perhaps such an episode was necessary to precipitate the partition of both India and Pakistan. The fact that the creation of Pakistan had gained support from the British military is referred to in an earlier chapter. We also know, however, that the British favoured a united Punjab. The riots in the Punjab created a wedge between Muslims and Sikhs that significantly diminished the chances of the Punjab remaining united. Thousands of Sikhs shifted to central and eastern Punjab and many of the younger lot began to organise themselves for battle with Muslims if the Punjab was partitioned in a way that did not satisfy them. Thus one of the consequences – intended or unintended – was that it provided the Sikh movement a corps of ethnic activists who carried with them the accounts of atrocities by Muslims wherever they went and settled. Such dissemination of anti-Muslim propaganda most certainly demonised and dehumanised the Muslims in the eyes of the Sikhs.

Based on my own reckoning, the Punjab administration anticipated rioting only in urban trouble spots. It was thus ill-prepared to respond quickly against raids in villages in the Rawalpindi, Attock (Campbellpur), and Jhelum districts. Moreover, the colonial government had probably already decided in March 1947 not to commit British soldiers to troubled areas but to keep them in Rawalpindi in order to safeguard European lives. That factor may have played some role in the slow response, if the military authorities in Rawalpindi were unsure of what brief they had in hand to deal with such a situation. Anyhow, the importance of the riots in the three districts of the Rawalpindi division cannot be underestimated.

One can also wonder if the news about communal killings in Calcutta and Bihar reached the Punjab and played some role in turning Muslims against the Hindus and Sikhs. The closest to an answer is the testimony of Dr Jagdish Sarin, who worked as a volunteer in a refugee camp in Jhelum and heard many victims narrate that Muslims from Bihar and UP had sought refuge in the Rawalpindi area. Accounts of the savagery practised against them by the Hindus and Sikhs probably inflamed the local Muslims of northern Punjab to seek revenge. Neither Sir Evan Jenkins nor General Messervy mentions this connection, though it is highly plausible that the news of events in Bihar and Calcutta could have played some role in fomenting anger among Muslims. There is ample evidence to suggest that demobilised Muslim army personnel were involved in planning and executing the attacks in the villages. It is possible that some of them had been enraged by what they saw in Bihar. In one case at least, in the case of Parial village, Attock district, one finds evidence that those who threw grenades into the Sikh *gurdwara* had recently returned from Bihar.

Could there have been a Hindu hand behind the events in Rawalpindi? In Pakistani propaganda, the Hindu hand existed by default in all that went wrong in the pre-Partition era; the same continued after Partition. With regard to the riots in northern Punjab in March 1947, the answer must be an emphatically negative one. The Hindus were a small minority in northern Punjab. They could not have been able to influence the events in the villages unless one believes that the Muslim raiders had been bribed by them, which borders on the absurd. The interim government in Delhi at that time included not only the Congress but also Muslim League ministers as well as Sikhs. Such a government had no power or authority to interfere in the Punjab. Under the 1935 act, executive powers in a meaningful sense were vested in the governor-general (who was also viceroy).

On the other hand, when the Congress came out on 8 March 1947 in support of the Sikh demand to partition the Punjab, it became clear that it was not only the Muslim League high command, but also the Congress, that were going to obstruct any resolution to the Punjab problem that did not meet their own objectives at the all-India level. Most certainly, such a move complicated matters in terms of the Muslim

League being able to muster a majority and forming the government in the Punjab. The Muslim League occasionally did approach the Punjab governor to let it form the government. This was, however, overruled by Sir Evan Jenkins both on grounds of administrative difficulties – as the Sikhs threatened violent action – as well as that the Muslim League's failure to gather a stable and reliable majority in Parliament. It remains a moot point what direction the Punjab would have taken if a Muslim League government had been installed in office; that, of course, was impossible without the support of Sikhs or the Congress, or both. On the other hand, since the Muslim League agitation had brought down the coalition government of Sir Khizr Tiwana, there was no moral reason why the Sikhs and the Congress would lend it support.

The Muslim League leadership did little to placate the fears of the minorities. Jinnah had issued a strong condemnation of the attacks on Muslims in Bihar but remained silent on the riots in the Punjab. Justice Munir mentions that Jinnah had instructed him to ensure that the attacks on the Sikhs ceased, but there is no recorded public statement that would confirm that. At the same time, there is evidence of the involvement of Muslim League cadres and local politicians in the attacks in northern Punjab on the Sikhs. In any case, the colonial order was still intact despite the declining impartiality and efficacy of the administration. By the end of March 1947, tensions and conflict subsided; the suspicions, fears and concomitant anxieties, however, remained undiminished and in fact were greatly exacerbated.

Such developments in the Punjab were also reflective of the failure at the all-India level of the British government to make the Indian leaders agree to a united India that Britain wanted to maintain even after colonial rule ended in the subcontinent. The Cabinet Mission was the last major effort in that direction but when it failed the result was the proliferation of organised violence that claimed thousands of lives in Calcutta and Bihar. It was only a matter of time before that contagion would afflict the Punjab where the election campaign and results had created a most explosive situation. The interim government that had been formed proved nothing more than a toothless ministry constituted by ministers representing irreconcilable interests. The end of the Wavell viceroyalty and the beginning of the last viceroyalty of Louis

Mountbatten coincided with the slight and temporary improvement in the Punjab situation.

Stage two

During the second stage in the partition of the Punjab, beginning in April 1947, the centre of gravity initially shifted to Delhi, where Mountbatten rather hastily came to the conclusion that since trust and goodwill did not exist between the Congress and Muslim League leaders, India could not be kept united. He, therefore, began to sound out the leaders of the two parties on their views on joining the British Commonwealth. He had probably been instructed by London to keep India united or divided in the British Commonwealth. In his private discussions with Jinnah, Mountbatten took the view that if India did not join the Commonwealth, it would be difficult to accept only Pakistan as a member. With Nehru, meanwhile, Mountbatten deployed the tactic that if India did not join the Commonwealth then India would be partitioned; Jinnah was determined that Pakistan should remain in the Commonwealth. Such pressure tactics ensured that both parties agreed to join the Commonwealth.

It was from such a vantage point that Mountbatten then sought to address the Punjab issue. The Punjab governors had been pleading that it should remain united as they could not find any natural cut-off point from where the Punjab could be partitioned neatly and would be acceptable to all parties. Mountbatten sponsored a number of meetings between Jinnah and the Maharaja of Patiala, and joined at least one of those meetings. Jinnah and the maharaja had brought with them their advisers. Jinnah was prepared to make very generous concessions if the Sikhs agreed not to demand a division of the Punjab. He proposed almost a Sikh state within the Pakistani state, but the Sikh leaders were not convinced. The Muslim–Sikh relations had never recovered from the adverse fall-out of the Masjid/Gurdwara Shahidganj conflict, and the carnage of Sikhs in northern Punjab only solidified the wall that had been rising between them. No doubt the Congress had also been cultivating the Sikhs and that most certainly impeded a Muslim-League–Sikh rapprochement. Moreover, the fact that a Hindu–Sikh composite identity was shared by many Khatri and Arora families of the Punjab probably created ethnic biases in favour of union with India. At the level of propaganda, historical memory of the persecution of the Sikh gurus by the Mughals acted as a wedge between Muslims and Sikhs.

The net result was that Jinnah's belated wooing of the Sikh leaders in May 1947 fell flat. In any case, Mountbatten had made an effort to facilitate talks between Jinnah and the Sikhs to reach an understanding on the unity of the Punjab. There is, therefore, no basis to suspect that Mountbatten was hostile to the Muslim League at that stage. It is only after those talks failed that Mountbatten made up his mind that the Punjab would also need to be divided. Jinnah's plea that the Bengalis and Punjabis were cultural nations that could not be divided was poor logic; it failed to carry the day because it contradicted his main stand that Hindus and Muslims comprised two separate nations.

Sir Khizr Tiwana proposed that, as one united entity, the Punjab could be considered directly for membership in the British Commonwealth without joining either India or Pakistan. Such a scheme did not receive any backing from the British government. It was a novel idea but probably too radical for the British to consider at that late a stage since they had developed the praxis of dealing only primarily with the Congress and Muslim League as representatives of 'Indian' opinion. The leadership of neither party would have supported such a scheme.

The most controversial move in the unfolding Partition drama was undoubtedly Mountbatten's decision to bring forward the date of Partition to mid-August 1947 instead of June 1948. Apparently, Mountbatten had taken Nehru into confidence about what he was thinking. For most other politicians the announcement of the imminent Partition date came as a shock. Therefore, while Mountbatten must be held responsible for the disastrous consequences, Nehru bears responsibility for not opposing it when it was mentioned to him in private. In any event, the June 3 Partition Plan prescribed not only the division of India but also of Bengal and Punjab, provided it produced according to procedure, the result that required that Bengal and Punjab be divided on the basis of contiguous Muslim and non-Muslim majorities, and 'other factors'. The Punjab Assembly voted to partition the province.

Concurrently, in the Punjab itself, communal violence had begun to rise again with some gruesome incidents taking place in Amritsar in April. It was the Muslims who were responsible for it. This much was acknowledged by Chief Secretary, Akhtar Hussain. The infamous bangle–henna incident which incensed the Muslim *badmashes* and *goondas* of Lahore was a provocation that originated with the Muslim criminal elements of Amritsar. It resulted in the escalation of assaults and arson in Lahore. From the middle of May onwards, the situation in Lahore deteriorated by the day. A Hindu–Sikh reprisal backed by the forces of the princely states of Nabha and Faridkot on the Muslim locality of Rajgarh outside Lahore, only exacerbated the processes of polarisation between Muslims and the Hindus and Sikhs. By the end of May, fires were raging mainly in the Hindu localities of the walled city of Lahore.

Sir Evan Jenkins noted that the announcement of the 3 June Partition Plan did not rouse much enthusiasm among the Punjabis. However, it made the task easier for the criminal elements and their political patrons and sympathisers in the administration to escalate violence. The conspiracy to set Shahalmi ablaze is a classic case of the way the violence was being carried out. The Shahalmi fire broke the back of the Lahore Hindus who till then seemed determined to remain in the city, notwithstanding their fewer numbers. The Congress leadership, including Gandhi, encouraged them to stay put. After the night of 21–22 June, when large portions of Shahalmi were set on fire, the Hindus panicked and their exit from Lahore began to assume significant proportions. The partiality and partisan role of the Punjab administration then took the form of direct complicity to actively side with one's co-religionists. In the case of Lahore, it meant that the Muslims enjoyed the upper hand and even services such as the fire brigade were no longer willing to play their role faithfully. Things continued as usual in the countryside. Some Sikh plan to make the Muslims of East Punjab pay the price for the wrongs done by their co-religionists to Sikhs in Muslim-majority areas may have gained greater relevance, but it was not time yet to implement it.

The authority of the Punjab governor was increasingly being flouted but the façade of a colonial power represented by civil servants, police officers and the Indian Army as well as British forces was still intact. That façade did constrain the Punjab degenerating into a Hobbesian state of nature, but it was only a matter of time when such power and authority would be gone. As noted earlier, the Hindus and Sikhs had begun to pull eastwards; housebreaking to loot was beginning to emerge as a strong motive for attacking Hindus and Sikhs. They were the most prosperous communities of the Punjab and the Muslims were most numerous. Such a lopsided reality was bound to generate mundane aims and objectives and produce a cumulative effect. The RSS did try to hit back in Lahore but it was no match for the resources that the Muslim League *badmashes* could muster with the help of a biased administration. Thus, June ended with the partition of the Punjab agreed through a constitutional process, but with a situation in which constitutional and legal bases for action were becoming increasingly irrelevant.

At the central level, the 4 July announcement by Jinnah that he would be the governor-general of Pakistan, and not Mountbatten, enraged the latter. The discussions on Partition had thus far been based on the assumption that Mountbatten would be responsible for its completion and that would mean him being the governor-general for both dominions. Jinnah's decision to award the governor-general position to himself was a slight that Mountbatten was not going to forgive easily. The record of the conversation between them brings that out vividly. The personal nature of the decision can be gauged from the fact that Jinnah decided to have British heads of the Pakistan armed forces as well as governors of the provinces. Many of the senior officers in the armed forces were also British. Mountbatten's alleged antipathy towards Pakistan probably originated after Jinnah's 4 July decision to make himself governor-general of Pakistan. However, as noted earlier, till at least 1 August 1947, Mountbatten was insisting that Pakistan should be given a fair share of the fighting services, including armament and other equipment. It seems more likely that his alleged bias against Pakistan began to influence his policies effectively after he became the Governor-General of India on 15 August 1947. From that time onwards, he represented the interests of the Indian state and government.

In any case, committees were created to supervise the division of territory and assets. Among them, undoubtedly, the most crucial was the Punjab Boundary Commission. An analysis of the Radcliffe Award is presented in earlier chapters; suffice it to say that considerable controversy surrounds it with regard to Mountbatten and Nehru allegedly conspiring to change its contents in a manner that three of the four *tahsils* of

Gurdaspur district were awarded to India and thus the road link to Kashmir via Pathankot *tahsil*. On the other hand, the fact remains that the Radcliffe Award was almost identical to the Wavell's Demarcation Plan of 7 February 1946. The only difference was appropriation of small portions of Kasur *tahsil* from the Lahore district in order to obtain a border that ran roughly equidistant between Lahore and Amritsar.

In the Punjab itself from July onwards, the locus of organised violent assaults on minorities began to expand eastwards. Sikh *jathas* that the Punjab administration had been warning about were waiting in the wings and started targeting Muslims on a rapidly increasing basis. The availability of troops under British officers was woefully inadequate and in case of further escalation, a total breakdown of law and order was most likely. The small Punjab Boundary Force became active from 1 August and took some punitive measures against Sikh marauders but such measures by no means could stem the communal attacks that were taking place in many parts of the Punjab. Awareness about the implications and ramifications of the partition of the Punjab, it seems, was not dispersed widely in the rural areas. Most people in the villages far away from Lahore and Amritsar remained poorly informed about it, if at all.

Consequently, while communication between the Hindu–Sikh groups and Muslims progressively diminished, that within the communities was poorly established from the very beginning and remained so till the time of Partition. Rural people of all communities suffered because of a lack of information and guidance from their leaders. Of all the people, the Muslims of East Punjab, especially those in the villages and the princely states, remained in the dark about the decision to partition the Punjab. Unlike the Hindus and Sikhs in the Muslim-majority districts of central, northern, and western Punjab, they were not attacked in a recurring manner till about the beginning of July. They were thus hardly aware of what could happen if the Punjab was divided.

On 12 August, the first large-scale movement of East Punjab Muslims westwards was noted by Jenkins. Up until then from March 1947, the outflow had been eastwards and that of Hindus and Sikhs. Then the whole of the Punjab was gravely disturbed. Jenkins' last FR and his telegrams on 13 and 14 August leave no doubt that the Punjab was descending into anarchy and chaos. He remarked that it was the responsibility of the administrations that come into power in the two Punjabs from

15 August onwards to bring the situation under control. Nevertheless, the continuation of an administration, albeit one that was losing control all the time, had meant that the casualties remained rather low: perhaps ten to fifteen thousand, though Jenkins gave a lower estimate.

Stage three

The final stage in the partition of Punjab briefly represented the Hobbesian nightmare, the State of Nature that exists when the State disappears, along with its law-and-order machinery. Being bonafide inhabitants of a place in the old Punjab became irrelevant. However, Hobbes did not discuss a scenario when an existing civil state disappears and society is plunged into chaos and anarchy, but the nightmarish situation gives way to something even far more sinister: the Partisan State which becomes complicit in the killing or forced expulsion of unwanted minorities. The administrations on both sides of the divided Punjab represented practically two independent entities although they were technically part of the new independent dominions of India and Pakistan.

At the all-India level, the final stage in the partition of the Punjab fully exposed the taboo nurtured in the viceroy's charmed circle of associates, left unchallenged by the native leaders: that a division of the Punjab would not entail a transfer of populations as well. Jinnah had, after the massacres of Muslims in Bihar, proposed, in November 1946, the transfer of populations between India and Pakistan. The Sikhs also floated that idea before colonial rule ended, but hardcore realism had no takers. Pluralism was the Congress's official ideology and the Muslim League had not rejected it, either, though the idea of a Muslim state was not exactly commensurate with pluralism. Moreover, Mountbatten had deluded himself into believing that whereas officialdom should have the right to decide which administration they wanted to serve ordinary people should stay put because a change of personnel will not affect the neutrality of the administration.

There was no empirical basis for taking such a position. On the contrary, all the evidence at hand pointed to the inevitability of a bloodbath. In particular, the intentions of the Sikh leaders were no secret. Neither India nor Pakistan have published official reports akin to the FRs that were written by the British governors or the chief secretaries. Under the circumstances, what happened in the two Punjabs can be gauged only with the help of first-person accounts as well as secondary sources, based also on first-person accounts, of the events that transpired in the Punjab from 15 August 1947 till the end of that year.

In the Pakistani Punjab, the exit of Hindus and Sikhs had been going on for months. An estimated half a million had already crossed the border to safety before the Radcliffe Award was made public. Others were put to flight as soon as power was handed over to the new administration. Punjab Governor Sir Francis Mudie did not mince words when he said that the Hindus and Sikhs had to be forced to leave in order to make room for the hundreds of thousands of Muslim refugees that headed towards Pakistan. It seems, however, that a grand plan to drive Hindus and Sikhs out of West Punjab did not exist, but that became inevitable as the influx from East Punjab not only created enormous problems of rehabilitating them but their stories of barbaric treatment in East Punjab infuriated the Muslims on the western side. Therefore attacks on the Hindus and Sikhs increased as did the pressure on them to leave.

On the other hand, there is no reason to doubt that the Sikh leadership involving the Akalis as well as some rulers of princely states had made up their mind to empty East Punjab of all Muslims. It was put into operation immediately after 17 August, when the Radcliffe Award became known to the general public. Next day, which coincided with the Islamic festival of Eid, proved to be the day when all hell broke loose on the nearly six million Muslim minority. Most of the Muslims were unarmed peasants, who had no clue that they would be forced to leave their ancestral abodes. The attacks on them, no doubt, had been planned much earlier, but remained in abeyance till such time that the conditions were ripe. The attacks took place much in the same way that Sikh villages were raided in March 1947; only the scale was many times bigger. No doubt Hindus were involved in financing the attacks but it was mostly Sikhs who took part in them. In the Hindi-speaking eastern districts, Hindu Jats also took part in the attacks on Muslims. The lawless Partisan State materialised in the fullest sense in the Sikh princely states, where preparations to expel Muslims had been underway for a long time. The PBF had no jurisdiction in the princely states and that made it easier to attack Muslims.

The evidence that has been provided on the conventional British territories of the East shows that although Ludhiana had also been included in the districts (initially it was not) there was no notable activity of the PBF in its rural areas, where the assaults on the Muslims were vicious, second only to those in Patiala state. Did the Muslims of Malerkotla escape the knife because the Sikhs would not attack them as Guru Gobind Singh had disapproved of it? Or is it because the Muslims inside the Malerkotla territory were armed and would have put up resistance? The truth must be a combination of both.

With regard to evidence of the involvement of the leadership of the three communities, while Master Tara Singh, the Maharaja of Patiala and the Crown Prince of Kapurthala were named by some eyewitnesses, we also learn that Sardar Patel was involved in financing bomb factories. He also goaded the Sikhs to kill the Muslims of Lahore – though by 12 or 13 August it was too late, because the Muslims had acquired the upper hand in that city. There is some evidence that the Pakistan government was involved in the attack at Kamoke on a train full of Hindu and Sikh refugees. The orders to attack its occupants had come from the central Cabinet, and that means that at least Prime Minister Liaqat Ali Khan was aware of it. The attack had been sanctioned as deterrence to the attacks that were going on in East Punjab on the Muslim minority. We also learn that Nehru and Gandhi used their influence to save Muslim lives. The Khaksars of Rawalpindi and Amritsar Communists played a leading role in saving lives.

Forewarned is forearmed

If we now analyse the events in the two Punjabs, the hypothesis that 'forewarned is forearmed' is confirmed in terms of the number of people available for targeting, their relative preparation to defend themselves and the preparations of those who wanted to attack them. We proceed on the assumption that there were 3.8 million Hindus and Sikhs in West Punjab and 5.9 million Muslims – M. Hassan, Secretary, West Pakistan Board of Economic Inquiry, gave that count in the end of October 1947 but was most certainly referring to the population strengths before the Radcliffe Award was announced. If, now, 500,000 Hindus and Sikhs had already moved to safe havens and the large-scale movement of Muslims took place only from 12 August 1947 onwards, as Sir Evan Jenkins reported, then potentially far more Muslims were available for violent assault than Hindus and Sikhs. More important to note is that whereas Sikhs bore *kirpans* as part of their religious right, this was not true of Hindus or Muslims. Thus, in both defensive and offensive roles, the Sikhs enjoyed an advantage. If now we remember that a Sikh network had already come into being in the aftermath of the attacks on them in Hazara and then in Rawalpindi, then the preparation among them to launch revenge attacks on Muslims were much more advanced than those of the Muslims.

It seems that the tales of attacks carried out in March 1947 on Sikhs in northern Punjab by Muslims, many of whom were also ex-servicemen, had become the model the *jathas* were determined to replicate on a scale that dwarfed those let loose against their co-religionists in the spring. The scale of attacks in West Pakistan, on the other hand, even after the announcement of the Radcliffe Award, never reached anywhere in that vicinity. There is no doubt that the preparation of the Sikhs to wipe out all Muslims from East Punjab was very thorough. Therefore once the restraints and constraints that the colonial state imposed were removed, the Sikhs enjoyed the upper hand in those areas where the vestiges of the colonial state did not exist at all – the Sikh states of East Punjab. Thus when comparing the two different theatres of violence there can be no doubt the organised violence on the unarmed Muslim minority of East Punjab was far more thorough and effective.

The context

The hypothesis that 'forewarned is forearmed', therefore, needs to be refined because the environment in which the attacks took place in the princely states was very different from that of East and West Punjab. No doubt, partisan administrations took over in both East and West Punjab but that did not mean that the restraints from the immediate British period ceased to exist altogether. With the exception of the rural areas of Ludhiana district in East Punjab, where the assault on Muslims seemed to have taken place without any hindrance – just as it happened in northern Punjab from the night of 6 March to 13 March 1947 – some modicum of a 'law and order' agency remained intact. However, in those princely states where the rulers had entered into the conspiracy to expel all Muslims from their territories, neither the PBF nor any other such body was present for at least a couple of months to monitor the situation, systematic genocidal attacks could take place in relative secrecy. Later, the joint rescue units of the Indian and Pakistan armies carried out rescue missions and we learn from Maj. General Syed Wajahat Husain that one such unit saved many Muslim lives in Kapurthala state, while Lt. General Aftab Ahmad Khan saved Hindu and Sikh lives in West Punjab, especially the areas around Montgomery (Sahiwal). However, such units were also not everywhere, and wherever foot convoys or people in trains were without armed escort, they were attacked on both sides of the border.

If 200,000–250,000 Muslims only from Patiala state were missing in November 1947, as Mian Iftikharuddin had reported, and they did not come over to Pakistan afterwards, then the loss of life in only one place almost equals the loss of life in West Punjab. The Muslims whose evidence has been presented in this book talk of the loss of life on a scale of thousands. The more neutral and scholarly Khosla report has provided convincing data to establish that between December 1946 and December 1947, Hindus and Sikhs in the western Punjab were subjected to recurring aggression by Muslims. If 250,000 Hindus and Sikhs died in West Punjab, then at least an equal number of Muslims must have died in East Punjab. This is admitted by both the Khosla and the patently partisan SGPC reports. In fact, both obliquely concede that more Muslims lost their lives in East Punjab.

This investigation was not designed to provide a conclusive empirical basis for establishing the total fatalities in the Punjab, but it cannot be denied in light of the observation of many other scholars that more Muslims perished in East Punjab than Hindus and Sikhs together in West Punjab. It is clear from the stories from East Punjab, especially Ludhiana district and the princely states, that the attacks on Muslims were large-scale and claimed thousands of lives. It therefore seems reasonable to assume that the Muslim loss of life in East Punjab was somewhere between 250,000 and 500,000. The total loss of life for the whole Punjab province, including the British territories and the princely states, would then be between 500,000–750,000, with Muslims suffering more losses, in spite of the fact that till the beginning of July 1947 the main victims were Hindus and Sikhs. A portion of all violent deaths included women and girls being killed by their own family members and co-religionists so that the enemy group did not get hold of them and defile family and community honour; as well as those women and girls who killed themselves for the same reason, usually by drowning themselves in water wells. However, the total loss of life from January to December 1947 was not the result entirely of violence but also due to nature's scourge in the form of torrential monsoon rains, floods and epidemics. Thousands perished on the way to, or in, the refugee and relief camps.

The three stages: a cumulative process

From the above analysis, it should not be difficult to identify linkages between the three stages – the preceding stage creating conditions for the next one. Social capital, deriving from a shared Punjabi identity, began to dissipate when political entrepreneurs and ethnic activists shifted emphasis on differences and conflicts from the real and imagined past as well as present. Communication failures between communities and parties, in turn, generated fear and angst among common folk. With the disintegration of state machinery and government, victims could be targeted both randomly or through selection. If we include the uncertainties that must have prevailed at the highest levels of the British administration in the Punjab, the outcomes of intended and unintended consequences of actions at the level of high politics, organised groups of ethnic activists and the people in general, it is not difficult to understand that the situation got out of control, creating situations of anarchy and chaos of different intensities. In particular, bands of armed men on both sides carried out the worst attacks. Already, from March 1947, nexuses comprising politicians, criminal gangs, and partisan officials in the administration collaborated to carry out crimes against humanity. Neighbours largely did not take part in attacks on neighbours, though rogue elements were found even among them. At no point did the pogroms and massacres degenerate into a war of communities. The transfer of power to the Indian and Pakistani administrations removed the constraining factor in the middle. Hence, ethnic conflict resulted in forced migration and, in turn, ethnic cleansing. During all the three stages we find ample evidence of people helping and protecting members of the demonised group. Such succour was rendered even to complete strangers, and at huge personal risk.

Motivations

The motivations for taking part in the attacks may have been ideological or religious, and even the survival instinct must have been a factor. However, the urge to loot and plunder and capture females of the enemy group most certainly animated many who took part in the raids. This way, it was not only grave economic loss that was inflicted on the enemy, but also loss of honour. The 'retributive genocide' that Paul Brass talks about was about both self-righteous ethno-centrism and an opportunity to get hold of the possessions of the demonised and dehumanised Other.

It is interesting to note that in Pakistan, only the so-called untouchable Hindus survived all over the Punjab – primarily to continue performing unclean tasks in West Punjab. On the other hand, during my visits to East Punjab, I heard that here and there Muslims from the working castes (non-landowning) had remained behind. Therefore, on both sides, capturing the land and other property was a very strong factor in joining the raids on the enemy. Equally, if the working castes wanted to remain, they were allowed to do so in some places. Therefore, the partition of the Punjab was most certainly a very attractive proposition for those seeking material benefit out of the crimes against humanity that they partook in.

Ethnic cleansing or genocide?

Which is the more appropriate description of what happened in the Punjab in 1947, ethnic cleansing or genocide? The answer is quite easy:

it was without any doubt the first case of ethnic cleansing after World War II. There is no evidence to support that either the Muslim League or the Sikhs upheld an ideology that required that a demonised and dehumanised pariah group of human beings must be rendered physically extinct to achieve their political objective. No doubt, planned genocidal attacks did take place in March 1947 against the Sikhs and again in the period August–November 1947, when the whole of Punjab was disturbed. Such attacks took place against whosoever was in a more vulnerable position. In particular, organised terror against the Muslims of East Punjab bore all the characteristics of retributive genocide. Yet the overriding intention seems to have been that of getting rid of unwanted populations; using force was the way to achieve it.

However, if there were no exit routes then ethnic cleansing could not have been achieved without genocide, which could include not only physical annihilation but forced conversions when possible. Therefore, if one looks at the end product we learn that some ten million Punjabis had become unwanted minorities, and force and terror were used to get rid of them. This was achieved through a loss of somewhere between 500,000 to 750,000 lives.

Concluding remarks

On the basis of the above discussion, we can now proffer some conclusions with regard to the question of a Muslim versus a Sikh plan of ethnic cleansing:

Was there a Muslim plan to eradicate Hindus and Sikhs from the Punjab or in case of its division from the Pakistani Punjab?

The SGPC report alleged that a grand plan to drive out all Hindus and Sikhs from pre-Partition Punjab existed from the time the demand for Pakistan was made in 1940. It consisted of ideological and political dimensions that produced a mindset in which systematic demonisation and dehumanisation of Hindus and Sikhs prepared the Muslims to attack them without mercy. Had the Muslim League won the whole of Punjab they would have forced the Hindus and Sikhs to flee so that no trace of such unwanted minorities remained in Pakistan.

Such a conclusion is not easily warranted. There is evidence that suggests that even in a divided Punjab, the Muslim League had no clear policy on how to deal with the minorities. Evidence from some Hindu and Sikh accounts also suggest that they believed that once the rioting was over they would be able to come back. Ram Parkash Kapur's account of the responses of some of the top Muslim League leaders in Lahore suggests that even after Pakistan had come into being, they were urging his father to stay on. They did reverse their advice a few weeks later, when Muslim refugees from East Punjab poured into Lahore. Such a decision was reflective of *realpolitik* rather than premeditated conspiracy. Also, in the outlying districts, where Hindus and Sikhs were present in insignificant numbers, the attacks on them did not take place till sometime in September. On the other hand, no doubt the assault on Sikh villages of northern Punjab were planned and carried out along military lines and some Rawalpindi-level Muslim League leaders took part in the mob attacks. Was all this part of an agenda that had already been agreed secretly by the Muslim League? No conclusive and incontrovertible evidence has been found in this investigation.

One can, of course, conclude that since the partition of India on a religious basis was unacceptable to the Hindus and Sikhs and they countered it by demanding the partition of the Punjab, the zero-sum game that ensued could not be resolved through rational argumentation. Under the circumstances, resorting to violence remained the main solution to such an impasse. In other words, even when no strong evidence exists to suggest that a grand plan was ever considered and implemented by the Muslim League to eradicate Hindus and Sikhs from the Punjab, the demand for a partition of India on a religious basis was inherently discriminatory. Since the Hindus and Sikhs were not willing to live in such a state that they perceived would be based on Islamic law, which would be inherently discriminatory against them, an armed confrontation to resolve the contest was inevitable.

One of the theoretical arguments set forth in Chapter One is that when two or more groups claim the same territory and neither is willing to concede defeat, the resolutions of such a dispute is likely through the weaker group being forced to flee such territory or, much worse, liquidated physically. Therefore, even if a grand Muslim League plot to eradicate all Hindus and Sikhs from an undivided Punjab was not hatched earlier, the ideas, ideology and politics it adopted in undivided Punjab created conditions that resulted in the partition of the Punjab, albeit demanded by Sikhs and backed by the Congress. Quite simply, if India was to be partitioned, the Sikhs and the Congress were determined that the Muslim League would not get the whole of Punjab. In other words, even without a proper plan and strategy to drive out Hindus and Sikhs from West Punjab, the Muslim League inevitably created conditions that would result in the breakup of the province and concomitant ethnic cleansing.

Moreover, the Muslim League leaders were fatuously complacent and irresponsible for not realising that their Pakistan scheme would inevitably imperil the lives of millions of unarmed Muslims. That a decision to divide the Punjab had already been taken in June 1947 and approved by the Punjab Assembly should have at least been circulated to the Muslims of eastern Punjab. One argument in defence of the Muslim League leaders could be that they continued to believe that there would be no need for the transfer of population. Considering that the Sikhs had been threatening with dire consequences if the Partition did not give them what they wanted, some advance warning should have been issued and circulated among the Muslims of East Punjab. On the contrary, in some places the Muslims were told to stay put. In Amritsar, this continued to be the policy which was followed till things spun out of control.

Was there a Sikh plan to eradicate Muslims from East Punjab?

One is almost tempted to answer: Yes, there was. This conclusion needs to be heavily qualified, however. The Akali leaders had been actively canvassing support from the Sikh princes for a Sikh state in eastern Punjab and at least the Maharaja of Patiala had begun to nurture such an ambition allegedly on the advice of an astrologer. Some other princes were also party to it. However, such a plan was a conditional or rather contingent plan. An undivided India would have made it irrelevant, but a divided Punjab conferred on it the urgency that resulted in a systematic onslaught on the East Punjab Muslims. Nevertheless, it is important to realise that the Sikhs must have been greatly worried about the failure in achieving the Sikh state. They were a minority in the Punjab, but also spread all over it. Any partition of the Punjab would have divided them if it remained peaceful. That is why even when they rejected Jinnah's generous offer in May 1947 as well as those that were brokered subsequently by Sir Penderel Moon in July, they kept on wavering till the very end, unsure of how to achieve their goal.

However, they did have a contingency plan if the Punjab was divided and it was based on the use of force and terror to make the Muslims run for their lives from East Punjab. Therefore, the Sikhs in particular had a special interest in expelling Muslims – if not Hindus at that time – in order to concentrate their co-religionists in those parts of the Punjab they wanted to become a Sikhistan or Khalistan. Such an objective necessitated the use of brutal force and the Sikhs had made preparations accordingly. The weapons they used in some cases included even machine guns and other automatic weapons. The transition from colonial to Indian rule provided the opportunity to quickly realise ethnic cleansing in a matter of a few months.

The SGPC report endeavours to prove that the Muslim League had a definite plan to drive Hindus and Sikhs out of the Punjab while the Sikhs were only reacting to it. This is reasonable but it does not preclude that the Sikhs had such a contingency plan in hand to react and when the occasion and opportunity arose they implemented it with far greater determination than the way the Hindus and Sikhs were forced out of West Punjab. Equally, it is reasonable to argue that the Muslim League had no grand plan from the beginning but its politics and ideology produced such explosive situations that every trigger pulled on the way intensified the processes of forced migration and ethnic cleansing.

Consequently, the significance of a Sikh plan with regard to the partition of the Punjab must be put in perspective. It does not prove that the Sikhs were hell-bent on the partition of the Punjab to attain a Sikh state; rather, if the Punjab were partitioned in a way that was unacceptable to them, they were going to resort to organised violence and force Muslims to vacate East Punjab.

Punjab: A plural or a pluralist-composite culture?

A careful examination of the accounts of pre-Partition Punjab does not warrant a definitive stand on the exact nature of inter-communal relations and interaction. Was it a province in which a number of religious communities lived side-by-side but without becoming part of a single Punjabi entity – a plural society as Kuper argues or, a pluralist-composite culture that despite the fact of religious differences also constituted a cultural whole which was not merely a sum total of the variegated population? The fact that the Punjab was severed and ruptured in a most gory manner would suggest that the distinctions and separate existence of the three communities was real – in other words, at least Muslims on the one hand and Hindus and Sikhs on the other lived in a plural order without cohesion and solidarity among them.

Such an inference does not follow automatically and in an unproblematic manner, though it seems that there is a grain of truth in it. After the partition of the Punjab, no comparable slaughter of citizens has taken place either in West or East Punjab, but then, a collapse of the state and structure of authority comparable to 1947 has not taken place either. However, West Punjab did not transform into a homogenous unit in terms of ethnicity and identity. As argued in the chapter on ethnic cleansing, identity, individual and collective, is both self-defined and other-defined. It is relational, not something given or fixed. Also, differences by themselves do not result in conflict. They have to be politicised. Consequently, homogeneity is not entirely a matter of objective description and fixed boundaries. Subjective feelings and inputs of political entrepreneurs play an important role in identity formation and perceptions.

Ethnic identity in West and East Punjab

West Punjab was emptied of Hindus and Sikhs in 1947. Except for a miniscule Christian minority and a handful of Parsees and others, West Punjab was formally a compact Muslim-majority province. However, having been created in the name of Islam and therefore under heavy debt to the clerics and *pirs* who had campaigned for Pakistan as an Islamic state once such a state had come into being, such elements were bound to demand that Pakistan be declared an Islamic state. These elements therefore started clamouring for an Islamic state from the very beginning. In early 1951, both Sunni and Shia ulema signed a twenty-two-point Islamist agenda for converting Pakistan into an Islamic state.

The problem was which particular doctrinal interpretation of Islam would become state ideology. Equally, who was a 'Muslim'? At that early stage the Sunni–Shia differences receded into the background as both groups joined ranks against the Ahmadis whom they considered holding beliefs contrary to Islam.

Thus in 1953, a virulent anti-Ahmadiyya agitation broke out in Lahore, masterminded by some Muslim League leaders in the Punjab who hoped to created enough anarchy so that the government of their own party at the centre could be destabilised. If that were to happen, Punjab Chief Minister Mian Mumtaz Daultana hoped to elevate himself to the position of Prime Minister of Pakistan (*Court of Inquiry,* 1954: 283). It may be recalled that Sir Muhammad Zafrulla Khan, a leading member of the Ahmadiyya community, presented the Muslim League case before the Punjab Boundary Commission with sterling competence. In 1947, the Ahmadis were included in government statistics among Muslims, and that alone had inflated the Muslim percentage of the Gurdaspur district to a bare majority of fifty-one per cent. In 1974 they were found to be holding beliefs contrary to the teachings of Islam and declared a religious minority by the Pakistan National Assembly.

From the late 1980s onwards, the Sunni and Shia communities were victims of sectarian violence and terrorism, partly because of Saudia Arabia and Iran's involvement but also because of the rise of fundamentalism among them, which dissipated the social capital accumulated over the generations. Once again, it was not common Sunnis and Shias who took part in terrorism but bands of armed men on both sides. They did not hesitate to kill people belonging to the other sect even when the other group was offering prayers or congregating to mourn a death. Desecration of each other's mosques, graveyards and such other places has taken place. Targeted killings of individuals from each other's group have also taken place (Ahmed, 2009: 159-65).

In the future, the Sunni–Shia divide might prove fatal to the homogeneity of West Punjab if the obsession for confessional purity is allowed to keep eliminating all anomalies. In recent years, even among the Sunni sub-sects, considerable bloodshed has taken place as a result of terrorism by the Deobandis against the Brelawis. Moreover, the Punjabi language was denied official patronage and literacy in Punjabi became a rarity. In the early 1990s the speaker of the West Punjab Assembly, Muhammad Hanif Ramay, allowed an MLA to make a speech in Punjabi in the Assembly. However, that did not get established as a regular practice. The neglect of Punjabi continues to be the consistent policy of all governments in Pakistan.

In East Punjab, the underlying exclusivist logic of religious nationalism continued to haunt Hindu–Sikh relations. In 1956, the former princely states of Patiala, Faridkot, Kapurthala and others were amalgamated into East Punjab, but this did not satisfy the Sikh leaders of the Akali Dal, who began to campaign for a compact Punjabi-speaking province – a demand which was actually purported to create a Sikh-majority province without the Hindi-speaking Hindu-majority Ambala division. In reaction, Punjabi Hindus, under the influence of various communal parties as well as the Congress party, declared Hindi and not Punjabi as their mother tongue. However, in the 1965 war with Pakistan, Sikh officers and soldiers in the Indian Army fought with distinction and the Sikh leaders came out forcefully in support of the war effort.

That paved the way for Prime Minister Indira Gandhi to give up opposition to the Punjabi Suba, which came into being in 1966. However, such an overture did not mean an end to Sikh nationalism. In the 1970s some Sikhs began to float the idea of Khalistan as a separate Sikh state. In the 1980s, the Khalistan movement became a major secessionist threat. It resulted in armed encounters between militant Sikhs and the Indian security forces and police. Ultimately, it was defeated through the use of excessive force in the early 1990s (Ahmed, 1998: 113-34). The conflict claimed thousands of lives. Gradually, with the revival of the democratic processes, the situation in East Punjab normalised. The veteran Indian journalist Rajinder Puri lamented the negative impact of the Partition on Punjabi in the following words:

'After partition the Punjabis disappeared. In West Punjab they became Pakistanis. In East Punjab they became Hindus and Sikhs. They also became Akalis and Congressmen, Arya Samajists and Jan Sanghis. Never Punjabis' (1985: 132).

Ethnic peace and amity

There is, of course, evidence in the other direction as well. Whenever the two governments have relaxed the restrictions on Punjabis visiting the other side, the encounters have been very emotional. The classic case in this regard was when the Pakistan High Commissioner to India allowed East (Indian) Punjabis to come to Lahore to watch a cricket Test match in early January 1955. Thousands of Hindus and Sikhs accepted that invitation and they were received with unprecedented warmth and generosity. Very touching and moving scenes of old friends and neighbours embracing each other could be seen. The high point of that rendezvous of estranged Punjabis was a *mushaira* (poetry recitation) in the main hall of the Lahore Municipal Committee. My brother, Mushtaq Ahmad, was among the audience. He remembers that when the people's poet Ustad Daman came onto the stage, the very first verse of his poem brought tears to people's eyes, some even crying out aloud. That verse was:

> *Lali ankhian di pai dasdi ay*
> *Roay toosi vi o roay asi vi aan*
> (The redness of the eyes tells us
> That both of us have wept)

I was told by a friend, Amjad Babar, who knew Ustad Daman very well and had spent a great deal of time in his company, that Daman had first recited this poem in Delhi, soon after Partition. Pandit Nehru had been present on the stage on that occasion and Daman had addressed him by name. Nehru had also cried.

Later, Pakistanis went to Amritsar a number of times to attend cricket matches and other sporting events. The reception from the other side has been equally warm. The last time such a rendezvous took place was during the cricket Test in Lahore in 2004, followed by another Test in Mohali, near Chandigarh, East Punjab. The interaction between East and West Punjabis confirmed that the Punjabi identity remained a very strong part of the cultural make-up of the people. The governments of the two Punjabs took some cautious steps to restore contacts, albeit on a very small scale. Thus it was agreed that a weekly bus service between Lahore and Amritsar would begin from 25 January 2006. (Maini, 2007: 69-70).

Chance encounters

The Indian diplomat, Moni Chadha, whose visit to Rawalpindi and his ancestral villages including Thamali are mentioned earlier in this book, narrated his emotions when landing at Lahore in the following words:

'I was emotionally overcome as the PIA plane touched down at Lahore, even though my acquaintance with the city had been limited. After a couple of hours I boarded the small, twin-engine plane for Rawalpindi. I was conspicuous because of my turban, and clearly an Indian. As we took off, the person in the window seat on my left spoke to me in Punjabi and introduced himself as Arif. I cannot recall his other name, but he told me that he had resigned from the position of Attorney General of (Pakistani) Punjab in 1979. I did not ask why, and he did not say.

'He had done his LLM in London and in time became the President of the Lahore Bar Council. When he learnt of my mission, Arif spoke to me about the tragedy of Partition. It came out in the conversation that, like me, he was born in 1937, but on the Indian side of the new border in Hoshiarpur. Like my family, his entire family were refugees. His mother and many other relatives were killed even as he escaped with his life.

'Like me, he was nostalgic about his birthplace. When I mentioned that I hoped to bring some soil back from my ancestral village on return to India, he talked about his own nostalgia for his village in Hoshiarpur, and said that he had been hoping to visit his own village one day with exactly the same thought. In those rare few minutes that we were together there was a close kinship between us, born of a shared tragedy.'

This chance encounter several thousand metres up in the skies, between two Punjabis with quite similar Partition tragedies haunting them since their childhoods, compelled me to embark on my last initiative to tell a story related to what had happened more than sixty-three years ago. I was determined to trace the man my friend Moni had talked to. The Internet searches did not lead anywhere. Finally, I requested friends in Lahore to see if someone fit the description Moni had given about Arif. After several days of email exchanges between us from Stockholm and

Lahore, the team that finally succeeded comprised my dear friends, Dr Hassan Amir Shah, Khawaja Tariq Masood and his son Khawaja Omer. Khawaja Tariq Masood practises law in Lahore and specialises on Labour Law and Rights. He believed that a senior lawyer, Arif Chaudhry, fit the description, though he did not know if he was born in Hoshiarpur. Another couple of days of detective work finally established that indeed Arif Chaudhry was born in Hoshiarpur. In that short conversation, Moni had probably confused some of the information he had in his mind about Arif. Arif did not serve as Attorney (Advocate) General of Punjab; also, he was not President of the Lahore Bar Council but President, Lahore High Court Bar during 1978–79. He became a judge of the Punjab High Court and later of the Pakistan Supreme Court. After retirement he served as Chairman Federal Services Tribunal. He is currently President and Founder-Patron of the Pak–India Friendship Society with branches in Lahore, Indian Punjab and London.

In the aftermath of the nuclear tests by India and Pakistan, I became active in the peace movement. Thanks to the Internet, I got into contact with Indians with a Lahore connection. Sat Paul Arora, a resident of Delhi and formerly of Kucha Mullomata, at the Pani Wala Talab in the walled city of Lahore, contacted me sometime in early 2001. I visited Delhi in October that year and met him at his home. Though he and his wife had many things to say about Lahore, I will narrate only one story:

'In 1995–96 a gentleman from Lahore, Syed Asad Husain, came to attend a conference in Bangalore. Later when he was in Delhi, he wrote a letter to *The Indian Express* in which he enquired about a Dr Khera, who had saved his life as a child in Lahore. As it happened, Dr Khera was my wife's uncle and we were very close to him, but he had died a long time ago. He had been a famous surgeon of Lahore. We went to meet the Pakistani gentleman who told us that all his life he had wanted to meet the man who had saved his life by performing an operation that was considered very dangerous at that time. He was very pleased to have met us.

'Meeting him kindled in me a desire to visit the city of my birth. We were able to do so last year. The problem was that I could not locate the house where we had once lived. The taxi driver proved to be an angel and went around making enquiries. After some time a crowd gathered and everyone tried to help us. Finally, we met an old man to whom I described my house, as also my father and family. He thought for a while, then he held my hand and took me into a corner of the street and then said: "Look in front now; isn't that your house?" For a moment all those years meant nothing, time simply stood still. Sure, in front of me was our house. It was clear to the crowd, that had become even larger, that we had come from India. Suddenly from somewhere, Coca Cola bottles were brought and we were treated to a drink.

'I stepped forward and knocked at the door. An elderly man came out to meet us. I explained to him that we had lived here once upon a time, and only wanted to see it from the inside, if it was all right. He had a flowing white beard and a very kind face. He said, "This is your house, please come in." The women and other members of the family were alerted about our presence and they let us go about as we wanted. I saw that one of the chairs in the house was the one we had left behind, which they confirmed. Nothing much had changed. I was overwhelmed and tears rolled down my cheeks. The current owner was also deeply moved by our presence. He embraced my son Rajinder and me. He was crying and said, "Now that you have seen your old house, promise that you will help me get a visa to India because I want to see my house in Jammu once before I die."'

On the same trip to India I went to visit Yuvraj Krishan, formerly of Purani Anarkali Lahore, whose story from 1947 appears earlier in this book. He lived in a locality called Vasant Kunj, a long distance from central Delhi. The taxi I was travelling in was driven by a Sikh who was not particularly well informed about the localities on the outskirts of New Delhi, so the search became longer and longer. Finally, I went into a merchant's shop and called Mr Krishan for directions.

When the conversation ended, a man, who might have been thirty, came out of the shop and asked me whether I was from Lahore. I was quite surprised and asked how he knew. He replied:

'My father had a shop in Said Mittha Bazar in the walled city of Lahore. You spoke a Punjabi which was identical to his and I knew you must be from Lahore.' He did not charge me the two rupees for the phone call, saying that his father's *atma* (soul) would be glad that some Lahori had visited their shop again (Ahmed, 2006).

On the whole, my conversations with old-timers from the Pakistani Punjab indicated that while nostalgia about old Hindu and Sikh friends always figures in their stories, simultaneously they expressed resentment against Hinduism's caste oppression, which always hurt them. Also, the more politically informed tended to argue that had the Hindus and Sikhs not left, the Muslims would have remained poor and deprived. On the other hand, nostalgia for old Muslim friends and abandoned homes and schools also figured in the conversations with Hindus and Sikhs, but since they were on the whole more prosperous, the partition of the Punjab is seen more as aggrandisement by Muslims to loot their property and possessions. They did, however, admit that the caste system created a chasm between them and the Muslims.

Homecoming

I have collected scores of stories about Punjabis getting a chance to visit their ancestral abodes on the other side of the border. The following is a selection from both sides:

Former Indian Prime Minister Inder Kumar Gujral

I met Inder Kumar Gujral in October 1992, in Delhi. I had come to attend a conference and used that opportunity to meet some people of West Punjabi origin, as my curiosity about the old Punjab has always been constant. He and his wife Sheil met me in their home and within minutes we were conversing in the familiar West Punjab Punjabi. To my pleasant surprise, Sheil Gujral turned out to be a former resident of the same Temple Road on which my ancestral house is located. Both told me many moving stories of their visits to Pakistan; how well they had been received and the emotional scenes that took place when they met old neighbours and friends. Mrs Gujral narrated a story about how, when she and Inder visited her old home on Temple Road, their next door neighbours, who still lived in the same place, insisted that they should stay with them. Another story, which I recall from my memory as I did not take any notes then, was about a loyal Muslim servant. He had kept as a sacred trust the jewellery that her sister had left behind when she fled to India. Later, when law and order was restored, he returned everything. In his autobiography, *Matters of Discretion* (2011), Gujral narrates at length his childhood in Jhelum and later his college days in Lahore. His was a family belonging to the Arya Samaj movement. His father Avtar Narain Gujral was a disciple of Mahatma Gandhi, while Inder went on to join the Communist movement while in Lahore. Inder and Sheil visited Jhelum and Lahore in 1982. He writes:

> As we were about to leave, I saw an aged Muslim lady, Khatajan Bibi, pushing her way towards me. I immediately recognized her, for she had served as a midwife when I and later my two brothers were born....Khatajan Bibi hugged me as a mother would. She was meeting Sheil for the first time. She gave her a small coin as her *shagun* (blessing) (Gujral 2011: 20).

Gujral's childhood friend, Ahsan Ali, his father's assistant, Muzaffar Hussain Shah and his father's colleague Mohammad Bashir all came to meet him and Sheil. They were invited to dinner at the Civil Club. The poet Jogi Jhelumi asked if he recognised him. Gujral answered that he could still recall him reciting anti-British poems at the Jubilee Ghat public meetings. Later, a *mushaira* was held where the deputy commissioner and other higher officials were present. Gujral, whose interest in Urdu poetry is proverbial was invited to preside. Sheil recited one of her poems. He writes in a highly charged emotional manner, 'After the mushaira was over, almost everyone invited us to come again soon with the rest of the family. I was moved, when they said: "Jhelum is still yours, don't forget it" (ibid.: 23).

Sunil Dutt

'Ever since my family left our village Khurd in Jhelum district in 1947, I wanted to visit it at least once. Great success as a filmstar, and being a Congress member of the Indian Parliament is one thing, but the soul always longs for the past and my roots were across the border in the Pakistan Punjab. In 1998, I got a chance to visit Khurd, thanks to the special interest taken in my plea by then Prime Minister of Pakistan, Mian Nawaz Sharif. I came along with Dilip Kumar. People in our village had been informed in advance. Some of the young men had even seen my movies. It was a feeling I can't describe when I set my foot on the soil where my childhood had been spent. The old women addressed me by my nickname "Bajjya" since my real name is Balraj. They wanted to know how my mother was. When I told them that she had died, they began to cry.

'My family had been saved by a friend of my uncle, Yaqub. I went to his village Nawan Kot to thank him exactly half a century late for saving my family members during those terrible days of 1947. He had died and his children also did not live there anymore. Anyhow, I met some people there and conveyed to them my regards. They promised to inform Yaqub's children. I came back thoroughly convinced that good and bad people are to be found in all communities and one should never judge harshly a whole people.'

Raj Babbar

'Yes, the success in Bollywood has been great for me, but at home my parents only talked about Jalalpur Jattan, which they left in 1947. So although I was born in Agra, I always felt that I had a lost home in Jalalpur Jattan. Some years ago I visited Pakistan to attend a Punjabi conference. The receptions at the airport and in the hotel were memorable. I felt that I was at home among my own people. I expressed a desire to visit my hometown and this was immediately arranged. The news spread quickly to Jalalpur Jattan. Some young men from there came to Lahore and escorted me to Jalalpur Jattan. They formed a caravan of motorcycles as we drove into that small town.

'The townspeople received me very warmly. Many elders remembered my family and also the exact house where we lived. I was told that a mosque had been built in the courtyard of our old house and therefore they were not sure if I would like to go there. I said to them, "I would be very pleased to go there if you have no objection. Now I know the secret of my success. If people are praying five times a day in the courtyard of my house then obviously their blessings help me become so successful." This pleased everybody and we quickly went on to see the old house. Quite frankly, the problem is not people. It is bad politics.

We must do everything to remove misunderstandings.'

Rachna Anand

During my three-year stay as a visiting research professor at the Institute of South Asian Studies, National University of Singapore, I had an opportunity to meet several Punjabis with their roots on the other side of the divided Punjab. One of them, Rachna Anand, told me this fascinating story about her visit to her ancestral Pind Dadan Khan (PDK). Her grandfather, Hakim Chunni Lal Kohli, was a highly respected practitioner of traditional medicine who was always accessible to people. Her father was in school when the Partition took place. He would never tire of talking about Pind Dadan Khan, although he had never visited it again after Partition. Rachna had married and moved to Singapore but Pind Dadan Khan continued to be part of her life even there. She told me that she visited Pakistan on 16 March 2007 as part of a goodwill mission from the Singapore Press Club. While in Rawalpindi, the Chief Eecutive Officer of the English daily, *Pakistan Post,* Raja Arshad Khan, helped her secure permission to visit PDK. He put Rachna in contact with Chaudhry Nazar Hussain Gondal, a member of the Punjab Assembly. She explained to him her burning desire to visit the place which her father never tired of talking about. The rest of the story is best presented in her own words. Upon my request she wrote it down and sent it to me by email:

'It was arranged by Raja Arshad that his driver will drive me to PDK the next day in his official car. So the following day I left for PDK in the wee hours of the morning. I was constantly in contact on the mobile phone with my dad in Delhi. We both didn't sleep a wink. We were talking almost through the night. I will always remember that night of anticipation. We reached PDK by around 9.40 a.m. and went straight to Chaudhry Gondal's home. He was there personally and met me with great affection. There I met a huge gathering of elderly men. After light refreshments I was taken towards my ancestral home.

'I had never visited here before, yet it all looked so familiar. I could tell where everything else was once I reached my father's school. Through the mind map, I could tell we were near the ancestral home. A big crowd was waiting there to receive me. As I came out they rushed forward to garland me. I was in shock from then onwards. As they were taking me on a tour of the street, an old friend of my father's eldest sister approached me and gave me a big hug, took me by the hand and told off the hordes of men around me that this lady has travelled this far not to walk around but to see her ancestral home! She then led me to our old house.

'When the old people learnt whose granddaughter I was, they showered love on me. It was too much for me to bear. I could only cry in return. Everyone wanted me to visit their home. They were giving me gifts, of whatever they could find in there homes. I was totally stumped by the affection shown.

'Someone brought my grandfather's old letters and later brought a wooden toy, which they were willing to part with only if I visited them in their home. So I went. I was told I could take the wooden toy if I could tell what it was for. It didn't take me time to realise whose home I was sitting in. It was the home of one of my grandfather's dear friends, Maulvi Abdul Aziz, head *maulvi* of the masjid and its *madrassa* (religious school). My grandfather and Maulvi Abdul Aziz were both Hafiz-e-Quran and used to discuss the Quran, Urdu poets and other books regularly

'My grandfather left Pind Dadan Khan some weeks before the worst atrocities began on boh sides. While in India he learnt that Maulvi Abdul Aziz was seriously ill. He prepared medicine for him and sent it in these wooden toys smuggled in through couriers at that time. Maulvi Abdul Aziz recovered fully after the taking the medicines sent by my grandfather. His children kept the wooden toys in memory of their friendship along with some of my grandfather's letters. So, I was given one of those wooden toys for giving the correct answer.

'Many spoke of his magical touch and medical practice. Many of his former patients visited me simply to thank me in person for my grandfather, Hakim Chunni Lal Kohli's healing touch, that had helped them. Some remembered him as a Hafiz-e-Quran, a lover of books and a philanthropist. He never charged the poor for consultation, instead gave them medicine and a sack of grain to eat along with his medicine, knowing they will not be able to afford food. To some he would give slips authorising them to get milk from the local *halvai*.

'To my very great surprise I met a practising Hindu Brahmin, a Dutt, who told me that he and his family lived in peace with the Muslims. My father, who was on the phone, talked to him and could remember his family. Chaudhry Gondal Sahib also talked to my father and invited him to visit Pind Dadan Khan. It warms my heart to discover families in PDK that are now a part of my family today, and that of our generations to come.'

Wasim Akram

On Tuesday, 3 May 2005, cricket legend and arguably one of the greatest left-arm fast bowlers of all times, Pakistan's Wasim Akram and his father Chaudhary Mohammed Akram, visited their ancestral village Chawinda Devi, Amritsar district. Chawinda Devi was a mixed village with Arain and Syed *biradaris* of Muslims and Sikh and Hindus constituting an equal population. Wasim's family belonged to the Arain section of Chawinda Devi.

Wasim and his father were given a rousing welcome by the young and the old. His father, who spent his childhood there before migrating to Pakistan in 1947, became emotional as he stood in the courtyard of the house where he had grown up. Some of his old friends were still living there. Bhagwan Singh, the occupant of their ancestral house, held him close and in chaste Punjabi said 'this house still belongs to you'. (*The Hindu,* 4 May 2005). When somebody urged him that he should come more often Wasim's father remarked, 'I could come every month if both governments let me' (Zee TV, India, 3 May 2005).

Dr Khushi Muhammad Khan

'I have already told you the story of how we reached Pakistan from Nabha as part of a foot convoy. We settled in Gujranwala. In 1949, I wrote a letter to Dr Girdhari Lal, the father of my playmate, Ashwani Kumar Sharma. Dr Lal, a Brahmin, was the only qualified medical practitioner in Amloh. He was kind and considerate and respected by everyone. A reply arrived and thus Ashwani and I began to correspond with each other. We remained in touch till 1958.

In the meantime, I received master's degrees in Economics and English Literature and began a career as a lecturer, which took me to different parts of West Punjab. In 1963, I went on a scholarship to Germany where I secured a PhD in Development Economics. I returned to Pakistan but failed to get a reasonable job as corruption and not merit had become the way to success. Back in Germany, I set up a family and began working as a researcher and university teacher. My professional engagements took me to many parts of the world, but my heart and soul continued to long for a visit to my place of birth, or as they say in Hindi, my *janam bhoomi*, Amloh. I revived my contact with Ashwani Kumar who insisted that I should visit them. But at that time East Punjab was in turmoil. The Khalistan insurgency was in full swing and getting a tourist visa was well nigh impossible for an ex-Pakistani. However, as luck would have it, a famous Indian academician, Prof A.M. Khusro, who had previously been the Indian Ambassador to Germany, came to do some research at the German Overseas Institute where I worked. I told him my story and requested his help in getting the visa. That kindly man helped me and I could visit India.

'I arrived back in Amloh in 1982, after thirty-five years. The small town had changed somewhat but its people were as good-hearted as before. I was given a rousing reception: one that is given only to long-lost sons-of-the-soil. Ashwani and other childhood friends took me through the main streets in a procession. Old men and women came asking about my family. A friendly competition ensued as to who should invite me for lunch and who for dinner. Old Hindu habits of Muslims being barred from the kitchen were no longer practised. I received real Punjabi hospitality wherever I went. A public meeting was arranged in which the speakers referred to the common Punjabi heritage deriving from the contributions of the great Sufis such as Baba Fariduddin Ganjshakar and the founder of Sikhism, Baba Guru Nanak, and other great souls. I requested that I should be permitted to sleep the first night in our old house where I was born. Its current owner was a Sikh refugee family from Lyallpur (now Faisalabad). They were only too glad to let me fulfil my desire.

'I felt I owed something to my hometown and its people. Consequently, I established an educational foundation "Munshi Ji" (the name by which my father was usually known and addressed). I deposited a sizeable amount of cash in the local bank. The procedure is that from the interest, which accrues annually, deserving students of poor background are given scholarships. Both boys and girls benefit from the programme. I have visited Amloh several times since. I always stay with my schoolmate, Ashwani Kumar, whose children treat me as their elder. With multiple visa entries in my passport granted by the Indian embassy in Germany, I now spend equal time in both Punjabs whenever I am in the subcontinent.'

Persona non grata for most Punjabis

The lucky few who have managed to go across the Punjab border always have stories of the warm reception that they have received. However, for most Punjabis, not only is the Right to Return out of the question, but even to visit their ancestral abodes is not possible. In 1998, when Indian Prime Minister Atal Bihari Vajpayee and Pakistan Prime Minister Mian Nawaz Sharif signed the Lahore Declaration which was to usher peace between India and Pakistan, it suddenly surfaced in media discussions that Punjabis from both sides wanted to visit their lost homes in the other half. An announcement in a Pakistani newspaper that visa applications for a visit to East Punjab can be submitted resulted in thousands of people applying for it. It turned out to be a hoax, as neither India nor Pakistan was willing to relax the controls. During cricket matches played in Lahore (2004) and Mohali (2005) both sides let fans cross the border. Thousands made use of that opportunity and were received with traditional Punjabi hospitality and care. Ordinarily, this is not possible. Two stories illustrate this pull of the native soil that never goes away.

Brigadier (Retd) Yasub Ali Dogar

'I was only an infant at the time of Partition. Therefore I do not have any personal memories of that area. The Dogars were settled in contiguous forty-four villages, together known as Dogar Chautalia in Punjab, since the times of the Mughals. My parents, aunts, uncles, and other elders – all talk about the *dess* or *desh* till the end of their lives, as if it was a paradise on earth. Its weather and climate, people, customs and traditions, brotherhood among families living together – all were exemplary, something not found in the new land they were forced to settle in. The one spot on earth they adored was our village Dhaddar, *tahsil* Dasuya, district Hoshiarpur.

'I visited Jullundur twice to attend the Bi-Annual Border Security Force Meeting Conference.The first time was on 14–15 December 1994 and the second time on 17–19 December 1995. On both occasions I requested permission to visit my ancestral village, where I was born on 8 December 1946. Both times my request was overruled for security reasons.

'Much worse was that on the first occasion in 1994 my *mamaji* Chaudhry Nur Karim Dogar sent some gifts for his classmate Lt Colonel (Retd) Hargurjit Singh Sandhu. Both were from the same village – *chak* 10-BL, Chichawatni, district Sahiwal [called Montgomery before Partition] in a canal colony. They studied together from class one to class ten and were very close friends. His wife was the daughter of the *lambardar* in the next village, 9-BL. The old colonel now lived a retired life in Model Town, Jullundur. I implored my counterparts to let me go and see them. Colonel Sandhu got to know about me the very first day when I expressed my wish to see him, because some people who were there heard me and informed him. He was living only a few kilometres away from where we were staying. Even that request was ignored. However, on the last day, I talked to a senior Sikh officer who was also a Sandhu. He somehow understood my feelings. However, instead of me being taken to them, Colonel Sandhu and his wife were brought to the place where we were staying. I met them and handed over the gifts and greeting of my uncle. They were deeply touched. The old Colonel had brought his wife, daughter and her two children also to meet me. He told me that he had asked them to specially come and meet me as I had come from his *watan* (homeland).

'My disappointment in not being able to give the good news to my mother (my father had died in 1989 when I was commanding the Siachen sector) that I visited our ancestral house, the graves of our ancestors, and other deeply emotional and spiritual feelings about our village are beyond description.'

Dr Ajay Mehra

'As I grew up in Dehri-on-Sone, a small but beautiful town in Bihar, and all over the state, I heard stories from my parental generation that my family comes from another beautiful town across the border – Chakwal. We Mehra Khatris believe that we originate from Chakwal. I understood the meaning of "across the border" a little later as I read and understood about "partition" in 1947, but could not gather much either about Chakwal, or about the circumstances that brought our ancestors from the Punjab to the Bengal, of which Bihar was a part then. Apparently, my great-grandfather had landed himself a job in the police in Bihar and later the whole family got settled there; none of my parental generation had seen Chakwal.

'Therefore, when I was invited for a conference by the Quaid-i-Azam University on "Communal Violence in South Asia" to be held in early 2003, I was delighted. I hoped that the desire to visit and see Chakwal, the land of my ancestors, would be fulfilled. But 2003 was a bad time for Indians and Pakistanis to visit each other; a terror attack on the Indian Parliament in December 2001 had led to banning of flights by India and Pakistan over each other's airspace. The diplomatic relations were reduced to the minimum. Obviously, it was not more difficult to obtain a visa than usual. Keen to visit Pakistan, I had to go around the high walls of the Pakistan High Commission in Chanakyapuri, Delhi's diplomatic enclave. Fortunately, I ran into the senior-most officer of the High Commission, who was perhaps pretty junior in the diplomatic service hierarchy. A polite gentleman, he said that they awaited the interior ministry clearance, which never came. Finally, appreciating the keenness of the three invitees to the conference, he decided to grant the visa the next day just before the High Commission closed down at 5 p.m.

'However, India and Pakistan are endangered by each other's citizens and show courtesy to them by granting visa only for specific cities. Our visa came with Islamabad stamped. I requested the officer to give me a visas at least for Chakwal and Lahore, explaining the reason for my keenness for Chakwal. He smiled, ***"Is bar Islamabad ho aiye, agli bar sara Pakistan ghuma denge"*** (Please visit Islamabad this time, next time we will take you to the whole of Pakistan).

'Our hosts were keen to take me to Chakwal, only 60 kms from Pakistan's capital, but were hesitant. If the police and security did check, it could lead to problems for both of us. So I could not go to Chakwal. I still hope that in my next visit, whenever it is, I will be able to go to Chakwal, about which I have read a lot from the Chakwalis.

'Unfortunately, people of "Pakistani origin" irrespective of whether they were born before Pakistan came into being in August 1947 or not, are no longer granted visa for India; multiple visa is out of the question ever since Pakistan-based terrorists carried out the carnage in Mumbai on 26 November 2008 that left at least 173 innocent people dead.'

Human nature and identity

In light of the above discussion, one can conclude that human nature is neither innately selfish, suspicious and aggressive as Hobbes believed, nor is it altruistic and trusting without any reservations; rather, the instinct to survive is paramount in all situations, and that can be realised through trust and solidarity as much as mistrust and conflict depending on the objective situation. If, now, one remembers that identity both at the individual and collective levels is multi-dimensional, one can argue that although Hindu, Muslim and Sikh religious identities were no absolute bar to relating to each other peaceably, the caste prejudices and economic inequalities that existed would have created tension. A democratic formula taking care of these factors could have helped surmount the difference and emphasise common culture and tradition, but in 1947, aggression and violence erupted instead as the leadership of the three communities failed to agree to a fair power-sharing formula.

The Punjab bloodied, partition and cleansed

The controversial international boundary fixed by the Radcliffe Award of 17 August 1947 created bitterness on both sides. The Liaqat–Nehru/ Nehru–Liaqat Pact of 1950 affirmed the irreversibility of not only impassable borders but also that the Right to Return no longer applied to the Hindus, Muslims and Sikhs who had lost hearth and home during the great upheaval of 1947. However, it was not until the 1965 and

1971 wars between the two states that relations completely ruptured: only a few times since then have common folk, with some ease, been able to visit the other side in connection with cricket matches. The weekly bus service between Lahore and Amritsar is also confined largely to Sikh pilgrims visiting their sacred sites in the Pakistani Punjab. On the whole, the official emphasis is on mutual rejection.

Nothing epitomises the officially sanctioned revulsion of the Other as much as the flag-lowering ceremony at the Wagah–Attari Border situated between Lahore on the Pakistani side and Amritsar on the Indian side. Every evening, border guards and soldiers symbolically seal the border by ramming the iron-gates with a fierce bang to indicate that an impassable barrier exists between the two countries and their peoples. Large crowds on both sides watch this awe-striking spectacle of mutual rejection. They add zest to the ceremony by nervous clapping and other gesticulations. In recent times, the egregiously aggressive features of the ceremony have been toned down and it has become more of an entertainment, but the two Punjabs remain inaccessible to each other.

References

Ahmed, Ishtiaq. *State, Nation and Ethnicity in Contemporary South Asia*, London and New York: Pinter, 1998.

———. 'The Lahore Effect', in *Seminar*, Number 567, November, New Delhi, 2006.

———. 'The Spectre of Islamic Fundamentalism over Pakistan (1947-2007)' in Rajshree Jetly (ed.). *Pakistan in Regional and Global Politics*, London, New York, New Delhi: Routledge, 2009.

Maini, Tridivesh Singh. *South Asian Cooperation and the Role of the Two Punjabs*, New Delhi: Siddharth Publications, 2007.

Puri, Rajinder. 'What it's all about?' in Amrik Singh (ed.), *Punjab in Indian Politics: Issues and Trends*, New Delhi: Ajanta Books International, 2000.

Official Documents

Mansergh, Nicholas and Penderel Moon (eds). *The Transfer of Power 1942-7, vol. XI, The Mountbatten Viceroyalty, Announcement and Reception of the 3 June Plan,*

31 May – 7 July 1947, London: Her Majesty's Stationery Office 1982.
Report of the Court of Inquiry constituted under Punjab Act II of 1954 to enquire into the Punjab Disturbances of 1953, Lahore, 1954.

Interviews

Inder Kumar Gujral, New Delhi, 9 October 1992
Sheil Gujral, New Delhi, 9 October 1992
Raj Babbar, Mumbai, 20 October 2011
Sunil Dutt, Mumbai, 20 October 2011
Sat Paul Arora, Delhi, 22 October 2001
Dr Khushi Mohammad Khan, Stockholm, 16 June 2003
Amjad Babar, Washington DC, 11 July 2009
Moni Chadha, from Delhi via email, 28 December 2010
Brigadier Yasub Ali Dogar, Lahore, via telephone and email, 13 January 2011
Dr Ajay K. Mehra, Noida, UP, via telephone and email, 13 January 2011
Mushtaq Ahmad, Stockholm, 20 February 2011
Rachna Anand, via email from Singapore, 21 February 2011

ACKNOWLEDGEMENTS

In the 11 years since the first edition of this book was published by Rupa Publication in 2011, the list of those institutions and individuals who have helped me has grown very long.

Thanks go first to the Swedish Research Council (Vetenskåpsrådet), which awarded me a very generous three-year research grant during January 2003–December 2005. This study would not have been possible without extraordinary help and assistance that I received.

The Department of Political Science, Stockholm University, from where I obtained my PhD and where I worked most of my life, provided time off for me to do fieldwork. I received encouragement and support from many colleagues. I would particularly like to mention Claes Linde who, despite being extremely ill, came to a seminar I gave on the findings of my research on the Punjab prior to publication.

Some names must be named in a special list because quite simply, without these fine individuals, there is no chance I would have single-handedly managed such a vast project. In Lahore, Ali Haroon Shah and Shireen Shah, Prof. Dr. Hassan Amir Shah and Rukhsana Shah and as Brigadier (retd) Yasub Ali Dogar went out of the way to help me. In Delhi, Pran Nevile, Moni Chadha, Yuvraj Krishan, Bhisham Kumar Bakshi, Vimal Issar, Satish Chopra, ambassadors Veena and Rajiv Sikri and Vimal Issar showered many favours on me. I have had the privilege of enjoying the hospitality of Yuvraj Krishan and B.K. Bakshi whenever I visit Delhi. Uma Vasudev put me in touch with her aunts. Professor Manchanda did me a great favour by interviewing on my behalf people from the outer rim of western Punjab, settled in Delhi after Partition. Ajay Mehra, a friend of many years, also helped a lot. Kirpal Dhillon helped with essential information regarding the first post-Partition East Punjab government. Commodore Uday Bhaskar came to my rescue by putting me in contact with an Indian Administrative Services officer, H.I.S. Gerewal. He called his father Bikram Singh Gerewal, whose phenomenal memory helped identify the ministers in the first post-Partition East Punjab government. Prof. Harbans Mukhia, Prof. Shamsul Islam, Prof. Partha Ghosh, Prof. Jagdishlal Dawar, Ravi Bhandari, Gautam Navlakha, Satish Chopra, Himashu Chawla, Ramesh Chandra Khanna, Brigadier (retd) Vijai and Doe Nair, Colonel (retd) Anand, Maninder Kaur Mattewal, Nirupama Dutt and Harkishen Singh Mehta in Chandigarh too have been steady supporters.

At Punjab University, Chandigarh, Professor Bhupinder Brar rendered crucial help to get me going with field research in the East Punjab countryside. Before submission for publication, the manuscript was read and commented upon by three benefactors of mine: Dr Peter Lomas, Reginald Massey and Tammy Swofford. Their suggestions and help greatly improved the manuscript. Mohammad Shahidul Islam contributed to this study with two graphs on the Punjab population that appear in the Introduction. Mian Saleem helped me get hold of the 1941 Punjab Census.

My sincerest thanks and gratitude to all those who volunteered to grant me interviews. Without their help the story would never have advanced much. Some of those experiences profoundly affected me. I will cherish those moments forever, even when we were discussing painful memories and reopening old wounds.

In Stockholm my elder brother Mushtaq Ahmad and the late Riaz Ahmed Cheema shared with me their reminiscences of Partition. Ajmal Butt, Ashok Bhasker, Khawaja Shahid, Ahmed Faqih, Masood Qamar and Rafiq Khan and Imran Mirza have been a group with whom I discussed my research all along and received their comments and suggestions.

In 2017, on the 70th anniversary of Partition, the Dr Hari Sharma Foundation and Gursharan Singh Memorial Committee invited me to deliver the annual Gursharan Singh lecture. I visited Vancouver, Winnipeg and Montreal where I gave talks and made many friends: the late Dr Chinnoy Banerjee, Ajay Bhardwaj, Sukhwant Hundal, Harinder Mahil, Sadhu Binning, Prabhjot Parmar, Mukhtiar Singh, Jasvir Manguwal, Dr Radhika Desai, Prof Dolores Chew, Shailendra Kumar Chaudhary, Babar Shaheen and Naushad Siddiqui Sahib.

This book has been translated and published into Urdu, Hindi and

Punjabi-Gurmukhi and a Punjabi-Shahmukhi edition is in the offing. I would like to especially thank Gurprit Singh from the bottom of my heart who while based in Kolkata translated the book into Hindi while the Punjabi-Gurmukhi edition has been translated by Sukhwant Hundal and Kanwal Dhaliwal who also edited it. In Pakistan, Zakria Khan left no stone unturned in procuring information on the deputy commissioners who served in the western districts. I must say that deputy commissioners of several districts and their staff went out of their way to help.

I take this opportunity to thank some new friends, Dr Sanjeev Chopra, Atul Singh, Arvind Saharan, Dr Vinod Mubayi, Prof. Lakhvir Singh, Dr Gurmukh Singh, Dr Dharamjeet Singh, Dr Jaspreet Kaur, Sukhdeep Singh, Prof. Dr Dipak Malik, Anand Vardhan, Vibhuti Rai, Raj Pal, Dinesh Mahajan, Rishi Kakar, Rajan Khanna, Dinesh K Vohra, Pavan Jha, Swati Bakshi, Meera Dewan, Rashi Puri, Oishika Roy, Dr Yaqoob Bangash, Dr Furqan Ali Khan, Dr Waqas Masood, Mujahid Hussain Sayed, Waheed Bhatti, Aamir Rana, Safdar Navaid Zaidi, Mansoor Alam, Asif Alvi, Arif Niazi, Naeem Arif, Dharam Rehani, Rias Saarim, Masud Mirza, Moin Ahmed Bijnori, Malik Ikhlaq Ahmed, Zahid Kardar, Mo Sadiq, Dr Najam Butt, Waqas Butt, Tahir Malik, Usman Shahid, Prof. Tariq Jatala, Ahmed Raza Wattoo, Rana Abdul Hameed Khan, Akmal Kalyar, and Ehtesham Hassan.

Last but by no means least, I would like specially to thank from the bottom of my heart Kapish Mehra, Yamini Chowdhury, Aurodeep Mukherjee, Oorja Mishra and Nishtha Kapil at Rupa Publications for publishing this new edition of my book to mark the 75th anniversary of Partition.

Ishtiaq Ahmed
Solna Municipality, Stockholm
7 June 2022

PUNJAB LEGISLATIVE ASSEMBLY 21 MARCH 1946 TO 4 JULY 1947

Speaker

Diwan Bahadur S.P. Singha, MA, LLB. (West Central Punjab – Indian Christian) (21 March 1946 to 4 July 1947).

Deputy Speaker

Sardar Kapur Singh, B.A., LLB. (Ludhiana East – Sikh, Rural) (26 March 1946 to 4 July 1947).

Premier

Malik Sir Khizr Hayat Khan Tiwana, KCSI, OBE (Khushab – Muhammadan Rural), (21 March 1946 to 2 March 1947).

Ministers

(Ministry dissolved after governor's rule imposed on 5 March 1947).

1. Chaudhri Lahri Singh, BA, LLB (Rohtak North – General, Rural) – Minister of Public Works.
2. Mian Muhammad Ibrahim Barq (Alipur – Muhammadan, Rural) – Minister of Education.
3. Mr Bhim Sen Sachar, BA, LLB (Lahore City – General, Urban) – Finance Minister.
4. Nawab Sir Muzaffar Ali Qizilbash (Lahore – Muhammadan, Rural) – Minister of Revenue.
5. Sardar Baldev Singh (Ambala North – Sikh, Rural) – Minister of Development.

LIST OF MEMBERS OF PUNJAB LEGISLATIVE ASSEMBLY TILL 4 JULY 1947

1. Abdul Ghafur Khan, Chaudhri (Shakargarh – Muhammadan, Rural)
2. Abdul Hameed Khan, Khan Sahib Sardar (Muzaffargarh – Muhammadan, Rural)
3. Abdul Hamid Khan, Rana, BA, LLB (Pakpattan – Muhammadan, Rural)
4. Abdul Hamid Khan, Sufi (Karnal – Muhammadan, Rural)
5. Abdul Haq, Mian (Okara – Muhammadan, Rural)
6. Abdul Sattar Khan, Mr (Mianwali North – Muhammadan, Rural)
7 Ahmad Jan, Maulvi (North-west Gurgaon – Muhammadan, Rural)
8 Ajit Singh, Sardar (South-west Punjab – Sikh, Rural)
9 Akram Ali Khan, Chaudhri (Taran Taran – Muhammadan, Rural)
10 Ali Akbar Khan, Chaudhri (Kangra and eastern Hoshiarpur – Muhammadan, Rural)
11 Allah Bakhsh Khan Tiwana, K.B. Nawab Malik, Sir, MBE (Sargodha – Muhammadan, Rural)
12 Allah Yar Khan Daultana, Khan Bahadur Mian (Mailsi – Muhammadan, Rural)
13 Anwar Khan, Rai (Jaranwala – Muhammadan, Rural)
14 Asghar Ali, Khan Sahib Captain Chaudhri (Gujrat East Muhammadan, Rural)
15 Ashiq Hussain, Major Nawab, MBE (Multan – Muhammadan, Rural)
16 Ashiq Hussain, Sayed (Dipalpur – Muhammadan, Rural)
17 Atta Muhammad Khan, Sardar, BA, LLB (Dera Ghazi Khan North – Muhammadan, Rural)
18 Aziz Din, Chaudhri (Lyallpur – Muhammadan, Rural)
19 Bachan Singh, Sardar (Ludhiana Central – Sikh, Rural)

20 Badlu Ram, Chaudhri (Rohtak Central – General, Rural)
21 Bagh Ali, Mian (Fazilka – Muhammadan, Rural)
22 Bahadur Khan Dreshak, Sardar, MBE (Dera Ghazi Khan South – Muhammadan, Rural)
23 Bahawal Bakhsh, Chaudhri (South-east Gujrat – Muhammadan, Rural)
24 Barkat Ali, Malik (Eastern Towns – Muhammadan, Urban)
25 Barkat Hayat Khan, Sardar (North Punjab – Labour)
26 Bashir Ahmad, Mian, Bar-at-Law (Ferozepore East – Muhammadan, Rural)
27 Behari Lal Chanana, Lala (South-east Multan Division – General, Rural)
28 Beli Ram, Thakur, BA, LLB (Kangra East – General, Rural)
29 Bhagat Ram Sharma, Pandit, BA, LLB (Kangra West – General, Rural)
30 Bhagwan Das, Lala (Commerce and Industry)
31 Budhan Shah, Pir (Khanewal – Muhammadan, Rural)
32 Dalip Singh Kang, Sardar (Lyallpur East – Sikh, Rural)
33 Dalip Singh, Thakur (Kangra South – General, Rural)
34 Daud Ghaznavi, Maulana (East Punjab – Labour)
35 Dev Raj Sethi, Mr (Lyallpur and Jhang – General, Rural)
36 Durga Chand Kaoshish, Pandit (East Punjab – Landholders)
37 Faiz Muhammad, Khan Bahadur Shaikh, BA, LLB, MBE (Dera Ghazi Khan Central – Muhammadan, Rural)
38 Faqir Chand, Pandit (West Lahore Division – General, Rural)
39 Fateh Muhammad Sayyal, Chaudhri, MA (Batala – Muhammadan, Rural)
40 Fazal Elahi, Chaudhri (Gujrat-north – Muhammadan, Rural)
41 Fazal Elahi, Mr (East-central Punjab – Indian Christian)
42 Fazal Haq Piracha, Khan Bahadur Sheikh (Bhalwal – Muhammadan, Rural)
43 Ganga Saran, Rai Bahadur Lala (Trade Union Labour)
44 Ghazanfar Ali Khan, Raja (Pind Dadan Khan – Muhammadan, Rural)
45 Ghulam Farid, Chaudhri, BA, LLB (Gurdaspur East – Muhammadan, Rural)
46 Ghulam Muhammad Shah, Syed (Jhang East – Muhammadan, Rural)
47 Ghulam Mustafa Shah Jilani, Khan Sahib Makhdum Sayed (Lodhran – Muhammadan, Rural)
48 Ghulam Rasul, Chaudhri (South-west Gujrat – Muhammadan, Rural)
49 Ghulam Samad, K.S. Khawaja (Southern Towns – Muhammadan, Urban)

50 Gibbon, Mr, C.E. (Anglo Indian)
51 Gopi Chand Bhargava, Dr (University)
52 Guest, Mr P.H. (European)
53 Gurbachan Singh Bajwa, Sardar, BA, LLB (Sialkot – Sikh, Rural)
54 Gurbachan Singh, Sardar (Ferozepore West – Sikh, Rural)
55 Gurbanta Singh, Master (Jullundur General – Rural, Reserved Seat)
56 Harbhaj Ram, Chaudhri (Lyallpur and Jhang – General, Reserved Seat)
57 Hari Lal, Munshi, BA (Hons), LLB (South-West Towns – General)
58 Iftikhar Hussain Khan, Nawab (Ferozepore General – Muhammadan, Rural)
59 Inder Singh, Sardar (Eastern Town – Sikh, Rural)
60 Isher Singh Majhail, Sardar (Amritsar North – Sikh, Rural)
61 Jagdish Chander, Mr (Karnal North – General, Rural)
62 Jagjit Singh Mann, Sardar (Central Punjab – Landholders)
63 Jahan Ara Shah Nawaz, Begum, MBE (Outer Lahore – Muhammadan, Women, Urban)
64 Jahan Khan, Chaudhri (North-west Gujrat – Muhammadan, Rural)
65 Jaswant Singh, Sardar (North-west Punjab – Sikh, Rural)
66 Jiwan Lal, Pandit (South-east Gurgaon – General, Rural)
67 Jogindar Singh Mann, Sardar, MBE (Gujranwala and Shahdara – Sikh, Rural)
68 Kabul Singh, Sardar (Jullundur East – Sikh, Rural)
69 Kale Khan, Raja (Rawalpindi East – Muhammadan, Rural)
70 Karamat Ali, K.B Sheikh, BA, LLB (North-Eastern Towns – Muhammadan, Urban)
71 Kartar Singh, Sardar (Lyallpur West – Sikh, Rural)
72 Kehar Singh, Sardar (Jagraon – Sikh, Rural)
73 Khair Mehdi Khan, Raja (Jhelum – Muhammadan, Rural)
74 Khan Muhammad Khan Kathia, Mehr (Montgomery – Muhammadan, Rural)
75 Kidar Nath Sehgal, Lala (Amritsar and Sialkot – General)
76 Krishna Gopal Dutt, Chaudhri (North-eastern Towns – General)
77 Lehna Singh Sethi, Dr (North-western Towns – General, Urban)
78 Man Singh Jathedar, Sardar (Sheikhupura West – Sikh, Rural)
79 Mangoo Ram, Chaudhri (Hoshiarpur West – General, Rural, Reserved Seat)
80 Manuel, P, Mr (Anglo-Indian)

81 Matu Ram, Chaudhri (Ludhiana and Ferozepore – General, Reserved Seat)
82 Mehr Chand, Chaudhri (Hoshiarpur West – General, Reserved Seat)
83 Mehtab Khan, Chaudhri (South-east Gurgaon – Muhammadan, Rural)
84 Mir Muhammad Khan, Rai (Samundri – Muhammadan, Rural)
85 Mohan Lal, Mr (Una – General, Rural)
86 Mohar Singh, Rao Sahib Rao, BA, LLB (North-west Gurgaon – General, Rural)
87 Mohy-ud-Din Lal Badshah, Sayed (Attock South – Muhammadan, Rural)
88 Mubarik Ali Shah, Major Sayed (Jhang Central – Muhammadan, Rural)
89 Muhammad Abdullah Khan Sahib, Mir (Mianwali South – Muhammadan, Urban)
90 Muhammad Abdus Salam, Mian (Jullundur North – Muhammadan Rural)
91 Muhammad Amin, K.S. Sheikh (Multan Division Towns – Muhammadan, Urban)
92 Muhammad Arif Khan, Khan (Jhang West – Muhammadan, Rural)
93 Muhammad Feroz Khan Noon, Malik Sir, KCSI, KCIE (Rawalpindi Division Towns – Muhammadan, Urban)
94 Muhammad Ghulam Jilani Gurmani, Mian (Muzaffargarh North – Muhammadan, Rural)
95 Muhammad Hassan, Chaudhri (Ambala and Simla – Muhammadan, Rural)
96 Muhammad Hussain, Chaudhri, B.A., LL.B (Sheikhupura – Muhammadan, Rural)
97 Muhammad Hussain, Sardar (Chunian – Muhammadan, Rural)
98 Muhammad Iftikhar-ud-Din, Mian, BA (Oxon) (Kasur – Muhammadan, Rural)
99 Muhammad Iqbal Ahmad Khan, Rai (Ludhiana – Muhammadan, Rural)
100 Muhammad Jamal Khan Leghari, Khan Bahadur Nawab Sir (Tumandar)
101 Muhammad Khurshid Khan, Rao, BA, LL.B. (Rohtak – Muhammadan, Rural)
102 Muhammad Nawaz Khan, Lt Col. Sardar Sir, KCIE (Attock Central – Muhammadan, Rural)
103 Muhammad Nur Ullah, Mian (Toba Tek Singh – Muhammadan, Rural)
104 Muhammad Rafiq, Mian (Outer Lahore – Muhammadan, Urban)

105 Muhammad Raza Shah Jilani, Haji Mukhdumzada Syed (Shujabad, – Muhammadan, Rural)

106 Muhammad Sarfraz Ali Khan, Raja (Chakwal – Muhammadan, Rural)

107 Muhammad Sarfraz Khan, Chaudhri (Sialkot Central – Muhammadan, Rural)

108 Mumtaz Ali Khan, Sardar, BA, LLB. (Attock North – Muhammadan, Rural)

109 Mumtaz Muhammad Khan Daulatana, Mian (Sialkot South – Muhammadan, Rural)

110 Narindar Singh, Sant (Montgomery East – Sikh Rural)

111 Narotam Singh, Sardar, BA, LLB (South-East Punjab – Sikh, Rural)

112 Nasar Din, Chaudhri, BA, LLB (Sialkot North – Muhammadan, Rural)

113 Nasarullah Khan Nasir, Rana (Hoshiarpur West – Muhammadan, Rural)

114 Nasarullah Khan, Chaudhri (Amritsar – Muhammadan, Rural)

115 Nau Bahar Shah, Sayyed (Kabirwala – Muhammadan, Rural)

116 Pancham Chand, Thakur, BA, LLB. (Kangra North – General, Rural)

117 Parbodh Chandar, Mr (Gurdaspur – General, Rural)

118 Parkash Kaur, Shrimati (Dr) (Amritsar – Sikh Women)

119 Partap Singh, Sardar, MA (Amritsar South – Sikh, Rural)

120 Piara Singh, Sardar (Hoshiarpur South – Sikh Rural)

121 Prem Singh, Chaudhri (South-east Gurgaon – Reserved Seat)

122 Prem Singh, Mahant (Gujrat and Shahpur – Sikh, Rural)

123 Prithvi Singh Azad, Sardar (Ambala and Simla – Reserved Seat)

124 Raj Muhammad Khan, Chaudhri (Hafizabad – Muhammadan, Rural)

125 Ram Sharma Pandit, Shri (Southern Towns – General, Urban)

126 Rameshawari Nehru, Mrs (Lahore City – General, Women, Urban)

127 Ranbir Singh Mehta, Mr (Ludhiana and Ferozepore – General, Rural)

128 Ranjit Singh, Chaudhri (Hissar South – General, Rural)

129 Rattan Singh Tabib, Chaudhri (Ambala and Simla – General, Rural)

130 Rattan Singh, Sardar (Ferozepore East – Sikh, Rural)

131 Rattan Singh, Sardar (Ferozepore North – Sikh, Rural)

132 Roshan Din, Khan Bahadur Chaudhri (Shahdara – Muhammadan, Rural)

133 Sadiq Hasan, Sheikh (Amritsar City – Muhammadan, Rural)

134 Sahib Dad Khan, Khan Sahib Chaudhri, BA, LLB (Hissar – Muhammadan, Rural)

135 Sahib Ram, Chaudhri (Hissar North – General, Rural)

136 Said Akbar Khan, Raja, BA, LLB (Gujar Khan – Muhammadan, Rural)

137 Sajjan Singh Margindpuri, Sardar (Kasur – Sikh, Rural)

138 Salah-ud-Din, Chaudhri (Gujranwala North – Muhammadan, Rural)

139 Samar Singh, Chaudhri (Karnal South – General, Rural)

140 Sant Ram Seth, Dr (Amritsar City – General, Urban)

141 Sant Ram, Mr (Jullundur General – Reserved Seat)

142 Sardul Singh, Sardar (Lahore West – Sikh, Rural)

143 Shahadat Khan, Rai (Nankana Sahib – Muhammadan, Rural)

144 Shanno Devi Sehgal, Shrimati (South-eastern Towns – General, Urban)

145 Shaukat Hayat Khan, Sardar (South-eastern Towns – Muhammadan, Urban)

146 Sher Singh, Chaudhri (Jhajjar – General, Urban)

147 Shiv SaranSingh, Sardar (Kangra and Northern Hoshiarpur – Sikh, Rural).

148 Shiv Singh, Sardar (Gurdaspur North – Sikh, Rural)

149 Sudarshan Seth, Mr (Eastern Town – General, Urban)

150 Sultan Ali Nangiana, K.B. Mian (Shahpur – Muhammadan, Rural)

151 Sundar Singh, Chaudhri (Amritsar and Sialkot – General, Reserved Seat)

152 Sundar, Mr (Karnal North – Reserved Seat)

153 Suraj Mal, Rao Bahadur Chaudhri, BA, LLB (Hansi – General, Rural)

154 Swaran Singh, Sardar, BA, LLB (Jullundur West – Sikh, Rural)

155 Tara Singh, Sardar Sahib Sardar (Ferozepore South – Sikh, Rural)

156 Tasadaq Hussain, Begum (Inner Lahore – Muhammadan, Women, Urban)

157 Tilak Raj, Professor, MA (Rawalpindi Division – General, Rural)

158 Udham Singh, Sardar (Amritsar Central – Sikh, Rural)

159 Ujjal Singh, Sardar (Western Towns – Sikh, Urban)

160 Virendra, Mr (West Multan Division – General, Rural)

161 Wali Muhammad Gohir, Chaudhri (Jullundur South – Muhammadan, Rural)

162 Waryam Singh, Sardar (Batala – Sikh, Rural)

163 Wazir Muhammad, Malik (Inner Lahore – Muhammadan, Urban)

164 Zafar-ul-Haq, Chaudhri (Rawalpindi Sadar – Muhammadan, Urban)

165 Zafarullah Khan Jhanian, Chaudhri (Ajnala – Muhammadan, Rural)

166 Zafarullah Khan, Chaudhri (Gujranwala East – Muhammadan, Rural)

GLOSSARY

Arain:	an agricultural tribe, overwhelmingly Muslim
Abaji:	father
Arora:	a trading caste of Hindus and Sikhs
Badmash:	rogue, used interchangeably with *goonda*; however, in Punjabi parlance, also someone who enjoys some prominence in the underworld hierarchy
Biradari:	patrimonial lineage; used interchangeably with caste or to indicate a closer group within a larger caste configuration
Brahmin:	priestly caste among Hindus, the highest in social ranking
Chacha/Chachaji:	paternal uncle; also used symbolically for elders
Chak:	village in the canal colonies
Dada/Dadaji:	paternal grandfather
Dadi/Dadiji:	paternal grandmother
Danda:	thick stick
Deira:	a sitting or socialising place associated with *pehlwans,* or prominent figures in a locality
Gujjar:	a pastoral-agricultural tribe, largely Muslim, but also includes Hindus and Sikhs
Gurdwara:	Sikh place of worship
Guru:	Sikh religious leader; traditional teacher
Haveli:	mansion
Goonda:	rogue, used interchangeably with *badmash;* however, in Punjabi parlance, slightly lower in hierarchy than a *badmash*
Imam :	Muslim prayer leader
Jat/Jatt:	an agricultural tribe in Punjabi-speaking eastern Punjab, largely Sikh; in the Hindi-speaking former

Ambala division, overwhelmingly Hindu; in central Punjab, both Muslim and Sikh; and in western Punjab, overwhelmingly Muslim

Jatha: Armed group, often on horseback

Jehad/jihad: Islamic holy war

Khala: mother's sister; aunty

Khatri: the dominant Hindu caste in the Punjab though theologically second to Brahmins

Kirpan: short curved sword carried by Sikhs

Lathi: long stick used in fighting or by police to quell an unruly crowd or mob

Mama/mamaji: maternal uncle

Mandir: Hindu place of worship

Masjid: Muslim place of worship

Maulvi: Muslim cleric

Mohalla: neighbourhood; locality

Panchayat: village council

Pind: village

Pir: Muslim spiritual guide

Pehlwan: wrestler; bodybuilder; a locality's strongman more feared than respected

Rajput: an agricultural tribe, often with larger holdings than Arains, Gujjars and Jats. In northern and western Punjab overwhelmingly Muslim, elsewhere belonging to all three – Hindu, Muslim and Sikh – groups.

Sarpanch: head of village council

Syed: putative descendent of Prophet Muhammad

Teli[s] : one who grounds mustard seeds to extract the oil

Thanedar: officer in charge of a police station

Tonga: horse-drawn buggy; horse-drawn carriage

Tahsil/tehsil: administrative and revenue sub-unit of a district

BIBLIOGRAPHY

Abisaab, R. *Converting Persia: Religion and Politics in the Safavid Empire*, London: I.B. Tauris, 2004

Adeeb, Y. *Mere Shehr Lahore* (My City of Lahore), Lahore: Atish Fishan Publications, 1991

Afzal, Muhammad. *Dastan-e-Sandham* (The Story of Sandham), Islamabad: Chaudhry Muhammad Ajmal (no date given)

Ahmad, Bashir. *Dil Bhatkay Ga* (The Heart will go Astray), Lahore: Ferozsons Ltd., 2003

Ahmad, Saeed. *Great Sufi Wisdom: Bulleh Shah,* Islamabad: Saeed Ahmad, 2004

Ahmed, Ishtiaq. *'Sikh Separatism in India and the Concept of Khalistan'* in Haellquist, K. R. (ed.), *NIAS Report 1990*, Copenhagen: Nordic Institute of Asian Studies, 1990

——— *State, Nation and Ethnicity in Contemporary South Asia,* London and New York: Pinter, 1998

——— 'The 1947 Partition of Punjab: Arguments put Forth before the Punjab Boundary Commission by the Parties Involved' in Ian Talbot and Gurharpal Singh (eds), *Region and Partition: Bengal, Punjab and the Partition of the Subcontinent,* pp. 116-167, Karachi: Oxford University Press, 1999

——— *Let's not forget Jallianwala Bagh,* Lahore: *Daily Times,* 13 April 2003

Akbar, M. J. *India: The Siege Within*, Harmondsworth: Penguin Books, 1985

Alhaq, Shuja. *A Forgotten Vision: A Study of Human Spirituality in the Light of the Islamic Tradition,* Chippenham, Wiltshire: Minerva Books, 1996

Anand, Som. *Lahore: Portrait of a Lost City,* Lahore: Vanguard Books Ltd, 1998

Ashraf, Agha. *Aik Dil Hazaar Dastan* (One Heart and a Thousand Stories), Lahore: Atish Fishan Publications, 1989

Ali, Chaudhri Muhammad. *The Emergence of Pakistan,* Lahore: Research Society of Pakistan, 1973

Ali, Ikram. *History of the Punjab (1799-1947),* Delhi: Low Price Publication, 1970

Ali, Imran. *The Punjab under Imperialism 1885-1947,* Karachi: Oxford University Press, 1989

Allana, G. (ed.). *Pakistan Movement: Historic Documents*, Lahore: Islamic Book Service, 1977

Azad, Maulana Abul Kalam. *India Wins Freedom,* Lahore: Vanguard Books Pvt. Ltd. 1989

Aziz, Khursheed Kamal (ed.). *Complete Works of Rahmat Ali,* Islamabad: National Commission on Historical and Cultural Research, 1978

_______ *The Murder of History,* Lahore: Vanguard Books, 1993

_______ *History of Partition of India,* Vol. I, New Delhi: Atlantic Publishers and Distributors, 1995

Bakshi, S. R. (compiler) *'Resolution adopted by Council of Action of the All-Parties Shia Conference',* held at Poona, 25 December 1945, in *The Making of India and Pakistan: Ideology of the Hindu Mahasabha and other Political Parties,* Vol. III, New Delhi, Deep & Deep Publications, 1997

Batalvi, Ashiq Hussain. *Hamari Qoumi Jidojehed* (Our National Struggle), Lahore: Pakistan Times Press, (no year of publication given)

Bell-Fialkoff, A. *Ethnic Cleansing,* New York: St. Martin's Press, 1999

Bhatia, S. *Social Change and Politics in Punjab: 1898-1910*, New Delhi: Enkay Publishers Pvt. Ltd. 1987

Brass, Paul. *Ethnicity and Nationalism: Theory and Practice,* New Delhi: Sage Publications, 1991

Browning, C. R. *The Path to Genocide,* Cambridge: Cambridge University Press, Canto edition, 1995

Burki, Shahid Javed. *Pakistan under Bhutto, 1971-1977*, New York: St. Martin's Press, 1980

Butalia, Urvashi. *The Other Side of Silence: Voices from the Partition of India,* New Delhi: Penguin Books, 1998

Chandra, Prabodh (compiler). *Rape of Rawalpindi*, Lahore: 'The Punjab Riots Sufferers' Relief Committee, 1947

Chaudhry, Nazir Ahmed. *Development of Urdu as Official Language in the Punjab (1849-1974*), Lahore: Government of the Punjab, 1977

Chalk, F., and K. Jonassohn, *The History and Sociology of Genocide: Analysis and Case Studies,* New Haven and London: Montreal Institute of Genocide Studies and Yale University Press, 1990

Chughtai, Hakim Muhammad Tariq Mehmood Abqary Mujadidi (compiler and editor). *1947 ke Muzalim ki Kahani khud Muzlumon ki Zabani* (The Story of the 1947 Atrocities from the Victims Themselves), Lahore: Ilm-o-Irfan Publishers, 2003

Collins, Larry and Dominique Lapierre. *Freedom at Midnight*, New York: Avon Books, 1975

Connor, W. *Ethnonationalism: The Quest for Understanding,* Princeton: Princeton University Press, 1994

Darling, S. M. *The Punjab Peasant in Prosperity and Debt,* New Delhi: Manohar Book Service, 1978

Farquhar, J. N. *Modern Religious Movements in India,* Delhi: Munshiram Manoharlal, 1967

Gardezi, H. N. *Chains to Lose, Life Struggles of a Revolutionary: Memoirs of Dada Amir Haider Khan,* New Delhi: Patriot Publishers, 1989

Geertz, C. (ed.) *Old Societies and New States,* New York: The Free Press, 1963.

Gellately, R. 'The Third Rech, the Holocaust, and Visions of Serial Genocide' in Robert Gellately and Ben Kiernan (eds). *The Specter of Genocide: Mass Murder in Historical Perspective,* Cambridge: Cambridge University Press, 2003

Gillmartin, David. *Empire and Islam: Punjab and the Making of Pakistan,* Delhi: Oxford University Press, 1989

Gopal, M. *Sir Chhotu Ram: A Political Biography,* New Delhi: B. R. Publications, 1988

Grewal, J. S. 'Historical Geography of the Punjab' in *Journal of Punjab Studies,* Vol. II, no. 1, Spring 2004

Gujral, Inder Kumar. *Matters of Discretion: an autobiography,* New Delhi: Hay House India, 2011

Gujral, Satish. *A Brush with Life: An Autobiography,* Delhi: Viking Books, 1997

Gutman, R. *A Witness to Genocide,* Shaftesburg, Dorset: Element Book, 1993

Hamid, Shahid (Maj. Gen [Retd]). *Disastrous Twilight,* London: Lee Cooper, 1986

Hansen, Anders Bjorn. *Partition and Genocide: Manifestation of Violence in Punjab 1937-1947,* New Delhi: India Research Press, 2002

Hasan, Mushirul. *India Partitioned: the Other Face of Freedom*, Vol. II, New Delhi: Lotus Collection, Roli Books, 1995.

Hobbes, T. *Leviathan,* London: Penguin Classics, 1985

Husain, Azim. *Mian Fazl-i-Husain: Glimpses of Life and Works 1898-1936,* Lahore: Sang-e-Meel Publications, (no date of publication given).

Husain, Syed Wajahat (Major General). *Memories of a Soldier: 1947 – Before During After*, Lahore: Ferozsons (Pvt) Ltd., 2010

Ibbetson, S. D. *Punjab Castes,* Lahore: Sang-e-Meel Publications, 1994

Iftikhar, Khawaja. *Jabb Amritsar Jall Raha Tha* (When Amritsar was Burning), Lahore: Khawaja Publishers, 1991

Jalal, Ayesha, *The Sole Spokesman*, Cambridge: Cambridge University Press, (1985).

Jetly, Rajshree (ed.) *Pakistan in Regional and Global Politics*, London, New York, New Delhi: Routledge, 2009

Jones, K. W. *Arya Dharm: Hindu Consciousness in 19th-Century Punjab*, Delhi: Manohar, 1989a

——— *The New Cambridge History of India: Socio-Religious Reform Movements in British India*, Cambridge University Press, Cambridge, 1989b

Josh, Bhagwan. *Communist Movement in Punjab (1926-47)*, Delhi: Anupama Publications, 1979

Khan, Fazal Muqeem Khan (Major-General). *The Story of the Pakistan Army*, Karachi, Karachi: Oxford University Press, 1964

Kholi, S. S. *The Life and Ideals of Guru Gobind Singh*, Delhi: Munshiram Manoharlal, 1986

Jonassohn, K., and Björnson, K. S. *Genocide and Gross Human Rights Violations*, New Brunswick and London: Transaction Publishers, 1999

Jonsson, G. (ed). *East Timor: Nationbuilding in the 21st Century*, Stockholm: Centre for Pacific Asian Studies, 2003

Kellas, J.G. *The Politics of Nationalism and Ethnicity*, New York: St Martin's Press, 1998

Kecmanovic, D. *The Mass Psychology of Ethnonationalism*, New York and London: Plenium Press, 1996

Khan, Muhammad Ayub. *Tarikh-i-Pakistan Aur Jullundur* (The Pakistan Movement and Jullundur), Lahore: Asatair, 2002

Khosla, Gopal Das. *Stern Reckoning: A Survey of the Events Leading Up To and Following the Partition of India*, New Delhi: Oxford University Press, 1989, first published in 1949

Kuper, Leo. *Genocide*, New Haven and London: Yale University Press, 1982

Lahori, Tahir. *Sohna Shehr Lahore* (The Lovely City of Lahore), Lahore; Sang-e-Meel Publications, 1994

Lake, D. A. and D. Rothchild, (eds). *The International Spread of Ethnic Conflict*, Princeton: Princeton University Press, 1998

Lamb, Alastair. *Incomplete Partition: The Genesis of the Kashmir Dispute 1947-1948*, Hertingfordburg, Hertfordshire: Roxford Books, 1997

Lang, B. *Act and Idea in the Nazi Genocide*, Syracuse: Syracuse University Press, 2003

Leigh, M. S. *The Punjab and the War*, Lahore: Government Printing Press, 1922

Maini, Tridivesh Singh. *South Asian Cooperation and the Role of the Two Punjabs*, New Delhi: Siddharth Publications, 2007

Malhotra, Dina Nath. *Dare to Publish*, New Delhi, 2004

Malik, M. A. *The Making of the Pakistan Resolution,* Karachi: Oxford University Press, 2001

Mann, M. *The Dark Side of Democracy: Explaining Ethnic Cleansing,* Cambridge: Cambridge University Press, 2005

Melson, R. *Revolution and Genocide: On the Origins of the Armenian Genocide and the Holocaust,* Illinois: University of Chicago Press, 1992

Menon, Ritu and Bhasin, Kamla. *Borders and Boundaries: Women in India's Partition,* New Delhi: Kali for Women, 1998

Mittal, G. *Lahore ka jo Zikr Kiya: Aap Biti* (Remembering Lahore: An Autobiography), Lahore: Book Home, 2003

Moon, Penderel. *Divide and Quit,* New Delhi: Oxford University Press, 1998

Munir, Muhammad. *From Jinnah to Zia,* Lahore: Vanguard Books Ltd, 1980

Nagina, Z. I. *Ghazi Ilam Din Shaheed,* (Lahore; Jang Publishers Press, 1988

Naimark, N. M. *Fires of Hatred: Ethnic Cleansing in the Twentieth Century Europe,* Cambridge Mass., London: Harvard University Press, 2001

Nevile, Pran. *Lahore, a Sentimental Journey*, Delhi and Karachi: Allied Publishers Ltd, 1993

Oren, Stephen. *'The Sikhs, Congress, and the Unionists in British Punjab, 1937-1945'*, *Modern Asian Studies*, Vol. VIII, No III, Cambridge: Cambridge University Press, 1974

Pandey, Gayendra. *Remembering Partition,* Cambridge: Cambridge University Press, 2001

Pirzada, Syed Sharifuddin (ed.). *Foundations of Pakistan: All-India Muslim League Documents, 1906-1947,* Vol. II, Karachi: National Publishing House Ltd, 1970

Rashid, Rao. *Jo Meiney Dekha: Pakistani Syasat aur Hukumrani ki Haqiqat* (What I Saw: The Inside Story of Pakistani Politics and Governance), Lahore: Jamhoori Publications, 2010

Robert, Andrew. *Eminent Churchillians*, London: Phoenix, 1995

Salim, Ahmad (ed). *Lahore 1947*, Lahore: Sang-e-Meel Publications, 2003

Seervai, H. M. *Partition of India: Legend and Reality*, Bombay: Emmanem Publications, 1989

Shahnawaz, Begum Jahan Ara. *Father and Daugher: A Political Biography,* Karachi: Oxford University Press, 2002

Sheikh, Majid. 'The 30-Year Rule of the 'Three Hakeems' in *Dawn,* Karachi, 25 June 2005

——— *'When the 'Wild' Proved More Educated'*, *Dawn,* Lahore edition, 24 January 2010.

Shils, E. *'Primordial, Personal, Sacred and Civil Ties'*, in *British Journal of Sociology*, 1957

Singh, Amrik (ed.) *The Partition in Retrospect,* Delhi: Aanamika Publishers & Distributors (P) Ltd, 2000

Singh, G. *Religion and Politics in the Punjab,* New Delhi: Deep & Deep Publications, 1986

Singh, Harbans and Barrier, N. Gerald (eds). *Punjab Past and Present: Essays in Honour of Dr. Ganda Singh,* Patiala: Punjab University, 1976

Singh, Khushwant. *A History of the Sikhs,Vol. I, 1469-1839*, Princeton: Princeton University Press, 1963

——*A History of the Sikhs,* Vol. II, *1839-1964,* Princeton: Princeton University Press, 1966

—— *Ranjit Singh: Maharajah of the Punjab 1780-1839*, New Delhi: Orient Longman, 1985

—— *Truth, Love and a Little Malice,* New Delhi: Viking, 2002

Singh, Kirpal. *The Partition of the Punjab*, Patiala: Patiala University, 1989

—— *Select Documents on Partition of Punjab – 1947*, Delhi: National Book Shop, 1991

Steinberg, S. *The Ethnic Myth: Race, Ethnicity and Class in America,* New York: Atheneum, 1981

Stone, Dan (ed). *The Historiography of Genocide,* Houndsmill, Basingstoke, Hampshire: Palgrave Macmillan, 2008

Taqi-ud-din, Hafiz. *Tarikh ki Adalat Mein,* (In the Courtroom of History), Gujranwala: Jeenay Do Publications, 1999

—— *Pakistan ki Syasi Jamaaten Aur Tehriken* (The Political Parties and Movements of Pakistan), Lahore: Classic, 2001

Talbot, Ian. *Khizr Tiwana: The Punjab Unionist Party and the Partition of India,* Richmond, Surrey: Curzon, 1996

Talbot, Ian and Gurharpal Singh, (eds). *Region and Partition: Bengal, Punjab and the Partition of the Subcontinent,* Karachi: Oxford University Press, 1999

Talbot, Ian and Shinder Thandi, (eds). *People on the Move: Punjabi Colonial, and Post-Colonial Migration*, Karach: Oxford University Press, 2004

Talha, Naureen. *Economic Factors in the Making of Pakistan,* Karachi: Oxford University Press, 2000

Talib, Sardar Gurbachan Singh. *Muslim League Attack on Sikhs and Hindus in the Punjab 1947,* New Delhi: Voice of India, 1991, first published in 1950

Tan, Tai Yong, and Gyanesh Kudaisya, *The Aftermath of Partition in South Asia,* London: Routledge, 2000

Tan, Tai Yong. *The Garrison State: The Military, Government and Society in Colonial Punjab, 1849-1947*, New Delhi: Sage Publications, 2005

Tanwar, Raghuvendra. *Reporting the Partition of Punjab: Press, Public and Other Opinions*, New Delhi: Manohar, 2006

Tuker, Sir Francis. *While Memory Serves*, London: Cassell and Company Ltd. 1950

Wali, Khan. *Facts are Facts: The Untold Story of India's Partition*, New Delhi: Vikas Publishing House Pvt Ltd, 1987

Warraich, Suhail. *The Traitor Within: The Nawaz Sharif Story in His own Words*, Lahore: Sagar Publishers, 2008

Westerlund, David and Svanberg, Ingvar (eds.). *Islam Outside the Arab World*, pp. 212-252, Richmond: Curzon Press, 1999

Williams, H. 'Freelance' in *Times Literary Supplement*, 13 February 2004.

Wolpert, Stanley. *Jinnah of Pakistan*, Karachi: Oxford University Press, 2002

Young, C. *The Politics of Cultural Pluralism*, Madison: The University of Wisconsin Press, 1976

Official documents

Carter, L. (ed. and compiler). *Punjab Politics 1936-1939, The Start of Provincial Autonomy: Governors' Fortnightly Reports and Other Key Documents*, Delhi: Manohar, 2004

——— (ed.). *Punjab Politics 1940-1943, Strains of War, Governors' Fortnightly Reports and other Key Documents*, Delhi: Mahohar, 2005

——— (ed. and compiler). *Punjab Politics 1 January 1944–3 March 1947: Last Years of the Ministries (Governor's Fortnightly Reports and other Key Documents)*. New Delhi: Manohar 2006

——— *Punjab Politics, 3 March–31 May 1947, At the Abyss, Governors' Fortnightly Reports and other Key Documents*, New Delhi: Manohar, 2007a

——— *Punjab Politics, 1 June–14 August 1947, Tragedy, Governors' Fortnightly Reports and other Key Documents*, New Delhi: Manohar, 2007b

Disturbances in the Punjab, Islamabad: National Documentation Centre, 1995

Mansergh, Nicholas and W. W. R., Lumby, (eds). *The Transfer of Power 1942-7, Volume I The Cripps Mission, January–April 1942*, London: Her Majesty's Stationery Office, 1970

——— *The Transfer of Power 1942-7, Volume II Quit India, 30 April–21 September 1942*, London: Her Majesty's Stationery Office, 1971.

Mansergh. N. and Penderel Moon, (eds). *The Transfer of Power 1942-7, Volume VI The post-war phase: new moves by the Labour Government, 1 August 1945–22*

April 1946, London: Her Majesty's Stationery Office, 1976
——*The Transfer of Power 1942-7, Volume VII The Cabinet Mission, 23 March–29 June 1946,* London: Her Majesty's Stationery Office, 1977
——*The Transfer of Power, 3 July–1 November 1946, Volume VIII The Interim Government,* London: Her Majesty's Stationery Office, 1979
—— *The Transfer of Power 1942-47,* Volume IX The fixing of a time limit, 4 November 1946–22 March 1947, London: Her Majesty's Stationery Office, 1980
—— *The Transfer of Power 1942-47,* Volume X, *The Mounbatten Viceroyalty, Formulation of a Plan, 22 March–30 May 1947,* London: Her Majesty's Stationery Office, 1981
—— *The Transfer of Power 1942-7,* Volume XI, *The Mountbatten Viceroyalty, Announcement and Reception of the 3 June Plan, 31 May–7 July 1947,* London: Her Majesty's Stationery Office, 1982
—— *The Transfer of Power 1942-47, Volume XII The Mountbatten Viceroyalty Princes, Partition and Independence, July 8–15 August 1947*, London: Her Majesty's Stationery Office, 1983
Note on the Sikh Plan, Lahore: Government Printing Press, 1948.
RSS (*Rashtriya Swayam Sewak Sangh*) *in the Punjab,* Lahore: Government Printing Press, 1948.
Sadullah, Mian Muhammad (compiler), The Partition of the Punjab 1947, Volumes I, II , III and IV, (official documents compiled for the National Documentation Centre, Lahore) Lahore: Sang-e-Meel Publications, 1993
The Journey to Pakistan: A Documentation on Refugees of 1947, Islamabad: National Documentation Centre, 1993
The Punjab Alienation of Land Act, 1901, Lahore: Government Printing Press, 1901
The Report of the Court of Inquiry constituted under Punjab Act II of 1954 to enquire into the Punjab Disturbances of 1953 (also known as *Munir Report*), Lahore: Government Printing Press, 1954
The Sikhs in Action, Lahore: Government Printing Press, 1948

Microfilms

Fortnightly Reports of Punjab chief secretary for 1946 (which also include reports of the Punjab governor) in the Political Department Miscellaneous (also known as Political and Judicial records) under the designation: L/P & J/5/249. London: British Library.
Fortnightly Reports of Punjab chief secretary for 1947 (which also include

reports of the Punjab governor) in the Political Department Miscellaneous (also known as Political and Judicial records) under the designation: IOR L/P & J/5/250.

Newspapers

Daily Times, Lahore, 13 April 2003.
Dawn, Delhi, 1947.
Pakistan Times, Lahore, 1947.
The Tribune, Lahore, 1947.
The Civil and Military Gazette, Lahore, 1947.

Journals, Magazines and Reports

Economic and Political Weekly, Vol. XXXIII, No. 12, 8 August 1998, Mumbai, 1998
Journal of Genocide Research, London: Taylor & Francis, Cartex Publishing, 2003
Journal of Sikh Studies, Vol. XXVII, No. 2, Amritsar: Guru Nanak Dev University, 2002
Middle East Journal, Vol. 4, No. 3 , July, Washington DC 1950
Modern Asian Studies, Vol. VIII, No. 4, Cambridge: Cambridge University Press, 1974
Modern South Asian Studies, Vol. XIII, No. 3, Cambridge: Cambridge University Press, 1979
Modern Asian Studies, Vol. XVII, No. 4, Cambridge: Cambridge University Press, 1983
Modern Asian Studies, Vol. XXXVI, No. 3, Cambridge: Cambridge University Press, 2002
NIAS Report 1990, Copenhagen: Nordic Institute of Asian Studies, 1990
Outlook, New Delhi, 28 May 1997
The Chronicle of Pakistan, http://therepublicofrumi.com/chronicle/1947_09.htm, downloaded on 13 December 2010.
Seminar, Number 567, November, New Delhi, 2006
The South Asian, http://www.the-south-asian.com/July-Aug2000/Chakwal_memories_4.htm, Delhi, downloaded on 7 August 2000
War in History, Vol. XVI. No. 4, London: Sage Publications, 2009

INTERVIEWS

1992

Recollection of conversation with Inder Kumar and Sheil Gujral, New Delhi, 9 October 1992

1997

Naqsh Lyallpuri, Mumbai, 2 January, 1997
B.R. Chopra, Mumbai, 4 January 1997
Abdullah Malik, Lahore, 9 December 1997
C.R. Aslam, Lahore, 15 December 1997

1999

Som Anand, New Delhi, 18 October 1999
Rattan Chand, Delhi, 19 October 1999
Ram Parkash Kapur, New Delhi, 20 October 1999
Jamna Das Akhtar, Delhi, 20 October 1999
Amarnath Sehgal, Delhi, 20 October 1999
Pran Nevile, Delhi, 21 October 1999
Harkishen Singh Surjeet, New Delhi, 21 October 1999
Yuvraj Krishan, Delhi. 21 October 1999
Prem Dhawan, Mumbai, 22 October 1999
Nanak Singh Broca, Mumbai, 23 October 1999
Dr Jagdish Chander Sarin, Delhi, 24 October 1999
Dr Prem Sobti, Delhi, 24 October 1999
Ramanand Sagar, Delhi, 25 October 1999 and again in Mumbai, 18 October 2001

2000

Mujahid Taj Din, Lahore, 2 and 25 February 2000

2001

Ramanand Sagar, (second interview), Mumbai, 18 October 2001
Raj Babbar, Mumbai, 20 October 2001
Sunil Dutt, Mumbai, 20 October 2001
Sat Paul Arora, Delhi, 22 October 2001
Bhisham Sahni, Delhi, 23 October 2001

2002

Mushtaq Ahmad, Stockholm, 12 April 2002
Aziz Mazhar, London, 18-19 May 2002
Chaudhri Riasat Ali, London, 18 May, 2002
Rashid Ishaq Khaksar, London, 18 May 2002
Hameed Akhtar, London, 19 May 2002
Syed Muhammad Islam, London, 19 May 2002
Syed Zia Mohiyuddin, Stockholm, 24 June 2002
Mrs Kanta Singh Luthra, Salem, Oregon, 15 July 2002
Professor Emeritus Shaukat Ali, Mansfield, Massachusetts, 29 July 2002

2003

Mian Maqsood Ahmed, Lahore, 3 April 2003.
Mian Muhammad Salim, Lahore, 4 April 2003
Arif Khokhar, Lahore, 4 April 2003
Col. (Retd) Nadir Ali, 5 April 2003
Mohammad Farid Mirza,Lahore, 7 April 2003
Hassan Din, Lahore, 13 April 2003.
Syed Afzal Haider, Lahore, 13 April 2003
Sheikh Anwar Ali, Islamabad, April 15, 2003
Khawaja Iftikhar, Lahore, 17 April 2003
Noor Bhari, Lahore, 17 April, 2003
Chaudhri Muhammad Bashir, Lahore, 18 April 2003
Rana Muhammad Rashid, Lahore, 18 April 2003

A. Hameed, Lahore, 19 April 2003
Professor Muhammad Sharif Kunjahi, Gujrat, 20 April 2003
Syed Aftab Hassan, Gujrat, 20 April 2003
Ahmad Bashir, Lahore, 22 April 2003
Mian Jalal Din, Lahore, 22 April, 2003.
Syed Ejaz Hussain Jafri, Lahore, 22 April 2003
A.T. Chaudhri, Lahore, 23 April 2003
Haji Muhammad Akram, Lahore, 23 April 2003
Begum Nasim Amir Hussain Shah, 25 April 2003
Tahira Mazhar Ali Khan, Lahore, 25 April 2003
Chaudhri Muhammad Siddiq, Lahore, 27 April 2003
Raja Tajammul Hussain, 27 April 2003
Sardar Shaukat Ali, Lahore, 3 May 2003
Dr Khushi Muhammad Khan, Stockholm, 16 June 2003

2004

Kamla Sethi, Delhi, 7 March 2004
Jagan Nath, Delhi, 8 March 2004
Kevel Krishan Tulli, Delhi, 8 March 2004; clarifications via telephone on 30 January 2006
Sampuran Singh Sachdev, Delhi, 9 March 2004
Kidar Nath Malhohtra, Delhi, 10 March 200
Professor V.N. Dutta, Delhi, 10 March 2004
Balraj Dev Aggarwal, Delhi, 12 March 2004
B.R. Lal, Delhi, 12 March 2004
Manohar Lal Sharma, Delhi, 12 March 2004
Ram Dayal Chopra, Delhi, 12 March 2004
Iqbal Singh, Delhi, 13 March 2004
Vimal Issar, Delhi, 13 March 2004
Mrs Vimla Virmani, Delhi, 13 March 2004
Amar Singh, (formerly of Rawalpindi) Delhi, 14 March 2004
Madanlal Singh, Delhi, 14 March 2004 and 15 March 2004
Amar Singh, Delhi, 15 March 2004
Dina Nath Malhotra, Delhi, 15 March 2004
Hari Dev Shourie, Delhi, 16 March 2004
Gurdev Singh (formerly of Jhang), Delhi, 16 March 2004
Hans Raj Khatri, Sidhwan Bet, Ludhiana district, 17 March 2004
Old Mr Arora, Kishanpura, Moga district, 18 March 2004
Pyara Singh Naulakh, Kishanpura, Moga district, 18 March 2004

Gurdev Singh (formerly of Lyallpur rural areas), village Galib Kalan, Ludhiana district, 18 March 2004.
Nashatar Singh, village Galib Kalan, Ludhiana district, 18 March 2004
Harkishan Singh Mehta, Chandigarh, 20 March 2004
Selja Saini, Chandigarh, 20 March 2004
Gurcharan Das Arora, Amritsar, 24 March 2004
Devi Das Mangat, Amritsar, 25 March 2004
Mohan Singh Rahi, Amritsar, 25 March 2004
Ripudamman Singh, Amritsar 26 March 2004
Giani Mahinder Singh, Amritsar, 27 March 2004
Sardar Kundan Singh Samra, Kotla Sultan Singh, Amritsar district, 27 March 2004
Moni Chadha, Delhi, 28 March 2004
Gurbachan Singh Tandon, Noida, 29 March 2004
Pushpa Goel, Delhi, 29 March 2004
Savitri Dutt-Chibber, Delhi, Noida, 29 March 2004
Pushpa Hans, Delhi, 31 March 2004
Col. Hans Raj Chopra, Delhi, 31 March 2004
Mahmooda Begum, 9 December 2004
Ameer Khan, Chak Beli Khan, Rawalpindi district, 11 December 2004
Haji Muhammad Hanif, Chak Beli Khan, Rawalpindi district, 11 December 2004
Khawaja Masud Ahmed, Rawalpindi, 12 December 2004
Sheikh Noor Din, Rawalpindi, 12 December 2004
Haji Muhammad Sharif, Parial, Attock (Campbellpur) district, 13 December 2004
Faiz Zaman, Parial, Attock (Campbellpur) district, 13 December 2004
Syed Nazir Hussain, Choa Khalsa, Rawalpindi district, 14 December 2004
Raja Muhammad Riasat Khan, Chou Khalsa, Rawalpindi district, 14 December 2004
Haji Sher Khan, Thamali, Rawalpindi district, 14 December 2004
Jan Dad Khan, Thamali, Rawalpindi district, 14 December 2004
Davender Bhardwaj, via email from USA, 14 December 2004
Chaudhri Roshan Din, Kallar Syedan, Rawalpindi district, 15 December 2004
Haji Sher Ahmed, Rawalpindi, 15 December 2004
Sheikh Muhammad Ishaq, Rawalpindi, 15 December 2004
Malik Muhammad Aslam, Lahore, 17 December 2004
Mustansar Husain Tarrar, Lahore, 17 December 2004

Ghulam Rasul Tanveer, Lyallpur (Faisalabad), 19 December 2004
Mujahid Al-Hussaini, Lyallpur (Faisalabad), 19 December, 2004
Abdul Bari, Multan, 20 December 2004
Chowdhry Abdul Wahid, Multan, 20 December 2004
Chowdhry Abdul Saeed, Bahawalpur, 21 December 2004
M. A. Shamshad, Multan, 21 December 2004
Syed Khurshid Abbas Gardezi, Multan, 21 December 2004
Arshad Multani, Multan, 22 December 2004
Ataullah Malik, Multan, 22 December 2004
Akram Warraich, email from Lahore, 22 December 2004
Mashkoor Sabri, Multan, 22 December 2004
Sheikh Abdul Wahab, Lahore, 24 December 2004
Kaleb Ali Sheikh, Lahore, 25 December 2004
Qamar Yurish, Lahore, 26 December 2004
Omar Saeed, Lahore, 27 December 2004
Sheikh Arshad Habib, Lahore, 27 December 2004
Sheikh Nur Muhammad, Lahore, 27 December 2004
Syed Qamurruzaman Shah, Lahore, 28 December 2004
Muhammad Ashiq Raheel, Lahore, 29 December 2004
Ali Bakhsh, Lahore, 30 December 2004
Haji Abdul Rahman Gill, Lahore, 30 December 2004; followed up by Ahmed Salim on 29 September 2005; and 15 October 2005

2005

Professor Kirpal Singh, Chandigarh, 2 January 2005
Tilak Raj Oberoi, Chandigarh, 2 January 2005
Mahinder Nath Khanna, Amritsar, 3 January 2005
Bhagwan Das, Batala, 3 January 2005
Inderjeet, Batala, 3 January 2005
Ranjit Singh Bhasin, Kapurthala, 3 January 2005
Mrs Rajnish Tandon, Hoshiarpur, 3 January 2005.
Professor Chaman Lal Arora, Jullundur, 4 January 2005
Baldev Verma, Ludhiana, 4 January 2005.
Maulana Habibur Rahman Sanvi Ludhianvi, Ludhiana, 4 January 2005.
Mohan Lal Jhanji, Ludhiana, 4 January 2005.
Ranjit Singh (Ajit Singh), village Nathu Majra, Ludhiana district, 4 January 2005

Vicky's classmate's father, village Nathu Majra, Ludhiana district, 4 January 2005.

Babu Khan, Malerkotla, 6 January 2005.

Chaudhri Abdul Shakoor, Malerkotla, 6 January 2005.

Dr Nizam Din, Malerkotla, 6 January 2005.

Amrik Chand Ahluwalia, Patiala, 7 January 2005.

Pandit Mohan Lal Balo, Patiala, 7 January 2005.

Raghbir Singh Sahni, Patiala, 7 January 2005

Sardul Singh Virk, Lakhmari, Kurukshestra district, 8 January 2005

Faqir Singh Virk, Lakhmari, Kurukshestra district, 8 January 2005

Shamsherjit Singh Virk, Lakhmari, district Kurukshestra, Haryana, 8 January 2005

Premchand Khanna, Delhi, 9 January 2005

Girdhari Lal Kapur, Delhi, 9 January 2005

Bhola Nath Gulati, Delhi, 9 January 2005

Aftar Singh Judge, Delhi, 10 January 2005

Lajpat Rai Seth, Delhi, 10 January 2005

Professor V. N. Dutta, New Delhi, 10 January 2005

Raskhat Puri, Delhi, 10 January 2005

Trilok Kumar Gulati, Delhi, 11 January 2005.

Ghulam Haider, Rajgarh, Lahore, 13 January 2005

Muhammad Munir, Rajgarh, Lahore, 13 January 2005

Lambardar Muhammad Hanif, Rajgarh, Lahore, 13 January 2005

Sheikh Muhammad Farooq, Rajgarh, Lahore, 13 January 2005

I.A. Rehman, Lahore, 14 January 2005.

Mian Muhammad Sharif, Lahore, 14 January 2005

Mian Mustafa Kamal Pasha, Lahore, 14 January 2005

Professor Vinay Kumar, Stockholm, 3 February 2005.

Professor Prem Singh Kahlon, Nashville, Tennesse via email, 15 June 2005

S. Jarnail Singh Pasricha interviewed by Mrs Inderjeet Kaur, Headmistress Montgomery Girls High School, Kapurthala and sent by email on 1 August 2005

Suleman Cheema, via telephone from Lahore, 13 October 2005

Hukum Qureshi, Lahore (by Ahmad Salim), 30 October 2005

Syed Ahmed Saeed Kirmani, Lahore, (by Ahmad Salim) 31 October 2005

Panditji, Karnal, Haryana, 28 November 2005

Basta Singh, village Adampur, Fatehgarh district, East Punjab, 28 November 2005

Naugurdial Singh, village Adampur, Fatehgarh district, East Punjab, 28 November 2005

Richpal Singh, village Adampur, Fatehgarh district, East Punjab, 28 November 2005

Teja Singh, Boran, Fatehgarh district, East Punjab, 28 November 2005

Des Raj, village Kakra, Patiala district, 28 November 2005

Karnail Singh, village Kakra, Patiala district, 28 November 2005

Ajaib Singh, Gujjarwal, Ludhiana district, 29 November 2005

Harmail Singh, Gujjarwal, Ludhiana district, 29 November 2005

Chhitru, village Dangoli, district Rupnagar, 29 November 2005

Amar Singh, village Dangoli, Rupnagar district, 29 November 2005

Naseeb Kaur born Azmat Bibi, village Phul Khurd, Rupnagar district, 29 November, 2005.

Chaman Lal Ahuja, Panipat, 30 November 2005

Sudharshan Kumar Kapur, Old Gargaon outside Delhi, 1 December 2005

Brig (Retd) Sarjit Singh Chowdhary, Delhi,1 December 2005

Ashwini Kumar, Delhi, 2 December 2005

Raj Rani Gosain, Noida, 2 December 2005

Sikander Lal Bagga, Delhi, 3 December 2005

Chaudhri Nazir Ahmed Virk, Sheikhupura, (by Ahmad Salim), 30 December 2005

Chaudhri Tawwakullah Virk, Sheikhupura, (by Ahmad Salim), 30 December 2005

Haji Mukhtar Ahmed Khan, Sheikhupura, (by Ahmad Salim), 30 December 2005

2006

Asaf Ali Shah, Lahore (via email) 3 January 2006

Ahad Malik, Stockholm, 13 January 2006

Dr Hafeez Ahmad Mughal, interview via email from Lahore, 16 January 2006

Riaz Ahmed Cheema, 16 May 2006

Jaspal Singh Kohli, London, 8 June 2006

Chaudhri Anwar Aziz, Lahore, 15 December 2006

Reginald Massey, Llanidloes, mid-Wales on 5 July 2006; also via email 4 August 2007

Ambassador Azim Husain, London, 8 July 2005

2007

Nasim Hassan, Hockessin, Delaware, USA (by email) 1 January 2007
Ayaz Khan, Linkoping, Sweden (via email), 14 January 2007
Lt. Gen. Aftab Ahmad Khan, letter from Lahore dated 2 February 2007
Muhammad Feroz Dar, Solna, Sweden, 18 February 2007
Col. (Retd) Ata Muhammad Dogar, Lahore, 10 May 2007
Bhisham Kumar Bakshi, via email from Delhi, 5 March 2007
Manmohan Taneja, interviewed by Professor Manchanda in New Delhi, on 7 and 10 March, sent on 10 March 2007
Dr. Satya Pal 'Bedar', interviewed by Professor Manchanda in New Delhi 11 March 2007, sent on 11 March 2007
Dr Teja Singh, Edmonton, Canada, 17 March 2007, via email
Gobind Thukral, Chandigarh, via email, 21 July 2007
Jagpal Tiwana, Dartmouth, NS, Canada, via email, 11 April 2007
Mrs. B.A. Choudhary, Lahore, (via email sent by her son Dr. Muhammad Farooq) 22 July 2007

2009

Amjad Babar, Washington DC, 11 July 2009

2010

Ian Talbot, email response from Southampton, UK of 19 March 2010.
Professor Narendra Mohan Vaid, Panipat, interviewed by Arvind Vaid who sent it by email on 14 April 2010
Kumar Chand, Singapore, 10 May, 2010
Moni Chadha, second interview via email from Delhi, 28 December 2010

2011

Nirmal Tej Singh Chopra, Singapore (via email) 5 January 2011
Brig. (Retd) Yasub Ali Dogar, Lahore, via telephone and email, 13 January 2011
Dr Ajay K. Mehra, Noida, UP, via telephone and email, 13 January 2011
Mushtaq Ahmad, second interview, Stockholm, 20 February 2011
Rachna Anand, via email from Singapore, 21 February 2011

Batool Begum, interviewed by her son, Brigadier Yasub Ali Dogar, in Lahore, 3 March, 2011

Grandmother of Saleem Haroon Bhatti, via email from Lahore, 5 March 2011

Kuldip Kumar Chopra, Stockholm, 20 April 2011

2012

Riaz A. Khan, London, (via email), 28 October 2012

2013

Satyendra Kumar, New Delhi, 17 March 2013

Visharda Hoon, via email from Chennai, 13 May 2013

2014

Upendra Kumar Pundit, via email from Amsterdam, 12 July 2014

2016

Rana Muhammad Azhar Khan, Lahore, 16 March 2016

2017

Sheikh Hamid Ali, Lahore, 15 April 2017

INDEX